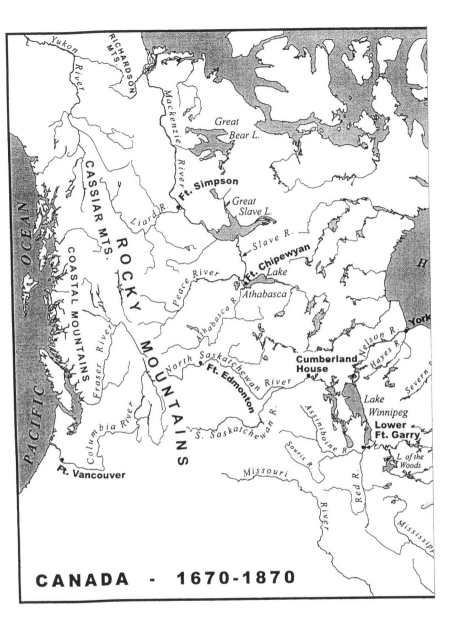

CANADA - 1670-1870

Let Them Be Remembered

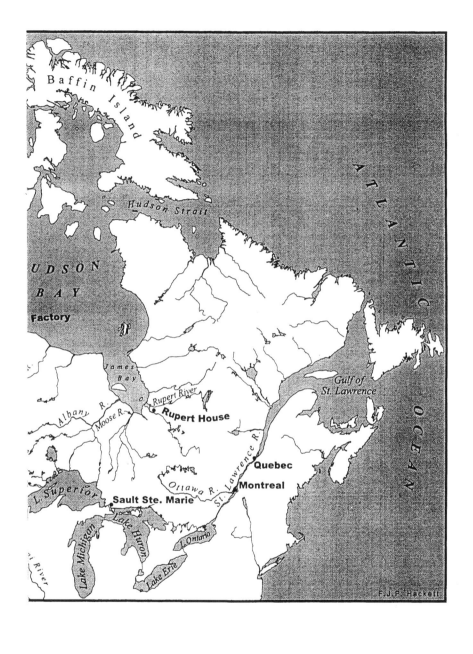

To Johnny
Elizabeth B. Losey
June 2003

Let Them Be Remembered

The Story of the Fur Trade Forts

Elizabeth Browne Losey

VANTAGE PRESS
New York

Published by Vantage Press, Inc.
516 West 34th Street, New York, New York 10001

Manufactured in the United States of America
ISBN: 0-533-12572-3

Library of Congress Catalog Card No.: 97-91114

0 9 8 7 6 5 4 3 2 1

To the memory of my dear husband, Everett, whose constant support, unfailing help, and cheerful companionship not only made this book possible, but also turned our quest for the fort sites as we journeyed through the land of the fur trade, into a most rewarding and joyous adventure.

To the native peoples of Canada who shouldered much of the heavy loads, manned the birch bark canoes and York boats, taught the fur traders how to survive in a strange and often hostile environment, and by showing the way along the waterways, across the vast prairies and through the mountain passes, enabled the traders to open up the country from the Atlantic to the Pacific oceans.

To the many government agencies, who through their farsighted programs of restoration and/or reconstruction of major fur trade posts, through their policy of marking with cairns or plaques sites important in the fur trade, and through their ongoing archaeological excavations and studies, are doing so much to make sure that the story of the fur trade is preserved for all people now and for the future.

Contents

List of Maps

Acknowledgments

This book would not have been possible without the interest and help from many people. In particular I am greatly indebted to Dr. Jennifer Brown, Alice Brown, Dr. David Burley, Robert Coutts, Richard P. Erickson, Kenneth Favrholdt, Dr. Renée Fossett, Dr. Russell Magnaghi, Lily McAuley, Dr. Michael Payne, C. S. "Paddy" Reid, Jacques Van Pelt and George A. Whitman for their generosity in sharing with me the results of their research and their knowledge as well as their kindness in reviewing parts of the manuscript for accuracy. Should there be any errors, I must assume responsibility for them. I also am grateful to Parks Canada and the provincial historic resources organizations that trusted us with information leading to the location of many of the fur trade sites. We were careful not to abuse their confidence. And lastly, I thank the many people scattered throughout Canada, most of them anonymous, who took the time and trouble to give us the directions we needed to find the sites, invited us into their homes, gave us gifts of food, and encouraged us with their friendly interest.

Introduction

Seldom, if ever, is a fad of fashion responsible for the exploration and early development of a country. But it is to just such a phenomenon that Canada owes much of its early existence.

Commencing in the late seventeenth century and extending to the mid-1800s, a universal craving for beaver hats swept through Europe. Ownership of a beaver hat became the hallmark of all who considered themselves gentlemen. Made from the dense underwool of lustrous beaver pelts and costing large sums of money, these hats were considered family heirlooms and as such were carefully passed on from father to son. To satisfy this demand required an enormous number of beaver pelts.

When early explorers discovered beaver in abundance in the New World area now known as Canada, enterprising individuals in England banded together to capitalize on this information. In 1670 they secured from King Charles II a Royal Charter incorporating them as "The Governor and Company of Adventurers of England Trading into Hudson's Bay," and granting them monopoly of all trade carried on through Hudson Strait and possession of all territory reached through the strait that they might occupy in the pursuit of their trade. In essence it was one huge blank check to ownership of all lands draining into the Hudson Bay watershed. Known as Rupert's Land after the new company's patron, Prince Rupert, it corresponded roughly to about one-third of modern Canada.

The Hudson's Bay Company, headquartered in London, established trading posts along Hudson and James bays as places for the Indians to bring their beaver pelts and other furs in exchange for trade items such as guns, powder, tobacco, beads, cloth, and ironware. After the passage of nearly 100 years, the company, although still maintaining their posts on the shores of both bays, found it necessary to extend their trading operations inland into the home territories of the native Indians.

All this activity on the part of the Hudson's Bay Company did not go unnoticed or unchallenged by the French. They, too, set out to stake their claim in the lucrative trade in furs. They had established their toehold in the New World in 1607 when Champlain founded the settlement of Quebec City on the cliffs above the St. Lawrence River. From that base and using the St. Lawrence River and the Great Lakes as their routes for penetrating into the interior, they pushed steadily westward in their pursuit of the beaver. By the mid-1700s they had reached beyond Manitoba's Lake Winnipeg and even down to the mouth of the Mississippi River. However, their defeat in 1759 by the British on the Plains of Abraham resulted in the fall of New France, thereby bringing an end to both their ventures and French colonialism in Canada.

The gap left by their disappearance did not remain unfilled for long. In 1774 a group largely composed of Scotsmen and French traders loosely organized into a partnership organization known as the North West Company took up the French route into the interior of the St. Lawrence River, moving aggressively into the trade for furs.

They soon encountered stiff opposition from the long-established Hudson's Bay Company. This rivalry, which continued for nearly fifty years, gradually escalated into a bitter no-holds-barred struggle for control of the fur trade. It ended only in 1821, when the older company was able to absorb the North West Company.

During this period of rivalry, the fur traders of both companies slowly penetrated ever farther into the heart of what was an unknown land to them. Because of the fact that it required only a few years for the region controlled by each trading post to become depleted of beaver, frequent relocation of the posts into new untrapped areas was necessary. Each trader, of course, tried to get the jump on his rivals, beating them to the new territory and erecting his fort ahead of and beyond his rivals' posts. As they each leapfrogged their way westward following the beaver-inhabited waterways, the geographical barriers of this as yet largely unknown country were gradually pushed back. So it was that before the end of the 1700s the traders with their fur posts had spread out along most of the major rivers, such as the Saskatchewan, the Athabasca, the Winnipeg, and the Assiniboine, which flowed through the central interior of the country.

By 1793 Sir Alexander Mackenzie of the North West Company had traveled the length of the Mackenzie River to the Arctic Ocean, and a few years later, by following the Peace River he broke through the barrier of the Rocky and Coastal Mountains to reach the Pacific Ocean. The mighty Fraser River had been conquered by Simon Fraser in 1808. David Thompson successfully completed his survey of the entire length of the Columbia River when he reached its mouth on the Pacific Ocean in 1812.

For nearly half a century after the absorption of the North West Company, the Hudson's Bay Company, enjoying the exclusive trading rights granted by their Royal Charter, was the dominant force in the fur trade. Eventually, however, the company was forced to bow to the increasingly strong antimonopolistic sentiments both of government and of the people. Their Royal Charter was deemed an anachronism that was no longer acceptable to the spirit of the times. In 1869 the Hudson's Bay Company signed a Deed of Surrender whereby they relinquished their Charter to the British Crown (in the person of Queen Victoria) and returned to Crown domain their vast holdings in Rupert's Land. A year later (1870) the Queen signed the Order-in-Council that transferred Rupert's Land to the newly formed dominion of Canada. In return for this voluntary action by the Hudson's Bay Company, they received monetary compensation and retention of ownership of large blocks of land. Sale of these properties to settlers and commercial entrepreneurs augmented the company's fur and retail sales in western Canada in the last decades of the nineteenth century.

Even though deprived of its trading monopoly, the company prospered over the next one hundred years and became one of the giants in Canadian merchandising. In the northern parts of the country they still engaged in their time-honored practice of buying furs from the native people. But the whims of fashion are nothing if not fickle. By this time beaver hats had long been replaced by silk ones. Nonetheless, the demand for fur for coats and jackets remained strong. Yet even this fashion trend was not destined to last. Beginning in the 1970s a rising groundswell of public opinion against trapping of all animals became so outspoken and widespread that the Hudson's Bay Company in the mid-1980s found it expedient to yield to public opinion. They cut completely their three-hundred-year-old ties to the fur trade, no longer buying new furs or handling fur garments in any of their stores. It appeared that the reign of the fur trade was ended.

Nonetheless, the beaver had done its work. It had been the catalyst that promoted the exploration and settlement of a great country. It had also been responsible for the founding of a company that had grown and prospered for 325 years, thus making it one of the oldest continuously operating businesses in the world.

This book is a look into the past as seen from today's perspective. It is an attempt to recapture—with the aid of a lively imagination—the scenes that confronted the fur traders during the period of their greatest activity, from 1670 to 1870.

In a very few instances the task is easy—the old building, weather-beaten and a bit sway backed, miraculously still stands in its original setting on riverbank or lakeshore. Much more often, the buildings have long disappeared. All that remains is the site itself; the river still flows by, the mountains still rise up against the sky, or the plains still stretch endlessly toward the far horizon. The imagination is called upon merely to supply the fort with its palisades and bastions. Finally, however, there are the many sites where a stone cairn, monument, or bronze plaque erected beside a busy thoroughfare, in the middle of a well-landscaped city park, or on the side of a museum building is all there is to serve as a reminder that a thriving fur trade post once stood in the general area. In many cases urban development has long since changed the landscape completely and effectively obliterated all traces of the past.

It is the purpose of this book to take a trip back into time, to show what the trading post sites, waterways, portages, and mountain passes look like today. The book tells the story of many of these fur forts. It includes a brief history of each establishment and short quotations from contemporary letters or journals that help illustrate a post's appearance and activities during its period of existence.

The order of presentation of the posts will, in general, follow chronologically these two main streams of westward movement. The same waterways, portages, and mountain passes used by the men of the Hudson's Bay Company and the North West Company as they struggled to establish their trading posts are followed in this present-day look into the past.

Let Them Be Remembered

Charles Fort/Rupert House

When my husband Everett and I began to discuss and develop plans that would guide us during our twenty-year search for fur trade fort sites, we concluded it was only logical to begin our quest at the birthplace of the fur trade: Rupert House, a small Cree village located at the mouth of Rupert River at the southeast corner of James Bay. This destination was easy to reach. The Polar Bear Express from Cochrane, Ontario, took us to Moosonee; from thence a short air flight across the southern tip of James Bay brought us to Rupert House. As we walked up the sloping dirt roadway leading from the riverside float dock to the gleaming white buildings of the Hudson's Bay post standing on top of the bank, we felt almost overwhelmed with a sense of history—for on this very spot over three hundred years ago, right here at Rupert House was where it all began.

At this place on September 29, 1668, the English ship *Nonsuch,* under the command of Captain Zachariah Gillam and guided by Grosseilliers after a nearly four-month voyage from London, dropped anchor, and here the Hudson's Bay Company's long saga of trading European goods for Indian furs in northern and western Canada began.

Intrigued and convinced by the glowing accounts of two French explorers, Radisson and Grosseilliers from Trois-Rivières, Quebec, of rich fur lands to be reached through Hudson's Bay, a few wealthy and enterprising Englishmen had decided to risk underwriting the cost of a trading expedition.

Charles Fort, as the small post was called, was quickly built. Located on a low sandy terrace on the south bank of Prince Rupert River, it consisted of one thatched-roof wooden house sufficient to house the men, their provisions, trading goods, and a twelve-foot deep cellar in which the supply of sea-beer was safely stored. In spite of six long icebound months under Captain Gillam's wise leadership, the crew survived well, using the ship's provisions for food, supplemented by the deer and fowl that they shot. No loss of life occurred nor outbreak of scurvy. In the spring a highly successful trade in beaver was made with the more than three hundred Indians who came to the fort.

When the *Nonsuch* returned to London in October 1669 with a cargo of 3,000 pounds of beaver that was promptly sold at a substantial profit, they were jubilant. Encouraged by the success of this first venture, eighteen of the original backers, headed by Prince Rupert, cousin of the King, formed a corporation and applied for a Royal Charter that would grant them exclusive trading privileges in all the lands draining into Hudson's Bay. On May 2, 1670, Charles II granted them such a charter, and thus was born the Hudson's Bay Company, officially known as "The Governor and Company of Adventurers of England Trading into Hudson's Bay."

During the next several years Charles Fort was enlarged and upgraded. First another house was built, then it was fortified with a log palisade and ditch. Finally in 1674 it was expanded by the construction of a bakery, a brewery and two more houses. However, in 1681, prompted by fears of an imminent French invasion, Charles Fort was abandoned because of its perceived military vulnerability. Its location, close to the riverbank overlooked by a high hill to the southeast, while convenient for trading, was not suited for defense.

The site for the new Charles Fort II was a short distance downriver on a high sandy knoll that overlooked both Rupert Bay and the river. The fort's purpose was primarily for military defense rather than for trade. It consisted of a three-story log tower with small aboveground bastions for cannon. In addition, there was a building used as a kitchen. In 1686 upright log defensive walls and earthen bastions with log reinforcements were built. Unfortunately, before the cannon could be transferred onto the new bastions, the French, led by de Troyes and Pierre Iberville, captured and destroyed the fort in a surprise attack. Only the kitchen building was left standing to house the English prisoners until they could be sent back to England. After that, it, too, was demolished, and no traces remained of English presence on Rupert River.

It would not be until 1776—nearly one hundred years later—that the Hudson's Bay Company returned to the river and established Rupert House, a trading post destined for a long existence that is still continuing.

We knew we had only about four hours for our visit before the southbound plane would pick us up. To our great good fortune, Father Provencher, the resident O.M.I. priest, who, along with many of the local people, gathered at the dock to meet the incoming plane, recognizing that we were strangers, had politely asked us (in French) if he could assist us. Drawing upon my long-dormant French, I thanked him and explained that we would like to see as much of the people and village as possible. He immediately took us in tow, and with him as our sponsor we were privileged to talk to many of the local Cree people, to watch a ninety-year-old lady laboriously scrape a moose hide, to peek into a canvas-covered pole tepee where meat was being smoked, to talk to a Cree carver from whom we were able to buy a beautifully crafted scale model of a Rupert House freighter canoe. We were taken into the home of a French-speaking family to share their noontime meal. We went to the Anglican church and were introduced to the resident priest. He told us how many of the parishioners were not able to support the church financially but supplied cordwood to heat the building.

It is in the cemetery beside their tiny church perched on a slight elevation overlooking the beautiful river and a bit isolated from the rest of the village that James C. Watt, Hudson's Bay Company manager at Rupert House, was buried in 1944. During his term as post manager, continuous overtrapping had almost completely wiped out the beaver in the area. Since they were the main source of income for the people of Rupert House, the beaver's disappearance meant economic disaster, indeed, actual starvation, for the entire community. In 1928 one occupied beaver house was found. It was then that Watts had his inspired idea. Instead of buying the pelts from the trapped beaver, he proposed that he would pay the same price as for a pelt but would instead buy the live beaver, which would then become his own property and as such be protected from trapping. Furthermore, he promised to do this for all subsequent beaver found. The Indians agreed to go along with his proposal. The plan worked. The Indians received the credit they so desperately needed, and the beaver were left to live and reproduce.

From this tiny beginning, twelve years later, the beaver population increased to over four thousand. Trapping could once more be resumed, only this time to ensure the stability of the beaver resource it was under a system of quotas putting the annual harvest on a sustained yield basis. It is no wonder that to this day the Indians of Rupert House burn a small piece of beaver meat in honor of Jimmy Watts each time they bring a beaver to camp.

After leaving the church and cemetery and knowing that the time for our visit was almost up, we headed back in the direction of the dock—the focal point of Rupert House. We walked along the dirt road that parallels the river some sixty feet below. On the day we were in Rupert House the sky was a clear blue reflected in the blue of the river; the white clouds were matched by the glistening white of the Hudson's Bay buildings. The flat expanse of dark green evergreen muskeg extended to the far horizon to the north. It was just this scene, little changed, that had greeted the eyes of Captain Charles Bayly, Grosselliers, and the crew of the *Nonsuch* over three hundred years ago.

We paused at the head of the roadway leading down to the river. There is a small, rather weather-beaten stone cairn with the simple inscription: "Hudson's Bay Company, Rupert's House Post, originally called Fort Charles, Established on this site 1668 by Medard Chouart des Grosseilliers."

On the other side of the dock roadway and opposite the Hudson's Bay Company post was a long building parallel to the river that served as the canoe shed. Here the Cree were constructing the well-known Rupert House freighter canoes famous throughout the entire north country. Many of the canoes in various stages of completion were stockpiled outside the building. The establishment of a canoe-building industry was another idea of Manager Watt in his attempts to improve the local economy.

Warned by the sound of our approaching airplane that we must leave, we hastened down to the floating dock. Before we climbed into the plane, there was time for our last look—a look that would always remain in our memory: the simple cairn at the head of the roadway commemorating the founding of Rupert House; the red-roofed white Hudson's Bay buildings and line of somberly dressed Cree men seated along a low concrete wall to the right; to the left the canoe shed and stockpiled canoes; and seated on the ground in a rough circle a group of men playing some kind of hand game.

We waved to the group of well-wishers gathered on the dock and in a few minutes were aloft and headed back southwest to Moosonee.

Moose Factory

Early in the morning we boarded the Ontario Northland train, familiarly known as the Polar Bear Express, at Cochrane, Ontario, to begin our journey to Moose Factory at the bottom of James Bay. Before long we emerged from the farming belt of fields and woodlands and entered the flat stunted spruce and muskeg country of the North. At mile 142 we reached Moose River Crossing, so named because of the long trestle railroad bridge spanning the river at this point. We left the train, climbed down the steep bank to the river, and found our small brigade of three canoes waiting for us. Then, just as Indians, fur traders, and explorers had always done for over three hundred years, we headed downstream toward Moose Factory, the only difference being that outboard motors had replaced paddles.

We were in the lead canoe. Our guide, a Métis of Cree-French ancestry, was head of our small flotilla (in fur trade days he would have been called the *bourgeois*; also in his capacity as steersman he would have been known as the *gouvernail* of his canoe).

In early September the Moose River was shallow in many places—our guide called it a dry river, and it required keen reading of the water and adroit maneuvering to avoid getting hung up on the sandbars just under the surface. To have done so would have been a serious blow to his pride and reputation. We passed the wide mouth of the mighty Abitibi River, one of the main tributaries of the Moose, flowing in from the east. A little later we reached the junction of the French and Moose rivers. Here was a Cree encampment built on a high bluff where we spent the night. We didn't exactly rough it—we didn't sleep on the ground in a tepee or eat dried moose meat; instead, we feasted on roast chicken and slept on comfortable cots in a cabin.

After supper we gathered outside on the high bank around a small campfire, content to absorb the peace and beauty of the scene before us. Shortly before twilight, far off in the distance we heard the faint cries of geese and eventually spotted a small flock flying toward the south. A Cree lad ten or twelve years of age stepped over to the edge of the bluff and, using nothing but his voice, began to call to the geese. Incredibly, they turned and headed toward us. Several times they veered back southward, but each time the boy's renewed calling brought them around headed in our direction until finally they circled overhead and dropped down among the boulders along the riverbank just below us. In an instant the young Cree had scrambled down the bank; then, very slowly worming his way flat on his belly, and using every boulder as a shield, he approached closer and closer to the unsuspecting birds. Finally, after what seemed an interminably long time, he rose, there was the sound of a gunshot, and a goose was killed. This was truly a remarkable demonstration of the Crees' well-known ability to call or, as they say, "talk down" the geese. During the fall goose season, when sportsmen from all over come to James Bay for the shooting, the Crees are in great demand as guides because of this talent.

Early the next morning, strengthened by a hearty breakfast, we embarked in our canoe and, aided by the swift current of the river, soon reached Factory Island—our final destination. This is where Moose Factory is located. The island is about eight miles long and two and one-half miles wide and is situated in the Moose River about twelve miles from James Bay.

Moose Factory was the second trading post established by the newly formed Hudson's Bay Company. Encouraged by the success of the first trading venture to the east side of the bay and the establishment of Rupert House, the company sent out other trading expeditions. In 1672 under Governor Bayly, a small post was built on an island in the Moose River. This fort consisted merely of a stockade with four bastions and a small house in the center of the enclosed courtyard.

A year later, the volume of trade and the superior merits of its location, which offered an easier and safer access for ships plus a closer proximity to the rich fur lands of the interior, resulted in Moose Factory superseding Rupert House as the principal post at the bottom of the bay.

During the next few years, reflecting this new status, the post was materially enlarged and strengthened, so that by 1683 it presented a most formidable defense to any would-be attackers. It consisted of a square compound 130 feet on a side, surrounded by a sixteen- to eighteen-foot-high palisade, with a bastion equipped with cannon on each corner. A strong redoubt, also mounting cannon, faced the river. The great gate, the main entrance into the fort on the river side, was half a foot thick, studded with large nails and reinforced with bars and hinges of iron.

As we stepped ashore in front of the Hudson's Bay store—the modern successor to all those previous posts stretching back three hundred years—we were confronted with a group of curious but friendly Indians, mostly children. We soon discovered that it was not our arrival that was the attraction; rather, it was the presence of an ancient fur press and two old cannon standing in the open grassy area between the store and the river. These relics, which historians (and ourselves) would view with a mixture of great interest and respect, were serving as an admirable substitute for playground recreational equipment—great for climbing over and on and under. Furthermore, throughout the North the Hudson's Bay Company store has always been and is to this day the focal point of the community—the natural place for people to gather and visit. So much for the presence of our "welcoming" committee.

After a brief stop at the Hudson's Bay store to buy film, of which we always seemed to be in need, we walked over to the post manager's (formerly known as the chief factor's) house close by. It was a neat white building, its plainness transformed by a backyard full of beautiful flowers. The profusion of vivid colors brightened up the entire area. We wondered who it was who had wrought such a miracle in the face of the harsh north climate.

Next door stands the venerable Hudson's Bay Company staff house, built in 1820. It is recognizable by its white clapboard exterior, small-paned windows, and traditional red roof. On a tall pole in front the three-century-old Hudson's Bay Company flag still proudly flies. We were delighted to be allowed to go inside this historic building and join others in the dining room for lunch. In our imagination, it was easy to picture the tables crowded with Hudson's Bay Company employees, "servants," as they were then called, traders, missionaries, ships' captains, and visiting dignitaries, the room ringing with the animated sound of conversation in English, French, and Cree.

A short distance from the Hudson's Bay Company complex is the old graveyard. Partially surrounded by a broken-down, weather-beaten picket fence, it is the last resting place for many of the company servants and their families and for the local Cree Indians. Age and weathering have rendered much of the lettering on many of the tombstones illegible, but we were able to decipher the headstone of Bishop John Horden, first Anglican bishop of Moosonee, and of Richard Robins, an early surgeon at the fort. The names and dates on the Thomas family stone read like a litany of sorrow and reflect the harsh conditions of life at Moose Factory: Edward, 1801–02; Mary, 1791–1802, lost on an ice floe; Richard, 1802–03; Jane, 1804–05. Yet in spite of the loss of all four of their children in the space of three years, the enduring and sustaining faith of their parents is affirmed in the final inscription: "The Lord giveth and the Lord taketh away. Blessed be the name of the Lord."

In an open field adjacent to the Hudson's Bay store and now designated as Centennial Park are two old buildings—relics from the busy fur trade days. The first is the forge, a small wooden building distinguished by its massive chimney. Inside is an immense open fire operated by twin bellows, one at each end. The other structure is the powder magazine, a windowless building of thick masonry walls with but one entrance.

Also in the park is a small museum containing interesting displays that graphically tell the story of Moose Factory from its founding in 1673 to the present.

One of the highlights of our visit to Moose Factory was attending a Sunday church service at St. Thomas Anglican Church. This lovely little church is perched beside the main dirt road that borders the river. It was built about 1860 of logs covered with clapboard and reflects the Gothic influence on architecture rather than the more restrained, balanced Georgian style of the Hudson's Bay buildings constructed a half-century earlier.

Inside, we were struck by the beauty of the altar, pulpit, and lectern frontals. Each was of moosehide, crafted by the local Cree women in lovely designs of wildflowers and waterfowl exquisitely wrought in porcupine quills.

We noticed numerous holes about one inch in diameter in the floor that had been plugged with wooden plugs. We learned that in the spring, when the water of the Moose River rises to great heights due to backup from ice jams, sometimes flooding the island, the floor plugs are pulled out. This allows floodwaters to drain out, which prevents the church from being washed off its foundation and swept out into the river, as indeed had happened some years earlier.

The resident priest was a Cree who conducted two services, one in Cree and one in English. As we sat on this Sunday in early September listening to his sermon on God's goodness toward his people by providing beasts of the field and fowl of the air for their food, the air outside was filled with the loud clamor of thousands of geese. These geese are the main source of food for the Cree. Each fall they gather on their traditional centuries-old feeding grounds in James Bay. It was a present-day reminder that God was, indeed, still providing for his people.

As we left the church and walked along the dusty road, we were overtaken by a car and offered a ride down to the dock where the Indians in their Rupert House freighter canoes vie with each other for passengers going to Moosonee on the mainland. During our brief ride, we learned that our kindly benefactors were Mr. and Mrs. J. J. Wood. Mr. Wood, a longtime Hudson's Bay employee, was the post manager at Moose Factory, a position he had held for more than twenty years. The mystery of the creator of the beautiful flower garden was also solved when, in response to our lavish praise, Mrs. Wood quietly admitted that she was the person responsible.

8

The next morning we woke up to a downpour of rain, gray skies, and a cold wind. We had made arrangements the previous evening with Chief Archibald of the Moose band to go with him on a fishing trip up the Moose River. I'm sure he expected us to back out, but we had no such intention. So, dressed in all the warm clothes and rain gear that we possessed, we soon left Moosonee behind us and were on our way up the river to some rapids reputedly good for walleyes. It was raining so hard we could see very little of the surrounding country, we caught no fish when we finally arrived at the rapids, and we were beginning to shiver with the cold. Chief Archibald, however, rose to the occasion magnificently. We landed on a narrow, sandy beach, and within an incredibly short time he had a cheerful fire blazing, a canvas canopy erected, and a big panful of beautiful walleye fillets he had caught the previous day sizzling over the fire. We could hardly wait to eat the fish and drink the steaming mugs of strong tea. What a feast! So, warmed, dried, and fed, we made the return trip still in the pouring rain in high spirits. During our day with Chief Archibald we talked about many things and learned much from him about the customs of his people—their beliefs, their problems, and their ways of hunting. In response to our real interest, he promised to give us one of his goose head decoys. As several days elapsed and no decoy, we thought he had forgotten his offer. But on our last day, just as we were about to board the southbound Polar Bear Express for our trip home, up he rushed with the decoy, his promise faithfully kept.

Albany House

We wanted to visit the site of Albany House, so we chartered a plane to fly the ninety miles up the west side of James Bay from Moosonee to Albany River. Here in 1679 the Hudson's Bay Company established their third post. It was one more link in the company's plan to encircle the bay with posts conveniently located for the fur trade with the Indians.

Originally it was simply a crude rectangular building in the center of a 100-foot-square cleared area surrounded by a palisade. Its defenses were substantially strengthened during the next several years, so that by 1685 it had become a well-designed structure consisting of a palisaded enclosure approximately one hundred feet by eighty-five feet with a bastion at each corner and two substantial buildings averaging forty-one feet by twenty-four feet whose rear walls formed part of the north and south palisade walls. Dr. Walter Kenyon of the Royal Ontario Museum, whose archaeological work at Fort Albany has uncovered the layout of the fort and revealed much of its long history, noted that "the entire . . . fort because of its shape, every inch of its outer walls could be covered by musket-fire from within."

We flew along the coast, the seemingly endless waters of James Bay on our right and on our left the flat muskeg country dotted here and there with scattered stunted black spruce along the many rivers slowly coursing through the lowlands toward the bay. Except for the long, straight lines crisscrossing the muskeg made by caterpillar tractors—lines that would remain as scars on the landscape for many years—the scene was unchanged from that first seen by the early English and French newcomers.

In response to our buzzing the tiny hamlet of Albany Fort, a decrepit rattletrap "car" came to pick us up and drive us the short distance into the settlement. We had been told to be sure to meet Bill Anderson, a real "old-timer" and an independent trader. As we stepped into his store, we entered the 1850s. The dark, low-ceilinged building had a long counter on one side; the rest of the area was totally filled with tables covered with piles of clothing, including coats and jackets; on the floor were boxes, barrels, and crates of all sizes and shapes. Shelves on the walls were loaded with housewares and miscellaneous items of all kinds. Rubber boots, tools, shovels, pails, and snowshoes hung from the ceiling beams. Bill Anderson's store was stocked to satisfy all the needs of his Cree customers. Indeed, he was even their banker. While we were in the store gazing in admiration at a pair of moosehide gauntlets trimmed with beaver and decorated with exquisite beadwork (which we subsequently bought), a number of the local Cree people began coming in. They had apparently just received their government allotment checks and wanted to cash them. Bill brought out an old-style battered cardboard suitcase, which he laid on the counter. He opened it up and to our astonishment, we could see both sides were crammed full with neat bundles of currency. One by one the people stepped up to the counter and handed their checks to Bill, who then in return counted out the equivalent in cash. It was apparent that Bill Anderson had their trust as well as much of their trade.

We needed a canoe to go the short distance up Fishing Creek to the site of Albany House. Unfortunately, a canoe was not available and, as our time was limited, we could not wait for one to return. However, our pilot was resourceful and after ascertaining the time of the tide change agreed to taxi us in the plane the short distance up Fishing Creek to our site. So back we went via the same rattletrap car to the plane, and soon we were slowly and cautiously taxiing up the narrow creek to the site of the old post. The physical evidence of the old fort was quite evident. Traces of a ditch surrounding a flat space of approximately one hundred feet square were visible, as were several depressions marking the location of old cellars and a concentration of bricks.

Alerted by the pilot that the tide in the river would soon turn to begin its ebb flow, we quickly slithered down the steep bank onto the plane floats, scrambled inside, and were soon airborne, headed back toward Moosonee, our mission successfully accomplished.

Historically, the establishment by the Hudson's Bay Company of three forts—Rupert House, Albany House, and Moose Factory —around the perimeter of the bay did not go unnoticed by the French of New France. They, too, were desirous of tapping the rich fur resources of the North. To meet the threat posed by the French traders, the Hudson's Bay Company transferred their posts built for trading purposes into fortifications strong enough to withstand attacks from both Indians and French.

The English fears of French aggression were soon realized. In March 1686 a force of one hundred men and five officers in thirty-five canoes under the command of Chevalier de Troyes and three of the illustrious LeMoyne brothers left Montreal on an expedition whose objective was to wipe out the English forts at the bottom of the bay.

Benefiting from the strong element of surprise, the French were first able to overpower Moose Factory. Quickly following up on their success, they moved eastward to Rupert House. Once again, daring coupled with surprise enabled them to capture not only the fort but also the English ship moored in the river directly in front of the post.

Before leaving the fallen fort, they burned it to the ground. Not until 1776, nearly one hundred years later, was Rupert House reestablished to begin its unbroken history down to the present day.

Next de Troyes and his men pointed their canoes up the west side of James Bay toward Albany Fort. Here luck and the total unawareness by the English of any enemy presence in the bay enabled the French to mount a well-placed battery overlooking the fort, which rendered resistance futile and surrender inevitable.

Thus within the space of four months the three Hudson Bay forts at the bottom of the bay, heavily fortified though they were, fell into the hands of the French.

For the next twenty-seven years the bay was the scene of an unceasing struggle between the French and English for control of the bay and its lucrative fur trade. Possession of the forts seesawed back and forth between them. Finally, in 1713, the Treaty of Utrecht, recognizing the English claim to prior possession, confirmed their title to the bay and restored it to them.

We had long wanted to see York Factory, the fourth bay post to be established by the Hudson's Bay Company. We knew there were but two ways to get there—air and water. We decided to go by water. This would give us an opportunity to retrace the historic waterway that linked York Factory on the bay to the interior at Lake Winnipeg.

This route via Hayes River and through Oxford, Knee, and Swampy lakes had been found, after much early trial and error by the fur traders, to be the most navigable. For nearly two hundred years over its waters and portages had gone countless tons of provisions and trade goods and thousands of bales of furs. It became the main highway from the bay into and out of the country and as such was used by voyageurs, explorers, Hudson's Bay Company "servants" and "gentlemen," missionaries, scientists, and early settlers. Every inch of this river would be peopled with the ghosts of these travelers. We looked forward with much anticipation to following behind them.

Fortunately, Jack Clarkson of North Country River Trips, Manitoba, was able to arrange such a trip for us. We agreed to yield to twentieth-century convenience by using a twenty-foot inflatable rubber raft instead of a canoe and a ten-horsepower motor instead of paddles. We began our journey at Norway House, a Hudson's Bay post at the northeast end of Lake Winnipeg, the traditional western terminal of the river.

Norway House

Norway House is of much interest as one of the major early Hudson's Bay Company posts. First built in 1796, it is still in operation today serving the needs of the local Indians. After two earlier sites had been successively abandoned, the third Norway House was built during 1826–28 in its present location on the east side of Jack River at its junction with Playgreen Lake. Its main purpose was primarily as a central distributing and transfer point for the company's transport system rather than as a post for trading of furs. It was strategically located at the crossroads of converging brigade routes to and from York Factory to the east, Red River to the south, Saskatchewan River to the west, and the Athabasca River country to the north.

In addition to being the hub of the company's transport system, its central location (considerably more convenient and accessible than York Factory) resulted in its inevitable emergence as an inland administration center.

Here, beginning in 1833, the Governor and the Northern Council, composed of all chief factors who were able to attend, as well as chief traders (the latter without voting rights), met in annual session. At this time decisions regulating the business for the ensuing year were made and punctiliously recorded in the company's Minute Books. Assignment of personnel to posts was made; the number of canoes and amount of goods for each post determined, arrangements for an adequate supply of provisions to fuel the brigades made, promotions in rank announced (these were subject, however, to approval by the London Committee), furloughs granted or refused, and policy decisions regarding the natives, the missionaries, the competition, and use or nonuse of liquor formulated. The Standard of Trade (i.e., the number of beaver pelts required to buy each trade item) was reviewed; complaints about any trade goods found to be of poor quality were voiced; discipline problems were resolved. The list of matters handled was a long one. But there was still time for fun—R and R, as we would term it today. Feasts and dances were popular and enjoyed by both the commissioned gentlemen and the men of the brigades.

Under the competent leadership of Chief Factor Donald Ross, who served as its manager for twenty-one years, Norway House with its many buildings reflected its position of importance. The major buildings were constructed around a rectangular grassy compound that was bisected by a raised wooden walkway connecting the archway warehouse on the west or river side to the principal residences on the opposite side. On the northern perimeter were the boatbuilding shop, fur store, storehouse, and guest house; facing these to the south were the provision store, sales shop, storage depot, and jail. To the north and to the south of the compound were extensive kitchen gardens.

Because of the skill of its carpenters in building York boats, Norway House early on became known as the center for the production of these craft. Indeed, this traditional activity continued uninterrupted until 1923, when the last two were built.

By the 1870s the importance of Norway House began to decline. The advent and rapid spread of railroads and steamboats with their cheaper rates soon made the old time-honored Hudson Bay–Hayes River–Norway House route obsolete. Trade goods no longer came down from York Factory. As a consequence, Norway House ceased to function as a primary transfer and distribution center and was reduced to becoming merely the central post in a relatively minor trading district, supplying the needs of the local inhabitants.

Although most of the original buildings of the Hudson's Bay post are now gone, one still survives—an impressive reminder of days past. This is the archway warehouse, so called because of the wide arched passageway through the center of the building. Erected in 1840, this seventy-foot-by-twenty-seven-foot building embodies the fine sense of proportion as well as soundness of construction that characterized many of the Hudson's Bay Company buildings wherever they were erected. The traditional red-hipped roof and red trim framing, the small-paned windows, and the white walls present a most pleasing appearance. Perched on top of the roof is a small belfry housing a bell of much historical interest. This bell bears the following inscription: "Ship 'Sea Horse', launched March 30th, 1782, Hudson's Bay Company." The bell was rung three times daily—morning, noon, and night—as well as on special occasions.

As we walked through the passageway, we admired the sturdy hand-hewn ceiling beams, the wide, well-worn floorboards, the warm patina of the spruce walls, the massive iron lock and hinges on the doors, and the graceful arch over the opening.

We stood in the opening of the passageway looking down the wooden boardwalk leading to the Jack River a few yards distant. The scene we were watching could easily have been a replay of 150 years ago. A steady stream of Crees of all ages was flowing between the modern Hudson's Bay store next to the ancient warehouse and the many boats lined up on the shore. To further complete the illusion, a York boat partially submerged but still colorful in its faded red paint was beached by the company dock. To be sure, white plastic shopping bags

14

and six- or twelve-packs had replaced burlap bales, wooden crates, and barrels, but the age-old pattern of trade was still continuing unchanged.

One other relic from the past still remains. Immediately to the rear of the warehouse is the jail, a small white-washed masonry structure with walls two feet thick. Built in 1855, it now serves as a storage place for the company's petroleum products.

In 1843 Augustus Peers, a young newly arrived clerk, wrote in his diary found in the British Columbia archives: "Norway House stands on the bank of Jack River at its junction with Playgreen Lake. The fort, which is built of wood, is enclosed with high stockades. The houses are all of one story high, and being whitewashed present a very neat and pleasing appearance. In front is a green enclosure, intersected by platforms, the main one leading down to the river through the principal store."

Life at Norway House in 1841 is well summed up by Robert M. Ballantyne in his book *Hudson's Bay, or Every-Day Life in the Wilds of North America*. He wrote:

> Norway House is also an agreeable and interesting place, from its being in a manner the gate to the only route to Hudson's Bay; so that, during the spring and summer months, all the brigades of boats and canoes from every part of the Northern Department must necessarily pass it on their way to York Factory with furs; and as they all return in the autumn, and some of the gentlemen leave their wives and families for a few weeks till they return to the interior, it is at this sunny season of the year quite a gay and bustling place; and the clerk's house in which I lived was often filled with a strange and always noisy collection of human beings, who rested here awhile ere they started for the shores of Hudson's Bay, the distant regions of M'Kenzie's River, or the still more distant land of Oregon.

There was another place nearby closely linked to the story of Norway House that we wanted to visit. This was Rossville, a small Cree village about two miles by water from Norway House. Here, in 1842, a Methodist mission with the Reverend James Evans as pastor was established. This minister is remembered chiefly for two things. First, he devised a system of writing known as Cree syllabics. He was able to represent all the sounds of the Cree language by fewer than fifty syllabic characters. Necessity being the mother of invention, Evans contrived to make a primitive printing press from an old fur press, cut out type from the lead lining Hudson's Bay tea chests, and made ink from chimney soot; for paper he used birchbark. Thus equipped, he printed

5,000 pages of religious material for the instruction of the Cree people of the region.

The second thing for which James Evans is remembered is his tin canoe. Lacking a birch bark canoe or the means to purchase one, he fabricated a canoe of sorts made from sheets of tin. In spite of its unconventional appearance, it proved seaworthy and he was able to travel the thousands of miles required by his missionary work to the Indians without serious mishap. His friend Chief Factor Donald Ross, however, called it a "Tin Machine" and said no amount of gold would ever induce him to step into it.

We were able to make arrangements with a local Cree who agreed to take us in his boat over to Rossville. Soon we were standing on the small windswept point that extends into Playgreen Lake. This point is bare except for the 1861 Rossville Church and, some distance away, a small weather-beaten cenotaph dedicated to the memory of the Reverend James Evans and to mark the site of his first church, erected in 1841. The inscription is almost beyond deciphering, and the likeness of Evans is nearly beyond recognition. However, a better and more lasting memorial and one that will always survive is his Cree syllabics system—the system that enables the Cree people to write and read in their language.

On our return to Norway House we passed the simple weather-beaten Anglican church on the west bank of the Jack River. Apparently service had just concluded, for a large number of people were still gathered outside. Our boatman explained that this was an important day for the local Crees. The Anglican bishop was making his annual pastoral visit, so everyone had turned out for the occasion. This explained the large number of small boats drawn up on the shore, boats being the only way of getting to the church. The bishop, on the other hand, arrived by the diocesan plane—perhaps the twentieth-century descendant of James Evans's tin canoe.

Three hundred and seventy-five miles and eleven days later, we ended our trip at York Factory on the western shore of Hudson Bay. During that time we traveled over the same lakes, down the same rivers, ran the same rapids, and made many of the same portages as the voyageurs before us. The sights we saw were virtually the same as those seen by them, for the country is little changed.

For example, there is Robinson's Falls. Here the waters of the Hayes, compressed into a narrow rock-walled gorge, thunder down a forty-five-foot drop. It is a place of great beauty. Large pines tower

16

above. The river flings its foaming white water over three descending terraces into a lovely pool below whose beauty (at the time we were there) was enhanced with an abundance of lovely white water lilies.

It is also still a place where a backbreaking portage must be made. As we plodded along a well-beaten path, worn deep into the moss, carrying our gear down to the lower end of the falls, it was easy to picture the husky voyageurs, bent under their load of two ninety-pound bales jogging across this self-same path 150 years ago. Here we were, indeed, literally following in their footsteps. In the mid-1800s the Hudson's Bay Company, because of the length and difficulty of this portage, constructed a mile-long tramway to facilitate the movement of goods and men around the falls. Traces of this old tramway are still visible.

Farther along we entered the picturesque mile stretch known as Hill Gates. Here the river is so constricted by eighty-foot-high rocky cliffs that the voyageurs in their ponderous York boats were unable to use their oars. In an early effort to improve the transportation system, for certain portions of the Hayes River route York boats, capable of carrying three tons of cargo, had replaced canoes. The York boats were large wooden craft, pointed at bow and stern, equipped with heavy oars of great length. Downstream the current would carry them through, but upstream was quite a different story. No wonder this section of the Hayes was often known as Hell Gates.

Midpoint of our trip was Oxford Lake, a large, very deep lake studded with a multitude of islands of all sizes and shapes. It was at this point that the sunny, pleasant weather we had been enjoying deserted us. It turned cold, windy, and rainy. Our provisions were nearly exhausted. Worse, the gauge on the gas tank was hovering near the empty mark, and Oxford House, our goal for supplies and gas, was about thirty miles away. We kept going, making our traverses from point to point on as straight a course as possible, so as to conserve every drop of gasoline. It was rapidly getting dark—rain dripped from the brims of our hats, down our backs, and through our so-called rainproof suits. The prospect of pitching a wet camp for the night loomed closer.

Just when our spirits were at low ebb, we saw racing down the lake, engine at full throttle, an Indian going out to check his fish nets. We managed to attract his attention, and he came over to our raft. Although he couldn't speak English, by means of signs, smiles, and Canadian currency we succeeded in getting three gallons of gas transferred from his boat to ours. Much relieved, we continued on our way, and just as it was getting really dark we saw the scattered lights of Oxford

House twinkling ahead and were soon tied up at the Roman Catholic mission dock. Here we received the warm hospitality that is so very typical throughout the north country. A hot bath, warm food, a place to dry our sodden clothes, a soft bed—things really looked rosy again.

Oxford House

The next morning, rested and refreshed, we proceeded down the lake the short distance to the Hudson's Bay store. Perched at the top of a gentle rise and overlooking the lake stretching away to the south, this post has been serving the needs of the local Crees and the fur trade traffic ever since its founding in 1798.

Oxford House, strategically located at the eastern outlet of Oxford Lake, was the major staging post on the Hayes River route midway between York Factory and Lake Winnipeg. In addition to being the chief storehouse and supply depot, it developed a flourishing agricultural operation, so that it was able to provide the fur trade with ever-welcome vegetables, grains, potatoes, and dairy products. It was a very popular stopping-off place with the men of the brigades. They took full advantage of the comforts and pleasures it offered.

Robert Ballantyne, a teenage clerk in the employ of the Hudson's Bay Company, described Oxford House as he saw it in 1845:

> It is built on the brow of a grassy hill, which rises gradually from the margin of Oxford Lake. Like most of the posts in the country, it is composed of a collection of wooden houses, built in the form of a square, and surrounded by tall stockades, pointed at the tops. These, however, are more for ornament than defense. A small flagstaff towers above the buildings, from which, upon the occasion of an arrival, a little red Hudson's Bay Company's flag waves its tiny folds in the gentle current of an evening breeze. There were only two or three men at the place; and not a human being, save one or two wandering Indians, was to be found within hundreds of miles of this desolate spot.

Isaac Cowie, making the trip from York Factory to Lake Winnipeg twenty years later in 1867, had the following to say about Oxford House in his book *The Company of Adventurers:* "We reached Oxford House on Holey (not Holy as it is often spelt) Lake that evening, and spent the next day there, refitting. The post stands on high ground at some distance from the water's edge, and commands a lovely view of the lake and its varied islands. There were fields off which fine crops of barley and potatoes had been taken, and a garden which produced all common vegetables of first-rate quality . . . Of course our boatman took advantage of their stay there to invite the belles from the bush to an all-night dance, and the thumping of their jigging feet reached our camp on the lakeside all through the stilly night."

Usually, regardless of the request, the Hudson's Bay store was able to supply all needs, but this time through some twentieth-century bureaucratic or perhaps computer mix-up the one item we desperately needed, i.e., toilet paper, although ordered by the store manager, had not been included in the weekly airlift of supplies from Winnipeg. Oh well, moss would have to do!

We spent several hours wandering around the small settlement. It was interesting to see the older generation represented by the elderly women wearing shapeless "Mother Hubbards," moccasins, and head shawls pulling little wagons loaded with their weekly supply of groceries down the dusty road from the store to their homes. In contrast, the younger generation, dressed in blue jeans, dashed about in beat-up, rickety pickups crammed to overflowing with kids, grown-ups, dogs, and groceries. I noticed a very pretty little Cree girl trying to balance a big box of Pampers on the handlebar of her bicycle and thought, *You've come a long way, baby* from the moss-filled diaper bags of olden days.

We were especially interested in seeing the newly erected modern shop where the Crees, utilizing their traditional skills, were manufacturing snowshoes. With the aid of some initial government funding for the building, steam-box, and necessary tools, they have organized into a company that at this time (1980) employed twenty men.

Twelve miles below Oxford House, we came to Trout Falls, a ten-foot waterfall of great beauty. We pitched our tents on the only suitable spot available—an expanse of flat, bare rock at the head of the falls. After supper as we sat around the campfire and watched the smoke from our cooking fire slowly ascending into the night sky, I wondered how many others had been here before us and had, like us, sat around their campfires and watched the smoke spiral upward to disappear among the bright stars above. Here, indeed, on this very rock ledge must have sat the nameless voyageurs, as well as the well-known people such as Sir George Simpson, Sir Alexander Mackenzie, Sir John Franklin, David Thompson, and Dr. John McLoughlin—almost a complete roll call of fur trade giants.

That night sleep would not come. For me, at least, the presence of too many spirits of the past was felt. Restless, I crawled out of my tent and, instead of encountering ghosts, saw a marvelous display of northern lights. Luminous curtains of pale green, yellow, and pink rose and fell, sometimes slowly and gently, sometimes with incredible speed racing across the sky. Often these swirling curtains seemed to swoop down and touch the earth. Awestruck, I watched and marveled, capturing this spectacle in my memory to last forever.

The next morning we carried our gear to the lower end of the falls,

Jack safely rode the empty raft down the chute, and after a breakfast augmented by freshly caught walleyes we were soon on our way.

Before long we reached forty-mile-long Knee Lake, so named because of a bend about midway where its waters are pinched into a narrows and its direction changed by nearly ninety degrees. The western half was full of lovely pine-and-spruce-covered islands of all sizes, each a potential place of refuge in the event of a storm. The eastern half offered no such protection. There were no islands on its vast expanse. We were fortunate—the sky remained blue, the sun continued to shine, and although the wind blew and waves often broke over the bow, we made the crossing without mishap.

Swampy Lake, merely a widening of the Hayes River, came next. We made a brief landing on the west shore and discovered a clearing and a trace of an old building foundation that might have been the site of Logan's Depot, a minor trading post established by the Hudson's Bay Company sometime between 1816 and 1819.

Under date of August 20, 1821, Nicholas Garry in his diary noted: "Entered Swampy Lake about 9 miles in length. Passed Logan's Depot on the west side, now deserted. Four wooded buildings in excellent order." In 1819 Sir John Franklin referred to it as "this cheerless abode."

The eastern extremity of Swampy Lake marks the beginning of the fifty-mile stretch where the Hayes, by means of almost continuous rapids, descends nearly five-sevenths of its total drop to the sea.

The going was fast, thrilling, and always beautiful. Each rapid was different and offered a new challenge. Some presented a simple straight run-through; others were wickedly deceptive. Each required the correct reading of the water and the necessary skill to keep the raft under control.

It was not always easy to determine which channel to follow, for in many places there was little to indicate the proper course. We followed the wrong channel just once, but that mistake cost us a half-day's loss of time and a lot of backbreaking work in retracing our way.

At about mile 250, with the long series of rapids behind us, the Hayes broke out of the rocky Precambrian shield country and entered the flat alluvial Hudson Bay lowlands. Steep banks of clay replaced the weathered lichen-covered rocky cliffs. Trees dwindled in size and number. Vigorous stands of pine, spruce, and poplar gave way to a sparse fringe of spindly black spruce bordering the unbroken reach of northern muskeg stretching back from the river. This was, truly, "the land of the little sticks."

Everywhere huge sections of bank had been sheared off, witness to the instability of the soil and to the terrific scouring power of the ice and river at the time of the spring breakup. Now the river broadened out, its volume augmented by the flow from two main tributaries, the Fox and God's rivers. This increased flow resulted in speeding the current to nearly eight miles per hour.

Late in the afternoon of the tenth day we reached tidewater. Here the struggle began. The force of the current carrying us downstream collided head-on with the incoming tide from the bay. In brief, we were caught in a powerful riptide made worse by strong head winds. Choppy waves continually broke over the raft, drenching us all. It seemed as though we were barely holding our own. However, slowly, ever so slowly, we did advance and finally, after about three hours, headed into the mouth of Ten Shilling Creek, a small tributary of the Hayes, just a couple of miles above our final destination of York Factory and the location of the well-known York Factory Goose Camp, where we found shelter and food.

York Factory

The story of York Factory spans two and one-half centuries. After a failed earlier attempt made in 1670, an expedition headed by Governor George Geyer succeeded twelve years later in building a post on the north bank of Hayes River about one and one-half miles upstream from the bay. This was the beginning of a settlement destined to last for 275 years, to be abandoned only in 1957.

The fort built by Geyer was a substantial one, for the danger of attack by the French was clearly recognized. There were four wooden bastions, one at each corner of a thirty-foot square enclosed by a palisade of vertical logs. A large two-story warehouse stood in the center. The trading store was in one bastion, the supply store in a second. Quarters for the garrison were in the remaining two. In addition, there were two other bastions—in one of which the officers lodged; in the other were the kitchen and forge. Firepower for the fort consisted of thirty-two cannon and fourteen swivel guns. Since no attack was anticipated from the woods and marshy muskeg in the rear, all the armament faced the river in the front.

In spite of the strength of the fortifications, Iberville once again proved to be the nemesis of the English. In 1694 he was able to approach from the rear, land his men, and mount batteries trained on the fort. After three days of bombardment, the English surrendered. French victory was short-lived, however, for two years later the English under Governor Knight recaptured the post, only to lose it the following year to whom else but Iberville.

This occurred in one of the most striking naval battles of the time. Iberville had reached the estuary of the Nelson River and was awaiting the arrival of his three companion ships, which had fallen behind due to a storm. Suddenly he was confronted with the sight of three well-armed English ships swiftly bearing down upon him. Outgunned and outmanned, the French commander attacked vigorously and by a brilliant display of courage, skill, and daring sank one of the enemy ships, captured the second, and put the third to flight. This exploit secured for Iberville a hero's renown in French Canada that endures to this day. When the French ships finally appeared several days later, York Factory could no longer hold out and it fell into the hands of the French, where it remained until sixteen years later, in 1713, when by the Treaty of Utrecht it, along with three other bay posts, was restored to the English.

Early the next morning, rested and refreshed, we quickly made the short trip from the goose camp to York Factory, situated on the north side of the Hayes River—the place we had worked so hard to reach. We beached our raft for the last time and eagerly scrambled up the steep, slippery clay bank. In front of us was what we had come so far to see—a solitary huge white structure, all that remains today of a once proud and busy fort complex crowded with buildings and people.

This building, now painted white with dark green trim, was known by the Cree as "Kichiwaskahegun," meaning "Great House." It is built in the shape of a 102-foot-by-106-foot square with an open courtyard in the center. It is two stories high, with the exception of a three-story central section surmounted by an enclosed hexagonal look-out tower. Out front, between the building and the rapidly eroding bank, is a tall flagpole rigged as a mast. Subsequent to our visit this flagstaff has toppled over and has not been reerected. An old ship's cannon is still in place maintaining its lonely vigil over the bay.

We opened one of the main doors, thick and nail-studded, noting as we did so the elaborate wrought-iron hinges and the huge hand-forged latch and escutcheon. As we stepped inside, the empty rooms echoed to our footsteps. Light filtered through the rows of small-paned windows, shedding a soft, warm glow on the spruce walls worn smooth with age and partially revealing the great square-hewn beams strengthened by huge hand-carved knees, which spanned the vast 100-foot-long halls. Massiveness, honesty, and soundness of construction were clearly evident throughout the entire building.

On the ground floor were the trading room; the ice room, with a dirt floor where frozen meat and fish were kept; and the receiving room, where the wooden boxes, bales, and kegs unloaded from the ship were stored until they could be sorted and repacked into outfits for the interior posts; as well as several other general supply and storerooms. The long lofts were on the second floor, where the furs were stored, graded, and pressed into ninety-pound bales.

We climbed the steep, narrow, well-worn stairway leading to the turret. From this vantage point the view over the surrounding muskeg and bay extended clear to the far horizon in all directions. From here, the arriving ships from England would first be spotted.

After the restoration of York Factory to the English in 1713, there was comparative peace for seventy years. Under the able leadership of a series of capable Governors such as James Knight, Henry Kelsey, James Isham, Ferdinand Jacobs, and Humphrey Marten, the fort was strengthened and enlarged. Their attempts to halt the incessant warfare between warring tribes (particularly the Chipewyan and Cree) that prevented their trapping beaver were successful. Slowly the Hudson's Bay Company people stationed at the post were learning to live on the local resources of game and fish instead of depending on the foods brought in at great expense by the ships from England. Finally, the policy of expecting the Indians to bring their furs down to the bay to trade was gradually changing to one of establishing posts inland, the better to meet the growing competition from the French traders who were increasingly successful in getting the furs from the Indians by intercepting them on their way down to York Factory.

In 1783 there occurred a brief setback—the last attempt by the French to gain possession of the bay. La Pérouse, encouraged by his capture and destruction of Prince of Wales' Fort at the mouth of the Churchill River, set sail for York Factory. Using the same approach as Iberville had done almost one hundred years ago, La Pérouse successfully attacked the fort from the rear. York Factory was burned to the ground, but it was a hollow victory. The Governor managed to outwit the French. He saved the bulk of his furs by smuggling them onto the company ship, which adroitly eluded the French and slipped safely away for England.

The Treaty of Paris in that same year (1783) brought hostilities to an end. York Factory was restored to the English and was quickly rebuilt. For the remainder of its existence, cannon were no longer needed for defense—their sounds were only heard as salutes to approaching and departing ships. The cannon used to salute ships were left at the post by the Sixth Regiment of Foot on their way to Red River in 1846.

For almost the next seventy-five years York Factory was the hub of the Hudson's Bay Company's operation. It was the port of entry for the yearly supply ship from England with its cargo of goods for the Indian trade as well as of provisions for the company's trading posts established throughout the interior of the country. It was also the port of shipment for the wealth of furs harvested each year.

The furs brought down from the far interior by the brigades had to be carefully sorted, graded, and then pressed into ninety-pound bales.

It was the company's accounting center, keeping many clerks busy from dawn to dusk handling the enormous amounts of paperwork that had to be completed, all painstakingly written by hand. Accounts had to be balanced, daily journals completed, invoices checked against cargo manifests, indents for next year's supplies prepared, and volumes of correspondence written (with at least one copy for each).

It was the great depot where supplies and trade goods were warehoused before being sorted and packed into outfits destined for the many posts scattered throughout the country. It was also for many years the place where the annual meetings of the Northern Council, the governing body presided over by Sir George Simpson, were held.

In its heyday (about 1850) York Factory usually had a complement of forty servants, five clerks, one postmaster, plus commissioned officers ("gentlemen," in Hudson's Bay Company parlance). This number was substantially increased during the summer months with the arrival of the brigades from the interior and during the brief periods of frenzied activity, usually in September, when the annual ship was in port.

Among the most able Governors were William Tomison, Joseph Colen (memorable because of his introduction of the York boat into the Hayes River transportation system), John Ballenden, John George McTavish, and James Hargrave.

Over fifty buildings made up the fort complex. They were originally laid out in an *H* shape with the warehouse, guest house, and summer mess forming the center bar. The wings of the *H* were composed of fur stores, provision shops, trading rooms, and officers' and servants' quarters. In addition, there were many other buildings scattered about, including a boat shed, oil store, lumber house, icehouse, cooperage, blacksmith shop, bake house, net house, hospital, school, library, doctor's house, clergyman's residence, and Anglican church. To the north of the fort were the massive stone-walled powder magazine and the graveyard.

By 1860 the importance of York Factory began to decline, its days of glory fading. The advent of steamboats on the rivers and the ever-increasing extension of the railroads were responsible. Instead of sending goods by sea to York Factory, a distance of 3,000 miles from London, goods were directed to the much closer eastern seaboard and thence westward by rail, a much shorter and therefore cheaper route. River steamboats on the Saskatchewan, Peace, Athabasca, and Mackenzie replaced the canoe and York boat. Economics dictated that York Factory's function as chief port and distribution center end. The last brigade left York Factory for the interior in 1874.

Soon, even York Factory's place as the chief accounting center was terminated when that function was transferred to Upper Fort Garry at the forks of the Red and Assiniboine rivers.

During the last seventy-five years of its existence, York Factory was reduced to handling only the coastal trade of the bay and serving the needs of the local Cree. For a brief time it serviced posts below Split Lake and for a few years even became the headquarters of the newly created Nelson River district. However, the end came in 1957 when A.

B. McIvor, post manager, closed and locked the main door into the warehouse for the last time, turned his back, and walked away.

After 275 years of existence, York Factory had ceased to be. But perhaps not quite. York Factory is a national historic site, and Parks Canada is attempting to preserve what little is left of the once-proud fort. It will be a costly and difficult undertaking, but we think York Factory well merits that the attempt be made.

Churchill River Post

It was during the winter of 1619–20 that the Churchill River witnessed the arrival of the first white men. The Danish navigator Captain Jens Munck and a crew of sixty-four were sailing the waters of Hudson's Bay in search of the illusive Northwest Passage. The approach of winter forced them to look for a place of refuge. Fortunately, they discovered a large river flowing into the bay. This they ascended about four and one-half miles, to where they found a location suitable for establishing their winter quarters. Their stay there was short-lived and tragic. By springtime, scurvy and exposure to arctic cold had done their deadly work. Only the indomitable captain and two of his men had survived. Undaunted, these three managed to rig up one of their vessels and successfully sail it back to Denmark. The only witnesses to their sojourn on the shores of the Churchill River were the bodies of their fellow shipmates and a few abandoned cannon.

Sixty-eight years later (in 1688), attracted by the possibilities of a lucrative trade in whale oil from the large number of beluga whales present in the Churchill estuary as well as the prospect of capturing the fur trade of the Athabascan Indians, the Hudson's Bay Company sent an expedition under Thomas Savage as chief with eight men (including the eighteen-year-old Henry Kelsey) to establish a post on the Churchill River. The spot chosen was about two and one-half miles farther upstream from Munck's winter camp. After an auspicious start—twenty-eight casks (ten tons) of whale oil were shipped to London—the post was completely destroyed by fire the following year. The ongoing war with the French and other difficulties prevented its reestablishment until twenty-eight years later.

In the year 1717 James Knight, a most enterprising Governor, was instructed by the Hudson's Bay London Committee to reestablish the post on the Churchill River. The site chosen was on the north bank of the river on high ground protected by a rocky ridge in the rear—in fact, the very same spot where the ill-fated Danes had wintered nearly one hundred years earlier. The spot selected lacked both wood and water. The mudflats strewn with boulders prevented the near approach of ships. It offered no ground suitable for cultivation. Nevertheless, outweighing all these disadvantages were its excellent defensive capabilities.

A picture of the location is given most graphically in Governor Knight's own words:

Wee pitch'd our tents & I Gott my bedding ashore but was Wellcom'd by Such a Quantity of Musketos that as Soon as they light or wherever they fix they Sting like great Wasps that wee are nothing in the World but knotts & bumps our flesh is.

Saty 20 July. I burnt and Cleard a place where I Design the ffactory for to Stand, wch I believe to be the very place where Capt Monk built upon when he Wintred here, by the brass Gun & the Square peices of Cast Iron as wee have found thare . . . The place is the best in this River both for Landing of Goods & the house Standing, but here is no Good place at all.

Such was the site as chosen by Governor Knight. In a short time a simple trading house was erected and enclosed by a palisade with a bastion at each corner. For nearly thirty years this new post, officially named Prince of Wales' Fort, was the center of a thriving trade in furs and whale oil. As many as forty or more cargoes of furs arrived each summer, brought down by the Chipewyan.

Prince of Wales' Fort

In 1731 the Hudson's Bay Company, vividly remembering the earlier successes of Iberville and still acutely apprehensive of potential threat from the aggressive French, decided to replace this wooden Prince of Wales' Fort of Governor Knight's with a fort on the Churchill River that would be invincible. The site chosen was at the tip end of the rocky promontory at the mouth of the river on the west side. This tongue of land is surrounded on three sides by water; on the fourth side is a narrow gravel ridge. The flat, barren terrain affords perfect visibility in all directions.

This mighty undertaking required nearly forty years to complete. Its building spanned the terms of Governors Richard Norton, James Isham, Ferdinand Jacobs, and Moses Norton. It demanded an incredible amount of backbreaking manual labor carried out under the harshest of working conditions.

The design embodied the latest, most advanced military engineering concepts. Local quarried stone was used throughout the entire fortification: for walls, bastions, and interior structures. It was intended to be fireproof, and it was.

Basically, the plan was a 300-foot square with a massive arrow-shaped bastion protruding from each corner. Rampart walls forming a stone curtain between each bastion were fifteen feet high and twenty feet wide at the top and were surmounted with a five-foot parapet with forty-eight gun ports. The massive gateway leading into the fort was defended by a ravelin commanding the approach from the river. In the courtyard within the fortress walls were quarters for the Governor and for the men; a large warehouse; craft shops for carpenter, shipwright, armorer, and cooper; and a fifteen-foot-deep well. The four bastions housed, respectively, a storage room, carpenter shop, stable, and powder magazine. An outside wooden palisade 25 feet from the walls of stone completed the fortification.

Now, at last, the Hudson's Bay Company had a post that was invincible—impregnable to any and all attacks from the French. And even though defects in design and in construction were evident, such as a lack of proper mortar in bedding the masonry blocks, their confidence should have been justified.

On the eighth of August 1782 Samuel Hearne, Governor of the new fort, was astounded by the appearance of three ships of the line flying English colors at the mouth of the Churchill River slowly working their way upriver. Not until they had landed 150 men and guns on the narrow peninsula close to the fort was their ruse discovered. English ships they were not. They were French warships under the command of Comte de la Pérouse. Governor Hearne recognized he was in a hopeless situation. He had only 39 men within the walls of his fort—no match for the 250 French rapidly approaching. Even worse, he had no trained crews to man any of the fort's forty-two guns, each of which required about ten men to operate. He was not given to useless heroics; he accepted the inevitable and surrendered the fort. And so the invincible, the fort impregnable to all attacks from the French, yielded without a shot being fired.

La Pérouse was determined to destroy the fort completely. The few wooden buildings were burned to the ground. The stone walls of the barracks were blown in; cannon were spiked, their undercarriages burned. At many places the massive stone walls were undermined and gaping breaches blown in them. But in spite of all that fire and explosives could do, much of the great stone walls and bastions remained standing when La Pérouse departed two days after his first appearance.

Although there were many who accused Samuel Hearne of cowardice in not putting up some kind of resistance, apparently the Hudson's Bay Company did not share this feeling, because he was sent back from London the following year to reestablish a trading post in the Churchill River area.

Fort Churchill

No attempt was made to rebuild Fort Prince of Wales' Fort. Instead, Hearne went upriver and on the site of Knight's old establishment built a new Fort Churchill. Here the Hudson's Bay post remained for the next 180 years. During that long period, it became less of a fur trading center and more of a distribution depot for food and trade goods coming in from England and a collection point for furs to be shipped out. In 1929 the railroad reached Churchill; a modern harbor was built equipped with grain elevators; and in 1933 the Hudson's Bay Company abandoned its old location on the west side of the river and moved to the east side, where the new town of Churchill had been established.

It took three trips to Churchill before we succeeded in reaching the sites of old Fort Churchill and Prince of Wales' Fort. However, we persevered and were well rewarded with some memorable experiences.

After three years of trying, we finally made arrangements with local tour operator Mike Macri to take us in his Zodiac rubber raft upriver to the site of old Fort Churchill. He cautioned us that the timing of our departure from Churchill would be governed by the incoming tide from the bay; otherwise, we would be stranded on the mud flats a considerable distance from shore. So late one afternoon Mike, his wife, Doreen, their dog, Mac, and we piled into the raft and started the four and one-half miles upriver.

En route we stopped to enjoy the sight of a pod of beluga whales cavorting about our raft. These graceful glistening white creatures seemed to be as curious about us as we were about them. Mike lowered an underwater microphone into the water, which enabled us to hear the beluga calls—an amazing repertoire of rather high-pitched chirps, whistles, and squeals. No wonder the old-timers called them sea canaries.

When we were abreast of the old Fort Churchill site, Mike headed toward shore. All too soon our raft gently bumped to a stop. A quarter-mile of glistening wet, slimy mud strewn with rocks and boulders of all sizes still intervened between us and the shore. However, this was no problem—or so I thought—for we had brought hip boots. My first step out of the raft onto the slippery mudflat warned me that this would be no mere pleasure stroll to shore. The mud was viscous, deep, and clutching, and my borrowed boots were several sizes too large for me. It followed, therefore, that my feet and the boots kept parting company. As I struggled along trying desperately to maintain my balance and keep from falling forward on my face in that terrible mud, I thought of

James Knight's comments made so long ago about the difficulties of reaching shore at this very same spot. What was true then was equally true today.

At long last dry land was reached. We thankfully changed from hip boots to walking shoes. Leaving the shore behind us, we climbed onto a rocky plateau. It was here, nestled at the foot of this protecting ridge, that Fort Churchill had stood. Today nothing remained but a few shallow depressions. It was all covered with a thick growth of impenetrable willow brush.

Away to the south stretched open muskeg country brightened at this season of the year (early September) with the gold of a few scattered tamaracks and the scarlet of bearberry and blueberry. Among the low sedges and on the mudflats to the south was a mantle of white—not of snow but of snow geese. Overhead, the sky was brilliant blue. Flocks of low-flying geese filled the air with their musical calling.

We walked to the lonely cemetery nearby. Only a few wooden crosses and small weather-beaten picket enclosures yet stood. Untended, they, too, will soon succumb to time and neglect, and then the last visible evidence of Fort Churchill will disappear.

Since we could not return to Churchill until the next day because of the time of the full tide, we headed toward the Macris' hideaway cabin to spend the night. There good food, good conversation, and pleasant companions provided a wonderful ending to a most memorable day. Not even the swarming hordes of mosquitoes "like great Wasps," as James Knight wrote so many years ago, could spoil it.

On our return downriver, we landed at Sloop's Cove. This is a small bay on the west side of the river where repair work on the ships was carried out by the ship's carpenters. It was also used for mooring the company's smaller craft. Iron mooring rings fastened into the granite rock still remained. Also still visible were the signatures of many of the early Hudson's Bay Company servants and sailors, including the most famous signature of all, S' Hearne July ye 1 1767, each painstakingly carved into the hard rock face.

Prince of Wales' Fort was, of course, one of the main reasons for our trip to Churchill. It was clearly visible on the west bank across the river estuary. We anticipated no difficulty at all in reaching it. We soon learned otherwise.

On our first trip to Churchill we were taken across the river to the fort and were just walking up to the impressive ravelin protecting the main gate when our Parks Canada guide received a warning by her walkie-talkie that a severe squall was rapidly approaching downstream. We had to return to Churchill at once. Greatly disappointed, we dutifully reembarked and were soon safely back, just moments ahead of heavy winds and rain.

The next time, several years later, we once more reached the fort and were not chased out by squall warnings or wandering polar bears. Unfortunately, however, the weather was dark and overcast—hardly ideal conditions for good photographs.

We returned to Churchill yet again after a lapse of a few years, and this time we hit the jackpot: plenty of time to see the ruins, and ample sunshine. Our first impression was one of great size, massiveness, and strength. The cannon still pointed their muzzles through the openings in the parapet wall. The outside walls were forty feet thick at the base and fifteen to twenty feet high. The fact that these walls still stand defiantly is largely due to a massive reconstruction project by the government begun in the late 1930s and completed twenty years later. You wondered how such a fort as this could ever fall. (But then they wondered that about Louisbourg as well.) Inside the large courtyard the signs of destruction were very evident. There were no roofs remaining, and only a small part of the barrack walls were still standing. The powder magazine in the northwest bastion lay open to the sky, its six-foot-thick stone vaulted roof completely destroyed. Fort Prince of Wales's length of existence was brief, only about twelve years (in its completed stage), but its memory as perpetuated by these stone ruins will undoubtedly last for centuries.

During our many trips to Churchill, in addition to achieving our objective of visiting the two Hudson's Bay posts, we enjoyed many other benefits. Of course, there were the polar bears, and we were fortunate enough to see many of these beautiful animals. There was the amazing beauty of the country: the characteristic smooth gray rocks bordering the shores of Hudson's Bay and, in the fall, the tundra aflame with scarlet and yellow.

Most important, however, were all the friendly people we met. The list is long. They each in their way contributed to the pleasure of our stay: Harry Dyal, Garnet Penwarden, Roy Bukowsky, Mike and Doreen Macri, Myrtle de Meules. Finally, but most definitely not least, were Lily McAuley and Wilf Van Steelandt. We first met Lily in her capacity as Parks Canada interpreter on our aborted trip to Prince of Wales' Fort. There a strong bond was forged between her and us by our common acceptance of a northern philosophy that says that the only way to treat the scourge of mosquitoes and blackflies is to, as Lily so succinctly put it, "just ignore them." From this beginning we became recipients of the generous, warm hospitality that is so typical of the North. Lily and Wilf's home, their table, their car, even their treasured cloudberry liqueur were freely offered to us. Even more important, however, their friendship was given, and that was the greatest gift of all. It is with great sadness that it must be here recorded that Lily, a true friend and interpreter of her beloved north country, finally lost her valiant fight against cancer. She died on November 16, 1994.

Fort Michilimackinac

Rivalry between the French and English for control of the fur trade was not confined to the shores of Hudson's Bay. The English traders from their base in northern New York on the Hudson River at Orange (present-day Albany) and the French *coureurs de bois* from their strongholds of Montreal and Trois-Rivières on the St. Lawrence penetrated the vast territory north and west of the Great Lakes—in fact, as far as the Mississippi River.

To halt the inroads of the English into this region, which the French regarded as theirs by right of prior discovery and exploration, Governor Denonville in 1686 ordered La Durantaye to build a fort on the northern shore of the strategic Straits of Mackinac. This fort, erected on the site of modern St. Ignace, lasted but fifteen years. During that time the fur trade got completely out of hand. Liquor, although expressly forbidden by law, was freely supplied to the Indians; illegal trading was carried on by both officers of the garrison and their men; drunkenness, gambling, and licentiousness were rampant. Discipline was almost nonexistent. Responding to pressure from the missionaries, Louis XIV in 1698 summarily issued drastic orders that canceled all trading licenses, forbade all trading by the military, prohibited all trade in the interior, closed all the western posts, and demanded that all *coureurs de bois* and traders return home to the St. Lawrence. Henceforth, furs must be brought out of the interior by the Indians to Montreal, where the trading would be done under the close scrutiny of government officials. Accordingly, the first Fort Michilimackinac was closed and its last Governor, LeMothe Cadillac, headed south in 1701 to build Fort Detroit, strategically located to command the waterway connecting the upper and lower Great Lakes.

However, this new policy was destined to failure. The Indians, accustomed to the traders coming to them, refused to make the long and arduous journey to Montreal; furthermore, without the restraining influence of the garrisoned posts, intertribal quarrels erupted into fighting, to the detriment of "making furs." So in 1715 the policy was abandoned.

The need for a post to dominate the straits area and to checkmate penetration by the English traders was still clearly recognized. It was decided that Fort Michilimackinac be reestablished. This time the spot chosen was on the south shore of the straits on a sandy point of land just slightly to the west of today's Mackinac City. There a palisade of vertical sharpened posts enclosing a small compound was soon erected, blockhouses were constructed, and six cannon mounted on bastion platforms. In addition, there were quarters and houses for thirty French families of soldiers and officers as well as a church built by the Jesuits. Outside the walls close by were the houses of thirty or more French traders.

For the next sixty-five years, until it was moved to Mackinac Island, this small palisaded fort was the hub of the fur trade for nearly a quarter of a continent. Its strategic location gave it absolute command over the fur trade traffic into and out of the *pays d'en haut*. Not a canoe, a boat, or a bateau passing through the straits could escape its surveillance. It was from this great entrepôt that the traders and explorers equipped from its storehouse with provisions and goods departed for the west toward the Mississippi and the far Saskatchewan in their journeys of exploration and trade, and it was to this post that they returned, sometimes with canoes heavy-laden with pelts, other times with canoes riding high in the water, empty of furs. In truth, Fort Michilimackinac was the French fur emporium of the west.

But suddenly it was over. Quebec fell to the British in 1759, followed by Montreal in 1760. The French were vanquished and all their settlements, military forts, trading posts, and religious missions were forfeited to the victorious English. When word reached Fort Michilimackinac of the French defeat, Captain Beaujeu quickly embarked the entire garrison in canoes and hastened toward French settlements in Illinois country. Charles de Langlade, his second-in-command, remained behind. It fell to him to yield the fort to the English when Captain Henry Balfour arrived in 1761.

Captain Balfour soon departed but left behind thirty men, first under Lieutenant Leslie and later under Captain Etherington, to garrison the depot. Their task was not easy. The French traders still remaining at the fort were resentful and embittered. The Indians, who hated the English, were surly and restless. During their first year of occupation, the British made changes at the fort: the stockade was enlarged; the French houses were torn down and replaced with soldiers' barracks and commanding officers' quarters.

The Indians did not accept the finality of the French defeat. United and inspired by the Ottawa Chief Pontiac, they carried out a plan that was nearly successful in wiping out all frontier British posts in the midwest area. The great Pontiac Conspiracy of 1763 began May 10 when in simultaneous attacks Forts Presque Isle, Sandusky, St. Joseph, Ouitanon, Miami, and Le Boeuf were overrun and destroyed.

Three weeks later it was the turn of Fort Michilimackinac. Utilizing a brilliantly deceptive stratagem, the Indians were able to overpower the fort. Under the pretext of celebrating King George's birthday, the Indians staged one of their rough-and-tumble ball games called *bagattaway* outside the fort walls close to the main gateway entrance. During the course of the game, the ball, as if by accident, was lofted over the wall. The players rushed inside to retrieve it and, once inside, grabbed the knives and hatchets that had been concealed under the blankets of the squaws who were conveniently standing by the gateway. Amid shouts and war whoops, they began killing and scalping the unarmed soldiers stunned by the onrush of over four hundred yelling Indians. In a short time it was all over. Twenty-one had been slain; of the sixteen taken prisoner, five were subsequently slaughtered; the rest were eventually released.

For better than a year after this debacle Fort Michilimackinac was abandoned except for a few French traders and the Jesuit priest. In September 1764, however, the British returned and immediately began repairing the destruction wrought both by the Indians and by neglect. In a short while the fort was restored to its former condition and ready to resume its position as the major headquarters for the trade of the entire Northwest.

Reflecting its importance, within the walls of the fort at this time, in addition to the Jesuit church, were soldiers' barracks, French and British traders' houses, a blacksmith shop, the King's storehouse, a commanding officer's house, a priest's house, and the powder magazine. The stockade walls had four corner bastions and four blockhouses. There were two main gates, one facing toward the land and the other leading to the water.

One of the most colorful of the British post commanders was Major Robert Rogers, leader of the famous Roger's Rangers and hero of the French and Indian Wars. His grandiose schemes to make Fort Michilimackinac the capital of an inland empire and complete disregard of any regulations relating to the fur trade (such as use of liquor, licensing) with which he disagreed soon brought about his downfall. After only one year as commander of the post, he was recalled to Montreal to answer charges of treason (charges of which he was subsequently acquitted).

Among the most successful of the British traders who used Fort Michilimackinac as their headquarters was John Askins. He arrived there in 1764 and soon established a prosperous business as a wholesale trader with his own vessels and warehouse. He outfitted not only his own agents and voyageurs but also other traders.

When Major Patrick Sinclair arrived in 1779 to take command of the fort, he found that much of it had been allowed to fall into disrepair.

Furthermore, he was convinced that the fort would be indefensible in the event of an attack by the Americans should the battleground of the American Revolution shift to the Great Lakes area. His solution was to relocate the fort on nearby Mackinac Island—a site possessing great natural defenses, a sheltered harbor, and an abundant supply of wood and stone for fuel and construction.

By the summer of 1781 his plan had not only been accepted, but Fort Michilimackinac had been partially dismantled, the salvaged materials transported to the island, and the new fort, to be known as Fort Mackinac, constructed on the high bluff overlooking the harbor and straits.

So on a day in midsummer 1781 the British flag was lowered for the last time and the garrison shouldered their packs and marched out the water gate to the canoes waiting to take them to their new fort on the island. With the departure of the garrison, most of the traders soon left, many of them also moving to the island.

Fort Michilimackinac lay abandoned. The raucous noises of a busy fur trade post were stilled—the quiet broken only by the cries of gulls flying overhead and the ceaseless waves washing on shore. Before long all traces of decaying walls and buildings were obliterated by time and windblown sand. Their location remained only as a dim memory in the minds of a few.

In 1960 Fort Michilimackinac awakened from its long sleep of nearly two hundred years. Spurred on by the interest of historically minded residents in the area and by the extremely fortunate discovery of a French map drawn of the fort in 1749, the Mackinac Island State Park Commission began its reconstruction of the fort, based on meticulous research of old records and careful archaeological excavations of the site.

Today a visit to the fort is, indeed, a journey into the past. Within the palisaded enclosure the French traders' homes with their small gardens, the commanding officers' and British traders' homes, the soldiers' barracks, the powder magazine, the King's storehouse, the blacksmith shop, the priest's residence, and the Jesuit church have all been accurately reconstructed. Aided by the magic of electronic displays, some of the most dramatic moments of the famous 1763 massacre are vividly and realistically portrayed. In the church the 1754 marriage of Charles de Langlade and Charlotte Bourassa is reenacted.

Once more the British flag flies proudly from the tall flagpole. Once more the fort is the scene of activity and life, even though it is now tourists instead of fur traders who throng the compound. Once more it is possible to stand as we did in the water gateway and look out over the straits and watch the boats pass by—to realize that except for the fact that long, majestic freighters have replaced canoes and bateaux and sailing sloops, nothing has changed. What met our gaze was exactly what the voyageurs, the fur traders, and the Indians saw as they, too, looked out through the water gate. The waters of the straits, deep and blue, still flow by, and the gulls continue to circle noisily overhead.

Fort Timiskaming

The story of Fort Timiskaming spans more than two centuries. The original post established by the French on the west side of Lake Timiskaming in 1679 was completely destroyed by the Iroquois nine years later. Thirty-two years elapsed before the French returned. This time they built their post on a peninsula on the east side of the lake at the Narrows. Lake Timiskaming is, in fact, merely a widening of the Ottawa River into a narrow lake seventy miles long enclosed by high tree-covered hills. About midway, two peninsulas extending into the lake from opposite shores constrict the lake into a narrow strait barely a quarter of a mile in width. From their new fort at this vantage point the French controlled not only the principal route to James Bay from Montreal but also several river systems penetrating the rich fur country to the east and west. Indeed, the site was so well chosen that it remained the location of the fort for the remaining 182 years of its existence.

The void left by the departure of the French after their defeat by the English in 1759 was soon filled—first by independent traders from Montreal and later, after 1788, by the North West Company. Under the able leadership of Aenas Cameron, Angus Cameron, and Alexander McDougall, the fur trade at Fort Timiskaming prospered. The Standard of Trade used was the marten instead of the more commonly used beaver at Hudson's Bay posts.

A contemporary account written by George Gladman of the Hudson's Bay Company in 1794 described Fort Timiskaming as follows:

> The Houses stand on a Point on the Et. side stretching into the Lake on a high Situation, another point projects from the opposite side making a Narrow Channel only 1/4 mile across, thro' which a strong current runs to the So-ward. The Houses consist of a Wholesale and Retail Warehouse, a House for a Master and Clerks and another for men all at right angles within Pallisadoes. Ten or Twelve Yards higher up on the Point there are two other commodious dwelling Houses one for the Master and the other Mr. Grant's in which they reside. Besides these they have some detached Buildings as a Smith's Forge, also a very complete Ice House, [and] a magazine but all in irregular situations.

Because of its location somewhat off the main arteries of the fur trade traffic, Fort Timiskaming largely escaped the violence and ruthlessness of the conflict being carried on in the Northwest between the rival North West Company and Hudson's Bay Company.

In 1821 the merging of the two companies into one—the Hudson's Bay Company—brought peace to the fur trade. Fort Timiskaming continued for many years as an important and profitable post. At the insistence of George Simpson, overseas Governor, it was incorporated into the traditional trading pattern of the Hudson's Bay Company, which meant the use of Moose Fort on James Bay instead of Montreal as the base both for receiving supplies and for shipping furs. This practice was continued in spite of constant difficulties in securing enough Indians willing to make the lengthy and arduous journey to James Bay; they much preferred their customary and easier route down the Ottawa River to Montreal. It wasn't until 1863 that improvements to the transportation system of the Ottawa River, plus the imposition of customs duty on English goods imported to Moose Fort, brought about a reversal of policy and Fort Timiskaming was returned to Montreal jurisdiction.

At about this same time, the lumbermen who had been working their way up the Ottawa River valley reached Lake Timiskaming. On their heels came independent traders and settlers. This influx of people spelled the end of the traditional fur trade economy based on barter and credit. Cash became the medium of exchange. The extension of the railroad first to Mattawa at the junction of the Mattawa and Ottawa rivers and later to the foot of Lake Timiskaming and the introduction of steamboats on Lake Timiskaming radically altered the old trading patterns.

Striving to meet the challenges posed by these changes, Fort Timiskaming gradually ceased to function primarily as a fur trade depot; instead, it became a trading store dealing in general merchandise supplying the needs of the lumber camps, the settlers, the petty traders, and the Indians. In 1887, in order to meet increasing competition and better serve the requirements of its customers, the Hudson's Bay Company moved its store from its rather isolated location at the Narrows to the nearby village of Ville Marie. Although the fort itself lingered on for a few more years, it finally closed its doors in 1901, after two hundred years of operation.

Today the only reminders that a busy and important fur trading post once flourished on this spot on the shores of Lake Timiskaming at the Narrows are three massive stone fireplace chimneys still defying ravages of time and weather and two small cemeteries nearby where several of the fort's chief traders lie buried.

The presence of the church at the fort is shown by the tall cross marking the site of the small chapel built by Father Poire in 1839. The Oblate priest Father Laverlochère, affectionately known as the "Apostle of Hudson's Bay," who ministered for many years within the Timiskaming and James Bay areas until his death in 1884, lies buried in the cemetery on the hill overlooking the fort site.

The site of Fort Timiskaming is one of peacefulness and beauty. In the fall when we were there, the poplar trees scattered on the sandy point with their golden leaves gleaming in the sunshine, the sparkling blue waters of the Ottawa River swiftly flowing by, and the deep green of the cedars on the hillside made a picture not soon forgotten. We agreed with the words of Chief Trader Thomas Anderson, who wrote in 1894: "Fort Temiscamingue was at one time the prettiest spot on the Ottawa River, many pleasant days I have spent at it."

Fort Michipicoten

The importance of the Michipicoten River as a major link in the chain of lakes and rivers connecting James Bay and Lake Superior was recognized early, not only by fur traders and explorers but also, well before them, by the native peoples. In fact, its strategic location at the junction of the water route north to Hudson Bay and east to the St. Lawrence River was probably the main reason for its two centuries of continuous existence as a fur trade post.

The French, probing ever farther into the country west of Montreal, by 1717 reached the north shore of Lake Superior and shortly thereafter in 1725 established a trading post at the mouth of the Michipicoten River. This post located on the south side of the river nearly opposite the mouth of the Magpie River remained in operation until 1763, when defeat by the British forced the abandonment by the French of their trading posts and withdrawal from the country.

The void thus created did not last long. The enterprising Alexander Henry the elder, undaunted by his recent harrowing experience during the massacre at Fort Michilimackinac, where he had miraculously escaped death, formed a partnership with Cadotte, a trader from Sault Ste. Marie, and in 1767 reestablished a trading post on the old French site on the Michipicoten River. In Henry's account of his travels and adventures written in 1809, he described the post site: "The lake is here bordered by a rugged and elevated country, consisting in mountains, of which, for the most part, the feet are in the water, and the heads in the clouds. The river [Michipicoten] which falls into the bay is a large one, but has a bar at its entrance, over which there is no more than four feet water." He continued: "On reaching the trading post, which was an old one of French establishment, I found the lodges of Indians." His next words give an interesting insight into his trading practices: "To ten lodges, I advanced goods to a large amount, allowing every man credit for a hundred beaver-skins, and every woman for thirty. In this I went beyond what I had done for the Chipeways, a proceeding to which I was emboldened by the high character for honesty, which is supported by this otherwise abject people."

In 1783 the North West Company took over the post on the Michipicoten. The importance of this post to the North West Company lay in its location. Not only was it athwart the main highway from Montreal to their rendezvous headquarters at the western end of Lake Superior, first at Grand Portage and later at Fort William; it was also astride the southern terminus of the water route via the Missinaibi-

Moose rivers to James Bay and, as such, was an excellent base from which to penetrate the rich fur country to the north.

The Hudson's Bay Company responded in 1797 by establishing a fur trade post on the north bank of the Michipicoten opposite the North West Company. The rivalry between the two concerns for control of the fur trade of the Missinaibi-Moose valley lasted until the union of the two companies in 1821. At that time the Hudson's Bay Company abandoned its post on the north side of the river and moved over to the former North West Company fort on the south side, and there it remained until 1904, when the post was closed.

In 1827 Michipicoten became the administrative headquarters of the Lake Superior district, and several annual meetings of the Southern Governing Council were held there. It also became the major entrepôt for the districts of Lake Superior and Lake Huron. Here furs were collected, graded, pressed, and packed for transport to Moose Factory and thence to England. And here the trade goods and supplies received from England via Moose Factory were warehoused for distribution.

By 1863 increased extension of the railroads and the introduction of steamboats on Lake Superior brought about the abandonment of the northern route to James Bay via the Michipicoten–Missinaibi–Moose river system in favor of the east–west route to Montreal via the Great Lakes and St. Lawrence River.

For many years the establishment consisted of a small house for the chief company official posted there, a couple of storehouses, a few servants' quarters, and various sheds and pens for livestock. Until about 1850, Indians camped around the post during the summer months. Defying official Hudson's Bay Company policy against elaborate structures, an impressive two-story building with many windows and a gallery on three sides was built in 1877 for P. W. Bell, Chief Factor from 1868 to 1888. It was quickly dubbed the "Big House," its grandeur in stark contrast to the rest of the fort.

In addition to fulfilling its primary function of trading goods for furs, Michipicoten carried on a thriving fishery. In the early spring during the migratory run, nets stretched across the mouth of the Michipicoten River consistently produced great numbers of whitefish and lake trout. Most of the catch was salted and barreled. Besides supplying its own needs, Michipicoten frequently furnished salt fish to other posts. Fish processing was an important part of company activities at Michipicoten and it is interesting to note that today, more than one hundred years later, fishermen still flock each spring to the mouth of the Michipicoten to enjoy phenomenal fishing.

During the winter months, boatbuilding and repair were a major activity at the fort. Suitable wood was obtained upriver, and the iron-work needed was produced by the fort's blacksmith. The post's carpenters were kept busy repairing and outfitting the Hudson's Bay Company schooners, which often docked at the post for the winter.

Another major activity carried on at the post during the winter months was the manufacture of "country-made goods," notably tin-ware of a superior quality, such as kettles, pots, teapots, lamps, and bread pans. In addition, the blacksmith was busy producing axes, fish spears, knives, and beaver traps. Whatever was not needed for the fort's own use became an item for trade.

Michipicoten was also used as a base for missionary endeavors in the Lake Superior area. The Hudson's Bay Company was unfailingly supportive of their efforts and freely offered hospitality to the missionaries as well as other concessions, such as considerable discount on supplies.

Throughout the nineteenth century, the fort provided supplies, provisions, and equipment for survey and exploration crews, commencing in 1827 with the Sir John Franklin Arctic expedition and continuing with the Dawson expedition of 1858, numerous mining company surveys, the Canadian Pacific Railway survey of 1881, and prospectors and miners operating in the Ontario Michipicoten Mining Division.

When the Robinson-Superior Treaty was signed in 1850, Hudson's Bay Company personnel at Michipicoten assumed the responsibility of distributing the annual annuities to the local Indians. This encouraged them to remain in the vicinity of the post and conduct their trading there.

By 1904 progress had brought many changes. The company closed the post's doors for good, its days of usefulness ended.

Today there are no buildings left standing in the large, open clearing pleasantly bordered by the Michipicoten River and wooded hills. Nothing remains to witness the existence of a once busy and important trading post except the stone foundations of a few buildings hidden in the tall grass. Somewhat apart are the tumbled-down stones of what were once the powder magazine walls. A few pilings along the river's edge mark the location of the dock.

The rustling of the tawny dry grass breaks the silence. The murmur of the river as it flows toward Lake Superior a short distance away can be faintly heard. The brilliant red of a single mountain ash tree heavy with berries stands out from the dark green of spruce and balsam. After nearly two hundred years of bustling activity, Fort Michipicoten now sleeps undisturbed.

Fort St. Pierre

Pierre Gaultier de la Vérendrye did more than any son of New France to extend its borders westward. He faithfully and doggedly, in spite of an array of misfortunes that would have thwarted most others, persevered in his quest of discovering a passage by river that would lead to the *Mer de l'Ouest* and give access to the riches of the China trade.

In 1726, when he was *Commandant des Postes du Nord* at Lake Nipigon, he picked up information from an Indian about a great lake beyond Lake Superior out of which flowed a river toward the west. To find and trace the course of this river became the goal he pursued for the rest of his life.

Through his friend and patron, the Marquis de Beauharnois, Governor of New France, La Vérendrye applied for funds to enable him to undertake this exploration, but Louis XIV had other uses for his money. La Vérendrye would have to finance his exploration himself. The only assistance offered was a fur trade monopoly in the country he would be exploring. Based on this monopoly, La Vérendrye secured the backing of some Montreal merchants motivated by the expectation of prospective profits.

So, in the summer of 1731, La Vérendrye, his three sons, his nephew, soldiers, and voyageurs, about fifty persons in all, set off in six canoes from Montreal. At Fort Michilimackinac a brief stop was made to pick up the Jesuit missionary Father Meisager, who was to accompany the expedition.

Because of the necessity of carrying on trade as they traveled, the party was encumbered with trade goods and supplies and therefore could not make the rapid progress a purely exploratory party could make. By the end of August, they reached the western end of Lake Superior. At this point the men refused to go farther, complaining of the lateness of the season and the length and difficulty of the nine-mile portage that bypassed the falls and rapids of the Pigeon River. After much persuasion, La Vérendrye was able to induce a few to continue under the leadership of his nephew, La Jemeraye, while he and the rest of his men wintered at the nearby French fort at the mouth of the Kaministiquia River.

La Jemeraye with one of La Vérendrye's sons and one other man struggled over the long portage, the first white men and forerunners of the long procession of traders, explorers, wintering partners, and voyageurs who would use this same portage, which quickly became known as the Grand Portage—Gateway to the West.

Following the rivers and lakes that today form the international boundary between Canada and the United States, La Jemeraye reached Rainy Lake before freeze-up. The site he chose for his fort was at the foot of a small series of rapids on the right bank of the Rainy River near its outflow from the lake. Here at the rapids was an excellent fishery, and close by in the marshes grew wild rice in abundance—welcome additions to their meager food supplies.

In a meadow surrounded by a grove of oak trees, La Jemeraye erected his post, calling it Fort St. Pierre. It was fifty feet long, with two opposing gates, the front one facing the water. Two bastions protected the gates. Additional defense was provided by an interior platform connecting the bastions. In one of the bastions were a storehouse and a powder magazine. Within the thirteen-foot-high palisade walls were two main buildings, each with two rooms and a double chimney.

Throughout the long winter, La Jemeraye carried on a trade with the local Indians, the Monsonis. In May he sent out his returns to La Vérendrye, who was still at Kaministiquia. From there, canoes were sent to deliver the furs to Fort Michilimackinac for forwarding to Montreal to satisfy La Vérendrye's impatient creditors and to pick up trade goods for the ensuing year.

By the beginning of June, La Vérendrye and his men left Kaministiquia for Fort St. Pierre, which they reached on July 14. After a short stay, the journey westward was resumed.

La Vérendrye returned to Fort St. Pierre on numerous occasions to hold council with the Indians in an effort to keep them from warring with one another and to secure the peace so essential for successful trading in furs. Like his illustrious predecessor the Comte de Frontenac, a former Governor of New France, La Vérendrye knew how to use pageantry, oratory, gifts, and councils in order to secure the loyalty of the Indians. His efforts made Rainy Lake a French inland sea with Fort St. Pierre as its headquarters. The post remained in operation until it was abandoned in 1758, shortly before the conquest.

Today Fort St. Pierre has been rescued from oblivion. Although all traces of the original fort had long disappeared, its location was remembered. Once again, after a lapse of 250 years, a reconstructed Fort St. Pierre stands at the outlet of Rainy Lake. The palisade walls, the bastions, the two double-room buildings, the elevated interior platform, and the massive gates have all been re-created. From its commanding site overlooking Rainy Lake it serves as a most fitting monument to a great French explorer and trader.

Fort St. Charles

The second of the forts erected by La Vérendrye, as he slowly advanced westward in his search for the ever-elusive Western Sea, was Fort St. Charles, so named after the patron saint of his sponsor, Governor Beauharnois.

In the summer of 1732 La Vérendrye left Kaministiquia for Fort St. Pierre and together with La Jemeraye paddled down the beautiful Rainy River out into the Lake of the Woods. They threaded their way through a bewildering maze of spruce- and pine-covered islands, narrow channels, across open water subject to treacherous winds, finally reaching a site on the far western side of the lake, which they deemed suitable for their post.

Here they constructed Fort St. Charles, which measured sixty by one hundred feet. The palisade consisted of a double row of fifteen-foot pointed stakes. There were two gates on opposite sides, one opening out to the lake in the front, the other to the woods in the rear. Four bastions and a watch tower guarded the gates. Within the enclosure were houses for the commandant and the missionary, four buildings with chimneys for the men, a storehouse, a chapel, and a powder magazine. These structures were of the usual construction of logs chinked with clay and roofs covered with sheets of bark.

The soil in the vicinity of the fort was found to be good. The surrounding woods were quickly burned, not only to prevent their being used as a protective screen for any hostile Indian attack, but also to prepare the ground for spring sowing.

One of the chief problems constantly plaguing La Vérendrye was the almost incessant warfare of the Crees and Monsonis against their ancient enemies the Sioux. Without peace, there could be no trade in furs, and without the profit from that trade, there could be no exploration.

Great councils with all the colorful trappings of pageantry, ceremony, gift giving, and feasting were held at Fort St. Charles. Speeches were made by the Indian chiefs, natural-born orators, and by La Vérendrye, who was similarly gifted. Typical of such a council is one that took place in January of 1734. In La Vérendrye's report to the Marquis de Beauharnois, Governor-General of New France, he wrote:

On the 2nd of January, all the Frenchmen being in my room, the six chiefs and the principal men entered. In the middle of the room I had caused to be placed 12 lbs. of ball, 20 lbs. of powder, 6 axes, 6 daggers, 12 Siamese knives, two dozen awls, needles, beads, vermilion, gunscrews, six dagger hatchets, six collars of beads, six flags, 24 fathoms of tobacco, six cloaks with gilt bands, six shirts, six pairs of breeches, six pairs of leggings, the whole of which I divided among the six chiefs.

After the bestowal of the presents I thanked them several times, according to their custom, in the name of our Father, for having come to see me. 'I am ashamed,' I said, 'to have only that to give you today, but, if you are clever, you will come back to see me with all the people of your villages after their hunting, so that you may be in a position to have your wants supplied by the trader. Don't come with empty hands as you did the first time.' This made them smile.

Promises of peace, pledges not to wage war, and promises to trade only with the French were made. But the promises were not always kept and the price was high. The gifts, the ammunition, the food for the feasts nearly drained La Vérendrye's scanty stock of trade goods and provisions. Furthermore, he entrusted one of his sons to accompany them on one of their warring expeditions against the distant Sioux of the prairies.

In May of 1734 La Vérendrye returned on the first of his many trips to Montreal and Quebec in order to present to Governor Beauharnois his plans for future exploration southward into the land of the Mandans and to try to arrange for additional credit to purchase supplies, even though he still owed for goods already received. The French Crown still was adamant in its refusal to provide any financial assistance, but Governor Beauharnois gave La Vérendrye permission to farm out his posts to merchants for a period of three years, receiving in return the license fees payable in goods and furs, with the stipulation that during that time he was to refrain from all trading and devote himself exclusively to the task of exploration and discovery. By September 1735, La Vérendrye was back at Fort St. Charles.

The year 1736 was one of disaster. First was the sudden death of La Jemeraye, La Vérendrye's nephew and most capable assistant. Next, the canoes with supplies that were to have been provided by the merchants under the new licensing agreement had not arrived. The post was almost totally destitute of provisions, goods, and gunpowder. It was crucial that supplies be secured.

So, on June 5, a party of twenty-one men, including Father Aulneau, under the leadership of La Vérendrye's oldest son, Jean-Baptiste, set off in three express canoes on the urgent mission of securing and bringing back the vitally needed supplies as quickly as possible. Their destination was Kaministiquia or even Fort Michilimackinac, if necessary.

The first night out, on an island (soon to be known as Massacre Island), camp was made. Here, surprised by a large band of Sioux, the entire party was massacred. There were no survivors to tell what happened. The slain were scalped and their heads hacked off from their bodies. Many of the heads were wrapped in beaver robes as a gesture of contempt for the value placed by the French on beaver robes. Even Father Aulneau was not spared. His body, when found, was in a kneeling position, an arrow in his side and a knife wound in his breast. The massacre was in retaliation for La Vérendrye's son's participation the previous year in a raiding party against the Sioux.

With the loss of his son, his nephew, and half his men within the short space of three weeks, La Vérendrye was, for the present, forced to abandon all current plans for further exploration and establishment of new posts.

An indication of La Vérendrye's resolute character and devotion to his goal is shown by his refusal to yield to the repeated demands of the Cree and Monsonis for an all-out war of revenge upon the Sioux. Rising above his personal grief, he first took measures to strengthen the defenses of Fort St. Charles, so that it could be successfully defended by a few men against any hostile force. He also recovered the bodies of his slain son and companions and buried them in the small chapel within the fort. Finally, he had to placate and put off his Indian allies, the Crees and Monsonis, who were insisting that he join them in a large-scale war of revenge against their common enemy. La Vérendrye well knew that such a war would make it impossible for any future journeys of discovery to be safely undertaken. Addressing the Indians who had assembled at Fort St. Charles for a grand council, La Vérendrye persuaded the Indians to give up their war plans—at least temporarily.

It was nearly two years before he felt he could leave Fort St. Charles and take the next step forward in his search for the Western Sea. Fort St. Charles continued as a subsidiary supply post for a few more years, until 1749, but after 1738 it no longer served as his headquarters.

Before many years had passed, the palisades and the buildings within had fallen down, their rotting timbers mixing with the rich humus of the forest floor. Fort St. Charles was lost to sight and to memory.

In 1889 letters written by Father Aulneau to his family in France came to light. This sparked a keen interest in the story of Fort St. Charles and a desire to discover its site. Under the leadership of the Jesuits of the Collège de St. Boniface at St. Boniface, Manitoba, several expeditions were sent to search the western shores of the Lake of the Woods. Finally, in 1908, their efforts were rewarded—they found the site of Fort St. Charles. Flat chimney stones, fireplaces, and old stockade stumps were uncovered. And most important, the bodies and skulls of the slain men were likewise discovered.

Under the sponsorship of the Minnesota Fourth Degree Knights of Columbus the site is being preserved and maintained. The palisade with bastions has been reconstructed; within the enclosure, the outlines of the buildings are demarcated by foundation timbers. The graves of Father Aulneau, Jean-Baptiste La Vérendrye, and the nineteen other men killed in 1736 have also been outlined and identified by markers.

Fort St. Charles is located in the southwest corner of Lake of the Woods, on that geographical anomaly known as the Northwest Angle. The post is on an island in Angle Inlet just south of the Canadian–U.S. border. From our base at the very pleasant resort of Angle Outpost we went by boat to Magnuson's Island, the site of the fort. It is in a beautiful spot—a small cove backed by tall trees and facing the open waters of the lake. Today it is a fisherman's paradise, renowned for its fabulous catches of walleyes and muskies. Pleasure boats of all sizes cruise the waters.

We left the twentieth century behind us as we entered the small palisaded enclosure and journeyed back in time 250 years. At this very spot Indians had gathered in grand council to hear the words of La Vérendrye. Here two dozen men existed under conditions of hardship and often hunger. Here their leader had endured constant disappointments and frustrations; here from the lookout in the bastion the long-awaited canoes carrying vital supplies had been watched for in vain day after day. Here, too, La Vérendrye had received the tragic news, first of the death of his nephew, and then, shortly afterward, of the massacre of his son, Father Aulneau, and their nineteen companions. As we stood and looked down at the simply inscribed stone slabs marking the graves of the slain, all the horror of the attack became heartbreakingly real.

Instinctively in our thoughts we paid homage to a man who could rise above all these tragedies and disappointments and carry on with his assigned mission. As Arthur S. Morton wrote, "Champlain made the East and La Vérendrye grasped the West for the French. Together they made the French masters of little short of a Continent—of a vast domain which smaller men were to lose."

Fort la Reine

After a lapse of two years following the tragic events of 1736, La Vérendrye resumed his role as leader of the search for the Western Sea. In September of 1738 he left Fort St. Charles and, tracing the course of the Winnipeg River, reached Lake Winnipeg within a few weeks. Here, near the mouth of the Red River, a brief stop was made at Fort Maurepas, a spot that La Vérendrye had ordered established by one of his merchant supporters four years earlier. After two days of paddling up the Red River, the great forks of the Red and Assiniboine were reached. Without hesitation, the party turned westward and began the ascent of the Assiniboine.

It was a difficult passage because of sandbars, strong current, shallow water, and tortuous channels. Finally, they could go no farther without risking severe damage to the canoes. So, at this point, forced by necessity, La Vérendrye selected a suitable site on the south bank of the river for his fort. The spot was well chosen. It was at the southern end of a long-established twelve-mile carrying place between the Assiniboine River and Lake Manitoba, used by the Indians on their way to the English post of York Factory on Hudson Bay. It was close to the rich beaver country north of the river. Also, it was on the northern edge of the prairies, which offered an open road to the country of the Mandans. A fort located here would divert the Indian trade from Hudson Bay, offer easy access to rich beaver lands, and serve as a suitable base from which all subsequent exploration to the south toward the Mandans as well as to the west could be carried on. Construction of the fort began immediately, and La Vérendrye recorded in his journal that within twelve days Fort la Reine and its houses were completed. At last he was free to renew his explorations—to begin his journey to the Mandans, which he successfully accomplished.

Upon his death a few years later in 1749 and the forced withdrawal of his sons from the trading posts they had struggled so hard to establish, the western posts were transferred to Le Gardeur de Saint-Pierre as Commandant. He, unfortunately, lacked the skill needed to deal successfully with the Indians, and he was unable to win their loyalty.

Trouble soon developed. The Indians became dissatisfied and resentful. In 1750 they burned down Fort la Reine. Saint-Pierre rebuilt the post, which according to his journal now consisted of a palisade with bastions, several adjoining buildings, and a powder magazine. Two years later the Assiniboines invaded the fort compound intent on plunder. Saint-Pierre, certainly not deficient in courage, grabbed a blazing brand and, standing in front of the open door to the powder magazine, threatened to throw it inside, blowing them all up, including himself. The bluff worked and the frightened Assiniboines fled the fort. Nevertheless, when four days later Saint-Pierre and his men left with the furs for the annual rendezvous at Grand Portage, the Indians returned and burned the fort to the ground. Upon his return, Saint-Pierre found nothing but charred ruins, so once again the fort was rebuilt. It was abandoned in 1756 when Saint-Pierre and his men returned to Quebec to aid in the defense of their country against the English. This marked the end of the French occupation of Fort la Reine—a fort that had been one of the most important French trading posts in the west.

Such a strategic location was not left long vacant. Traders of the North West Company and the Hudson's Bay Company soon established themselves in the area. Almost immediately upon the withdrawal of the French from Fort la Reine, the Hudson's Bay Company moved in and took possession of the post. Later in 1796 they built a new fort at or near the same site, and this post, now called Portage la Prairie, remained in operation until it was closed in 1870.

The North West Company by 1794 also had a post built at the portage. Daniel Harmon of the North West Company in his journal entry for June 13, 1805, noted: "Portage la Prairie, or Plain Portage. Here the North West Company have a miserable fort, the local situation of which is beautiful, beyond any thing that I have seen in this part of the world. Opposite the fort, there is a plain, which is about sixty miles long, and from one to ten broad, in the extent of which, not the least rise of ground is visible,—To this place, the Natives resort every spring, to take and dry sturgeon."

Alexander Henry the younger in his journal gave a more favorable picture of conditions at the fort: "July 9th [1806] at Portage la Prairie we have an excellent garden, well stocked with potatoes, carrots, corn, onions, parsnips, beets, turnips, etc., all in forwardness and good order. Cabbages and melons do not turn out so well as at Panbian [Pembina] river—the soil here is too dry and sandy."

Today, just south of the modern city of Portage la Prairie, near the bank of the Assiniboine River, a pyramidal rock cairn with an appropriately inscribed bronze plaque marks the site of La Vérendrye's Fort la Reine. It is off the beaten path, and asking for directions and careful map reading are required to locate it.

We were glad we made the effort and happy to realize that the site of this fort, which played such an important role in La Vérendrye's search for the Western Sea and in the annals of the fur trade, will be forever preserved.

Fort Dauphin

Fort Dauphin, one of the oldest trading posts in the Northwest, was first established in 1741, when La Vérendrye sent his son Pierre to build a fort to the north and west of Lake Manitoba. The spot chosen was, according to J. B. Tyrrell, about three-quarters of a mile up the Mossy River from its outlet into Lake Winnipegosis. Other historians locate the post either at the mouth of the Waterhen River or at or near the eastern end of Meadow Portage. In any event, Fort Dauphin was situated in the general area of the southern end of Lake Winnipegosis and the extreme northwestern part of Lake Manitoba. This location enabled the French to intercept the flow of Indian trade headed for the Hudson's Bay Company at York Factory.

In spite of the 1763 Trade Proclamation, which was drawn up to safeguard and reinforce the monopoly rights of the Hudson's Bay Company in the vast lands covered by their charter, independent traders found ways to circumvent the proclamation. Major Robert Rogers, Commandant at Fort Michilimackinac, quick to seize any opportunity to enhance his prestige and that of his post, defied the proclamation and issued trading licenses for the Indian territory. The traders—French-Canadians and Pedlars (a derisive term used by the Hudson's Bay people for French and English fur traders from Montreal)—outfitted and licensed at Fort Michilimackinac soon spread throughout the forbidden territory.

Numerous trading posts, all bearing the name of Fort Dauphin, were established in the general area of Lake Dauphin. Although their specific location changed frequently, they always remained in the good hunting grounds in the vicinity of the lake.

There is much uncertainty regarding the exact location of many of the posts, but based on discovery of ruins and interpretation of contemporary records it appears probable that the Pedlars had a post at the mouth of Mossy River by 1769, Peter Pond had his at the northwest end of Lake Dauphin by 1775, the North West Company had its post on the southwest shore of Lake Dauphin near the mouth of the Valley River by 1797, and the Hudson's Bay Company had a trading post near the mouth of the Mossy River. In 1821 when the Hudson's Bay Company and the North West Company merged, the Hudson's Bay Company abandoned its Mossy River post and took over the North West Company fort on the Valley River, which was operated until 1870.

The sites of these various forts were shrewdly chosen in order to secure locations most favorable for Indian trade and for eliminating competition from rival traders. At Meadow Portage, a narrow strip of land separating Lake Manitoba from Lake Winnipegosis over which the traders traveled to reach their posts, the Indians often assembled, sometimes as many as 200 tents, to meet the brigades in order to trade their furs.

In a pleasant little park on the south shore of Lake Winnipegosis close to the mouth of the Mossy River stands a cairn commemorating the building in 1741 of the first Fort Dauphin by Pierre La Vérendrye in this vicinity. As we stood on the shore looking out across the wide expanse of water bounded only by clouds and sky, we tried to picture the small brigades of canoes, laden with goods, speeding across the lake, paddles moving in unison, as they headed unerringly toward the mouth of the river where we stood. Once this was reached, they would quickly disappear from sight as they ascended the river toward their trading post.

Nowadays there are dock facilities at the outlet of Mossy River where small commercial fishing boats tie up. We wondered if it would be possible to find a portion of the river untouched by modern developments. So, leaving the town behind us, we followed some dirt back roads inland for a few miles and to our delight, just as the sun was setting, came to a narrow wooden bridge over the river. From this vantage point we could see what a lovely stream the Mossy was. It flowed placidly through land of gentle beauty. A few trees, bushes, and open fields bordered its banks. The tops of the trees glowed in the setting sun. Just below us a small grebe quietly swam off, quickly disappearing in the encroaching shadows. Truly the traders had a lovely stream upon which to build their posts.

Fort Paskoyac

By the time of his son Pierre's return from the Mandan country on the Missouri, La Vérendrye had reached the conclusion that the Saskatchewan River was the key to the discovery of the Western Sea. To further his explorations in that direction, in 1743 he arranged for the first Fort Paskoyac to be built. The site chosen was on a small island near the outlet of the Saskatchewan River into the west side of Cedar Lake. It was at the crossroads of Indian trails and was long used as a traditional camping place. However, this fort remained independently active for only one year and probably was closed due to a shortage of supplies. For the remainder of its existence it was a minor outpost of Fort Bourbon, which had been established, also by Pierre La Vérendrye, on the north bank of the Saskatchewan River just below the foot of the Grand Rapids.

La Vérendrye, discouraged, frustrated, and practically bankrupt, resigned his commission and returned in 1744 to eastern Canada, where he died five years later. The claims of his sons, who meanwhile had been faithfully carrying on his work in the west, were completely ignored; they were summarily dismissed from their posts and were even prevented from regaining possession of their own trading goods stored at the posts or collecting from the Indians indebted to them. It remained for future generations to appreciate the La Vérendryes—father and sons—and give them the accolades they so richly deserved.

The French leaders who followed La Vérendrye had orders to continue the westward expansion and exploration as well as to compete with the English for the Indian fur trade. Accordingly, sometime between 1751 and 1753 a new Fort Paskoyac was built, this time on a site on the Saskatchewan River that was strategically located to divert the Indian trade away from the English posts on Hudson's Bay. In addition to its function as a fur trading post, it was intended as a base for future westward exploration in search of the elusive Western Sea.

This post, located where the modern town of The Pas now stands, was visited by Anthony Henday during his journey of exploration into the interior from York Factory in 1754. On May 29, 1755, he described his experience as follows:

> Paddled 60 miles, then came to a French House I passed last Autumn; there were a Master & 9 men. On our arrival they gave the Natives 10 Gallons of Brandy adulterated, and they are now drunk. The Master invited me in to sup with him, and was very kind: He is dressed very Genteel, but the men wear nothing but thin drawers, & striped cotton shirts

ruffled at the hands & breast. This House has been long a place of Trade belonging to the French, & named Basquea. It is 26 feet long; 12 feet wide; 9 feet high to the ridge; having a sloping roof; the Walls Log on Log; the top covered with Birch-rind, fastened together with Willows, & divided into three apartments: one for Trading goods; one for Furs, and the third they dwell in.

Henday continued:

The French talk Several Languages to perfection: they have the advantage of us in every shape; and if they had Brazile tobacco, which they have not, would entirely cut off our trade.

At about this same time, Fort Bourbon was relocated to the west side of Cedar Lake, probably on the same island as the first Fort Paskoyac. It existed until 1758, when it was pillaged and burned by the Indians.

In 1759 on the Plains of Abraham in Quebec, the defeat of the French by the English brought to an abrupt end all the French plans and dreams of western expansion and exploration. They left the country. Their posts, established with so much effort and hardship, were closed. The French era was over.

Yet the coals in the fireplaces of the abandoned forts had scarcely grown cold before a few enterprising free traders, such as Alexander Henry and Benjamin and Joseph Frobisher, moved into the deserted country. The site occupied by Fort Paskoyac became important once again, as independent traders established their trading posts there.

The junction of the Pasquia and Saskatchewan rivers has always been a traditional gathering place for the Indians. Here was located an important fishery for whitefish. Also, it was a very convenient spot for aggressive Indian chiefs to levy tribute on traders passing by.

In his journal, Alexander Henry gave a colorful account of what happened to him when he arrived at Pasquia in October of 1775:

On our arrival, the chief, named Chatique, or The Pelican, came down upon the beach, attended by thirty followers, all armed with the bows and arrows, and with spears. Chatique was a man of more than six feet in height, somewhat corpulent, and of a very doubtful physiognomy. He invited us to his tent; . . . Chatique presently rose up, and told us, that he was glad to see us arrive; that the young men of the village, as well as himself, had long been in want of many things of which we were possessed in abundance; that we must be well aware of his power to prevent our going further; that if we passed now, he could put us all to death on our return; and that under these circumstances, he expected us to be exceedingly liberal in our presents; adding, that to avoid misunderstanding, he would inform us of what [trade goods] it was that he must have. The men in the canoes exceeded the Indians in number; but, they were unarmed, and without a leader: our consultation was therefore short, and we promised to comply.

Pasquia, controlling as it did one of the main river approaches to the English forts on Hudson's Bay, continued as a site of great importance to the traders of the North West Company. It was the farthest point they could reach in one year when outfitted at Fort Michilimackinac. Not until the center of the bitter struggle between the North West and the Hudson's Bay companies had moved farther up the Saskatchewan did its significance decline.

Pasquia, or The Pas as it is known today, is a most interesting place to visit. There is a small, pleasant park on the south bank of the river. Here has been erected a monument to Henry Kelsey, a Hudson's Bay Company fur trader and explorer who in 1690 reached The Pas on his journey from York Factory on Hudson's Bay to the prairies of Saskatchewan, where he became the first known white man to see the great herds of buffalo roaming the plains.

Close by is Christ Church, a modest white building built in 1840. It is notable because some of its furnishings and pews were made by two ships' carpenters belonging to the relief expedition of 1847 sent out to search for Sir John Franklin, lost somewhere in the Arctic.

The Indians who have occupied this land for countless generations now live mostly on the north side of the river. Their community in addition to their neat homes contains a large, modern shopping mall and a sports arena.

Today there is very little left to show that an important trading post once stood on the banks of the river. There is no trace left of the French fort, no ruins remain to indicate the site of the Pedlars' posts, nothing to mark the spot from whence Indian chiefs descended upon the brigades to levy their tribute. All have disappeared.

As we slowly walked along the pleasant pathway bordering the south side of the river, pausing now and then to enjoy the view of the river, we could just see upstream the mouth of the Pasquia River. Downstream, the river disappeared from sight into the bordering marshlands. We suddenly realized that, indeed, there was something here that remained as a witness to the days of Fort Pasquia. It was the Saskatchewan River itself, unchanging and timeless, flowing silently on its appointed course eastward to lose itself in the water of Lake Winnipeg.

Henley House

The French conquest of the Hudson's Bay Company forts on Hudson's Bay and James Bay was nullified by the terms of the 1713 Treaty of Utrecht, which mandated that these posts be returned to the English company. The French, in spite of this setback, were not completely thwarted. With great energy and shrewdness, they moved swiftly to close the back door approach to the bay forts. They established small log-tent outposts at strategic points in the hinterland that enabled them to meet the Indians on their way to the bay and secure their furs in trade.

In 1743 three Frenchmen from their outpost up the Albany River were able to intercept Indians journeying to Albany Fort and trade for all their prime pelts. When the Indians eventually reached the Hudson's Bay post, they had nothing but inferior skins to offer for trade.

Joseph Isbister, master of the fort, chagrined and alarmed by this disturbing evidence of the French presence, immediately decided that the only way to counter this threat to his trade was to establish his own inland post.

Without wasting any time, he organized and led a small party up the Albany River that same summer (1743). The trip was a difficult one due to the shallowness of the river and the presence of many rapids and falls.

Isbister and his men passed the spot where the French had had their small outpost. Farther on, about 160 miles upstream from the bay, they reached the junction of the Albany and Kenogami rivers. Quickly recognizing the strategic value of this location, Isbister erected his new post, named Henley House, on the north bank of the Albany directly opposite the mouth of the Kenogami.

The prime purpose of Henley House was not to trade furs but rather to safeguard from French interference the trade coming to Albany House from the interior. It was to function as a sort of modern-day "pit stop" where the Indians could pause on their long journey to the bay and secure provisions to help them continue on to Albany Fort. Since trading for furs was not its objective, Henley House needed only a small complement of men and a very limited supply of trading goods.

In 1755, twelve years after its establishment, disaster struck the small post. Apparently, two Indian women were being forcefully kept by the master, William Lamb, within the post against the wishes of their husbands. Encouraged by the nearby French, who skillfully fanned their resentment and anger, the Indians succeeded in murdering not only the master but also the three other company servants stationed at the fort.

According to the account written by Andrew Graham in his book *Observations on Hudson's Bay 1767–91:* ". . . in the morning when the three men were out a hunting they murdered the master, and shot the three men from out the windows of the house as they came to the gate, not suspecting what had happened. They throwed the dead bodies amongst the willow-bushes, carried off what would be most useful for them, leaving the doors and windows open."

When Chief Factor Isbister at Albany Fort learned of the massacre, he pursued and captured the murderers. After consultation with fellow officers and with the council at Moose Fort, he ordered that the three men be hanged for their crime. Because of this act, Isbister was dismissed by the Hudson's Bay Company. In Graham's words, "the Company lost a good Factor, he knowing their affairs in the Bay thoroughly well."

The fort, defenseless and plundered, was soon burned to the ground by the Indians. Within a short time, however, Henley House was rebuilt on the same site. Andrew Graham described the fort in his *Observations:* "It is built of wood with four bastions and curtains, and has a few small cannon for its defence. It is subordinate to Albany, and is situated a hundred miles up that river, which is so shoal that it is with the utmost difficulty provisions are conveyed up thither in flat-bottomed boats . . . The number of men are fifteen, draughted from the complement of its mother settlement."

For greater security, the number of men assigned to the post was increased. But if the company was persistent, so, too, were the Indians. Four years after the first disaster, in 1759, the Indians struck again. They took advantage of the period when the strength of the post was reduced due to the absence of many of the men on their annual trip to Albany Fort for provisions and trading goods.

Once again Graham described the incident:

They [a band of Canadians and Indians from Nipigon led by Louis Menard] formed themselves in a body, and in the night-time come and concealed themselves under the river bank until the morning. When the master [George Clark] went out to take his morning walk they fired and killed him dead before the gateway, and wounded another man in the thigh at the same time, who had the presence of mind to run in and lock the gate, where he and his two companions fired upon them all day from the upper windows, which was returned by the cowardly savages in platoon, firing from under the bank, continually whooping and making a most frightful noise after their savage manner; not having courage to come upon the bank. In the evening the three men agreed that one of them should go out of the back window, and if they within should hear the report of a gun to conclude that the savages had discovered and shot him; but if not, they were to follow. By this conduct they got clear off, travelling for three days and nights, assisting the wounded man along, until they came to a home Indian's tent, where they were used very civilly. And next day the men with the boat came up, when they informing them with what had happened, they all returned back to Albany.

When some time later men from Albany Fort returned to the scene of the disaster, they found that the post had been torched and completely destroyed, "the unfortunate master laying on the plantation naked, and scalped, with his dog laying dead by him."

In spite of this disaster, after a delay of six years, steps were taken in 1765 to reestablish Henley House, even though the upland Indians threatened to destroy it yet again.

This time the site chosen for the fort was on a gravelly island in the Albany River opposite the mouth of Henley River and ten miles below the mouth of the Kenogami River, where the first Henley House had been built twenty-five years earlier. The new post was completed in 1768.

The proper function of Henley House was not completely resolved. The Governor and London Committee still felt that the purpose of the post was only to assist the Indians on their long journey to the bay, not to trade for furs, thereby diverting them from Albany Fort. The London Committee repeatedly reiterated their policy that Henley House was to be a "transit post" and no more, that it had been established "solely with the design of assisting the Indians in the Course of their Journey and not with any motive to prevent the Trade being brought to Albany Fort in the usual manner." The Committee declared quite categorically that Henley House was to be subordinate to Albany. It was not to be provided with the usual wide range of trading goods—only guns, flints, powder, shot, and a small supply of brandy.

Gradually, however, some of the more enterprising factors of the bay posts, such as Ferdinand Jacobs at York Factory, Humphrey Marten at Albany Fort, and, eventually, a somewhat reluctant Andrew Graham, began to accept the need for inland posts. They felt that trading posts established inland from the bay were essential if the Hudson's Bay Company interests on the bay were to be protected from the encroachments of the Pedlars from Montreal. They recognized that these inland posts were an effective check to the independent traders,

65

providing encouragement to the Indians to resist the Pedlars' often-times high-handed methods of trade.

These factors also knew that the Indians had to spend at least two months each year on their journey to and from Albany Fort and that this arduous trip required a large amount of powder and shot and provisions both for themselves and their families back home. It was not surprising to the factors that the Indians regarded the Hudson's Bay Company's insistence that they come to the bay to trade as "a deceit" and chose whenever they could to trade with the Pedlars at their inland posts.

It was also recognized that the establishment of these subsidiary posts far from the direct supervision of the factors at the bay posts opened the door to the practice of private trading, to the uncontrolled use of liquor in the trade, and to the opportunity for the Indians to cheat the company by getting goods on credit at one post and then evading their debts by taking their furs to another.

However, it was not until 1775 that the Governor and London Committee reversed their long-held policy regarding the status of Henley House. In a complete about-face, they directed that Henley House was no longer to function as a mere assistance post for Indians traveling to Albany Fort. Henceforth it was to operate as an independent trading post—"a large Mart of Trade." Henley House quickly justified its new status by showing a return of 2,000 Made Beaver. (Made Beaver was a Hudson's Bay Company accounting term. It set one prime winter beaver skin as the standard unit of value by which all other furs, as well as each item of trade goods, were evaluated. Their value was then expressed in terms of "Made Beaver.")

The Hudson's Bay Company initiated a second major policy change. They decided to adopt the Nor'Westers' use of numerous temporary and mobile outposts set up in the Indians' own homelands. They ordered that the bayside forts—Moose, Albany, and York—were to function primarily as factories for the supply of the inland posts. These inland posts were, in turn, to set up and outfit small temporary outposts—mere log tents—which could easily and quickly be moved according to the prospects of trade and in response to movements of the competition. Henceforth the location of the inland posts would be determined by the needs and convenience of the Indians as well as by the presence of the fur-bearing animals. No longer were the factors to remain within the walls of their bayside forts; mobility and aggressiveness were to be the new order of the day. In the much-quoted (but not completely accurate) words of Joseph Robson, the Hudson's Bay Company had finally emerged from its eighty years' sleep "at the edge of a frozen sea."

The task of supplying posts upriver from Albany Fort was always a difficult one due to the many shoals, falls, and rapids in the river. To solve this problem a superintendent of boats was stationed at Albany Fort. It was his responsibility to maintain the flow of goods and furs on the river. A system was devised utilizing both boats and canoes according to their best capabilities. The boats had greater carrying capacity and better stability. They could be made of fir, which was available around the forts. However, if repairs were required, they could only be done by the boat repairman at Albany Fort. They could not navigate the falls unassisted. Canoes, on the other hand, were indispensable for rapid travel over the falls, rapids, and shallow river stretches. In addition, they were easily portaged. Henley House was chosen to receive and warehouse all the supplies and goods from Albany Fort. It then supplied Gloucester House (established in 1777, 234 miles farther upriver) as well as all the interior log-tent outposts in the area.

In addition to its new role as a fur trading fort and a supply depot, Henley House was now to serve as a base for expeditions into the interior designed to explore and map the country and to determine the precise location of the company's trading posts. Philip Turnor, a young surveyor, was brought over from England by the company in 1778 to accomplish this task.

During one of his journeys inland from Albany Fort, Turnor stopped at Henley House. He wrote a detailed description of the post in his journal dated August 6, 1780:

Henley House stands upon an Island on Northside the River a small branch of about 70 or 80 Yards wide running round the North side of the Island and a small creek falling into it on the North side (called Chickney Creek) the Island is about 3/4 Mile long and near 1/4 Mile wide the House stands about 150 Yards from the west or upper end of the Island . . . I think Henley House the worst building I have seen in the Country both as to Convenience and Workmanship the Flankers all given way from the sheds that both Flankers and Sheds are obliged to be shored the platforms of Sheds and tops of the Flankers all rotten the Flankers neither Wind nor Water tight and was a Person to begin to Repair it I am of Opinion he would find more Labour than in Building a Substantial good new House . . . I should think it would be much better to build a House upon the heighest ground as it would not be subject to damage by deluges and in that case I should think it most prudent to let the present House stand untill the new one is tenantable as I should not think any of the materials of the present House worth puting into a new one except the Brickwork.

Two years after this description was written, Henley House was completely destroyed by an accidental fire. A new fort was immediately erected on the same site based on plans drawn up by Philip Turnor.

For the next seventy-five years Henley House remained in operation serving the needs of Indians drawn from a large area. By 1880, however, all vestiges of the fort had completely disappeared.

Originally we had planned to reach the Henley House site by paddling the time-honored river route of the Albany River from James Bay, but the unexpected death in 1994 of my husband, the faithful companion of all my journeys in search of the fur trade forts, rendered this impossible.

So one day in early autumn, Jeff Martin, the pilot, and I flew in a Cessna 185 from his float plane base at Forde Lake, thirty miles west of Hearst in northern Ontario, straight north to the Albany River. The muskeg was a beautiful sight. It was carpeted in shades of light green, dark green, and chartreuse, brightened with the golden color of aspen and a very few spots of red. Everywhere shining through the vegetation, water sparkled reflecting the blue of the sky. Presently we reached the broad Albany, its brownish-tinged waters flowing smoothly to the east.

Using the information detailing the location of the two Henley House posts contained in Philip Turnor's journal and our large government topographic maps, Jeff had no problem in flying directly to both sites.

The location of Henley House I was indeed a strategic one. It was situated on the north side of the Albany River directly opposite the mouth of the Kenogami River. The post was erected along the flat bordering the river, backed by a slightly higher bluff covered with an unbroken expanse of trees. From this vantage point all canoe traffic on the Albany River, as well as on the Kenogami River, could be monitored.

Ten miles downstream was the site of Henley House II. Directly in front of the mouth of the small Henley River draining into the Albany River from the north is a small elliptical island. It is encircled by a low, flat zone with a thick growth of trees at a slightly higher elevation occupying the center. Here on the south side of the island next to the Albany River was the site of Henley House II.

Both sites of Henley House shared the atmosphere of remoteness, loneliness, and strange beauty that characterizes the north muskeg country. Even as we flew over this vast country, we, too, felt this special spell.

Fort Coulonge

During the third quarter of the seventeenth century, when the English were establishing trading posts on the shores of James and Hudson Bay, the French from their bases at Montreal and Quebec were pushing westward, building posts along the St. Lawrence and Ottawa rivers and the north shores of lakes Huron and Superior.

Even as early as 1650 the prominent d'Ailleboust family of Quebec had erected a stockaded trading fort on the Ottawa River between Calumet and Allumette islands. They gave the name of their seigneury, *Bois de Coulonge,* to both the fort and the nearby river. Nicolas d' Ailleboust de Manthet, a well-known and adventurous member of the family, spent the winter of 1694–95 at the fort. From its founding until the British conquest in 1760, Fort Coulonge was held and operated by the d'Ailleboust family.

With the withdrawal of the French from New France, Fort Coulonge, as well as many of the other trading posts established by the French, was abandoned and soon fell into disrepair. Alexander Henry the elder, while traveling the Ottawa River on his way to Fort Michilimackinac in 1761 referred to Fort Coulonge in his book *Travels and Adventures in Canada and the Indian Territories* as follows: "On the morning of the 14th, [July] we reached a trading fort, or house, surrounded by a stockade, which had been built by the French, and at which the quantity of peltries received was once not inconsiderable."

Fort Coulonge was so advantageously located that it was not overlooked when the fur traders of Montreal, organized into the North West Company, began taking over and rehabilitating many of the posts vacated by the French.

Forty years after Henry's reference to the deserted Fort Coulonge, Daniel Harmon on his first trip from Montreal to the western fur country wrote in his journal: "May 11, Sunday [1800]. We are encamped on a small Island opposite to where the North West Coy. have a Fort [Coulonge] and the Person who has it in charge came to invite my fellow travellers and me to go to sup with him, to which invitation I readily agreed and was treated with all the politeness of which a Canadian is master (which is not a little) and they in that, as well as in many other respects resemble their ancestors the French."

According to W. Kaye Lamb, editor of Harmon's Journal, it is quite probable that some of the last buildings erected by the French were still standing at the time of Harmon's visit there.

One of the more colorful masters of Fort Coulonge during its years as a North West Company post was Joseph Godin. He began his rather checkered career as an illiterate voyageur. However, an ability for shrewd—even unscrupulous—trading not hampered by the niceties of ethical standards, nor burdened by any loyalty except to his own interests, coupled with his reputation as a powerful fighter of great physical strength, enabled him to successfully crush all competition from other traders. Consequently, his deceptions and questionable practices were conveniently overlooked by the North West Company, which rewarded him with an extraordinarily generous salary.

At the time of the union of the North West Company and the Hudson's Bay Company in 1821, Fort Coulonge, along with several other trading posts on the Ottawa River, was entrusted to the Montreal agents McGillivray and Thain for outfitting. Because of the forts' location, it was decided that their provisioning could be better handled by these agents than by the Hudson's Bay Company's southern department headquarters at Moose Factory.

In 1823 John McLean was sent to Fort Coulonge to replace Joseph Godin, who had remained there after its takeover by the Hudson's Bay Company. In his *Notes of a Twenty-five Years Service in the Hudson's Bay Territory*, McLean described his arrival at the fort: "We arrived at Fort Coulonge early the next day, when a portly old gentleman, bearing a paunch that might have done credit to an Edinburgh baillie, came puffing down to the landing-place to receive us. We soon discovered that Mr. Godin was only 'nominally' in charge of the establishment, for that his daughter, a stout, masculine-looking wench, full thirty summers blown, possessed what little authority was required for the management of affairs."

McLean had been in charge of Fort Coulonge but a few months when, to his chagrin and surprise, John Siveright arrived with authorization to take over as bourgeois of the post. McLean was relegated to running the fort during the summer months in Siveright's absence while on his annual trip to Montreal with the year's accumulation of furs.

Siveright, an employee of the North West Company since 1805, came to Fort Coulonge from his post at Sault Ste. Marie, where he had been clerk in charge since 1815. Most of his subsequent twenty-eight years with the Hudson's Bay Company were spent in the Ottawa River districts of Fort Coulonge and Fort Timiskaming. In 1828 he was appointed chief trader, and eighteen years later he attained the rank of chief factor. John McLean remained at Fort Coulonge for only three years before being transferred to a post on Rivière aux Lièvres, a tributary of the Ottawa River.

In 1825 McGillivray, Thain and Company went bankrupt and the supervision of the Ottawa River posts was assumed by George Simpson, who in that same year was named Governor of both the Northern and Southern departments by the Hudson's Bay Company.

At the time of its greatest expansion, the trading post proper consisted of eight buildings: a warehouse, the master's residence, distinguished by an enormous stone chimney, and the clerk's house, all three joined to each other and sharing a large kitchen; a canoe shed, an ice-house, a blacksmith forge, servants' quarters, and a small hostelry. Squared logs, peaked roofs, narrow windows, and doors painted red characterized the fort's construction. Later, as increasing attention was devoted to farming, numerous sheds, barns, and stables were erected.

Fort Coulonge began to experience troubled times. Trade was falling off. The surrounding country was becoming depleted of fur-bearing animals. Competition from opposition trading establishments was fierce and unrelenting. Settlers and shantymen (i.e., loggers) were moving into the country in increasing numbers, and all were indulging in small-scale trading whenever possible. Siveright reported in 1830 "that during the winter he had met much business opposition from the shantymen and traders, including some Americans, who lumbered, cleared land, sold liquor and other articles and dealt in furs." He added that "expenses were keeping at a high level, but the beaver were rapidly decreasing. Fly-by-night taverns continued to be set up."

To meet the challenge, although trading for furs was still vigorously pursued, attention was turned to supplying the needs of the settlers and lumbermen. Under Siveright's direction, farms were developed where peas, oats, and barley were grown and cattle raised. In 1827 new buildings and a store were built by the post carpenter, Jean B. St. Denis. For a time the large quantities of hay raised on the fort's farm for use by the shanties represented a profitable undertaking. However, when the British preferred duty on colonial timber was drastically reduced in 1842, ninety percent of the shantymen were forced to close down their operations.

The stream of settlers moving into the country continued relentlessly, and soon all the arable lands along the Ottawa as far up as Fort Coulonge were taken. This settlement of the land made furs increasingly difficult to obtain. In a letter written to the Hudson's Bay Company London Committee on June 20, 1841, Simpson expressed his views regarding the prospects for the Ottawa River posts.

On my way up the Ottawa, I touched at the posts of Lake of Two Mountains, Fort Coulonge, Lac des Allumettes, and Matawa, where I found things in a regular state, with evidence that the persons in charge gave their best attention to the business; but from the exhausted state of the country I am sorry to say the trade is by no means as prosperous as could be wished. A small profit is nevertheless made at all these establishments by the sale of supplies in the neighbourhood, and while they thus cover their expenses I think it is necessary and proper that the posts should be maintained, as they check in a greater or less degree the encroachments of petty rival traders on our more valuable inland districts . . .

Nevertheless, only three years after this letter was written Simpson decided to close Fort Coulonge. The large 675-acre farm with all its buildings was sold. The small sales shop, however, was kept open and operated under a succession of clerks. Finally, in 1855, this, too, was sold, with Thomas Taylor, the last clerk, becoming the new owner.

So, after nearly two hundred years of existence, under the aegis of first the French, then the North West Company, and finally the Hudson's Bay Company, the trading post of Fort Coulonge passed out of existence.

As late as 1873, of the fort proper, the three contiguous buildings, the icehouse, and the forge were still standing. In 1892 even these lonely survivors disappeared, consumed in the flames of a disastrous fire.

It was an old picture in the Spring 1966 issue of the *Beaver* magazine of some of the buildings still standing on the site of Fort Coulonge that provided us with the clue we needed to locate the fort.

We entered the province of Quebec from Ontario by crossing the Ottawa River in the vicinity of Allumette Island. We soon reached the small French-speaking village of Fort Coulonge, situated on the south side of the Coulonge River a short distance upstream from its junction with the Ottawa River.

Here we began our inquiries at the local restaurant, gas station, and *épicerie*—usually our best sources for information. We drew nothing but polite "je ne sais pas" responses. No one recognized the area shown in our picture. Apparently, even the memory of the old trading fort had been completely lost.

Late in the day, discouraged but still determined, we headed down a dusty side road to find our campground for the night. And there our perseverance was rewarded. When we showed the *Beaver* magazine to the owner of the campground and explained our hopes to find the place shown in the photo, he summoned his wife, a longtime resident of the area. After examining the picture closely, she said she thought she recognized the place and could direct us to it.

So, early the next morning, our hopes high, we left the campground. Following the directions given us, we drove out of Fort Coulonge northward and along a side road that closely paralleled the Coulonge River. Within a short time we came to a large clearing instantly recognizable as the place portrayed in our picture. The buildings, their placement, the wooded area—all corresponded closely. We had, in truth, found the site of the old trading post of Fort Coulonge.

It was a large open field by the side of the road just a few yards back from Coulonge River at its junction with the broad Ottawa River. A thick fringe of trees and bushes bordered the field on the far side. Also toward the rear the few remaining buildings, roughly constructed, timeworn, and weathered, were clustered. In spite of a luxuriant growth of grasses, wildflowers, and sumac bushes, foundation ridges and cellar depressions of buildings that were once part of Fort Coulonge were faintly discernible.

A tall white wooden cross on the riverbank directly across from the clearing marked the location of the early fort cemetery where traders, settlers and natives alike, were buried.

As we stood by the river and surveyed the peaceful scene before us, we tried to re-create in our minds the activity that once characterized this busy trading post; to see the river's edge lined with canoes, boats and bateaux; to hear the voices of the Indians, the French, the Scots, the British, the Americans as over the years they filled their respective roles of trapper, trader, shantyman, farmer, and settler.

At last we abandoned our reveries into the past and left Fort Coulonge to slumber on, undisturbed and remembered by only a few.

Fort Sault Ste. Marie

The French were not slow in recognizing the enormous strategic value of the rapids at the outlet of Lake Superior. In 1670 they erected a tall cross on a hill overlooking the turbulent rapids in the river below and, in a formal ceremony, took possession of the land in the name of Louis XIV, King of France. The Indians assembled for the occasion were impressed by the colorful pageantry but totally uncomprehending of its significance for them. To them, the rapids were simply where they gathered every year to take advantage of the phenomenal whitefish run. For several weeks their tents lined both banks of the river and men, women, and children were hard at work reaping the bountiful harvest of fish. Soon drying racks would be full of hanging fish neatly gutted and split, tails pointing skyward, slablike sides exposed to the sun and air.

To the French, possession of the rapids meant control of all traffic—upstream and downstream. The rapids formed a formidable barrier stretching across the river and could only be passed by portaging around them. The advantages of the site were many and obvious. The presence of the fishery as an unfailing source of food was also of great importance. Accordingly, a French military post as well as a Jesuit mission were established on the south bank of the river. This first Fort Sault Ste. Marie was built just west of today's St. George Island. The fort was surrounded by a palisade 100 feet on a side; enclosed within were several buildings and a redoubt. By 1750 what had been simply a trading station and mission was changed into a military post with the arrival of a small garrison.

Alexander Henry, who visited the fort in 1762, described it as follows: "Here was a stockaded fort, in which, under the French government, there was kept a small garrison, commanded by an officer, who was called *the Governor,* but was in fact a clerk, who managed the Indian trade here, on government account. The houses were four in number; of which the first was the governor's, the second the interpreter's and the other two, which were the smallest, had been used for barracks."

The capitulation of the French in 1760 resulted in their abandonment of Fort Sault Ste. Marie, and the fort stood empty for two years, until it was regarrisoned by the British in 1762 with a small detachment from Fort Michilimackinac. Unfortunately, it was almost totally destroyed by fire that same year; the garrison was transferred back to

Fort Michilimackinac, where several of them were destined to lose their life in the massacre that occurred there the following year.

It was not until after the close of the American Revolution that a second Fort Sault Ste. Marie was built. This time it was established on the north side of the river and was the base from which, first, the North West Company and, later, the Hudson's Bay Company conducted their fur trade.

The North West Company quickly took advantage of the strategic location of the rapids of Ste. Marie. They were the gateway to the great Northwest, and through them their St. Lawrence route from Montreal to their headquarters at the west end of Lake Superior must pass. Accordingly, they spared no effort in establishing a well-equipped post there. Situated at the foot of the rapids, their establishment consisted of numerous storehouses, warehouses, and dwellings as well as a sawmill and a boatyard.

The old portage trail around the rapids was replaced by a forty-foot-wide roadway. A little later a more ambitious project was undertaken. A half-mile canal with one lock thirty-eight feet long, 8'9" wide, a lift of nine feet, and a parallel towpath for the oxen to track the boats were completed. This enabled loaded canoes and batteaux to bypass the rapids without discharging their canoes.

At Pointe aux Pins, a few miles above the rapids, the company built several schooners suitable for navigation on the Great Lakes. One, the *Otter,* was used primarily on Lake Superior. A sheltered harbor formed by a pier built out from a small island provided safe mooring for the schooner *Otter* so cargo could be safely received and discharged.

In 1812 war between the United States and Great Britain erupted and the security of the North West Company post at the rapids was threatened. In July 1814 this danger was realized when an American force pillaged and burned not only the entire North West establishment but also the company's schooner on Lake Superior. In addition, they destroyed the canal lock. The only thing that escaped destruction—and this was considerable—was the annual return of furs from Fort William. The brigade of forty-seven large canoes manned by 135 well-armed men carrying a cargo valued at $1 million slipped behind the islands of the North Channel and successfully eluded the American warships.

After the 1821 merger of the two rival fur companies, Fort Sault Ste. Marie declined in importance somewhat as the old North West Company route to Montreal via the St. Lawrence was gradually supplanted by the Hudson's Bay Company's Albany River route to York

Factory. However, the Hudson's Bay Company, in recognition of the strategic importance of the rapids, continued to maintain a post there for many years. John McLean, who spent the night at the company fort while on his way to his new post in New Caledonia in 1833, characterized the fort as "a large depot of provisions for the purpose of supplying the canoes passing to and from the interior and the surrounding districts." A final improvement was made when about 1850 a tramway operated by horses was built at the old portage, replacing the single horse-drawn cart used previously.

Today the area of the two Sault Ste. Maries is rich in reminders of the fur trade days. A very attractive riverside park has been created along the south shore. At the upper end the sites of the first Fort Sault Ste. Marie, established by the Sieur de Repentigny in 1751, and Fort Brady, built on the same location in 1822, are suitably marked by appropriate cairns and tablets. Close by is the small white house of John Johnston.

The story of John Johnston is an interesting one. This son of a prominent Irish family immigrated to Canada as a young man of twenty years. Intrigued by the tales of the fur trade, he decided to become a fur trader and so in 1792 purchased his stock of trading goods, hired five voyageurs, and set up shop at La Pointe on the Madeline Island off the south shore of Lake Superior. There he fell in love with the daughter of the Chippewa chief Wabogish (White Fisher) and subsequently married her. Before long Johnston moved to Sault Ste. Marie, where he soon built a comfortable home, complete with extensive library and surrounded by flourishing vegetable and flower gardens. His home, reflecting his superior educational background, soon occupied an important place in the life of the small community of Sault Ste. Marie. From here he carried on his prosperous business as an independent fur trader.

During the War of 1812, he participated in the successful capture of Fort Mackinac by the British. Two years later he further aided the British cause by outfitting at his own expense about one hundred of his voyageurs and sending them to reinforce the British garrison holding Fort Michilimackinac threatened by American efforts to recapture the fort. It is no wonder that when, a bit later, American ships arrived at the Sault they did not spare Johnston's property. In addition to the North West Company establishment across the river, they completely destroyed his home, stables, and all other buildings. All were burned to the ground. Nothing daunted, when the war ended Johnston rebuilt and resumed business.

In 1823 his daughter, Jane, who had received the benefits of an excellent education both from her father and from schooling in Ireland, married Henry Rowe Schoolcraft, well-known as Indian agent, historian, explorer, and writer. The home they built and lived in has been moved from its original site downriver to a new location within the park next to Johnston's house. The name Portage for the street that parallels the river perpetuates the memory of the old portage around the rapids.

Of the rapids themselves, one portion still remains untamed, free to race and tumble over the rocky ledges of the river. The rest of the rapids and all the beautiful tree-covered islands but one are no more. They have been swallowed up by the five cavernous locks through which all the traffic to and from Lake Superior must now pass—700-foot freighters carrying 20,000 tons of cargo have replaced the thirty-six-foot *canots du maître* (the freighter canoes of the fur trade days) whose carrying capacity was about sixty-five carefully loaded ninety-pound *pièces,* for a total of three tons.

One last remnant of the early days lingers on. Miraculously, whitefish in large numbers are still caught each year in what rapids yet remain. Across the river on the Canadian side, there are numerous reminders of the fur trade days. One of the most outstanding, still on its original 1814 location close to the river below the rapids, is the magnificent stone mansion of Charles Oakes Ermatinger, a prominent fur trader and one-time partner of the North West Company. He was a shrewd trader and managed to operate profitably as a Nor'Wester, as an independent trader, and as a Hudson's Bay Company official. He, like John Johnston, aided the British attack on Fort Mackinac, but unlike the latter, when retribution came some two years later his property was spared by the Americans. Charles Ermatinger and Charlotte, his Ojibway wife, kept open house for all who came—North West Company and Hudson's Bay Company officials, artists, missionaries, scientists, and voyageurs all enjoyed their hospitality. Invitations to their annual dinner were eagerly sought.

Upriver, at the head of the rapids on the grounds of the St. Mary's Paper Company, is a restoration of a small portion of the canal and lock built by the North West Company in 1797. What a dramatic contrast between it and the giant Canadian lock just a few yards distant. As we stood and looked at this small stone-lined lock with its wooden gate, it was hard to realize that it played as important a part in the smooth passage of freighter canoes bypassing the rapids as does the huge concrete Canadian lock to the mighty freighters of today.

Near the locks and also on the grounds of the St. Mary's Paper Mill stands a building whose many changes have almost completely obscured its original appearance. Built in 1814 as a powder magazine by the North West Company, it had massive walls of stone and no windows. Over the years subsequent drastic alterations and additions caused it to lose its identity, and it came to be known, erroneously, as the Hudson's Bay Company blockhouse. Close scrutiny revealed the thick stone walls of the original powder magazine.

One last spot should be visited. A replica of the tall cross erected in 1671 by Sieur de St. Lusson has been raised on a bluff overlooking the city. We stood there, and just as the French had done more than three hundred years ago, we, too, looked down on the rapids and river that have made the "Sout de Sainte Marie" a place of such great strategic importance.

Fort du Traite, Portage du Traite/ Frog Portage

The lull in fur trading that followed the conquest of Canada by the English did not last long. Among the first traders to arrive in the old French territories were Joseph and Thomas Frobisher from Montreal. They were determined to penetrate the unexplored country to the west and north. By 1774 Joseph Frobisher reached the Churchill River and was one of the earliest traders to use the portage that connected the waters of the Saskatchewan with those of the Churchill.

The Indians had used this portage for generations—to them it was known as Frog Portage. This name, according to Alexander Mackenzie's explanation as recorded in his *General History of the Fur Trade,* reflected the contempt of the Cree for the ignorance of the northern natives (the Chipewyan) in the hunting of beaver as well as in preparing, drying, and stretching the skins. To show their derision, the Cree stretched and dried the skin of a frog and placed it at the portage.

Frobisher had moved into a log hut built earlier by Louis Primeau on the Churchill, close by the portage, where he was able to intercept the Indians on their way down to Fort Churchill on Hudson's Bay with their annual harvest of furs. A large number of these pelts were owed to the Hudson's Bay Company as payment for credit extended to them the previous fall. Frobisher, not hampered by ethical niceties, by one means or another managed to secure the furs from the reluctant Indians. He only stopped when he had as many furs as his canoes could carry. Elated at his success, he hurried down to the annual rendezvous at Grand Portage. After this "coup" the portage was henceforth known as Portage du Traite (Trade).

The following year, 1775, he and his brother, Thomas, along with Alexander Henry the elder pooled their trading goods and headed back to the Northwest. They reached Amisk Lake in November, and there they built a fort on the west shore near the mouth of the Sturgeon–Weir River, in which to spend the winter. Early next spring Thomas Frobisher and six men left the fort, ascended the Sturgeon–Weir River, and crossed over the Portage du Traite to the Churchill River. On the north shore where the river broadens into a five-mile-wide lake known today as Trade Lake they constructed a trading post called Fort du Traite.

Joseph Frobisher and Alexander Henry followed several months later. Here once again their trade with the Indians was highly profitable, and they made a rich haul of furs. From their fort, so strategically

80

located, they were effectively cutting off the Indian trade destined for Fort Churchill.

How the trading was conducted is rather vividly described by Alexander Henry. He wrote:

> While the lodges of the Indians were setting up, the chiefs paid us a visit, at which they received a large present of merchandise, and agreed to our request, that we should be permitted to purchase the furs of their bands.
>
> They inquired, whether or not we had any rum; and, being answered in the affirmative, they observed, that several of their young men had never tasted that liquor, and that if it was too strong it would affect their heads. Our rum was in consequence submitted to their judgment; and, after tasting it several times, they pronounced it to be too strong, and requested that we would *order a part of the spirit to evaporate.* We complied, by adding more water, to what had received a large proportion of that element before; and, this being done, the chiefs signified their approbation . . .
>
> The Indians delivered their skins at a small window, made for that purpose, asking, at the same time, for the different things they wished to purchase, and of which the prices had been previously settled with the chiefs.
>
> On the third morning, this little fair was closed; and, on making up our packs, we found, that we had purchased twelve thousand beaver-skins, besides large numbers of otter and marten.

In 1777 Joseph Frobisher returned to his Churchill Fort for one last year. This time the Hudson's Bay Company had sent a man, Robert Davey, upriver to meet and protect the Indians coming down the Churchill for Cumberland House. Frobisher followed him and eight days' travel upstream he met not only his associate Primeau, coming down with four canoes of furs from Frobisher's brother, Thomas, but also twenty-eight canoes of Indians headed for Cumberland House. Although Frobisher tried to lure these Indians with liquor and gifts to trade with him, Davey successfully thwarted his efforts and safely escorted the Indians to Cumberland House for trade. Joseph Frobisher's final returns, however, were still substantial—seven canoes of furs, including four of his brother's.

Fort du Traite was not occupied for long. As the fur trade moved ever westward in its search for untapped beaver country, the fort was soon left behind, its usefulness ended.

However, its memory is perpetuated in the name of both Trade Lake, where the fort was located, and the Portage du Traite, where the famous—or infamous—trading was done. This carrying place, whether known as Frog Portage, Trade Portage, or Portage du Traite, remains today as it always has been, a vital connecting link between the two great Saskatchewan and Churchill river systems. Over it canoeists, trappers, hunters, and Indians still travel.

There are but two ways to reach Portage du Traite: water and air. We chose to go by air; accordingly, we drove to Pelican Narrows, about forty miles southeast of the portage, where a float plane base was indicated on our map. Upon arrival at Pelican Narrows, we soon spotted the dock with a Cessna 185 moored to it. But here our luck ran out. The weather turned sour—rain and high winds moved in from the north. There would be no flying on this day. Dejectedly we drove around the little Cree village, which was almost totally obscured by the heavy rain squalls. The waves of Pelican Lake were thundering up onto the shore. A few fishermen were pulling up their boats to higher ground for safety. The Hudson's Bay store was undergoing a face-lift. The traditional white siding and red roof, the hallmark of company stores for generations, were being replaced by modern nondistinctive metal siding.

It was not until two years later, in early October, that we tried again to reach the portage. This time we decided to make the attempt from Flin Flon because of its large modern float plane base. As we drove north from Winnipeg, we soon encountered snow and sleet. The farther we went, the worse it was. We wondered if we were making this long drive only to be disappointed yet again. Upon arrival in Flin Flon, we checked with the air base and were told that all planes had been grounded, but that clearing weather was forecast for the next day; also, although skim ice was forming on some of the lakes to the north, a few float planes were still in service. We were to report at the base the next morning at 10:00.

The next day was not encouraging. It was cold, windy, and overcast, but at least the snow had stopped. We waited anxiously at the air base one hour, two hours. Finally, the welcome news was received—it was clearing to the north; we could take off. We had told our pilot that we wanted to follow as closely as possible the route used by the voyageurs in traveling between the Churchill and Saskatchewan river system, so instead of heading directly toward the portage, he flew due west to pick up the Sturgeon–Weir River before turning north.

The ground below was snow-covered, skim ice fringed the shores of many of the smaller lakes, and occasional brief snow squalls obscured our vision. Would we be able to get clear aerial photos of the portage, the main purpose for our flight? We watched and photographed the Sturgeon–Weir River, now a narrow, twisting channel broken by the stretches of whitewater rapids that had earned it the name Maligne (Bad) River; now widened into island-dotted lakes. Suddenly the waters of the great Churchill River, broadened at this point into Trade Lake, appeared ahead. The snow squalls, which had been intermittently plaguing us, stopped as if in answer to our prayers, and there below us in perfect clarity was that 335-yard ribbonlike trail stretching from the Churchill River to the small lagoon, the source of the Sturgeon–Weir River.

After a skillful landing in the small bay and taxiing as closely as possible to the shore, we climbed out and slipped and scrambled over the rocks to shore. The next hour went by quickly. Even though today a tramway equipped with a small flatbed car runs the entire length of the portage, it was easy to block that out of our mind and picture the voyageurs and *engagés,* their backs bent under the weight of at least two ninety-pound *pièces* (bales) or carrying the upturned canoes, jogging along this very pathway; to imagine the traders and *bourgeois,* unencumbered by baggage, striding along, no doubt welcoming this opportunity to stretch their legs after the rather cramped space in the canoe. Their names would be like a roll call of all the giants in the fur trade.

With our footsteps in their footsteps we walked the portage from end to end. It is quite level and goes through a rather open stand of spruce and poplar. At the Churchill end there is a small area of exposed granite bedrock. We speculated whether this could be where the Crees so many years ago placed their dried frog skin in mockery of the Chipewyans' way of dressing beaver. Also at this end is a cairn marking the site of the portage as a national historic site.

The Frobishers' Fort du Traite is thought to be on the north shore of the Trade Lake expansion of the Churchill River directly across from the portage. Recent search suggests that Primeau's log tent was on the south side of Trade Lake on a little point just to one side of the portage.

We were reluctant to leave this spot. To us, for a short while, the past had come alive and we had somehow bridged the centuries between fur trade days and the present. David, our pilot, perhaps sensing our feelings, when we were airborne, instead of heading directly back to Flin Flon, circled the area several times to give us a final view and a chance to say good-bye to the famous Portage du Traite.

Cumberland House

The establishment of Cumberland House was the direct result of the Hudson's Bay Company's realization that the posts of independent traders strategically located along the major rivers leading to Hudson's Bay were effectively preventing the Indians from coming down to the bay to trade. No longer was it sufficient to follow their century-old policy of remaining in their bayside forts depending upon the Indians to make the arduous and frequently dangerous journey to exchange their pelts for European trade goods.

Therefore, in 1774 Samuel Hearne was ordered to proceed inland and establish a post somewhere on the Saskatchewan River, strategically located to command as many as possible of the traditional travel routes used by the Indians. After careful search, Hearne selected the site for his fort. On the third of September 1774 Hearne wrote in his journal:

> Fine pleasant weather as above, sot out early in the Morning and Paddl'd about 10 Miles up the above little River then came into Pine Island Lake, we then went about 2 Miles to the Westward on the South side, when we came to a fine Bay, which seem'd very Comodious for building on, so we landed and I Pitch'd on the part I thought would be most convenient. The People Empd the Remainder of the Day in Clearing a spot of Ground to Build a log Fort on for the Present. The Spot I Propose to build the Proper house on is fine and Levle, and tho not very high has seldom or Ever ben known to overflow by any of the Indians in Company . . . It has a Commanding view of Pine Island Lake for several miles Each way and is said to have some good fishing Places near, also plenty of Grass, Spring and Fall.

This location had Pine Island Lake (also known as Cumberland Lake) in the front, Bigstone River to the west, Saskatchewan River to the south, and Tearing River to the east. It was at the hub of a network of water systems giving access into the interior in all directions. It was, indeed, strategically located. In fact, it was so well chosen that Hearne's post, named Cumberland House, continues in existence to the present day—the oldest permanent settlement in Saskatchewan.

Under Hearne's energetic leadership, a log tent caulked with moss, sufficient for their winter lodging, was erected within four days. Shortly afterward a temporary storehouse was added to the east end of their quarters, making a building twenty-eight feet by fourteen feet overall.

Cumberland House was located in the forest belt, too far from the plains to benefit from the herds of bison as a source of food. It was largely dependent upon fish from the lake, supplemented by ducks and geese from the surrounding marshes and occasional moose and deer. Fortunately, the fishery seldom failed.

After one year, Hearne was recalled to serve as Governor of the mighty stone fortress, Prince of Wales' Fort, at the mouth of the Churchill River, and Matthew Cocking was sent as his replacement. Cocking, in turn, was succeeded by William Tomison in 1778. For the next twenty-six years Cumberland House served as the administrative center for the inland posts. Tomison labored to develop and organize trade from York Factory westward along the Saskatchewan River to effectively meet the competition from the North West Company. He also was careful to continue company policy of civil treatment of the native people, thereby winning their respect. That this policy was a wise one is proved by the fact that the company forts staffed by few men were not attacked and their men traveled throughout Indian country without loss, of either their trading goods or life.

At Tomison's instigation, gardening was commenced, which slowly expanded to include milk cows and a large vegetable garden—the source of milk, butter, and fresh produce, welcome additions to the monotonous diet of fish.

Sixteen years after the founding of Cumberland House, the North West Company built a post beside the company's Cumberland House. Over a period of years, the North West Company had developed a remarkably effective system of provisioning their brigades for their rapid journeys. The forest belt through which they traveled could offer only fish for sustenance. As a main source of food this was frequently unreliable. It was highly perishable, and procuring it consumed time that could not be spared. However, this problem was early solved. The ample supply of buffalo meat, procured from the plains and rendered into the highly nutritious and easily transportable pemmican, became the staple that fueled the northern brigades. Depots for the storage of this essential commodity were established at suitable intervals along the North West Company's main travel routes. It was the loss of one of these caches of pemmican in the vicinity of The Pas that led the North West Company to build their own Cumberland House post in order to provide safer storage for the pemmican and other supplies essential for the smooth functioning of the brigades.

Alexander Henry the younger noted in his journal in 1808 that "This post [Cumberland House] is kept up by us less for the purpose of trade than for the convenience of a depot to supply our northern brigades. In the spring we bring down the Saskatchewan to this place from 300 to 500 bags of pemmican, and upward of 200 kegs of grease; part of the latter is taken to Fort William, while the whole of the former is required for our people going out in the spring and coming back in the fall."

About 1790, the Hudson's Bay Company constructed a new post to replace Hearne's fort. This one was located on the opposite side of the small bay from the North West Company depot. Here, for the next thirty years, these two small fortified forts became something like the Grand Central Station of fur trade traffic. Here the paths of the Hudson's Bay Company chief factors and chief traders and of the North West Company wintering partners, each accompanied by his brigades of *voyageurs, engagés,* and Orkneymen, converged. Here in the brief respite allowed, they rested, perhaps celebrated a bit, exchanged news, overhauled canoes, and, restocked with provisions and trading goods, sped off to their far-off destinations.

Although mutual assistance and friendly cooperation between the two competing posts usually prevailed, that did not in any way influence each trader's zealous and single-minded pursuit of trade for his own company. With the merging of the two companies in 1821 a new era began. At Pine Island Lake, the North West Company's depot was abandoned in favor of the Hudson's Bay Company's post.

Cumberland House at the time of the 1821 union was described as "log-houses built without much attention to comfort, surrounded by lofty stockades, and flanked by bastions." Parchment instead of glass was used in the windows. The complement for the post included thirty men and nearly the same number of women and children. However, improvements were made, for several years later Alexander Ross could record his impression of the post as "large and tolerably well built, with a handsome dwelling-house, having glass windows, and what is still more uncommon in these parts, a gallery in front—the only instance of its kind I have yet seen in the country."

From about 1830 Cumberland House declined in importance, its days of glory ended. It still continued for many more years to serve as a pemmican depot and a supply center for the fur brigades. But its role as administrative center was transferred by Governor George Simpson to Norway House, which took over as the new center of power and decision making.

The introduction of paddle-wheel stern-wheelers on the Saskatchewan River in 1874 pumped new life into the small community, providing a temporary reprieve to its economy. Once again, Cumberland House renewed its role as a distribution point for goods and supplies. But this was not destined to last. In 1925 the railroad, penetrating northward, rendered steamboats obsolete, so they, too, along with the canoes and York boats, passed into oblivion, and once more Cumberland House relapsed into isolation.

Today, Cumberland House affords easy access to the modern traveler—easy, that is, if rain has not turned the road into a slippery morass of mud. On our first trip, we were not lucky—it had rained the previous day. We slithered along, sliding from one side to another, narrowly escaping the ditches on each side. Finally, we could go no farther. Directly in front, crossways of the road, was a huge freight truck mired in the mud. Fortunately, the relief crew was ahead of us and, after an hour, the truck was extricated and we could creep by. The road ended at Pemmican Portage, where a cable ferry carried cars and passengers over the Saskatchewan River to Pine Island. There were several signs posted at the river crossing. One warned: "Bears spotted in the Community. Please do not leave your Children unattended." Another informed that the river froze during the months of October and November, making ferry operations impossible. Service would be resumed the following year when the river would be free of ice.

We drove the few miles from the ferry crossing to Cumberland House, parked our motor home in a grove of magnificent spruce trees, and then, donning low rubber boots to combat the mud that was everywhere, happily roamed about the small community. We spent considerable time walking over the large field where once stood the Hudson's Bay Company Cumberland House post. Historically, the waters of the lake extended to the clearing, but now a broad half-mile zone of willow and alder brush, the result of a drastic drop in the lake level, separates the area of the old post from the lake. Indeed, the lake can no longer even be seen from this spot.

One venerable relic of the very early days still remains, however. That is the powder magazine. Foursquare and sturdy, its massive white-washed rock walls capped with a hipped roof, it has weathered both the elements and vandalism for nearly two hundred years. What tales its rocks could tell if they could but speak!

Until fairly modern times the Hudson's Bay Company's buildings and their extensive gardens filled the clearing. Today all but one have been demolished—only numerous cellar holes and foundation ridges remain to mark their location. And these, too, will soon be swallowed up by the rapidly encroaching growth of grasses, goldenrod, asters, and berry brambles. The one building that escaped destruction was the typically white-sided, red-roofed Hudson's Bay Company home of the post manager.

We walked a short distance down the wide pathway through the brush from the clearing toward the lake. Try as we could, it was almost impossible to imagine that once a busy waterfront existed right here where we were walking; wharfs extending into the lake; canoes, York boats, stern-wheelers; lines of men loading and unloading cargoes; all the noise and confusion of a busy post at the crossroads of major trade routes. Today the quiet is broken only by the rustling of the dry marsh grasses, the familiar "konk-a-ree" of the red-winged blackbirds, and the sharp cries of the terns and gulls flying over the lake some distance away.

In a small park under a protecting stone canopy, the two boilers from the stern-wheeler *Northcote* are displayed. The *Northcote,* a Hudson's Bay Company vessel, was the first of several stern-wheelers to be used on the Saskatchewan River. They ran from Grand Rapids at the mouth of the river at Lake Winnipeg to Edmonton. Cumberland House was their main distribution and warehousing port of call. In 1875 the fickle and constantly changing flow of water in the Saskatchewan, which resulted in the diversion of water from the main river channel, eventually rendered this portion of the river impractical and virtually impossible for navigation.

In 1875 the *Northcote* played a brief and rather inglorious part in the Battle of Batoche. Attempting to carry out its mission of bringing reinforcements to General Middleton, it was effectively and speedily eliminated from the conflict by the Métis forces. By 1886 the *Northcote,* stranded by low water, was permanently beached at Cumberland House. Before too many years the two boilers, along with some rusting iron machinery, were all that remained of the once-doughty vessel.

Dwarfed by the two huge *Northcote* boilers is the small Hudson's Bay Company cannon mounted close by. Marked on the cannon is the name KINMAN and the date 1812. It probably was used chiefly for ceremonial occasions, such as saluting approaching and departing brigades and vessels.

Cumberland House was the home of the parents of our friend Lily McAuley. We had promised Lily when we were with her at Churchill some time earlier that we would contact them when we visited there. This we did, and what a wonderful experience for us!

Lily's father, Joseph Richard McAuley, a mild, gentle-speaking, eighty-eight-year-old man of Scottish descent, by means of his reminiscences led us back to the days when the Hudson's Bay Company was the dominant force affecting the lives of all who lived in Cumberland House. Mr. McAuley remembered as a young boy pushing the heavy-loaded flat-wheeled trucks up the inclined ramp from the boats to the warehouses above—all for the wages of a handful of candy. Later he freighted for the company, manning the heavy York boats, carrying 240-pound loads over the portages. He came from a long line of Hudson's Bay Company employees—servants, as they were called in those days—which included both his grandfather and father.

A generation later a McAuley was manager of the Hudson's Bay Company post of Red Earth on the Carrot River southeast of The Pas. Joseph McAuley's maternal grandfather, the Reverend John Richards Settee, was a native Anglican clergyman. From his base at Lac la Ronge, beginning in 1846, he served in the remote areas of northern Saskatchewan and Alberta.

We kept refilling our guest's teacup, hoping that a constant supply of the hot beverage would induce him to continue his stories and patient responses to our many questions. He chuckled with quiet satisfaction when he spoke of his success at fishing for sturgeon—thirty-seven in one week—worth $3.75 per pound. He rather proudly admitted that he had been successful each year in getting his moose and was hoping to be lucky in the current year's drawing for licenses so that he could go moose hunting yet again.

Finally, the teapot was drained, the cookies all eaten, and our visit with Mr. McAuley and the past was over. We shall always remember what a fine, courteous gentleman he was, and we considered ourselves extremely fortunate to have had the opportunity of spending an evening with him.

Grand Portage
Fort Charlotte

During the third quarter of the eighteenth century, while the Hudson's Bay Company was not only consolidating its position on Hudson Bay and James Bay but also beginning its first penetration inland with the establishment of Cumberland House on the Saskatchewan River, Henley House on the Albany River, and Missinaibi Lake House in the Missinaibi-Michipicoten river system, the North West Company was developing its post at the western end of Lake Superior into its major inland depot.

Grand Portage, situated at the extreme western end of Lake Superior, was the gateway to the *pays d'en haut*—the upper country. Though this area had been known to Indians for countless centuries, the first white man to use it of whom we have a written record was the great French-Canadian explorer Pierre La Vérendrye, who crossed it in 1731, while on the first of his many exploratory trips into the interior in search of the Western Sea. From that time until the fall of New France to the English, French traders and explorers regularly traveled over it in their ever-widening penetration into the Northwest.

Grand Portage, called by the French *Le Grand Portage,* i.e., the Great Carrying Place, is an eight-and-one-half-mile detour, bypassing the lower twenty-mile section of the Pigeon River, which is rendered impassable by a continuous series of waterfalls and rapids. The eastern or lower end of the portage begins in a small sheltered bay of Lake Superior, a few miles south of the mouth of the Pigeon River. It ends upstream on the river after gaining an elevation of 630 feet. Pigeon River is a link in the chain of rivers and lakes leading to Rainy Lake, Lake of the Woods, and thence to Lake Winnipeg.

The hiatus following the withdrawal of the French from the upper country was of short duration. By 1765 the adventurous and daring Alexander Henry the elder had extended his trading to Lake Superior, and within a few years he began to use the Grand Portage as he pushed ever farther into the rich fur lands to the west and north.

He commented in his journal in June of 1775: "The transportation of the goods at this *Grand Portage, or Great Carrying-place,* was a work of seven days of severe and dangerous exertion, at the end of which we encamped on the river Aux Groseilles [Pigeon River]. The Grand Portage consists in two ridges of land, between which is a deep glen or valley, with good meadow-lands, and a broad stream of water.

The lowlands are covered chiefly with birch and poplar, and the high with pine."

The importance of Grand Portage increased as more and more traders used it on their way to the Northwest. By 1778 it is estimated that goods and furs valued at approximately £40,000 sterling passed over it each year, requiring the labor of about five hundred people for approximately a month during the summer. It was to Grand Portage that the partners of the North West Company who had wintered in the remote fur country far to the west and north came each year with their canoeloads of furs, and it was likewise to Grand Portage that the business agents of the company came from their headquarters in Montreal with their cargoes of trading goods and provision for the ensuing year. During the brief period of a few weeks, the partners and agents were busily engaged in making all the arrangements necessary for the following year's trade: for each post allocation of supplies and trading goods as well as assignment of personnel had to be determined, provisioning of the brigades provided, employees' wages paid, and a general accounting of the company's financial position rendered.

All the furs brought down from the interior were pressed into ninety-pound bales ready for shipment to the company's warehouse in Montreal. The trade goods and supplies brought from Montreal were sorted and repacked according to each post's allocation for the ensuing year. Then they were transported across the portage to the canoes waiting on the Pigeon River at the upper end.

For three or four weeks there was a steady stream of men, like a line of ants, moving in opposite directions over the long portage, their backs bent under their heavy loads. They had divided the nine-mile distance into sixteen *poses,* or resting places, where they would pause for a few moments before resuming their half-trotting pace. They normally completed the round-trip of eighteen miles in about six hours.

The appearance of the North West Company establishment at Grand Portage is well described in John Macdonell's diary. In July of 1793 he wrote:

> The Grand Portage is situated in the bottom of a shallow Bay perhaps three miles deep and about one league and a half wide at its mouth from *Pointe aux Chapeaux* to *Pointe a la Framboise* having a small Island just opposite the fort about halfway from one of these points to the other; on a low spot which rises gently from the Lake. The pickets are not above fifteen to twenty paces from the waters edge. Immediately back of the Fort is a lofty round Sugar loaf mountain the base of which comes close to the Picket on the North West Side . . .

All the buildings within the Fort are sixteen in number made with cedar and white spruce fir split with whip saws after being suquared [sic], the Roofs are couvered with shingles of Cedar and Pine, most of their posts, Doors, and windows, are painted with spanish brown. Six of these buildings are Store Houses for the Company's Merchandize and Furs &. The rest are dwelling houses shops compting house and Mess House—they have also a warf or kay for their vessel to unload and Load at.

All their buildings were within a fifteen-foot-high palisade enclosure twenty-four by thirty rods in size.

The northmen who brought down the furs and the wintering partners from the interior made their camp west of the small creek that runs by the fort, while the Montrealers camped on the beach east of the creek. There was little tendency for the two groups of canoe men to fraternize, particularly since the northmen considered themselves to be greatly superior in every way to the Montrealers, whom they rather contemptuously called pork eaters (*mangeurs de lard*) because of the inclusion of salt pork in their rations.

Alexander Mackenzie described the manner of living at Grand Portage: "The proprietors, clerks, guides, and interpreters, mess together, to the number of sometimes an hundred, at several tables, in one large hall, the provision consisting of bread, salt pork, beef, hams, fish, and venison, butter, peas, Indian corn, potatoes, tea, spirits, wine, & and plenty of milk, for which purpose several milch cows are constantly kept."

At the end of the rendezvous when the ledgers were closed, the outfits distributed to the north canoes, and the bales of fur safely stowed in the Montreal vessels, there was always time for celebration. The ball was the highlight of the rendezvous, a fitting climax to the end of one trading season and the beginning of the next.

Daniel Harmon's journal entry for July 4, 1800, described the event in quite favorable terms: "In the evening, the gentlemen of the place dressed, and we had a famous ball, in the dining room. For musick, we had the bag-pipe, the violin and the flute, which added much to the interest of the occasion. At the ball, there was a number of the ladies of this country; and I was surprised to find that they could conduct with so much propriety and dance so well."

But the days of greatness for Grand Portage were drawing to a close, as the continuance of the North West Company's post there was threatened. The terms of Jay's Treaty, which stipulated that all British must withdraw their posts on American soil by 1796, were finally beginning to be enforced. Furthermore, all goods brought into the United States were to be subject to custom duties.

The North West Company yielded to the inevitable and made preparations to abandon their post, which was on American soil. Fortunately, they remembered from French discoveries that the Kaministiquia River, some thirty miles to the north, offered an alternative route into the interior, so it was at the mouth of that river (well above the international boundary) that they established their new headquarters. First named Fort Kaministiquia, it was later called Fort William in honor of the principal North West Company partner William McGillivray.

The year 1802 was the last that Grand Portage saw the excitement and frenzied activity of the North West Company rendezvous. From then on, although the XY Company maintained a post there for a few years, and still later the American Fur Company established a short-lived fish-processing station at the portage, Grand Portage quietly faded into relative obscurity.

We chose the perfect time of the year to cross the Grand Portage. It was the middle of May; the air was clear and crisp; the trees were in full bud, not yet leafed out; a few of the northern birds, such as the winter wren, had returned and were filling the woods with their music; in places the ground was carpeted with the delicate blossoms of spring beauty; and best of all, the pestiferous clouds of mosquitoes and black-flies had not as yet made their appearance.

The nine-mile portage bisects the reservation of the Grand Portage Band of the Minnesota Chippewa tribe. It is administered and maintained by the U.S. National Park Service. Thus the preservation of this historic link in fur trade history is permanently assured.

The trail is of wagon-width and on most of its length presents fairly level walking through a mixed woods of spruce, balsam, poplar, birch, and an occasional lofty white pine. The large beaver pond near the upper end supported a huge beaver lodge in the center, which appeared to be in active use.

The ease with which we strode along, unencumbered by nothing more than a small packsack carrying our lunch and water canteen and enjoying the convenience of boardwalks that spanned the creeks and beaver pond, we knew was not what the voyageurs had experienced. For them, the crossing consisted of heavy loads—180 pounds minimum—muck and mire, slippery rock ledges; no plank walkways; and swarms of mosquitoes and blackflies. The miracle of DDT would still be unknown for many years yet to come.

The trail ends at a small clearing on the bank of the Pigeon River.

Here is the site of Fort Charlotte, built by the North West Company shortly after their establishment at Grand Portage. This was a stockaded post enclosing several buildings used to store the trading goods brought over the portage until they were loaded into the canoes ready for the return journey back to the wintering grounds. Furs brought down from the interior were temporarily stored here as well. During the summer months, Fort Charlotte was a busy place. It played an important role in the smooth transport of goods and furs over the Grand Portage; as was the case at the Lake Superior end of the portage, the rival XY Company also had erected a stockade post adjacent to that of the North West Company.

John Macdonell's diary entry for the fifth of August 1793 described his brief stay at Grand Portage en route west to his assigned post on the Assiniboine River:

> I left the lake Superior and walked over the Grand Portage to Fort Charlotte accompanied by Mrss. Cuthbert Grant and John Bennet the sailing master of the otter. The Portage is full of hills [and] is divided by the voyageurs into sixteen Poses or resting places, its soil is cheifly composed of copper coloured clay the cheif vegetable production of which is spruce, fir and other evergreens. Mr. Donald Ross has been so long in charge of Fort Charlotte that he has acquired the respectable name of Governor. Next day I assisted my Bourgois in sending off fourteen canoes for the Red River. These N.W. Canoes are about half the size of the Montreal or Grand River Canoes and when loaded to the utmost can carry a Tun and a half. The number of men required to navigate them is four to five . . . A head clerk or Bourgeouis is allowed by the concern to have an extra man in his canoe to wait upon him . . . I set out after the fourteen Canoes above mentioned to winter in the Red River.

We found nothing to mark the site either of the fort or of the riverside dock except a few bramble-covered mounds and a crumbling commemorative rock cairn.

The brigades of canoes arriving and departing, the steady stream of voyageurs, backs bent under their heavy loads, the warehouses, the clerks busily checking their invoices and bills of lading, the colorful confusion, noise, and activity—all these are no more. The quiet murmur of the river as it flows by and the rattling call of a kingfisher are the only sounds to break the silence.

Yet, as we stood quietly on the bank of the river, looking upstream toward the west, we became aware of the sound of singing far off in the distance, faint at first but steadily growing louder. Suddenly from around the bend of the river a brigade of canoes swept into view, paddles flashing in perfect unison; closer and closer they came; louder resounded the voices raised in joyous song. Then just as abruptly as they had appeared, they were gone, completely vanished from sight. It was quiet once again. Had it all been just our imagination? Who can say?

Fort Lac la Pluie

Fort Lac la Pluie was a most important link in the chain of posts the North West Company had forged between their interior headquarters at Grand Portage (or after 1802 at Fort William) and the Athabasca country in the far Northwest. It appears to have been established sometime between 1775 and 1787.

The Nor'Westers soon discovered that the distance from Lake Athabasca to Lake Superior was too great to permit the Athabasca brigade during one navigation season to bring out the furs and return with the trade goods and provisions before the freeze-up of the rivers. To solve this problem, they established a depot on the Rainy River a short distance downstream from Rainy Lake for the use of the Athabasca brigade. A picked crew of voyageurs from Montreal, after depositing their trade goods at Grand Portage, hastened on to Fort Lac la Pluie with the Athabasca allotment of goods, received the rich cargo of furs already brought down, and then immediately returned to company headquarters on Lake Superior. Eliminating the round-trip from Rainy Lake to Lake Superior enabled the Athabasca brigade to speed back north with a head start of several weeks. These few weeks were crucial—often spelling the difference between reaching their northern posts before freeze-up or being stranded short of their destination. As Arthur S. Morton so aptly put it, "That goods leaving Montreal in May and furs leaving Athabasca at about the same time should meet year after year without fail on the shores of Lake Superior, or at Rainy Lake, and be exchanged and the crews reach their winter houses at the two extremes almost with the regularity of ocean liners was surely a triumph of human organization over the inescapable obstacles and vagaries of nature."

Trading for furs was a minor activity at Fort Lac la Pluie. In addition to being a depot for trade goods, its chief function was to provide the provisions necessary to fuel the Athabasca brigade on its long journey back to its wintering post. These, along with small amounts of meat, consisted chiefly of wild rice procured from the Indians from the marshes around Rainy Lake where it grew abundantly.

Fort Lac la Pluie was situated on a high bank on the north side of Rainy River a short distance below a series of falls and rapids that had to be portaged at the outlet of Rainy Lake. The large size of the post reflected its important status. Two wooden bastions flanked the main gate in front. Within the stockade was the usual complement of warehouses, storage sheds, men's dwelling houses, cooper's house, carpenter's shop, stables, and icehouse. In addition, one large building known as the "Athabasca House" was reserved exclusively to handle the equipment, supplies, provisions, and trading goods for the Athabasca brigade.

The fort is described by an early visitor, John J. Bigsby, in his book *The Shoe and Canoe* as follows: "The fort is a set of timber dwelling-houses, stores, stabling, &, forming a hollow square, protected by strong picketing and heavy gates. Near to these last is a small hole in the picket, through which to pass articles in unsafe times. High above all is a wooden platform, ascended by a ladder, and used as a look-out."

The entry for August 2, 1800, in the journal of Alexander Henry the younger recorded his stopover at the fort on his way to his post on the upper Red River. He wrote that after passing through Lac la Pluie and proceeding down the Rivière du Lac la Pluie past the Chaudière portage, he reached the fort where he was met by Mr. Grant, one of the proprietors of the North West Company. Henry commented on the "good garden, well stocked with vegetables of various kinds—potatoes, in particular, which are now eatable."

Judging from journals kept by the fort's proprietors, it is probable that at least thirty men were permanently employed there. This was in addition to the Indian women and their numerous offspring.

Fort Lac la Pluie was a busy place. Coopers made the many barrels and kegs needed for the wild rice, corn, and maple sugar and the fish (principally whitefish and sturgeon) from the excellent fishery near by. Carpenters and sawyers, in addition to erecting new buildings as need demanded, had the never-ending task of maintaining and repairing the existing structures. Logs for building had to be cut, hauled to the fort, and squared or whip-sawed into planks. In a rather unprecedented innovation, they split 5,000 shakes to be used for roof covering instead of utilizing the customary more primitive sheets of bark.

From early days Fort Lac la Pluie was known for its output of canoes. The birch trees used for their making grew abundantly in the nearby forests. One man skilled in the art of canoe making was charged with the sole task of producing as many of these craft as possible to satisfy the never-ending demand for them.

After the union of the North West and the Hudson's Bay companies in 1821, Fort Lac la Pluie remained a headquarters, but its importance was greatly diminished. No longer did it serve the Athabasca brigades. Henceforth, York Factory on Hudson Bay was the depot that supplied their trading goods and provisions and in turn received their annual harvest of furs.

Today a short dead-end street off the main highway at the western edge of the modern city of Fort Frances leads to Rainy River and the site of Fort Lac la Pluie.

We walked over the well-tended lawn to the large granite boulder with the commemorative bronze tablet that stood in the center of this small level clearing. The tablet affirmed that this was the site of Fort Lac la Pluie. It was a lovely place. The river flowed quietly by at the foot of the clearing; a few trees were scattered about the opening. Flowers had been planted around the base of the boulder. Nothing here suggested that a busy *entrepôt* where traders, voyageurs, and Indians met, lived, and worked once occupied this spot. The buildings have disappeared long ago; the many voices are stilled; even the rapids a short distance upstream are now quiet, drowned by waters of the nearby paper mills' holding ponds.

However, it is yet possible to stand at the top of the bank and look downstream to the west and, almost incredibly, see exactly what the inhabitants of Fort Lac la Pluie saw—a beautiful river bordered by meadows and trees flowing swiftly along, unmarred by any evidence of modern intrusion, no summer cottages, no factory smokestacks. Truly, it is a minor miracle!

Henry–Frobisher Fort

On the tenth of June 1775, the indomitable Alexander Henry the elder left Sault Ste. Marie headed for the Upper Country. His brigade consisted of twelve small (North) canoes and four large (Montreal) canoes carrying a cargo of goods and provisions valued at £3,000 sterling. At Grand Portage he had to replace his Montreal canoes with the smaller ones required for the shallow rivers of the interior. Seven days were consumed in getting his canoes and goods over the portage.

As he proceeded up the west coast of Lake Winnipeg toward the mouth of the Saskatchewan River, he was joined by other traders, including Peter Pond and Joseph and Thomas Frobisher. The augmented brigade, now numbering thirty canoes and 130 men, moved on up the Saskatchewan River toward Cumberland House. There the traders separated, each going to his own chosen area. Henry and the two Frobishers, however, decided to pool their resources and winter together in the forest belt to the north where Joseph Frobisher had traded such a rich harvest of furs the previous year.

Their combined force, which numbered forty men and ten canoes, pushed onward with all speed, for the days were getting shorter, the nights colder—the time of freeze-up was fast approaching. They headed north across Cumberland and Namew lakes and ascended the notorious Sturgeon–Weir River (most appropriately called *La Rivière Maligne* because of its wicked rapids and falls) to Amisk Lake. Henry noted in his journal: "We crossed Beaver [Amisk] Lake on the first day of November; and the very next morning it was frozen over. Happily, we were now at a place abounding with fish; and here, therefore, we resolved on wintering."

Peter Fidler, Hudson's Bay Company surveyor, on his map of Amisk Lake prepared in 1792 showed a house on the western shore in a bay south of the mouth of the Sturgeon–Weir River. This quite probably could indicate the site of the fort built by Henry and the Frobishers sixteen years earlier.

Henry's journal continued: "The . . . party was employed in building our house, or fort; and, in this, within ten days, we saw ourselves commodiously lodged. Indeed, we had almost built a village; or, in soberer terms, we had raised buildings round a quadrangle, such as really assumed, in the wilds which encompassed it, a formidable appearance. In front, was the house designed for Messrs. Frobisher and myself; and the men had four houses, of which one was placed on each side, and two in the rear."

Curious to visit the plains country south of the Saskatchewan River, Alexander Henry left the relative security and comfort of the fort on January 1 and spent the next three months in the dead of winter wandering around the plains, visiting numerous Indian villages, observing native customs, and participating in their hunts and feasts. His attitude regarding this rather remarkable journey is revealed by his comment that "long journies, on the snow, are thought of but as trifles, in this part of the world."

Early the next spring Thomas Frobisher, followed several weeks later by Henry and Joseph Frobisher, left their base fort on Amisk Lake and journeyed to their new post on the Churchill River opposite the Portage du Traite, where they carried on a highly profitable trade with the Indians.

For the next two years, until he left the *pays d'en haut* for good, Joseph Frobisher maintained the post on Amisk Lake as a base from which to advance into the Churchill River country to the north. By 1778, however, there was no further need for the post, so it was abandoned. Before long all traces of it had disappeared. Its site lay forgotten and unknown for the next 175 years.

In 1953 Henry Moody, a lifelong resident of Denare Beach, on the east shore of Amisk Lake, succeeded in locating the site of the Henry–Frobisher fort. It was, just as Fidler had shown it on his 1792 map, on the western shore in a small bay just south of the mouth of the Sturgeon–Weir River.

When we learned of this discovery, we made plans to drive to Amisk Lake and rent a boat so that we could visit and photograph the site. We stayed at the T and D Resort, a very pleasant place on the southeast side of the lake, the only side with highway access. We had arranged for a boat for the next morning. However, "the best laid plans of mice and men . . ." Amisk Lake is a large body of water, subject to periods of strong winds that produce such high waves that no one, not even the hardiest fisherman, dares venture out. The next morning we awoke to high winds, foaming whitecaps, rolling waves, and the realization that our trip could not be made.

We tried again several years later. We returned to the same resort and once again arranged for a boat. This time we drew a beautiful day. The trip across the lake following the south shore to the western side was delightful. Brilliant red cliffs crowned with luxuriant forest border the south shore, which is broken into a series of promontories and bays. Wooded islands of all sizes dot the surface of the lake. The western shore is low, wood-covered, with extensive marshy areas bordering the

Sturgeon–Weir River, which enters Amisk Lake about midpoint on the western side.

We headed directly across the lake, our goal the small bay fringed with a white sandy beach just a short distance south of the mouth of the Sturgeon–Weir River. We were soon there. A well-worn portage trail leads directly westward from the bay to a small inland lake known for its excellent fishing. Our site, however, was a short distance to the north of the trail. Here on level ground on top of a fifteen-to-twenty-foot bank was where the Henry–Frobisher fort once stood. Thick brush grew along the base of the bank at the edge of the lake, while trees covered the upper level. There was no cairn here to mark the site—only a few brush-covered mounds, and depressions along with scattered chimney stones.

We stood for a while on top of the bank lost in reverie, almost oblivious to the magnificent view that confronted us. In our thoughts was pictured the procession of brigades passing close by, for the way to that El Dorado of fur lands—the Athabasca country—lay right past this very bank on which we stood. We wondered, too, if the fur traders had enjoyed the same beauty of the lake with its islands and red cliffs—a scene unchanged from their days to ours—just as we were doing.

Fort Sturgeon

As early as 1775, following the customary route from Montreal via Grand Portage, Rainy Lake, and Lake of the Woods to Lake Winnipeg, independent "Pedlars" established posts on the lower Saskatchewan River in the general area of Fort à la Corne. The next year (1776) they abandoned these houses and moved upriver above the forks of the North and South Saskatchewan rivers and built Fort Sturgeon. This fort, also known as Peter Pond Fort and Fort Sturgeon River, existed only five years, but during that brief period it occupied a position of considerable importance in the fur trade.

Fort Sturgeon was situated on the north bank of the North Saskatchewan on a level plain in the poplar parklands just below the mouth of the Sturgeon River and about four miles above the modern city of Prince Albert. The fort was ideally located. To the south across the river lay an extension of the prairies that would provide easy access to the buffalo country and an assured supply of buffalo meat. The wooded parklands extending to the river from the north would be a source of furs.

Realizing that competition among so many would be ruinous, they decided to pool their resources and form a "common concern" for one trading year. Among the traders included in this group were Joseph Frobisher, Peter Pond, Peter Pangman, Nicholas Montour, William Bruce, and Bartholomew Blondeau.

After spending two winters operating under this arrangement, Peter Pond was convinced that greater profits would be realized if he, unaccompanied by any other Pedlars, could advance into the hitherto-unexplored Athabasca River area and tap the fur from that country. He secured the backing of the other traders at the fort who agreed to provide his outfit. So, in the spring of 1778, he set off from Fort Sturgeon with five canoes of goods and provisions and a crew of twenty men and headed for the far-off Athabasca country.

He established a post about thirty miles south of Lake Athabasca, and there he spent the winter. During that period the amount of furs he traded was twice what he could bring out in his canoes, so he was forced to cache some until the following year.

A year later, to his backers' relief and great satisfaction, he returned with a cargo of magnificent furs that not only greatly exceeded all expectations but also established the reputation of the Athabasca country as a source of the finest furs imaginable.

Relations between the traders housed at Fort Sturgeon and the Indians were not always peaceful. In 1777 an Indian was murdered by a French-Canadian employed at the fort. During that same year, three men sent out from the fort to trade and live with the Indians were killed. Two years later an Indian dropped dead from overdrinking at the fort. Fearful of reprisal, the traders were forced to keep all their men concentrated at the fort in order to be prepared for any possible attack. In 1780 the climax came when the Indians completely destroyed the fort, burning it to the ground.

The Pedlars' reckless use of rum in their trading as well as their high-handed manner in dealing with the Indians accounted in large part for these acts of hostility and vengeance that occurred. Alexander Mackenzie observed "the improper conduct of some [of the Pedlars] which rendered it dangerous [for them] to remain any longer among the natives."

Peter Fidler was at the site of Fort Sturgeon on September 23, 1792. His journal entry for that date reads: "An old Canadian House, or Houses burnt down, that no less than 6 different companies remained here, in separate Houses, but all within the same stockades. All the Houses are not burnt down, and nobody has been here these several years past."

Fort Sturgeon was not too difficult to find. About five miles west of Prince Albert we spotted a small side road marked "Peter Pond" leading south toward the Saskatchewan River. This was the clue for which we were searching. We drove down the dirt road, crossed a railroad track, and, following the road to the end, came to the site of Fort Sturgeon. It is marked by a rock cairn with bronze tablet.

There are no visible signs at all to indicate that a stockaded fort once stood in this small clearing at the edge of the woods on the bank of the river. Any traces of building foundations, cellar holes, or chimney stones disappeared years ago, undoubtedly because of the constant erosion of the north bank caused by the action of the river.

In the quiet of the late afternoon we stood on the edge of the bank watching the broad Saskatchewan smoothly flowing eastward. It was somewhat difficult to realize that it was actually from this very rather insignificant spot that Peter Pond embarked with his twenty men in five canoes and headed upstream to begin his long and remarkable pioneering journey—a journey that led him over the Portage du Traite and the Methye Portage down the Athabasca River as far as the shores of Lake Athabasca. His achievement opened the way for the many others who would follow him as they, too, sought to garner the rich fur harvest from that land of promise.

Fort Île à la Crosse

From the primitive trading post established by Louis Primeau and Thomas Frobisher in 1776 right down to the modern Hudson's Bay Company store of today, Île à la Crosse has been continuously occupied. Its location along the route to the Athabasca country enabled it to play a key role in the supply and transport system that evolved in support of the fur traders' penetration into that area.

The first to recognize the strategic importance of Île à la Crosse, Frobisher and Primeau established contact with the Athabasca Indians and from them secured a rich cargo of furs of premium quality. Other traders quickly followed in their footsteps, and for many years the Athabasca country became the "Promised Land"—the "El Dorado" of the fur trade.

During the three-year period 1782–85 traders representing three different trading interests established themselves at Île à la Crosse. By 1789, however, the North West Company emerged as the sole survivor. It made Île à la Crosse the headquarters for its Churchill River department, now governed by William McGillivray, nephew of Simon McTavish and a newly made wintering partner. One of the chief functions of this post was as a storage depot for the supplies of pemmican brought in from the upper Saskatchewan posts that were so vital to provision the Athabasca brigades.

In 1799 at Île à la Crosse an event of importance in the life of David Thompson, the celebrated explorer-surveyor who had just recently left the service of the Hudson's Bay Company and entered that of the North West Company, took place. This was his marriage *en façon du nord* to Charlotte, the fourteen-year-old Métis daughter of Patrick Small. This union ended only with the death of Thompson in 1857 at the age of eighty-seven, followed by that of his wife three months later.

The year 1799 also marked the appearance of the Hudson's Bay Company at Île à la Crosse. William Auld left William Linklater with six men to establish a trading house there as an outpost of Fort Churchill on Hudson's Bay.

Within a short while competition between the two rival trading companies became intense and at times even violent. The North West Company felt that by right of prior occupation and discovery Île à la Crosse was well within their jurisdiction, and they fought bitterly and savagely to maintain their monopoly there and drive out the Hudson's Bay Company.

John Duncan Campbell, aided by Samuel Black and Peter Skene

Ogden, headed the campaign of harassment. Since the Nor'Westers greatly outnumbered the Hudson's Bay servants, some years by as many as twenty-six to eight, their depredations went largely unchallenged. Peter Fidler, as well as Robert Sutherland, successively in charge of the Hudson's Bay post, had to stand by helplessly as the Nor'Westers shot at the post's weathervane and the company flag, carried off their firewood, destroyed their garden, stole their fishing lines, and cut their nets. In addition, the North West Company built a watchtower at the very gates of their opponents' fort for the purpose of preventing the Indians from entering the Hudson's Bay post for trade. Finally, the Nor'Westers issued an ultimatum forbidding the Hudson's Bay people from leaving their quarters. This was the last straw. The North West Company had succeeded in completely terrifying the Indians and in cowering the Hudson's Bay Company servants.

Peter Fidler in his journal entry for January 21, 1811, wrote: "Some people in reading this journal might very naturally suppose, that many of the ill actions that has been done was by people in a state of inebriety—but they are very sober people—it is a systematic plan that has been laid at the Grand Portage to harass and distress us and determined to expel us from these posts of the country where they get the greater part of their very prime furs at very little expense . . ."

As soon as the ice was out in the spring of 1811, Peter Fidler abandoned his post and jubilant Nor'Westers climbed over the stockades and set fire to the deserted fort. The Hudson's Bay Company refused to admit defeat, however, and they rebuilt the post in 1814. A year later they established a new post at a slightly different location with John Clarke in charge. Although harassment from the North West Company continued unabated, Clarke was able to maintain control of his post and to make a satisfactory trade during the winter.

The years of 1817 and 1818 were marked by escalating violence. The Hudson's Bay post and goods were captured; their establishment was even encircled with a fence on the landward side in an attempt to prevent the Indians from trading there. Nevertheless, the Hudson's Bay and John Clarke rebuilt yet again, calling their new post Fort Superior.

The bitter strife at Île à la Crosse ended only in 1821 with the merger of the two companies. As a consequence, only one of the two trading forts established there was retained. Île à la Crosse kept its position as the supply depot for the Athabasca brigades. However, reflecting a major change in the transportation system of the newly organized company, all goods coming in and furs going out passed through York Factory on Hudson Bay. Norway House serviced the

Athabasca and Mackenzie brigades in the same way that Rainy River had formerly done under the North West Company.

Lac Île à la Crosse is a large Y-shaped body of water formed by the widening of the Churchill River. The river flows from its source in Churchill Lake in a southeast direction in a forty-mile-long arm, known as the West or Aubichon Arm, before abruptly changing direction and flowing northeast for forty miles in the East Arm. At the base of the V thus formed by the two arms is the tail of the Y—a deep, narrow bay about thirty miles long.

Île à la Crosse today, like the early fur trade posts, occupies a site at the junction of the two arms and leg of the Y. We spent a pleasant afternoon wandering around photographing the lake and the buildings of the St. John the Baptist Mission, some of them over one hundred years old.

In front of the modern gold-colored, metal-sheeted Hudson's Bay store is a historical marker commemorating the long occupation of this area, first by the native Indians and then by the North West and Hudson's Bay Company trading posts. In the rear of the store stands a lone survivor of earlier days. This is the sturdily built gleaming white warehouse topped with the traditional Hudson's Bay red-hipped roof and dormer. Its back to the highway, it faces the lake from whence its trade and traffic formerly came.

Toward dusk we walked along the shore until we found a convenient resting place on a sand-scoured log washed up from the lake. We sat there for a long time marveling at the vast expanse of water spread before us.

To our far right was the mouth of the Beaver River, which gives access to Green Lake, the Saskatchewan River, and the prairies; closer on our right was the South Bay extension of the lake; to our left was the Aubichon Arm of the Churchill River, which leads to the Methye Portage and the Athabasca and Mackenzie rivers; and directly to the north in front of us stretched the open expanse of the great East Arm of the Churchill, which leads through the Canadian Shield country to Fort Churchill on Hudson Bay or, via Frog Portage, to the Saskatchewan River and Lake Winnipeg. It is no wonder that this spot became a crossroad of major importance in the fur trade.

As the twilight deepened, the local fishing craft and speedboats came in to shore and the lake appeared deserted. Then, masked by the shadows of the gathering darkness, the ghosts of the intrepid fur traders and their brigades appeared, silently and swiftly paddling their canoes over this historic water highway.

Missinaibi Lake House/
New Brunswick House

By 1776 diminished fur returns forced the Hudson's Bay Company to the realization that they could no longer depend upon their century-old policy of relying upon the Indians to come down to their posts on the bay with their furs for trade. The company decided upon the Missinaibi-Michipicoten waterway system leading to Lake Superior for one of their first experimental probes inland.

In 1777 E. B. Kitchin, chief at Moose Factory on James Bay, sent John Thomas with four men and three Indian families to establish a trading post on Lake Superior at the mouth of the Michipicoten River. His instructions read: "... the Company does not mean for you to Strive to Trade such Indians as does already Trade to Moose Fort but that You will with all Diligence pursue and Endeavour to intercept all those Indians whom Trade with the French Pedlars at Meshipicoote."

After an arduous trip Thomas reached Missinaibi Lake, where he left his men while he proceeded on to Michipicoten on Lake Superior. Assured by the Indians there that Missinaibi Lake was "rich in geese, fish and rabbits" and undoubtedly dismayed and influenced by the stretches of shallow water and numerous portages that intervened between Missinaibi Lake and Lake Superior, he decided he could compete against the French just as successfully at Missinaibi Lake as at the mouth of the Michipicoten River. He therefore returned to Missinaibi Lake and on the northeast end of the lake close to the river's outlet built his post, which was named Missinaibi Lake House.

This extension southward toward the Height of Land by the Hudson's Bay Company did not go unnoticed or unchallenged by the Canadian traders. They were able to influence the Indians and prevent them from transporting supplies or hunting for the company. For several years troubled relations with the Indians, as well as scarcity of provisions, forced Thomas to return to Moose Factory each fall, only to reappear each spring to try once again to operate his post. Finally in 1780, during his absence, the post was burned to the ground.

The site remained unoccupied until 1817, when the post was rebuilt in an effort to counter the trading activities of the North West Company, which was advancing northward over the Height of Land. With the union of the two companies in 1821, this was no longer necessary, so the site was abandoned once again and remained unoccupied until the early 1870s.

At that time a post was built on the site for the third time. It was so successful that the post on nearby Brunswick Lake was forced to close in 1879 and not only its trade but also its name were transferred to Missinaibi Lake House. Henceforth, the post on Missinaibi Lake was known as New Brunswick House. It controlled the trade of the route to James Bay until 1912–13, when the C.N. Railroad was constructed just north of the lake. The town of Peterbell was established on the rail line, and the Hudson's Bay Company set up a post there. This, of course, rendered their post on Missinaibi Lake obsolete. So, in 1914, New Brunswick House, the last of the Hudson's Bay posts in the Missinaibi-Michipicoten valley, was permanently closed.

We only reached the site of New Brunswick Lake House on Missinaibi Lake after two attempts. The first time, when we were about two-thirds of the way along the fifty-mile rough dusty road leading from Chapleau to Missinaibi Lake, the spring shackle of our boat trailer, jarred by the pounding of the horrible road, broke in two. All we could do was leave the boat and trailer by the side of the road and continue on to Missinaibi Lake. There we found help in the person of a very resourceful park manager who was able with the proverbial "haywire and hairpin" to wire together the trailer so successfully that we were able not only to bring it the remaining distance to Missinaibi Lake but also to drive it the 300 miles on our return trip home.

With much enthusiasm we set off for the northeast end of the twenty-seven-mile-long lake where New Brunswick House had been located. We had been warned by people familiar with the lake that a quarter-mile wide, very shallow sandbar extending across the lake would prevent our reaching our destination at the northeast end several miles beyond the bar.

We soon reached the bar, jumped out into about three or four inches of water, and started to drag the boat. It quickly became obvious that it simply was not possible to drag it across the bar—there just wasn't enough water. So, both crestfallen and frustrated at getting so close to our goal without being able to reach it (we could see the peninsula barely two miles ahead where the post had been located), we returned to our campsite.

It was several years before we could make a second attempt. This time we had an eleven-foot inflatable rubber raft, which we knew we could pull across the sand bar. So, in high spirits, we started up the same rough dusty road leading to Missinaibi Lake. But once again the rough road took its toll. The engine in our motor home seemed to lose all power on each hill. We were past the midway point when this trouble developed, so we decided to continue forward. Alternately coasting downhill and vigorously accelerating uphill, we managed to limp into the Missinaibi Lake campground. There close inspection of the motor revealed the trouble. The rough road had jiggled loose two sparkplug wires. This, of course, was easily fixed.

The next morning, we set off for the northeast end of the lake confident that this time, in our rubber raft, we would be able to get across the sand barrier and reach our goal. And this we did. We pulled the raft over the bar quite easily and so had no further difficulty in completing our trip to the New Brunswick House location.

The site of New Brunswick House is an elevated finger of land that extends into the lake from the east side close to the narrows that lead to the commencement of the river. Offering water access on three sides, the site was not only strategically located for trading, but also possessed great scenic beauty. The unobstructed view up the long lake, framed by pine-covered hills on each side, was magnificent. Even the fur traders must surely, on occasion, have marveled at its grandeur.

Today many cellar holes and deep pits as well as a few collapsed portions of old buildings are all that survive of the once-bustling trading house. Scattered among the rank growth of grasses and wildflowers were bits of rusted iron, old pails, broken tools, and stove parts. A close examination of the fallen-down buildings showed the careful dove-tailing that characterized nineteenth-century carpentry.

We were reluctant to leave this beautiful and historic spot. We took one last look from its commanding elevation and then went down to the beach below and were soon afloat in our rubber raft headed for our campsite halfway up the lake.

As we sped along toward the sandbar, we commented on how fortunate we had been to have such a perfect day—blue sky with only a few fleecy clouds (good for photography). Barely over the sandbar on the homeward stretch, however, we noticed big black clouds suddenly boiling up from the south with a curtain of rain in front moving rapidly in our direction.

We were well aware of Missinaibi Lake's reputation as a very dangerous body of water subject to sudden squalls accompanied by winds of tremendous velocity. We quickly realized the storm would be upon us within minutes and that we could not possibly outrun it, so we headed our raft toward the closest shore, about half a mile distant. Our outboard motor was doing its best, but the shore seemed to get no closer. And then suddenly we couldn't see the shore. The rain squall enveloped us—waves six to eight feet high tossed our raft like a leaf in all directions. Sometimes our motor was completely out of the water; the next moment it was almost totally submerged. The violent wind picked up water from the waves to add to the deluge pouring down.

Throughout it all we clung tightly to the raft ropes, knowing that our safety depended upon our hanging onto them, for even if the raft capsized, it would still float. We felt we were making no progress but hoped we were still headed toward land. Finally, after what seemed like an eternity (we realized afterward it was about fifteen minutes), our raft grounded on the pebbly beach of shore and we realized that we had survived the storm—that we were safe.

In about half an hour the squall passed on, the waves subsided and the blue sky and sun reappeared, all vestiges of the storm gone except for the water still dripping from the trees and from us. We quickly drained the raft and got ready to shove off, headed for our campground.

However, the lake had one last trick to play on us. As I went to step into the raft, one foot stuck in the wet sand, throwing me off balance, and the next thing I knew, I was sitting on the lake bottom in water up to my shoulders, but like the Statue of Liberty, my camera with the precious film was held aloft, safely above the water. This was only a minor setback, which we both greeted with hilarious laughter. Once more we boarded the raft—successfully this time—and before too long arrived at our motor home, where we were soon enjoying the comforts of dry clothes, warmth, and a good "bracer or two."

Wapiscogamy House/Brunswick House

Missinaibi Lake House was not the only trading post established by the Hudson's Bay Company in the Missinaibi-Michipicoten valley. In 1776 Thomas Hutchins, chief at Albany Fort on the west coast of James Bay, as a step toward realizing the company's goal of establishing a post on Lake Superior, sent Thomas Atkinson, surgeon, with four men and two Indian families in four canoes with instructions "to Build an Halfway House as a more sure means of facilitating the other."

After traveling about two hundred miles, they reached "Wapiscogamy, a Creek on the North Shore [of the Missinaibi River]." There on the west bank of the Missinaibi and a half-mile upstream from Wapascogamy Creek, they quickly put up a log tent in which to spend the winter of 1776–77. The following summer they constructed their permanent post.

A report written in 1781 by John Thomas describing conditions at Wapiscogamy House does not present a very favorable picture: "Wappiscogamy House in its present form will never be able to contain Trading goods or provisions safe it being so ill contrived that *I am obliged to keep the Gunpowder directly under the fireplace.*"

Construction of a larger and better-designed fort to replace the original post was begun on the same site in 1781. The resulting fort was named Brunswick House. Philip Turnor, company surveyor, was master of the post during the 1782–84 seasons. John Thomas, chief at Moose Fort, sent Turnor a letter dated October 9, 1783, instructing him to "endeavour to enlarge the Trade at Brunswick House by treating the Indians with Civility & dealing Justly and equitably with them. To Encourage dilligence and Sobriety in the Men under your Command and discountenance the Contrary which will be a means of the Company's affairs prospering under your management and will entitle you to their Esteem as well as that of Your Friend & Servant John Thomas."

The Brunswick House post operated until 1791, when the establishment of another company post in a more strategic location on Brunswick Lake rendered it unnecessary. It reopened briefly in 1800 to counter competition from a post of the North West Company established nearby. However, when that company withdrew from the area in 1806 Brunswick House was closed permanently.

After Jeff and I completed our aerial survey of the Henley House sites on the Albany River, we flew south up the Missinaibi River as far as Wapiscogamy Creek. Its outlet into the river is marked by a promi-

111

nent sand delta. About one-half mile farther upstream we reached the fort site location on the west bank of the river. There are no really distinctive features characterizing the spot. Unbroken shoreline extends in both directions into the far distance. On gently rolling terrain rising slightly back of the low riverbank is a zone of trees that extends a short distance to the nearby extensive marshy tundra. The creek as it cuts its path in loops and curves winds around in such a way that between it in the rear and the river in front the general area of the fort site is almost completely encircled by water. The chief advantage of the fort's rather unprepossessing location was its capacity of unimpeded surveillance of the Missinaibi River.

Micabanish House/New Brunswick House

Continuing their efforts to secure and maintain control of the Missinaibi-Michipicoten river system and to have a base as close as possible to the Height of Land, William Boland with ten men in 1788 was sent to establish Micabanish House on a lake of the same name. This location proved extremely advantageous and profitable, so much so that Brunswick House on Wapiscogamy Creek was abandoned in 1791.

Eight years later, both the name of the trading post and of the lake were changed respectively to New Brunswick House and Brunswick Lake. It became the company's chief post in the Missinaibi-Michipicoten river valley and until 1871 was the only post in operation in that area. However, by 1879 the post that in the early 1870s had been reestablished for the third time on Missinaibi Lake was showing such profitable returns that the company closed down its New Brunswick House on Brunswick Lake.

Continuing our flight farther down the Missinaibi River to Brunswick Lake (formerly Micabanish Lake), we soon arrived at the site of New Brunswick House (formerly Micabanish Lake House). The fort was located on a slightly elevated rounded point in the northwest corner of the lake. A vast forest extended in all directions, but the large clearing where the fort buildings once stood was still clearly visible. Today it was hidden from the lake by a large border of trees. We were enjoying the beautiful weather—ideal for photography—and reveling in the golden color of poplar and tamarack, which did much to brighten up the somber green of pine and spruce. Some of the rocks that formed the fort's dock could be seen in clear shallow water close to the shore. The location of this fort was both strategic and scenic. It faced the water of a most beautiful lake, and it was close to water passageways into the interior.

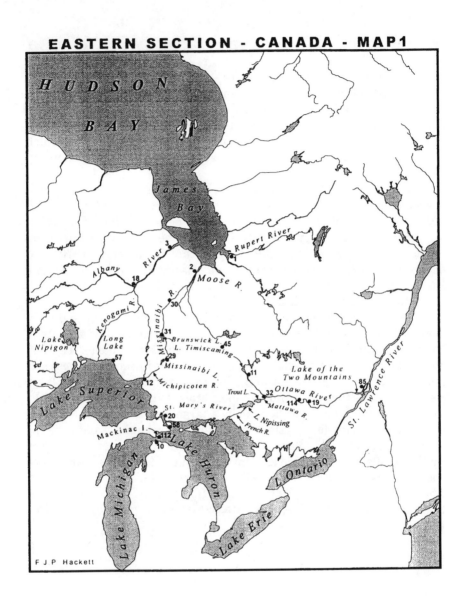

HUDSON

BAY

James
Bay

Rupert River

Albany   River 3
                    1
                 2   Moose R.
        18
              R.
Kenogami R.   30
Missinaibi R.
Long   31
Lake   Brunswick L. 45
Lake   L. Timiscaming
Nipigon   29
              Missinaibi L.
         57   11   Lake of the
              12 Michipicoten R.   Two Mountains
Lake Superior   Trout L. 32 Ottawa River   85
              St. Mary's River   Mattawa R. 114
                    20   L. Nipissing   19
         Mackinac I. 58   French R.
              12 10
              Lake Huron
Lake Michigan
                    Lake Ontario   L. Ontario

St. Lawrence River

Lake Erie

F J P Hackett

114

Fur Trading Forts—Eastern Section Canada

1. Charles Fort/Rupert House
2. Moose Factory
3. Albany House
10. Fort Michilimackinac
11. Fort Timiskaming
12. Fort Michipicoten
18. Henley House
19. Fort Coulonge
20. Fort Sault Ste. Marie
29. Missinaibi Lake House/New Brunswick House
30. Wapiscogamy House/Brunswick House
31. Micabanish House/New Brunswick House
32. Mattawa House
45. Frederick House
57. Fort Pic
58. Fort St. Joseph
85. Fort Lachine
112. Fort Mackinac
114. Fort William (Lac des Allumettes)

Mattawa House

Mattawa House, at the junction of the Mattawa and Ottawa rivers, was built by the North West Company about 1784 and was one of the first forts built by the recently organized company. It was an important post in the company's main water highway from Montreal to the *pays d'en haut*—a route pioneered by the French during the first half of the eighteenth century. It was operated as an outpost of Fort Timiskaming, some thirty-five miles up the Ottawa River.

Mattawa House continued to be operated after the union of 1821. In 1840 it was removed from the Fort Coulonge district and transferred to the Timiskaming district in an attempt to meet the competition and act as a check on the activities of the petty traders who were infiltrating the upper Ottawa River. However, eight years later it was returned to Lac des Allumettes (formerly Fort Coulonge) in order to meet the needs of the increasing number of lumbermen who were rapidly spreading throughout the Ottawa River valley. Colin Rankin who later (in 1879) rose to the rank of chief factor, was sent as postmaster by George Simpson to take charge of the Mattawa post.

Settlement and the appendages of civilization continued to move up the Ottawa. The telegraph reached Mattawa in 1871 and was followed nine years later by the arrival of the Canadian Pacific railroad. Mattawa not only became the railhead for the lower Ottawa valley but also replaced Fort Timiskaming as administrative headquarters for the outlying fur posts in the Timiskaming district. Gradually, however, the post declined in importance and was finally closed about 1915.

Today nothing remains of the buildings that comprised Mattawa House. However, the long point of land marking the junction of the Mattawa and Ottawa rivers where the post was located has been made into a lovely little park. A large white cross as well as a historic plaque has been erected to commemorate the trading post.

From the vantage point of the park we could enjoy sweeping vistas both up and down the Ottawa as well as up the Mattawa to the west. With the exception of a railroad bridge crossing the Ottawa just below the mouth of the Mattawa, the scene remains virtually unchanged from what it was two hundred years ago, when all the brigades to and from Montreal passed this very point on their way to or from James Bay or going to or returning from the western interior.

This small tongue of land was, indeed, a most important landmark to the hardy voyageurs of the fur brigades. It is very fitting that it be forever preserved as a memorial both to them and to the fur trade era.

116

Pine Island Fort
Manchester House

Pine Island was a scene of intense activity during the fall of 1786. This island or peninsula located on the east bank of the Saskatchewan River about one-half mile north of the entrance of Big Gully Creek into the river is about three-quarters of a mile long, with an average width of nearly four hundred feet. The river at this point (including the island) is approximately nine hundred yards wide. Originally it was covered with pine, but the construction of five trading posts and the need for an abundant supply of firewood soon destroyed much of the forest growth.

The first to erect a trading post on Pine Island was Donald McKay, an independent trader. A few weeks later he was followed by Peter Pangman, representing Gregory, McLeod Company, trading agents from Montreal; Robert Longmoor, sent by William Tomison, inland chief for the Hudson's Bay Company; and William Holmes of the recently organized North West Company. The last to arrive was the Frenchman Champagne.

It was inevitable that with five competing trading houses all located cheek by jowl on this small island a great deal of friction would occur. Competition was keen and ruthless. No trick or stratagem, however dishonest, was left untried. "Get the Indians' furs by whatever means necessary" was the traders' motto.

Tomison complained: "It is not possible to please the natives when there is so many houses to go to, the Canadians giving the same quantity of Liquor for 20 skins that they used to give for 50." Each trader endeavored not only to disrupt his competitors' trading with the Indians but even to divert to himself furs that had been already pledged to one of the other traders as repayment for credit. In such a competitive situation it was a wonder that outright violence and bloodshed did not erupt.

Perhaps partly as a result of the chaotic and turbulent conditions that prevailed the first year, in the following season (1787) Donald McKay relinquished his independent post and joined forces with William Tomison. Also in that same year Gregory, McLeod merged with the North West Company, so Peter Pangman united with William Holmes. Champagne abandoned the area completely. Henceforth, there were but two trading forts on the island: Hudson's Bay Company's Manchester House and the North West Company's Pine Island Fort.

William Tomison, as inland chief for the Hudson's Bay Company, was committed to the better organization of trade on the upper Saskatchewan River in order to mount successful opposition to the North West Company. To that end he established Manchester House, which at that time (1786) was the westernmost post of the Hudson's Bay Company. It was well placed to tap the furs of the rich parkland to the north as well as the Battle River valley to the south. The first boat to be used by the company on the Saskatchewan was built at Manchester House in 1788. Known as a York boat, it was pointed at both ends, which enabled it to navigate successfully the Saskatchewan River with its many sandbars. It was used to take pemmican downstream to the company's depot at Cumberland House.

The North West Company's Pine Island Fort was built at the downstream end of the island, nearly one mile from Manchester House. A. S. Morton in his *A History of the Canadian West to 1870–71*, described the fort as follows:

Pangman's post, as the ruins indicate, was about 160 feet square. It would have the usual two gates; as it was on an island each would face its branch of the river. The Wintering Partner's house was in the centre. Between it and the north palisade was the store and a glaciere, a house in which fresh meat was heaped up in the winter and finally covered with water, which immediately froze and thus gave the post a supply of fresh meat up to the departure of the brigade for Grand Portage. From the line of the palisades the houses on either side ran chequer-board fashion diagonally across the fort to the western gate. Thus there was a triangular open space within the palisades and in front of the Proprietor's house. Here the Indians would gather, but would be under observation, and if the occasion called for it, as was the case one day, would be under fire from the huts on every side. At the ceremonial entry of a band, the chief and his councillors would be received with a fusillade and pass from the gate to the 'Indian Hall' before them to smoke the pipe of peace and hold a council with the Wintering Partner in his own home. Here also the ceremony of clothing the chiefs whose bands had brought in a satisfactory quantity of furs would take place in the spring.

Trade with the Crees from the north and with the Fall (Gros Ventres) Indians from the plains was carried on at both trading forts for the next six years. Gradually the beaver, marten, and other high-value furs traded by the Crees enabled them to acquire considerable superiority in weapons over the Gros Ventres, whose wolf and fox skins, being of far less value, could only be traded for a much smaller number of firearms. Thus the Gros Ventres became the underdogs, subject to terrorization by the Crees. The Gros Ventres held the traders to blame for their plight, feeling that the traders had become allies of the Crees. Their resentment and frustration steadily increased until finally, in November of 1793, it boiled over, resulting in their attack on the Pine Island forts.

John McDonald of Garth in his *Autobiographical Notes* gave a vivid description of what happened:

A war had broke out in Sumr. between the prairie Crees & the Tribe of Mandans & Fall Indians in the Missouri. Several had been killed on both sides. The Missouri Indians knowing that the Crees were in league with the Whites on the Saskatchewan determined war upon them also. They killed an old man who went to the Plains to look for his Horses. It was not known first who comitted the act i.e. what tribe; when a numerous band of those tribes came to Mr. Finlay under pretence of Trade . . . [The Indians] as usual walked into the Fort & began after a short time to Trade what little they had; when they began to be insolent Mr. Finlay soon perceived their intentions to overpower himself and men, & murder them & then to pillage the goods. This was at last apparent to all, but poor Mr. Finlay was too great a Coward to take any effective steps tho' they told him they had killed his Old Man, saying he would pacify them by presents, when Mr. Hughes though a Novice exclaimed Presents will not do. To arms men—when he seized his own arms the men followed his example, The Indians seeing his resolution fled out of the House & pell-mell—man and woman—swam across the River, Mr. Hughes & his men followed & fired & it is supposed some were killed. Thus Mr. Hughes as brave a fellow (which I often experienced since) as ever trod soil saved Mr. Finlay—his men & property, by his daring conduct.

Manchester House, at the upper end of the island, did not escape the attention of the Gros Ventres. It is not certain whether it was attacked just before or shortly after the attempted raid on the North West Company fort. Joseph Colen, Chief Factor in charge of York Factory, wrote in 1794 in a letter to the Governor of the Hudson's Bay Company in London that "the natives attacked Manchester House last Fall, where only seven resided, plundered the house of every article of trading goods, which they carried away. The men escaped only with the clothes on their backs."

A final reference is made to them in an entry Duncan McGillivray made in his journal for September 25, 1794: "We arrived at Pine Island Fort about Sunset. The men regret the friendly reception that used to await them at this place after the fatigues of the Voyage, but it is now in a ruined condition, the buildings are consumed to ashes and in a few years no traces will remain, to shew that it has ever been inhabited by Christians."

Pine Island was not easy to find. Even a representative of the Saskatchewan Department of Parks and Renewable Resources, to whom we wrote for help in our search, replied that "Pine Island does not have a marker—I cannot give you an exact location." Nevertheless, we persisted. We knew it was on the Saskatchewan River about one-half mile north of the mouth of Big Gully Creek. We utilized a Saskatchewan grid map and our car compass and put our trust in our four-wheel-drive vehicle to get us through roads that successively deteriorated from gravel to long-abandoned lanes whose wheel ruts were almost obliterated by encroaching brush to a faint trail that eventually dead-ended in an open field at the base of a high grass-covered hill.

We scrambled up the hill, and there below us flowed the Saskatchewan and over against the opposite side was Pine Island. The scene that stretched before us was one of great pastoral beauty. The gentle rolling hills on the far side of the river were clothed with fields of green, dotted here and there with small groves of trees. Pine Island, long and narrow, was once more covered with a thick stand of pines.

We sat for a long time on the top of the hill enjoying the magnificent view spread before us. Against such a backdrop of peace and serenity it was difficult to imagine the violent scenes of that time in November two hundred years ago when the Gros Ventres carried out their raids against the two trading forts.

With some reluctance we finally descended the hill, pausing frequently to admire the lovely prairie flowers that carpeted the hillside and the field below. We even speculated whether this protected field might just possibly have been the very place where the Indian boys guarded the horses left behind by the warriors while carrying out their attempted raid across the river.

Of course, that we will never know. What we did know was that we had been 100 percent successful in our quest to discover historic Pine Island.

Fort Resolution

The establishment of the North West Company's Fort Resolution was marred by tragedy. In 1786 Cuthbert Grant (Sr.) and Laurent Leroux were sent by Peter Pond on behalf of the North West Company to establish a trading post at or near the mouth of the Slave River on Great Slave Lake. The party paddled down the Athabasca River across the western end of Lake Athabasca to enter the Slave River. Halfway down this river they encountered the first of four rapids that effectively barred (and do today) further progress on the river. Utilizing the small streams to the east of the main river, as well as portaging, they successfully bypassed the first three rapids, known today as Cassette, Pelican, and Mountain. When they reached the fourth and last one, Cuthbert Grant ordered the other canoes to wait while he reconnoitered to determine whether it could be safely run. He instructed his men that if he decided it was feasible to run the rapid, he would fire his gun as a signal for them to proceed. Unfortunately, just as he was realizing the rapid could not be run, one of his men, forgetting the signal arrangement, fired at a duck flying low overhead. Immediately the men waiting at the head of the rapid shoved off into the river and within seconds were caught in the powerful surging grip of the rapid. The two canoes were swamped and five men drowned. From then on this rapid was called the *Rapides des Noyés* (Rapids of the Drowned).

The North West Company post was erected first on the left bank of the Slave River a few miles from the mouth. A short time later it was moved to Moose Deer Island, a short distance off the mouth of the river.

From 1815, when the Hudson's Bay Company established their Fort Resolution on the west shore of Great Slave Lake about four miles south of the mouth of the Slave River, until 1821, when the two rival companies merged, competition for the Indian trade was keen. The Hudson's Bay Company as a latecomer to the area operated at a considerable disadvantage.

According to George Simpson, who analyzed the problem in a lengthy report to the London Committee written in early 1821, this disadvantage was the result of the company's handicap of late arrival coupled with its ignorance of the country and its resources and its ill-preparedness for basic survival, as evidenced by its nonprovision of hunters, fishermen, and nets. In addition, its post was severely undermanned and understocked. This was in great contrast to the North West Company's superabundance of men and well-chosen goods. This fact was quickly noted by the Indians, causing them to look upon the

Hudson's Bay Company as "contemptible." Simpson felt that the only way to improve this situation was for the company to provide a sufficient quantity of goods properly assorted and selected for the trade plus a greatly enlarged complement of men and officers. Recognizing the importance of maintaining the company's presence in Great Slave Lake, he concluded his report by writing: "While opposition continues little profit can be expected from this District, it is however necessary to keep up the chain of communication throughout the Country and the establishment of Gt. Slave Lake is absolutely required, as the Key to McKenzies River, a very Rich and valuable tract of Country."

After the union in 1821, the present Hudson's Bay Company fort was constructed on the same site as its original post. Also at this time the rival North West Company fort was abandoned in favor of the Hudson's Bay post.

Today, after 175 years, the Hudson's Bay trading post continues as an important element in the life of Fort Resolution. Its white buildings with the traditional red roofs still stand on the south shore of Great Slave Lake close to the mouth of the Slave River. Nearby, Alexander Mackenzie camped while impatiently waiting for the ice to clear from the lake so that he could proceed with his epic 1789 voyage of discovery down the Mackenzie River—the river he called River of Disappointment, since it led only to the Northern Sea and not to the Western Sea as he had hoped and anticipated.

When we visited Fort Resolution in 1975 it was a small settlement of about 450 people. The languages spoken were Chipewyan and English. A large proportion of the inhabitants gained their livelihood by trapping, supplemented by fishing in the Great Slave Lake for *inconnu,* lake trout, walleye, and whitefish. Recently a sawmill operation utilizing the abundant supply of timber has provided additional employment.

Fort Resolution, one of the oldest communities in the North West Territories, seemed to have been, to a large degree, bypassed by many of the trappings of the twentieth century. Old-style houses of squared timbers with dovetailed corners had not as yet been totally replaced by the assemby-line matchbox houses of modern manufacture.

In 1975 the era of the snow machine had apparently not arrived, for instead of the Ski-doo or Moto-ski now so common in the north country, every backyard almost without exception had at least several sled dogs, each chained to its own small shelter. Indeed, from the howling and barking of the dogs, particularly when the noon whistle is blown, it was very easy to believe the claim frequently made that Fort

Resolution has the highest per capita sled dog population in the entire North West Territories.

The tall spire of the Roman Catholic church rises high above the surrounding buildings and symbolizes the important place the church occupies in the lives of the people. St. Joseph's Mission was founded by the Oblates of Mary Immaculate in 1852 under Father Faraud.

Fort Espérance
Fort John

It was soon realized by the partners of the North West Company that they must have a dependable source for pemmican—that staple item of food needed to fuel their brigades in their increasingly distant penetration into the fur country. Therefore, in 1787 Robert Grant, partner, ascended the Assiniboine River to the mouth of the Qu'Appelle, up that stream to a spot about one-half mile below the outlet of Big Cut Arm Creek. There on the flats on the south side of the river he erected his post.

Called Fort Espérance, the post was located on the prairies in the heart of the buffalo country. From its bastions enormous herds of these animals were commonly seen. Although some trading for furs was done, Fort Espérance, in addition to being the headquarters for the entire district of the Qu'Appelle-Assiniboine rivers, existed chiefly as a provision post. Its function was to secure the buffalo meat, both fresh and dried, and "grease," i.e., fat rendered from the backs of the buffalo, needed to make the enormous amounts of pemmican required by the fur trade. During the winter months trade was brisk with the Plains Indians (mostly the Assiniboines).

Since the buffalo supplied all their basic survival needs, it was only the lure of the tobacco, liquor, guns, and ammunition available at the trading post that induced the Indians to bring in the buffalo (meat and hides), wolf skins, and beaver and otter pelts required to obtain these "luxury" items. A journal entry made by John Macdonell for Tuesday, March 24, 1795, illustrates a typical trading exchange: "*Grand Diable* arrived and made me a present of 6 buffalo robes and 10 wolves;—gave him, in return, a large keg and a chief's clothing in consideration of his bringing and sending his band to trade here all winter, and in recompense for his giving the Fort a good name and sending every person who would listen to him to trade."

The journal entry for March 26 is of interest: "Le Grand Diable went away after making me a tender of his wife's favors and seemed surprised and chagrined at my refusal, but the Lady much more so, and I thought it prudent to make her some trifling presnts to pacify her."

During the spring the men at Fort Espérance were busy making pemmican. The buffalo meat was first dried and pounded to powder. This was then put into buffalo-hide bags of a uniform size called *taureaux*. To this was added melted buffalo grease. Each bag when full weighed approximately ninety pounds. Sometimes dried berries were added to the mix, thereby improving the flavor, but plain or deluxe, pemmican was a highly concentrated food of great nutritional value. When properly prepared, it lasted almost indefinitely.

Each spring Fort Espérance sent down its pemmican to the North West Company's supply depot at Bas de la Rivière near the mouth of the Winnipeg River, where it would be available for the brigade going into the fur country via the Athabasca or Saskatchewan river. This made Fort Espérance a vital link in the whole transport and supply system as developed by the North West Company. A typical year's output for this post (1795) was 275 *taureaux* of pemmican, forty-two bales of mixed furs, forty-five of buffalo robes, and four of dressed skins.

For the twenty-three years of its existence on the flats of the south bank of the Qu'Appelle, Fort Espérance had five masters: Robert Grant, William Thorburn, John Macdonell, Poitras, and John McDonald.

During this period, the fort, which was 150 feet square, was enclosed by a stockade with bastions. Its situation on the low flat at the edge of the river rendered it vulnerable to flooding. In the spring of 1795 John Macdonell recorded in his journal that "half of our garden under water from the over-flowing of the river, [and] three corners of the fort inundated from the same cause."

Frequent repairs were needed, such as a new chimney to the master's dwelling. A garden was cultivated, and the potatoes, onions, and parsnips it produced made a welcome supplement to the mainstay daily item of buffalo meat. Routine activities for the men included hunting, fishing, building maintenance, cutting firewood, keeping track of inventory of trade goods, salting buffalo tongues, and making candles. The women, in addition to routine chores of cooking and cleaning, were kept busy lacing snowshoes, making moccasins, dressing buffalo skins, and sewing *taureaux*.

Relations with the Plains Indians became rather strained. Indicative of the growing mistrust is the following entry for October 20, 1793: "The warriors traded a few skins brought upon their backs, and went off ill-pleased with their reception. After dark, the dogs kept a constant barking, which induced a belief that some of the warriors were lurking about the fort for an opportunity to steal. I took a sword and a pistol and went to sleep in the store. Nothing took place."

In the summer of 1810 the caretaker of the horses belonging to Fort Espérance was murdered by the Indians. Additionally, there is some evidence to indicate that the fort was successfully stormed and its people killed. Alexander Henry the younger, in his journal entry for

Sunday July 29, 1810, wrote: "They [Assiniboines] also informed us of a report from below that our establishment on Riviere Qu' Appelle had been destroyed and abandoned; but they knew not by whom, nor how it happened."

So after twenty-three years Fort Espérance was abandoned. A new post was reestablished somewhere on one of the Qu'Appelle lakes and operated for four years. Relations with the Indians did not improve. McDonald's spring brigade had barely left the new post on the small lake en route east to the North West Company depot of Bas de la Rivière when it was ambushed and many of his men either killed or wounded.

It was decided to relocate the post once again. This time the spot chosen was on the north side of the Qu'Appelle River about one-half mile west of Big Cut Arm Creek. The new establishment, named Fort John after John Macdonell, was erected near a spring at the crest of a gentle slope a mere 100 yards from the Hudson's Bay post built the previous year (1813) on the riverbank. Fort John, as the North West Company headquarters for the Assiniboine region, housed a large complement of men. The numerous buildings comprising the fort complex occupied an area 200 by 160 feet, all enclosed by a strong palisade.

The intensified and increasingly bitter competition between the North West Company and Hudson's Bay Company and particularly the resentment felt by the Nor'Westers at the attempts being made to confiscate their pemmican were reflected in the events that ensued at these two neighboring posts.

Alexander Macdonell, now in charge of Fort John, was determined to force John Richard MacKay, master of the Hudson's Bay post, to abandon the Qu'Appelle valley. When MacKay and his brigade of twelve men arrived back at their fort in the autumn of 1815, they found only blackened and charred logs. Their post had been burned down by the men of Fort John. MacKay, undaunted, immediately began to rebuild his post.

About one week later Macdonell and his brigade of thirty-six men arrived at their post of Fort John for the season's trade. Losing no time, Macdonell sent Cuthbert Grant down to MacKay demanding that he relocate his fort some other place. Should he refuse, he (Macdonell) "would come down with his own men and cut the few stockades" that MacKay had already erected. MacKay was not cowered by this threat and refused to move. A second peremptory order followed, reinforced by warlike activity at Fort John, including training two cannon on the English post below. In this tense situation, some Indians rallied to the support of MacKay, and their presence enabled him to carry on at his post throughout the winter trading season.

However, in the spring of 1816 when MacKay and his brigade were travelling downstream to the Hudson's Bay post of Fort Douglas on the Red River, Alexander Macdonell struck. His men, augmented by many half-breeds whom he had recruited, took the men in MacKay's brigade prisoner and confiscated their cargo of furs. Once again MacKay's post was burned to the ground.

Alexander Macdonell, along with Cuthbert Grant and their *bois brûlé* followers, proceeded on their way down the Qu'Appelle and Assiniboine rivers headed toward the Red River. Reaching Brandon House, they successfully overpowered it and seized its stores of pemmican. They then continued their journey, which was to culminate so tragically on June 20, 1816, on Frog Plain in the affair at Seven Oaks.

In spite of their setback at the hands of Macdonell and his men, the Hudson's Bay people did not give up. They simply moved to a new location about one and one-half miles above the mouth of Beaver Creek on the Assiniboine. There on the river flat they built a new trading fort.

The North West Company, well aware not only of the increasing hostility of the Indians toward them but also of the escalating struggle between the two rival trading companies, abandoned Fort John, probably partly because of its poor defensive capabilities. They moved back down to the south side of the Qu'Appelle. There on a high knoll overlooking the river flats below and only 300 yards to the west of the site of their first Fort Espérance, they erected Fort Espérance II. This new post with its advantageous location was capable of strong defense. Sturdy palisades enclosed the fort area, which was about 150 feet square. Between 1816 and 1819 it served not only as the North West Company's administrative center but also as its major source of pemmican.

However, at the close of the 1818–19 season, after thirty-two years of operating in the Qu'Appelle valley, the North West Company decided to withdraw from the area. The buffalo were no longer as plentiful. Furthermore, they wanted a location where they could not only compete more effectively with the Hudson's Bay Company but also have a strategic base near the junction of the Qu'Appelle and Assiniboine rivers.

The life of this new North West post was very brief, for after the union of the two trading companies in 1821 it was absorbed by the neighboring Hudson's Bay Company's Beaver Creek House.

Our quest for the sites of Forts Espérance I and II and Fort John, all within the beautiful Qu'Appelle valley, was a most happy experience. It is true that directional signs were almost nonexistent, but with the aid of our indispensable car compass and with the Qu'Appelle River as a highly visible point of reference, in addition to friendly help from several local people, we succeeded in finding each of the three fort sites.

A large field of lush waist-high ripening grain separated from the river by a border of thick brush covered the river bottom flat where Fort Espérance I had been located. Since we did not wish to damage the crop by trampling through it, we walked around the periphery only, but even from there we were able to discern some slight depressions marking old cellar holes.

We walked about three hundred yards to the west to the high knoll, site of Fort Espérance II. Quickly ascending to the top, we were rewarded with a magnificent view of the entire Qu'Appelle valley. To the north the bare gently rounded hills, each separated by a ravine filled with trees and brushy undergrowth in the flaming colors of fall, bordered the mile-wide green valley floor. The narrow ribbon of the river wound in sinuous curves through this verdant bottomland, its course marked by the low bushes bordering its banks. Above, a prairie hawk screamed as it circled in mounting spirals high overhead.

To mark the sites of Fort Espérance a most unusual and impressive monument has been erected by the Historic Sites and Monuments Board of Canada on a small knoll between the larger knoll to the south (site of Fort Espérance II) and the river flat to the east (site of Fort Espérance I). A large bronze buffalo head, set in a square concrete frame, faces the northwest, the direction from whence the great herds used to come; opposite is a bronze beaver hide embellished with Indian pictographs set in a concrete stretcher. Between these two sculptures is a concrete rectangular column on which is affixed an appropriate descriptive plaque.

We crossed the Qu'Appelle and, turning west on a narrow dirt road paralleling the north side of the river, soon came to the simple provincial tablet marking the site of Fort John. As we surveyed the peaceful scene before us, idyllic in its serenity and beauty, we found it very difficult to picture the violence and strife that once prevailed at this spot.

But all that is in the distant past. Today the lovely Qu'Appelle valley, no longer disturbed by the turbulent events of 175 years ago, is at peace, content to offer serenity and beauty to all who are fortunate enough to travel through it.

Swan River Valley
Upper Assiniboine River

The last twenty years of the eighteenth century witnessed an invasion of the Swan River valley by the North West and Hudson's Bay companies as well as independent traders. Apparently they all had discovered that the Swan River offered relatively easy and direct access to the plains country, home to the enormous herds of buffalo.

The river, which varies in width, was free of obstructing rapids. Near its outlet at Swan Lake the low banks were swampy and muddy. However, upstream poplar and pine suitable for building construction were available. Fish were abundant and ample numbers of moose, red deer, and buffalo were present.

For the Hudson's Bay Company traders coming from York Factory on Hudson Bay, the way lay via northern Lake Manitoba, Cedar Lake, Mossy Portage, Lake Winnipegosis, and Shoal River to Swan Lake.

To the Nor'Westers it offered an alternative route into the interior. Instead of the long, arduous journey from the forks at Red River up the twisting, shallow Assiniboine, fighting the current and the many shifting sandbars, they could travel up the western side of Lake Winnipeg, then by means of Dauphin River, lakes St. Marten, Manitoba, and Winnipegosis, and the Shoal River reach Swan Lake.

The first to appear in the area was William Bruce, an independent Pedlar from Montreal, and it is thought that he established his post on the Shoal River, the outflow of Swan Lake. His rough and violent treatment of the Indians earned for him such enmity that only a devastating outbreak of smallpox among the natives prevented them from attacking his post.

In 1787 the North West Company moved into the Swan River area. Robert Grant, partner, built Swan River Fort on the north bank of the river about ten and twelve miles above Swan Lake. For about three years he was unopposed by other traders, but in 1790 the Hudson's Bay Company sent in Charles Isham, half-breed son of James Isham, former chief factor at York Factory, with orders to establish Swan River House on the river one-half mile above the North West fort.

A description of their fort is found in the booklet *The Fur Trade in the Swan River Region* published by Manitoba Historic Research Branch. Swan River House: ". . . consisted of a large central house flanked by some smaller out-buildings and was surrounded by a [twelve-foot] palisade. As at most inland posts, fort components were built in the Red River frame style: walls were framed with log uprights at frequent intervals, and joined by horizontal logs. Thatch was used for the roof and sawn logs for the floor. Wooden partitions divided the building into rooms. Exterior walls were plastered with mud and covered with pine bark. Oiled parchment served as windowpane material."

Isham, in spite of being outnumbered by his North West trading rival, as well as hampered by a shortage of goods, by inferior tobacco (that most basic item of trade), and by a lack of well-trained men, managed to survive and conduct a successful operation.

Isham, being an astute trader, decided in 1793 to outdistance the competition and establish a post on the upper Assiniboine River. Utilizing the well-known and relatively short land portage between the waters of the upper Swan and upper Assiniboine rivers, he built Marlboro House near the elbow of the Assiniboine. The North West Company immediately replied to this challenge by establishing a post midway between the two rivers.

During the next few years, trading forts proliferated in the Swan River valley. The leapfrogging of posts was done on a large scale. Cuthbert Grant of the North West Company in 1793 established Bird Mountain House fifty miles farther upstream near the mouth of Thunder Creek to cut off the flow of furs to the Hudson's Bay Swan River House. The following year, Isham retaliated by building Somerset House about two miles above Grant's newly established house. Isham's fort was located on the northwest side of an open plain used by the buffalo during the winter months. Its trade was so successful that even during its first year the earlier-established Swan River House was reduced to little more than a supply depot.

In 1795 the North West Company, pursuing its customary aggressive policy, erected posts immediately next to Hudson's Bay Swan River House and Somerset House. Countering this hostile move, Isham and Peter Fidler in that same year ascended the Swan River, crossed to the Assiniboine, and ascended to a point some fifteen miles west from the elbow, where they built Carlton House.

Isham realized that by having a house on the upper Assiniboine, which could be reached from the Swan River via a short overland portage, he would be able to reach his post and commence trading a month earlier than his rivals, thus gaining a considerable advantage over them.

John Macdonell of the North West Company in his *Some Account of the Red River* referred to the adverse effect this advantage had on his operations: ". . . trade [in beaver and otter] has been almost ruined since the Hudson Bay Company entered the Assiniboil River by the way of Swan River, . . . who by that means and the short distance between Swan River and their factory at York Fort, from whence they are equiped, can arrive at the *Coude de l'homme* [elbow], in the Assiniboil River, a month sooner than we can return from the Grand Portage, secure the fall trade, give credits to the Indians and send them to hunt before our arrival."

Traders for both companies soon realized the ruinous effect of the fierce competition. Peter Fidler in 1808 compared the state of the many trading posts on the Assiniboine with the success achieved by Grant, who entered the area in 1783 and within a ten-year period that was free of competition was able to amass the comfortable sum of £23,000.

The Swan River valley soon became trapped out, and the Indians moved on to more productive areas. Betweeen 1796 and 1799 Hudson's Bay Company returns had fallen from 2,110 to 795 Made Beaver. In response to this decline, the Hudson's Bay Company temporarily closed their Swan River and Somerset Houses. Swan River House was briefly reopened for the 1807–08 season with Peter Fidler in charge.

The North West Company continued to operate their Swan River posts in spite of declining returns, but with the union of the two companies in 1821 the posts in the Swan River valley ceased to operate. Henceforth the area (still retaining its name of Swan River district) was administered from Fort Pelly, the new headquarters established in 1824 on the Assiniboine.

We were not able to find any of the sites of the Swan River forts—if indeed the precise location of any of them is known. We had to content ourselves with photographing the river approximately thirty miles from Swan Lake. It is a pretty little stream, wandering at this point through aspen parklands, and there is a well-worn trail still very visible along its bank. The nearby log trading post museum in the town of Swan River serves as a reminder of the many fur forts that once dominated this now-tranquil valley.

Fort Alexandria

The North West Company was not caught unawares by the Hudson's Bay Company's advances on the upper Assiniboine. Indeed, it was already in the process of building its Fort Alexandria when Charles Isham and Peter Fidler arrived in October of 1795.

Fort Alexandria, where Daniel Harmon was to spend the better part of five years, is well described in his journal entry for the twenty-third of October 1800:

> The fort is built on a small rise of ground, on the bank of the Assiniboine, or Upper Red River, that separates it from a beautiful prairie, about ten miles long, and from one to four broad, which is as level as the floor of a house. At a little distance behind the fort, are small groves of birch, poplar, aspin and pine. On the whole, the scenery around it, is delightful. The fort is sixteen rods in length, by twelve in breadth; the houses, stores, &, are well built, are plaistered on the inside and outside, and are washed over with a white earth, which answers nearly as well as lime, for white washing.

Archibald Norman McLeod, North West Company partner, spent the winter of 1800–1801 at Fort Alexandria. Many of his diary entries reflect the great importance of the buffalo in the daily life of the fort. On March 3, 1801, he wrote: "Some of the men at work making horse sledges, others melting or Boiling back (Buffaloe) fat to put in the Pimican, all the women at work sewing Bags to put the Pimican into. Roy, Girardin, & E. Ducharm came home with the last of the meat, & brought home the Lodge & now we have finished hauling meat, for this Season, we have now about eighty five Buffaloe Cows in the Meat house. Collin very busy making kegs to put Grease into, old Parrant, making nails for the Sledges, & Plante hanging up the meat & tongues he put in salt ten days ago, to day."

The manufacture of pemmican was the primary activity at Fort Alexandria due to its proximity to large herds of buffalo. Despite its location, however, there were times when food provisions at the fort were nearly exhausted. In January of 1805 Harmon wrote in his journal that "for nearly a month, we have subsisted on little besides potatoes; but thanks to a kind Providence, the last night, two of my men returned from the plains, with their sledges loaded with the flesh of the buffalo."

At the end of May 1805 Fort Alexandria was briefly closed, but it was reopened in 1807 and remained in operation until the 1821 union of the two rival companies. At that time it and all the other posts that were clustered on the upper Assiniboine River were permanently abandoned, and the region was left without a trading post for the next three years, until the first Fort Pelly was built in 1824.

As was the case with the posts on the Swan River, we were not able to locate the precise site of Fort Alexandria. The best we could do was photograph the Assiniboine from a bridge that crossed the river only a few miles upstream from the fort's location. The river at this point was a quite unpretentious stream flowing quietly along between its brushy borders, showing no evidence of the part it had once played in the turbulent events that had taken place on its banks.

Fort Chipewyan
(1788–1821)

In 1788, only ten years after Peter Pond established his fur trading post known as the Old Establishment on the Athabasca River just forty miles south of Lake Athabasca, thereby opening up and revealing the richness of the Athabasca fur country, Fort Chipewyan I was built by the newly formed North West Company.

Peter Pond, the first European to penetrate this country, believed that the Pacific Ocean was only 150 miles west of Lake Athabasca. "There remains," he wrote, "no more than 74 degrees between Arabasca [Athabasca] and Bearing [Bering Strait] which is nothing to the distance between the great carrying place [Grand Portage] and Arabasca. This I know to be a fact. Could the exact distance be come at I would not believe [it] to be more than 60 degrees." Modern measurements show that the actual distance from the valley of the Slave River to the Pacific is approximately twenty degrees (520 miles) and to Bering Strait is sixty-six degrees (1,716 miles).

Pond felt the Pacific could be reached by a river system beginning with the Slave River, the northward extension of the Athabasca River, and terminating on the Pacific Ocean at the inlet discovered by Captain Cook in 1778, which, because of its rapid current, was assumed by him to be the estuary of a large river flowing from the east. Pond believed that this river (named Cook's River) must be the one flowing westward from the western end of Great Slave Lake. Based on scientific observations and astute inferences he drew many maps reflecting his conclusions. It is interesting to note that his earliest maps, based largely on information received from the natives, show the Slave River flowing out of Great Slave Lake northward to the Polar Sea. His later maps, however, incorporating the reported discovery of Cook's "River" (which was not until 1794 proved to be merely an inlet), show the Slave River emptying into the Pacific.

In 1787 Alexander Mackenzie, a mere youth of twenty-three years, was appointed to replace Pond in the management of the Athabasca district, so that Pond could devote his time to further exploration. He traveled the Slave River, Great Slave Lake, and the headwaters of the mighty river flowing to the west, i.e., the river known today as Mackenzie River, establishing its exact location at sixty-two degrees north latitude.

The following year, Pond turned over to the young Mackenzie the results of his explorations—all his notes, observations, conclusions, and maps relating to a possible route to the Pacific. By May he had left the Northwest, and in the following year, 1789, plagued by personal problems including charges of murder (which were never proved), he retired from the North West Company.

Mackenzie, like Pond, was primarily a fur trader and as such was motivated by two objectives in his search for a practical way to the Pacific: participation in the lucrative marine fur trade of the coast and discovery of a route utilizing the westward-flowing streams to eliminate the long, costly, and difficult route to and from Montreal. He lost no time in capitalizing on the information given him. First, he realized that a post located on Lake Athabasca was just about at the limit of the distance a canoe brigade could travel to reach the rendezvous at Grand Portage in summer, exchange furs for supplies, and return in the fall before freeze-up. Second, he decided that a post on Lake Athabasca would be more advantageous as a base from which to conduct his explorations than the one on the Athabasca River. Accordingly, he arranged for his cousin Roderick Mackenzie to be transferred from the Churchill to the Athabasca district in order to oversee the moving of Pond's old post to a new location on Lake Athabasca. On a point on the south shore about eight miles east from the mouth of the Athabasca River in 1788 Fort Chipewyan I was built.

In his *Reminiscences* Roderick Mackenzie wrote:

> On my arrival at our destination, I looked out for a suitable spot for a new establishment to replace the old one of Mr. Pond. After making every possible enquiry and taking every measure of precaution, I pitched on a conspicuous projection that advances about a league into the Lake, the base of which appeared in the shape of a person sitting with her arms extended, the palms forming as if it were a point.
>
> On this point we settled and built a fort which we called Fort Chipewean. It is altogether a beautiful, healthy situation, in the center of many excellent and never failing fisheries . . .

In fact, the fishery could be relied upon to yield 50,000 whitefish, trout, pike, perch, and golden-eye annually. For years, each man's daily allowance of fish was eight pounds.

Fort Chipewyan soon became the most important fort in the North. Roderick Mackenzie was pleased to provide the fort with all the refinements possible. He even painted the interior of the post buildings, much to the astonishment of not only the natives but the voyageurs as well. In addition, reflecting his own cultured and studious interests, he amassed a collection of over two thousand books and periodicals, which earned for the fort the name "Little Athens of the Hyperborean Region." As historian L. R. Masson wrote: "The shelves of the fine library of the Fort sagged under the weight of the numerous well-chosen books."

Such was the fort from which Alexander Mackenzie departed on his justly famous journeys of discovery. The first, in 1789, following the river that, though first seen by his predecessor, Peter Pond, was named Mackenzie River, led to the Arctic instead of the hoped-for Pacific Ocean. The second, in 1793, although it reached its goal of the Pacific Ocean, traced a route quite impracticable for fur trade transportation.

By 1800 it was realized that a more advantageous location for Fort Chipewyan would be on the northwest shore of Lake Athabasca. The early breakup of the Peace River and the resultant reversed flow of its waters flushed the ice eastward into the lake, so that it often became lodged against Old Fort Point, forced both by current and the prevailing winds. This same phenomenon was responsible for opening up the northwest corner of the lake considerably earlier in the spring, affording access to rivers and fishing grounds. A further point in favor of the new location was the rocky cliffs to the north, which gave protection from the strong north and west winds.

So, sometime around 1800, Fort Chipewyan was moved across the lake to the site it has occupied ever since. The old fort was allowed to fall into decay and was totally abandoned by 1820, even though it retained its function as a fishing station for many years.

Fort Chipewyan II was situated on a rocky point on the northern shore of Lake Athabasca. Backed by high pink cliffs, it commanded an uninterrupted view over the lake. The fort, about 160 yards square, contained about fifteen buildings within the palisaded enclosure, ranging in size from the largest, sixty by twenty feet, to the smallest, the sixteen-by-fourteen-foot blacksmith shop. The summer and winter house held the stores and the officers' quarters, while the summer depot contained the Indian hall. Clerks' rooms containing the barest essentials were twelve feet square; married officers had rooms ten by fourteen feet. After 1815 a watchtower was constructed in response to the killing by the Indians of the inhabitants of Fond du Lac, a small post at the eastern end of the lake.

This fort was the great North West Company emporium of the north. Presiding over its destiny were some of the company's most capable and distinguished wintering partners—men such as James McKenzie, Edward Smith, George Keith, and John George MacTavish. It was the distribution hub of the highly efficient and superbly organized transport system involving outward delivery of furs and inward receipt of goods and supplies for the entire Athabasca district.

Here the brigades were formed, provisioned with the essential pemmican, and sent with their annual harvest of furs to Fort la Pluie on Rainy Lake, there to deliver the furs and receive in exchange the provisions and trading goods for transport back to Fort Chipewyan. These then had to be tallied and repacked for further distribution according to their ultimate destination for the posts on the Peace River, the Mackenzie River, and the district of New Caledonia west of the Rocky Mountains. And all this had to be accomplished between breakup in late spring and freeze-up by October 1.

The lustrous furs of the Athabasca region were considered well worth the tremendous effort and cost required to acquire them, and the North West Company would tolerate no intrusion on its monopoly of the area. Therefore, in 1799, when the newly formed but short-lived XY Company established a post on Little Island, and three years later, in 1802, when Peter Fidler of the Hudson's Bay Company built Nottingham House on English Island—both posts within a mile of Fort Chipewyan—the North West Company reacted immediately and ruthlessly. To keep watch over the activities of the Pothies, as people of the XY Company were called, James McKenzie, in charge of Fort Chipewyan, posted a sentry on the high ground behind the fort. Intimidation and bribery were routinely used to prevent any trading between the XY and the local Indians.

Competition with the XY Company was terminated in 1804 with the amalgamation of the two companies. Competition from the Hudson's Bay Company, however, was much more formidable and sustained, lasting until the merger of 1821.

Nottingham House

From the time of his first arrival on Lake Athabasca and the establishment of Nottingham House until its abandonment four years later in 1806, Peter Fidler and his men were subjected to a campaign of intimidation, humiliation, terror, and violence deliberately planned by the North West Company in its efforts to drive them out of the country.

Soon after his arrival in 1802 Fidler sent Swain, his assistant, up the Peace River to trade for buffalo meat needed to make the pemmican required to provision his canoes for the outward trip in the spring. Swain was forced to return empty-handed. The North West Company by a combination of bullying, threats, cajolery, and liberal gifts of liquor had successfully prevented the Indians from trading with him.

Each succeeding year the harassments not only continued but increased in severity. Still Fidler kept doggedly returning to his post. Except in spirit, he was no match for the North West Company. He was outnumbered five to one in men; he had but two or three canoes and only a small stock of trading goods. He did not have enough men to go to the Indian tents to trade *en derouine* as the Nor'Westers were able to do but instead had to wait for the Indians to come to him at Nottingham House. This the Indians didn't dare do because of the threats of the North West Company. Consequently, his returns in beaver were woefully small.

Shortly after the news reached Fort Chipewyan in May of 1805 that the North West and XY companies had amalgamated, Peter Fidler received a note from James McKenzie of the North West Company:

> —desiring my co'y to tea—but on purpose to tell every bad thing they could in order to make us leave this 1/4—and among many things Mr. McLeod told me that we had no right to come into this 1/4 for the purpose of Trade & they would act with the greatest vigor towards us in order to expel us from hence, & afterward said Proprietors of the NW Co were resolutely determined that the Servants of the Hudson's Bay Company should walk over their Bodies rather than they would allow an Indian to go into the H B Co House.
>
> Two days later "The French [N W Co.] set fire to all our wood that we had collected with great labor and carried down to the water's edge ready for rafting to build a new house with.

But worse was to come. Fidler's fourth season at Nottingham House (1805) was marked by sustained harassment from his competitors from nearby Fort Chipewyan. In order to intimidate and watch Fidler's every move, the Nor'Westers, led by Samuel Black, "took down their watch house they had all summer near here, & rafted it over to our house, . . . putting it up before the Door & within 10 yards of it . . ." The Nor'Westers' threats prevented the Indians from bringing their furs and meat to Fidler's fort. If his men attempted to go to the Indians' home camp, the Nor'Westers "threatened to break their canoes in pieces." Their efforts to hunt geese were thwarted because Black and his men were always able to scare them away. The fort's vegetable garden was destroyed. A disastrous fire was barely averted when their tormentors "tore a large piece of Bark from the roof of our dwelling house—& put it upon the top of our chimney which soon took fire, and was very near setting the whole house on fire . . ."

Rendered desperate by these tactics and the threat of starvation, Fidler entered into an agreement with James McKenzie whereby he would refrain from all trading with the Indians; in return McKenzie would give him 300 large beaver and other skins equivalent to 200 Made Beaver at the time of his departure in the spring, plus enough moose meat and pemmican to carry him over the winter. However, when spring came, McKenzie refused to hand over the skins as promised. Fidler, disheartened and discouraged, had to leave for York Factory, his season a complete failure. His journal entry reflected his helplessness: "We were so very few—they were so numerous." This brought to an end Fidler's attempts in the Athabasca area, as Nottingham House was abandoned.

Fort Wedderburn

After the final departure of Peter Fidler and the closing of Nottingham House, the North West Company remained unopposed in the Athabasca district for nearly ten years. Then in 1815 the Hudson's Bay Company renewed their attempts to penetrate the area. John Clarke was chosen to head this venture. He successfully established Fort Wedderburn immediately opposite Fort Chipewyan on an island (first known as Coal Island, now called Potato Island). His post was hastily constructed; it was not fortified and had no enclosing palisade.

Clarke set off for the Peace River country to trade with the Indians for furs and buffalo meat. Ensuing events proved his bravery but also showed his reckless lack of planning and foresight. An appalling lack of provisions, coupled with the Nor'Westers' successful intimidation of the Indians, prevented them from giving any assistance to the Hudson's Bay men. The frightening off of game in the area by the Indians resulted in total disaster for Clarke's expedition. Sixteen of his men perished from starvation; and as a final humiliation, he was forced to surrender to the North West Company the few goods he had in return for enough food to enable him to return to Fort Wedderburn.

In spite of this disaster, Clarke returned to his post the following year (1816). Once again he experienced the full force of the North West Company's hostile tactics, which culminated in January 1817 when, taking advantage of their superior numbers, the Nor'Westers seized Fort Wedderburn and arrested Clarke.

Almost incredibly, Hudson's Bay people doggedly returned to Lake Athabasca the next year (1817), determined to prove that the Indians could depend on their continued presence—that they would not be driven away.

In the fall of 1818 their venture was under the leadership of a new man. This was Colin Robertson, an ex-Nor'Wester, aggressive and wily, well aware of all the strategems and tricks used by his former colleagues. Robertson had some twenty-two canoes manned by five or six men each, and he was ready to meet force with force; to fight fire with fire. His motto was: "When you are among wolves, howl!"

His first impression of conditions at Fort Wedderburn was quite unfavorable. He wrote in one of his letters:

> The first object that presented itself to my view was fifty or sixty Indians, clothed in the choicest goods, strutting about the Fort with long calumets and scarlet fire bags in their hand as if engaged for the sole purpose of parade, their joint hunts during the winter not exceeding two

hundred made beavers. Then turn your eyes to the company's servants, thirty in number marshalled out in red belts and feathers, complaining of their master and their master of them, still you would suppose the business of the Fort was closed and the men ready to embark. No! Not a single canoe ready to be put in the water.—Such was the state of affairs on my arrival at Fort Wedderburne.

But Robertson soon changed all this. When the men from Fort Chipewyan began swaggering around, trying their usual tactics of intimidation and bullying, they found, to their surprise, that the Indians, bolstered by a new confidence in the Hudson's Bay men, refused to be intimidated and that the men of Fort Wedderburn were ready and eager to stand up and "give as good as they got."

However, veteran Nor'Wester Samuel Black was not to be thwarted. At a time when many of the men from Fort Wedderburn were away in search of furs and provisions he went over to the fort and managed to instigate a fracas. In the ensuing struggle, complete with pistol shots (which missed their mark), Colin Robertson was captured, dragged into a canoe, and taken over to Fort Chipewyan, where he was kept prisoner for eight months in a barred-off section of the fort's privy.

Robertson's own account of his capture reads like a page out of an adventure thriller. In a letter from Fort Chipewyan dated February 12, 1819, he wrote:

On the morning of the 11th October about an hour before day, my servant entered my bedroom, and informed me a canoe had just arrived from the fishery with the body of one of our servants who was accidentally shot the night before. . . . Sleep at this early hour therefore out of the question, I rose and ordered an early breakfast, but just as we were sitting down to our repast, one of the men entered, and mentioned that Saucisse had arrived from the N.W. Fort and was calling to Bushe to come out and fight. I got up, went to my bed room—,put a pistol as I thought into my pocket, and went towards the place where the man was standing, where I saw Mr. Simon McGillivray. I was relating to him what happened—; at this time Black with eight or ten men made a rush from behind, and in a moment I was surrounded. In the struggle my pistol dropped down and got entangled in my clothes and in the attempt to find it, went off. At the report of the pistol they rushed and closed on me, and dragged me to the beach, where I happened to disengage myself and made some resistance by laying about with the empty pistol. At this juncture I am rather surprised our people did not come up to my assistance, for it was no easy task to embark me although held by some of the strongest men belonging to their fort. When placed in the canoe, I made an attempt to upset it in the hopes of making my escape by swimming,

141

when Black drew his pistol upon me. This had little or no effect, and as I did not succeed it was owing to my strength being exhausted.

Robertson turned his captivity to his advantage, however. By his close and keen observation of North West Company activities from within he was able to learn of the weaknesses, dissension, and dissatisfaction besetting the company. In addition, Robertson by means of an ingenious cipher system conveyed in kegs of liquor, managed to outwit his captors and maintain his control of the trade at Fort Wedderburn so successfully that twenty-five packs of furs were traded for the season. On his way to Montreal to stand trial, Robertson was able to effect his escape at Cumberland House.

For the season 1819–20 the Hudson's Bay post with Dr. William Todd in charge operated without any harassment from the North West Company. Dr. Todd had a constable with him at his fort with a warrant for the arrest of Samuel Black but was unable to serve it.

September 20, 1820, marked the arrival of a man who was destined to mastermind the affairs of the Hudson's Bay Company for the next forty years. George Simpson, shrewd, capable, courageous, and determined, as well as ruthless in his own way, trained in commercial methods and efficiency, was assigned to Fort Wedderburn. His instructions were to avoid collisions with the North West Company if possible but, at the same time, maintain and defend the rights, interests, property, and persons of the Hudson's Bay Company by all and every means within his power.

Simpson's presence was immediately felt. Discipline was tightened; economy instead of extravagance was stressed; morale was boosted. The planting of a garden was encouraged, and potatoes, cabbages, and the like were successfully grown. The watchtower built by the Nor'Westers overlooking the Hudson's Bay post was quickly matched by one erected by Simpson close to the Fort Chipewyan stockades.

When Simon McGillivray (mixed-blood son of William McGillivray, chief partner of the North West Company) and his colleagues, attempting to carry on the harassment tactics of previous years, occupied the watchtower overlooking the Hudson's Bay post, Simpson immediately responded by putting up a stockade tall enough to prevent those in the watchtower from spying on his fort. Undaunted, McGillivray, ignoring the accepted line of demarcation between the North West blockhouse overlooking the gate to Fort Wedderburn and the Hudson's Bay property, brazenly began to extend his blockhouse beyond this boundary line to the very palisade surrounding Fort Wedderburn. At this point, a constable from Montreal came forth from Fort Wedderburn, served McGillivray with a warrant, arrested him, and took him prisoner in the Hudson's Bay post. Although McGillivray subsequently escaped, further provocation from the North West Company was largely suspended.

At long last the bitter struggle between the two companies ended. News of their union was learned by Simpson on his way out to York Factory in the spring of 1821. Peace at last was to reign in the fur trade, and Fort Wedderburn was abandoned in favor of Fort Chipewyan. Henceforth, the old North West Company emporium would be the sole trading post on Lake Athabasca.

Fort Chipewyan
(1821)

Fort Chipewyan, repaired and refurbished with lumber salvaged from Fort Wedderburn, continued to be the headquarters for the Athabasca district and the distributing center of supplies for the Athabasca and Mackenzie river area. The meat provisions (mainly buffalo and moose) were supplied from the Athabasca and Peace rivers; potatoes came from potato fields on Potato Island; but the chief source of food was, as always, the fish procured in the prolific Lake Athabasca fishery, especially at Old Fort Point on the south side of the lake.

At the Northern Council meeting of July 5, 1823, at York Factory, Simpson named Chief Factor James Keith and Chief Trader Peter Warren Dease to be in charge of Fort Chipewyan. Before many years, the traditional construction of canoes at Fort Chipewyan was gradually phased out in favor of the larger, stronger York boats, capable of carrying three times the lading of the old Northwest canoe (i.e., about eighty bales) and far safer and better adapted for travel on the large bodies of open water in the district.

A sketch of Fort Chipewyan made in 1823 by Chief Factor James Keith showed that it was laid out in the traditional manner of most fur posts. There were the usual buildings for stores with cellars underneath, the interpreters' and guides' house, the men's houses, the fort's summer and winter house and kitchen, the blacksmith shop, two outside ovens, woodyards, a boat store, a canoe store, a stable, a dog kennel yard, a lookout, and a watch house observatory. All this was enclosed by a high palisade with a main front gate and five bastions at the corners. Squared logs *poteau sur sol* used for the foundations were laid on the sandy rock base on the northwest shore of the lake. The log buildings were put together as post houses. Wooden pegs were used in place of nails. Clay, sand, and grass were used as caulking between the logs, and shingles made of bark covered the roofs. These shingles had to be renewed every year. Parchment covered the windows in all the buildings except the factor's house, which had glass panes. Fireplaces provided both heat and light. These were made of clay and stone, which became as hard as cement.

A few years after the union, in 1828, during the course of an inspection trip from York Factory to the Pacific Ocean, Governor George Simpson spent two days at Fort Chipewyan. Archibald McDonald, who accompanied him, noted in his journal that "all the buildings about this place [Fort Chipewyan] are in a state of decay. Gardens not very extensive." He recorded that James Heron was to replace William McGillivray as head of the fort.

Fort Chipewyan continued its long tradition of active support for the many scientists, explorers, and fur traders who used the fur fort as the base from which to take off on their daring journeys. The list of such men is a long one, beginning in 1789 with Alexander Mackenzie and including surveyors Philip Turnor and Peter Fidler; geographer David Thompson; fur trader and explorer Simon Fraser; Arctic explorers Sir John Franklin, Dr. John Richardson, Lieutenant George Back, and Robert Hood; fur traders Peter Warren Dease, Thomas Simpson, and Dr. John Rae; and scientist Captain John Henry Lefroy, who spent the winter of 1843 at the post and noted a population numbering sixty people.

Fort Chipewyan was gradually losing its preeminence as the most important fur trading post in the North, for the center of fur activity was shifting to the west. The buildings of Fort Chipewyan were old; many had become obsolete. So, in the 1870s, Chief Factor Roderick MacFarlane completely rebuilt the aging fort, with the single exception of the blacksmith shop. He erected his new fort on the original site of the North West fort and in a large measure followed the same layout. Even though by this time palisades and bastions were no longer considered necessary, MacFarlane nevertheless retained them in his new reconstruction, and, as always, they fulfilled their traditional function of enclosing the compound, which now consisted of thirty buildings such as the store, warehouse, great house of the chief factor, and mess hall. Many of the new buildings were constructed utilizing the Red River style, commonly used by the Hudson's Bay Company for their trading posts.

The passing years brought changes. In the 1880s the first steamer used in the North, the 135-foot stern-wheeler SS *Grahame,* was built at Fort Chipewyan, bringing to an end the era of the York boat and a transportation system based on the famous Methye (La Loche) portage and inland rivers.

The tall fort palisades were replaced by picket fences; the council chamber was ignominiously used as a cow stable. But still the white buildings of the Hudson's Bay fort stood proudly on the same promontory the company had occupied ever since 1800. Yet inevitably the fact had to be accepted that the trading of furs was no longer the sole and dominant activity of the area.

Finally the end came. The Hudson's Bay business was transferred to a retail store located in the village, and first in 1939 and then in 1950 the buildings of the company's Fort Chipewyan were torn down. The chief factor's house, the last to go, was demolished in 1964. The "Great Emporium of the North" was no more. The noise and bustle of trading activity ceased. Silence fell over the rocky point.

Today there are no highways leading to Fort Chipewyan (if you except the rather hazardous winter road made each year over frozen water and marsh to Fort McMurray, 175 miles to the south). Steamboats that used to service the community no longer operate. Open skiffs powered with outboard motors are used by everyone for local travel on the lakes and rivers. Fortunately, the construction of a modern airport in 1966 now makes Fort Chipewyan accessible by air.

One beautiful day in July 1984, we boarded the plane at Fort McMurray for the flight down the Athabasca River, across the west end of Lake Athabasca, to land at Fort Chipewyan forty minutes later. There we were met by Sally Whiteknife, a very attractive and soft-spoken Cree from the local band office. It was she who shepherded us around during our four-day visit, who arranged that we meet the people we wanted to meet and see the places we wanted to see. We shall always be most grateful to her for her friendly help.

Through Sally, we were introduced to Mr. Horace Wylie and were privileged to spend an entire afternoon with this most interesting gentleman. Mr. Wylie was the great-grandson of Colin Fraser, the young Scotsman who accompanied the great Sir George Simpson on many of his travels as his personal piper. From the 1820s through the 1850s, Simpson's arrival at any of the forts within his vast domain was always attended with much pomp and ceremony. A most important part of this was the procession into the post headed by the piper playing lustily on his bagpipes. Colin Fraser's bagpipes were handed down by him to his son, Colin Fraser, Jr., who operated a trading post in Fort Chipewyan during the late 1800s; from him they came eventually to his grandson, Horace Wylie. Well aware of the very great historical significance of these bagpipes, Mr. Wylie very unselfishly, in a most public-spirited act, donated the bagpipes to the Provincial Museum in Edmonton. Thus this valuable and personal link with the fur trade days is now safely housed—available for all to see.

During the period when the Hudson's Bay buildings were being demolished, Mr. Wylie managed to salvage many artifacts that otherwise would have been destroyed or lost. To us the most interesting was the company bell, which hung in the belfry and was used to signal time for the daily activities as carried on within the fort. This bell is inscribed with the words: "J. Warren & Sons, London 1881. Omnia fiant ad Gloria Dei."

To the rear of Horace Wylie's home are two long rectangular storage sheds, obviously very old. We noticed the decided nautical curvature of the roofline. Mr. Wylie explained that the material used for these buildings came from the scows used on the downriver run on the Athabasca. When they reached Fort Chipewyan, they were broken up and the lumber utilized for construction, since it was never attempted to return them upriver.

As we sat in Mr. Wylie's comfortable home with its big picture window overlooking Lake Athabasca and Potato Island and listened to him reminisce about bygone days at Fort Chipewyan, we felt as though somehow, through him, we were being granted a rare glimpse backward into time—into the world of George Simpson, of the chief factors, of life at Fort Chipewyan as it was during the fur trade days.

When we admitted that we had been unable to find any trace of Peter Fidler's Nottingham House on nearby English Island, Mr. Wylie immediately offered to take us back there in his boat, for he knew exactly where the old chimney stones were that marked the site of the fort. Of course we gratefully accepted, and within a very short while we had covered the half-mile distance from his home to English Island. We beached the boat in a small bay on the southeast side of the island. Without hesitation Mr. Wylie ascended the sloping bank and, walking directly to a small clearing, pointed to a pile of tumbledown stones half-hidden by the tall grasses. These rocks are all that remain of Nottingham House—a rather pathetic monument to the four-year valiant but fruitless efforts of Peter Fidler to break the North West Company's hold on the Athabasca fur trade.

If these stones could but speak, what tales they could tell of bravery, humiliation, frustration, terror. Now, however, as we wandered around the clearing, it was indeed difficult to imagine the violent scenes that took place. Today the island is quiet and peaceful, the silence broken only by a couple of native children playing at water's edge and the sounds of their parents setting up their summer camp a short distance away.

All too soon our afternoon with Horace Wylie came to an end. His courtesy, his generosity in sharing his knowledge of the past with us, his helpfulness will always be gratefully remembered. Our visit to him was one of the highlights of our stay in Fort Chipewyan.

Sally made arrangements for her brother George (who incidentally, as we found out one evening a little later, is a masterful cribbage player) to take us over to Potato Island—the large island directly opposite Fort Chipewyan and the site of Fort Wedderburn.

"Snowbird" Martin, a lifelong resident of Fort Chipewyan, accompanied us as guide. We ascended the sloping path to a modest clearing on the north side of the island, where "Snowbird" assured us the fort had once stood. Just as Simpson had described it in 1821, "its aspect is Northerly and eclipsed from the Sun about one half the year, by a huge Rock behind the House; the soil thin and sterile—." Although we found no visible traces of the fort buildings, we were confident we were standing on the very ground where the stirring events of 1819–20 had taken place. In our imagination we could see the mighty Colin Robertson being overpowered by the Nor'Westers, dragged down to the beach, and forced into a canoe beached perhaps at the very spot where our skiff was now moored. Here, too, George Simpson, diminutive though he was in physical stature, successfully countered all attempts by his boisterous adversaries to intimidate him. Now, 170 years later, all is quiet. People came here for picnicking and berrypicking. Perhaps, though, if one listens closely enough, the strident threats and shouts of the two rival companies may yet be faintly heard in the whispering of the aspen leaves.

We spent many happy hours wandering around Fort Chipewyan photographing the old landmark houses. The names of their owners read like a roster of Hudson's Bay time-honored servants: Flett, Fraser, Wylie. We even located a few small surviving Hudson's Bay white buildings with the traditional red hip roof that antedated the present modern metal-sided store.

At the western end of town we found the one hundred-year-old trading store operated by Colin Fraser, Jr. This building, solidly built of squared timber, though empty today, is silent testimony to his success as an independent trader in competition with the Hudson's Bay Company. For example, in one year (1894) he sold 8,022 pelts and forty-eight pounds of castoreum, for which he received $20,000. This Colin Fraser, son of Colin Fraser, George Simpson's bagpiper, lived to be ninety-one years old and was regarded as outstanding among the independent traders of the North. This building is but a few yards away from Little Island, site of the short-lived XY trading house.

And, of course, we found our way to the place at the eastern end of the village where the North West and Hudson's Bay Company's Fort Chipewyan had once been located. We walked along the old dirt roadway that paralleled the lakeshore, past the Anglican church toward the rocky promontory now crowned only with the cobblestone cairn erected by the Historic Sites and Monuments Board of Canada to mark the site once occupied by the fort. Foundation stones and rotting timbers, depressions and cellar holes, plus an occasional rusty bolt or nail, a broken piece of old stove—that is all that is left of the once proud and mighty post. And even these slight traces will soon be lost to sight completely, hidden by the encroaching growth of grass and wildflowers.

For over 150 years the shore just below was lined successively with canoes, York boats, scows, and stern-wheelers bringing the trading goods and provisions required to supply the needs of the vast Athabasca-Mackenzie region and taking out its rich harvest of furs.

Here on this now lonely and deserted embankment were once clustered the numerous buildings and service facilities. Here lived and worked the many servants, the artisans, the laborers, the accountants, the clerks, the commissioned "gentlemen." Here were all the bustle and activity that characterized this most important fur trading post—the "Grand Emporium of the North." Perhaps all will not be totally lost. Canadian archaeologists have recently been excavating this location. We hope this will result in preservation and perhaps some type of simple restoration of the site. Fort Chipewyan should not be allowed to pass into oblivion.

As a step in this direction in the late 1980s the people of Fort Chipewyan, under the sponsorship of the Fort Chipewyan Historical Society, erected a full-size authentic replica of a Hudson's Bay Company's warehouse at the edge of the old company fort compound to be a musem and repository for fur trade artifacts and memorabilia.

Sally took us to the Roman Catholic mission at the western end of Fort Chipewyan, where we were privileged to enter the beautiful Our Lady of the Nativity Church. Examples of native craftsmanship adorned the interior. Particularly striking was the use of diamond willow and caribou antlers to form an impressive free-standing cross. A thriving vegetable garden and a pen containing several fat white geese were ample testimony to the Oblate priests' traditional skill and dedication to gardening and the raising of poultry.

Later, at the opposite (eastern) end of the community, adjacent to where the buildings of the Hudson's Bay post had stood, we visited the simple white Anglican church. Built in 1880 and consecrated by Bishop Bompas, St. Paul's has remained largely unchanged and still serves the needs of the many Anglicans in the community.

Sally arranged a special treat for us. We were invited to a cookout at Doré Lake, a spot much frequented by the people of Fort Chipewyan for swimming, fishing, and picnics. We were lucky enough to be the guests of Marjorie Wylie, who prepared the food—barbecued chicken and salads, all delicious, but surpassed by her hot bannock cooked over the campfire, dripping in butter and smothered with Saskatoon berry jam. Even now, many years later, we still dream about it! Marjorie is a superb cook and, as we were to discover on the last day of our stay in

Fort Chipewyan, always had food for extra "drop-ins" at her bountifully laden table.

Arrangements had been made for us to travel up the Athabasca River as far as Embarras, believed to be in the general vicinity of Peter Pond's post of 1778, and then to visit Old Fort Point on the south shore of Lake Athabasca, site of Fort Chipewyan I. We were very fortunate that Larry Mercredi, a Chipewyan from Fort Chipewyan, had agreed to be our guide. His skill and versatility were amply demonstrated during our two-day trip.

After loading camping gear, sleeping bags, food, and gasoline into our open skiff, we left Fort Chipewyan early in the morning, crossed the western end of the lake, and were soon threading our way through the Athabasca delta, a maze of waterways of the mighty river. Marshland, vast and endless, stretching to the far horizon, bordered the river. On the occasional low ridge, trees, mostly cottonwoods, grew. Overhead, ducks were ceaselessly flying in all directions. And from the marsh itself came a constant cacophony of bird sounds of all descriptions. The majestic bald eagle was commonly seen; in fact, we had a "close encounter" with ten of these beautiful white-headed, white-tailed birds.

After several hours of travel, we came to the camp of a group of native boys employed in a band-sponsored project of cleaning up and repairing the ravages caused by weather and neglect to the many native cemeteries in the area. Larry hailed the project leader, whom he knew, and we were instantly invited to join the group, who were taking a midafternoon tea break. The big black kettle was quickly put to boil over the campfire, and in a few minutes we, too, were enjoying mugs of hot tea. We were made to feel very welcome and thoroughly enjoyed our visit. When it was time to leave and continue our journey, one lad quietly hastened down to the water's edge in order to be there to assist me in climbing over the several boats between the river's edge and our boat. His thoughtful assistance was much appreciated.

We continued on up the river and soon reached the general area where it is believed that in 1778 Peter Pond established his trading post, the first in the Athabasca country and the one that amply demonstrated the region's enormous potential for furs.

We ended our journey up the Athabasca at the tiny trading post and government post office of Embarras Portage, fifty miles south of Fort Chipewyan. This small, isolated post was situated atop a steep bank on the east side of the river and run by a nonnative couple. Here no hospitable gesture of a cup of coffee was made. We visited for a short while but soon left to begin our return trip down the river to the lake and our camping site for the night.

Larry had chosen Little Poplar Island, a tiny island just off Old Fort Point. Within an incredibly short time our tent was set up and sleeping bags spread out; a large tarp erected over the kitchen area and delicious moose steaks were sizzling over the fire and bannock was baking. What a feast we had!

Afterward, we sat around the campfire and, to our amazement and delight, superchef Larry pulled out his harmonica and entertained us with a melody of Métis jigs and Western cowboy songs that set our toes to tapping. By now the campfire had burned down to glowing embers; a full moon shining over the lake cast its golden light and held each of us within its spell. We talked of many things and felt privileged that Larry shared some of the Chipewyan beliefs and legends with us. His skill as a raconteur held us spellbound. Finally, as though reluctantly, the last spark in the fire flickered out—this most memorable evening was over.

The next morning, after a hearty breakfast and more of Larry's good bannock, we broke camp and traveled the short distance to Old Fort Point. This small point curving around a tiny bay is about fifteen miles east of the mouth of the Athabasca River. It was on this point that Roderick Mackenzie at the request of his cousin Alexander Mackenzie built the first Fort Chipewyan in 1788. And it was from this fort, from this small bay, that Alexander Mackenzie both departed on and returned from his two famous journeys of exploration—the one in 1789 to the Arctic down the Mackenzie River and the second, in 1793, to the Pacific Ocean.

Today there are no visible traces left of this early fort. Only two things remain unchanged from what they were in Mackenzie's day: the view to the north encompassing the broad open waters of the lake with its few scattered islands, and the nearby prolific fishery.

Several snug little houses, along with the remains of a few tumbled-down log buildings and cellar holes now nearly totally obliterated by rank growth of grasses and brambles, in addition to a simple cemetery nearby, show that the Chipewyans have inhabited this area for many years. Larry told us it was his birthplace, where he grew up, and where he wished to return to be buried.

It was now time to make the twenty-mile crossing of the lake from Fort Chipewyan I on the south side to Fort Chipewyan II on the north side. The wind had increased steadily throughout the morning, so that now whitecaps tumbled and tossed over the turbulent water and five-to-six-foot waves pounded the water's edge. Encouraged by Larry's calm assurance but still a bit apprehensive, we embarked. It quickly became evident that Larry was a superb navigator. By skillfully riding the crest of the waves we arrived back at Fort Chipewyan several hours later, not only safely but also bone dry instead of drenched by waves and spray as we had fully anticipated.

Sometime earlier in the day, I had made the discovery—horrifying for a photographer—that I was nearly out of film. Since the following day was Sunday, I knew I must get to the Hudson's Bay store before closing time on this day. So as soon as we landed, I hastily grabbed a ten-dollar bill from our common kitty and set off as fast as I could jog toward the Hudson's Bay store a mile away. Fortunately, I was given a lift by a kind-hearted lady who was headed for the same place. Breathlessly I rushed into the store, picked up my film, and handed the ten dollars to the clerk. Unfortunately, the amount needed was $10.75. I offered to sign a slip—as countless other customers were doing for their rather considerable purchases. I gave local references; I pleaded; but to no avail. The clerk was adamant. In desperation I looked around in the forlorn hope that I might see a familiar face. Just about ready to accept defeat, I suddenly spotted two men to whom we had briefly talked while on our Athabasca River trip the previous day. Emboldened by my desperate need, I walked up to them and asked if they would please lend me seventy-five cents. I'm sure they were as astonished at this bit of panhandling as I was myself, but they laughingly handed me a dollar. After fervent thanks and promise of repayment, I raced over to the unsmiling clerk, who was just about to close the till for the day, handed her the money, retrieved my film, and marched triumphantly out of the store.

Later, when I was recounting my experience, the humor of the situation struck us. Here we were, friends on a first-name basis with one of the members of the Hudson's Bay board of directors in Toronto as well as one of their top officials at the company's headquarters in Winnipeg. We had been awarded a bronze medal as one of the Hudson's Bay Company of Adventurers. We were gathering material for a book concerning Hudson's Bay trading forts. And yet we couldn't get credit for seventy-five cents! It was really a good joke on us. However, perhaps it just might be that this control of credit is the secret of the Hudson's Bay Company's success for over three hundred years.

The next day, although our flight was due to leave in the afternoon, it was rescheduled for early evening. Faithful Sally, ever mindful of our welfare, at suppertime took us over to Marjorie Wylie's house. Here a family reunion and celebration were under way—tables loaded with food were set up on the porch and on the lawn. We were immediately welcomed and urged to sit down and "help yourselves." So once more we were lucky enough to enjoy the warm hospitality and wonderful cooking of Marjorie Wylie.

The extra time given us by the plane's delayed departure gave us the opportunity to once again climb Monument Hill, there to stand on the site of Fort Chipewyan to enjoy the magnificent view from this vantage point. We wanted to make sure that along with the memories of all the friendly people we had met, our journey on the Athabasca, and our seeing sites so significant in fur trade history, we would always be able to recapture in our mind's eye the wonderful panorama of blue lake, green wooded islands, and pinkish rocky cliffs spread before us.

Reluctantly we turned away and walked down the hill. It was going to be hard to leave Fort Chipewyan. One thing was certain. We knew someday we would return.

Frederick House

In 1778 Philip Turnor, surveyor, was engaged by the Hudson's Bay Company for a three-year period. Turnor was ordered by the company to determine the exact longitude and latitude of their various posts in Rupert's Land and their respective distances from one another in order to discover the shortest practical travel routes between them. At the expiration of his contract, it was renewed for another three years. During this time Turnor made an extensive survey of the region south of Moose Factory, in particular the Abitibi River country.

Based on his report, the Governor and London Committee decided to set up a permanent establishment in the area as a means of blocking the threatening push northward toward James Bay by the Canadian Pedlars.

Turnor left Moose Factory in June 1784 and the next year established a post on the southeast shore of a lake now known as Frederick House Lake. This fort, called Frederick House in honor of Frederick, Duke of York, was erected on a little gravel hill in a small bay today called Barber's Bay. Temporarily closed in 1795, it was reopened in 1798 and continued in operation for the next fourteen years.

Frederick House was in a remote and rather inaccessible region where fur-bearing animals were fairly plentiful. In addition, the Frederick House Lake fishery provided a dependable source of food to supplement the potatoes and barley that were successfully grown at the post.

Turnor spent the next two seasons at Frederick House. During that time, in addition to carrying on a trade in furs he did considerable traveling, following the rivers and portages between Lake Timiskaming, Abitibi Lake and River, and Frederick House Lake. His attempt to find an overland trail that would bypass the difficult navigation of the Frederick House River was unsuccessful.

Frederick House proved to be somewhat of a disappointment to its Moose Factory base. Its fur returns were not great, it was both difficult and expensive to supply, and competition from the Pedlars was both constant and vigorous.

From Moose Factory the rivers leading to Frederick House (the Abitibi and Frederick House) were notoriously treacherous. Canoes, with their small cargo capacity, instead of boats, had to be used. The securing of a sufficient number of canoes as well as Indians willing to undertake the arduous journey to Frederick House was always a problem. The Pedlars were adept in stratagems designed to intercept the

Indians from coming to a rival's trading fort. At Frederick House they had adroitly stationed four of their men with two log tents. In addition, the Canadians extended liberal credit to the Indians, which the Hudson's Bay Company refused to do.

In January of 1812 a proposal was made whereby the Hudson's Bay Company would agree to give up their post of Abitibi House on Abitibi Lake in return for the Canadians' withdrawal from Frederick House Lake, thus leaving the Canadians once more in control of Lake Abitibi and the Hudson's Bay Company unopposed on Frederick House Lake. However, before this arrangement could be carried out an event at Frederick House rendered it unnecessary.

In December 1812 an Abitibi Indian named Capascoos massacred the Frederick House master, Alexander Belly, and two laborers, Robert Sabiston and Hugh Slater, plus nine Indians. To this day the story of what actually took place remains a mystery.

The disaster at Frederick House was first discovered by two men from a nearby Hudson's Bay post. They found the trading house completely deserted. It had been thoroughly vandalized and its warehouse and storage cellars cleaned out of guns, ammunition, and European goods. Later, with the disappearance of the snow, twelve bodies, all shot, were found scattered about the post.

The most likely explanation suggested by the evidence is that after the initial massacre had secured the post, any person who came there during the winter was killed in order to conceal the crime and allow the murderer (or murderers) to remain unmolested, free to enjoy the comforts and the food available at the post. Although a reward was offered for the capture of Capascoos and his accomplices (if any), they were never apprehended. Frederick House was never reestablished but was allowed to fall into ruin.

In 1911 the post was vividly brought back to life. At that time the Timiskaming and North Ontario Railway (now the Ontario Northland) was being constructed. A steam shovel working in the general area of Barber's Bay was excavating a gravel ridge to obtain ballast for the track. Suddenly its big bucket began scooping up musket barrels, copper kettles, broken and empty barrels, and other artifacts. A short distance south several skeletons in shallow graves were unearthed. These relics and gruesome remains rescued the old fur trading post from one hundred years of oblivion.

To perpetuate the memory of Frederick House, a provincial plaque was erected on the dramatically rediscovered site. The monument stands beside busy Highway 101 several miles east of Timmins. It is no longer close to the shore of Frederick House Lake, because in 1909 the south half of the lake was drained as a result of a diversion of the Frederick House River. Today, what was the south half of Frederick House Lake is a sand and clay flat covered with grass and sedges through which the river winds.

Perhaps few people, as they speed past the marker, know the story of the site that it commemorates. It is eminently appropriate, however, that places of historic significance be permanently marked and not allowed to be forgotten, that they be made an indestructible part of our historical heritage.

Hungry Hall House
Asp House

On the north bank of the Rainy River a few miles upstream from Lake of the Woods, traces of old trading post foundations are visible. Close to shore a weathered dock piling still embedded in the river bottom extends several feet above the water surface. Archaeological work at the site has uncovered artifacts from the fur trade period.

There are a few tantalizing references to a Hudson's Bay trading post at the mouth of Rainy River in the journals of some of the early traders. For example, Alexander Henry the younger, leaving Rainy Lake for Lake of the Woods in August of 1800, noted in his journal that the party "passed the old H.B. Co. establishment, which has been abandoned for several years" and later that day "passed another old H.B. Co. establishment." David Thompson in 1797, in his notes on his journey down the Rainy River, mentioned that on the stretch between Long Sault and Lake of the Woods there were two trading posts located in close proximity and identified them as the houses of Mr. McIntosh and Mr. McKay, the latter "from Albany" (i.e., the Hudson's Bay Company). This reference may be a clue to the identity of the second post noted by Alexander Henry in his journal entry of August 4, 1800.

Rainy River was off the regular route used by the Hudson's Bay Company to reach the fur country. However, by the third quarter of the eighteenth century they were gradually beginning to push more boldly from their bay bases into the interior.

In 1793 John McKay was outfitted with trading goods and provisions at Fort Albany and sent inland to Rainy River with instructions to build a trading post that would not only be profitable for the Hudson's Bay Company but would also pose a competitive threat to the North West Company, already well established on that river. In September of 1793 McKay ascended the Rainy River and built his post a little below Manitou Falls and twelve miles below the North West Company's important post Lac la Pluie, then in the charge of Charles Boyer.

Conditions in the Lac la Pluie area were not too promising. The previous year (1792) four North West men had been killed by two Indians while fishing. The animal population had declined, forcing many of the Indians to go elsewhere to trap and hunt, with a consequent decline in trade. McKay was quite pessimistic over trading prospects, and the season's results confirmed his fears. His trade was eighteen packs of furs, the equivalent of 1,163 Made Beaver; that of Boyer five packs.

In 1794 McKay decided to build a second post, this time at the mouth of Rainy River, since the Indians from Lake of the Woods with whom he wished to trade refused to travel up the river to his fort at Manitou Falls. This second post, called Asp House, was situated at or very near where the Hudson's Bay's Hungry Hall House of the 1830s was later located. Both of McKay's Rainy River posts were supplied with European provisions from Albany Fort, but country food such as wild rice, moose, deer, ducks, rabbits, and fish was also required as a supplement.

At the end of October, Boyer and seven men came down from his Lac la Pluie post and built a trading house a mere 200 yards below McKay in the hope of intercepting the Indians on their way to the Hudson's Bay Company's Asp House. In spite of this maneuver, relations between the two traders were friendly, extending to mutual assistance in times of food shortages and to reciprocal hospitality on numerous occasions. This cordiality, however, was never allowed to obscure, or hinder, their keen rivalry for pelts.

In April of 1795 Boyer closed his post after enduring a winter of extreme scarcity of food and a disappointing trade. He realized too late that locating beside Hudson's Bay Company's Asp House at the mouth of the river had been a mistake. However, returns from his Lac la Pluie post at the head of the river continued to be satisfactory, since debt, or credit, extended to the Indians was rarely lost. Any unpaid balances remaining at the end of the season were worked off by the Indians building canoes for the post.

McKay's returns from his two posts for his second season (1794–95) were 1,309 Made Beaver, but the furs were costly since many of the debts extended by him to the Indians remained unpaid. In fact, in McKay's opinion, the returns were not sufficient to cover wages and food, even if the trading goods cost nothing.

However, McKay and ten men returned once again to Rainy River in the fall of 1795. Since the hunters in the Lake of the Woods area still refused to journey upriver to Manitou Falls, he made no attempt to reopen his fort there but wintered at Asp House, near the mouth of the river. Here he faced stiff competition from the Nor'Westers from all directions. He wrote: "I am almost sure that their is more Canadians within two Hundred miles round me than Indians."

Today Oak Grove Resort occupies the very spot where McKay's Hudson's Bay Company's Asp House and the company's later Hungry Hall House were located. In 1984 the owners, Larry and Linda Boudreau, traced their ownership back through their parents and grandparents, who acquired twenty acres from the Hudson's Bay Company and the remaining acreage from the local Indians. One of the Boudreaus' most prized possessions is a copy of the original land deed and bill of sale from the Hudson's Bay Company in London, which was on display in their office. Also to be seen there is the glass case containing their collection of artifacts found during archaeological excavations made on their land. Among the items are an ink bottle, a fork, buttons with the Hudson's Bay crest, pieces of blue-and-white Staffordshire china (Honeysuckle pattern), shot, a clay pipe, a lidded copper pail used by Hudson's Bay Company for measuring each man's monthly issue of liquor, an iron ax head, a soapstone ceremonial pipe, and arrowheads.

We parked our motor home at the edge of a magnificent grove of enormous oak trees that bordered the clearing on the riverbank. After a hasty supper, we walked over to the opening by the river where a historical marker stood, marking the site of Hungry Hall. Here the faint depressions and slight ridges formed by the cellars and foundations of the early fort buildings were plainly visible in the lengthening shadows cast by the setting sun. We climbed down the bank and out onto the resort dock. Close to shore the one piling, slanting above the water, all that remained of an early fort dock, was easily spotted and duly photographed.

Then, as probably others had done who once manned the trading posts built here, we looked down the river in the direction of Lake of the Woods. We, however, were not anxiously and hopefully watching for the appearance of canoes bringing the Indians with their furs for trade; we were merely enjoying the placid beauty of the river quietly flowing by and the spectacular sunset in the western sky.

South Branch House

William Tomison, in overall charge of Hudson's Bay inland operations in the late eighteenth century, was a strong and consistent advocate of establishing and organizing the company's trade on the Saskatchewan to meet the ever-increasing competition from the North West Company. Therefore, in 1785, in response to the construction of trading forts on the South Saskatchewan by two rival interests (Peter Pangman, an independent trader, and William Holmes of the North West Company), Tomison sent Mitchell Oman up the South Saskatchewan with instructions to construct a fort there.

The site chosen for South Branch House was on the right bank of the river, on a beautiful plain with a hill in the background. It was strategically located near a well-used Indian track fording the river, later known as Gardepuy's Crossing, and was close to the border between parkland woods and open prairie plains. It was also sited so as to effectively cut off the native traders from the rival posts of Pangman and Holmes. In recognition of this, these two traders abandoned their newly built posts and hastily constructed new ones on the opposite bank of the river a mere 400 yards below the Hudson's Bay Company's South Branch House.

For the next few years relations between the Indians and the traders were friendly and nothing occurred to disrupt normal trading. However, trouble was brewing. For many years the rich harvest of beaver, otter, marten, and other prized furs brought to the posts by the Cree had enabled them to acquire an ample supply of guns and ammunition. In contrast, the Indians from the plains, such as the Gros Ventre, who could bring in only wolf and fox skins, which were little valued by the traders, were not able to secure the weapons they wanted. The Cree were not slow to take advantage of their superiority in armaments. They ruthlessly waged war against the poorly armed tribes, killing many and driving the remainder out of their traditional homeland.

In 1793 a band of Cree came upon a band of Gros Ventre in the vicinity of the South Saskatchewan River. What occurred next was described by Duncan McGillivray in his journal entry for March 1795: "They watched their opportunity and, when the others retired to rest unsuspicious of danger, they fell upon them like hungry wolves and with remorseless fury butchered them all in cold blood except a few children whom they preserved for Slaves." It was natural for the Gros Ventres to seek revenge, but without weapons they were powerless.

Accordingly, they schemed to attack and plunder for their military stores the two trading posts on Pine Island in the North Saskatchewan River. In their minds these traders must be allies of their enemies, since it was from them that the Cree obtained their guns. In the summer of 1793 the Gros Ventre attacked the Pine Island forts and were able to capture some horses and carry off a considerable amount of trading goods.

Emboldened by this success, in July of the following summer they suddenly descended upon the trading posts on the South Saskatchewan. South Branch House was the first target. It was ill-prepared to repel any hostile attack. Its palisades had neither inside shooting platforms nor bastions. In addition, on this fatal day company officers James Gaddy, Magnus Annal, and Hugh Brough were absent from the post and only two company men (J. C. Van Driel and William Fea), and a small handful of Indian men, women, and children were within the fort. The first intimation of danger was the appearance of one or two hundred Gros Ventre galloping toward the fort. As soon as they were seen by the interpreter, he recognized their hostile intent and urged Brough to flee with him to the safety of the nearby woods, but Brough remained behind, probably not able to believe that the erstwhile "friendly" Gros Ventre had any hostile intentions toward anyone from the Hudson's Bay Company. His credulity cost him his life, for he was quickly shot down and scalped. When Annal returned from his visit across the river, he, too, met the same fate. By this time the gates to the fort had been shut and barred. Van Driel and Fea each sought safety by hiding in old cellars. The Indians set fire to the palisades and were soon swarming into the doomed fort.

Duncan McGillivray's journal entry for August 29, 1794, based on an account received from Louis Chattelain, gives a vivid account of what then took place: "The Savages finding no resistance—broke into the Fort and began a Scene full of horror and destruction. After they became masters of the booty which amounted to 60 or 70 Ps [i.e., pieces of about ninety pounds each]; they made a deligent search for the unfortunate people; Butchered every soul that came in their way in a most inhuman manner; even the Women and children did not escape the merciless cruelty of the miscreants who destroyed every age and sex with the most indiscriminating fury that can actuate the mind of a savage." Fea was discovered in his hiding place and killed. However, Van Dreil was lucky enough to escape in a small canoe. Next the victorious Gros Ventres turned their attention to the North West post across the river. Once again McGillivray's journal gives a graphic account of what happened.

161

... Jacques Raphael an interpreter had gone out a riding in the morning, and after ascending the side of a hill to view the Country arround he found himself on the summit fronting the enemy at the distance of a few yards coming in an opposite dirrection.—The Savages instantly gave the War hoop by which he discovered their hostile intentions and being well mounted he immediately turned about and rode full speed to the Fort pursued closely by 5 or 6 Cavaliers who instead of entering with him amused them-selves with taking a few Horses without the Piquets; whilst he gave the alarm and bolted the Gates. The Men got quickly under arms and stationed themselves in the Block Houses before the arrival of the Savages who advanced boldly up to the fort as if they derived confidence from the Success that attended their attempt on Pine Island last Winter, or wished to intimidate the People within by a shew of intrepidity which they did not possess; for the first discharge from the Fort discouraged them so much that they retired in confusion behind a rising ground, that effectually covered them from the Shot of the Beseiged. From this situation they kept up a continual fire upon the Fort for half an hour, when their ammunition began to be exhausted, and their war Chief L'Homme de Callumet a brave and undaunted Indian disparing of success from the mode of attack, which did not agree with his fiery nature, advanced a second time towards the Gates encouraging his Warriors to follow him; but he was interrupted in the midst of his harrangue by a Shot from the Before mentioned interpreter which Stretched him breathless on the ground, and the miscreants after recovering his body, retreated with mournfull lamentations for loss of their leader and threatening vengeance against the authors of his death.

Although the fort had been saved, Louis Chatelain, the master, recognizing the implacable hostility of the Indians and the impossibility of conducting further trade, decided to take advantage of this reprieve and withdraw from the area. Accordingly, he and his men loaded all their trading goods, supplies, and equipment into canoes and abandoned the post.

It was not until eleven years later that trading posts were reestablished on the South Saskatchewan. In 1805 both companies rebuilt within a few hundred yards of each other about six miles farther upstream from their previous forts. After their merger in 1821, the Hudson's Bay Company took over the North West post and operated it until about 1870.

With the aid of a sketch map kindly furnished us by the Saskatchewan Historic Parks, the site of Hudson's Bay Company's South Branch House was not difficult to find. It is only a few miles north of Batoche, where the tragedy of the Northwest Rebellion of 1885 came to its bloody end. In a small copse of young poplars on the bank of the river a provincial marker has been erected on the spot where South Branch House once stood.

On the warm summer day that we were there, the only sounds disturbing the peaceful quiet were the murmuring of the river steadily flowing toward its junction with the North Branch about sixty miles downstream, the faint rustling of the poplar leaves, and the steady drone of the cicadas, interrupted occasionally by the pure, clear, bubbling music of the western meadowlark. In such a tranquil setting it was difficult to picture the carnage, the flames, the smoke, the cries and screams of the victims, the blood-curdling war whoops of the Indians that took place on that day in June almost two hundred years ago.

Today nothing is left of the forts except a few mounds of rubble and faint cellar depressions. Only the river, timeless and unchanged, and the adjacent plains and woods remain as they were during the days when the two trading posts stood on the bank of the river.

Portage la Loche/Methye Portage

In 1778 Peter Pond discovered the key that unlocked the door to the rich and untapped fur country of the Athabasca. Guided by local Indians, he was the first recorded white man to cross the twelve-and-a-half-mile Methye (also known as La Loche) portage over the divide that separates the waters of the great Athabasca and Mackenzie rivers flowing into the Arctic Ocean from the Churchill-Saskatchewan rivers leading to Hudson Bay. Alexander Mackenzie, his cousin Roderick, and others from the recently organized North West Company soon followed in Pond's footsteps.

Aggressively and promptly taking advantage of this access to the Athabasca country provided by the portage, the North West Company soon was able to establish a virtual monopoly of the trade in the area, which remained practically uncontested for almost twenty years but, when finally challenged by the Hudson's Bay Company in 1802, was ruthlessly and vigorously defended.

During the days both of the North West Company supremacy and later of the long period of Hudson's Bay Company dominance, the southward flow of furs funneled through the bottleneck of the Methye portage was fabulous. Perhaps less glamorous but equally important was the incredible amount of goods and supplies essential to the fur trade that came northbound over the portage. For more than one hundred years the Methye portage served as the key link in the fur trade transportation system.

However, by 1883 the railroad had reached Calgary. From that point freight and passengers moved by oxen- or horse-drawn wagons north to Edmonton and on to Athabasca Landing on the banks of the river of the same name. There brigades of scows (later supplanted by stern-wheelers) took aboard both people and cargo for the run downriver to Fort McMurray. This combination of train, wagon, and scow by successfully bypassing the portage had rendered it obsolete. No longer would the voyageurs have to backpack the countless bales of furs and tons of goods and supplies over the long portage. Henceforth the once-busy Methye portage would be quiet and deserted, used only by an occasional Indian, a solitary hunter or trapper. Its days of glory lay in the past, when it was the one and only way to reach the riches of the famed Athabasca fur country.

The Methye portage extends twelve-and-a-half miles from Wallis Bay on the northwest side of La Loche Lake to the Clearwater River at a point about eighty river miles east of its junction with the Athabasca

River at Fort McMurray. Its course lies in a general northwest-southeast direction and, with but one major exception, follows fairly level terrain. The portage traverses typical north country character-ized by sandy ridges covered with jack pine, spruce, and poplar, inter-spersed with numerous small ponds, grassy sloughs, and extensive pockets of muskeg.

From its southern terminus on La Loche Lake, the trail follows the very small, crooked La Loche Creek for a short distance, winds through a wet, swampy area, and crosses the upper reaches of La Loche Creek and one small stream before reaching the higher ground of the sandy ridges. Following these low ridges, the portage continues on through the woods for about seven miles before reaching a small body of water known as Rendezvous Lake. The trail skirts the western side of the lake and begins a very gradual ascent for two miles to attain the actual height of land, at an elevation of 1,690 feet. From this point, the port-age commences a gradual descent through the woods for a short dis-tance until, with quite startling abruptness, it reaches the rim of the escarpment bordering the Clearwater River valley far below. The next mile is the infamous and dreaded backbreaker facing those making the portage southbound. For here the trail, in a scant mile, drops 690 feet in elevation, equivalent to a 13 percent grade. After descending to the valley floor, the portage continues for a half-mile across a wet, mucky floodplain overgrown with a tangled thicket of vines and willows over-shadowed by giant poplars and spruce, before emerging onto the large grassy clearing on the banks of the Clearwater River—its northern ter-minus.

Because the Athabasca country was so distant from the major sup-ply depots of the North West Company at Rainy Lake and the Hudson's Bay Company at Norway House, in the brief period of time between ice breakup in early summer and freeze-up in early fall it was not possible to complete round-trips between these points in one season. In order to overcome this obstacle, a system was worked out whereby the men from the north bringing out the year's trade of furs across the Methye portage as far as Rendezvous Lake would rendezvous with the men from the south packing in the trading goods and supplies across the portage to the same lake. There, in scenes of frenzied activity, the bales of fur were exchanged for the goods and supplies. Little time was left for comraderie around the campfire. Each man knew he was in a race against time and realized the necessity to complete the return trip without becoming ice-bound en route. So in an incredibly short time, the transfers were made and each brigade carrying its exchange cargo sped homeward.

For many years everything transported across the portage was carried on the backs of men. As a part of his employment contract each man was required to carry two ninety-pound pieces (bales). Some earned premium pay for carrying an extra piece. Until the 1820s, canoes also were carried across the portage. However, after that time, as canoes were replaced by York boats, this practice was discontinued.

Eventually the portage was improved and widened so that oxen-drawn Red River carts, each carrying an eight-hundred-pound load, were used on the eleven-mile portion of the trail between La Loche Lake and the top of the Clearwater escarpment. Between that point and the river below, stoneboats pulled by men were used. To facilitate the handling of the goods and furs and to store provisions needed by the brigades for their return trip northward, a large warehouse was built in the clearing by the river. Also, a York boat terminus was established at each end of the portage. The oxen were overwintered at Bull's House, near the mouth of La Loche River. Eventually both the North West and the Hudson's Bay companies built small posts near each end of the portage.

The men who packed the furs and goods across the Methye portage were an elite group who considered themselves superior to all others. They and they alone had the right to wear the single feather in their headband, to lay claim to the proud words: *je suis un homme du nord* (I am a northman).

In addition to the nameless voyageurs, almost everyone prominent in the fur trade passed over the Methye portage at one time or another: Peter Pond, Alexander Mackenzie, Roderick Mackenzie, Peter Fidler, Daniel Harmon, George Simpson, the McGillivrays, Colin Robertson, David Thompson, Philip Turnor—to list but a few. Almost without exception, each of these men recorded in his journal or in letters an account of his experiences in crossing the famous portage.

Ever since we had become interested in fur trade history, we had dreamed that one day we, too, would walk the Methye portage. Finally, in September of 1984, our dream became a reality. We drove to the little village of La Loche, located in the far northwest corner of Saskatchewan. There we made arrangements at the local float plane base to fly the next morning to Wallis Bay and be dropped off at the mouth of La Loche Creek by the southern terminus of the portage.

On the following morning, undaunted by low-hung clouds, overcast leaden sky, and misty rain, we loaded packsacks, cameras, and ourselves into a Cessna 180 and within a few minutes had flown across Lac la Loche to Wallis Bay, the southern terminal of the Methye portage. The pilot taxied slowly toward shore, but several hundred yards away the plane came to a stop as the pontoons gently grounded on the hard sand bottom. We stifled our misgivings, took off our boots, and, burdened with our gear, opened the plane door, climbed out onto the floats, and jumped in. As we waded toward shore, the firm bottom gave way to oozy muck and muskeg liberally "enriched" with fresh, succulent droppings from many geese. Removing this muck from our feet was not accomplished easily, for we had to do it while standing, since there was no place anywhere on which to sit, but finally, with our boots back on, we turned away from the lake and took a few steps toward the clearing visible close by where we knew the portage trail began.

And then it struck us—the clearing was on the east side of La Loche Creek; we were on the west side! And the creek, though shallow, had a soft, mucky bottom. At this point our sense of humor came to our rescue. In between howls of laughter, we assured ourselves that, in spite of the muck and the still-falling rain, we really were having a wonderful time. So once again, we took off our boots and waded across the creek, with each step sinking deep into the ooze. At long last we walked the few rods to the grassy opening—the southern end of the portage where once had stood Methye Lake Post. Today a rock cairn has been erected by the Historic Sites and Monument Board of Canada to mark this historic spot.

We had no difficulty finding the portage track leading out of the clearing. For the first mile or so the trail went through scattered marshy spots and areas of spongy sphagnum moss and over, by means of pole bridges, the upper reaches of La Loche Creek and one other small stream. Shortly after crossing this second creek, we reached higher ground, and the drier well-worn trail along the sandy ridges made for easy walking. From this point onward for the next seven miles the portage wound through a variety of northern forest types. Sometimes the trail was bordered by dense stands of tall, spindly spruce and jack pine, both festooned with long streamers of grayish moss of ghostly appearance; other times the forest gave way to brush-free open areas of scattered jack pine, many of which, deformed and grotesque in shape, bore in their branches thick bunches of parasitic growth known as "witches' brooms." These clearings were usually carpeted with yellowish caribou moss. For much of the way, the trail led through mixed stands of tall, slender poplar, spruce, and jack pine.

After an hour of steady walking, we took a brief ten-minute rest (the first of many). At this same time, to our great delight, the misty drizzle stopped, the clouds lifted, and the sun came out. So, rested and in high spirits, we continued on our way. The silence of the forest was broken only by the chattering of the numerous red squirrels or the nervous clucking of the spruce grouse. The closest we came to seeing any wild animal were the abundant wolf and bear droppings on the trail and an old moose skull and antlers left by a hunter obviously more interested in meat than in a trophy rack.

At times the path led through areas where the forest floor was ablaze with the vivid red berries of the low-growing bunchberry. The sunshine filtering through the gold of poplar leaves and tamarack needles onto this carpet of scarlet created a picture of unforgettable beauty.

We were fascinated by the infinite variety of mushrooms we found growing in abundance by the trail. There were white, orange, yellow, scarlet, and brown ones ranging in size from small to very large. Many were smooth-surfaced; others were etched in featherlike patterns, or were dotted with scattered spots resembling sesame seeds. We marveled at their unique beauty.

Finally at about five o'clock we reached the south side of Rendezvous Lake, our destination for the night. Here was where the voyageurs before us had made their camp. It was, indeed, a historic spot. A mantle of pale yellow-green caribou moss covered the dry, sandy ground beneath the scattered scrubby jack pine and poplar growing in the clearing. This area was almost completely devoid of underbrush or firewood—the result of its continuous use as a campground for more than one hundred years. Accordingly, we had to go some distance to find sufficient wood for our campfire. We lost no time setting up camp. Soon supper was cooking over our fire, our tarp stretched over a line between two trees, and our sleeping bag rolled out.

After supper we walked along the edge of the lake and marveled at the large number of caribou, bear, and wolf tracks clearly imprinted in the sandy beach. A few mallard ducks were quietly feeding in the lake shallows. Tired though we were, we sat by our campfire enjoying the peaceful silence, the beauty of the sunset, and the brilliance of the sun's last rays as it sank behind the low hills surrounding the lake.

As twilight deepened, the air became steadily colder. Eventually the full moon appeared, its silvery light reflected on the calm waters of the lake. The deep slow hoot of a great horned owl broke the silence. And once or twice a loon laughed far out on the lake.

Still we sat, loath to leave the warmth and glow of the slowly dying embers. Even though neither of us would ever admit it, perhaps we were waiting, hoping the irrepressible spirits of those voyageurs who had camped on this very spot so many years ago might return and we would be able to catch a glimpse of them or perhaps hear a faint whisper of their songs and merriment. At last we could wait no longer. We crawled under our tarp and burrowed into our sleeping bag. We knew nothing further until we awakened the next morning to find a world covered with glistening white frost. Did our voyageurs come? We would never know. Moving briskly to keep warm, we soon ate breakfast, broke camp, and by nine o'clock were on our way to cover the last four miles of the portage.

The trail led along the south shore of the lake on a narrow sand ridge nearly a mile before striking the main portage path on the west side of the lake. It was from this western terminus that the southbound voyageurs usually loaded their packs into canoes and paddled across the lake to the campground on the southeast side, thereby saving a mile of portaging. The portage continued for a mile or so through a rather dense stand of spruce and jack pine before breaking out into a more open woods of young birch, spruce, and poplar.

And here, at a point about ten miles from the southern end, we finally reached the highest point on the portage, an elevation of 1,690 feet, which marks the height of land—the great divide—that separates the waters flowing to the north from those flowing to the south and east. For the next mile the portage wound through sunlit woods, the golden yellow of the poplars and birch contrasting with the dark green of scattered spruce.

We knew our way was now closely paralleling the rim of the Clearwater escarpment, even though it was still effectively screened from our sight by the trees. With almost startling abruptness, we reached a 100-foot cleared strip along the north side of the trail, which made it possible to see the Clearwater River and valley one thousand feet below; to enjoy the view that never failed to cause all who saw it to write of its beauty in their journals. It was, indeed, truly breathtaking. Gently rolling green-clad hills rising to a height of about one thousand feet enclosed a three-mile wide wooded valley through which the Clearwater River wound in graceful loops. This magnificent valley stretched in either direction as far as we could see. The colors of autumn did much to enhance the scene: overhead a brilliant blue sky, broken only by a few slow-moving white clouds; below the soft gold, pale orange, and yellow of the poplars and birch brightening the somber greens of spruce and jack pine, the silver ribbon of the stream sparkling and glittering in the sunlight.

Alexander Mackenzie's account written in 1801 vividly records his impressions of the scene as he saw it:

> Within a mile of the termination of the Portage is a very steep precipice
> . . . This precipice, which rises upwards of a thousand feet above the

plain beneath it, commands a most extensive, romantic, and ravishing prospect. From thence the eye looks down on the course of the little river,—beautifully meandering for upwards of thirty miles. The valley which is at once refreshed and adorned by it, is about three miles in breadth, and is confined by two lofty ridges of equal height, displaying a most beautiful intermixture of wood and lawn, and stretching on till the blue mist obscures the prospect. Some parts of the inclining heights are covered with stately forests, relieved by promontories of the finest verdure, where the elk and buffalo find pasture.

Some years later, in 1808, Daniel Harmon likewise referred to the beauty of the view over the valley. He wrote that "as we arrive at this end of the Portage, we have from a high hill an extensive & beautiful prospect of the level Country that lies before us as well as of the different windings of a small River that we are to descend."

In September of 1820 George Simpson, not one to rhapsodize over scenery, included in his journal account of the crossing of the portage the observation that "the summit of the precipice commands a very charming and extensive view of the surrounding country . . ."

After we had sat for many minutes silently enjoying the beauty of the panorama spread before us and had photographed it from every possible angle, we reluctantly took up our packs and began the last leg of the portage. The trail was long and quite steep as it wound down the side of the valley wall. It took us nearly an hour to reach the river flat at the bottom. From here until the end, the portage was across wet, swampy bottomland and through tangles of vines and thick willow brush. Overhead towered giant poplars, and here, for the first time, we encountered one of the curses of the north—swarms of voracious mosquitoes. After walking about half a mile, we broke out of this wetland and ascended a slight rise, and there before us was the large clearing on the south side of the Clearwater—the northern end of the Methye portage.

We had about an hour before our plane was due to pick us up, so we had ample time to explore this interesting and historic area. At one edge of the clearing was an Indian camp, obviously still being used, although uninhabited at the moment. A green canoe was propped against a tree; tent poles, a number of stretching hoops for beaver, numerous pots, pails, and cans were lying on the ground.

At last we heard a plane. It flew high overhead, quickly disappearing from sight. A bit later it returned, but still high above us. We quickly grabbed an orange rain parka out of our pack, and when the plane came back yet again we vigorously waved the parka back and

170

forth. This did the trick, for the pilot spotted us and began circling lower and lower, carefully examining the river before setting down some distance upstream.

In the few minutes remaining before the plane taxied down to us where we were waiting on top of the sandbank, we quickly but ceremoniously dipped our hands into the Clearwater River, splashed a few drops of water on each other, and joyfully and proudly echoed the ancient boast *je suis un homme du nord,* to which our crossing of the Methye portage had entitled us.

Fort Montagne à la Bosse

Fort Montagne à la Bosse, built by the North West Company about 1790, was located on the upper Assiniboine River close to the wintering grounds of the buffalo. It remained in operation until 1805 or later.

As the Nor'Westers moved ever westward in their pursuit of furs, the already-overextended supply line from Montreal was stretched to the utmost. It became necessary to establish posts whose primary function was to provide the supplemental provisions their brigades required.

The North West Company with its large number of employees and abundance of goods was able to establish posts at will, thereby forcing its rivals to undergo the expense of doing likewise. Responding to fluctuating opposition from its competitors, Fort Montagne à la Bosse was frequently reestablished and as often abandoned. In 1794 it was reopened by John Macdonell.

Fort Montagne à la Bosse traded an average of sixty packs a year, mostly wolves and buffalo. However, its chief and most important return was the meat of the buffalo—fresh, dried, beat, the grease and the marrow. These were the ingredients needed to make the pemmican—that indispensable item of food needed to fuel the north- and west-bound brigades. The bulk of the Assiniboine provisions (i.e., buffalo meat) came from this post and from the North West Company's Fort Espérance, located about a week's travel farther west.

The post was situated on a high bank and was enclosed by a stockade 200 feet by 250 feet, within which were the numerous buildings typical of a fort complex.

Daniel Harmon, who spent eight days at the fort, gave the following description in his journal entry for October 26, 1804: "The fort is well built, and beautifully situated, on a very high bank of the Red River [Assiniboine], and overlooks the country round to a great extent, which is a perfect plain. There can be seen at almost all seasons of the year, from the fort gate, as I am informed, buffaloes grazing or antelopes bounding over the extensive plains, which cannot fail to render the situation highly pleasant."

We had little difficulty finding the site of Montagne à la Bosse. A few inquiries at a truck stop and restaurant on the busy Trans-Canada Highway at Virden gave us the necessary directions. After driving north for a few miles on a dusty gravel road, we came to the prominent rock monument bearing a suitably inscribed plaque that marks the site of the fort. The view out over the plains and river valley below is no

172

longer visible. A thick growth of trees and bushes effectively screens it from sight. And even if we could see through the trees, there would be no grazing buffalo, no bounding antelope to watch with delight. Today such scenes can only be seen in our imagination.

Grant's House/Aspin House/(Fort de la Rivière Tremblante)

By 1791 the Nor'Westers had advanced westward as far as the upper reaches of the Assiniboine River. In that year Robert Grant, partner in the company, built a fort on the left bank of the river near the mouth of the Rivière Tremblante. This post, called Grant's House, was also known as Aspin House and as Fort de la Rivière Tremblante. It was located in prime fur country, and from it came the bulk of the beaver and otter pelts for the Assiniboine district. Two years later, Cuthbert Grant took over the post when he was placed in charge of the district, and from then on it became his favorite place of residence. This fort not only was a major source of furs, but also served as an important provisioning post for brigades traveling to the Athabasca country.

The post faced formidable competition from rival trading companies. An entry written by Duncan McGillivray dated March 4, 1795, reads: "His [Cuthbert Grant Sr.'s] Department is entirely ruined by different interests:—his opponents this year are very numerous having no less than 14 forts to oppose, which with 7 belonging to the Company amounts in all to 21 forts in R.R. [Assiniboine River]."

John Macdonell of the North West Company in his *Some Account of the Red River* mentioned still another problem that confronted Grant's House.

This [Rivière Tremblante Fort], and the temporary posts established above it, furnish most of the beaver and otter in the Red River returns, but this trade has been almost ruined since the Hudson Bay Company entered the Assiniboil [Assiniboine] River by the way of Swan River, carrying their merchandise from one river to the other on horseback,—three days' journey,—who by that means and the short distance between Swan River and their factory at York Fort, from whence they are equiped, can arrive at the Coude de l'homme [elbow], in the Assiniboil river, a month sooner than we can return from the Grand Portage, secure the fall trade, give credits to the Indians and send them to hunt before our arrival; so that we see but very few in that quarter upon our arrival.

With Grant's departure from the Assiniboine in 1798 Grant's House was closed. For the period of its existence, this fort, the "Upper Post," built by Robert Grant and operated by Cuthbert Grant, was the great fur fort of the North West Company in the Assiniboine department throughout the 1790s; their pemmican, on the other hand, came from their forts on the prairies to the south.

Historians have identified the site of Grant's House on the left bank of the Assiniboine River just above the point where the Rivière Tremblante flows in from the east. The ruins were found in the bottom of the valley 500 paces east of the Assiniboine and 50 paces from the foot of a wooded bank, at the mouth of a dry ravine, on slightly sloping land thirty-five feet above the river.

We were not able to visit this precise location but had to be content with seeing and photographing the Assiniboine River valley in the general area of the fort's location. A short distance west of the small village of Togo, the bridge on Highway 357 crosses the Assiniboine not far from the mouth of Rivière Tremblante. We felt confident that this section of the river valley that we photographed from the bridge was very similar to that occupied by Grant's House close by and that it would, therefore, serve to show the general appearance of the area where the fort had once stood.

Fort Bas de la Rivière
Fort Alexander

The area around the mouth of the Winnipeg River was of great importance to the early fur traders, since it was on the main canoe route from Montreal to the west by either the Saskatchewan River or the Red and Assiniboine rivers. From 1733, when the eldest son of La Vérendrye built on the right (northeast) bank of the river, his second Fort Maurepas, one or more fur posts have always been located here.

Toussaint Le Sieur in 1792 erected a trading fort for the North West Company on the south side of the river about six miles below and opposite the site of the old Fort Maurepas. His post was known as Le Sieur's Fort, but more commonly as Fort Bas de la Rivière. Probably one of the first North West Company's forts built west of Fort William, it served as a major provision depot.

The impossibility of carrying large amounts of provisions in the canoes made necessary the establishment of numerous provision posts at suitable intervals along all the routes. It was to Fort Bas de la Rivière that the enormous amounts of pemmican needed to provision the brigades for their long voyages into the Athabasca country were brought down every spring from the posts on the Red and Assiniboine rivers in buffalo country.

By 1800 the Hudson's Bay Company had established Fort Alexander within a few rods of the North West Fort Bas de la Rivière. Built by either John or Donald McKay *le malin,* it was supplied from Fort Albany on James Bay. In addition to trading for a few furs, it was intended both to serve as a provision post and to maintain surveillance over the North West post. The few men stationed here had the responsibility for proper storage of the pemmican, making sure it was kept dry and free of mold; in addition, they transported it by boats to Hudson's Bay Company Brandon House, a distribution post up the Assiniboine River. Alexander Henry the younger, who spent two days at Fort Bas de la Rivière in August of 1800, wrote that "the H.B. Co. have an establishment at this place near the N.W. Co. They have a clerk and two men who pass the summer here, but talk about throwing it up this fall, as a post will not pay expenses."

Nicholas Garry, a director of the Hudson's Bay Company, while making a joint tour with Simon McGillivray of the North West Company of both companies' trading posts after the merger of 1821 commented in his diary: "arrived at Bas de la Riviere where the North West had a trading Post, now become Hudson Bay's.—The Post is placed in a very beautiful Situation and surrounded by cultivated Land where they grow Potatoes, Wheat And Vegetables. At the Moment we were there there were 50 Women and Children living at the Expense of the Company. This is an immense Expense and some Steps should be taken to avoid it. This was a Sort of resting Port for the Athapascan Canoes."

As a result of the merger, the Hudson's Bay Company closed down its own post and transferred operations to Fort Bas de la Rivière, which, before long, became known as Fort Alexander. It remained a district post for Lake Winnipeg for some time. However, it soon lost its importance as a provision depot because after 1821 the majority of shipments passed through Norway House and York Factory; the old North West Company route through Fort Bas de la Rivière to Fort William was seldom used.

In our quest to find the sites of Forts Maurepas, Bas de la Rivière, and Alexander, we drove north on Manitoba Highway 11, which closely follows the southwest side of the Winnipeg River. We knew the many dams obstructing the free flow of the river had forever altered its appearance by drowning its formidable rapids. Happily, there are yet many stretches free of cottage and industrial development to delight the eye as the river winds through the beautiful Canadian shield country of bare rock, spruce, pine, and birch.

At one particularly scenic spot we ate our lunch, picnic style, on the gently sloping bare rock at river's edge. There were a few small riffles visible—too minor to be called rapids. Otherwise, nothing disturbed the quiet, strong flow of the river as it neared its final destination in Lake Winnipeg. A solitary white pelican roosted on an exposed rock in midstream. This river, a continuation and integral part of the Rainy Lake–Rainy River–Lake of the Woods fur trade highway, had carried the canoes of explorer, trapper, and trader for well over a hundred years. Its rapids and chutes had claimed their toll of lives and cargo. Its waters had echoed to the voyageurs' chansons. The thrusting canoe bow, the powerful paddle strokes had broken its surface.

We continued toward the small hamlet of Fort Alexander, located in an Indian reserve that encompasses both sides of the river at its junction with the lake. From this point onward, the river widens considerably as it nears the lake, the country on both sides flattens out, and woods are replaced by marshes.

After only one stop for information, we found what we sought. In a large level field near the edge of a low bluff bordering the river, we found the rock cairn erected by the Historic Sites and Monument

Board of Canada to mark the location "in this area" of the North West and Hudson's Bay posts of the 1790s—i.e., Forts Bas de la Rivière and Alexander.

A bit disconcerting was the statement on the plaque that La Vérendrye's second Fort Maurepas had also stood "nearby," since it was our impression gained from early journals that it had been built on the right hand, i.e., the northeast side, of the river—in other words, on the opposite side of the river from where we were standing. This, perhaps, is merely an indication of the many difficulties and uncertainties that still exist regarding the precise location of many of the early fur forts.

At any rate, this field where we stood, knee-deep in prairie wildflowers and grasses, the air full of the fragrance of clover and goldenrod and the hum of bees, was indeed, as Palliser had described it in 1857, "fine fertile flat, elevated 40 feet above the river." We were satisfied, even if this location were not the exact site, that it was on some such flat as this that the great pemmican depots of Fort Bas de la Rivière and Fort Alexander had once stood.

Fort Forks

Undeterred by the failure of his 1789 voyage down the Mackenzie River to reach the Western [Pacific] Sea, which ended disappointingly on the shores of the Arctic Ocean, Alexander Mackenzie was determined to try again, this time, however, by way of the great Peace River.

So, in 1792 from his post at Fort Chipewyan on Old Fort Point on the southwest shore of Lake Athabasca, as the first step in his preparation for his journey he arranged to have a fort built far up the Peace River, which would serve as an advance base from which to launch his second attempt the following year.

Early in the spring two men from Alexander McLeod's fort at the mouth of the White Mud River were sent some forty miles upriver to prepare the site and cut and square the timbers needed for construction of the fort. The spot chosen was on the right bank of the Peace River about six miles above the forks formed by its junction with Smoky River. The fort was called Fort Forks, although sometimes it was known as Smoky Forks.

On October 10, 1792, Mackenzie, accompanied by two canoes laden with the necessary articles for trade, set off on the first leg of his great journey. Three weeks later, on November 1, he reached the spot that had been selected for his fort to find that his advance party "had formed a sufficient quantity of pallisades of eighteen feet long, and seven inches in diameter, to inclose a square spot of an hundred and twenty feet; they had also dug a ditch of three feet deep to receive them; and had prepared timber, planks, &. for the erection of an house."

By the sixth of November the river began to run with ice, marking the end of navigation, and by the twenty-second ice had formed thick enough to allow safe passage across the river, a condition that would last until the end of next April. Mackenzie noted that "on the 27th [November] the frost was so severe that the axes of the workmen became almost as brittle as glass."

By the end of April, trading for the winter's furs had been completed; canoes had been repaired and new ones built. Mackenzie engaged his hunters for the ensuing season and closed the business of the year by writing his dispatches and balancing his ledgers. On May 8 six canoes heavily loaded with furs and provisions set off down the Peace River for Fort Chipewyan. The next evening at seven o'clock Mackenzie and the nine men who had agreed to accompany him on his voyage of discovery, along with provisions, goods for presents, arms, ammuni-

179

tion, and baggage, embarked in their twenty-five-foot canoe and headed upstream against the strong current.

Mackenzie's return to his Fort Forks in August of 1793 at the completion of his triumphant voyage to the Pacific Ocean is best described in his own words: "At length, as we rounded a point, and came in view of the Fort, we threw out our flag, and accompanied it with a general discharge of our firearms; while the men were in such spirits, and made such an active use of their paddles, that we arrived before the two men whom we left here in the spring, could recover their senses to answer us. Thus we landed at four in the afternoon, at the place we left on the ninth of May."

Mackenzie soon continued down the Peace to return to Fort Chipewyan. After spending the winter of 1793–94 there, he gave up his life as an explorer-trader and left the fur country, never to return.

His successor at Fort Forks was Alexander McLeod, who remained there until he retired in 1799. For the final few years of the fort's existence it is thought that John Finlay and then Archibald Norman McLeod were in charge. David Thompson, the eminent geographer, spent the year 1803 conducting meteorological observations. By 1805 the fort was closed down, superseded by the North West Company's Fort Dunvegan, newly established some sixty miles farther up the Peace River.

A major mud slide blocking the main highway leading into Peace River Crossing from the south delayed our arrival until late in the afternoon. Fortunately, however, even after checking into an RV campground close by and eating our supper we still had sufficient time before twilight to drive up to the overlook on top of one of the hills above the town.

The view spread out below us was magnificent. Low wooded hills rose from each side of the river valley. A short distance upriver the waters of the Heart, the Smoky, and the Peace converged into one mighty stream. Here was the famous Forks—the point of departure for Alexander Mackenzie's historic journey to the Pacific. We realized that we were, in truth, looking at a very historic spot.

Early the next morning we drove upriver on a secondary road that closely followed the left bank of the Peace. We soon came to the familiar Historic Sites and Monument stone cairn that we sought. The monument was enclosed by a neat white fence, and at one corner was a tall pole flying the flag of Canada.

The actual location of Mackenzie's Fort Forks was on the right side of the river—that is, across and, in the words inscribed on the bronze plaque, "opposite this spot" from where we were standing. As we looked across the river to the other side, to the rolling hillside of openings and scattered groves of trees, it was difficult to imagine that a substantial fort once stood there; to realize that it was from this very spot on the swiftly flowing river before us that nearly two hundred years ago a frail birchbark canoe of twenty-five feet loaded with 3,000 pounds of cargo and carrying ten men not only had departed but also had returned 107 days later, after successfully completing the very first crossing of British North America, and thereby laying justifiable claim for Canada's proud motto: "A Mari Usque Ad Mare."

Fort George (North Saskatchewan River) Buckingham House

Forced by the declining supply of beaver available at their Pine Island forts, the North West Company and the Hudson's Bay Company advanced about 120 miles farther upstream in order to reach an area where beaver were still abundant. During the year 1792 they each erected a fort almost side by side on the north bank of the North Saskatchewan River.

Angus Shaw of the North West Company was the first to build his post, which was called Fort George. His clerk, John McDonald of Garth, wrote in his *Autobiographical Notes* that "the new fort was upon the margin of a fine hummock of pine, upon a rising hill or bank, with the noble Sascatchewan in front, its banks covered with strong wood for perhaps a mile in breadth and twenty in length along the river."

Although no detailed description of the fort exists, archaeological work at the site suggests that there were two gates in the stockade, one to the south facing the river and one to the north opening out to the woods. Within the enclosed area, which measured approximately 187 by 194 feet, directly opposite the south gate was the main house, twenty-four by seventy-six feet. This structure contained living quarters for the wintering partner and the Indian hall used for receiving the chiefs with the required customary ceremony. Other buildings were storehouses, a blacksmith shop, clerks' houses, men's quarters, and an icehouse, all ranged along the east and west walls.

During most of its eight years of operation, Fort George was under the charge of Angus Shaw. He had as assistants two clerks, Duncan McGillivray and John McDonald of Garth, as well as a crew of sixty to eighty men. In addition, there was an almost equal number of women and children who likewise lived within the fort.

Because of its location on the North Saskatchewan, which formed the approximate boundary between the northern forests, home of the furbearers, and the parklands and prairies to the south, home of the buffalo, Fort George served both as a fur trading fort and as a provisioning post. For example, its returns for the 1794–95 season were 325 bales of furs and 300 bags of pemmican.

Fort George was but one of the several forts along the North Saskatchewan known as Forts des Prairies. In order to obtain the buffalo meat on which much of their trading system depended, these posts had the difficult task of maintaining trading relations with Plains Indians, who were always fiercely independent, usually truculent, and frequently hostile.

The traders and their men lived in a constant state of tension. It was for this reason that quite often rival companies built their posts next to each other—indeed, sometimes within a common stockade. Such an arrangement not only provided a common defense but also, as an added benefit, gave each company the opportunity of keeping its neighbor's trading activities under close surveillance.

When news of the Indian destruction of Manchester House on Pine Island in 1792 and the massacre at South Branch House the following year reached Fort George, the men remained within the fort compound for six weeks, not daring to venture outside the palisade walls. Their Hudson's Bay neighbors and competitors from Buckingham House abandoned their post and moved into Fort George for protection.

Friction and rivalry among various Indian tribes as they congregated near the forts during the trading season frequently erupted into conflict that threatened the traders and their men. And finally the use of rum, demanded by the Indians as a prerequisite for any trading, increased the danger of violence.

Fort George remained in continuous use until 1800, when forced by depletion of the beaver, it was finally closed in favor of a new post (Fort de l'Isle), which had been established about twenty miles farther upriver. As early as the fall of 1799 the post had been partially abandoned, for David Thompson, who spent the winter there, wrote in his journal that on his arrival September 5 he "found the fort without doors or windows, and otherwise dilapidated."

According to his journal entry for September 30, 1809, Alexander Henry the younger sent several of his men upriver to the abandoned post to salvage some of its stockades and other wood and raft them down for his use at Fort Vermilion. A final glimpse of the old fort appears in Henry's journal under date of October 27, 1809: "Passed the ruins of old Fort George, only the chimneys of which are now to be seen."

William Tomison, chief of the Hudson's Bay Company's inland operations, lost little time in following Angus Shaw up the Saskatchewan that same year (1792). By the middle of October Tomison arrived at the spot chosen for his fort. It was on a high plateau, the upper of two benches almost four hundred yards back from the river one hundred fifty feet below. Only a small brush-fringed gully lay between his fort site and Fort George a few hundred yards to the east. Stretching back from the plateau were dense woods and areas of open pines—an ample source of building material. Tomison quickly set his twenty-eight men to constructing the numerous buildings, erecting a strong stockade, digging a well in the bottom of the small creek that trickled down the gully, and constructing the main house, which measured sixty-three by twenty-six feet.

Relations between the leaders of the two opposing forts, while not overly cordial, were, nevertheless, quite civil. Matters concerning trade were discussed and amicably settled, as it was important that they agree on the price in trade goods they would pay for furs and meat. They also had to determine to which company each Indian was indebted. A vigilant watch was kept by each trader to make sure that an Indian who had received credit from one company did not trade his furs at the rival company. When any such gambit was detected, swift retribution would follow.

On the whole, the men from the two rival forts tried to minimize friction. They no doubt realized that in view of their isolation and their small numbers, which made them vulnerable to hostile Indian attacks, they had to depend on each other for support. And, too, sheer loneliness and perhaps the dreary monotony of their life throughout the long winter months fostered some social contacts between the two posts.

An entry in Duncan McGillivray's journal described an incident when the men at his post rushed to the assistance of their neighbors:

22nd March [1795].—An accident happened this morning which has again renewed our intercourse with our neighbours:—retiring from breakfast we were alarmed with a sudden cry of fire! and rushing immediately out we perceived clouds of smoke ascending from the English House; forgetting at that instant our former animosity we obeyed the dictates of humanity by running to their assistance & the Fire, after having consumed part of the roof, was happily extinguished. Soon after, we received a letter of thanks and an invitation to pass the evening at Mr. Tomisons, where all our differences were accomodated over a dish of tea, whilst the Canadians and his men diverted themselves with dancing and drinking plentifull draughts of what they call delicious punch.

A less friendly episode involving the two forts was described by John McDonald of Garth. During a period of drought Tomison, fearing that his well at the foot of the gully might dry up, withdrew the permission he had previously given to the men of Fort George to draw water from it. Vigorous protests from the Nor'Westers were of no avail. However, Tomison reversed his decision when he was told by McDonald "if he would not give us our wants that either of us must pay a visit to the bottom of the well." As McDonald observed, "This argument rather startled him & we got our share of the water ever after."

Buckingham House was at a continual disadvantage in its competition with Fort George. Its complement of men was invariably smaller; its stock of trade goods was less. It had experienced men in charge such as Peter Fidler, George Sutherland, James Pruden and Henry Hallett, but they could not overcome these serious handicaps. As early as 1795, the area around the two rival forts had been virtually trapped out. In McGillivray's words: "The Country arround Fort George [as well as Buckingham House] is now entirely ruined. The Natives have already killed all the Beavers, to such a distance that they lose much time in coming to the House, during the Hunting Season."

So once again it was necessary to move farther upriver to reach new sources of fur. A new fort was built at the mouth of the Sturgeon River; however, Buckingham House continued to operate for a few more years, until finally in 1800 it was completely abandoned.

We set off for Fort George and Buckingham House in high spirits, confident we would have no trouble in locating their sites, but as so often was the case, with no directional signs to point the way we soon were hopelessly lost amid the maze of backcountry roads. Fortunately for us, a friendly farmer who happened to drive by not only knew the location of the forts but also offered to lead us to them.

Within a short time we had reached our goal. There on the upper of two terraces sloping up from the North Saskatchewan was the place where once had stood Fort George. The one-acre site at the time of this our first visit in 1983 was overgrown with thick brush and prairie grasses. It was enclosed by only a four-strand wire fence, within which was a simple provincial marker identifying the site as Fort George.

Although thick coniferous forest covered the area at the time the fort was built, it is now all gone, replaced by extensive grassland openings, isolated clumps of trees, and numerous brush-bordered ravines leading down to the river. The entire river valley spread out below us in all its peaceful beauty—gently rolling hills of open fields and patches of woods and the river quietly flowing eastward.

We spent considerable time examining and photographing the numerous depressions and the many rock piles still plainly visible scattered throughout the area—tangible evidence of the buildings that once stood here. We walked down through the knee-high grasses bright with the yellow and white of prairie flowers, the pink of the wild rose, to the lower terrace and over to the tree-fringed ravine to the west. As we crossed over the gully, now bone-dry, we recalled that it was right here at the lower end of this streambed that Tomison's well had once provided water for the two forts.

We followed a well-worn path leading up out of the gully, probably the very same one used by the traders before us, and soon reached the level flat of the high plateau. Here, likewise enclosed by a wire fence, were the site of Buckingham House and the provincial identifying marker. This area had been leveled for cultivation, so lacked the visible surface evidence of the fort's existence.

As at Fort George, the view from this site was magnificent. We walked a few yards to the edge of this plateau high above the river. Below us was a lower bench that sloped gradually to the river some 550 yards distant. We, like the traders of both Buckingham House and Fort George, could look far in all directions. But unlike them, who had to be constantly on the alert to catch the first glimpse of distant brigades, friendly or rival, the unexpected approach of Indians, friendly or hostile, the appearance of grizzly or buffalo, we could be content merely to enjoy the beauty of the scene spread before us. As McGillivray nearly two hundred years ago had so aptly written: "It was a Grand Sight to me to see such a Grand River."

Ten years later (1993) we returned to Fort George and Buckingham House and were amazed at the changes that had taken place. A magnificent interpretation center housing excellent displays pertaining to the history of the two forts and the culture of the native peoples of the area has been erected close by the fort sites.

It was here that we met Louise Crane, the affable manager, who made our visit so very worthwhile and enjoyable. Under her guidance we walked the short distance to the Fort George site. The overgrown brush-covered area that we remembered from our first visit had all been cleared, so that the old cellar holes, foundation ridges, rock piles, and depressions were now clearly visible. The careful archaeological work that had followed the clearing of the site had resulted in the determination of the layout of the fort's buildings and their function.

A proposal to delineate each of the major structures with heavy squared timbers spiked to the ground had been accepted by the province of Alberta and technical help provided. A work bee to implement this plan had been scheduled for the day following our visit. The Friends of the Forts, a volunteer organization dedicated to the welfare of the two posts, had offered to provide the man—and woman—power.

We were caught up in the general enthusiasm for the project and offered to stay over a day and join the work crew. Our offer was promptly accepted. What a rewarding experience we had! It was hard work—lifting and carrying heavy timbers, digging post holes, pounding spikes with a heavy maul, sawing beams—but aided by laughter, good camaraderie, and abundant food, it was fun. Later, gathered for a bountiful spur-of-the-moment supper at the home of one of the volunteers, we all enjoyed the delicious food, the hospitality, and the great sense of accomplishment we all shared. We ourselves felt very privileged and grateful to be included with such a wonderful group of people.

We really hated to leave the next morning but were happy to know that both Fort George and Buckingham House are in good hands and that the Friends of the Forts will make sure that these two forts, at least, will always be remembered, their sites preserved, and the unforgettable view of the peaceful Saskatchewan valley and beautiful river protected forever.

Fort Pic

The strategic importance of the Pic River was recognized quite early. Its mouth, on the north shore of Lake Superior, was the southern end of a major navigable canoe route that by means of the great Albany River and tributaries reached its northern terminus at Fort Albany on James Bay.

Gabriel Cotté, who had previously operated as an independent trader and outfitter at Michilimackinac for a number of years, in partnership with John Grant and Maurice Blondeau, established a trading post on the west bank of the river near its outlet into Lake Superior sometime prior to 1789. A profitable thirty bales of furs were traded during the 1790 season.

John Macdonell, following the north shore of Lake Superior on his way to his post at Fort Qu'Appelle, wrote in his diary on July 5, 1793: "Twelve to fifteen leagues further on we found the entrance of the Pic River where there is a Trading Post belonging to Mr. Cote and associates situated within half a mile of our encampment. This was the coldest night ever I felt at this time [of] the year, and in the vicinity of our encampment there are eleven Crosses in memory of that number [of] men that are buried here most of whom perished last winter by various casualties."

In 1795 Cotté was succeeded by another independent trader, St. Germain, who had previously owned the post at the mouth of the Michipicoten River.

At this time Fort Pic consisted of a cleared area approximately 193 feet by 145 feet, surrounded by a nine-foot stockade. Within the compound were three buildings: a 136-foot-by-12-foot warehouse, constructed of horizontal cedar logs and roofed with layers of cedar bark; living quarters thirty feet by twenty feet of similar construction; and a small stable.

Four years later [1799] Baptiste Perrault of the North West Company took over the post, and for the next sixteen years the fort enjoyed its greatest prosperity. Additional buildings were constructed, such as a forty-foot-by-twenty-one-foot "Great House" of five rooms with a fireplace and eight glass windows, a forty-eight-foot-by-eighteen-foot warehouse, a forge, and a powder magazine. The normal complement of men now needed to operate the post included the resident wintering partner, three clerks, an interpreter, and ten voyageurs. A census taken during 1805 showed that there were sixteen men, two women, and three children living at the fort, while the Indians in the immediate vicinity numbered forty-four men, forty-five women, and fifty-eight children. In 1805 five canoes carrying seventy-eight pieces of trading goods and eighty-two pieces of provisions were dispatched to Fort Pic from North West Company headquarters at Fort William. Returns from Fort Pic for the following year were eighty-six packs of furs. Fort Pic remained an important post not only as a source of fur but also as a harbor of refuge for brigades when threatened by the perilous waters of Lake Superior.

The fort was taken over from the North West Company by the Hudson's Bay Company at the time of the union of the two companies in 1821. For the next forty-four years several factors were in charge of the post, beginning with Alexander McTavish and including Thomas McMurray and Charles Begg. Apparently, the fort soon assumed the appearance of a typical Hudson's Bay Company post, for Louis Agassiz, who visited it in 1847, wrote that the buildings formed a hollow square and were single-storied, whitewashed, and trimmed with red; the square was planked and a plank roadway protected by a picketed palisade led from a river gate to the river. Numerous contemporary references indicate that farming of some sort was carried on, requiring additional cleared land.

After 1865 only a very minimal operation was maintained, and sometime before 1914 even that was terminated. Fort Pic was abandoned and left to fade into oblivion.

The site of Fort Pic was easy to find. We were able to drive to the tiny Indian village of Heron Bay, located on the west bank of the Pic River just a short distance above its outlet into Lake Superior. In the middle of the common, a grassy field bordered by houses and a large church, an informative sign summarizing the history of Fort Pic has been erected by the Ontario government.

We continued on a narrow dirt road paralleling the west side of the river for nearly a mile until we reached its mouth flowing into Lake Superior. Here on the west bank of the river, about 150 yards from its mouth, had once stood Fort Pic. The site was in the area of sand dunes on a flat sixteen feet above the normal water level—high enough to escape spring floods. The steep bank that borders the flat curves to form a wide beach area downstream to Lake Superior.

Unfortunately, in 1930 a paper company's boom camp was set up right over the site of the old fort, causing extensive damage and alteration to the original surface features. However, in spite of this destruction, archaeological excavations conducted in 1964 were successful in uncovering traces of the fort's stockade and vestiges of three buildings, thought to be the "great houses" built by Cotté and by St. Germain. The well, still in use, appears to be the original one. At the time when it was widened and deepened, several artifacts, such as copper trade pails and an ax head, dating from the fur trade period were retrieved from its bottom.

Today Fort Pic has disappeared completely. Its existence is preserved by a government marker, references in traders' journals and diaries, a few rotted planks and timbers, and a handful of hand-wrought nails hidden beneath the surface of the ground. That is all. Only the river with its bordering wood-covered sand dunes and hillsides and the mighty unpredictable Lake Superior flinging its powerful waves upon the shore remain unchanged.

From the high bank where we stood on the fort site we looked upstream and saw not canoes coming swiftly down the river with their rich cargo of furs, but log booms lining each side of the river—a reminder that it is logs that now come down the river each spring. We saw fishing tugs tied up along the bank and realized that they are the ones, not the big Montreal canoes laden with supplies for the fort, that now leave treacherous Lake Superior and turn up into the safety of the river. The beach below us, once crowded with canoes and men, is now deserted; voyageur footprints and keel marks have long since been erased from the sand by the waters of the river.

Fort St. Joseph

When Fort Mackinac was lost to the British by the terms of the 1783 Treaty of Paris concluded at the end of the American Revolution, they were forced to find another location that would give them the same strategic advantage of a fort situated at the crossroads leading into the fur country. After considerable reconnoitering, it was decided that St. Joseph Island would be a suitable substitute for Mackinac Island. In the words of Lord Dorchester, it was designed to be "within our Frontier a Rendezvous for the Indian Traders (returning with Furs from their wintering grounds round Lake Michigan and near the Mississippi) where they meet the merchants or their Agents from Lower Canada, discharge past credits with their Peltries and receive a fresh supply of goods for the ensuing winter; this commerce has hitherto been carried on at Michilimackinac during the whole month of June . . ."

Accordingly, preliminary work on a new post was commenced, and in 1796, when the British post on Mackinac Island was transferred to the United States as mandated by the terms of Jay's Treaty, the British flag was first raised over the infant Fort St. Joseph. Even before this, however, the North West Company in 1792 had established a small fort at the foot of St. Joseph's Island, where they constructed canoes for use in the interior.

Daniel Harmon, newly engaged clerk for the North West Company, on his first trip from Montreal to Grand Portage, company headquarters at the west end of Lake Superior, reached St. Joseph Island on May 28, 1800. He recorded his impression of the place in his journal:

To this place the British troops came and built a fortification, when the Americans took possession of Michilimackinack. There are stationed here one Captain, one Lieutenant, one Ensign, and thirty nine privates. The fort is built on a beautiful rise of ground, which is joined to the main island by a narrow neck of land. As it is not long since a settlement was made here, they have only four dwelling houses and two stores, on the other parts of the peninsula; and the inhabitants appear like exiles. The North West Company have a house and store here. In the latter, they construct canoes, for sending into the in-teriour, and down to Montreal. Vessels, of about sixty tons burden, come here from Detroit and Mackana and Soult St. Maries. The whole island is computed to be about twenty miles in circumference; the soil is good it is distant, nearly nine hundred miles from Montreal, and forty-five from Mackana . . .

From their depot on St. Joseph Island, which became a sort of way station on the Montreal–Grand Portage route, the North West Company furnished trade goods and supplies to their partners wintering in the *pays d'en haut* northwest of Lake Superior.

During the next decade, construction of Fort St. Joseph continued. Based on archaeological excavations carried on in 1963 and 1964, a rather clear picture emerged of the buildings and the palisade that constituted the fort. A rectangular two-story wood-frame blockhouse occupied the highest point of ground within the fort enclosure. The upper floor contained two rooms for officers' quarters. The lower part was divided into four compartments, one for each of the different type of stores: ordnance, provision and commissary, Indian department, and regimental. Also built was a wooden guardhouse that contained guard-rooms for officers and men and three solitary cells. A bakery constructed close to the blockhouse was a wooden building with a chimney at each end. The interior was divided into two compartments: the commandant's kitchen and the bakery. Finally, a storehouse was erected that both housed the engineer's stores and served as a workshop and office. Traces of the foundations of a small building adjacent to the storehouse not as yet investigated may be the remains of the Indian council house. Surrounding these buildings was a palisade complete with curtain walls, bastions, ravelins, and two gates.

Gradually relations between the United States and Great Britain began to deteriorate on all fronts. Jefferson's Embargo of 1807, which prevented the importation of British goods into the United States, had a major impact on the fur trade. The Montreal firms tried to circumvent the embargo by forming a business partnership with the American John Jacob Astor. By 1811, as a result of governmental control and the embargo, large amounts of British trade goods had accumulated in the storehouses at the fort, the agents unable to forward them into American territory.

On June 18, 1812, war was declared between America and Great Britain, and by July 8 the news had reached Fort St. Joseph. In the incredibly short time of eight days, a British force of forty regulars augmented by 160 voyageurs and men from the North West Company and 300 Indians had embarked in the North West Company's sailing brig *Caledonia* and were on their way to the successful capture of the American fort on Mackinac Island. As a result of their victory, Fort St. Joseph was practically deserted by the British in favor of the newly conquered island and fort, which became their major stronghold and base of operations.

Two years later there was no one left to offer resistance to American forces when they landed on St. Joseph Island. Fort St. Joseph was put to the torch, as well as all the storehouses and other buildings belonging to the North West Company. However, the cluster of civilian houses and the warehouses belonging to John Jacob Astor's South West Company were left intact.

Nicholas Garry while on his trip to the posts of the Hudson's Bay Company and North West Company at the time of their union wrote in his diary: "Sunday 24th June [1821].—At six o'clock we passed the site of the Village of St. Joseph upon an Island of the same Name. The Ruins of the old British Fort are still standing. The Situation is very commanding. A Corporal's Guard is now on the Island for the Protection of the Powder Magazine which has been sent from Drummond Island."

The British occupation of Mackinac Island was short-lived, for it was restored to the Americans in 1815 by the Treaty of Ghent. The British, rather than rebuild the completely destroyed Fort St. Joseph, decided on Drummond Island, just to the south of St. Joseph Island, as the location for their new fort. This choice was an unfortunate one, for Drummond Island was later granted to the United States by the Joint Boundary Commission. Once again (in 1828) the British had to withdraw, this time to Penetanguishene, where they were able to establish a permanent post. By 1829 Fort St. Joseph had ceased to exist. It had been completely abandoned by the military forces, the Indian Department, and the fur traders.

Today Fort St. Joseph is easily reached by a modern bridge crossing the North Channel at the upper end of Lake Huron and paved and well-marked roads lead to the southern tip of the beautifully wooded island where the fort was located during its brief eighteen years of existence. We spent considerable time in the excellent interpretive museum just outside the fort site. We particularly enjoyed the life-size diorama realistically showing a trader with his supply of goods temptingly spread out on the ground before him and the Indians offering their lustrous peltries in trade.

Of the fort itself almost nothing remains but piles of stone rubble marking the location of the major buildings. The powder magazine located in what was once the north bastion is the best preserved. Three of its stone-and-cobble walls are still standing. In addition, a second structure still retains vestiges of its stone walls. This was the new bakery that replaced the original bakery destroyed by fire in 1802. Elsewhere the outlines of the various buildings have been delineated with stones and identified by informative markers.

The prospect from where we stood on the site of the blockhouse on the highest point of ground in the center of the low hill was a most pleasant one. Just below us and following the shoreline the foundations of the numerous small traders' homes clustered around the periphery of the fort were clearly visible. In this same area close to the shore, the warehouses and workshops of the North West Company, as well as those of the other fur-trading companies, had been located.

To the east, the south, and the west the blue waters of Lake Huron sparkling in the sunshine stretched clear to the far horizon. Truly, as both Harmon and Garry had written 175 years ago, Fort St. Joseph had occupied a site that was both "beautiful" and "commanding."

Pine Fort/Fort des Épinettes

The large horseshoe bend of the Assiniboine River just east of the mouth of Épinette Creek was a favored location for the establishment of early trading posts. It possessed numerous natural advantages. The nearby creek furnished water year-round; there was a sufficiency of spruce for *watape* and gum and of birch—all needed for canoe repairs—the flat, level plain on the north bank seventy-five feet above the river afforded excellent visibility both up- and downstream; and the twenty-foot-wide flat at the toe of the bank provided a suitable landing for the loaded canoes. However, one drawback was the lack of large, mature trees. The sandy soil that characterized the area could support only a rather meager growth of small balsam, spruce, and poplar, hardly suitable for fort construction.

More important, the location, situated as it was in buffalo country, guaranteed a dependable supply of meat, both fresh and dried. Furthermore, it was on the direct route to the upper Missouri River, home of the Mandan Indians, with whom an active trade was carried on for their corn, squash, beans, and tobacco as well as horses. Finally, since it was close to the upper limits of the Assiniboine's navigability for canoe travel, it served as transfer point where cargo from the canoes was transferred to horses for overland transport to posts farther upstream.

Within a very few years after the conquest of New France by the British in 1763, enterprising free traders from Montreal began moving into the Northwest fur trade, following in the footsteps of their French predecessors. One of these was Thomas Correy, who, it seems likely, in 1768 built the first Pine Fort on the horseshoe bend near the mouth of Épinette Creek. This post encountered considerable resistance and threats of reprisal from local Assiniboine Indians who were determined to preserve their status as middlemen—go-betweens—in the trade between the traders at the post and both the western Indian tribes and the Mandans to the south. Finally, a devastating smallpox epidemic, which decimated the native people and struck down some traders, brought about the abandonment of Pine Fort in 1781.

The horseshoe bend did not remain unoccupied for long. In 1785 a trading post was built by the North West Company about three-quarters of a mile upstream from the earlier post. Known as Pine Fort or Fort des Épinettes because of its location close to the Épinette Creek, this post was not only one of the earliest forts established by the North West Company, but also its most important one in the area of the middle Assiniboine River.

Because of its location in the heart of buffalo country, Pine Fort quickly became a major provision post. Its chief function was to secure the enormous amounts of pemmican needed to provision the brigades of voyageurs on their journeys into and out of the fur country. A lively trade both in fresh buffalo meat, which was made into pemmican at the fort, as well as pemmican already made by the Indians, was carried on with the local Assiniboines. In addition, trade was maintained with the Mandan and other tribes of the Missouri region to the south, who traded not only their agricultural products, such as corn and beans, but also their horses for European guns, ammunition, and kettles.

Pine Fort served also as a major supply and distribution depot, servicing other North West Company forts farther up the Assiniboine and on the Qu'Appelle, Shell, and Swan rivers. As such, it probably remained open throughout the year, instead of being closed during the summer months as was customary for most trading posts.

Since navigation beyond Pine Fort was often uncertain and sometimes impossible because of the shallowness of the river, goods, and supplies brought up in twenty-five-foot canoes (*canots du nord*) from the North West Company headquarters at Grand Portage at the western end of Lake Superior were unloaded and stockpiled at Pine Fort for further distribution.

Troubled relations with the Indians were a continuing and constant source of worry for the traders at Pine Fort. This was largely due to intertribal frictions and jealousies, as well as to resentment among the Assiniboine, who saw their lucrative position as middlemen between the traders and the Mandan threatened. One example occurred in July 1794 when McKay, master of Pine Fort, by giving trade goods to the value of 200 beaver skins managed to ward off an attack on his fort by 600 Sioux who considered him responsible for providing their enemies, the Assiniboine, with ammunition.

By 1794 the effects of the wars in Europe were being felt throughout the fur trade. Not only were fur prices falling, but also the demand was greatly reduced. The North West Company's attempts to diversify had not been successful. To minimize its losses, a policy of retrenchment and economy became necessary. During the previous year (1793) the company had been forced to establish a new post—Fort Assiniboine—only thirteen miles above their Pine Fort, in order to meet the competition there from posts built both by the Hudson's Bay Company and by free traders. This new post had rendered Pine Fort superfluous; it was, accordingly, closed down at the end of the summer of 1794.

By this time, the center for trading activity on the middle Assiniboine had shifted upstream to the area around the mouth of the Souris

River. Here for the next ten years traders from the North West, the Hudson's Bay, and XY companies competed, each trying to outmaneuver and outtrade the other. In 1805 the North West and XY companies amalgamated, and as a result, the North West Company moved out of Fort Assiniboine and occupied the former XY Company's Fort la Souris, which was located directly across the river.

Acting under instructions of John Macdonell, a North West partner, François Antoine Larocque dismantled the buildings of their recently occupied Fort Rivière la Souris, loaded them onto a raft, and floated them downstream back to the familiar horseshoe bend on the Assiniboine, where they were laboriously reerected on the Pine Fort site. Once again Pine Fort resumed its role as a distribution, provisioning, and pemmican center. It also became an important service center. Among its employees was a blacksmith who was kept busy at his forge supplying the nails, ax heads, chisels, and many other items of iron needed by the trade.

This second Pine Fort remained in operation for but a few years, probably only until 1811. At that time it was abandoned and the company moved on upstream, this time six miles above the mouth of the Souris to a new location of the north shore of the Assiniboine in order to compete with Hudson's Bay's Brandon House, newly established directly opposite on the south side of the river.

Archaeological excavations made at the site of Pine Fort during the summers of 1971–74 indicate the existence of two stockades, two bastions on diagonal corners of the stockades, and two buildings within the enclosure. The evidence of two distinct palisades suggests that there were probably two construction phases, with the outer stockade being of later date.

The traditional French-Canadian method of posts-in-ground (*poteaux sur sole*) was used in the construction of the two buildings. The larger structure, approximately seventy-eight and three-quarters feet by nineteen and three-quarters feet, contained the forge as well as the main living area. The second building, much smaller, measured only nineteen and three-quarters feet by seventeen and three-quarters feet. An abundance of artifacts typical of the fur trade period was recovered. These included glass seed beads, brooches, rings, bells, buttons, tinkling cones, metal arrowheads, kettle parts, gun parts, pipes, bottles, textiles, knives, scissors, and files.

For many years after the last traces of the trading post had disappeared, the large horseshoe bend along the Assiniboine lay deserted until eventually farmers moved into the area and the native grassland was turned under by the plow.

When we commenced our search for the site of Pine Fort, we didn't have much to guide us. All that we knew for certain was that it was on the north side of the Assiniboine River near the mouth of Épinette Creek. Fortunately, our road map showed Épinette Creek. The attendant at Spruce Woods Provincial Park, where we had spent the night, told us that there was a narrow dirt road that more or less paralleled the north side of the river and led toward our goal of the junction of Épinette Creek with the Assiniboine.

After driving across the Assiniboine, we turned onto the obscure farm road that ran through scattered copses of small birch and poplar and open sandy fields and then along the high bank overlooking the river below. Eventually we crossed an insignificant river bottom with just a trickle of water, which we assumed was Épinette Creek. Almost immediately afterward we came out onto a large open plateau of many acres high above the river. The bank curved in a long, gradual horseshoe bend. We felt we were in the right area—but where precisely had the fort been located? We wandered around through the tall prairie grasses looking for clues, such as any evidence of shallow trenches indicating a stockade, depressions suggesting a cellar, or piles of stone, possible remains of a chimney. We found nothing.

At the far end of this open area some distance away, we saw a huge mechanized tiller or disker moving back and forth working up the plowed field. We walked over to question the operator, who turned out to be a young Hutterite lad. He assured us, "Yes, there had been people digging in the area some years back, but he didn't know anything much about it." We talked to him for a considerable time and learned many interesting facts about Hutterite customs and beliefs but, unfortunately, nothing to help us pinpoint the site of Pine Fort.

Finally, we very reluctantly reached the conclusion that we would have to be satisfied with finding and photographing only the general area where the fort had been located, rather than its specific site.

Shortly after leaving the big field on our way back to the campground, we noticed two people harvesting Saskatoon berries from the heavily laden bushes that were growing everywhere in great profusion. On a sudden impulse we stopped, left our vehicle, walked over to the berry pickers, and inquired if they, by any possible chance, might happen to know the site of Pine Fort. To our utter amazement and great delight, they not only did know its location but very kindly also offered to turn back and lead us right to it. By an astonishing stroke of good fortune, one of our berry pickers turned out to be a daughter of the Snart family, who had owned the horseshoe bend area for many years and on whose farm the archaeological work had been done that had successfully discovered and identified the location of Pine Fort.

The spot to which they led us was just past Épinette Creek, almost exactly where we had earlier parked our motor home and commenced our search. However, the remains of the fort were not in the big field on the north side of the farm road where we had looked, but rather on the very small brushy area between the road and the river.

Here had stood the important post of Pine Fort. Over the years the action of the river has eroded and sloughed off much of the bank and along with it a large part of the fort. At one time, particularly after spring breakup, artifacts and stockade timbers had been noticed protruding from the steep banksides. It is believed that some part of the north and west area of the fort, still unexcavated, lies under the gravel road. One of the biggest changes occurred in 1979, when the river drastically shifted its course, cutting a new channel, so that now only a small intermittent flow remains in the old riverbed, which is slowly filling up with willow brush.

Despite this major change, the site still conforms to the description given of it by the eminent Canadian historian J. B. Tyrrell in 1890. He described the setting of the fort as "north of the river on a level grassy flat which breaks off towards the stream in a steep-cut bank twenty-feet high. To the north the ground rises in several poplar-covered terraces to the main bank of the valley, which is a mile and a half distant, while to the south, across the shallow river, is a low bottom land a mile wide."

It was with a wonderful sense of "mission accomplished" that we finally left the great horseshoe bend and headed back to our campground. Thanks to a combination of perseverance, luck, and the kindness of people willing to help us, we had been successful in our quest for the site of the North West Company's Pine Fort.

Fort Assiniboine (Assiniboine River)
Fort Rivière La Souris
Brandon House

During the last decade of the eighteenth century, the center of fur trade activity moved upstream from the middle Assiniboine to the area surrounding the mouth of the Souris River. To meet the challenge from free (independent) traders who had penetrated this region, the Nor'Westers, Cuthbert Grant, Sr., and John Macdonell in the fall of 1793, while en route to their winter headquarters farther upstream, chose a site for the new fort on the north bank of the Assiniboine close to Ranald Cameron's small post established earlier by Nor'Wester Peter Grant. The location was about two miles above the mouth of the Souris River. Joseph Augé, commonly referred to as "Old Augé," was charged with its construction.

At the same time, close on the heels of the North West canoes led by Cuthbert Grant and John Macdonell, came the cumbersome York boats of the Hudson's Bay Company under the leadership of Donald McKay (nicknamed *le malin*, i.e., the mad one) and John Sutherland. Their destination was the same: the area near the mouth of the Souris, and likewise their purpose was the same: establishment of a post in buffalo country that would provide the large amounts of pemmican required for the fur trade.

The spot selected by McKay for the erection of his fort was directly opposite the mouth of Five Mile Creek and very close to the site chosen by the recently arrived Nor'Westers for their post. In fact, following the common practice of locating trading posts within sight of each other, so as to maintain surveillance over the competition, the foundations for McKay's fort, which was named Brandon House, were probably only about one hundred yards above Augé's Fort Assiniboine.

Normally, relations between the men of the two posts were marked as often by ready tolerance, rough good humor, and reciprocal hospitality as by blustering threats and harassment. Donald McKay, however, was not nicknamed *le malin* without reason. As a former Nor'Wester, he was schooled in the more aggressive tactics pursued by that company. Frequently pugnacious and belligerent, he was not liked by his fellow traders. He quickly became embroiled with Augé, his counterpart at the neighboring post of Fort Assiniboine. His exploits included shooting at Augé, fighting off Indians and throwing them downstairs, and challenging his opponents to a duel.

McKay's behavior, however "mad" though it was and, as such, unacceptable to the Hudson's Bay London Committee, did not prevent him from having a shrewd and farsighted grasp of the strategic necessity for the Hudson's Bay Company to penetrate the Assiniboine area—that stronghold of the North West Company—the source of their rival's pemmican. McKay proposed achieving this by advancing southward from the Albany River and by utilizing York boats for transportation.

In 1795 Robert Goodwin, who succeeded McKay as chief at Brandon House, commented in his journal entry for January 6, 1795: "We are four houses [i.e., trading posts] here, and very little made at any of them yet." Competition amongst the traders was keen. Sometimes the traders from Brandon House found themselves competing against not only other opposing companies but also rival outposts of their own company.

In November of 1797 David Thompson, who in May of that year had severed his connection with the Hudson's Bay Company and entered into the employ of the North West Company, reached Assiniboine House, of which John Macdonell was then in charge. Thompson wrote in his *Narrative:* "We remained with Mr. John McDonell twelve days: in which time I put my journal, surveys and sketches of the countries that were in black lead into ink; and having sealed them up directed them to the Agents of the North West Company."

Shortly after he had accomplished this task, accompanied by nine men, a few horses, and thirty dogs he set off in a southwesterly direction toward the Missouri River for the dual purposes of establishing the exact positions of the Mandan villages on that river and inducing some of the Indians to engage in regular trade with the North West Company.

In 1798, competition in the Souris-Assiniboine area was intensified with the arrival of the newly formed XY Company. They built their Fort La Souris on the east bank of Five Mile Creek at its junction with the Assiniboine. This placed it directly opposite the North West's Fort Assiniboine and the Hudson's Bay's Brandon House. John Pritchard was the trader in charge.

To more effectively meet this challenge to their Souris mouth trade, the North West Company in 1801 moved across to the west side of the river and set up a small post just north of Five Mile Creek, a mere half-mile above XY's Fort La Souris.

About 1800 McKay's younger brother, John, of a more equitable temperament, was given charge of Brandon House. He was described in grateful terms by his neighbor John Pritchard of the XY Fort La

Souris, who, after becoming hopelessly lost for several days during the summer of 1805, was found by Indians and brought back to his own fort in an exhausted and weakened condition. Pritchard wrote: "The news was soon at my neighbors. They and their men came running breathless to see me, my friend John McKay of the Hudson's Bay Company (at B.H. a gunshot away) brought with him flour, sugar, coffee and tea with a couple of grouse and immediately set acooking himself as I believe the people were so transported that no one would have thought to provide for me. Having taken a little refreshment they washed, shaved and clothed me. McKay dressed my feet and he became both my surgeon and my nurse."

By 1804, however, the North West Company had successfully absorbed the XY Company, so it no longer continued to exist as a separate company. As a result, the North West Company, convinced that the south side of the Assiniboine was a more favorable location, was able to move into the XY's empty fort. It also undoubtedly enlarged the post by erecting new buildings to better handle the anticipated increased volume of trade from the combined companies.

In May of 1805 Daniel Harmon stopped at the North West fort on his way east from his post of Fort Alexandria on the upper Assiniboine. He wrote: "Here are three establishments, formed severally by the North West, X.Y. and Hudson's Bay companies. Last evening, Mr. Chaboilly [North West post manager] invited the people of the other two forts to a dance; and we had a real North West country Ball. When three fourths of the people had drunk so much as to be incapable of walking straightly, the other fourth thought it time to put an end to the ball or rather bawl! This morning we were invited to breakfast at the Hudson Bay House with a Mr. McKay, and in the evening to a dance. This, however, ended more decently than the one of the preceding evening."

The journal entry of Alexander Henry the younger, written a year later (in 1806), established beyond any doubt that the North West's fort was now on the south side of the Assiniboine.

July 12th, [1806]—At two o'clock we proceeded, and soon came to Montagne du Diable, the tops of which we had seen at Wattap River—Having passed them we traversed a level plain for about 15 miles, when we arrived opposite our establishment of Riviere la Souris, which is situated on the S. side of the Assiniboine. I was therefore under the necessity of applying to the H.B.Co. people to ferry us over, which they very willingly did. Their fort stands on the N. side, where also ours formerly stood. The gentlemen of the N.W. Co. are so fond of shifting their buildings that a place is scarcely settled before it is thrown up and planted else-where.—Mr. F. A. Larocque has this post in charge for the summer.

Larocque's journal for the winter of 1806–7 reflects a pleasant existence, particularly since "there were plenty of books at the place." He commented that Thomas Vincent of the Hudson's Bay post (Brandon House) had fifty-three men in his employ, whereas, in contrast, he had fifty-two women and their families to support, with an insufficient number of men to provide a bare subsistence for such a large number.

The North West Company occupied their post on the south side of the Assiniboine for only two or three years. In 1807 Larocque was ordered to demolish the fort buildings and raft them downstream back to the old site of Pine Fort on the horseshoe bend where they were to be reerected.

With the disappearance of the XY Company and the removal of the North West Company downstream to its old location of Pine Fort, the Hudson's Bay Company post remained as the only trading concern in the Souris-Assiniboine area for the first time since 1793. Relations between the two companies were correct and even friendly. In fact, on occasion the men at Brandon House were able to avail themselves of the services of the blacksmith at Pine Fort.

However, this latest move of the North West Company was destined to be of short duration. Sometime after 1811 they closed Pine Fort and, in order to better meet competition from the Hudson's Bay Company, moved upstream six miles beyond the mouth of the Souris to a spot that was directly opposite the Hudson's Bay's Brandon House II which had been newly established on the south side of the river in May 1811.

Here, on top of a high bank, Fort La Souris was constructed. On the landward side the terrain was so marshy that the construction of a corduroy road was required in order to reach the fort. This inconvenience was considered but a minor one when weighed against the strategic advantage the site possessed of a clear and unobstructed view of the rival Brandon House across the river only 200 yards away.

At this same time that the North West Company was moving upstream to their new location on the north side of the river, the Hudson's Bay Company was likewise determining that it was time for them to push farther up the Assiniboine. Accordingly, Yorstone was busy making arrangements for buildings to be dismantled and moved and supplies ferried to the new site on the southwest bank of the Assiniboine more than three miles from their old fort.

Shortly after Brandon House II had been established in its new location, Peter Fidler, a longtime Hudson's Bay employee and a capable and highly competent surveyor and trader, was sent there as its new master. Under his leadership, affairs at the fort prospered. The men were kept busy trading with the Indians for furs and provisions, making kegs, repairing guns and making wheels for the carts that were gradually beginning to replace canoes, along with performing the multitude of other routine daily tasks required for living in a fur fort.

These two posts of the rival companies were destined to be the scene of the first overt hostile acts of the so-called Pemmican War. It all started back in 1811 when Lord Selkirk of Scotland, a major shareholder in the Hudson's Bay Company, acquired from that company a huge tract of land (116,000 square miles) encompassing much of the Red and Assiniboine watersheds. His purpose was to establish a farming colony at the forks of the Red and Assiniboine rivers for people evicted from their lands in Scotland. This introduction of agriculture into what had always been considered fur country was perceived as threatening the fur trade and thus not well received by either the North West or Hudson's Bay traders.

When, moreover, Miles Macdonell, the new colony's first Governor, in an effort to secure food for his settlers issued a proclamation forbidding the removal out of the area of all supplies of pemmican, the reaction was immediate and vehement. An abundant supply of pemmican was essential for the successful operation of the fur trade. It was the one food that fueled the brigades in their long journeys. Without it, the fur trade would collapse. The Hudson's Bay traders, largely because of Lord Selkirk's close relationship to their company, halfheartedly and begrudgingly complied with the embargo to some extent. The Nor'Westers, on the other hand, refused to recognize Macdonell's authority to issue such a proclamation and completely ignored it.

By June of 1814 most of the North West's supply of pemmican had been brought down from the upper Assiniboine and Qu'Appelle rivers and had been stockpiled at their Fort La Souris. Macdonell correctly surmised that this pemmican was not going to be turned over to him but rather would be secretly conveyed to the Nor'Westers' important pemmican depots of Cumberland House on the North Saskatchewan and Fort Bas de la Rivière on the Winnipeg River. Accordingly, he sent his sheriff, John Spencer, accompanied by Joseph Howse from the Hudson's Bay Company and three men from Lord Selkirk's Red River colony, to seize the pemmican stored at Fort La Souris.

When this party came to the fort gates and flourished their warrant, demanding entrance, John Pritchard, clerk in charge, promptly refused their request and shut and bolted the heavy gates. Sheriff Spencer thereupon broke into the fort by force. By removing three pickets from the stockade he gained access into the fort compound. He quickly moved to the storehouse, where, by pulling the staples from the locked doors, he was able to enter the building and seize the pemmican stored within. In all, he obtained 479 bags of pemmican, 865 pounds of dried meat, and ninety-three kegs of fat, equivalent to thirty tons of food supplies. Most of this he carried across the river to the Hudson's Bay Brandon House; the remainder was taken down to the settlement on the Red River.

It could only be expected that this forcible invasion of Fort La Souris and seizure of its supply of pemmican would result in prompt retaliation on the part of the enraged Nor'Westers. And so it did. Early in May of 1816 Métis forces headed by Cuthbert Grant surprised and seized Hudson's Bay factor James Sutherland and his brigade of six bateaux loaded with pemmican and furs as they were descending the Assiniboine from Fort Qu'Appelle. The Nor'Westers rendezvoused with their own pemmican boats and then in a large flotilla augmented by the boats captured from Sutherland began the long journey down the Assiniboine toward their ultimate destination of Fort Bas de la Rivière at the mouth of the Winnipeg River.

Grant split his force into two columns of mounted men, who rode along, one on each side of the river, keeping abreast of the canoes. What happened next when they neared the two forts (Fort La Souris and Brandon House II) is best told in the words of Peter Fidler:

That on the evening of the 31st day of May last 1816, Alexander Macdonell, a partner of the North West Company accompanied by Several Canadians and men commonly called half breeds—arrived at the Trading house of the North West Company called <u>Riviere la Sourie,</u> and situated opposite Brandon House at the distance of about two hundred yards. That on the following morning a body of about 48 men composed of Canadians, Halfbreeds and a few Indians armed with Guns, Pistols, Swords, Spears, and Bows and Arrows, appeared on Horseback in the Plain near to the Hudson's Bay Company's trading house (called Brandon House) of which he the deponent [i.e., Peter Fidler] was then Master and Trader for the said Hudson's Bay Company, that this body of men, beating an Indian drum, singing Indian Songs and having a Flag flying rode towards the North West Company's trading house, that on a sudden the said body of men turned their horses and rode on a gallop into the yard of Brandon House, where they all dismounted, erected their flag over the gate of the house and deliberately tied their horses to the stockades.

That then Cuthbert Grant, a halfbreed and clerk in the service of the North West Company who appeared to be the leader of the party, come to the Deponent and demanded the keys of the House that on the deponent refusing to deliver up the keys, a halfbreed called McKay (son of the late Alexander McKay formerly a partner of the North West Company) assisted by several of his companions broke open the doors of the Hudson's Bay Company's Warehouse and plundered the property consisting of trading goods, furs and other articles to a considerable amount, which together with two boats belonging to the H.B.Co. they carried away. The deponent further saith that when the said McKay and party had finished plundering the Houses of the Hudson's Bay Company the whole body of Canadians, halfbreeds and Indians, crossed the River and went to the North West Company's House taking with them the plundered property . . .

The pillaged and plundered Brandon House suffered another disaster the following year when it was almost completely destroyed by fire. In the fall of 1817 Fidler returned to the fort and began the arduous task of restoration. Gradually relations between his post and the North West Fort La Souris became more amicable and cooperative. The two masters agreed to send men from each company in a joint trading venture to the Mandans, pooling their goods and sharing equally in the profits. They even agreed to conduct their trade according to a common schedule of prices set for furs and meat. And concluding that it was becoming too expensive to equip men to travel to the Indians for trade, they instead required the Indians to bring their furs and provisions to the posts for trade.

The struggle between the two companies, while continuing with increasing ruthlessness, had now largely shifted to the Athabasca country. The two trading posts on the Assiniboine were left relatively untouched by it. Fidler was free to carry out his plans for constructing a new storehouse and for undertaking the cultivation of additional land to produce increased crops. He noted in a report written in May of 1819: "At Brandon House [the soil is] still more sandy but in wet or rainy seasons produces abundant crops."

By the fall of that year Fidler left Brandon House, never to return. Two years later the bitter struggle between the two companies ended with their union in 1821. Henceforth there would be no need to maintain two forts at the same location. Brandon House was largely abandoned and trading operations were moved across the river into the former North West Company's Fort La Souris, now renamed Brandon House III. It is possible that the location of this fort on the north side of the river closer to the cart trail, which by now had largely replaced the river as a route for transportation, plus the desire to have the river as a barrier between the fort and the increasingly hostile Indians to the south, may have been largely responsible for this decision.

Three years later, in 1824, as a result of Governor George Simpson's evaluation of the Souris-mouth–Assiniboine trade, Brandon House III was closed. But the post was destined to reappear one more time. In Simpson's words, ". . . the autumn of 1828, when it was considered expedient to re-occupy the post of Brandon House during the winter as a means of protecting the trade, otherwise the Indians would have taken their hunts to the nearest market, which was that afforded by our opponents, who had recently established themselves at Pembina . . ."

Accordingly, in 1828 Chief Trader Francis Heron with a complement of twelve men was instructed to reestablish the post of Brandon House. He recorded in his journal: "At 10 a.m. I arrived at this station, accompanied by three men with horses and carts employed in transporting the Outfit hither from Fort Garry. The place selected for the post is situated about twelve miles above the old Brandon House. I was prevented from fixing upon the site of the old establishment owing to the want of wood there. The situation chosen on the contrary possesses superior advantages on that score, being well stocked with timber of every description required at an establishment in these parts . . ."

Heron built his fort, Brandon House IV, on a high knoll about half a mile north of the Assiniboine. It was surrounded by a stockade, with a gate in the middle of the south side. The area enclosed measured 110 feet by 100 feet and contained three or four buildings. During its first two years of operation, the post made large returns in "white rats" (muskrats?), but when these animals disappeared the trade fell off so drastically that expenses were barely defrayed. Furthermore, because of its location, the post was exposed to the constant danger of attacks by Gros Ventre and the Mandan of the Missouri. For these reasons the post was closed permanently in 1832. Henceforth, after a nearly uninterrupted presence on the river stretching back to 1793, there would be no more trading houses on the Assiniboine bearing the name Brandon House.

We would never have been able to find the North West and Hudson's Bay forts on the Assiniboine in the Souris mouth region without the help of Mr. and Mrs. Morley Brown of Wawanesa and David Hems of the Manitoba Culture, Heritage and Recreation Department. That agency kindly arranged for David to spend a day with us. He, in turn, introduced us to the Browns, who are intimately acquainted with the area and who have done so much to unravel the complicating identifications of the various forts in the vicinity.

So, one very, very hot day in early July of 1988, led by the Browns, we set off for the site of Brandon House II (1811–21). After driving down numerous farm lanes and along the edges of plowed ground, we reached a large open field bordering the south side of the Assiniboine, about three miles upstream from the mouth of Five Mile Creek. A thick fringe of trees on a raised bank hid the river from sight. The field, which had been under cultivation for many years, was quite level. It had been planted to a green cover crop that had now reached a height of six to ten inches. The soil was very sandy (just as noted by Fidler); in fact, there were numerous sand blow-outs scattered throughout the field. Of course, all traces of man-made above-surface features had long since been obliterated by plow and harrow. However, in the bare sandy areas we did see numerous tiny fragments of bone, shell, and ceramics—all indicators of the fort's earlier presence.

In spite of the increasing heat, which was rapidly becoming almost unbearable—particularly to the two of us, who were accustomed to the cooler climates of northern Michigan—we penetrated the thick growth of trees along the rim of the bank, and with clouds of mosquitoes buzzing and biting, and nearly blinded by perspiration streaming down our faces, we scrambled down the still visible old trail leading to the river.

We looked across the river to the site of the North West's Fort La Souris (1811–21). A thick growth of trees along the rim of the riverbank hid the clearing from our view. As we stood at the river's edge, fighting an almost overwhelming urge to plunge into the river, clothes and all, in order to enjoy a few moments of coolness, it was difficult to imagine that the peace and quiet of this pastoral scene before us with its river flowing tranquilly by had once, back on June 1, 1816, been disrupted by cries and shouts, gunfire, and splashing of horses, as the Nor'Westers and Métis, loaded with their plundered goods from Brandon House, noisily charged across the river back to their fort on the opposite bank.

While walking back to our cars parked at the edge of the big field, we realized that if it were not for the journals and writings of the early traders and post managers chronicling the happenings at their forts, the field that we were crossing would be just that—a big field growing a crop. But because of these written records, the archaeologist was provided with the clues needed to unlock the secrets hidden underground. Today we can, in large measure, know not only what happened at Brandon House but also its location and appearance.

Next we turned our attention to the two fort sites at the mouth of

Five Mile Creek on the south side of the Assiniboine, three miles downstream from the Brandon House site. Here again, we followed a farmer's lane that ended at the river. To the south of the lane was the site of the XY Company's Fort La Souris (1801–05) with John Pritchard as master. At the edge of the cultivated field in the thick fringe of trees bordering the river we found several cellar holes, now partially filled in and obscured by vegetation.

A few yards to the north, on the other side of the lane, we saw numerous clusters of stones scattered about on a bare area bordering a planted field—telltale indicators of a fort's existence there.

Once again we braved the heat and mosquitoes and pushed our way down through the thick tangle of trees, vines, and brush to reach the mouth of the small Five Mile Creek where it trickled into the Assiniboine. To the north, directly across from us, shielded by the ever-present screen of riverbank trees, was the location of Brandon House I and Fort Assiniboine—sites we were to visit in the afternoon.

First, however, we were welcomed back to enjoy the warm and gracious hospitality of Mr. and Mrs. Brown and their daughter. Their home, sheltered in a grove of beautiful old oak and cottonwood trees, close to an old oxbow of the Assiniboine, was a perfect oasis of beauty and coolness from the sweltering heat and sun of the day. Inside, in addition to much stimulating and informative conversation regarding the history of the Souris-mouth group of forts and the often conflicting and contradictory evidence regarding their location, we were refreshed and revitalized with tempting and delicious food and drink. It was with some reluctance that after most heartily thanking the Browns for their help and kindness we drove away to continue our quest, with David as our guide, for the remaining two fort sites we hoped to find.

We crossed to the north side of the Assiniboine on the small cable-drawn ferry just north of Treesbank, a few miles above the mouth of the Souris. We went west a short distance, then turned onto a car-wide woods road. This old trail, David told us, was once the Yellow Quill trail used for centuries by Indians traveling along the north side of the Assiniboine.

When stopped by an impassable bog, we continued on foot for perhaps another mile through a stand of second-growth poplar and maple before reaching a large clearing of four or five acres surrounded by a grove of young poplars. This field is under the ownership and protection of the province of Manitoba. It has never been disturbed by cultivation. Consequently, the numerous ridges, depressions, and rock piles, still plainly evident, are there for the archaeologist to interpret. This was the site of Brandon House I (1793–1811).

We enjoyed wandering around the clearing, photographing the area from all possible angles. We noted the ridge running across the clearing on which many of the fort buildings had been erected. We examined some of the more obvious surface features, such as mounds and depressions, and tried to understand their significance.

Although it was partially obscured and much overgrown by grass and brush, we were able to follow the old trail worn deep into the side of the bank that led to the traditional fording place over the river. Looking to the south, we could just detect the mouth of Five Mile Creek. From where we stood on the bank of the river, the general locations of three trading posts were visible—all, as Pritchard had said in 1805, "just a gunshot away."

Just to the east of the Brandon House clearing among the scattered small poplars are evidences of a neighboring trading fort, quite possibly one of the earlier North West posts. The North West's Fort Assiniboine is known to have been on a well-used Indian trail about one-quarter mile north of Brandon House. Its location has been suggested by discovery of evidence of a fort on the tree-covered bank top close to the river on the old trail at the one-quarter mile distance from the Brandon House clearing.

In retracing our steps along the old Yellow Quill trail through the woods toward our car, we passed by this site, now completely overgrown with brush and trees and with little left to indicate its presence, but of special interest because of David Thompson's sojourn there for a few months during the winter of 1797–98.

We were elated that we had been successful in locating and photographing so many of the trading posts of the Souris-Assiniboine area. In addition, we realized that we had been greatly privileged to actually see and walk on the very sites where so much of fur trade history had been made during the exciting years between 1793–1821. We had had, indeed, a most eventful day and one we would not soon forget.

Fort Red Deer River/
Fort Rivière la Biche

During the last decade and a half of the eighteenth century, the Nor'Westers were steadily extending their penetration into the fur country beyond Lake Winnipeg. By ascending the Assiniboine and crossing over on the centuries-old portage into Lake Manitoba, they gained ready access to the lakes and streams lying to the west and north.

Red Deer was one such lake, and it was on the river of the same name near its junction with the Etomami River about twenty miles from its outlet into the lake that in 1794 the North West Company built Fort Red Deer River. Hugh McGillis, who became a partner in the company in 1801, was in charge.

Fort Red Deer River was one of several outlying forts included in the company's Swan River Department. For the years 1800–02 Archibald Norman McLeod was head of this department. His journal for that period contains many references to Fort Red Deer River. McLeod had a number of plans for the expansion and improvement of the trade in his district but was forced to cancel them, as he explained in the first entry made in his journal: "November 1800.—but the last of these plans—was knocked in the head,—by the arrival of Mr. Harrison from River a la Biche [Red Deer] with a letter from Mr. McGillis wherein he mentions if he has not sent [to] him one half of the goods & Liquor originally brought to Swan River, (for his demands amount to that) &. a number of men, the opposition (or the XY) will make as many packs [of furs] as he will, &. as every other consideration must give way to that it of course superseded the idea of makeing so many establishments."

McGillis kept up a constant barrage of demands for additional goods, particularly high wines, (i.e., brandy) cloth, blankets, guns, and rum. McLeod, whose supplies were limited, did his best but could not always satisfy McGillis's requests. As McLeod wrote, "God knows I am by no means in a situation to furnish him much . . ."

We had no difficulty locating the site of Fort Red Deer River. We knew from our road map that Highway 9 crossed the Red Deer River just below its junction with the Etomami, a short distance south of the little town of Hudson Bay, where we planned to spend the night. The next morning, the owner of the local RV campground where we had spent the night gave us the directions we needed. Undeterred by the falling rain, we set off on our quest.

The only obstacle we encountered was the steep roadway of wet, greasy clay leading down to the level flat by the river where the town ballpark was located. We slid down easily, almost too easily. I resolutely pushed the thoughts of how we were going to get back up the hill to the back of my mind.

We parked our motor home at the foot of the hill and continued on foot around the edge of the ball diamond toward the river. The slippery clay clung to our feet and made walking quite precarious, but we struggled on and soon reached the small clearing down by the river where, according to a provincial marker erected there, Fort Red Deer River had once stood.

At this season of the year (autumn) there was so little water in the river that in many places the rock-strewn bottom was completely exposed. The surrounding country was quite flat. It supported a luxuriant growth of trees and bushes that threatened to engulf the small clearing.

The site of this fur fort, in contrast to many we had seen, possessed little in the way of scenic beauty. In fact, its whole appearance was rather depressing; perhaps the steadily falling rain contributed to this impression. At any rate, we were not reluctant to leave the spot and head back to our vehicle—ready to face the challenge of the slippery hill. By the most adroit handling of gears, pedals, and throttle and with only a minimum of slipping backward, we reached the top of the hill and the main highway—our venture once more happily concluded.

Rocky Mountain Fort
Fort St. John

Alexander Mackenzie of the North West Company was the first white man to push up the mighty Peace River during his epic journey of discovery that ended on the shores of the Pacific in July of 1793. Mackenzie commented while passing the mouth of the Sinew River (present-day Pine River) that "this spot would be an excellent situation for a fort or factory, as there is plenty of wood, and every reason to believe that the country abounds in beaver. "

John Finlay, another Nor'Wester, likewise advanced up the Peace on his way to explore its northern branch (now known as the Finlay). It has been proposed that as early as 1794 Finlay may have built a post in the area favorably noted earlier by Mackenzie either as an advance base from which to undertake his own journey or perhaps in 1797 as a post warranted by the results of his explorations.

At any rate, no later than 1798 a post called Rocky Mountain Fort was built on the south side of the Peace River just west of Moberly River and only twelve miles above the mouth of Mackenzie's Sinew River. The little that is known about this North West Company fort is gained from an anonymous journal kept there covering the period October 5, 1799, through April 20, 1800. Some tentative evidence has been advanced to suggest that Simon Fraser was in charge of the post at this time and would, therefore, have been the writer of the journal.

The fort consisted of a shop that might or might not have included the "Big House," men's quarters sufficient to house twelve men, four women and five children, at least one storage shed, a fifty-five-foot flagpole, and a fur press. No fewer than five Indian lodges were pitched nearby.

At that time, not only was Rocky Mountain Fort the earliest permanent European establishment on mainland British Columbia; it was also the most westerly English- or French-speaking outpost on the continent of North America. Life at the isolated post was not easy. Conditions were hard and bleak. The journal briefly mentioned a voyageur who became deliriously insane, a bitter fight between two of the men, and an incident on New Year's Day when a shot was fired through the window of the chief trader's bedroom by an employee who had apparently been "celebrating" too long and too much.

Early in March 1804, after an arduous 150-mile walk up the ice-bound Peace from Fort Forks, David Thompson arrived at Rocky Mountain Fort. It was Thompson's meticulous course descriptions and latitudinal calculations that nearly 175 years later enabled archaeologists to locate the site of the fort.

By 1805 Rocky Mountain Fort was closed down and the site abandoned. It was not until fifteen years later, at the height of the conflict between the North West and Hudson's Bay companies, that trading activity returned to the area for a very brief time. In 1820 the Hudson's Bay Company established a small post, known as Fort de Pinette, or Yale's House, back where Rocky Mountain Fort had once stood. Its purpose was to offer competition to the North West's Fort St. John which in 1806 had been established twenty miles downstream. The North West Company immediately countered this move of the Hudson's Bay Company by erecting their own fort—a "nuisance post" called MacIntosh's Post—adjacent to the rival establishment. When the union of the two companies took place in 1821, both these posts were deemed redundant by Governor George Simpson and closed down. Their trading operations were transferred to the former North West's Fort St. John.

In 1806, shortly after Rocky Mountain Fort was closed, a replacement post called Fort St. John was established by the North West Company. It was built on the north bank of the Peace River just downstream from the Beatton River confluence. This fort, as shown by the intensive archaeological work done in 1975 and 1976 by F. Finlay, K. Fladmark, and B. Spurling, consisted of an area approximately 98 feet by 108 feet surrounded by a stockade. Within the enclosure there were three main buildings arranged to form a small central quadrangle about forty-five feet square. On the north side of this inner courtyard facing the river was the "Big House," which functioned as the chief trader's residence, the store, and the mess hall. The men's house occupied the west side of the quadrangle, while on the opposite east side was a building that probably served as a storehouse or trading store. During its early years, some of the men responsible for the management of the post were Fred Goedike, J. Clarke, and Archibald McGillivray. Daniel Harmon, who was stationed at Fort Dunvegan 120 miles downriver from Fort St. John during the years 1808–10, made frequent reference in his journal to the men passing by or stopping off at his post on their way to and from Fort St. John.

After fifteen years of existence as a North West post, Fort St. John buildings had deteriorated and were in need of major repairs. Hugh Faries recorded in his post journal, which covered the period of October 1822 through May 1823 "All fallen in ruins, the wood of the buildings being perfectly rotten." He undertook a vigorous program of renovation that included replacing decayed flooring, rebuilding fallen-down chimneys, installing new windows, and "mudding" all the buildings with a "yellow earth" found along the banks of the Peace River. In addition to repairing the fort, Faries's men were busy making pemmican from the buffalo meat received in trade, most of which was sent to supply the posts west of the Rocky Mountains. From the birch trees, which grew in abundance to a good size along the Peace, they obtained the sheets of bark required for both making and repairing the company's canoes. Much of this material was likewise destined for the posts beyond the Rockies—areas that were devoid of birch trees.

Following orders from Governor Simpson, who stressed the need for making each fort as self-sustaining as possible by growing its own foodstuffs, the men undertook the cultivation of an extensive garden. The grains, vegetables, and potatoes produced contributed substantially to their food supply.

Along with the daily tasks of cutting firewood (fifteen cords was each man's quota) and hauling water, the men at Fort St. John had to build a stable and cut hay to house and feed the horse they had brought from Fort Dunvegan in 1822—the first such animal to reach northern British Columbia. From numerous references in Faries's journal, it was apparent that game was becoming increasingly difficult to find and that the local Indians in the fort area were on the verge of starvation.

After the union of the Hudson's Bay and North West companies, Fort St. John was renamed Fort d'Épinette. By the spring of 1823, diminishing resources in the immediate area and the need to establish a new post farther west, better located both to handle the increasing traffic to company posts beyond the Rocky Mountains and to accommodate the Sekanni Indians, led to the decision by the recently amalgamated Hudson's Bay Company to close down Fort d'Épinette and transfer its trade to Fort Dunvegan downstream and to reestablish the Rocky Mountain Portage Fort sixty miles upstream.

However, as soon as the local St. John Indians learned of this plan, they vigorously expressed their objections—indeed, their outright refusal to take their trade to Fort Dunvegan. They declared "that however wretched they might be rendered for want of those necessaries they had hitherto been accustomed to receive from the traders,—they were unanimously determined not to barter at Dunvegan."

They insisted that they and the Indians attached to Fort Dunvegan "were generally on bad terms even when they traded at different posts." Moreover, they added that if they were both to meet for trade at Dunvegan "their quarrels would daily become more frequent and serious, and in all probability would eventually tend to the destruction of many on both sides." They maintained that "the country about Dunvegan was not their lands and that they were not Beaver but Rocky Mountain Indians, and as such be entitled to trade at the newly-reopened Rocky Mountain Portage fort."

However, these strongly voiced objections did not change the company's decision. Francis Heron, who had arrived to take charge of Fort d'Épinette, began to make preparations for the dismantling of the fort and the move upriver. On the twenty-eighth of October, he and his men set off up the Peace with two boatloads of building materials and goods, leaving Guy Hughes, the clerk, alone at the fort.

Several theories have been advanced to explain what occurred next. One is that Hughes, while seeking to find an Indian to employ as a guide, patted the shoulder of one in a friendly fashion while assuring him he would be fairly paid. That Indian, apparently in good health, suddenly took ill and died the same night. As retribution, the Indians, believing Hughes responsible for this death, shot and killed him the very next day as he unsuspectingly walked along the riverbank. One day later, four of Heron's men returning to the fort on their way to Fort Dunvegan were ambushed and shot as they stepped out of their canoes and their bodies thrown into the river. The remaining three men, on their way back to pick up another load of supplies, damaged their canoe and so were forced to walk to the fort. Their approach by land enabled them to see the unmistakable evidences of pillage and killings and to flee to safety before being detected by the murderers.

The second theory explains the murders as simply the venting of the rage, frustration, and revenge of the Indians at being forbidden to trade at the reestablished Rocky Mountain Portage Fort and offered Fort Dunvegan as their only choice. Whatever the reason, the murders, which constituted some of the most violent events to take place in the interior of British Columbia involving fur trade personnel, resulted in the immediate closure of all Hudson's Bay Company posts on the upper Peace River.

A few years later Archibald McDonald, while accompanying Governor George Simpson on a canoe voyage from York Factory to the Pacific, wrote in his journal: "in [August of 1828] dined about 500 yards below Fort d'Epinette: near the same distance above it, the same side, is Riviere d' Epinette (Pine River) a stream of some size. Encamped within a short distance of Mr. Yale's House on the left hand. Did not land at St. John's were the people were murdered. Saw the houses and a cross or two on the beach."

It was not until 1860 that the Hudson's Bay Company moved back into the area. Fort St. John II was built on the south side of the Peace a short distance upstream from the South Pine River. In 1874 the fort was moved almost directly across to the north side of the river onto river flats at the base of the bare rolling hills to the north.

Philip Godsell, a free trader, described a visit he made to the post (Fort John III) in 1912, when F. W. Beatton was factor:

> Shortly after my arrival I paid a visit to the Hudson's Bay fort perched upon the bank just south of the Revillon post. It was the usual square of unpretentious squared log buildings, whitewashed, with a flagpole and a wooden fur press in the courtyard. I received a decidedly cool reception from F. W. Beatton, the factor, an old Orkneyman and a very loyal if bigoted servant of the company, who was married to a Cree woman and had lived at Fort St. John for thirty years or more. Close association with natives had made him far more Indian than white in his outlook upon life, while his one pet aversion was free traders. Against such fancied usurpers of the Company's one-time glory and monopoly he harboured an inveterate hatred and for years at a time he would not set foot upon the soil of Revillon's post, neither would he step aboard an opposition steamer. He was a Hudson's Bay man first, last and always.

Fort St. John III made one more move, this time into the modern city on the top of the hills. Here, shedding its ancient name of Fort St. John and known today as "The Bay," it continues to carry on as a "post" of the Hudson's Bay Company.

Our quest for the sites of Rocky Mountain Fort and Fort St. John resulted in one of the most enjoyable days we had ever experienced. It all began several weeks earlier in Vancouver, in the office of Dr. David Burley of Simon Fraser University. Under the threat of potential destruction of historic sites along the Peace River downstream from the great Bennett Dam posed by the proposed construction of yet another huge dam, Dr. Burley and his students and associates (particularly F. Finlay, K. Fladmark, and B. Spurling) had done a great deal of archaeological exploratory work in the area, seeking to identify sites connected with the fur trade. Their search paid off, for they hit "pay dirt," so to speak.

Based on David Thompson's accurate and detailed observations and recorded courses, they were able to locate Rocky Mountain Fort of 1794, as well as the adjacent 1820 forts of Yale House and MacIntosh Post. Amazingly, these sites had suffered no man-made disturbance or destruction. Likewise, the locations of both Fort St. John (Fort d'Épinette) at the mouth of the Beatton River and Fort St. John II were successfully determined and detailed archaeological investigations conducted at the sites.

Dr. Burley most generously shared with us the wealth of information he had accumulated. He gave us maps showing location of the sites, as well as detailing the features of the forts as revealed by the excavations. In addition, he furnished us the names of several people in Fort St. John who he thought would be able to help us get to the Peace River sites. The best (and probably only) way to reach the sites, he said, was to find someone who owned a jet boat (river rats they were called) and would be willing to take us to the desired locations along the river.

So, armed with all this information, we headed for Fort St. John. As soon as we arrived there, we contacted Ms. Brenda Rudrud, curator of the Fort St. John Museum. She willingly agreed to help us and after many telephone calls was able to locate one Brian Clarke, who, to our great good fortune, agreed to take us the next day in his jet boat. He, in addition to being an expert pilot (we learned later that he raced his jet boats in competition all over the world), had frequently transported the people working at the sites during the excavations some years earlier, so knew exactly where we wanted to go.

Happy in the knowledge that our problem of reaching the Peace River sites had been solved, we devoted the rest of the afternoon to searching for the site of the Hudson's Bay Company's Fort St. John III, located somewhere on the river flats below the bluff where the city of Fort St. John is now located. We had an old picture showing Fort St. John III on the flats along the river, with the hills rising behind, their summits silhouetted against the sky, one rather sharply conical peak a prominent feature. As we drove slowly along the road at the foot of the bluff, we tried to find a match with the profile of the hills as shown in our picture.

Eventually we encountered a young couple who, when they learned of our quest, promptly took us in tow and led us back to their family home, which was directly across the road from the site of the fort. We found out, in fact, that this field where Fort St. John III once stood, during the days when Frank Beatton was manager, was now owned by their family. Until quite recently, one of the original buildings was still standing. Unfortunately, fire set by mindless vandals destroyed it, removing forever a priceless piece of history.

The next day, we met Brian and within a short time had the jet boat launched and were soon speeding downstream, barely touching the water it seemed, on our way to the site of the North West Company's Fort St. John—Hudson's Bay Company's Fort d'Épinette—just east of the mouth of the Beatton River.

The site is in a clearing on the low river floodplain terrace. Today it is completely covered with a dense understory of plants and bushes beneath aged cottonwoods. A tangle of fallen trees lies crisscrossed on the ground. This rank vegetative growth masks most of the surface features belonging to the fort, although one large hole was still easily discernible.

We looked beyond the flat sedge-covered shore to the wooded hills rising from across the river and were impressed with the beauty of the scene. We couldn't help wondering if the unfortunate Guy Hughes was likewise enjoying the view of rolling hills and peacefully flowing river as he walked along this bank the last night of his life just before he was brutally shot and killed. And the other four men—they, too, were shot and their bodies rolled into the river from this same spot where we were standing. Now, there is nothing left to mark these events—even the crosses on the bank are long gone—save men's memories and journal records.

Next, turning upstream, we skimmed along the surface of the river for about five miles. At a river bend on the south shore opposite the present city of St. John, we beached the boat and climbed up to the low flat above us. Dr. Burley's map had indicated that Fort St. John II had been located on this spot. The old abandoned square-hewn log building used by the Mounted Police many years ago, and which was marked on our map, was a useful point of reference to orient us to the fort site.

Sure enough, in a scattered grove of small poplars growing on the grass-covered low terrace just above the river and on the margin of a large plowed field we saw the faint mounds and depressions, indicators of the fort's existence here.

As we headed out into the river, we looked across toward the north side—and to our delight, we spotted the sharply pointed conical hilltop prominently silhouetted against the sky. At its base below was the small clearing bordering the river where Fort St. John III had stood and where we had been the previous afternoon.

Happily, we continued on up the river. The ride was exhilarating, the scenery truly beautiful. A range of rolling rounded hills and ravines, some quite bare, others tree-covered, rose on each side. Frequently we flushed small flocks of Canada geese who had been resting on the numerous sand- and gravel bars that we passed. These gravel bars, according to Brian, contain enough "color" to make it worthwhile, or at least interesting enough, to pan. We stored that interesting bit of information in our memory bank for possible future use!

Eventually we passed Moberly Creek emptying into the river on the south side. The outlet was almost totally hidden from our view by trees and brush. Just beyond and on the same side was the place we sought. We beached the jet boat at the edge of the sandy sedge-covered flat extending from the base of the bank. With keen anticipation we quickly walked toward the terrace, not even pausing to examine the numerous signs of wildlife so plainly imprinted in the damp sand—tracks of geese, shorebirds, mink, and moose.

We walked up the short sloping path to the top of the terrace. Before us was a semicleared area extending perhaps six hundred feet covered with a luxuriant growth of herbaceous plants overshadowed by scattered spruce and poplars. Here and there the bright red berries of bunchberry, the purple of aster and violets, the orange of rose hips brightened the green of the thick plant growth. On top of this low riverbank terrace were the sites of Rocky Mountain Fort, Yale House, and MacIntosh Post.

Guided by Dr. Burley's map, we walked along the well-worn path bordering the terrace edge toward the western end of the clearing. Here we were able to see a few low mounds and pits and the remains of a stone fireplace. It is probable that much of this site has disappeared due to bank erosion. The outlines of one building were traced in the course of archaeological work done under the supervision of F. Finlay. Based on her findings, it is suggested that this site was the location of the North West Company's nuisance fort MacIntosh Post of 1820–21.

Returning downstream about 325 feet, we came to a well-defined trench clearly visible, cutting through the thick hip-high plant growth. It was rectangular in shape and measured approximately eighty-five feet by ninety-eight feet. We had no difficulty walking its entire perimeter. Archaeological evidence suggests that this was a stockade trench, perhaps either never filled or from which the pickets were later removed. It is thought that this stockade trench enclosed the 1820–21 Hudson's Bay Company's Yale House.

Continuing downstream another 100 feet toward the eastern end of the clearing, we came to the area adjudged to be the site of the North West Company's 1794 Rocky Mountain Fort. Here the indications of a fort's existence were both numerous and unmistakable. Markers and plastic protective coverings still remained from the archaeological fieldwork conducted some years ago. We were able to find, even though they were partially hidden by the plant and brush growth rapidly encroaching on the clearing, several of the stone chimney mounds, some cellar depressions, and other smaller mounds and hollows. The large number and rich assortment of artifacts uncovered at this site confirm that it was occupied for a considerable period of time.

This site is of special significance and importance. It is probably the only fur trade fort site dating as far back as 1794 that is so well preserved and has remained untouched—so far—by man-made distur-bances. It is truly a remarkable find for all interested in the history of Canada's fur trade. It should be protected and preserved at all costs!

Lengthening shadows and failing light warned us that it was time to begin our trip back to Fort St. John. So, after taking a few last over-all shots from the boat of this very historic stretch of riverbank, we headed downstream, once more skimming along, following the bends and curves of the mighty Peace. What a lovely trip it was! What a great pilot we had! When it came to "settling up" for Brian's time, gasoline, and use of his boat, he adamantly refused any reimbursement. He did yield enough, however, to accept our invitation to dinner. So our won-derful day was extended to include not only a shared meal but also sev-eral hours of good conversation—enough to cement a friendship among the three of us.

Fort Augustus
Edmonton House

The steady advance of the fur trade posts up the North Saskatchewan River, necessitated by the depletion of the fur animals, continued. Neither the North West Company nor the Hudson's Bay Company practiced sustained-yield principles in their pursuit of furs. Their rivalry was too unrelenting to permit any conservation measures, such as the preservation of seed stock for future harvest. "Trap an area clean—if you don't, your competitor will—and then move on" was the universal policy. It is not surprising, therefore, that it took only three or four years after a fort's establishment for the surrounding area to be trapped out.

By 1795 Angus Shaw of the North West Company, who had built Fort George only three years previous, decided it was time to move farther upriver. The Fort George journal entry for May 11, 1795, reads: "Mr. Shaw has projected a plan of erecting a House farther up the River, in the course of the Summer. For this purpose mr. [James] Hughes has received directions to build 12 or 14 days march from this by water, on a spot called the Forks, being the termination of an extensive plain contained between two Branches of this River [the Saskatchewan and the Sturgeon River]. This is described to be a rich and plentiful Country, abounding with all kinds of animals, especially Beavers & otters, which are said to be so numerous that the Women and Children kill them with sticks and hatchets. The Country around Fort George is now entirely ruined."

Shaw hoped to be able to carry out this project without the knowledge of his close neighbor and rival William Tomison of the adjacent Hudson's Bay Buckingham House.

By the end of the summer of 1795 the Nor'Westers' new post, named Fort Augustus, was erected and ready for the fall trade. They did not enjoy their exclusive occupation of the new location for long. When William Tomison returned to Buckingham House in early fall and discovered he had been outmaneuvered by Shaw's stratagem, he wasted no time in following his rival upriver. Building on a site within a musket shot of the North West post, Tomison and his men constructed their fort with such speed that within a month, by November 7, the main building had been erected and its roof covered with sod.

When locating fur posts in the country of the Plains Indians, rival companies usually resorted to several measures designed to give them as much protection as possible from the ever-present threat of hostile action from Indian tribes. First, if posts were located on the north side of the Saskatchewan, any attacking bands from the plains to the south would face exposure when crossing the river. Second, by building the posts close enough so that they could be enclosed by a common stockade of massive vertical logs extending fifteen feet above ground greater defensive strength was ensured.

The two new forts conformed to these measures. Separated from each other by an interior wall, the traders and their men conducted their trading with reasonable harmony. Trading was brisk, and the land lived up to its reputation of abounding in beaver and otter. However, after seven years the supply of easily available firewood was exhausted, and the men were forced to spend an increasingly large share of their time hauling wood ever greater distances. Accordingly, in 1802 James Bird of the Hudson's Bay Company agreed to move some twenty miles farther upstream.

The location they chose was, as would be expected, on the north side of the river, on the flats below a prominent bluff on which the future city of Edmonton was destined to rise and flourish. There Edmonton House II and Fort Augustus II were erected, side by side, enclosed within a common stockade.

During the next eight years the two forts increased in importance, partly due to their strategic location at the upper limits of easy navigation on the Saskatchewan River. Their influence extended over a large area. Trading for pemmican became a major priority, as both companies needed more and more of this concentrated food to fuel their brigades traveling ever-increasing distances. The problem of preventing fights between the Plains Indians, such as the Blackfeet, and the Crees whenever they met at the forts for trade was never completely resolved. It required all the ingenuity of the traders to keep the peace between these ancient and volatile enemies.

After eight years at this location, the decision was made to move yet again. Alexander Henry the younger, in charge of the North West's Fort Vermilion, wrote in his journal in February of 1810: "Mr. Hughes [of Fort Augustus II] and myself determined to abandon both Fort Vermillion and Fort Augustus, and to build at Terre Blanche. The latter, being a more central place, will answer the same purpose as the two present establishments and save the expense of one of them; it will also draw all the Slaves [i.e., Blackfeet, Bloods, Piegans] to trade at one place, where we can better defend ourselves from their insults."

Preparations for abandoning Fort Vermilion and Fort Augustus were commenced on May 5, when the canoes were gummed and everything packed for the move to Terre Blanche. By the end of the month this had been accomplished. Progress was rapid on the construction of the two new establishments. Within the short space of little more than two months both the common stockade enclosing both sites and the interior stockade separating the two forts had been erected as well as the other usual complement of buildings such as bastions, main house with two wings, kitchen, Indian house, storehouse, and shop.

Within the space of a couple of years, James Hughes and James Bird, in charge of Fort Augustus III and Edmonton House III respectively, realized that moving their forts downriver to the mouth of the Terre Blanche River had been a mistake. The advantages they had hoped to gain had not materialized, so the decision was made to move back upstream to their previous site.

In 1813, therefore, back they went and the process of constructing the two forts was undertaken once again. As before, the forts were reerected side by side and enclosed by a common stockade. At this time Fort Augustus, under John McBean and John Rowand, was staffed by fifty-nine men, in addition to a small caretaker crew for the summer months; Edmonton House, with Francis Heron and Hugh Munroe in charge, had only thirty-one men plus its summer skeleton crew.

For the next eight years the forts coexisted. At first relations between them continued on "tolerable good terms," but this soon was replaced by antagonism and suspicion resulting from the escalating intercompany rivalry, intensified by the violent events occurring at the Red River settlement to the east. When Francis Heron undertook to reach some mutual understanding with his counterpart John McBean, in an effort to keep their trading practices within reasonable limits, negotiations had to be conducted by letter, since neither man dared walk through the gate in the common dividing wall into the other's fort enclosure for fear of being physically detained. When a mutually acceptable agreement was finally reached, the actual signing of the document could only take place on neutral ground outside the massive stockade that enclosed both forts.

Finally all the strife and bitter competition were ended with the union of the two companies in 1821. At the direction of Hudson's Bay Company's George Simpson, newly named Governor of Rupert's Land, James Sutherland was named chief factor of the Saskatchewan district, which included Edmonton House and Fort Augustus. One of the men assigned to assist him was John Rowand, given the rank of chief trader. Sutherland decided to make Edmonton House headquarters for the Saskatchewan district and to demolish the North West post. Within a few years its buildings were torn down and Fort Augustus was no more.

224

To John Rowand was assigned the charge of Edmonton House—a charge he retained for the next thirty-three years. During that period the names John Rowand and Edmonton House became almost synonymous. Under his astute direction, Edmonton House gradually evolved into a well-run and profitable post. It became the nerve center for trading activities over the prairie region stretching to the Rocky Mountains. Its location midway on the Saskatchewan River—the trans-Canada highway of the 1800s—made it a universal stopping-off place, a popular rendezvous for traders and brigades on their yearly trips to and from York Factory, Norway House, or the Red River, and later for explorers, scientists, missionaries, and wealthy dilettante travelers.

Relations with the Plains Indians remained troublesome and required forceful measures and eternal vigilance. For nearly the entire period of its existence Edmonton House was considered a post of great hazard—one that at any moment was subject to attack from the fiercely independent Indians of the Blackfoot Confederacy. It was a post that only the boldest and most resourceful could fill. Fortunately, John Rowand was such a man.

Horse stealing on a large scale, in spite of the most determined efforts to prevent it, continued almost unabated. As James G. MacGregor wrote in his book *John Rowand, Czar of the Prairies:* "To them [i.e., Indians], stealing horses was honorable, exhilarating, and practical; to the traders it was humiliating, discouraging, and costly. But as it had always been since the first Edmonton House had been built, so it was to continue throughout John Rowand's lifetime. The traders might rant and swear but the Indians, winking at each other and smirking, always protested their own innocence and their utter ignorance of who could conceivably have driven the horses away."

Sometime around 1830 the much-moved Edmonton House was relocated from the flats—always vulnerable to spring flooding—to the heights above the river. The old fort buildings were deteriorating and in need of not only major renovation but also widespread replacement. So, during the early years of the 1830s, a new Edmonton House was erected on the bluff overlooking the Saskatchewan River, a magnificent site and one that would eventually be claimed eighty-five years hence by the Legislative Building of the province of Alberta.

In keeping with the post's position of importance, Rowand decreed that the new buildings should reflect that status. His residence, quickly dubbed the "Big House" or "Rowand's Folly," was of three stories in addition to a full above-ground basement. It measured thirty by eighty feet, making it the largest such building west of York Factory on

Hudson's Bay. Along its entire length both front and back on the second-story level was a magnificent gallery. An imposing flight of steps led to the main doorway in the center of the building. A prominent feature of this imposing structure was the large number of windows—each paned with seven-by-eight-inch pieces of glass, an item of luxury not usually available for trading posts. On the second floor of the "Big House" were the living quarters for the chief factor, chief trader, and their families and guest rooms for important visitors. On the first or main floor were the principal reception room, the gentlemen's dining room, the ladies' dining room, and offices for the chief factor and the clerk. The kitchen, steward's and house servants' quarters, interpreter's room, rum room, and storage area were located in the basement.

The clerks' quarters, kitchen, and large mess hall or "Great Hall" occupied a row of connected rooms to the east of the "Big House." Opposite on the west side of the open square was the Indian house—a row of rooms containing the trade room, store, interpreter's room, storage area, and fur loft. Completing the square on the south side opposite the "Big House" was the row housing the servants' and artisans' quarters, the carpenter's shop, the blacksmith forge and quarters, and special quarters for the Orkney families who assisted the boatbuilders. In addition, various other structures such as icehouse, meat store, bake oven, stable, boat shed, and watchtower were all located within the massive fifteen-foot high stockade.

Paul Kane, the Canadian artist renowned for his paintings of native Indians and who had visited Edmonton House, wrote a vivid description of the large mess hall or "Great Hall" in the clerks' quarters on the occasion of Christmas Day, 1847: "The dining-hall in which we assembled was the largest room in the fort, probably about fifty by twenty-five feet, well warmed by large fires, which are scarcely ever allowed to go out. The walls and ceilings are boarded, as plastering is not used, there being no limestone within reach but these boards are painted in a style of the most startling barbaric gaudiness, and the ceiling filled with centre-pieces of fantastic gilt scrolls, making altogether a saloon which no white man would enter for the first time without a start, and which the Indians always looked upon with awe and wonder."

The Christmas dinner included boiled buffalo hump, boiled buffalo calf, a dish of *mouffle* (dried moose nose), whitefish, buffalo tongue, beaver tail, and wild goose, plus potatoes, turnips, and bread. In the evening the hall was the scene of the dance to which all inmates of the fort were invited by the chief factor. The hall soon filled up with the gaily dressed guests. In Kane's words: "Indians, whose chief ornament consisted in the paint on their faces, voyageurs with bright sashes and neatly ornamented mocassins, half-breeds glittering in every ornament they could lay their hands on; whether civilized or savage, all were laughing, and jabbering in as many different languages as there were styles of dress.—The dancing was most picturesque, and almost all joined in it.—I danced round her with all the agility I was capable of exhibiting, to some highland-reel tune which the fiddler played with great vigour, whilst my partner with grave face kept jumping up and down, both feet off the ground at once, as only an Indian can dance."

Edmonton House was the hub of constant activity year-round. The trading year opened with the arrival in late September or early October of the brigades from York Factory carrying the year's supply of provisions and goods for the entire district. This initiated a peak period in the annual cycle and required all hands to work at top speed night and day sorting and repacking the goods into "outfits" as requisitioned by the various forts two years previously; these then had to be speeded on their way in order to reach their destination before freeze-up. The first to leave were the brigades for Jasper House, on the east side of the mountains, where horses were waiting to carry the men and goods over the mountains to the canoes on either the Columbia or Fraser River, which would then be used to convey them to their final destinations in the Columbia or New Caledonia districts. The next to leave were the brigades of pack horses headed for Lesser Slave Lake, followed by the one for Fort Assiniboine on the Athabasca River. Finally, the last to go were the canoes with the outfit for Rocky Mountain House farther up the Saskatchewan. It was only after the last brigades had been dispatched that the fort gates were opened to the impatient Indians and half-breeds for trading.

The men at Edmonton House were seldom idle. The fields of barley, oats, potatoes, and hay required constant care. The enormous amounts of firewood needed to heat the fort buildings had to be cut and rafted downriver; lumber for building construction had to be whipsawed; buffalo had to be hunted to provide not only sufficient fresh meat for the table but also enough for the making of enormous amounts of pemmican. Men went west regularly to the fishery at Lac Ste. Anne to catch the thousands of fish needed to supplement the fort's food supply. The blacksmith's forge and anvil were kept busy; the carpenter and his crew not only kept the fort buildings in repair but also had the additional responsibility of building the York boats needed by Edmonton House, as well as those required by the other posts along the Saskatchewan.

The second peak of activity occurred in the spring. Trade in pemmican, dried meat, and grease continued at a brisk pace. The fort's fields had to be plowed and seeded. The voluminous journals had to be completed, ledgers balanced, and requisitions for the supplies needed two years hence prepared. With the breakup of the rivers, the canoes and packhorses began arriving from the outlying posts, bringing the furs traded during the past winter. All these had to be inspected and sorted; then, using the fort's large wooden fur press, the lustrous pelts were pressed into ninety-pound bales of uniform size.

Finally, about the middle of May, the work completed and the hectic days of activity over, the chief factor and many of the men from the fort embarked in the canoes and set off down the Saskatchewan headed for York Factory, nearly a thousand miles away. For the next several months there was little to disturb the quiet existence of the fort. The few men left behind as caretakers cultivated the fields, guarded the gates, and kept vigilant watch for any marauding Indians.

In 1854 Rowand's long and productive reign at Edmonton House came to an end. Reluctantly he had accepted the fact that it was time for him to retire. On his way down the Saskatchewan for the last time, headed for a new life in Montreal, he stopped off at Fort Pitt, where his son was stationed. There, the next morning, as he typically jumped in to break up a fracas between two voyageurs he fell to the ground struck down by a fatal heart attack.

Chief Factor William Sinclair, Rowand's longtime friend and associate, was appointed to succeed him at Edmonton House for a few years, until he was replaced by Chief Factor William J. Christie, who remained in charge of the post from 1858 to 1871. During that period, the fort continued to be the headquarters for the district. Trade for furs and provisions (i.e., pemmican) was carried on as usual. It became an increasingly popular place for visitors of all kinds, priests, ministers, and scientists.

In 1870 a large number of Blackfeet, in retaliation for the killing of some of their people by Crees and Assiniboines, threatened to attack Edmonton House. Father Lacombe, well-known to the Blackfeet as their friend and a frequent visitor to Edmonton House, strode around the outside of the fort's stockade, speaking to the angry Indians in their own language, and was able to persuade them to call off the attack. By morning the Indians had all disappeared. This was the last time the fort was ever threatened by hostile Indians.

Two years after this, in 1872, Richard Hardisty took over as chief factor of Edmonton House. He built a new "Big House" outside the

228

stockade higher up on the hill behind the fort, and in 1874 Rowand's "Big House" was torn down.

By this time the Hudson's Bay Company no longer had monopoly of the trade. Indian unrest, increasing competition from free traders and Métis, and the unrestricted use of liquor in the trade all resulted in unusual conditions and heavy expense to the company, so much so that Edmonton House, once the most successful and profitable of the inland forts and the model to which others were compared, was no longer showing a profit. In fact, the ledgers for Edmonton House showed mounting losses.

Times were changing. No longer was the company fort the sole destination for those climbing the steep bank to the top of the bluff. In increasing numbers it was the town of Edmonton that was sought. Reflecting this change, the Hudson's Bay Company in 1892 built a retail store outside the walls of the fort. Four years later, the chief factor moved out of Hardisty's "Big House," and this building, which had for twenty-two years been a dominant feature on the bluff, a proud symbol of the once all-powerful Hudson's Bay Company, was taken over by the Edmonton Golf Club as a clubhouse. A few years later, it was used by the city of Edmonton as a pesthouse for the confinement and treatment of victims of the recent smallpox epidemic. When that need ceased in 1906, the town burned it to the ground. However, like a phoenix rising from the ashes, the magnificent new Legislative Building was erected on the same site within a few years.

Meanwhile, the weather-beaten old buildings of the fort located on the edge of the bluff directly in front of the gleaming new provincial Capitol were increasingly regarded as an anachronism as well as an offensive encroachment on the beautifully landscaped Capitol grounds. The inevitable end came in 1915 when the historic old square-log buildings within the fort, one by one, were torn down. Within two days the work of destruction was completed—Edmonton House was no more.

A little more than fifty years after the bulldozers had completed their work of destruction and the dust settled over the pile of rubble that once was Edmonton House, ground was broken on the south side of the Saskatchewan, two bends farther upstream from the old post, for the re-creation of a new Edmonton House. This project was instigated by the historically minded citizens of Edmonton. Its goal was to recreate an accurate replica of Edmonton House as it was in the 1840s, when Chief Factor John Rowand was its master. Accomplishing this required a tremendous amount of enthusiasm, intensive scholarly research, and large sums of money. Completed in 1974, Edmonton House opened its main gate to welcome a steady stream, not of traders, Indians and missionaries, but of camera-carrying tourists—the voyageurs of the twentieth century.

It was to this Edmonton House that we, too, went early one morning in the late summer of 1986. The moment we passed through the main gate and emerged onto the fort's open courtyard, we stepped out of the present into the past. To our left was the Indian House, a range of connecting rooms forming the west side of the compound. Here was where the actual trading with the Indians was reenacted. In the first room, the Indians would have brought their furs, which were examined and appraised by the company clerk, who then issued tokens representing the value of their furs. The Indians exchanged these tokens for goods stocked in the trade store in the adjoining room. Here today the shelves were loaded with pots, kettles, ironwork of all kinds, beads, cloth, tobacco, vermillion, powder, bullets—all items required for the native trade. A fort living history interpreter, representing the company clerk and suitably dressed in smock and pants and sporting a most luxuriant and appropriate beard, knew his furs and his stock of trade goods. Extremely well versed in the history of the fur trade, he enacted his role of storekeeper with great spirit and realism. Beyond the trade store was duplicated a tiny cubicle assigned for the use of the interpreter when he was at the fort. The remainder of the Indian House was a storage room for baled furs and trade goods of all kinds. In the big loft upstairs, the furs were sorted, graded, pressed into bales, and stored, awaiting shipment in the spring. The sturdy iron balance scales and the fur press were almost hidden by the large number of skins hanging from the ceiling rafters. Traps of all sizes were everywhere. Bales of the pressed furs filled the shelves along the wall.

The huge three-story building forming the north side of the compound—a reconstruction of Rowand's "Big House"—was well named. It is indeed big. Its height and size enable it to dominate all the other buildings within the fort. We admired the long gallery stretching across the entire front of the building at the second-story level, the many attractive small-paned windows breaking up the somberness of the facade, the symmetrical placing of the roof dormers, and the imposing central stairway leading to the main entrance.

We ascended the steep flight of steps. At the top we were welcomed by "John Rowand" himself. He wore a high beaver hat, white shirt, *ceinture fléchée,* and beaded moccasins as befitted his rank of chief factor. However, his tall, somewhat cadaverous appearance was not that of John Rowand, who was actually round of face, short, and stocky. Obviously, there are limits to what even the most meticulous reproductions can achieve.

To the right of the main entrance is re-created a spacious room dominated by a massive stone fireplace where the chief factor, chief trader, chief clerk, and any male visitors of importance would have dined in rather regal splendor. In the rear are the smaller dining room where, in the isolation imposed by the fort's rigid protocol of sex (as well as class) segregation, the chief factor's wife and daughters ate, and the chief factor's office. On the opposite side of the main entrance is another room of immense size, likewise with its massive fireplace, which was used for meetings and gatherings of all kinds as well as for storage and, once a year, the annual New Year's dance. On the back side are the chief trader's office and a guest room reserved for important visitors.

On the second floor are the living quarters for the chief factor and chief trader and their families, as well as several small rooms for visiting dignitaries. As befitted his rank, Chief Trader John Rowand and his family enjoyed a spacious sitting room, large master bedroom, and two smaller bedchambers for his three daughters. The chief trader had one large room assigned for his use.

All the rooms on both floors are sparsely furnished: simple straight-backed wooden chairs, harvest tables, open-shelved dressers, low four-post rope beds, frequently with a buffalo robe as coverlet, a plain washstand. A few double stone fireplaces on the first floor served to warm the largest rooms.

As yet, the new boards that completely sheathed the walls and ceilings of all the rooms had not attained the soft patina produced by age and wood smoke. We managed by recourse to our always-vivid imagination, to overcome this sense of newness and populate the empty rooms with living people—the "gentlemen" of the Hudson's Bay Company (those always addressed and referred to as "Mr."), their Métis wives, the children, the servants, the missionaries—in fact, all the great diversity of people who constituted fur trade society in the 1840s.

We even thought we saw, in the early-evening dusk, John Rowand emerge onto the gallery and stand there, looking down over his fort complex. Was he, perhaps, enjoying a moment of private satisfaction, contemplating what he had accomplished thus far? Did he know that George Simpson had already written to the company's London Committee: "Mr. Rowand's very superior management at Edmonton which is without exception the most troublesome post in the Indian country does him much credit; he and the situation he holds seem made for each other, and the high order in which I found every thing connected with his charge as I passed this spring excited both my surprise and admiration."

We next descended to the above-ground basement where the great kitchen, the steward's and house servants' quarters, the rum and spirits room, and various storage areas are located. As we walked through these rooms, we were impressed with the atmosphere that had been created by the low ceiling supported by huge rough log beams, the heavy hand-hewn timbers for sill plates and joists, the massive stone fireplace, the small windows. All that was lacking was the hustle and activity of the large staff of servants busily carrying out their duties under the watchful eyes of the steward.

The kitchen is well equipped with all necessary cooking utensils as well as an assortment of wooden mixing bowls, including the gigantic ones needed for bread making. A big wooden barrel with spigot holds the water supply. Against one wall is a large open-shelf dresser for dishes; on a long deal table wooden plates and bowls are set for the servants' mess. The steward has a small room of his own furnished with bed, washstand, and desk. The rum room is well provided with small kegs, large barrels, and demijohns of rum and spirits. We noticed that the only access to this room is through the steward's quarters, probably a necessary precaution. The household servants were also housed on this floor.

We left the "Big House" and walked over to the clerks' quarters, a row of connecting rooms that formed the east side of the courtyard. Here the twenty to thirty bachelor clerks would have been housed and fed. They had their own separate kitchen in the rear where servants prepared their food. The clerks, along with interpreters, servants, old retainers, and transient hunters, ate in the large mess hall—the "Great Hall." This is a room of noble proportions, largest in the entire fort. It re-creates the scene of the Christmas dinner and dance of 1847 so vividly described by Paul Kane. It was also where the chief factor would have received the chiefs of the visiting tribes with much colorful ceremony and dignified ritual, followed by the traditional exchange of presents. Only after these preliminaries had been completed would trading commence the following day.

The gaudy and striking decorations that covered walls and ceiling of that vast room were a never-ending source of wonder and amazement to Indian and white man alike. If Rowand's intent was to awe and astonish the Indians, he was completely successful. Unfortunately, in today's reconstructed "Great Hall" the colorful decorations that so impressed the Indians are totally lacking. As we gazed about the room, we noticed its very pleasing proportions and the well-balanced placement of doors and windows—evidence of the innate sense of good design that characterized many of the builders of the early fur trade forts. Ceiling beams are massive, as are the fireplaces, one at each end of the room.

Today the room was quiet—the only noise the drone of countless flies buzzing around the windows. Once, however, the original room was alive—filled with the chatter and laughter of the bachelor clerks and those others entitled to eat at this mess, the clatter of dishes and of knives and forks, as jokes were played, as experiences and adventures were recounted. And on the nights when a dance was held, the rafters echoed with the sound of the indefatigable fiddles, and the floor resounded with the thump, thump of the moccasined feet of Indian and white man alike.

We left the bachelors' quarters and walked over to the range of rooms comprising the servants' and tradesmen's quarters. This forms the south side of the courtyard. In one-half the married men lived, two or three families to a room. The walls are hand-hewn squared timbers, the windows covered with parchment. Furnishings of tables, benches, bunks, and cradles are roughly made by hand. Tables are set with wooden bowls and plates—no china here. Clothing—capots, leather smocks, jackets with beautifully beaded designs, tuques—as well as skin parfleches, hunting knives encased in beaded scabbards, and snowshoes all hang from pegs on the walls. In one of these rooms we encountered two of the Métis wives who, while enjoying a social visit by the fire, were keeping busy ornamenting their husbands' moccasins with their skillful needlework.

The remaining half of the row is occupied by living quarters for the tradesmen so vital to a fur fort: the carpenter, cooper, boatbuilder, and blacksmith, along with the carpenter shop and the blacksmith forge. Finally, one room was reserved for three families brought over from the Orkney Islands to assist the boatbuilder in constructing the many York boats required by the trade.

As we wandered in and out of the various reconstructed rooms in this south row, all realistically furnished, cheerful fires burning in each fireplace, people busy at their tasks, we felt we were, indeed, getting a tiny glimpse of what life was like for these artisans and their families. It seemed almost incredible to us that it was the normal and customary arrangement for two or three entire families to live together in apparent harmony within the confines of a single room. It could not have been easy.

Outside the courtyard but still within the high stockade walls is the small building containing the tiny chapel, study, and bedroom for

233

the Reverend Rundle, one of the first missionaries to come to Edmonton House. The stark severity of his quarters reflects his Spartan existence.

Another interesting building is the meat house. Here are the wooden tubs and barrels, the heavy mallet, huge iron kettles, meat hooks, and scales—all the equipment used in the making of pemmican and the storing of salted tongues and dried meat.

And finally, there is one more small building essential to any fort. Built over a deep pit lined with ice blocks cut from the river, its double walls and sod roof provided sufficient insulation to preserve year-round the fish and buffalo carcasses stored in the pit.

By this time, the sun was low in the western sky and our visit into the past was nearly over; furthermore, our feet were screaming in protest at any further walking. Nevertheless, after leaving the fort enclosure we followed a path a short distance to the banks of the Saskatchewan River. There, moored by the bank, almost as though a voyageur had just stepped out of it, was a York boat, weather-beaten but still strong and sturdy, ready to take on a cargo of furs and head downstream for far-off York Factory. Somehow, for us, the sight of boat and river made the perfect ending for our day.

Before we left the city of Edmonton, we drove to the bluff overlooking the river where Alberta's Legislative Building is located. We walked around the beautifully landscaped grounds in search of certain historical markers. Finally we found what we sought: a simple bronze tablet on a low concrete slab along a main path leading to the Capitol Building paid homage to John Rowand, citing his bravery, integrity, and powerful influence in maintaining the peace with the Plains Indians in this region, where he spent most of his life. Close by was a second marker. It was a bronze tablet on a modest vertical slab marking the location of the northeast bastion of Edmonton House.

As we stood on this magnificent site, high upon the bluff rising above the great Saskatchewan River flowing powerfully eastward, we reflected that from this very site the Hudson's Bay Company had, in effect, ruled for many years a vast region stretching far beyond the borders of present-day Alberta. Their reign ended and their buildings were torn down. But today the site is once again occupied—this time by the Legislative Building, the seat of government for the province of Alberta. This is, indeed, a place of history both past and present.

Fort Pembina

As early as in 1793 the junction of the Pembina and Red rivers had been recognized as an advantageous location for a fur trading post. The Pembina, a pleasant little stream cutting through the prairie flatlands to the west, gave access to the enormous herds of buffalo, while the Red with its tributaries rich in beaver led directly to Lake Winnipeg and York Factory to the north or Montreal to the east.

Peter Grant of the North West Company was the first to establish a toehold in this area. His post built on the east side of the Red River opposite the mouth of the Pembina lasted but a brief period. By 1801 it had disappeared and could only offer a suitable location for a garden, as Alexander Henry the younger noted in his journal: "planted my potatoes and sowed a few garden seeds on the spot where Mr. Grant's fort stood."

Charles Jean Baptiste Chaboillez of the North West Company was the next trader to build at the junction of the two rivers. He erected his fort in 1797 on the west side of the Red, on the south bank of the Pembina. His fort, like Grant's, lasted but a year or two. The Indians who traded there were chiefly Chippewas, also known as Saulteux or Ojibwa. An excerpt from the post's journal faithfully records typical activities at the trading post:

[December 1797] Wednes: 13 The Indians still at the Fort they called me in Council to their Tents it was to ask if I would do them Charity to give them a large Keg Mixd Rum—as that I had all their Skins & that they were Pityful I told them if they were wanting to Drink that they might go & work the Beaver—& returned to the House—they were very much Displeased—In the Evening they all went to the English [Hudson's Bay Company] & prevailed on Mr. Miller to give them Liquor, which he did, I Suppose to avoid Quarrels, he having but few Men with him & all out in the Prairie—he gave them Twenty four Pints Mixd Rum—& on their living the House they robbed him of a New Gun—In the Night an old Woman came to the Door of the Fort & informed us of the Indians Intending to make a Trial to Pilladge—gave them Men each a Gun—Twenty Balls & Powder—& desired the People to discharge one Round, only with Powder—they immediately Came to the fort Door & asked what was the Matter, I told them that I was Inform that the Dogs wanted to bite us, & that I was preparing to receive them—They went to their Tents & were very quiet all Night—

In 1801 Alexander Henry the younger decided to locate at the Pembina–Red River junction. After selecting a proper site for his fort he "remained for the night and slept in the old [Chaboillez's] fort on the S. side. Fleas and wood lice made me very uncomfortable; the former always abound in our old buildings and are very troublesome."

Henry's Fort Pembina was erected on the west side of the Red River, on the north bank of the Pembina directly opposite Chaboillez's fort. It was on a tongue of land between the two rivers about one hundred paces from each. In his journal entry for May 17, 1801, Henry described the site as follows: "The ground was so encumbered with large fallen trees, and the underwood so intricate, that we could not see ten yards before us; however, I drew out the place as soon as possible. Between this spot and the plains on the W. are great numbers of fine large oaks, very proper for building, and on the N. side, between this and a small rivulet, are plenty of fine large bois blancs, proper for flooring and covering. The stockades must be hauled from some distance below, where there are fine patches of poplar."

Henry remained in charge of Fort Pembina for seven seasons (1801–08). During that time he was constantly enlarging and upgrading the post buildings. The storehouse, one hundred feet by twenty feet, was solidly constructed of oak. His house and the smaller buildings were whitewashed with white earth brought in from the Hair Hills. His large stable accommodated fifty horses. The original stockade, built of poplar, was soon replaced by a more durable one of oak. Even the dwelling houses were replaced by the second year.

Fifty sleighloads of ice and 400 kegs of water fitted the icehouse for storage of meat and fish. Blockhouses at the corners of the stockade provided for defense. A watchtower overlooking the front gate of the nearby XY post provided a means for constant surveillance of this rival's activities.

From the very first year of his arrival at the mouth of the Pembina River, Henry devoted much time and attention to the establishment of a garden. His journal is full of references to this activity: "[April] 14th. Men working at the new ground, and manuring the garden. [May] 7th. I planted potatoes, turnips, carrots, beets, parsnips, onions, and cabbage-stalks for seeds. Sowed cabbage seed. 10th. We finished planting eight kegs of potatoes. . . . [October] 20th. I took in my potatoes—420 bushels, the produce of 7 bushels, exclusive of the quantity we have roasted since our arrival, and what the Indians have stolen, which must be at least 200 hundred bushels more. I measured an onion, 22 inches in circumference; a carrot, 18 inches long, and, at the thick end, 14 inches in circumference; a turnip with its leaves alone weighed 25 pounds."

Relations with the Indians (principally the Saulteux and Assiniboines) were always unpredictable, while the Sioux (Dakota) usually represented a real threat not only to the fort but to the other Indians as well. Henry attributed much of this trouble to the unrestricted availability of liquor provided by the trading companies. He wrote in his journal in February of 1803: "But the Indians totally neglect their ancient customs; and to what can this degeneracy be ascribed but to their intercourse with us, particularly as they are so unfortunate as to have a continual succession of opposition parties to teach them roguery and destroy both mind and body with that pernicious article, rum? What a different set of people they would be, were there not a drop of liquor in the country! If a murder is committed among the Saulteurs, it is always in a drinking match. We may truly say that liquor is at the root of all evil in the North West."

Henry himself, like most other traders, was not above resorting to behavior that could scarcely be called honorable. He made no apologies for his actions as recorded in his journal for April 1, 1804: "I went to the upper part of Tongue river to meet a band of Indians returning from hunting beaver, and fought several battles with the women to get their furs from them. It was the most disagreeable derouine I ever made; however, I got all they had, about a pack of good furs; but I was vexed at having been obliged to fight with women. It is true it was all my neighbor's debts."

During Henry's seven-year tenure at Fort Pembina, the returns in pelts and pemmican were the highest in the Lower Red River department, averaging thirty ninety-pound bales of furs and eighty ninety-pound bags of pemmican per year. However, by 1805 the beaver had been almost completely exterminated due to incessant trapping and the onslaught of an epidemic disease.

The Hudson's Bay Company, also, had not been slow to recognize the strategic importance of the Pembina–Red River junction. By 1793 it had established on the east side of the Red River a small post, which it later rebuilt in 1801. At the same time, the newly organized XY Company moved in and built a fort close by, so that for the period 1800–1805 there were three rival trading concerns, all within sight of each other, vying by whatever means possible for the Indian trade. In 1805 this number was reduced to two when the XY Company merged with the North West Company, and in 1821 it was further reduced to one with the takeover of the North West post by the Hudson's Bay Company at the time of their union.

The Pembina location continued to be of great importance for many years. First, it was the traditional place of rendezvous for the fifteen hundred or more Métis who assembled there each year to organize their great buffalo hunts out on the plains to the west. Second, its location so close to the international boundary made it a center of illegal entry of goods from the United States, as well as the illicit export of furs. This was a direct violation of the Hudson's Bay Company's monopoly, based on its 1670 charter, to exclusive trade rights within Rupert's Land Territory, which included the Red River valley. George Simpson, the shrewd Governor for the Hudson's Bay Company, by giving lower prices and better range and quality of goods was able by 1854 to buy out or freeze out of this lucrative market all competitors, including not only the private independent traders but also the more powerful American Fur Company as represented by Norman Kittson. The Hudson's Bay Company was left in sole possession of the Pembina location. As late as 1870, even though it was admittedly a couple of miles south of the international boundary, at its own request and by the courtesy of the United States it was permitted to continue in operation until the final readjustment of the boundary.

The day we visited Pembina was quite overcast; a gentle rain was falling. The area where Chaboillez's Fort Pembina once stood is today the Pembina State Park. It is a most pleasant place—an open grassy area free of underbrush, a few large trees giving summertime shade, the tree-bordered bank of the Pembina River on the north side, and the high levee along the Red River on the east. An impressive granite boulder bearing an appropriately inscribed bronze tablet marks the site of the fort.

We walked along the top of the levee. The river flowing peacefully below us was partially shrouded by mist and fog. We remembered that in Chaboillez's and Henry's time there was no levee to protect their forts from the periodic floodings they frequently experienced. Beyond the fringe of bare-limbed trees standing like sentinels along the riverbank, the flat prairie lands extended on each side. From this one spot where we stood at the mouth of the Pembina River we could see across the broad Red to this east shore where Grant's fort of 1793 and the Hudson's Bay Company post had once stood. We could also look to the north, across to the clearing where Henry's Fort Pembina had been located on the north side of the Pembina River. Today, probably both because of the rain and the lateness of the season, the area was completely deserted and quiet—no picnickers using the park grills, no children running and shouting, no bicycles riding the pathways. What a contrast to the noises and the activities of fort life, to the movement and commotion of the throngs of Métis buffalo hunters astride their high-spirited horses, which once characterized this busy crossroads two hundred years ago. The buffalo have disappeared from the plains, the fur traders and their Indian customers are no more. Only the two rivers remain flowing in their ancient courses, but even they have been tamed by man-made structures.

Red Deer Lake House/Fort Lac la Biche Greenwich House

Motivated by a desire to find a feasible route to the upper waters of Athabasca River, which led to the great barrier of the Rocky Mountains, first David Thompson in 1798 and then Peter Fidler in 1799 paddled, poled, and portaged along the lengthy and arduous Beaver River track that led from the Churchill River at Lac Île à la Crosse to Lac la Biche and the waters of the Athabasca River.

David Thompson, who the previous year had left the service of the Hudson's Bay Company and entered the employ of the North West Company, pioneered the way. On August 19 he left Cumberland House on the Saskatchewan River. Ascending the Sturgeon–Weir River, he passed through Amisk Lake, continued up the upper Sturgeon–Weir River, and by means of the Frog Portage crossed over into the Churchill River five days later. He ascended this river, reaching the southern end of Lac Île à la Crosse on September 6. After spending two days at the North West post located there, he commenced the ascent of the Beaver River, surveying as he went, to Lac la Biche (also known as Red Deer Lake), which he reached nearly a month later, on October 4. He proceeded westward along the south shore of the lake for about a mile before finding a suitable location to erect his Red Deer Lake House.

He spent a busy winter trading with the local Indians and making numerous astronomical observations. Referring to the Indians who traded at his fort, he wrote: "The natives that traded at this House, were about thirty Nahathaway [Crees] and the same number of Swampy Ground Stone [Assiniboine] Indians who still continue to prefer their ancient mode of life to living in the Plains, where the rest of their Tribes are: The languages of both these people are soft and easy to learn and speak, that of the Stone Indians is so agreeable to the ear, it may be called the Italian Language of North America; . . . All these people are superior in stature and good looks . . ."

The Hudson's Bay Company, well aware of Thompson's exploration of the Beaver River and erection of a trading post on the south shore of Lac la Biche the previous year, quickly decided to oppose this post with one of their own. Accordingly, men were sent overland from Buckingham House on the Saskatchewan to Lac la Biche to build a trading post there close to Thompson's establishment. In August of 1799 orders reached Peter Fidler at Cumberland House to proceed west on the Beaver River track to Lac la Biche and there operate the company fort in competition with Thompson.

The Beaver River is a winding, sluggish stream with many tribu-taries forming an intricate and confusing maze of waterways lying be-tween the Athabasca watershed to the north and the Saskatchewan watershed to the south. At this time, except to the Indians the area was largely unknown. Fidler admitted in his journal that "we have unluck-ily no Indian to pilot us there and none of us have ever been at that place before." Many times he followed the wrong branch of the stream and had to backtrack, thus losing much time. Furthermore, provisions were running very short. To add to his difficulties, whenever possible the Nor'Westers whom he occasionally encountered endeavored by all manner of harassments to induce him to give up and turn back. Fidler recorded in his journal that "Mr. McTavish of the old company [North West] used every mean and rogish method in his power to persuade our pilot to leave us" and again he wrote: "A Canadian [Nor'Wester] canoe with 2 men passed us on their way to Green Lake we suppose to tell the master there of our unexpected arrival and to get all the Indians out of the way if possible." One of the Canadians went so far as to draw a map of the Beaver River for Fidler that was deliberately misleading.

In spite of all obstacles and hardships, Fidler persevered and at last found the Little Divide Portage leading from Beaver River to the small creek entering Lac la Biche at the south end. From the mouth of this creek he followed the shoreline westward for about half a mile and then north three-quarters of a mile, arriving at his destination, where he was welcomed by the builders of the fort, which had been given the name Greenwich House.

Thompson and Fidler and their men at their respective posts, probably located within gunshot distance of each other, lived and car-ried on their normal trading activities in a spirit of reasonable har-mony. Both men, in addition to their duties as post managers, devoted considerable time whenever possible to mapping and surveying and to making astronomical observations. Even though difficult and unpre-dictable, the Beaver River system was routinely used for many years. However, when George Simpson on his way to the Pacific coast in 1824 found the upper stretches of the river practically dry and consequently was forced to make long and circuitous detours involving numerous time-consuming portages to bypass sections impassable for canoes, he decided that the Beaver River as a link in the Athabasca River trans-portation system was impractical and should be abandoned. As its re-placement, he proposed that the Saskatchewan River be used as far as Edmonton House; thence travelers could go overland by horse brigade on a trail to be constructed that would lead to Fort Assiniboine on the Athabasca River.

Simpson in some detail and considerable vividness described in his journal the difficulties encountered in using the Beaver River route: "Left our Encampmt on Portage La Biche . . . and fell on River La Biche which we decended and a more disagreeable navigation or piece of Road I never travelled; the River itself was nearly dry so that it became necessary to carry the Baggage at least four fifths of the way, two men took down the Canoe light with great difficulty and Mr. McMillan and I walked the whole way and most abominably dirty Walking it was, the banks of the River having been recently overrun by Fire and while still smoking a light rain had fallen so that we were up to the knee every step in Charcoal and ashes, and by the termination of each Days March as black as Sweeps."

The two rival posts under Thompson and Fidler continued in active operation for only a few years. However, with the union of the two companies in 1821 the Hudson's Bay Company took over the North West fort and for the next ninety-one years maintained a post that served the Crees and Métis who had formed a settlement on the south shore of the lake.

During the turbulent days of the Riel Rebellion of 1885, the local people, influenced by messages sent to them by the insurgent Cree leader Big Bear, looted the Hudson's Bay post. Father Faraud, the O.M.I. priest in charge of the Lac la Biche mission, wrote in a letter to a brother priest, Father Fabre: "Men, women and children poured into the store, and into the house. In less than a quarter of an hour there wasn't a pin, a bit of merchandise, comestible of any sort, or fur left—everything had disappeared. Then, like all revolutionaries, they broke the windows, the doors, the tables, the window frames were chopped up with axes, books of every sort were torn into a thousand pieces and blown away by the wind; the women were having fun tearing lengths of cloth and dividing among themselves." The Hudson's Bay post survived this disaster for another quarter-century before finally closing its doors in 1912.

Today there is little left to recall the existence of Red Deer Lake House or Greenwich House. The province of Alberta has erected a large wooden sign beside the dusty gravel road leading to Lac la Biche stating that these two trading posts erected respectively by David Thompson and Peter Fidler had once stood on the south shore of the lake. Unfortunately, all vestiges of these forts have long since disappeared—their precise location unknown. However, one thing does remain largely unchanged from the days when Thompson and Fidler viewed it from the gateway of their fort. Lac la Biche still stretches to the far northern horizon, its broad expanse broken only by a few islands and narrow promontories. From its waters, just as in the day of Thompson, comes an abundance of fish of many kinds. The white pelicans continue to make their spectacular plunges into its depths for food, while in the fall it harbors thousands of waterfowl who rest and feed on its surface.

We spent several hours at the Lac la Biche mission located on the south side of the lake only a few miles west of the modern town of Lac la Biche. Established in the 1850s by the Oblate priests of Mary Immaculate, it is regarded as their Canadian birthplace. The mission complex consists of an imposing church, a combination rectory-seminary building, and the nuns' residence. This mission was a major training center for young priests of the order in preparation for posting to far-off places where they served with selfless dedication.

Today this mission is the nucleus of a large Métis population, who faithfully contribute from their earnings and labor toward the mission's support. Several of the buildings are in desperate need of repairs. We were told by one young Métis guide that money, happily, has been promised by the government for renovation.

Lac la Biche mission through the work of its priests exerted—and continues to exert—a most important influence on the lives of many peoples of the North. We look forward to returning and, we hope, seeing these historic mission buildings fully restored and fulfilling their important functions once again.

Lesser Slave Lake Fort
Fort Grouard

As a result of the favorable information gained from David Thompson's extensive 1798 explorations in the Beaver River-Lesser Slave Lake area, the North West Company established a trading post at the west end of the lake on the shores of the shallow bay known today as Buffalo Bay. Peter Fidler, who had recently arrived at his post on Lac la Biche, noted in his journal on October 5, 1799, that "20 Canadians in 5 canoes embarked from this place [Greenwich House] to erect a settlement at the Slave Lake to the SW of the Peace River and very near it."

Thompson visited the North West post in November of 1802 and again in the following year. He observed that the surrounding countryside was burnt and still smoldering from a recent fire. Travel on land was difficult because of the tangle of fallen trees. Nevertheless, game appeared to be abundant, and the drying racks at the post were heavy with split whitefish and pickerel. He further commented that the soil surrounding Buffalo Bay was poor and attempts to raise garden crops to supplement the fort's food supply were not very successful. To the north, however, the soil appeared to be excellent (surely a prophetic observation subsequently proved by the rich fertility of the Peace River country). He also noticed that periodically the shallow water of Buffalo Bay evaporated, leaving an expanse of muck and marsh grass. John McGillivray, a partner of the North West Company, was in charge of the fort from 1801 to 1810.

The location of the post provided a shorter communication between the Athabasca and the upper Peace rivers. It was in rich fur country and was a convenient outlet for the Beaver Indians to trade their pelts.

In 1815 the Hudson's Bay Company as part of their plan to penetrate the Athabasca country—the Nor'Westers' stronghold—sent François Decoigne to Lesser Slave Lake to build a trading post in opposition to the North West Company. Decoigne was well chosen for this assignment. As a former Nor'Wester, considered one of its best—though extravagant—traders, Decoigne knew the stratagems that would likely be employed against him. He was able to bring out twenty-five packs of prime furs for the 1815–16 season. The results for the next year, however, were dramatically different. By that time, the rivalry between the two companies throughout the Athabasca country had escalated to violent and deadly proportions. On December 1 of 1816 the Hudson's Bay post was overrun and destroyed by the men from the neighboring North West post, robbed of its furs and provisions, and many of the officers and men made prisoners. Decoigne himself and a few others escaped into the bush, where they spent the winter with the Indians. By spring, when it was time to return to Norway House on Lake Winnipeg, he had managed to accumulate four canoeloads of furs.

Undaunted by this disaster, the Hudson's Bay Company attempted once again to establish their post on Lesser Slave Lake. This time John Lee Lewes was entrusted with the task. Fort Waterloo was built in the summer of 1818 on the shore of Buffalo Bay, 600 feet from the North West post. The Nor'Westers responded to this reappearance of their rivals by building a watchtower only fifty yards distant from the Hudson's Bay fort, so that all movement of the traders and their Indian customers was under constant surveillance. The resulting harassment and opposition were bitter and relentless. The Nor'Westers were able to temporarily lure the Indians away from Lesser Slave Lake to their post on Lac la Biche. Lewes persevered, however, and by the 1819–20 season he had succeeded in putting Fort Waterloo on a secure footing. When the two rival companies amalgamated in 1821, his fort was abandoned in favor of the North West's post, henceforth known as Lesser Slave Lake House.

By the mid-1800s this post was the largest settlement beyond Athabasca Landing. George Simpson's decision in 1825 that the Peace River country would be reached from Edmonton House rather than via the long Churchill–Methye portage route, reinforced Lesser Slave Lake as a major link in the new communication system. As a part of this new route, an overland portage from Lesser Slave Lake House to the Peace River, known as the Grouard Trail, had to be constructed and maintained by the company. Attempts to prevent any but company people from using the track were unsuccessful. The irresistible pressure of public use resulted in escalating costs for maintenance and repairs, which the Hudson's Bay Company was forced to assume. In spite of diligent efforts, the trail was strictly a dry-weather road used by the cart brigades in the summer months only. The rest of the year it was virtually impassable. Notwithstanding this handicap, each year tons of freight and an enormous number of bales of furs passed through Lesser Slave Lake House to and from Edmonton and the Peace River. In 1878, for example, 800 pieces were forwarded from Edmonton to Lesser Slave Lake House for transport over the Grouard Trail to Peace River and Athabasca by cart brigade. At the same time Edmonton had to furnish thirty bags of pemmican, fifty *taureaux* (ninety-pound-capacity bags made of buffalo skins) of grease, and thirty bags of flour to provision the brigade. The large number of Red River carts required for the overland portage were kept at the post. The inevitable damage done to the carts by the extreme roughness of the portage made the necessary repair work a major activity at the fort.

In 1886 this post had become so important that it succeeded Fort Dunvegan on the Peace River as the company's northwest headquarters.

In the early 1840s the Weslyan-Methodist minister Robert T. Rundle, who was serving as the company's chaplain at Edmonton House as well as instructor for the fort's children, in his capacity as missionary to the Indians made yearly trips to Lesser Slave Lake House to conduct services and minister to the local Métis and Crees, who had settled around the post. Although his dedicated efforts had some initial success, he was unable to establish a permanent following there.

Thirty years later, in 1871, the local people, traditionally and predominantly Catholic, welcomed the arrival of priests of the Order of Mary Immaculate. Their Bishop Grouard was able to found a permanent mission and build St. Bernard's mission church on a low hillside overlooking the waters of Buffalo Bay.

Just as was the case of the fur trading posts on Lac la Biche, there are today no traces left of either the North West or the Hudson's Bay post. Instead, again just as at Lac la Biche, the mission is the only tie yet remaining that stretches back to the time when trading was still being conducted from the posts at the west end of Lesser Slave Lake.

St. Bernard's mission is a peaceful place of quiet serenity. We entered the spacious church and marveled at its beauty. The large painting of the Crucifixion was the work of Bishop Grouard himself. A large tepee of spotless white, its entrance flaps open to reveal the Tabernacle within, occupied the center of the altar. Off to the left was a freestanding cross of local diamond willow, impressive in its stark simplicity. These objects reflected the culture of the people whom the mission served.

We left the church and walked the short distance to the simple cemetery on the gentle slope above the bay. Here the Order of Mary Immaculate maintains a cemetery for priests and nuns, their earthly work completed. A large granite cross surmounts Bishop Grouard's simple headstone. The remaining graves, precisely spaced side by side in orderly rows, are all marked alike with identical headstones, simply inscribed with name, year of birth and death, and the precious letters *O.M.I.*

An air of tranquillity pervades this bit of ground. The wind sighs softly in the tall spruce trees bordering the cemetery. The waters of the bay just beyond reflect the bright sunshine. After the turbulence and hardships of their lives given to God, they are at peace.

Likewise, all the bustle and movement centered at the trading posts once located on the bay, the shouts of the workers, the cries of the brigades coupled with the creaking of the Red River carts, and the bellowing of the oxen, have long ceased. The shores of Buffalo Bay lie quiet, their peace interrupted only by the strident cries of birds flying over the water and the happy noises from nearby vacationers.

McLeod's Fort
(Peace River)

Alexander McLeod, a nephew of Norman McLeod of the firm of Gregory, McLeod and Company, Montreal agents for the North West Company, was closely associated with Alexander Mackenzie during the years 1787–93, first at Fort Chipewyan and later on the Peace River. In 1790 he went up the Peace River as far as the mouth of the White Mud River, where he built a fort that remained in operation for only a brief span of two or three years.

Upon Mackenzie's return to the Fort of the Forks in 1793, after his successful journey to the Pacific Ocean, the explorer soon continued on down the Peace River, leaving the country never to return. Alexander McLeod, highly regarded by Mackenzie, was named to take over Fort of the Forks and the trade of the upper Peace River. Within a short time, McLeod moved from Mackenzie's old fort to a more suitable site on the opposite side (i.e., northwest) of the river a few miles downstream closer to the forks. There he established his new post, known as McLeod's Fort. It had a palisade enclosing a square of approximately one hundred feet and contained at least two large buildings. From this quite substantial post Alexander McLeod remained in command of the upper Peace River until 1799. In the spring of that year he embarked with his fur returns and headed down the river on his way to attend the annual meeting of the North West Company wintering partners at Grand Portage. He never returned west.

For a brief period McLeod's Fort and the upper Peace River were entrusted first to James Finlay and then to Archibald Norman McLeod. However, by the fall of 1805 the center of the trading activity on the Peace River had moved upstream from the Forks to the North West Company's newly established Fort Dunvegan. The once-important McLeod's Fort was abandoned, its buildings neglected and falling into disrepair. Only its garden spot was still used. Each year men from Fort Dunvegan returned to the old fort to sow their seeds and plant their potatoes.

Traces of McLeod's Fort can still be seen today. Leaving Peace River, we drove a short distance along a secondary road that followed the north side of the river. Soon at the edge of a large open field high above the river we spotted a provincial marker that identified the place as the site of McLeod's Fort. We walked over the area and had no difficulty in detecting the telltale ridges marking the palisade perimeter. The grassy mounds, vestiges of collapsed chimneys and buildings, and depressions left by cellars all were quite clearly visible. The view from the fort site was impressive. As far as the eye could see, we were able to look off to distant horizons in every direction while below us, timeless and unchanging, lay the Peace River valley in all its beauty.

Rocky Mountain House
Acton House

The North West Company, ever in the vanguard of those opening up new country to the fur trade, determined to advance to the upper limits of practical navigation on the North Saskatchewan within sight of the great mountain barrier of the Rocky Mountains just to the west and there build a fort. Their objective was twofold. First, they anticipated establishing a lucrative trade with the Kootenays from the beaver-rich country on the west side of the mountains, who were prevented from trading with forts farther east because of the implacable enmity of the powerful Blackfeet. Second, this fort would serve as a convenient base from which the company explorers could probe the mountains in their search for a feasible pass through the mountains leading to the Columbia River valley.

So, in mid-September of 1799, a force of Nor'Westers led by the redoubtable John McDonald of Garth embarked from Fort Augustus and headed upriver. McDonald had hoped to slip away unnoticed by his competitor in the adjoining Hudson's Bay fort, but James Bird was not caught napping. He, too, organized a force, and the two parties, some on horseback and some by boat and canoe, proceeded westward up the Saskatchewan. The two companies selected sites on the north bank of the river just above its confluence with the Clearwater. There on a high terrace a short way back from the river, the North West Company built Rocky Mountain House. Upstream, a mere musket shot away on a lower bench, the Hudson's Bay Company erected Acton House.

Even though written eleven years later, in 1810, Alexander Henry's description of the site of Rocky Mountain House—equally applicable to Acton House close by—was an accurate one:

> Our establishment stands on a high bank on the N. side of the river; the situation is well adapted for defense, as the blockhouses command the fort for some distance. This spot was formerly covered with aspen and pine, which have been cut down for the use of the place, leaving a large open space. Frequent fires have aided much in clearing away the wood and brush, so that we now have a grand view of the Rocky Mountains, lying nearly S.W.,—. Opposite the fort the river is 180 yards wide, while the distance from the bank on which the fort stands to the opposite bank is 250 yards; at high water the whole of this space is covered, and flows with a strong, rapid current. The channel in its ordinary state, as it was when we arrived last fall, was only 30 yards wide, and interrupted by a strong rapid, where the water rushes among some large stones, forming

a cascade whose perpetual roaring makes it a dismal neighbor in this solitary spot. This rapid is the first interruption of any consequence in approaching the mountains.

Each company knew that trading with Indians considered enemies by the Blackfeet would probably provoke hostile retaliation. Therefore, both forts were heavily fortified with massive palisades and bastions. Constant vigilance was the order of the day.

Within the walls of the high stockades and occupying about half of the area, the buildings of Rocky Mountain House were laid out on four sides of an inner courtyard. On the east was a long rectangular structure housing the master's dwelling, the storeroom, and the icehouse; the Indian and trade house occupied the south side; on the west was the men's house; completing the square to the north were the men's houses and the blacksmith shop. The remaining space was an open area containing the workshop and stable. Sturdy bastions on the northeast and southwest corners, as well as one on the center south wall overlooking the river, provided means of surveillance and defense.

Hudson's Bay Company's Acton House was laid out in a somewhat similar pattern. Its buildings were arranged to form an inner courtyard. The largest structure was the main house, where the chief factor or chief trader had his quarters. This formed the east side of the quadrangle. To the south was a combined stable and warehouse; on the west were two buildings: one served both as the men's residence and as a workshop, and the second housed the Indian trade room. The storehouse formed the courtyard's north side. Massive bastions at the southeast and northwest corners and on the west wall of the formidable stockade completed the fortification.

Trade with the Piegan Indians was carried on at both forts. Surviving records for Acton House show returns of 2,289, 3,551, and 1,368 Made Beaver respectively for their first three seasons of operation. The Nor'Westers tried hard to realize the two objectives that had been responsible for the establishment of their new fort. In both they failed. Despite valiant efforts by David Thompson and Duncan McGillivray (wintering partners), they were not able to induce the Kootenays in any number to cross the mountains and brave the hostility of the Piegans, who were fiercely determined to prevent them from coming in to trade and thereby acquire guns and ammunition. Both men penetrated the mountains looming so majestically to the west, probing and searching for a usable pass, but none was found. So, after only three years of operation, Rocky Mountain House closed its doors in 1802. Acton House did likewise.

251

Three seasons later both companies decided to try a second time, and the two neighboring forts were re-activated. Once again efforts were made to persuade the Kootenay to make the trip over the mountains in enough numbers to assure sufficient profits for the traders. But again these efforts failed.

Undeterred, the North West Company, bold and venturous in their thinking, resolved that "if the hill will not come to Mahomet, Mahomet will go to the hill." In the summer of 1807 David Thompson, indefatigable explorer and trader, pushed up the Saskatchewan to its headwaters and there discovered a pass that led through the mountains to the Columbia River. This pass was later quite unfairly called the Howse Pass after a Hudson's Bay Company man, Joseph Howse, who merely followed the route through the mountains blazed by Thompson two years earlier. Thompson ascended the Columbia as far as Windermere Lake, located deep in the heart of Kootenay country. On the west side of the lake he built a trading post that he named Kootenay House. The Kootenays came in large numbers to trade there, and each fall Thompson's brigade crossed back over the mountains with heavy loads of the precious furs. The success of Kootenay House eliminated the need for Rocky Mountain House, so in 1807 it was closed down. Again Acton House followed suit. However, unlike Rocky Mountain House, it had no new fort replacing it.

By 1810 the two companies were ready to make yet a third attempt to reestablish their forts on the upper Saskatchewan. Alexander Henry the younger, an experienced trader of many years with the North West Company, was sent to take charge of Rocky Mountain House.

Upon his arrival at the fort, he soon discovered that a blockade put up by the Piegans had prevented Thompson's Columbia brigade from following their customary route up the Saskatchewan and across the mountains to the Columbia River and Kootenay House. Henry, by a series of ingenious stratagems, succeeded in getting Thompson's canoe brigade past the watchful Piegans, who were camped by the fort. His plans backfired, however, when he discovered that Thompson, instead of being above Rocky Mountain House, was below it.

In desperation, the harassed explorer decided that somehow he would have to bypass the watchful Piegans. He resolved to strike north to the Athabasca River and follow it to the mountains. He knew that many miles of heavy forest, interlaced with a maze of rivers and streams, lay before him. Nevertheless, he and his men did not hesitate. They resolutely plunged ahead and, after a journey of much hardship, finally emerged on the banks of the Athabasca. This they ascended for five days before coming to the mouth of the Whirlpool River. Here they were forced to leave their horses and resort to snowshoes and dogsleds. Struggling up this small stream to its upper limits, they eventually reached the pass at the height of land. It was bitterly cold and the snow was so deep it seemed bottomless. But Thompson and his men survived. The next day, they began the precipitous descent down the west side following a stream identified today as Wood River, which flowed into the Columbia. There, at a place to be known henceforth as Boat Encampment, Thompson stayed long enough to build the canoes needed to continue his passage on the Columbia. Thus Thompson's journey, made out of desperation, had resulted in his discovery of the Athabasca Pass.

This northern route to the Columbia via the Athabasca Pass soon proved to be superior to the southern Howse Pass route and quickly became the principal and preferred route used in the fur trade for crossing the mountains. As a result, Rocky Mountain House would no longer be used as a base for mountain trade and exploration. Henceforth, the future of the two competing houses would depend solely on their trade with the Plains Indians—in particular that of the Piegans.

The 1810–11 season was a busy one at both forts. During the three years they had been closed, the buildings had deteriorated greatly. Consequently, much repair work had to be done to put them back into shape. As Alexander Henry wrote in his journal, "The rotten old buildings are falling to pieces . . ."

Trade with the Blackfeet was lively. It was often quite turbulent as well, for the liberal use of liquor, an integral part of trading, frequently resulted in violent confrontations in the trading room. Henry described the coldly calculated measures he took to prevent any trouble:

I repaired the bastions, and made a number of loopholes in the shop and garret bearing directly upon the Indian hall, where, if there should be any quarrel, it would of course begin. We should thus be able to destroy a good many before they could get out of the house, and then the guard in the bastions could take them in their retreat toward the gates, where also the bastions bore full upon them, and many could be killed as they crowded through. Furthermore, the bastions would bear upon those who should get out of the fort until they retreated beyond the reach of our guns.

Men at both posts were kept busy completing the fort buildings, trading with the Indians and carrying out the daily round of routine tasks, such as hunting for food, caring for the horses, and obtaining sufficient firewood for the voracious fireplaces. Christmas and New Year were welcome breaks in the post's yearly routine. Everyone looked forward to the festivities. Reflecting the generally pleasant relations between the two forts that existed at this time, a joint Christmas dinner was held at Acton House; a week later Rocky Mountain House reciprocated by hosting the New Year's dance.

At the beginning of the year, both forts were alarmed by persistent reports that they were going to be attacked by large numbers of Gros Ventre Indians. Defenses of each post were improved, and a constant alert was maintained. En route to Rocky Mountain House to launch their assault, the Gros Ventres were intercepted by the Piegans, who bluntly told them that if they attacked the fort they would, in turn, be attacked by the Piegans. Faced with this ultimatum, the Gros Ventres gave up and withdrew to the south. The Piegans had not come to the rescue of the forts out of any particular regard for the traders. They simply realized that if the forts were destroyed they would then be obliged to trade at Fort Augustus and Edmonton House, located downstream in the territory of their traditional enemies, the Assiniboine and Cree. It was to prevent this that they had faced down the Gros Ventres.

Rocky Mountain House and Acton House remained open for the following season. Then they were closed down once more—this time for a period of seven years. The North West Company and Hudson's Bay Company had both decided, in the interests of economy, to consolidate the trading at their respective Fort Augustus and Edmonton House. Cree and Assiniboine were already coming there to trade. It was thought that trade with the Piegan and other members of the Blackfoot nation could be carried on there as well. However, as might have been anticipated, this arrangement did not work out. The enmity between Cree and Assiniboine, on the one hand, and members of the Blackfoot nation (Blackfeet, Bloods, and Piegans), on the other hand, was so strong and deep-seated that they could not meet at the same trading post without the likelihood of violent confrontation and bloodshed. Such violence, of course, was not conducive to profitable trading.

Finally, recognizing the futility of trying to keep peace between the two hostile factions and in order to keep them apart, the two companies reopened their forts on the upper Saskatchewan in 1819. John Rowand from Fort Augustus, a Nor'Wester of many years' experience, was the man sent to Rocky Mountain House.

In the summer of 1821, news was received that the two companies had merged into one organization. With this unification, it was obvious

254

that only one of the two trading posts would need be retained. Would it be Hudson's Bay Company's Acton House or North West Company's Rocky Mountain House? Opinions differ among historians, and so far there has not been sufficient archaeological work to provide a definitive answer. However, after 1821 the name Acton House no longer appears in any records. The remaining fort (whichever one it was) was known as Rocky Mountain House for the rest of its existence.

George Simpson, the head of the new company, feeling that the Saskatchewan district was not only depleted of beaver but also losing a considerable sum each year, decided after the 1822–23 season to close Rocky Mountain House. He was induced to reconsider this decision by the actions of the Piegans, who did not bring their trade to Edmonton House, as had been expected, but instead took their furs to company posts west of the Rockies. They never ceased, however, in requesting that Rocky Mountain House be reopened.

Finally, in 1825, this was done. For the next six years, under John Rowand and Henry Fisher, the post, benefiting from the important Piegan trade, prospered, contributing substantially toward making the Saskatchewan the most profitable district of the company. For example, in one visit in the fall of 1829 the Piegans traded 2,000 beaver at the fort. In the winter of 1830–31 they were bringing a like number of skins when they were attacked by the Crow Indians. Fifty-seven Piegans were killed and all their furs stolen. This disaster, combined with the opening of a more accessible American fort, marked the end of the Piegans' coming to Rocky Mountain House. In 1832, after a disastrous season, the post was closed.

But the company's relations with the Piegans were not ended. In an effort to recapture their trade, the company finally agreed to grant their request for a post on the Bow River in the heart of their hunting territory. The new fort was built, but the Piegans failed to appear, so after two disappointing seasons it was permanently abandoned and trading activity was returned to Rocky Mountain House.

By this time Rocky Mountain House was over thirty years old, and in spite of periodic repairs and renovations it had reached the state of such dilapidation that further "patching up" was no longer possible. Therefore, in 1835, the capable and effective Chief Trader (and later Chief Factor), J. E. Harriott, built an entirely new post a short distance downriver but still within sight of the old one. This Rocky Mountain House, with the exception of one season when it was closed because of Blackfoot threats, remained in operation for the next twenty-six years as a wintering post, trading for fur and meat with the Indians of the northern plains.

At length the company accepted the fact that the Piegan trade had been irretrievably lost in favor of the Americans and concentrated, therefore, on encouraging the tribes of the Blackfoot Confederacy to come to Rocky Mountain House for trade, hoping thereby to keep them away from Edmonton House, where their enemies, the Cree and Assiniboine, traded. This policy was largely quite successful and helped avoid bloody clashes between the two hostile factions.

In April of 1848 Paul Kane, the noted artist, traveled to Rocky Mountain House for the purpose of studying and painting the Blackfeet whom he hoped to find there. He recorded his arrival at the fort as follows:

> We arrived at Rocky Mountain Fort on the 21st of April. This fort is beautifully situated on the banks of the Saskatchewan, in a small prairie, backed by the Rock Mountains in the distance. In the vicinity was a camp of Assiniboine lodges, formed entirely of pine branches. It was built for the purpose of keeping a supply of goods to trade with the Blackfoot Indians, who come there every winter, and is abandoned and left empty every summer. It is built like most of the other forts, of wood, but with more than ordinary regard to strength, which is thought necessary on account of the vicious disposition of the Blackfoot tribe, who are, without exception, the most warlike on the northern continent.

Henry John Moberly, who succeeded J. E. Harriott in charge of Rocky Mountain House in 1854, gave a detailed description of the fort in his book *When Fur Was King:*

> Mountain House was surrounded by the usual 28-foot pickets, with a block bastion at each corner and a gallery running all round inside about four and a half feet from the top, each bastion containing a supply of flintlocks and ammunition. Within was a square formed by the officers' houses, men's houses, stores and general trading-shops, a square between this and the pickets for boat-building, with forges and carpenter-shops, another square for horses and a fourth for general purposes.
>
> There were two gates, the main gate on the north and a smaller one on the south side leading through a narrow passage the height of the stockade into a long hall. In this hall, amid much speech-making, the Indians were received, the calumet passed and two glasses of rum of medium strength were given to each Indian. They were then turned out and the gates closed against them, the only means of communication being through two port-holes some twenty inches square opening through the stockade into a small blockhouse through which the trade in rum was conducted.

Under the wise rule of J. E. Harriott, Rocky Mountain House prospered. Not only his staff but the Indians as well both liked and respected him. Even though the demand for beaver dropped off due to the replacement of the beaver hat by the silk hat, the steadily increasing market for buffalo robes resulted in a profitable trade for the fort. The meat for the vast amount of pemmican required by the company continued to be a major item of trade.

Escalating violence erupting at all levels—between tribes as well as between tribes and traders—was the inevitable result of the uncontrolled availability of liquor, demanded by the Indians and provided by the traders. As a consequence of all the violence and unrest, trade at the fur forts suffered, and Rocky Mountain House was no exception.

In 1853 Harriott was transferred to the Red River settlement. Reflecting the diminishing importance of the post, a series of minor clerks were sent to replace him. The situation was becoming quite grim. No longer was the fort showing a profit.

The Hudson's Bay Company, long aware of the evils brought about by the use of liquor in trading, the most important of which was its negative effect on trade resulting in lowered profit margins, had finally decided to put a stop to it. No longer would it be available at their posts. In angry retaliation, the Indians refused to bring in any provisions to the fort; they even were able to prevent the fort hunters from making any successful hunts. As a result, there was no trade in provisions, and the people of the fort were going hungry. Starvation was a real possibility. The situation was so desperate that in the fall of 1861 no one was sent up the river to reopen the fort in preparation for the winter season. Later, when the Blackfeet arrived and found the fort standing silent and empty, they surged across the river, torched the fort, and watched the buildings blaze up and burn to the ground.

During the ensuing three or four years Chief Factor William Christie, head of the Saskatchewan district, was content to write off Rocky Mountain House from any further consideration as a viable post. However, in 1864 events occurred that induced him to change his mind. Gold had been discovered in Montana, and the American traders were quickly realizing that more profit could be made selling their goods to the influx of prospectors and miners than trading them to the Indians for furs. Christie reasoned that the Indians thus deprived of their American outlets would head back north ready to resume trading at their former posts on the Saskatchewan. In addition, the need to provide a trading fort for the Blackfeet away from Edmonton House, used by the Cree and Assiniboine, was, as always, most important. Therefore, in 1864 a crew was sent up the river under the leadership of

Richard Hardisty, and construction of a new Rocky Mountain House was begun.

William Francis Butler visited Rocky Mountain House in 1870. He made some rather astute observations about the post in his narrative *The Great Lone Land:*

> The Rocky Mountain House of the Hudson Bay Company stands in a level meadow which is clear of trees, although dense forest lies around it at some little distance. It is indifferently situated with regard to the Indian trade, being too far from the Plain Indians, who seek in the American posts along the Missouri a nearer and more profitable exchange for their goods; while the wooded district in which it lies produces furs of a second-class quality, and has for years been deficient in game. The neighboring forest, however, supplies a rich store of the white spruce for boat-building, and several full-sized Hudson Bay boats are built annually at the fort. Coal of very fair quality is also plentiful along the river banks, and the forge glows with the ruddy light of a real coal fire—a friendly sight when one has not seen it during many months.

The building site chosen was close to the river edge, only a few yards above the remains of the recently burned fort. Christie had decreed that this fort was to be built on an imposing scale, and so it was. The fort proper was a square surrounded by the usual sturdy palisade with a bastion at each corner. There was a gateway in the center of each side. The buildings within the stockade wall were arranged so as to form an inner square courtyard. Forming the north side and facing the main gate leading to the river was the chief factor's house, a scaled-down version of John Rowand's "Big House" at Edmonton. It was a two-story building with galleries extending its entire length on both levels, front and back. Heat was supplied by two massive double stone chimneys. The long, narrow building containing the men's quarters bordered the courtyard to the east, while on the opposite western side in a similar structure was the storehouse. To the south on either side of the passageway leading from the front gate to the inner courtyard were the interpreter and men's house and the Indian trade house. The blacksmith shop was located outside the courtyard by the northeast corner of the stockade. The fort's garden was enclosed by an adjoining palisade.

Both W. F. Butler in *The Great Lone Land* and H. M. Robinson in *The Great Fur Land* described the elaborate devices installed by the builders of the fort to prevent any surprise attempt by the Blackfeet during the bartering to overpower the fort. Bars, bolts, locks, sliding doors, and places to fire down upon the Indians were installed and, as an additional precaution, the area where the Indians gathered and where trading was done had no connection whatsoever with any other part of the fort.

This new fort was a brave—and expensive—beginning, but unfortunately, all the old problems that had beset the earlier fort continued undiminished. The Blackfoot trade did not return from Edmonton House. The American traders from their various whiskey forts kept the way open for the Indians to trade everything they possessed to satisfy their strong desire for liquor. No more did the Indians come in with buffalo robes or buffalo meat. Rocky Mountain House was destitute of provisions. Whereas formerly it was a major source of meat and provisions for other posts, now, in a complete reversal of roles, it had to rely on food from Edmonton House to enable it to survive. Even the fort's vegetable gardens failed, destroyed by a succession of heavy frosts. The only activity that continued as usual was the building of the fort's quota of York boats.

In 1874 the appearance of the North West Mounted Police put an end to the whiskey traders and their forts. Like the Arabs of old, they folded their tents and "silently stole away." With their disappearance and the presence of the Mounted Police, law, order, and quiet came to the plains. The Hudson's Bay Company responded by moving into the area. There, in the heart of Blackfoot territory, they built the post so frequently requested by these Indians. This removed the chief reason for maintaining Rocky Mountain House for their trade. Furthermore, no longer was the post able to provide any provisions. Its days of usefulness were over. Accordingly, at the close of the 1875–76 season Rocky Mountain House was shut down for good—never to be reopened.

A few miles west of the town of Rocky Mountain House are the sites of the old fur trading posts of Rocky Mountain House and Acton House. On a sunny afternoon in early September we drove to this lovely spot on the north bank of the Saskatchewan River. Just as Paul Kane had described it 130 years ago, the fort was "beautifully situated on the banks of the Saskatchewan in a small prairie, backed by the Rock Mountains in the distance." Two massive stone fireplace chimneys dominate the opening, the only obvious remains of what was once a busy fur fort. They alone have survived the ravages of time, weather, and man. Still defiantly erect, they maintain their lonely vigil.

A slight breeze rustled the leaves of the few scattered poplar trees. From some distant field we could hear the faint bubbling song of the western meadowlark. We sat on the edge of the bank for a while, enjoying the peace and beauty of the scene, fortunate in having the place all to ourselves. By now the autumn sun was casting a golden glow that spread over the smoothly flowing river at our feet, the dry prairie grasses, and the poplar trees. We looked across the river to the south in the direction from which the fierce Blackfeet, proud and unpredictable, had once made their appearance as they came to trade. On this day we saw no Blackfeet; instead, to our great delight, far downstream, an elk—the red deer of the traders—cautiously stepped out of the woods, slowly walked down to the water's edge, and began to drink.

Ten years later we returned to Rocky Mountain House. We were amazed at the changes that had occurred. A beautiful reception center complete with exhibits and a theater for interpretive slide presentations had been erected. Reflecting the significant amount of archaeological work that had been done, the sites of the four forts had all been identified and labeled with informative plaques as well as numbers keyed to a guide map.

We first walked to the site of the last fort built (1865–75). The two impressive fireplace chimneys, once the source of heat for the chief factor's "Big House," still dominate the site, although they are now somewhat obscured by a growth of slender poplar trees that have invaded the site. The various clearly visible depressions can now be identified as storehouse, men's quarters, and Indian trade room. A few yards away is the area occupied by the 1835–61 fort. This is a closely mowed grassy field undisturbed by any noticeable depressions or mounds. It is surrounded by tall prairie grasses and a profusion of sweet-smelling clover and goldenrod.

A walk along a trail leading through the woods of the river bottom and emerging about half a mile upstream onto the lower terrace led us to the site of Acton House (1799–1835?). Here the outlines of the fort buildings and the bastions are delineated by squared timbers. Carefully protected by glass, a small section of an original timber, still in place, can be seen.

From the site of Acton House it is a short walk through a lovely prairie meadow to the upper terrace where the North West Company's Rocky Mountain House (1799–1835?) had once stood. Here the grass is closely mowed so that the mounds, pits, depressions, and stone piles are clearly visible. It was a challenge to match these surface features with the fort buildings as shown on the guide map. From this upper terrace Acton House on the lower bench is easily visible.

The protection and identification of the fort sites of the Rocky Mountain House complex will ensure that this place, so important in the history of the fur trade, will always be remembered.

In addition, when we looked to the west we saw mountaintops above the trees, just as did Henry, Thompson, Rowand, and all the other men who lived at these forts. The "strong" rapids we passed as we followed the trail leading to Acton House are still rushing and tumbling over the stones of the riverbed. These are the very rapids whose "perpetual roaring," according to Henry, made them "a dismal neighbor in this solitary spot." These things are unchanged. They, too, can help preserve the memory of Rocky Mountain House and all those who worked there.

Athabasca Pass

We knew we would never be content until we could stand on the edge of the tiny pond known, even today, as Committee Punch Bowl lying at the height of land at Athabasca Pass. To reach this historic spot had been our goal for many years—in fact, ever since we began our quest for places important in the fur trade. Our determination was intensified by our recent visit to Rocky Mountain House, the place from which David Thompson's successful discovery of the pass had been launched.

We investigated existing ways of reaching the pass—on foot, by horseback, by helicopter. A realistic appraisal of our physical capabilities ruled out the first two choices. This left the third alternative, frightfully expensive but, as we were to conclude at the end of our trip, well worth the cost.

Early one cloudless morning in August of 1986, we lifted off from the helicopter base at Valemont, British Columbia, on the west side of the mountains and began our journey to retrace by air the route over the Athabasca Pass along which the fur traders had struggled with so much difficulty. We flew over a sea of jumbled massive mountains, their jagged peaks rising on all sides of us. The sheer faces of rock, bare of all vegetation, were broken only with patches of snow glistening a dazzling white in the sunlight.

Soon we reached the junction of the Whirlpool River with the Athabasca, known to the fur traders as *La Trou* (the Hole) because of its great depth of water at this point. Here the way to the pass lay along the valley of the Whirlpool River. On October 16, 1824, Governor George Simpson recorded his impression of the route up this valley: ". . . as we proceed the Road gets worse and the Mountains rise perpendicular to a prodigious height; the scenery Wild & Majestic beyond description; the track is in many places nearly impassable and it appears extraordinary how any human being should have stumbled on a pass through such a formidable barrier as we are now scaling and which nature seems to have placed here for the purpose of interditing all communication between the East and West sides of the Continent."

To us, looking down from the comfort of the helicopter, the river appeared sometimes as only a tiny ribbon of water almost hidden by the dense forests of fir and spruce through which it flowed, other times as a wide braided stream of many channels (known as *battures* to the traders) stretching across the entire valley floor. The icy water of these *battures* had to be forded, not only once but many times.

262

Governor Simpson's 1824 journal records the hardships imposed by these *battures:*

We forded the River about a Doz times to Day. . . . Proceeded through deep Snow and along the Bed of the River in some places Waist deep in Iced Water until 6 P.M. when we put up on the Grand Batture; every Man of the party knocked up. . . . Never did exhausted travellers turn out less disposed to renew a toilsome Journey than we did at 3 o'clock this Morng, every man of the party requiring the aid of a Walking Stick our feet being much blistered and Lacerated by the rough Travel on the Battures and in the Bed of the River; we—continued a Steady pace until 10 O'Clock having by that time forded the River 27 times when the joyful shout was given by one of the people that the Horses were in sight;

At length as the Whirlpool shrank to a small trickle, the valley opened up into a small mountain meadow of striking beauty. Cradled in this opening were three tiny pools of emerald green water strung like beads across the center of the meadow. On either side massive walls of granite towered toward the sky. It was hard to realize that this lovely little alpine meadow spread out below us at an elevation of 5,736 feet was actually the summit of the Athabasca Pass.

The helicopter gently set down at the western side of the clearing, which was just within the eastern boundary of British Columbia and thus outside Jasper National Park, where such landings are not permitted. The next hour was one of sheer joy and enchantment. We walked along the edge of the center pool, oval in shape and a mere 200 yards in diameter. Here, through the middle of this tiny tarn, the Continental Divide passes. From its northern side, its waters drain via the Whirlpool River northward to the Athabasca River and ultimately to the Arctic Ocean, while from its opposite side its waters run southward down Pacific Creek into Wood Creek and thence via the Columbia River to the Pacific. This was the Committee Punch Bowl, so named by Governor George Simpson on the occasion of his 1824 westward crossing of the pass. As he wrote in his journal, "That this basin should send its Waters to each side of the Continent and give birth to two of the principal Rivers in North America is no less strange than true both the Dr. [John McLoughlin] & myself having examined the currents flowing from it east & West and the circumstance appearing remarkable I thought it should be honored by a distinguishing title and it was forthwith named the 'Committee's Punch Bowl'."

Of course in addition to taking photographs, we had to dip our hands into each of these two infant rivulets at this, the very place of their birth—the start of their long journey in opposing directions to the far-off seas.

On the Governor's return crossing eastward the following spring, he recorded observing a ritual that has been honored by most travelers ever since: "Monday, April 25th [1825] Left our Encampt at 1/2 past 3 this Morng, the Snow very deep and the Walking most laborous. At 6 A.M. got to the Committees Punch Bowl where the people had a Glass of Rum each and ourselves a little Wine & Water which was drunk to the Health of their Honors with three Cheers." We, unfortunately, had neglected to provide ourselves with the necessary liquid spirits and had to be content with making our toast with the cold water of the Committee Punch Bowl.

The bare crests and peaks of the mountains rise to great heights above the spruce forests that cover the lower slopes up to the tree line of about sixty-five-hundred-foot elevation. Snow still covered many of the mountaintops and filled the ravines and crevices. The massive wall of McGillivray Ridge, which rises 8,850 feet just to the east of the Committee Punch Bowl, had been stripped of its trees by an avalanche or rock slide many years ago. A healing mantle of green vegetation is slowly creeping over the denuded area, obliterating the scars. Just visible over the top of the southern flank of McGillivray Ridge, the ice-field of the Kane glacier sparkles white and unsullied. Most of the alpine flowers that brightened the meadow earlier in the summer had withered away. The pinkish rose of the late-blooming Indian paintbrush and the yellows of ragwort, arnica, and hawkweed still provided bits of color here and there, and everywhere the shaggy white seed head balls of the anemone were conspicuous.

Knowing that in all probability we would never be returning to this magical spot, we tried to capture as much of it as we could on film. We boxed the compass with our camera, beginning with the headwaters of the Whirlpool winding through the shallow pool and wet marshy meadow to the north; the massive rock wall of McGillivray's Ridge to the east; the southernmost pond and Pacific Creek trickling down through the valley opening to the south; to the west the peaks of the Mount Brown range rising above their forest-covered bottom slopes to a height of 9,183 feet; and in the center of this panorama the blue-green waters of the middle pond—the Committee Punch Bowl—the tiny patch of water through which runs not only the height of land dividing the waters from the Arctic Ocean from those of the Pacific Ocean, but also the boundary line between the provinces of Alberta and British Columbia.

At length, most reluctantly, we realized it was time to go and allow the ghosts of David Thompson, George Simpson, John McLoughlin, and all those other hardy men to return in peace to the shores of the Committee Punch Bowl, disturbed no longer by our intrusion.

We were quickly airborne and able to enjoy our last bird's-eye look at Committee Punch Bowl and its two tiny flanking pools. As we flew toward the southern outlet of the pass, we could see very plainly vestiges of the old Athabasca trail winding through the trees to emerge at the eastern edge of the south pond. The voyageurs, backs bent under their heavy packs, are no more. Only their trail, beaten deep into the forest floor, remains as lasting reminder of their passage.

Soon we came to the brink of a forest-covered precipice. The ground below just dropped away. From the lip of this "hanging valley," Pacific Creek plunged down in its rocky bed to the river bottom of the Wood River 2,000 feet below. We realized we were at the top of the Grand Côte—that most dreaded part of the route over the Athabasca Pass. Whether ascending, if eastbound, or descending, if westbound, the Grand Côte was a formidable challenge. Tremendous obstacle as it was, it was routinely overcome by the tough people who engaged in the fur trade.

We followed the Wood River to its mouth, but now no longer does it empty into the Columbia River. Now its waters are swallowed up in the mighty man-made Kinbasket Lake, the result of the construction of the Mica Dam, the last in a series of dams built to harvest the power provided by the Columbia River.

Today, in addition to the confluence of the Wood River with the Columbia, the junction of Canoe River that flowed into the Columbia from the north near Boat Encampment, located at the Columbia's great north bend and the place of meeting and transfer for the east and westbound brigades before or after crossing the Athabasca Pass, is likewise gone forever—drowned by the waters of Kinbasket Lake.

These sites of such importance in the history of the fur trade have now vanished, victims of twentieth-century developments. Hopefully, however, the Athabasca Pass and its three small tarns on top of the Continental Divide will remain inviolate, safe from obliteration or destruction by man's intrusive activities, and continue to survive as visible reminders of a past both colorful and significant.

Rock Depot

Not too many years after the Hudson's Bay Company began to extend its operations inland from its posts on Hudson's Bay, the advantage of reaching the Indians in their camps, outfitting them (that is, giving them "debt," thereby assuring their take of furs), and getting them off into the bush to begin trapping before the arrival of the Nor'Westers (their major competitors) was soon realized.

A plan to shorten the time required for the passage of the Hayes River, the principal route from York Factory to Lake Winnipeg, was devised by Joseph Colen, chief factor of York Factory, and William Tomison, chief of inland posts. Basically, it called for boats to supplement canoes and for a storage-transfer depot near the last downstream rapid. For the last 120 miles of its course to York Factory on the bay the Hayes River flowed freely, unimpeded by any obstacle. Boats could be used on this stretch. Upriver, beyond this point where the river consists of a nearly continuous series of rapids and falls, it would be necessary to resort to canoes. A warehouse depot to handle the transfer of cargo from boats to canoes would be erected.

To put the plan into effect, Colen in 1794 ordered the erection of the depot. It was located on a point of flat land between White Mud Creek to the south and its junction with the Hayes River to the west. It was a short distance above the rough and boiling waters of Rock Rapids, the last obstruction in the river downstream. From the very first year, the plan proved to be practical and a time-saver. Colen brought outfits for the ensuing year upriver in boats from York Factory to Rock Depot. There he received the furs that Tomison had brought down in canoes from the interior. Their cargoes were exchanged, and Tomison was able to speed back to the interior without the necessity of making the trip to York Factory and return. A week's time was saved—an advantage of considerable importance in the race to reach the Indians before the competition.

The establishment of Rock Depot resulted in a saving not only of time but also of money by requiring less men and, in particular, fewer of the highly skilled and costly bow and stern men who handled the canoes. By 1798 Colen had his Hayes River transport system so well organized that thirty-two men at low wages were able to carry in four boats the cargo that had formerly required the labor of seventy-two highly paid men. Boats had even been successfully used to bring furs from the upper settlements of the Saskatchewan River, across the northern end of Lake Winnipeg, and up the Hayes River system as far as the headwaters of Trout River, a distance of some twelve hundred miles. Rock Depot remained an important and integral link in this increasingly efficient system of transportation. It also served as a rendezvous where company men frequently met in informal council.

In September of 1811 the first of several contingents of people from Scotland arrived at York Factory en route via the Hayes River to their new settlement at the Forks of the Red and Assiniboine rivers. It was almost immediately apparent to Lord Selkirk, founder and promoter of the colony, and to Miles Macdonell, his first Governor, that in order for the new venture to succeed, the river transportation system to and from Hudson's Bay had to be greatly improved. Lord Selkirk, a major shareholder of the Hudson's Bay Company, proposed that the portages be improved, way stations be established along the route, a winter road laid out, and a depot for the exclusive use of his Red River colony be established at the Rock. It was vital for the existence of the colony that people and goods be able to move freely and easily to and from the bay. Undoubtedly responding to pressure exerted by Selkirk, the depot for the colony was established at the Rock the following year.

Ever since its establishment, Rock Depot served as the rendezvous where canoes and boats from the Athabasca district and other inland posts met the heavier boats from York Factory, discharged their cargo of furs, and then loaded goods and supplies for the return trip to the interior. The depot was established strictly as a storage and transfer point in the transportation system based on York Factory and never intended to serve as a trading post for the Indians.

When Governor Simpson visited the Rock Depot in 1820, he was very critical of the way in which it operated. As a remedy he proposed the Burntwood River as an alternative to the Hayes. If this were accepted, he thought, "the business may be conducted with about 2/3ds of the people now required, it will entirely supercede the use of Canoes for this District . . . and enable us to introduce European Servants instead of Canadians, which would be a most important advantage."

In May 1821 Simpson submitted to the London Committee his evaluation of Rock Depot. He felt that the facilities there were totally inadequate for the orderly transaction of business and that the officers in charge were forced to work under extremely adverse conditions. They had "no other accommodation than a miserable confined Store where no more than one gang of them can properly work at a time." Furthermore, they were "compelled to make up their writings in Tents, either drenched with Rain or broiling under a vertical Sun, annoyed by Drunken Canadians and tormented by miriads of Musquitoes, Bull and Sand Flies; Books accounts and property scattered about, and ei-

267

ther lost, mislaid or Stolen, so that the affairs get involved in a laby-rinth of confusion." Accordingly, he recommended that the "business of this Department [Athabasca] should in future be conducted at the York Factory instead of the Rock Dépôt." In his opinion, "it will reduce the Expenses materially, the arrangements gone into with system, regularity and one half the trouble . . . ."

In 1821, at the time of the union of the North West Company and Hudson's Bay Company, Nicholas Garry of the Hudson's Bay Company came from England to arrange many of the details necessitated by the new coalition. In his diary covering his trip, he wrote in August of 1821: "At five o'clock we arrived at the Rock Dépôt, found Mr. Thomas Bunn in Charge. This Fort is beautifully situated, on the East side of the Hill [Hayes] River, which is here, about 300 Paces broad. Dwelling House, large Hall, Warehouses, all in excellent Order. Behind the House is a very excellent Garden, Cabbages and Potatoes; small Trout Stream, with Cane Work to catch the Fish. This Post will now be given up and the Goods sent direct from York. (The whole Country may now be sup-plied with Boats. . . .)"

With the establishment of Norway House in 1826, Rock Depot quickly declined in importance. The new post, more centrally located on the trade route, became the depot for the Athabasca brigades; even-tually the company's Northern Department Council meetings were held there instead of at York Factory. As Arthur S. Morton wrote in his *History of the Canadian West to 1870–71,* "Rock House, on Hill River, had rejoiced in its little day, but it was too distant for the dépôt of the outermost Districts."

Our float trip down the Hayes River from Norway House to York Factory gave us the opportunity to reach the site of Rock Depot. Com-fortably carried along in our large rubber raft, we had descended the rapid-filled section of the Hayes (usually called the Hill River in the early days). The rapids and falls over which we slid and plunged with so much ease and only an occasional drenching were formidable barri-ers to the canoe brigades. Many could only be overcome by the labori-ous portaging of cargo and canoe over slippery rocks and through mosquito-infested woods.

After passing the landmark known as Brassy Hill, its 392-foot height rendering it conspicuous against the surrounding flat terrain, and descending five more rapids, we came to White Mud Creek flowing in from the east. Here, at this confluence, Rock Depot had been estab-lished. The tongue of land embraced by the two streams is now over-grown with thick brush and tall spruce trees, although some yards toward the interior there is a more open area, possible evidence of an earlier clearing. Towering over the junction with the Hayes is a steep 100-foot clay bank rising abruptly from the south side of White Mud Creek. A short distance inland, the terrain flattens to the typical spruce-covered muskeg. We followed the creek inland a short way. It was a pleasant stream, its water clear, its depth shallow, and its flow quiet and steady.

As we walked over this spot now reclaimed by trees and brush, it was difficult to imagine that once, nearly two hundred years ago, men lived and worked here; that canoes and boats lined the banks of the two streams; that canoes of goods, provisions, and furs were loaded, unloaded, and stored here. It was rather astonishing to realize that the first marriage ever performed by a Protestant minister in western Canada took place here at this remote post. On September 9, 1820, the Reverend John West married Thomas Bunn, accountant in charge of Rock Depot, and Phoebe Sinclair.

We continued our trip down the Hayes and in less than half an hour arrived at Rock Portage, the last rapid in the river downbound. This was a most scenic spot. Across the smooth glistening ledge of tumbled rocks stretching across the river white cascades of water foamed and raced. On each side of the river, sand hills covered with spruce rose to heights of 150 to 200 feet. This was the rapid that Governor Miles Macdonell of the Red River Colony had said (not very realistically) that although difficult to improve, "a canal of fourteen yards cut through a solid rock behind this point would serve."

We, with much glee and some expert maneuvering by our helmsman at the outboard to avoid getting our rather unwieldy raft wedged between rocks, plunged through a narrow break in the ledge and, drenched with spray, emerged safely in the quiet waters below. We had overcome the last obstacle lying between us and York Factory. As we sped down the Hayes toward the bay, we instinctively knew that the men of the canoe brigades with the toilsome passage of all the rapids behind them must have shared the very same sense of elation that we were now feeling. In a strange way, it forged a bond of kinship between us.

Carlton House

When the Hudson's Bay Company post on the South Saskatchewan 120 miles above the Forks was destroyed by the Gros Ventres in 1794, William Tomison, chief of the company's inland posts, lost no time in building a replacement the following year. This time the post was located downstream from the Forks on the north bank of the river, just below the mouth of Peonan Creek. Built by James Sandison, canoe builder and carpenter, and two men and supplied with one canoeload of goods, Carlton House, as the new post was named, remained in operation for nearly nine years under the management of a series of capable men, such as James Bird, Joseph Howse, and J. P. Pruden.

In 1796 James Bird wrote to William Tomison:

> The Indians of this place have made no fall hunt worth mentioning. I have only traded about 300 beavers since you passed and have but a poor prospect of getting anything considerable this season owing to a scarcity of beaver (of which there is a universal complaint) and such a number of our traders having left this quarter, an account of whose debts I have enclosed, as also to the improvements the Canadian traders have made in the quality of their goods. A few years since, many Indians who from the great quantities of spirituous liquors given them were induced to go to the Canadians Houses, the superiority of our cloth, guns, etc. tempted to trade these articles from us; but they are now as well supplied by the Canadians. I find our guns this year very indifferent both in their locks and stocks, these are in general a dark red, and of course not much fancied by the Indians; our neighbours' guns far surpasses them in appearance.

In February of 1797 Bird complained: "I am sorry to inform you that Trade at this place continues amazingly small, not exceeding 900 MBr." He referred to trading relations between himself and his North West competitor as follows: "The amicable manner in which you & Mr. Shaw carry on the Trade at Edmonton appears enviable, particularly when contrasted with the method of conducting here. Mr. Finlay seems determined to get all the Furrs he possibly can regardless of the expence he may be at in procuring them, the large quantity of Goods he brought here (according to his own Account 150 Pièces), enables & perhaps in some measure urges him to persevere in this plan."

In August of 1801, on orders from William Tomison, Bird closed down Carlton House because of the "great waste of goods there" during the two preceding seasons.

In the fall of 1805, in a renewed attempt to establish a post on the

South Saskatchewan, Carlton House II was built about six miles farther upstream from the location of the earlier fort destroyed by the Indians in 1794. J. P. Pruden and Joseph Howse were the men stationed at this post during the five years of its existence. Daniel Harmon, in charge of the North West Company's South Branch Fort, noted in his journal on September 21, 1805: "Mr. William Smith and myself, together with fifteen labouring men, &c. are to pass the winter here; and a few hundred paces from us, the Hudson Bay people have a fort."

By 1810 both companies decided to abandon the South Saskatchewan and move to the northern branch. Here on a fertile river flat about three miles long by one-quarter mile wide on the south side of the North Saskatchewan, the Hudson's Bay Company built Carlton House III and the North West Company built its Fort La Montée, both forts enclosed within a common stockade.

The advantages of this site were many. Nearby were large stands of poplar and birch, while a few miles downstream spruce and tamarack grew in abundance, thus guaranteeing materials for building and canoe making. Numerous springs provided water, and limestone, an essential item for fort building, was available close by. The extensive prairies to the south were home to vast numbers of buffalo; across the river to the north were the woodlands, home to beaver, mink, and other furbearers. There were even sloughs nearby, a potential source of hay for cattle and horses. Of paramount importance was the forts' location at a well-used ford—the Great Crossing Place over the North Saskatchewan. Here was the junction of several of the major fur trade routes: one going north toward Green Lake and Île à la Crosse, another heading west to Fort Edmonton.

However, there was one serious drawback that could not be overlooked. The forts' location on the south side of the river made them particularly vulnerable to assault by hostile Indians. The threat of attack, especially by the Gros Ventres and the Crees, was always present in the minds of the traders and their men. Because of this and for better protection, the two posts submerged their mutual rivalry and distrust sufficiently to operate within a common palisade, built of stout logs, with bastions at the corners and thick gates.

Although the North West post had only twelve men, compared to the twenty-four for Hudson's Bay Company's Carlton House, it managed to capture 50 percent more of the trade. By 1816 the rivalry between the two posts had intensified so greatly that the sharing of one enclosure became impossible. The Nor'Westers moved out. Eventually, two years later, they established their La Montée post II on the north bank of the Saskatchewan about three miles upstream from Carlton.

During this period the defenses of Carlton were strengthened with the construction of two watchtowers and a new stockade.

For most of the first twenty-five years of its existence, Carlton House III was under the efficient management of J. P. Pruden, who was promoted to chief trader in 1821. It was his responsibility not only to carry on a profitable trade with the Indians but also to make sure that the vast quantity of pemmican needed to provision the northern brigades was obtained and shipped on schedule to the warehouses of Cumberland and Norway House.

The planting and cultivation of a large garden were major activities. Routine tasks of cutting and hauling firewood, harvesting hay for the fort's livestock, and constant repairing of buildings and stockade also kept the men busy. In addition, there was always work for the skilled craftsmen of the fort such as the tailor, blacksmith, cooper, and carpenter.

It was obvious after the union of 1821 that only one trading post in the area was needed. Carlton House was the one chosen to be retained. Accordingly, the North West's La Montée was dismantled and whatever could be salvaged of its building materials was rafted downriver to help in the enlargement and strengthening of Carlton House. For the next several years trading flourished, and by 1826 the volume of furs traded at Carlton House and in the Saskatchewan district was second only to that of the Athabasca district. Increasingly, however, Carlton House became more important as a major supplier of pemmican rather than as a source of fur.

Attacks by Indians remained a constant threat to the fort. On October 10, 1824, Chief Factor John Stuart wrote in his journal:

About 3 P.M. a large war party of Plain Indians made their appearance on the Hill behind the Fort, at first I could scarcely believe them to be enemies but nevertheless ordered the Gates to be shut and I was not long left in doubt they killed a poor old woman not above three hundred yards from the pickets on the alarm being given and the Gates Shut I got the people armed as quick as possible and the Bastions manned. But there was such a bustle in the Fort what between the Cree men, women and children that I could not readily be understood consequently was not much obeyed however with the assistance of Mr. Harriott and Bird who were quite cool and assiduous order was restored and as the war party was approaching I ordered the Swivels to be fired from the upper Bastion but was not perfectly understood and it was the Blunderbusses that was fired however it had much the same effect. The war party scampered off and were soon out of sight we kept a strict watch all night but saw nothing more of them and it was a mercy they did not surprise us.

By 1835, the fort buildings had fallen into such a state of disrepair that they were abandoned and a totally new fort complex was built about two hundred yards to the west. The new stockade was laid out in the form of a hexagon rather than the more traditional rectangle. It had four bastions and a lookout tower over the main gate facing the river. Within the twenty-five-foot-high walls the "Big House," men's house, store, Indian house, and provision store enclosed an inner courtyard. Beyond this were the stable and blacksmith shop.

Paul Kane, the artist, visited Carlton House in 1846. He wrote in his diary on September 7:

> The country in the vicinity of Carlton, which is situated between the wooded country and the other plains, varies much from that through which we had been travelling. Instead of dense masses of unbroken forest, it presents more the appearance of a park; the gently undulating plains being dotted here and there with clumps of small trees. The banks of the river rise to the height of 150 or 200 feet in smooth rolling hills covered with verdure. The fort, which is situated about a quarter of a mile back from the river, is enclosed with wooden pickets, and is fortified with blunderbusses on swivels mounted in the bastion. This fort is in greater danger from the Blackfeet than any of the Company's establishments, being feebly manned and not capable of offering much resistance to an attack. Their horses have frequently been driven off without the inmates of the fort daring to leave it for their rescue. The buffaloes are here abundant, as is evident from the immense accumulation of their bones which strew the plains in every direction.

After the passage of another twenty years, the ravages caused by the use of green timber in the fort's construction, coupled with inadequate maintenance, had reduced the post once again to a condition of disrepair. So between 1855 and 1858 a replacement fort was erected only a few yards east of the original 1810 site. The Earl of Southesk, who visited the post in 1859, when Richard Hardisty was the chief trader in charge, described the fort as "a large palisaded enclosure, with square bastions at each of the four corners; most of the houses tolerably good, but some not quite finished. It stood about a quarter of a mile from the river, at the foot of a bank, which had been cleared of wood immediately behind the buildings."

For the next twenty years Carlton House flourished. Its strategic location by the well-used ford across the river, as well as at the crossroads of major trails leading in all directions, made it an important distribution and provisioning center in the Hudson's Bay Company's transport system. The brigades of canoes and boats following the river, the Red River carts creaking across the plains, the paddle-wheel steamboats battling the river current and shifting sandbars—all stopped at Carlton House. Its warehouses received and stored goods for further transshipment to outlying posts. Here a large remuda of oxen and horses was maintained and carts were available. From this bustling *entrepôt* the outfits for the company's distant forts were packed and forwarded.

Carlton House became a mecca for travelers of all kinds and, with traditional company courtesy, offered hospitality to all. In addition to the Earl of Southesk, Dr. Walter Cheadle and Viscount Milton of England were among the visitors there. During these years Carlton was the meeting point for the company's winter mail express. Men carrying mail and dispatches from the far-off posts in the Saskatchewan, Athabasca, and Mackenzie districts to the north and west and men from the Red River colony in the east met here and exchanged mail pouches before racing back to their own districts before spring breakups made travel impossible.

Carlton House did not escape the devastating epidemic of smallpox that spread over the prairies in 1869. Records show that thirty-two of the sixty people living in the fort died of the disease. Captain William Butler, in the course of his journey from Upper Fort Garry on the Red River to Edmonton House for the purpose of carrying medicines and vaccines to all the trading posts and missions that he could reach, arrived at Carlton House in early November of 1870. He commented:

Another hour's ride brought us to a high bank, at the base of which lay the North Saskatchewan. In the low ground adjoining the river stood Carlton House, a large square enclosure, the wooden walls of which were more than twenty feet in height. Within these palisades some dozen or more houses stood crowded together. Close by, to the right, many snow-covered mounds with a few rough wooden crosses above them marked the spot where, only four weeks before, the last victim of the epidemic had been laid. On the very spot where I stood looking at this scene, a Blackfoot Indian, three years earlier, had stolen out from a thicket, fired at, and grievously wounded the Hudson Bay officer belonging to the fort, and now close to the same spot a small cross marked that officer's last resting place. Strange fate! He had escaped the Blackfoot's bullet only to be the first to succumb to the deadly epidemic. I cannot say that Carlton was at all a lively place of sojourn. Its natural gloom was considerably deepened by the events of the last few months, and the whole place seemed to have received the stamp of death upon it. To add to the general depression, provisions were by no means abundant, the few Indians that had come in from the plains brought the same tidings of unsuccessful chase—for the buffalo were 'far out' on the great prairie, and that phrase 'far out,' applied to buffalo, means starvation in the North-west.

About 1875 Carlton House was enlarged to accommodate a small detachment of the North West Mounted Police, who were stationed there for a short time to negotiate Treaty Six with the Indians. Samuel B. Steele of the police force, who spent a week at Carlton House in 1874 en route to his posting at Fort Saskatchewan, wrote: "Here perfect discipline existed. The offices and stores were neat, and over each door was painted in French and English the names of the store and office together with the class of goods in the buildings." As a military man, Steele would have noticed the defensive features of the fort such as the bastions and the firing gallery on the inside of the twenty-foot-high palisade. He would also have spotted the fort's weakness: the result of its location on the river bottom flat, which exposed it to enemy fire from the higher benchland in the immediate rear.

The appearance of paddle wheels on the Saskatchewan in 1874 made Carlton House such an easily accessible midway point on the river that for the next eight years the annual meetings of the Hudson's Bay Company's Northern Council were held there.

As had happened so many times before, the fort was showing unmistakable signs of deterioration. Much of the protecting palisade had rotted away and had not been replaced; only the north section built during the fort's enlargement in 1875 remained standing. The twenty-three buildings once safeguarded by a sturdy stockade were now completely exposed and defenseless. In the 1870s, in what proved to be a rather premature feeling of security, Chief Factor Lawrence Clarke's house as well as that of the Indian agent, in addition to a blacksmith's shop and stables, were built outside the fort walls. By 1880 the fort was maintained primarily as a storage place for grain, flour, and other bulky goods and as the center for payments made to the Indians as mandated by Treaty Six.

Riel's Rebellion erupted in 1885. The defeat at nearby Duck Lake of the small force of North West Mounted Police from Carlton House threatened the security of the fort. Recognizing the utter futility of trying to defend the post in its dilapidated and defenseless condition, the decision was made to abandon the fort and retreat to Prince Albert. True to his responsibility, Chief Factor Lawrence Clarke hastily began taking inventory of the company's goods as they were loaded into sleighs for the trip to Prince Albert. Much had to be left behind because of lack of room in the sleighs. Bags of flour were split open, their contents dumped onto the ground in the fort's courtyard and drenched with coal oil to render the flour useless.

Meanwhile, some of the men were making hay mattresses to put in the sleighs that were to carry the wounded brought back from Duck Lake. The inevitable happened. The straw accidentally caught fire from a nearby old wood-burning stove, and in moments the building was ablaze and the fire spreading uncontrollably to other structures. What escaped destruction by fire was pillaged and destroyed by the Indians and Métis the next day. This was the end of Carlton House. It was never rebuilt by the Hudson's Bay Company.

Carlton House, in contrast to many of the fur trade post locations that we sought, was easy to find. A modern paved highway and a sufficient number of directional signs led us to the site. When we came to the top of the upper bench forming the south wall of the Saskatchewan River valley we left our vehicle, so we could more fully enjoy the full scope of the panoramic view spread below. Beside us on an elevated grass-covered knoll stood a gigantic wooden cross—most impressive in its stark simplicity. It is a collective memorial to the many who had perished and been buried at the fort. Below on the open river bottom plain lay Carlton House, the rooftops of its buildings barely showing above the high walls of the palisade, its four bastions prominently visible. To the north about four hundred yards beyond the clearing in which the fort is located and which is broken only with scattered small groves of trees flows the broad Saskatchewan. Woods and grass-filled open areas cover the gentle hills that rise some distance back on each side of the river.

Leading down to the fort below from where we stood is the old roadway of the Carlton Trail. Once rutted and muddy (or dusty, depending upon the season of the year), traveled by horse, oxen, cart, and moccasined feet of Indians and whites alike, it is now paved (to the dismay of sentimentalists like ourselves) and traversed by automobiles, motor homes, motorcycles, and even the boots of a few hikers.

As part of a centennial project in 1967, the province of Saskatchewan undertook the reconstruction of the 1875 Carlton House. Much painstaking archaeological work was undertaken at the site to ensure the authenticity of the reconstructed fort complex. Four of the fort's buildings and the enclosing stockade with bastions and interior firing gallery have been reconstructed. The foundation outlines of other buildings have been delineated with narrow cement bands to show their original shape and location. In the open grassed enclosure are a Red River wooden cart and a massive lever-type wooden fur press.

Within the stores building is an array of the usual items of trade.

At the suggestion of the jovial clerk in charge, we entered into the spirit of the period and agreed to model the dress of a typical Métis couple, complete with shawl and long full skirt, tall hat, capote, *ceinture fléchée,* and the ever-present clay pipe, for the benefit of spectators gathered outside. We posed, grinning a bit self-consciously; cameras clicked and flashbulbs popped. Everyone was happy—the tourists had an amusing snapshot; we had a brief moment in the limelight!

Today the traders, the Indians, the canoemen, the carters, the steamboat captains—all those whose activities centered around the fort—have long since vanished. Peace and quiet have replaced noise and busy movement. Fortunately for those of us who like to make visits into the past, the panorama of wooded hills and fields rising above the smoothly flowing river and the palisaded fort standing alone in the middle of the clearing remains unchanged from 150 years ago, when Carlton House was one of the most important and active posts on the Saskatchewan.

Setting Lake House

Setting Lake House was one of the many short-term trading posts that the Hudson's Bay Company set up during the 1790s in the so-called *Le Pays du Rat* (i.e., muskrat country). This was a vast area extending westward from Hudson Bay through which flowed the mighty river systems of the Churchill, the Burntwood, the Grass, and the Nelson. It was country abounding in fine furs and affording excellent hunting and fishing.

The Hudson's Bay Company's first purpose was, of course, as always, to counter competition from the North West Company, who were threatening to intercept the Indians on their way to the company's forts on Hudson Bay. They proposed to do this by establishing and maintaining trading posts in the heartland of the Cree Indians, who were long accustomed to trading with the company's York Factory post on the west shore of Hudson Bay.

To reach the greatest number of natives, the company followed a policy of operating a post for only one or two seasons at one location before moving it to another part of the area. For example, small trading posts were established in the region as follows: 1791–93: Wintering Lake; 1792–93: Sipiwesk Lake; 1793–94: Wekusko Lake; 1794–95: Reed Lake; 1795–96: Setting Lake (upper end); 1796–97: Split Lake; 1798–99: Setting Lake (lower end). These spots were all provisioned from York Factory and, since they were within a relatively short distance from the depot, could be supplied with goods at a correspondingly lower rate. More important, the traders could reach the Indians ahead of their North West competitors. This enabled them to give the Indians their debt—i.e., to outfit them for the season's trapping on credit.

As Sir Alexander Mackenzie wrote regarding trading in the muskrat country before 1801, "The traders from Canada succeeded for several years in getting the largest proportion of [Indians'] furs till the year 1793, when the servants of that company [Hudson's Bay] thought proper to send people amongst them, (and why they did not do it before is best known to themselves) for the purpose of trade—From the short distance they had to come, and the quantity of goods they supplied, the trade has, in great measure, reverted to them, as the merchants from Canada could not meet them upon equal terms."

Setting Lake Post was located at the tip end of a small peninsula at the northwest corner of Setting Lake. After one year of operation (1795–96), it was abandoned in favor of a new location on Split Lake farther east, where the waters of the Burntwood, Grass, and Nelson rivers converged. To prevent its being used by the Nor'Westers, the Hudson's Bay trader burned the post to the ground before moving on to his new location.

We learned of the existence of Setting Lake Post by lucky chance. We were eating breakfast in the small dining room of the Kelsey Trail Hotel in Flin Flon on the day we were scheduled to fly to the Frog Portage on the Churchill River. In keeping with the friendliness and lack of formality that characterize the north country, we were soon chatting with the other people at the nearby tables. When we happened to mention our forthcoming flight and our ongoing search for the sites of early fur trading posts, one of our listeners, J. F. Dent of Manitoba Hydro, asked if we were aware of the existence of the remains of a post on Setting Lake. We replied that this post was unknown to us, but that we most certainly would be much interested in getting any information about it. Mr. Dent kindly promised to send us pictures of the site. A year later, he fulfilled his promise, sending us two excellent pictures of the Setting Lake Post site along with a summary of the facts regarding the post as compiled by an archaeologist working at the site for the province of Manitoba. We are most grateful for this help, which enables us to include Setting Lake post in our roster of fur trade sites of *Le Pays d'en Haut* revisited.

Bolsover House

The Hudson's Bay Company, as a part of its continuing effort to oppose the Nor'Westers on each and every lake on which the latter had established a trading post, sent their trusted employee Peter Fidler, competent surveyor and trader, to the Beaver River to set up a trading fort there to meet the competition from the North West Company. From the very beginning of his trip from Cumberland House, Fidler experienced all kinds of harassment from the Nor'Westers in their attempts to hinder or even prevent his progress up the Beaver River to Meadow Lake, where he planned to build his post. On August 30, 1799, he reached the mouth of Meadow Lake River. This tiny stream that flowed from Meadow Lake to the Beaver River was "so very crooked" and narrow that Fidler almost despaired of being able to navigate it successfully. Finally he reached Meadow Lake, which was so shallow and swampy for his heavily laden canoes that he had to proceed *demi-chargé* (i.e., carry only half his cargo at one time). This, of course, necessitated covering the same distance twice in order to transport his full cargo. Well aware of the far-reaching influence of the North West Company, in order to forestall any desertion by his Indian guides instigated by the Nor'Westers, as Fidler recorded in his journal, he "gave the pilot 3 quart keg of liquor to hunt well and induce the others to do so."

A few days later Fidler began his search for a site suitable for his trading post. Describing his attempt, Fidler wrote: "Mr. Isham, myself with 4 men in a large canoe went nearly all around the lake but could not find a convenient place for both wood and water—went to the very bottom of the lake and close along the south east side—at 10-1/2 a.m. we returned and embarked the goods in the canoes and went up the river about half a mile and carried everything 1120 yards across a fine plain on the north side the head of the river to a few pines where we shall build as it is the best place we have as yet seen—the worst inconvenience is the great distance to fetch water."

Fidler wasted no time in beginning construction of his post, which he named Bolsover House in honor of his hometown in England. Aided by Hugh Sabeston, the skilled carpenter and boat builder, progress was rapid. When J. P. Pruden arrived on September 22, he found that the store building had been completed and that Sabeston and seven men were hard at work constructing a house.

Meadow Lake had been chosen as the location for a fur trading post on the advice of Indian guides, who assured Fidler that ample provisions and furs could be obtained there. The post's location so far from both water and wood for building and heating continued to be a major drawback. Moreover, the fur returns proved very disappointing, amounting to only 190 Made Beaver for the first season (1799–1800), by far the lowest returns for any of the interior posts under James Bird's supervision. Accordingly, in 1801 the decision was made to close Bolsover House and transfer its remaining inventory of goods to nearby Green Lake Post.

Today there is little to perpetuate the memory of Peter Fidler and his Bolsover House. In the heart of Meadow Lake in a small park is a simple, unadorned monument of stone blocks bearing the traditional bronze plaque of the Historic Sites and Monuments Board of Canada, which cites Peter Fidler's accomplishments as a surveyor and fur trader in the service of the Honorable Hudson's Bay Company. There are no words of praise on this plaque, but if ever a man deserved such praise because of his long and faithful service, often under conditions of extreme hardship, his unfailing loyalty to his employer, and his major achievements as a surveyor, it is Peter Fidler. We suggest that the inscription: "Well done, thou good and faithful servant" would be appropriate.

Of the short-lived Bolsover House erected on a small stream a short distance above its entry into Meadow Lake there is no trace. Indeed, its actual site has not been precisely determined.

Fort de l'Isle

After the neighboring forts of the North West Company's Fort George and the Hudson's Bay Company's Buckingham House had been in operation about eight years—the normal life of the average fur fort—the two companies decided in 1800 that it was time to move their respective establishments some twenty miles farther up the Saskatchewan River in order to reach areas that had not as yet been trapped out of furs.

The site chosen was an island that would provide a measure of protection from enemy attacks, and the two companies lost no time in implementing their decision. Henry Hallett was responsible for the construction of Island House, the Hudson's Bay Company's post. It consisted of a twenty-four-foot-by-sixteen-foot storehouse and a forty-six-foot-by-twenty-three-foot dwelling that were completed by November 12, when thick ice was forming on the Saskatchewan. The enclosure of the buildings with a stockade had to wait until the following spring, when the river opened up and logs could be obtained and floated down from farther upstream.

The building of the North West Company's new fort, named Fort de l'Isle, was no less rapid. François Decoigne, whom John McDonald of Garth referred to as "a clever young man," was sent down from Fort Augustus to Fort Island, where he, again according to John McDonald, "made some progress building." By fall, when Duncan McGillivray and James Hughes returned from the North West Company's headquarters at Fort Kaministiquia with the year's supply of goods, Decoigne had the "stores ready for the goods; the men had to put up their own houses, six to a mess."

John McDonald of Garth was in charge of Fort de l'Isle for the first two years of the post's existence. He referred in his *Autobiographical Notes* to the three-way competition that existed on Fort Island: "We had now a strong, fresh opposition, with Sir Alexander Mackenzie at their head, from Forsyth, Richardson and Company. A Mr. de Rocheblave for the new Company [i.e., the XY Company], a gentleman of family, on one side and the Hudson Bay Fort on the other; I was thus placed between two fires."

In 1802 a fatal shooting occurred involving men from the North West and XY posts on Fort Island. The Nor'Wester James King left to pick up furs from Indians in payment of their debts to his company. Lamothe, a young clerk from the neighboring XY post, also left for the same purpose. Before reaching the Indian camp about five days' march away, they had mutually agreed to respect each other's claim to the furs due their respective companies. However, after King had picked up his furs from Indians indebted to the North West Company, he entered the lodge where Lamothe was and tried to browbeat him into giving up the furs that he had gathered on behalf of his company. Lamothe steadfastly refused to be frightened into doing this. Angry words were exchanged. King attempted to seize the furs, Lamothe fired his pistol, and King fell dead.

This deed of violence was the catalyst that resulted in the enactment of the Canada Jurisdiction Act of 1803, which provided that "all offenses committed within any of the Indian Territories—not within the limits of either of the Provinces of Upper or Lower Canada or of the Hudson's Bay's Chartered Territory—shall be tried in the same manner and subject to the same punishment as if the same had been committed within the Province of Lower or Upper Canada."

As for Lamothe, a Grand Jury brought in a true bill against him, and he came to Montreal ready to stand trial. However, to avoid a lengthy stay in jail while the matter of determining whether the Canadian courts had jurisdiction in his case was resolved, Lamothe simply returned to the Upper Country, thus effectively placing himself beyond the reach of the law.

Fur returns for the Hudson's Bay Company's Island House were 1,208 Made Beaver for 1800–1801 and 1,071 Made Beaver along with eleven bags of pemmican for the following year. The trading posts on Fort Island were occupied for only a few years before being abandoned in favor of the increasingly important Fort Augustus and Edmonton House farther upstream.

David Thompson's narrative of his travels referred to the island as "Isle of Scotland, North-West Company, 1800 and 1801," but eight years later (in 1808) as he paddled by he called it "Old Island Fort," which implied it was no longer in operation.

When we started our search to find Fort de l'Isle, we knew only that it was located on an island in the North Saskatchewan River in the vicinity of Myrnam. That small town was easily reached, and as was our custom, we sought the local gas station not only to "fill 'er up" (our motor home *always* needed gas) but also to seek information that would help us in our quest. To our surprised delight, we hit the jackpot. R. Tkachuk, a young man who happened to be standing by the gas pump, heard our inquiries regarding Fort de l'Isle. He not only knew where the fort had been located; he also promised to send us a picture of the provincial marker that had been erected on the site. He said he would have to wait until the river was frozen, so he could snowshoe across to the island. He told us further that if we drove north out of Myrnam a few miles we could see the western end of Fort Island from the highway bridge crossing the North Saskatchewan. This we did, and with the aid of our telephoto lens we were able to secure some photos showing the head of the island in the far distance. Incidentally, our pictures captured the amazing sight of hundreds of eave swallows flying over the river from their densely packed mud nests built under the bridge in pursuit of insects. And in due time we received the Fort de l'Isle picture as promised.

Four years later, in 1988, we were back at Myrnam. This time we were equipped with an inflatable rubber raft that we proposed to use to reach the island in order to obtain closer and more satisfactory pictures of the general area. Before inflating and launching our raft at the foot of the embankment close to the highway bridge, we noticed across the river a narrow dirt road winding along the river on the north side. We decided to follow this old road toward the east as far as we could, realizing it would bring us closer to the island and thus cut down the distance we would have to navigate in our raft.

It was a wise decision in many ways. First, it led us right opposite the western end of the island before ending in a homesteader's farmyard. Second, it allowed us to meet Nora Wyman and her young son, Thomas, owners of the homestead. We became so engrossed in our conversation with them that we nearly forgot our own objective.

In order to build up their ranch and put it on a sound "paid-up" basis, Mrs. Wyman's husband was working in the highly paid logging business in British Columbia, leaving her, aided by her son and daughter, to run the ranch in his absence. This involved rearing and training horses, keeping cattle, goats, and chickens, and planting and harvesting crops—quite a formidable challenge, but one that Mrs. Wyman seemed more than able to meet. Well-placed bullet holes in the car radiator of would-be poachers, previously warned, gave ample evidence of her resolute spirit.

Mrs. Wyman's mother was the third white child to be born in the North West Territories, while her father was the medical doctor who accompanied "Wop" May in the famous aerial search for Albert Johnson, the "Mad Trapper" of Aklavik. With such a background, it was no wonder that Nora Wyman was able to rear two children while coping successfully with the hardships of living in an isolated area on a ranch that was only slowly and laboriously being created out of the "bush." To us, she exemplified the true pioneer, and we felt privileged to have had the opportunity of meeting and talking to her.

As soon as we had explained our purpose in following the road leading to their ranch, Mrs. Wyman gave us permission to go through her gates, which would enable us to walk along the north shore of the river opposite the entire length of Fort Island. Both she and her son dissuaded us from using our raft to cross over to the island, pointing out that our small outboard motor was not sufficiently powerful to combat the strong current of the river.

We were reluctant to end our visit, but the sun was getting low in the west, and we had pictures to take and miles yet to travel. The walk along the riverbank brightened with the yellow and purple of goldenrod and asters was delightful. We were able to photograph the north side of Fort Island from its western tip to its eastern end. It was, as John McDonald of Garth had said nearly two hundred years ago, "a pretty island." For us, the day had been a complete success.

Jasper House
Henry's House

Jasper House, originally known as Rocky Mountain House, was built about 1800 by François Decoigne and Jasper Hawes of the North West Company. It was located near the mouth of Moose Creek on the northwest shore of a widened section of the Athabasca River known as Brûlé Lake. Its principal function was to serve as a convenient way station for brigades crossing the mountains by either the Athabasca or the Yellowhead Pass. It was also maintained as a winter post for the Iroquois who came into the country as hunters and trappers for the company.

Gabriel Franchère on his way east in 1814 described the post in his *Narrative of a Voyage to the Northwest Coast of America:*

> The post of the Rocky Mountains, in English, Rocky Mountain House, is situated on the shore of the little lake—in the midst of a wood, and is surrounded, except on the water side, by steep rocks inhabited only by the mountain sheep and goat. Here is seen in the west the chain of the Rocky Mountains, whose summits are covered with perpetual snow. On the lake side, Le Rocher a Miette—is in full view, of an immense height, and resembles the front of a huge church seen in perspective. The post was under the charge of a Mr. Deçoigne. He does not procure many furs for the Company, which has only established the house as a provision dépôt, with the view of facilitating the passage of the mountains to those of its employees who are repairing to, or returning from, the Columbia.

Three years later, when Ross Cox reached Rocky Mountain House (i.e., Jasper House) on his way east after retiring from the North West Company, he recorded his impression of the post as follows: "This building was a miserable concern of rough logs, with only three apartments, but scrupulously clean inside. An old Clerk, Mr. Jasper Hawes, was in charge, and had under his command two Canadians, two Iroquois, and three hunters."

In 1824, three years after the merger of the Hudson's Bay Company and the North West Company, Governor George Simpson stopped at Jasper House en route to Fort George, at the mouth of the Columbia River. Simpson was not slow in recognizing the problem caused by the presence of a significant number of "freemen" (independent trappers, mostly descendants of the Iroquois brought in by the North West Company) who, under the leadership of Jaco Finlay, a Métis trapper and formerly an interpreter for the North West Company, were engaged in trading with the natives. This was a direct violation of the monopoly rights of the Hudson's Bay Company and as such could not be tolerated or overlooked by sharp-eyed Simpson. He wrote: "I gave them notice that that practise must be discontinued as we should not allow Freemen interfere with and impose on the Natives . . . that no supplies of any description be given to them. These freemen are a pest in this country, having much influence over the Natives which they exert to our disadvantage by inciting them against us, but if such measures as I have recommended . . . are followed up they will soon be quite at our disposal as their very existence depends on us . . . their present independence and high toned importance is very injurious and in my opinion frought with danger to the concern."

By 1825 the main transportation route between Fort Edmonton and forts on the western side of the Rocky Mountains had been established. The ninety-mile land gap between Fort Edmonton on the Saskatchewan and Fort Assiniboine on the Athabasca was crossed by packhorse brigades; then canoes were used from Fort Assiniboine to the head of navigation on the Athabasca at Jasper House. Here canoes were replaced by horses, which carried the brigades over the mountains, either via the Whirlpool River and Athabasca Pass to the Columbia River at Boat Encampment or via the Miette River and the Yellowhead Pass to the Fraser River at Tête Jaune Cache. From these two points, travel was once again by canoe to reach the various posts along the two river systems.

The primary function of Jasper House, both under the North West Company and later under the Hudson's Bay Company, was to serve the needs of the brigades crossing the mountains. Its broad valley afforded excellent forage for the large number of horses required by the brigades. The chief activities at the post centered around the care and surveillance of the large herd of horses, often numbering as high as 350, that roamed at will throughout the valley. Hunting of game, such as mountain goat and sheep, moose, and deer for provisions and food, as well as fishing for the abundant whitefish were full-time occupations. Any trading done with the local Indians was usually for provisions rather than for fur.

Jasper House was a post characterized by its loneliness, frequent scarcity of food, and primitive quarters. Only a handful of people were stationed there. After his 1824 visit to the post, Simpson concluded that there was sufficient work there to warrant the addition of a clerk to assist the trader. Michael Klyne was put in charge of Jasper House in 1825. Five years later he moved the post upstream a few miles to the next widening of the river, known as Jasper Lake, where it remained until its final abandonment fifty-four years later. Klyne was described by Alexander Ross as "a jolly old fellow, with a large family."

Klyne was followed as master of Jasper House by Colin Fraser, a young man brought over from Scotland by George Simpson to serve as his piper. Fraser, the piper-turned-trader, remained at this post for fourteen long years. Finally, in response to his request for a transfer from Jasper House, where he had "been now fourteen years and going about every summer through a very rough country with a large family," Simpson sent Fraser to take charge of Fort Assiniboine farther downstream on the Athabasca River.

Paul Kane, the eminent Canadian artist, described his brief stay at Jasper House in November of 1846 in the account he wrote of his journey in the west:

> Jasper's House consists of only three miserable log huts. The dwelling-house is composed of two rooms, of about fourteen or fifteen feet square each. One of them is used by all comers and goers: Indians, voyageurs, and traders, men, women, and children being huddled together indiscriminately; the other room being devoted to the exclusive occupation of Colin and his family, consisting of a Cree squaw, and nine interesting half-breed children. One of the other huts is used for storing provisions in, when they can get any, and the other I should have thought a dog kennel had I seen many of the canine species about. This post is only kept up for the purpose of supplying horses to parties crossing the mountains.

In the mid-1850s game practically disappeared from the valley, and starvation threatened the very existence of the post. Not infrequently men were forced to depend on horse meat for survival. In an effort to encourage wild game to repopulate the valley, Simpson issued an order prohibiting any hunting by the freemen within thirty-five miles of the post.

By 1857 the decision was made to close Jasper House. Accordingly, the horses were rounded up and driven to Fort Edmonton to join the large herd maintained at that post. However, a year later it was reopened with Henry J. Moberly in charge. He had convinced Chief Factor W. J. Christie at Fort Edmonton that the Iroquois would return to the post to trade if it were reestablished. Moberly set off for Jasper House with a forty-horse brigade carrying his outfit, a cook and his wife, a French-Canadian horsekeeper, and six young Iroquois.

Upon his arrival at Jasper House, Moberly found that much work was required to make the post habitable. He wrote that "the dwellings were in a most dilapidated state—mud chimneys down, no windows, and some roofs fallen in—. It looked remote, unfriendly, and slow, and we felt exceedingly melancholy." Under his energetic direction, the buildings were repaired, the Iroquois sent out to hunt for game, and provisions made for the care of the horses, which once again pastured in the valley. At the conclusion of his first year, Moberly was able to bring down to Fort Edmonton eighteen ninety-pound packs of furs, leather, and provisions.

In 1861 Moberly left the service of the Hudson's Bay Company, and Jasper House, after its brief three years of renewed activity, soon became once again a seldom-used post of little importance. Dr. Walter Cheadle passed it by in the summer of 1862 and referred to it in his journal: "The Fort is merely a little house, surrounded with low paling, very clean looking & pretty, on the west side of the river, the ground around covered with wild-flowers." He also added the significant remark: "Short commons at Jasper House in winter."

One of the last references to Jasper's House is in the Reverend George M. Grant's diary covering Sandford Fleming's expedition through Canada in 1872. Grant wrote:

This station is now all but abandoned by the Hudson's Bay Cy. It was formerly of considerable importance, not only from the number of fur-bearing animals around, but because it was the centre of a regular line of communication between Norway House and Edmonton on the one side, and the Columbia District and Fort Vancouver on the other. An agent and three or four men were then stationed at it all the year round. . . . Now there are only two log houses, the largest propped up before and behind with rough shores, as if to prevent it being blown away into the River or back into the Mountain gorges. The houses are untenanted, locked, and shuttered. Twice a year an agent comes up from Edmonton to trade with the Indians of the surrounding country and carry back the furs.

Finally, in 1884, after fifty-four years of existence at its location on the shores of Jasper Lake, "embosomed in the mountains whose peaks are rising round about it on three sides," Jasper House, dilapidated, decayed, and deserted, was closed down and the site permanently abandoned.

The complete success of our visit to the site of Jasper House in 1986 was due to the helpful interest of many people. As the result of a letter written by our friend Donna Bland, formerly of Parks Canada, Churchill, Manitoba, to Mr. D. C. Stewart, then assistant superintendent of Parks Canada, Jasper, Alberta, detailing our interest in fur trade history, Carol Boyle, Parks Canada interpreter, was assigned to take us to the site of Jasper House, where archaeological work under the direction of Rod Pickard from Parks Canada was in progress. We could scarcely believe our good fortune!

We met Carol at the Parks Canada office in Jasper. She is a tiny person packed full of exuberant energy, enthusiasm, and knowledge. After a preliminary briefing in her office, she drove us along a very narrow winding road on the west side of the Athabasca downstream for several miles from the town of Jasper. At road's end we left the car and walked a short distance through scattered spruce to emerge onto a large open field. Spruce trees surrounded the clearing on three sides; on the fourth, to the east, was the swiftly flowing Athabasca River. In the background, to the rear of the evergreen trees, the massive wall of jagged mountain peaks rose high toward the blue sky, forming a truly spectacular backdrop. Across the river, the stupendous massif of Miette Rock, some fifty-eight hundred feet high, rose almost directly from the water's edge.

As we stood and surveyed this scene of grandeur, it was easy to understand why all travelers to Jasper House commented on the beauty of its location. Even George Simpson, usually too prosaically business-like to pay much attention to scenic beauties, was moved to describe the situation of Jasper House as "beautifully Wild & romantic."

At the northern side of the clearing and about 150 yards from the river, the top covering of sod and soil had been removed, exposing the site of the main building that was Jasper House. Hearth and chimney stones as well as some foundation timbers were clearly evident. The young people working at the dig were applying their brushes and trowels with meticulous care and attention. Off to one side was the rocker cradle where all soil removed from the site was carefully screened and sifted in order to capture any item that had escaped detection by the workers. Ron Pickard, project leader, explained that when the site had been completely uncovered and all photos, measurements, and pertinent data obtained it would be restored to its original natural condition by replacing the sod covering, after first protecting the excavated area with a plastic sheeting in the event of future studies being made at the site.

We crisscrossed the clearing, photographing it from every angle, rejoicing in perfect light, blue sky, fleecy clouds. We zoomed in on the details of the excavated building site and even captured the image of a large animal (buffalo?) leg bone protruding from the soil. A short distance away, we stumbled upon a few of the old weather-beaten hand-carved pickets lying on the ground half-hidden by the grass. These pickets had once formed part of the fence that enclosed the small cemetery adjacent to the post. Unfortunately, thoughtless souvenir hunters had long ago removed most of them.

It was with much reluctance that we left this spot—so beautiful and so important in the fur trade—a place where before our very eyes the past was actually revealed, bringing to life the words contained in the traders' journals.

In December of 1810 before leaving his temporary camp near the north end of Brûlé Lake in the Jasper valley, preparatory to his attempt to cross the mountains, David Thompson arranged that during his absence his young assistant, William Henry, clerk in the North West Company, should remain behind to care for the horses. In addition, he was instructed to construct a base camp somewhere in the valley conveniently located to serve the needs of the brigades crossing the mountains. The purpose of this small outpost was to provide storage facilities for provisions and sufficient pasturage for the brigade's horses.

Henry built his outpost on the east bank of the Athabasca, a short distance below the mouth of the Miette River, near the head of navigation by canoe. During the next two years Henry's post served as a support base, shuttling supplies over the mountains to Thompson, who was trading and exploring along the Columbia and Kootenay rivers. Early in September of 1811, Henry sent packhorses loaded with goods over the pass to Thompson at Boat Encampment on the Columbia River.

In May of the following year Thompson left the Columbia River and the great Northwest, crossing the Athabasca Pass for the last time. He described this crossing in his narrative:

At the height of land, where we camped in January last year and where my Men expressed their fears of an avalanche coming on them, and which then appeared to me not likely to happen from the direction I supposed they would take, we found an avalanche had taken place, and the spot on which we then camped was covered with an avalanche, which had here spent its force, in heaps of snow in wild forms round which we walked. On the 11th May, early the Men sent forward arrived with three Horses which relieved us of carrying our baggage, and the same day [we] arrived at the House of Mr. William Henry, who had everything in good order.

With Thompson's departure, William Henry was transferred to a post on the Willamette River in Oregon, and his post remained unoccupied, serving only as a temporary shelter for passing brigades.

Gabriel Franchère passed by Henry's House in 1814 on his way down the Athabasca after crossing the Athabasca Pass. He wrote in his journal: "We all presently arrived at an old house which the traders of the N.W. Company had once constructed, but which had been abandoned for some four or five years. The site of this trading post is the most charming that can be imagined."

After the Hudson's Bay Company took over the posts of the North West Company at the time of their merger in 1821, Henry's House was maintained as a winter establishment serving the brigades crossing the mountains by the Athabasca or Yellowhead Pass.

The morning following our day at the Jasper House site, once again led by our capable guide, Carol Boyle, we visited several areas of possible association with Henry's House. The precise location of this post has not been determined. Latitudinal observations of Thompson and others plus conflicting written descriptions have placed it on the east bank of the Athabasca, from directly opposite the mouth of the Miette to downstream almost as far as the modern Maligne Lake road.

Miette River, just south of the town of Jasper, was our first destination. This is such a pretty stream, its green water clear and sparkling, the rounded stones of its riverbed plainly visible, its banks bordered with spruce and fir. At the early morning hour of our visit, the air rang with the song of veery and northern water thrush. We walked over a trail through scattered pines along the edge of a high sandy ridge that bordered the north side of the river to its confluence with the Athabasca. Directly opposite on the east side was the prominent bald knob known locally as "Old Fort Point."

Here was the very place where the brigades headed for Yellowhead Pass and the posts of New Caledonia, left the Athabasca, and turned west up the Miette River valley. We tried to picture the scene—the heavily laden packhorses and the more spirited mounts ridden by the traders all plunging across the water, plodding along trails, brush snapping noisily under their iron-shod hooves, shouts of the drivers, creak and jangle of saddle and bridle, barking of accompanying dogs. These sights and sounds, long since vanished, can now exist only in our imagination.

We next crossed over to the east side of the Athabasca and followed a trail that led through bottomland woods before gradually climbing up to a ridge through scattered pines that culminated on top of the bare knob of Old Fort Point. From this vantage point, we could look far off in all directions. Directly below us flowed the broad Athabasca, dotted with many islands and gravel bars. Upstream to our left lay spruce forests as well as open areas along the river, known to the traders as *Prairie de la Vache*, where the brigade horses were pastured. Opposite us on the far side of the Athabasca was the mouth of the Miette River. Downstream to our right on the west bank lay the town of Jasper. On the east bank spruce forest extended to the north, broken only by the blue waters of Lac Beauvert, with Jasper Lodge on its shore and several other lakes scarcely visible farther north. Behind us stretched forest-covered foothills and valleys. Our broad panoramic view was confined in all directions by the embrace of a wall of lofty mountains that encircled the entire valley.

This magnificent sight that we were enjoying was ample reward for the rather long and somewhat fatiguing climb required to reach this spot. We also had the satisfaction of knowing that, somewhere within the scope of what we were seeing and photographing was the place where Henry's House had once stood.

Fort Providence

Peter Pond, that intrepid Canadian Pedlar, was the first, in 1778, to crack open the door leading into the rich fur lands of the Athabasca country. From his base on the Athabasca River some thirty miles upstream from Lake Athabasca, he pushed and probed ever farther north following the Slave River to Great Slave Lake.

Alexander Mackenzie, benefiting from Pond's notes and maps, carried on the work of exploration. In 1789 he set out from Fort Chipewyan on the south shore of Lake Athabasca to follow the river flowing out of Great Slave Lake to its ultimate outlet. He was accompanied by Laurent Leroux, a North West Company clerk who was familiar with the natives of Great Slave Lake from previous years of successful trading with them. Mackenzie was desirous of establishing permanent contact with the Yellowknives and so had supplied Leroux with a canoe "that I had equipped for the purpose of trade" and instructed him to "construct a fort on a point of land situated at the mouth of the river flowing out of Lac de la Marte."

So in 1789 near the upper end of the North Arm of Great Slave Lake the post known as Fort Providence was built. On the twenty-third of June of that year Mackenzie described the circumstances in his journal:

> We landed on the main land at half past two in the afternoon at three lodges of Red-Knife Indians, so called from their copper knives. They informed us, that there were many more lodges of their friends at no great distance; and one of the Indians set off to fetch them:
> Wednesday, 24. M. Le Roux purchased of these Indians upwards of eight packs of good beaver and marten skins; and there were not above twelve of them qualified to kill beaver.
> In the afternoon I assembled the Indians, in order to inform them that I should take my departure on the following day; but that people would remain on the spot till their countrymen, whom they had mentioned, should arrive; and that, if they brought a sufficient quantity of skins to make it answer, the Frenchmen [i.e., Le Roux] would return for more goods, with a view to winter here and build a fort, which would be continued as long as they should be found to deserve it. They assured me that it would be a great encouragement to them to have a settlement of ours in their country; and that they should exert themselves to the utmost to kill beaver, as they would then be certain of getting an adequate value for them.

The next day, saluted with "some vollies of small arms which we returned," Mackenzie left to continue on his journey. Two months later, on his return, he rendezvoused with Le Roux at Great Slave Lake. He described their meeting as follows:

> He [Le Roux] had seen no more Indians where I had left him; but had made a voyage to Lac la Marte, where he met eighteen small canoes of the Slave Indians, from whom he obtained five packs of skins, which were principally those of the marten. There were four Beaver Indians among them, who had bartered the greatest part of the above mentioned articles with them, before his arrival. They informed him that their relations had more skins, but that they were afraid to venture with them, though they had been informed that people were to come with goods to barter for them. He gave these people a pair of ice chisels each, and other articles, and sent them away to conduct their friends to the Slave Lake, where he was to remain during the succeeding winter.

Fort Providence remained at this location on the north side of Great Slave Lake for thirty-one years, until it was closed down in 1820.

It was from this post, shortly before it was shut down, that Sir John Franklin left on the first of his exploratory journeys into the Arctic. W. F. Wentzel, the clerk in charge of Fort Providence, experienced both in handling Indians and in the harsh realities of northern travel, was assigned by the North West Company to accompany Franklin's expedition. It is probable that had Wentzel's suggestions been more closely followed, the hardships and deaths Franklin's party experienced might have been avoided.

About 1830 the Hudson's Bay Company moved into the area and established Big Island Fort on Big Island at the western outlet of Great Slave Lake close to the beginning of the Mackenzie River. There, too, in 1858 Father Grollier established the Mission of the Immaculate Heart of Mary for the benefit of the Slavey Indians. However, three years later, this mission on Big Island was abandoned, due to the inconvenience of its location and the potential hazard from storms and floods.

Monsignor Grandin found a more suitable site about forty miles downriver from Big Island. This was a promontory on the right bank of the river, covered with rank growth of grasses indicating fertile soil; forests were nearby, sufficient for fuel and building; at the base of the promontory was a backwater forming a small bay providing safe anchorage for boats; and shoals of fish were visible swimming close to shore. In a fortuitous meeting with Donald Ross, chief Hudson's Bay Company official for the Mackenzie district, Monsignor Grandin was able to seek permission to erect his mission at this spot. His request was granted, and within a short time the Oblate priests began the construction of their mission, which they named *Notre Dame de la Providence*. It soon became the mother house of their most northerly missions and eventually included, besides the church, an orphanage, school, and hospital.

Soon so many Indians settled around the mission that the Hudson's Bay Company closed down its post on Big Island and built a new trading post named Fort Providence next to the mission. To this day it continues in operation, after more than one hundred years, trading furs as well as supplying much of the needs of the local community, still nearly 80 percent Slavey Indian.

Fort Providence was one of several settlements along the Mackenzie River that we were privileged to visit during the course of our week-long trip along the entire length of the river in the 103-foot MS *Norweta.* The first indication that we were nearing Fort Providence was our distant glimpse of the tall steeple of the church silhouetted against the predawn sky. Within a short time, Captain Don Tetreault, genial owner of the ship, had expertly eased the *Norweta* into a landing close to the very backwater inlet noticed by Monsignor Grandin well over one hundred years ago.

The 150-year-old Oblate mission complex of *Notre Dame de la Providence* covers a large area and is closest to the small bay where we moored. Here are the imposing Catholic church whose lofty steeple we had seen from downriver, the large three-story hospital, the orphanage and school operated by the pioneer Grey Nuns, who first came to the mission in 1867. Clustered close by are other buildings, their small-paned windows, pleasing proportions, and simple architectural style evidence of their venerable age and the French origin of their Oblate builders. Extensive fields stretching back from the river reflect the important place that agriculture once had in the life of the mission. At one time a herd of forty cattle was maintained here.

Farther along the road we came to the Hudson's Bay Company tract. One building dating from the early days is still standing, its red-hipped roof and neat white siding clearly identifying it as a company structure. The store itself, however, is now housed in a typical utilitarian metal-sided twentieth-century building.

Next down the road are the Snowshoe Motel, lounge, café, and craft shop. The attraction for us, and indeed for all the other passengers of the *Norweta,* was the excellent display of native crafts in the shop. The Slavey Indians are renowned for their skill in moose-hair tufting, and when we visited the post in 1975 they were almost the only native people who still practiced the art. We were happy to be able to purchase some beautiful examples of this tufting, as well as some lovely pieces of porcupine quill embroidery on caribou skin.

Various government and service buildings are located at the end of the road, while stretching back behind it almost to the woods are the homes of the local Slavey Indian inhabitants. As we retraced our steps over the dirt road on our return to the *Norweta,* we somehow felt close to all the many who had walked on this very road before us—the Oblate missionaries, the selfless and devoted Grey Nuns, the Hudson's Bay Company traders, the trappers, the Slavey Indians, to all of whom Fort Providence, situated so beautifully on the banks of the Mackenzie River, was home. And it seemed most appropriate that on the shore of the river had been placed a large, imposing granite boulder bearing a bronze plaque commemorating Alexander Mackenzie's achievement of traveling the length of the Mackenzie River in 1789.

Fort Lachine

While the Lake Superior forts of Grand Portage and later Fort William served as the great depots for the western end of the long inland water route from Montreal into the interior, from the time of its founding by Sieur de la Salle in 1666 Lachine's strategic location at the head of the turbulent rapids in the St. Lawrence River approximately ten miles west of Montreal made it, for nearly two hundred years, the natural eastern terminal and *entrepôt* for the fur trade to the Northwest—the *pays d'en haut*—used successively by the French, the North West Company, and the Hudson's Bay Company. The King's Post, i.e., the warehouses and stores belonging to the French King, was located here as early as 1671.

Its existence was threatened only once, when, in 1689, the Iroquois in a sudden ferocious attack indiscriminately massacred two-thirds of the inhabitants—men, women, and children—and burned the tiny settlement to the ground. The few survivors bravely rebuilt upon the blackened ashes of their former homes, thus enabling Lachine to escape permanent destruction.

All during the French period when the traders of New France such as La Salle, Le Moyne, Le Ber, and La Vérendrye were active, Lachine remained the major depot. But it was only after the loss of New France to the British in 1759 and the subsequent formation of the Montreal-based North West Company that it achieved its greatest importance.

Goods and provisions imported from England and France by agents on behalf of the traders were received and stockpiled over the winter in Montreal. As soon as the rivers and lakes were free of ice, usually by the middle of May, these goods and supplies were transported by cart over the nine-mile road that bypassed the rapids to the warehouses at Lachine. For the next several weeks Lachine was the scene of intense activity. Cartloads of goods from Montreal arrived daily; clerks were busily checking invoices, bills of lading, equipment lists; voyageurs were impatiently lining up to sign their contracts, which were quickly and duly executed by a notary; the priest was present to give his blessing to the new recruits; arrangements had to be made for the baggage and comfort of the company officials who would be traveling in canoes.

The canoes used to transport the goods from Lachine to the company inland headquarters at the western end of Lake Superior were *canots de maître,* or Montreal canoes. These craft were made completely of sheets of birchbark about one-quarter inch in thickness covering ribs of cedar. They were about thirty-six feet long, with a beam of six feet. They carried a cargo of three tons (which was equivalent to sixty-five ninety-pound bales) plus an additional ton of provisions needed en route, personal gear of crew and passengers, and spare emergency repair equipment. When one was loaded to capacity, freeboard was a mere six inches. The number of voyageurs needed to navigate these canoes varied from six to twelve. An average crew consisted of one *gouvernail* (steersman), one *avant* (bowman), and six to eight *milieux* (middlemen).

The voyageurs who manned these large canoes were commonly referred to as *mangeurs de lard,* or "pork eaters," since their rations included salt pork, a luxury item not available to the crews of the smaller "north canoes" used on the inland lakes west of the Great Lakes. Their basic fare consisted of pemmican.

These big freighter canoes were designed to handle the open waters of the Great Lakes, with their storms, strong winds, and huge waves. As sturdy as these canoes were, they had to be loaded with extreme care. Nicholas Garry recorded the process in some detail:

> The first Part of the Loading is to place 4 Poles or long Sticks at the bottom of the Canoe which run the whole Length. These support the whole weight and prevent the Bottom being injured. The Pièces or Packs which weigh about 90 lbs. each are then placed in the Canoe and with wonderful precision, each Pièce seeming to fit. The most weighty Goods are put at the Bottom, the Provisions, Cooking Utensils, Liquor, &, are likewise put in; at the Bow is placed a large Roll of Bark in case of Accident, with a supply of Wattape, Gum, &. A Canoe takes 60 Pièces and this with the Weight of Provisions, &, bring the Gross weight to about 4-1/2 Tons, an immense freight when this frail Conveyance is considered. When loaded you wonder where the Men are to sit but at the Word of Command they at once place themselves, the Guide at the Bow, the Steersman at the Stern; then the Canoe sinks into the water and the space between the Water and the Gunwale is not 1/2 a Foot.

Finally the last bale had been carried out of the warehouse, checked by the clerk, and loaded into the waiting canoe. The voyageurs take their places, their paddles poised for the first of the thousands of strokes that lay before them, the gentlemen, distinguished by their brushed beaver top hats and frock coats, carefully seat themselves amidships, prepared to endure their cramped position for endless hours, the signal is given, and with shouts of farewell and Godspeed from the throng of friends and relatives on the bank the canoes speed off, red paddles flashing in precise unison. Calm and quiet descend upon the now almost deserted warehouses, not to be broken until the brigades return in August, bringing out the rich harvest of furs from the *pays d'en haut.*

A short distance up the St. Lawrence brings the brigade to the confluence of that river and the Ottawa. There on a point at the head of the island of Montreal once stood the little Church of St. Anne. No canoe passed this spot without the men stopping to make an offering and invoke the saint's help and protection during their voyage. Peter Pond described this custom in his narrative as follows:

> —as you Pass the End of the Island of Montreall to Go in a Small Lake Cald the Lake of the Two Mountains thare Stans a Small Roman Church Aganst a Small Rapead this Church is Dedacateed to St Ann who Protescts all Voigeers heare is a Small Box with a Hole in the top for ye Reseption of a Lettle Muney for the Hole father to Say a Small Mass for those who Put a small Sum in the Box Scars a Voigeer but Stops Hear and Puts in his mite and By that Meanes thay Suppose thay are Protacted while absant the C[h]urch is not Locked But the Munney Box is well Sacured from theaves after the Saremoney of Crossing them Selves and Rapeting a Short Prayer—

The major route of travel from Lachine to the west end of Lake Superior—the gateway to the *pays d'en haut*—used by both French and Nor'Westers followed the Ottawa and Mattawa rivers, crossing over the height of land via a series of small beaver ponds (collectively known as La Vase Portage) to Lake Nipissing and then down the French River to Lake Huron. From this point, the way lay along the north shore of the lake through the North Channel to the formidable rapids of St. Mary's River at Sault Ste. Marie. Once this major obstacle was bypassed, at first by a portage around the rapids, later by means of a small canal and locks built by the North West Company, the remainder of the journey followed the north shore of Lake Superior.

After the union of the North West and Hudson's Bay Companies in 1821, this route gradually lost much of its importance, as Montreal was replaced by the Hudson's Bay Company's depot of York Factory on Hudson Bay as the chief emporium through which trading goods and furs flowed.

In 1833 the Hudson's Bay Company took over the North West Company's stone warehouse that had been built at Lachine thirty years earlier by Alexander Gordon, a former North West Company clerk. Strategically located on the recently constructed canal built to bypass the Lachine Rapids, it continued to be used as their fur trade depot until 1859, when it was purchased by the religious order of the

Sisters of Sainte Anne, who converted it into a residence for their employees.

Even though much of the movement of goods and furs had shifted to York Factory on Hudson Bay, Lachine remained a place of importance, because it became the official residence of George Simpson as well as the Canadian headquarters of the Hudson's Bay Company. The imposing mansion that served this dual purpose was the largest building in the area. It was located directly opposite the company's stone warehouse across the canal and was occupied by Governor Simpson from 1833 until his death in 1860.

Over the next one hundred years links that tied Lachine to the fur trade disappeared. Simpson's mansion was sold by the company and eventually torn down in 1880. The old stone warehouse was converted to residential apartments and became so altered in appearance as to be unrecognizable. Even the canal fell into disuse, replaced by the locks of the St. Lawrence Seaway.

However, in 1977 Parks Canada acquired the venerable stone warehouse, rescuing it from oblivion, and restored it to its original condition. To our great good fortune, we were in Montreal in 1985 for the Fifth North American Fur Trade Conference and were able to attend the colorful ceremonies marking the official dedication of the restored building. We walked from the site of Simpson's mansion across the highway to the footbridge over the canal leading to the warehouse, just as the governor must have done many times. The building now looks as it did when it was completed nearly two hundred years ago. Its appearance is solid, uncluttered, and massive; its lines are straight and true. The impression it gives is one of durability and agelessness.

Inside, the rather dim interior was filled with a great assortment of bales, barrels, and boxes containing the wide variety of goods needed for the fur trade. Stacks of colorful "point" Hudson's Bay blankets, yard goods, guns, traps, rope, clothing, beads of different colors and sizes, and tobacco in various forms were piled on the floor and shelves. This array of goods reflected the enormous diversity of items that the trading companies had to keep in inventory.

The formal dedication ceremony took place outdoors on the lawn extending from the front of the building to the river's edge. At the conclusion of the obligatory speeches and remarks and the unveiling of a Historic Sites and Monuments Board of Canada plaque, the colorful ceremony of the contract signing of the voyageurs took place. At a table set up in front of the warehouse, a notary was seated with the local curé standing close by. One by one, each voyageur, colorfully and appropriately dressed in moccasins, gartered pants, homespun or leather smocks, and *ceinture flêchée,* stepped up to the table, where he made his mark on his contract, thus binding himself to a three- or five-year term as voyageur. As soon as the crew of each canoe had signed, they lined up side by side to receive the blessing bestowed upon them by the black-robed priest. Eventually the signing was completed.

The voyageurs made ready to leave in their brightly decorated canoes, each an authentic replica of a Montreal *canot de maître* or a smaller North canoe. With the voyageurs' unfailing flare for showmanship, their departure was marked with a brief display of precise and complicated paddle handling before, singing lustily, they finally headed west upriver—could it be toward the *pays d'en haut?* With their disappearance, our trip back in time to the adventurous days of the fur trade had ended, but what an unforgettable experience it had been.

Fort Norman

Although a vast new territory had been opened up by Alexander Mackenzie's 1789 journey down the Mackenzie River, the North West Company did not react with any overwhelming enthusiasm to his discovery. Seven years elapsed before the first attempt was made to build a trading fort on the river.

However, during the first five years of the 1800s several forts were established at various points along the waterway. The first of these was Fort Norman, built in 1800 by John Clarke. It occupied a strategic location opposite Great Bear Mountain at the mouth of Great Bear River. During its long years of existence, its location was changed several times. Finally, in 1872, a third move brought it back to its original site at the outlet of Great Bear River and there it remains to this day.

After the union of 1821 Governor George Simpson planned to expand operations in the Mackenzie district. He optimistically assessed the area as one of considerable promise, commenting: "... the Trade [in the district] is however very profitable as it conducted at a triffling expense, few Men and Goods being required, and the Standard very high. Starvation is the only danger to be apprehended in this District."

In a report written in 1821 to the Hudson's Bay Company in London, Simpson wrote: "Great Bears Lake is the most certain place of procuring sustenance, as with the necessary precaution an abundant Stock of Fish may be taken in the Fall, for the Winter consumption, but the Fur bearing animals are not so numerous as in many other parts of the Country, having been hunted for a long series of Years while the North West Coy. had a post there and since it has been withdrawn very few Indians remain. It is however supposed that if we did establish a post there the Natives would return and it is more than probable that the Game is considerably encreased as they have been undisturbed for many years."

Unfortunately, the means to carry out his plans for long-term expansion were seldom available. The annual outfit of goods sent by the company for the Mackenzie district was woefully inadequate, barely sufficient to equip the Indians, with little remaining for the needs of the company's servants. The returns from Fort Norman for 1828, representing trade with about 120 Indians, were sixteen packs of furs valued at between £1,200 and £1,500.

Eight years later Chief Factor Edward Smith, in charge of the Mackenzie River district, wrote to Simpson calling his attention to the fact that because of the lack of trade goods, the company was incurring heavy indebtedness to the natives each year. Unless this situation could be corrected, he feared that this recurring balance due them "will ultimately destroy that confidence the Natives of late years have so unboundedly placed in the Company."

Another difficulty was the periodic disappearances of game throughout the area. These were linked to the now well-known ten-year cycle of rabbit population decline. At these times hunger, even famine, was suffered by all, traders and Indians alike. Winter was long and harsh. Men did not welcome a posting to the Mackenzie district and if once sent there would seldom renew their contract of employment. Although Governor Simpson viewed the Mackenzie as "the most advantageous wintering ground in the Indian Country," realities not only slowed down but frequently prevented the carrying out of his proposed plans for expansion there.

In the spring of 1830 Fort Norman was destroyed by the streams and creeks flooding the countryside and overflowing the banks of the still ice-bound Mackenzie. Its inhabitants narrowly escaped being swept away.

A few years later two Métis from Fort Norman attacked and killed a group of Indians fishing in a nearby lake. Murdock McPherson, chief trader in charge of the Mackenzie district, in a letter written to his friend James Hargrave at York Factory in 1836 described the outrage:

> You will hear I dare say, something this season of a most atrocious murder that was committed this Winter on a small party of the Fort Norman Indians by three of the Company's Servants—Half Breeds—of course, and of course, on account of Women.—In this unfortunate affair 3 men, 1 woman and 7 children were massacred. two young men made their escape and the lives of two Women were spared to crown the villany of the atrocious murderers.—Two of the men (La Graisse & Cadieu) passed the fall fishing at a Lake 3 or 4 days march from the Fort, some Indians were living in their vicinity whom they no doubt often visited & difficulties ensued between them on account of the Women. Our men returned to the Fort and in Decr they were sent accompanied by Jourdin to take home the fish. The poor unfortunat Indians were still in the vicinity of the Fishers and our Bucks paid them this hostile visit. They seized upon the arms of the poor unsuspecting Indians and then had them at discreation.

The natives reacted to these murders by ceasing to come into Fort Norman with their provisions and furs. Trade at the fort fell off sharply. In an effort to placate the Indians and restore normal trading relations, McPherson sent Robert Campbell to the post with a fresh supply of goods and with instructions to apprehend Cadieu, the chief perpetrator of the crime, bring him back to Fort Simpson for trial, and assure the Indians that justice would be done.

The winter of 1841–42 was one of starvation throughout the Mackenzie district. Simpson's policy of strict economy had long since put an end to the importation of luxury food items. The posts were now largely dependent on country food—that is, the game and fish that could be procured locally, supplemented by whatever could be grown in the post gardens. Flour, for example, would no longer be supplied to the forts. In the garden at Fort Norman barley, potatoes, turnips, cabbage, and beets were successfully grown. In many cases it was only these meager post gardens that made the difference between survival and starvation.

Fort Norman was the starting point for several important journeys of exploration, such as the 1837–39 expeditions of P. W. Dease and Thomas Simpson to the west and to the east of the Mackenzie River delta along the coast of the Arctic and Adam McBeath's 1843 westward penetration into the Mackenzie Mountains along the Keele River.

Fort Norman was one of the native settlements we visited during our cruise up the Mackenzie River in the MS *Norweta*. It occupies a strategic location on the east side of the Mackenzie just above the mouth of Great Bear River. The massive mesalike bulk of Great Bear Mountain towers 1,500 feet above this confluence and serves as a prominent landmark visible from all directions for many miles. After reaching the Mackenzie, the blue waters of Great Bear River flow for many miles, keeping their separate identity, before finally merging with the brown waters of the Mackenzie.

Fort Norman is built on a series of three terraces. The first, close to the river level, is a muddy bank occupied only by the many canoes and river skiffs belonging to the local people. Here also is the seasonal floating dock used by large vessels, such as the *Norweta*. On the second terrace, which is about forty feet above the first one, the small cabins of the Slavey Indians are built on one side of the narrow dirt road that runs along the terrace edge for the full length of the village. Behind most of these simple dwellings are tepees made of slender tall poles covered with canvas or skins and used for smoking game and fish. One of the most interesting structures on this road is a small wooden Anglican church made of hand-squared logs, complete with a small belfry in which the original bell still hangs. The windows and door are boarded over, but we managed to find a crack or two through which we could peer into the interior. A few pews, not in orderly rows but haphazardly scattered about, and lots of dust and cobwebs were all we could see.

The bell no longer tolls to call people to come to the little church. The silence is now broken only by the sound of an occasional mouse scurrying over the bare wooden floor and by the rustle of the tall grasses growing outside. Built about 1860, this was the first church erected on the entire river. It has managed to withstand neglect as well as the battering of arctic storms. Perhaps someday it will be restored and once more serve the spiritual needs of the village.

As we walked slowly along the dirt roadway, we noticed several small garden plots in which vigorous potato plants were growing. Apparently, the people were still recognizing the wisdom of Governor George Simpson's 150-year-old dictum about the need to produce locally grown vegetables. There were few native people around. Most of them were off in the bush either at the fishing lakes, at their traplines, or hunting. A few of the hunters had returned after a successful moose hunt, for behind their houses hanging over clotheslines, just like large quilts, were hides that had been scraped and fleshed.

On the third, or upper, terrace, which rose thirty feet above the second one, were the main buildings of the settlement. These faced the river and were strung out along one side of the roadway. They included in 1975 the government staff housing, the modern Bay store, post office, Royal Canadian Mounted Police post, nursing station, schools, and Roman Catholic and Anglican missions.

At the extreme southern end of this upper terrace and extending to the bluff rising from the river are the buildings belonging to the early Hudson's Bay Company's Fort Norman. They are characterized by their neat appearance, characteristic red-hipped roofs with dormers, narrow white clapboard sides, and small-paned windows. Although a surrounding fence and gate are no longer present, the placement of the buildings suggested the customary square and open courtyard layout of the early post.

As we left the dock and continued up the Mackenzie, our last view of Fort Norman was of the white, red-roofed buildings of the Hudson's Bay Company, shining in the late afternoon sunshine, still occupying their commanding position on the bluff above the river, a highly visible reminder of the days when the fur trade was the major activity and the reason for Fort Norman's existence.

Fort of the Forks/Fort Simpson

Seven years after Alexander Mackenzie's 1789 voyage of discovery down the river that now bears his name, the North West Company moved into the area. A post was built on the Mackenzie near the mouth of Trout River by David Livingston. For three years trading was carried on here with considerable success, until Livingston was murdered by Inuit in 1799. This tragedy resulted in the immediate abandonment of his fort.

The next year (1800) John Thomson, clerk in the company, established a trading post farther downstream on the east bank of the Mackenzie at the Camsell Bend opposite the mouth of the North Nahanni River. This post, called Rocky Mountain Fort, operated until about 1804. At that time the North West Company, strengthened by its amalgamation with the short-lived XY Company, expanded and reorganized its operations in the area. It constructed several new trading posts, such as Fort Good Hope and Fort Liard. In addition, it closed down Rocky Mountain Fort and replaced it with a new fort located farther upstream at the junction of the Liard and the Mackenzie rivers.

This new fort, appropriately named Fort of the Forks, was located on an island on the west side of the Mackenzie just below the mouth of the Liard. Its situation was a most beautiful one. In front, the mighty Mackenzie, nearly a mile wide at this point, flowed swiftly toward its ultimate outlet into the Arctic Ocean. Upstream, the far-reaching view stretching beyond the mouth of the Liard bringing down its muddy waters to the clear stream of the Mackenzie, all encompassed by the bordering bluffs, was a majestic one. Benefiting from the advantages of its highly strategic location, Fort of the Forks for the next seventeen years operated not only as the North West Company's principal fur trading post but also as its headquarters for the Mackenzie district.

The merger of 1821 resulted in the takeover of the Nor'Westers' Mackenzie posts. Quickly demonstrating its new position of dominance, the Hudson's Bay Company replaced the abandoned Fort of the Forks with a newly constructed trading post that they called Fort Simpson in honor of Governor George Simpson. The once-familiar name Fort of the Forks, thus discarded, soon became only a fading memory. It is as Fort Simpson that this new post, now a thriving village, continues to exist to this day. Indeed, it has occupied the same site longer than any other settlement on the Mackenzie River.

Chief Factor Edward Smith, capable and well liked, was in charge of Fort Simpson for its first nine years, until 1832. He was succeeded

307

by experienced and seasoned chief factors and chief traders including John Stuart, Murdo McPherson, John Lee Lewes, and John Anderson. In 1882 Julian Camsell, father of one of Canada's most famous geologists, Charles Camsell, became the chief factor at Fort Simpson, where he would serve for eighteen years, until his retirement from the company in 1900.

Fort Simpson served the Hudson's Bay Company as its administrative and distribution center for the Mackenzie district, just as Fort of the Forks had done for the North West Company.

Immediately upon the spring breakup in the Mackenzie River, the brigade left Fort Simpson for the Mackenzie posts to pick up the winter's catch of furs and to deliver the supplies and trading goods for the forthcoming season. It first went down to Fort McPherson on the Peel River and then worked its way back up the Mackenzie, stopping en route at Forts Good Hope and Norman. Once back at Fort Simpson, the brigade continued south to Fort Chipewyan on Lake Athabasca. Here another brigade took over and carried the furs via the Athabasca River as far as Rendezvous Lake on the Methye Portage. At this point the northern brigade met the provision-laden brigade from Norway House on Lake Winnipeg, the furs were exchanged for supplies and trading goods, and each brigade, loaded with their new cargo, quickly commenced their long return journey.

In 1826, at Governor Simpson's direction, canoes were replaced by the larger and more sturdily constructed York boats. These boats not only were safer—an important factor in crossing the open waters of Great Slave Lake and Lake Athabasca—but also had a much greater cargo capacity. For the next sixty years, until the appearance of steamboats in 1888, York boats were the "workhorses" of the Mackenzie waterway. Fort Simpson was their wintering base and the home port for their captains.

Since Fort Simpson functioned as administrative headquarters for the entire Mackenzie district (which by 1856 numbered eleven posts), its staff, in addition to the regular complement of personnel required for trading, included a surgeon, postmaster, and chief accountant.

Likewise, the fort itself, as befitted its status of importance, was constructed on a far more pretentious and permanent scale than what was customary for the usual fur post. The fort buildings were laid out along three sides of a large courtyard, the open end facing the river. In the early days, the entire complex was enclosed with a palisade. Within the square were six major buildings, all of about equal size, rectangular in shape, and constructed of massive hand-squared timbers. On the left side was the storehouse, whose upper story in later years housed an excellent natural history museum amassed under the encouragement of Captain Bell of the steamer *Wrigley*. Next came the provision house where the bales of dried meat and fish were stored. Here when the bell rang at five o'clock marking the end of the day's work the engaged servants went to receive their daily ration of dried meat and fish carefully weighed out for them on a huge set of old-fashioned balance scales. Directly to the rear of this building was an enclosure protected by a high fence, where the winter's supply of the thousands of split frozen whitefish consumed by both men and dogs was hung in the fall. Across the back of the square was the warehouse where the large inventory of trading goods brought each year by the York boat brigade was housed. The rear building on the right side of the courtyard was the sales shop. This was where the Indians bartered their furs for trade goods. It was here that the trust and honesty established over the years between the Hudson's Bay Company and the Indians were tested. The trader's appraisal of the furs, his prices established by the company's Standard of Trade, his measurements, and weight of goods and supplies all had to be fair and equitable. Likewise, the Indians who received goods and supplies on credit against their future take of furs had to honor their debt. Fair play, honesty, respect for promises made—these were the basis for successful trading relations.

The building in front of the sales shop was the "Big House," home to the senior officers and their families. It was well named, for it was truly big, containing twenty rooms. It was two stories high, with a gallery across the entire front at the second-story level and reached by a flight of outside stairs. On the ground floor at each end was a suite of bedrooms and a sitting room. The great dining hall occupied the central portion. Here the whole staff gathered for their meals. It was also where the dances, receptions, and holiday celebrations took place. Behind this hall were the pantries and two kitchens. One of the kitchens was equipped with a wood-burning range. The other had only an open fireplace that was used by visiting Indians who were accustomed to preparing their meals before an open fire. In addition to the six bedrooms on the upper floor, there were a billiard room (equipped with a billiard table brought over in sections from England), a general recreation sitting room (today it would be called a family room), a library room, and a so-called Ivory Room, which housed a collection of mammoth fossil tusks, bones, and teeth accumulated by some of those traders and visiting explorers interested in natural history.

Fort Simpson, just like Fort Chipewyan, was famous for its library. As early as 1850 the officers of the Mackenzie district established a free library of between two and three thousand books to be housed at the fort. It was a circulating library. Each man in charge of a post was entitled to borrow for his winter reading, a supply of books which were to be returned the following spring. The volumes were all well bound and covered a wide range of interests, particularly those of a philosophical, classical, and biographical nature.

A little more than fifty years later, in 1909, Agnes Deans Cameron, an intrepid and pioneer traveler of the very early twentieth century, had the great good fortune to visit Fort Simpson when most of the buildings of the fort complex were still standing. Her account of her visit to the fort's library as recorded in her book *The New North* reads:

> An outer stairway leading to the second story of a big building invites us. Opening the door, we find ourselves in the midst of an old library, and moth and rust, too, here corrupt. We close the door softly behind us and try to realise what it meant to bring a library from England to Fort Simpson a generation ago. First, there arose the desire in the mind of some man for something beyond dried meat and bales of fur. He had to persuade the authorities in England to send out the books. Leather-covered books cost something six or seven decades ago, and the London shareholders liked better to get money than to spend it. We see the precious volumes finally coming across the Atlantic in wooden sailing-ships to Hudson Bay, follow them on the long portages, watch them shoot rapids and make journeys by winter dog-sled, to reach Simpson at last on the backs of men. The old journals reveal stories of the discussion evoked by the reading of these books afterward as, along with the dried fish, deer-meat, and other inter-fort courtesies, they passed from post to post. Was never a circulating library like this one. And now the old books, broken-backed and disembowelled, lie under foot, and none so poor to do them reverence.
>
> What are the books which this sub-Arctic library sent out? We get down on the floor and gently touch the historic old things.—Here is a first edition of "The Spectator," and next to it a "Life of Garrick," with copies of "Virgil," and all "Voltaire" and "Corneille" in the original. A set of Shakespeare with exquisite line drawings by Howard shows signs of hard reading.

Situated in the center of the open courtyard was the administrative building—domain of clerks, accountants, and postmaster. Here the records were meticulously kept for the entire Mackenzie district. Journals, ledgers, invoices, indents, ladings, and copies of all correspondence both sent and received were compiled to undergo Governor George Simpson's careful scrutiny.

Fort Simpson was often referred to as the "Garden of the Mackenzie." It well deserved this title. Its soil of silty loam, free of stones, yielded abundant crops of potatoes, carrots, cabbages, rutabagas, beans, peas, and barley. The eight months of cold weather were more than offset by the long warm days of summer. In addition to producing a variety of vegetables to augment its table, the company successfully raised cattle, which not only furnished dairy products but also provided the oxen so useful for plowing and hauling hay and firewood.

In addition to being the administrative center for the Mackenzie district, Fort Simpson was the seat of a flourishing trade in furs. The major furs handled were beaver and marten. In the year of the coalition (1821), only 111 bales of fur were brought out of the Mackenzie country. Ten years later its output had increased by one-third. For the three-year period of 1853, '54, and '55, a staggering total of 137,132 martens came out from the Mackenzie River posts.

Intimate glimpses of life at the post are provided in Chief Trader McPherson's journal for 1837. By May 2 oats were sown and "Mosquitoes begin to become annoying." A little later plowing was commenced using the post bull, but since "this is the first time he has been yoked, the days work is found to be but poor." Flies continue to be "very numerous and troublesome to the Cattel." By the end of July the barley was ripening, "but small birds nip off the ends of the stalks as fast as it ripens." A month later the "bull broke into one of the gardens where oats was sown and eat the whole up." But not all the entries recorded misfortunes. On the November 30 anniversary of Scotland's titular saint the regular fare for dinner was supplemented with "a roasted swan and a moose-nose, a rice pudding, a cranberry tart, and a glass of wine." New Year's Day was celebrated according to long-established tradition. "The morning was ushered in by a salute fired by our people at the windows and doors, after which they came to wish us Happy New Year—and in return . . . they were treated, the men with a half a glass of brandy each, and the women with a kiss, and the whole of them with as many cakes as they choose to take and some raisins." The day concluded with a supper in the hall when each man was given "a fathom of twist tobacco and a clay pipe."

Our first visit to Fort Simpson was made in 1975 during the course of our trip up the Mackenzie River in the vessel *Norweta*. If we had hoped to find any traces of the early buildings of the Hudson's Bay Company's Fort Simpson, we soon had to accept the fact that we were not to be as fortunate as Agnes Deans Cameron, for none were left. We had to be content with photographing two warehouses standing behind the modern Hudson's Bay Company store, which still reflected to a slight degree their lineage. They had the pleasing proportions, the hip roof with center dormer, small-pane windows, and red siding—all features that characterized Hudson's Bay Company buildings prior to the metal-sided windowless structures of the present.

We stopped at the granite boulder erected at the south edge of the village on top of the riverbank, commemorating the founding of Fort Simpson. From this point can perhaps best be seen the grand view stretching far upriver beyond the mouth of the Liard as well as downstream for many miles. Behind the monument, on a slight rise of ground overlooking an extensive flatland close to the confluence of the Liard and Mackenzie, is the site of the early Hudson's Bay Company post. Today the only building occupying this quite commanding location is a small squared log house of ancient vintage long since abandoned.

We found our way to the justly famous craft shop where an impressive collection of the beautiful items hand-crafted by the Slavey Indians was displayed. After much deliberation, we finally selected a pair of moccasins made of home-tanned moosehide banded with beaver fur and decorated with exquisitely lovely beadwork. It was really a great pleasure to see this amazing assortment of baskets, moccasins, jackets, mitts, bags, and jewelry, all exhibiting the Slaveys' careful workmanship and superb sense of color and design. What great talent these people have! What things of beauty they have created from skins, beads, quills, and fur.

The next time we visited Fort Simpson was nine years later, in 1984. We had decided to spend a day there before proceeding on to Yellowknife, where we were to catch our flight to Bathurst Inlet for a week's stay at Glenn and Trish Warner's Bathurst Lodge. Shortly before we reached Fort Simpson, our vehicle developed serious motor trouble. We limped into Fort Simpson and there, to our good fortune, found Gary Allen, an auto mechanic from Detroit, who knew his business. Our problem was diagnosed as a burned-out wheel bearing. The necessary part had to be flown in the next day on a scheduled flight from Yellowknife. This was no serious problem, since we had a leeway of the several extra days we had allotted for sightseeing in Yellowknife prior to our departure date for Bathurst Inlet.

So we spent the next day walking the streets of Fort Simpson, chatting with the people, seeing the town's impressive school complex, their modern hospital, the venerable Anglican Church of St. David, and the Roman Catholic church. We admired the flourishing vegetable and flower gardens beside many of the houses.

We walked along the bank above the river and soon came to the small white cabin belonging to Albert Failie, the legendary explorer and trapper of the Nahanni River country. One of his flat-bottomed square-ended Nahanni skiffs was still lying at one side of his front yard.

We spent several hours sitting on a bench on top of the bluff watching the activity on the river: boats passing up and down, float planes taking off and landing. The riverbank below was crowded with both scores of red fuel drums and the many flat-bottomed riverboats pulled up on shore. But it was the river itself that fascinated us. We could almost feel the force of its strong, powerful current as it flowed steadily and irresistibly northward.

In the evening we went to a local softball game. The game was already under way when we climbed onto the bleachers. We asked a friendly man sitting next to us what the score was. He replied, "Twenty-seven to nothing." A bit startled at such a lopsided score, we next asked why the opposing team hadn't been able to get any runs. Our friend said he didn't know—the other team had not come to bat as yet! That was some game, but lots of fun. I don't remember the final score.

The next day our new bearing arrived at noon and Gary immediately commenced the necessary work of installation and we began to get ready for a quick departure. But we were destined to spend yet more time in Fort Simpson. Gary discovered that the damaged wheel bearing had scored the wheel hub so badly that a new hub assembly was required. So once again telephone calls had to be made to locate the necessary replacement. This time none was available in Yellowknife. What about Edmonton? Yes, one was finally located there, and the dealer promised to rush it out to the airport by taxi in an effort to make the flight to Fort Simpson, which was the last one for the next two days.

Meanwhile, we were rapidly running out of our "extra" days. We had to be in Yellowknife by departure time the morning of July 2 or we would forfeit our $3,000 week's stay at Bathurst—the culmination of a dream of many years' standing. Our nervousness increased—especially mine. The thoughts of horrendous airfreight, taxi, and repair bills did not sweeten my dreams. Would the new part arrive as promised? Would it fit? At two o'clock on the afternoon of June 30, the big plane from Edmonton landed. Our part was on board! Gary quickly went to work and soon was able to tell us that everything was OK—the new hub assembly fit perfectly. By 4:30 we were on our way, knowing that barring any further misfortune and by driving most of the night we would be able to reach Yellowknife in time. This we did, in spite of several further mishaps along our way, but that is another story.

In 1988 we returned to Fort Simpson in order to fly from there to visit the majestic Virginia Falls of the Nahanni River. The spectacular scenery, the incredible beauty of the rugged landscape, cliffs, gorges, and river culminating in the awesome splendor of the falls, the thundering white curtain of water pierced by a towering pinnacle of rock, plunging 385 feet to the river below, will be forever imprinted in our memory. It was truly a once-in-a-lifetime experience and made even more memorable by the skill of our pilot, Jaques Harvey, who knew exactly how to position the plane so that the best light and viewing angle were available to us as we strove to capture this spectacle on film.

As we walked around Fort Simpson, we were delighted to see many familiar faces and greet old acquaintances, such as Gary Allen still busy at his garage. In addition, we spent a delightful evening at the home of Tony and Julie Randall of the Royal Canadian Mounted Police, whom we had met along the Dempster Highway several years earlier while en route to Inuvik. Tony had introduced us to the joys of grayling fishing in one of the streams bordering the highway, and we had been able to lend a helping hand when his vehicle had a flat tire farther down the highway. Such experiences forge a friendship, and when we learned he had been transferred to Fort Simpson we looked forward to seeing him there.

To our great good fortune, the annual celebration of Deh-Cho Day took place during our stay in Fort Simpson. This was a day of games, contests, and feasting for all the peoples of Fort Simpson. It was held on the large flat at the southern edge of town, just below the high ground once occupied by the early Hudson's Bay post.

To prepare for the eagerly awaited visit of Pope Paul to Fort Simpson some years before, the hitherto-empty flats had been transformed into a well-maintained and attractive gathering place for the people. In order to provide an appropriate shelter where the Pope and the various native leaders could hold their discussions and deliver their addresses to the huge throng outside, a permanent open structure formed of the massive ribs of a huge tepee had been erected. Elsewhere, at the edge of the field, a small symbolic concrete memorial to peace and friendship complete with circular fire pit for the traditional burning of the sacred sweetgrass had been constructed and was dedicated by the Pope. And finally, a large drum dance circular pavilion had been built.

Throughout the day-long celebration there were canoe races, tug-of-war, wood-chopping and sawing contests, softball games, and drum dances. Close to the pavilion a row of barbecue grills had been set up. Here everyone was grilling his own succulent slab of whitefish or a big piece of caribou or moose meat. If you had no fish or meat of your own to bring (as was our case), that was no problem—there was plenty for all. Just pick out what you wanted from the ample supply heaped on a table. When we inquired whom we should pay for all this bounty, we were told there was no charge. This was an Indian feast and celebration—everyone shared and all were welcome. What a contrast to the white man's usual practice! So we entered wholeheartedly into the spirit of the day, and although we did not compete in any of the games, we joined in the laughter and fun and cheers of encouragement to the various contestants. Moreover, we did full justice to the barbecue meat and fish using our fingers and licking them clean *à la façon du nord.*

Toward dusk as we slowly headed back toward our motor home, we paused for a moment on the high rise of land once occupied by the Hudson's Bay Company so many years ago. From this vantage point overlooking the flat below, the cars and trucks, barbecue grills, and all the large recently erected structures vanished. In their place, for a few seconds in our imagination we saw tepees of Indians who had come to the fort to trade; we saw and could almost smell the smoke curling upward from their many cooking pits; we saw their birchbark canoes lined up on the river's edge; we heard the barking of dogs, the shouts of children.

Our glimpse into the past was but momentary, but we instinctively felt how appropriate it was that this piece of flatland below us, lying beside the Mackenzie and Liard rivers and used by the Indians for so many years, should still, even today, be continuing to serve as the traditional place of gathering not only for the natives but for all people in peace and friendship.

Fort William
(Kaministiquia River)

The treaty of peace concluded at the end of the American Revolution in 1783 established the boundary between the new republic and British Canada as far as the Great Lakes. Eleven years later, Jay's Treaty extended the international boundary westward as far as the Rocky Mountains. According to the terms of these treaties, the North West Company's depot of Grand Portage, located at the western end of Lake Superior, was found to be within the domain of the United States. It was, therefore, necessary to move the company's headquarters northward to British soil.

Fortunately, Roderick Mackenzie in 1798 rediscovered the old route along the Kaministiquia River from Lake Superior to Lac la Pluie that had been used by the early French explorers and traders. This route bypassed Grand Portage and was wholly within British territory. He described the incident in his *Reminiscences* as follows:

> After a long absence in the Indian territories, I paid this year [1798] a visit to Canada. Returning the following Spring, on my first trip from Grand Portage to Lac La Pluie, I met a family of Indians at the height of land from whom I accidentally learned the existence of a water communication a little way behind and parallel to this, extending from Lake Superior to Lake La Pluie, which is navigable for large canoes and, if adopted, would avoid the Grand Portage. . . . This apparently new route, being at the door of Grand Portage, and formerly used by the French, it is most astonishing that the North-West Company were not acquainted with it sooner. In 1784, at the establishment of the North-West Company, the Directors—despatched an expedition to survey a water communication said to exist between Pays Plat, on Lake Superior through Nipigon to Portage de l'Isle in River Winipic, which, after two months of hard labour, was reported impracticable, so that the North-West Company were left awkwardly situated, without one opening for their trade, until the present discovery. . . . In consequence of this discovery, measures were adopted for the removal of the establishment of Grand Portage to Caministiquia, and in 1801, the necessary preparations having been made, Caministiquia became the head quarters of the North-West Company for ever after.

The North West Company quickly took advantage of Roderick Mackenzie's discovery. A short distance from Lake Superior, the Kaministiquia River splits into three channels. The site chosen for the new fort was on the mainland side of the northernmost channel, close to the river's mouth. Here was a safe and protected anchorage as well as sufficient depth of water to accommodate the company's vessels used on the lake. Accordingly, in 1799 the North West Company purchased from the Indians the necessary land at this location for the establishment of their new depot.

The new headquarters was to be built on an elaborate scale, reflecting the confidence of the partners and agents in the strength and success of their company. Everything was to be done on a grand scale, and the amount of labor and materials required was enormous. At the height of the construction between 1802 and 1804 over one thousand men were employed, supervised by William McGillivray, one of the principal officers of the company. By 1805 most of the buildings had been completed, although several were not added until 1811. The final two structures (the stone powder magazine and the stone store) were not completed until 1815.

In 1802 the partners and agents, the voyageurs (both "pork eaters" from Montreal and "winterers" from the northern interior) gathered at Grand Portage for their last rendezvous there. During the following year the move was made to the new headquarters, even though it was still far from complete. Alexander Henry the younger recorded his arrival at the new fort in his journal entry dated July 3, 1803: "We found great improvements had been made for one winter—fort, store, ship, etc. built, but not enough dwelling houses. Only one range was erected, and that not complete; here were the mess room and apartments for the agents from Montreal, with a temporary kitchen adjoining. . . . Building was going on briskly in every corner of the fort; brick kilns had been erected and were turning out many bricks, so that we shall have everything complete and in good order before our arrival next year."

Known first as Fort Kaministiquia or simply as the "New Fort," in 1807 it was officially named Fort William in honor of William McGillivray, head of the North West Company.

In 1814 Gabriel Franchère, clerk of the North West Company, spent six days at Fort William during the course of his return journey to Montreal from Fort Astoria at the mouth of the Columbia River. In the narrative he wrote later, he described in considerable detail this magnificent North West Company headquarters, which was then at the peak of its splendor:

Fort William has really the appearance of a fort, with its palisade fifteen feet high, and that of a pretty village, from the number of edifices it encloses. In the middle of a spacious square rises a large building elegantly constructed, though of wood, with a long piazza or portico, raised about five feet from the ground and surmounted by a balcony extending along the whole front. In the center is a saloon or hall sixty feet in length by thirty in width decorated with several pieces of painting and some portraits of the leading partners. It is in this hall that the agents, partners, clerks, interpreters, and guides take their meals together at different tables. At each extremity of the apartment are two rooms; two of these are destined for the two principal agents; the other two to the steward and his department. The kitchen and servants' rooms are in the basement. On either side of this edifice is another of the same extent, but of less elevation; they are each divided by a corridor running through its length and contain each a dozen pretty bed-rooms. One is destined for the wintering partners, the other for the clerks. On the east of the square is another building similar to the last two and intended for the same use, and a warehouse where the furs are inspected and repacked for shipment. In the rear of these are the lodging-house of the guides, another fur-warehouse, and finally, a powder magazine. The last is of stone and has a roof covered with tin. At the angle is a sort of bastion or look-out place commanding a view of the lake. On the west side is seen a range of buildings, some of which serve for stores and others for workshops; there is one for the equipment of the men, another for the fitting out of the canoes, one for the retail of goods, another where they sell liquors, bread, pork, butter, & and where a treat is given to the travellers who arrive. This consists in a white loaf, half a pound of butter, and a gill of rum. The voyageurs give this tavern the name of Cantine salope. Behind all this is another range, where we find the counting-house, a fine square building, and well-lighted; another storehouse of stone, tin-roofed; and a jail, not less necessary than the rest. The voyageurs give it the name of pot au beurre—the butter-tub. Beyond these we discover the shops of the carpenter, the cooper, the tinsmith, the blacksmith, &; and spacious yards and sheds for the shelter, reparation, and construction of canoes. Near the gate of the fort, which is on the south, are the quarters of the physician and those of the chief clerk. Over the gate is a guard-house. . . . As the river is deep at its entrance the Company has had a wharf constructed, extending the whole length of the fort, for the discharge of the vessels which it keeps on Lake Superior.

Three years after Franchère's visit, Ross Cox, likewise on his way east from the Columbia River, stopped for a short time at the great North West headquarters on the Kaministiquia. As part of his description of the fort, he wrote:

The dining-hall is a noble apartment, and sufficiently capacious to entertain two hundred. A finely executed bust of the late Simon M'Tavish is placed in it, with portraits of various proprietors. A full-length likeness of Nelson, together with a splendid painting of the battle of the Nile, also decorate the walls, and were presented by the Hon. William M'Gillivray to the Company. At the upper end of the hall there is a very large map of the Indian country, drawn with a great accuracy by Mr. David Thompson, astronomer to the Company, and comprising all their trading-posts, from Hudson's Bay to the Pacific Ocean, and from Lake Superior to Athabasca and Great Slave Lake.

Fort William was, indeed, the nerve center of the North West Company's vast fur trading enterprise. It was the grand depot for their interior posts—the place to which each year during the Great Rendezvous the furs were brought and from which the supplies and trading goods were procured. It was also the place where each summer the wintering partners from the inland posts of the *pays d'en haut* and the agents from Montreal gathered to conduct the business of the company. The roster of participants most frequently included Angus Bethune, Simon Fraser, John Haldane, John McDonald, Daniel McKenzie, Kenneth McKenzie, Roderick McKenzie, Hugh McGillis, Archibald Norman McLeod, Dr. John McLoughlin, Angus Shaw, Simon McGillivray, William McGillivray, and Thomas Thain.

The returns from each trading post were carefully analyzed, the quality and supply of their trade goods as well as the changing demands and preferences of the Indians thoroughly discussed and evaluated, policies formulated for the ensuing season, the year's profits determined and distributed to each of the wintering partners based on his number of shares, and assignment of personnel to each fort made. While partners and agents were deliberating these matters in the Council House, over in the Counting House a battery of clerks was compiling the figures, drawing the balances, balancing the ledgers, checking invoices, indents, bills of lading—in short, assembling all the information impatiently required by those in the Council House.

Fort William was chiefly active during the relatively short period each summer of the rendezvous. At that time as many as two thousand people crowded into the fort and surrounding area. They included gentlemen partners and agents, clerks, guides, interpreters, skilled artisans, canoemen, laborers, and Indians. They were of many races but were primarily Scotsmen, French, Canadian, Métis, and Ojibwa.

While the partners and clerks were occupied with their deliberations and with their account books, the laborers and canoemen were busy sorting the bales of furs and goods and loading the canoes preparatory to their return journey—some bound for the inland posts of the *pays d'en haut* carrying the wintering partners and the year's supply of provisions and goods, the others headed for Montreal bearing the agents and the year's harvest of furs. In the meantime, the workshops of the cooper, blacksmith, armorer, canoemaker, and carpenter were busy day and night completing the work that had to be done before the departure of the brigades.

In spite of the hectic schedule that characterized the rendezvous, there was some time for relaxation and merriment. In the evening the partners and agents, clerks, interpreters, and guides assembled in the Great Hall, where they feasted on delicacies such as fresh beef, ham, fish, vegetables, butter, milk, tea, and coffee supplemented with a liberal supply of various liquors and wines, much of which had been brought to the fort all the way from Montreal. No doubt inspired by David Thompson's great map of the company's vast empire and stimulated by frequent recourse to a copious supply of spirits, many tales were told by these men as they reminisced about their experiences in the *pays d'en haut*. Frequently after the feasting the long tables were pushed back to the walls, bagpipes, flutes, and violins were brought out, and all abandoned themselves to the joys of the Highland fling and the Métis jig. Of course the revelry was not confined to the Great Hall. The campfires of the voyageurs and Indians outside the palisade walls were likewise the scenes of boisterous celebrating and merriment.

Finally the rendezvous was over. The brigades departed to the shouts and loud *feu de joie* of the fort's muskets and cannon. Fort William then settled back to a period of quiet and a more leisurely routine until the next summer. From a transient population of 2,000 the fort's staff dropped to a skeleton crew comprising the resident wintering partner, a clerk, and about two dozen artisans and laborers, such as blacksmith, joiner, canoe maker, cooperer, tinsmith, armorer, and farmer.

Kenneth McKenzie, who was the resident wintering partner from 1806 to 1816, lived in the house immediately behind the palisade and just to the west of the main gate. He was not only in charge of Fort William itself but was also responsible for the district that comprised the north shore of Lake Superior and extended inland as far west as Lac la Pluie. Also housed in this building was the captain of the North West Company's schooner, who often wintered at the fort. Immediately to the east of the gate were the quarters for Dr. John McLoughlin and his apothecary. The Doctor not only was a partner but when at the fort served in his capacity as medical doctor. James Taitt, year-round superintendent and overseer of the fort's laborers, lived in a small house outside the main palisaded square, close both to the naval shed and to the barns and stables. Farming was an important activity of the fort.

Nearly 350 acres were under cultivation with potatoes and corn, the major crops, followed by barley, peas, cabbages, and rutabagas. Cattle and horses were raised as well as sheep, pigs, and poultry. The routine maintenance of fort buildings, building of canoes, making barrels and casks, cutting and hauling hay, and gathering firewood were among the major tasks that kept the small force of laborers busy year-round.

Washington Irving in his book *Astoria,* written in 1835, drew quite a graphic and compelling picture of the Nor'Westers and their company as they were perceived by their contemporaries.

According to Irving, "Most of the clerks were young men of good families, from the Highlands of Scotland, characterized by the perseverance, thrift, and fidelity of their country, and fitted by their native hardihood to encounter the rigorous climate of the North, and to endure the trials and privations of their lot." The principal partners, or agents, on the other hand, all of whom resided in Montreal, "formed a kind of commercial aristocracy, living in lordly and hospitable style." Each year in midsummer a great meeting was held at Fort William. Two or three of the leading partners came from Montreal, and as many as possible of the wintering partners journeyed from their distant posts in the interior "to discuss the affairs of the company during the preceding year, and to arrange plans for the future." Each wintering partner, "whose forms and faces had been battered and hardened by hard living and hard service, and whose garments and equipments were all the worse for wear," nevertheless "felt like the chieftain of a Highland clan, and was almost as important in the eyes of his dependents as of himself." The Montreal partners "ascended the rivers in great state, like sovereigns making a progress . . . They were wrapped in rich furs, their huge canoes freighted with every convenience and luxury, and manned by Canadian voyageurs, as obedient as Highland clansmen."

The council meetings were conducted with great dignity and ceremony, for "every member felt as if sitting in parliament, and every retainer and dependent looked up to the assemblage with awe, as to the House of Lords." Ample time was allowed for feasting and revels. "The tables in the great banqueting room groaned under the weight of game of all kinds . . . There was no stint of generous wine, for it was a hard-drinking period, a time of loyal toasts, and bacchanalian songs, and brimming bumpers." At the same time as the chiefs were making "the rafters resound with bursts of loyalty and old Scottish songs" outside the Great Hall, the "Canadian voyageurs, half-breeds, Indian hunters . . . feasted sumptuously . . . on the crumbs that fell from their table, and made the welkin ring with old French ditties, mingled with Indian yelps and yellings." Irving concluded his account of the Northwest Company by commenting that "such was the Northwest Company in its powerful and prosperous days, when it held a kind of feudal sway over a vast domain of lake and forest."

On August 12, 1816, the normal routine of Fort William was abruptly shattered. It received a devastating blow from which it never recovered. The increasingly bitter struggle between the North West Company and Lord Selkirk of the Hudson's Bay Company and his Red River colony, which had been escalating for the past several years, had culminated in the unfortunate tragedy at Seven Oaks when Robert Semple, Governor of the colony, and twenty-two of the settlers had been killed by a group of Métis led by Cuthbert Grant. In retaliation, Lord Selkirk determined to cripple the North West Company, which he held solely responsible for the attack on his colony, by seizing its Fort William headquarters.

Armed with warrants for the arrest of the wintering partners and backed by a force of sixty soldiers of the disbanded De Meuron regiment, Lord Selkirk succeeded in surprising and occupying Fort William. Upon being served with the warrants, the partners offered no resistance but acted with dignified restraint. They were forced to give up their own quarters and move into one large building where they were kept under close guard by their captors. The fort buildings were ransacked, and as many of the partners' papers as could be found were confiscated. Finally, after a week of repeated questioning during which time the Nor'Westers were treated with no courtesy but rather like common criminals, Lord Selkirk announced that he was sending all of them east to stand trial on charges of "high treason, conspiracy, robbery and murder."

Accordingly, William McGillivray and all the wintering partners (eight in number) except Daniel McKenzie (whom Lord Selkirk detained), plus many of the company employees, were herded into three canoes. Selkirk, callously disregarding McGillivray's urgent warning that the canoes were dangerously overloaded, would not permit larger or additional canoes to be used, although many were readily available. Unfortunately, McGillivray's fears were fully justified. One of the canoes carrying twenty-two persons swamped and overturned in the stormy waters of Lake Superior. Kenneth McKenzie was drowned, as were eight others; Dr. John McLoughlin, virtually insensible, was washed ashore and only escaped death through prompt resuscitation.

Fort William was occupied by Selkirk and his men for nine months, until May of 1817. During that time he utilized and enjoyed all its facilities and supplies. Emboldened by his earlier appointment as a

Justice of the Peace for Upper Canada, he sent out detachments arresting North West Company employees and confiscating furs, supplies, and trading goods at most of the forts within the North West Company's Lake Superior district. He kept Daniel McKenzie under close guard. Also, aware of his well-known addiction for liquor, Selkirk kept him so well supplied with that commodity that he had no difficulty negotiating an agreement of sale with him in his state of drunkenness for the dispossession of Fort William—its stores, goods, and furs. Such a deal was entirely illegal, since neither Selkirk nor McKenzie had the necessary authority. In the spring of 1817 a decree issued by Lord Bathurst, British Colonial Secretary, directed both Lord Selkirk and the North West Company to restore all property and goods that had been seized to their original owners.

Although by this decree the North West Company regained possession of Fort William as well as its Lake Superior district forts, irreparable damage had been done. The effects of stoppage of trade, lack of furs, disruption of regular pemmican shipments to inland posts, and loss of face before the native people severely affected their operations and threatened their financial stability. It would take more than a year to recoup these losses and regain their former strong competitive position.

This litigation between Selkirk and the North West Company, which spread over three years and required that William McGillivray and the wintering partners (all of whom were on bail) remain in the east for their trials—trials that were endlessly postponed for lack of witnesses or of the accuser, Lord Selkirk—effectively prevented them from returning to their posts in the *pays d'en haut* to carry on the business of the company. As a consequence, the affairs of the company were severely hampered. In effect, Selkirk, by means of the lawsuits, had succeeded in practically putting the great North West Company into a straitjacket.

Coinciding with this period, the conflict between it and the Hudson's Bay Company reached a climax with renewed acts of violence on both sides. Still weakened by the Selkirk affair, the North West Company was forced in the spring of 1821 to agree to union with the Hudson's Bay Company, which ended the strife and brought peace.

To carry out the details of this amalgamation, Nicholas Garry, one of the directors of the Hudson's Bay Company, journeyed to Fort William, accompanied by William McGillivray and his brother, Simon. To William McGillivray fell the hard task of presiding at the last meeting of the North West Company wintering partners ever to be held at Fort William and informing them of the merger of the two companies. He indicated its far-reaching implications and attempted to explain how each one would be affected. Although many of the wintering partners were to be given the rank of chief factor or chief trader in the new concern, the inescapable fact remained that the North West Company had ceased to exist. No longer would the fur trade flow from Montreal through Lower Canada via the St. Lawrence–Lake Superior route to Fort William. Henceforth, it was to be directed to York Factory, the Hudson's Bay Company's great emporium on the west shore of Hudson Bay. Rivers far to the north of the St. Lawrence, such as the Hayes, would now carry the furs and goods. Obviously, this change would have a serious adverse effect on the financial prosperity of Montreal and Lower Canada. Finally, as a consequence of its replacement by York Factory, Fort William, stripped of its role as a major depot, would function merely as a minor trading post.

At last, after three weeks of meetings and discussions, often painful and strained, the business was concluded. The newly named chief factors and chief traders (now no longer partners) departed for their wintering posts. Nicholas Garry and Simon McGillivray left for York Factory by way of Lake Winnipeg and Norway House "to inspect the dépôts and inventories of property," to meet the new chief factors and chief traders and to decide which of the North West or Hudson's Bay posts were to be retained and which were to be abandoned. Garry's feelings at his departure from Fort William were tersely expressed in his diary: "Saturday the 21st [July]. Left Fort William and never in my Life have I left a Place with less Regret."

William McGillivray remained behind to oversee the virtual dismantling of his former company's showpiece, now nearly deserted. The famous paintings of Lord Nelson and of the Battle of Trafalgar, which had graced the walls of the Great Hall, were removed from their gilt frames, rolled up, and sent to York Factory along with many other objects, mute witnesses to the Nor'Westers' days of splendor and power. All traces of their imprint upon the fort were to be removed as completely as possible.

However, there was yet hanging on the wall of the Great Hall one item that McGillivray could not and would not surrender. This was the great map prepared by David Thompson—the map that covered the northwest quarter of the North American continent, the map that showed the seventy-eight forts of the North West Company, as well as the rivers, lakes, mountain ranges, and oceans that had been discovered and explored with so much toil, hardship, and daring by the men of the North West Company. This map was proof of a legacy and of a tremendous achievement that McGillivray felt compelled to protect and preserve. Accordingly, when at the end of July he stepped into his canoe to leave Fort William for the last time, never to return, the precious map, rolled and secured in a container, was safely stowed in his baggage.

The appearance of Fort William soon reflected its decline in importance. In 1833 John McLean wrote in his *Notes of a Twenty-five Years' Service in the Hudson's Bay Territory:* "We found the grand dépôt of the North-West Company falling rapidly to decay, presenting in its present ruinous state but a shadow of departed greatness. It is now occupied as a petty post, a few Indians and two or three old voyageurs being the sole representatives of the crowded throngs of former times." Washington Irving's much-quoted words written in 1836 in his book *Astoria* provide an eloquent obituary for both Fort William and the North West Company: "The feudal state of Fort William is at an end; its council chamber is silent and deserted; its banquet hall no longer echoes to the burst of loyalty, or the 'auld world' ditty; the lords of the lakes and forests have passed away."

Fort William continued in existence for sixty more years as a minor supply depot and important fishing post for the Hudson's Bay Company. By the time Chief Factor John McIntyre, who had been in charge of the fort since 1855, retired in 1878, the post was deemed obsolete, and in 1881 it was closed. Two years later all but one of the fort buildings had been torn down to make room for the Canadian Pacific Railway freight yards. Only one building, the stone powder magazine, remained, but finally it, too, in 1902 was demolished to accommodate further expansion of the freight yards. With its destruction, the last remaining vestige of this once-mighty fort disappeared forever.

The real significance of the North West Company's downfall accompanied by the eclipse of Fort William as a major fur fort is quite compellingly stated by W. Stewart Wallace in the introduction to his book *Documents Relating to the North West Company:*

> The names of the North West Company partners sound like a roll-call of the clans at Culloden. These men were hardy, courageous, shrewd, and proud. They spent a good part of their lives travelling incredible distances in birch-bark canoes, shooting rapids, or navigating inland seas. They were wrecked and drowned. They suffered hunger and starvation. They were robbed and murdered by the Indians, and sometimes by one another. They fell the victims of smallpox, syphilis, and rum. Yet they conquered half a continent, and they built up a commercial empire, the like of which North America at least has never seen.
> It is one of the ironies of history that this gallant enterprise should have been brought to nought through a compatriot of those Scots who

formed its backbone. Lord Selkirk may deserve the credit for establishing in the Canadian West the first colony of real settlers; but he deserves just as well the opprobrium of having ruined the first great industry that Canadians, by means of fortitude and foresight, had developed. The fall of the North West Company, for which Lord Selkirk was mainly responsible, was a blow to both Canada and its commercial centre, Montreal. It meant that the fur-trade was diverted from Montreal to Hudson Bay. It meant that large numbers of Canadian people, who had relied on the fur trade for their livelihood, were robbed of their means of support.

All traces of Fort William had completely disappeared by the beginning of the twentieth century, but now, nearly ninety years later, Fort William has risen from oblivion and once again stands in all its splendor on the banks of the Kaministiquia some few miles upriver from the fort's original location. This miracle is due to the dedicated efforts of the people of the Lakehead area and the Thunder Bay Historical Society, who in 1971 succeeded in securing the support and necessary funding for the reconstruction of the fort from the province of Ontario. Insisting on authenticity in layout, appearance, and furnishings as well as construction methods, the project proceeded slowly, but gradually, one by one the forty-eight buildings of the fort complex were built and furnished, the fifteen-foot palisade with bastions erected, and the long dock face along the river's edge constructed. Next the fort was brought to life by the superb talents of the people impersonating the Indians, voyageurs, farm laborers, guides, interpreters, artisans, and tradesmen with their families, clerks, wintering partners, and Montreal agents who had once occupied Fort William.

Today Fort William is once again the magnificent busy headquarters for the North West Company—just as it was during its halcyon days of 1804–21. To be sure, the rebuilt fort does not stand on its original site (that is now occupied by the Canadian Pacific Railroad freight yards and marked by a stone monument), but it is still on the north bank of the Kaministiquia, only nine miles upstream from its original location.

From the moment we walked through the main gateway leading to the large open main square flanked by impressive buildings on all sides, we stepped backward in time into the hectic days of the Great Rendezvous. Everyone from the wintering partners to the humblest voyageurs, through the magic of skillful and animated portrayal, was realistically carrying on the regular operation of the fort's business, oblivious to us, the intruders from the twentieth century.

In their well-equipped shops to the rear of the main inner courtyard, the coopers, the tinsmiths, the armorers, the carpenters, the tailors, and the blacksmiths were busy at work. Over in the northeast corner the skilled canoe makers were carefully crafting the birchbark canoes that played such a vital part in the fur trade transportation system.

Close by are the hospital and the guide's quarters. The doctor with obvious pride showed us through his hospital. It consists of a large, airy six-bed ward as well as an operating room that is equipped with a sheet-draped table and a cabinet containing various medical supplies and surgical instruments, such as were used in the 1810s. In one corner of the building is a tiny windowless room, bare except for a narrow table in the center and a cross on the wall. This small cubicle served as the morgue. Unfortunately, at the time of our visit a voyageur had just died in spite of the best efforts of the doctor. We glimpsed, through the partially opened door, the sheet-covered body lying on the table.

When we entered the guides' dwelling, we were hospitably greeted by a voluble flow of French-Canadian. Three or four of the guides were smoking their pipes and relaxing after their long journey to reach the Great Rendezvous. Their quarters are one large room simply furnished with rough tables and benches. The double-decker bunk beds ranged along the walls are covered with wool blankets or bearskins. Scattered throughout the room are their possessions: paddles of various sizes and shapes, axes, rifles, packs.

We followed a number of homespun-clad workmen who were headed for the Cantine Salope. This is a busy place thronged with people and noisy with the tongues of French, Scottish, and Ojibwa. We found a place on a bench in front of a bare trestle table and soon were enjoying a bowl of hearty stew and thick slices of dark, crusty bread. A Métis fiddler strolled through the crowded low-ceilinged room, providing the delightful music that was so typical of life in the fur trade.

Our appetites fully satisfied, we wandered over to the barns and stables of the farm area outside the palisade to the west. The cattle, horses, sheep, and pigs looked contented, sleek, and fat. The mangers were full of hay and the troughs full of feed. Some men were busy working in the garden, while others were harvesting hay. We stepped inside the small creamery building, permeated with the pervasive smell of sour milk and cream. The dairy master, intent on his task, was carefully stirring the cream in the large rectangular vat with a long wooden paddle. Before long the butter he was making, a truly luxury item in the *pays d'en haut,* would be enjoyed by those who ate in the Great Hall.

As we walked back toward the main courtyard, we passed the naval shed where ships' carpenters were busy at work framing one of the small vessels for use on the Great Lakes. In this same area is the small dwelling where James Taitt and his family lived. He was the permanent supervisor of the year-round employees—the farmers and all the various artisans.

Back within the main square, we were caught up in the bustle and confusion of the rendezvous. In the two great warehouses on the west side, each filled to the rafters with a vast array of trade goods, men were sorting and packing, preparatory for shipment to the inland posts. Opposite on the eastern side were the equally vast pack stores where clerks were hard at work sorting, grading, and pressing into bales of uniform size and weight (ninety pounds) the rich harvest of furs destined for shipment to Montreal and thence overseas to London.

Enclosing the square on the south are the huge storehouses required to hold the large quantities of provisions and corn required both by the voyageurs on their long journeys and by all the company's fur forts scattered throughout the *pays d'en haut*. Behind these storehouses and just within the southern wall of the palisade are two substantial buildings. The one to the east of the main gate was the residence and apothecary of the fort doctor whenever he was not wintering at nearby posts. This was where Dr. John McLoughlin lived during the years he was stationed at the fort. The building to the west of the main gate, known as the Wintering House, was occupied from 1806 to 1816 by Kenneth McKenzie, the year-round resident wintering partner. He was one of the nine North West men who were drowned in Lake Superior while on their way to Lower Canada as prisoners of Lord Selkirk.

Suddenly we began to hear cheers and shouts from outside the palisade and, within a few minutes, were swept along with everyone from inside the fort out through the gate and onto the long wharf extending the length of the fort. We soon saw the cause of all the excitement. Two canoes were rapidly approaching from upstream, the paddles dipping and stroking in quick and perfect unison. As they neared the fort, they were greeted with the traditional *feu de joie* of musket fire and a salute from the cannon. In a short while the North canoes reached the wharf and the wintering partners disembarked and were welcomed by company officials. As they stood chatting for a moment at the dock landing, we could see that all wore the tall lustrous beaver hat, the distinguishing mark of the gentleman. Each looked quite resplendent in his long frock coat of plum, fawn, or blue, his waistcoat ornamented with gilt buttons, topped by a frilly white jabot and colorful cravat. Soon, to the skirling of the fort bagpiper who marched before them, they walked through the gate and across the grass-covered courtyard to the Great Hall in the center of the north side of the square. Quickly mounting the steps to the long veranda, they disappeared through the central doorway into this imposing building. Wasting no time, we hurried after them and were soon privileged to eavesdrop on their animated discussion of the problems and policies affecting the fur trade that had to be settled during this rendezvous. What to do about securing a supply of Brazil tobacco was one of the items brought up. This was a subject of utmost importance and was heatedly debated. It was painfully apparent that their trade was suffering because of the lack of this item. The Indians, who greatly preferred Brazil tobacco, were taking their furs to the Hudson's Bay Company posts where it was always available. Throughout the sometimes vigorous expression of opinions, a manservant unobtrusively made sure that the partners' wineglasses were kept well filled.

Eventually the conference of the partners and agents broke up, and we were free to wander about the Great Hall. The room with its well-placed windows was a splendid example of the perfect proportions so typical of Georgian architecture. Walls and ceilings were paneled with cream-colored wainscoting. At one end was a fireplace surmounted with a simple mantel. On the walls hung the paintings of the Battle of Trafalgar and of Lord Nelson as well as portraits of various of the chief officers of the company. That of William McGillivray had the place of honor over the fireplace. At the opposite end of the long room hung David Thompson's great map of the *pays d'en haut*. This was the map that Lord Selkirk scornfully and petulantly called "a piece of quackery"—surely a comment that reflected little credit on his judgment. The mahogany dining table at which the partners and agents gathered was flanked by mahogany Chippendale chairs, beautiful examples of the cabinetmaker's art. Silver candelabra, English crystal, and fine porcelain graced the table. Those lower down in the social scale, the clerks, interpreters, and guides, were content with benches and simple trestle tables. Opening off at each end of the hall were two bedrooms that were reserved for the senior officers of the company. The southeast chamber was William McGillivray's room. It was appropriated by Lord Selkirk for his own use during the nine months of his occupation of the fort. We left the Great Hall and walked over to the nearby Council House. This was a small hip-roofed white clapboarded building just behind the main square. In spite of its small size, it was one of the two most important buildings within the fort. (The other was the Counting House where the clerks kept the books and records and determined each season's profit or loss.) In the Council House the part-

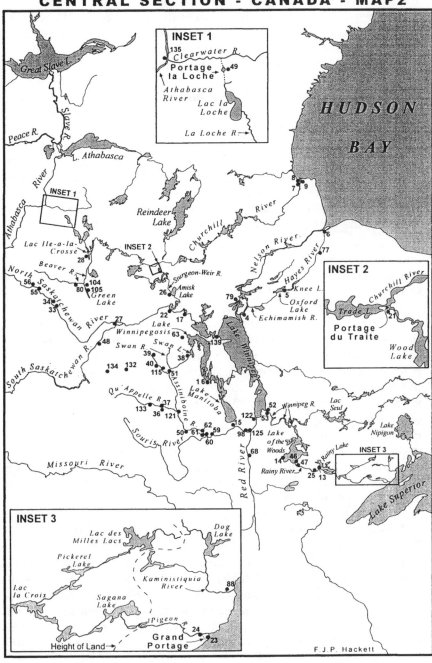

INSET 1

135
Clearwater R.
Portage
la Loche
49
Athabasca
River
Lac la
Loche
La Loche R.

Great Slave L.

Peace R.

Slave R.

Athabasca River

L. Athabasca

HUDSON

BAY

Reindeer
Lake

7 9

INSET 1

Lac Ile-a-la-
Crosse
28

Beaver R.

INSET 2

Churchill River

Nelson River

River

6

77

North Saskatchewan River
56
55
34
33
80
104
105
Green
Lake
Surgeon-Weir R.
26
Amisk
Lake
79
Hayes River
Knee L.
5
Oxford
Lake
4
Echimamish R.

INSET 2

Trade L.
Churchill River
21
Portage
du Traite
Wood
Lake

27
22
17
Lake
Winnipegosis
63
Swan L.
139
48
Swan R.
39
38
134 132
40
115
51
Assiniboine
Qu'Appelle R.
37
133
36 121
R.
62
50
61
59
60
98
125
Lake
Manitoba
16

Lake Winnipeg

South Saskatchewan R.

Souris River

Missouri River

Red River

52
122
53
15
68

Winnipeg R.
Lac
Seul

Lake
Nipigon

Lake
of the
Woods
14
46
47
25 13
Rainy River
Rainy Lake

INSET 3

Lake Superior

INSET 3

Lac des
Milles Lacs
Dog
Lake

Pickerel
Lake

Kaministiquia
River
88

Lac
la Croix

Sagana
Lake

Pigeon
24
Grand
Portage
23
Height of Land

F.J.P. Hackett

Fur Trading Forts—Central Section Canada

4. Norway House
5. Oxford House
6. York Factory
7. Churchill River Post
8. Prince of Wales' Fort
9. Fort Churchill
13. Fort St. Pierre
14. Fort St. Charles
15. Fort la Reine
16. Fort Dauphin
17. Fort Paskoyac
21. Fort du Traite—Frog Portage/Portage du Traite
22. Cumberland House
23. Grand Portage
24. Fort Charlotte
25. Fort Lac la Pluie
26. Henry-Frobisher Fort
27. Fort Sturgeon
28. Fort Île à la Crosse
33. Pine Island Fort
34. Manchester House
36. Fort Espérance
37. Fort John
38. Swan River Valley
39. Upper Assiniboine River
40. Fort Alexandria
46. Hungry Hall House
47. Asp House
48. South Branch House
49. Portage la Loche/Methye Portage
50. Fort Montagne à la Bosse
51. Grant's House/Aspin House
52. Fort Bas de la Rivière
53. Fort Alexander
55. Fort George (North Saskatchewan River)
56. Buckingham House
60. Fort Assiniboine (Assiniboine River)
61. Brandon House
62. Fort Rivière la Souris
63. Fort Red Deer River/Fort Rivière la Biche
68. Fort Pembina
77. Rock Depot
79. Setting Lake House
80. Bolsover House

88. Fort William (Kaministiquia River)
98. Fort Gibraltar
104. Green Lake House
105. Essex House
115. Fort Pelly
121. Fort Ellice
122. Lower Fort Garry
125. Upper Fort Garry
132. Touchwood Hills Post
133. Fort Qu'Appelle
134. Last Mountain House
135. Fort McMurray
139. Grand Rapids

ners and agents met to discuss and formulate the policies that would determine their operations for the ensuing year. Since at the moment the chamber was not in use, we were courteously invited to enter by a fine-looking young Scotsman dressed in Scottish kilt and sporran. Simple elegance was reflected in the furnishing of the room. The central baize-covered table around which the gentlemen gathered supported an array of silver candlesticks, crystal decanters, wineglasses, clay pipes, inkwell, and writing materials. At one end of the room was a large double-decker Caron-type iron stove, and against the wall were Sheraton and Windsor chairs as well as a small table bearing a beautiful Canton tea service. This was, indeed, the true nerve center of the fort. And it was undoubtedly into the blazing interior of that iron stove that the partners, on the night of that fateful day of their arrest by Lord Selkirk, stuffed their documents and letters to prevent them from falling into his hands.

As we headed back toward the main square, we suddenly became aware that the noise and bustle of fort life had ceased, the workers had closed their shops, and the farmers had left the fields, their work done for the day. The throngs of visitors had disappeared; only a few voyageurs hurrying to the *cantine* remained.

We slowly walked through the main gate out onto the now-deserted wharf. The fort lay still and quiet behind us. Before us the Kaministiquia River, unchanging, flowed toward its union with Lake Superior. The moment had come when we, too, had to leave Fort William and return to the twentieth century. Although the "lords of the lakes and forests have passed away," they will not be forgotten. They continue to live again each summer, as they gather for the Great Rendezvous in the magnificently re-created North West Company headquarters of Fort William. The epic story of their deeds and accomplishments will be safely preserved forever.

Fort Dunvegan

The North West Company quickly took advantage of the opportunity to penetrate the new and potentially rich fur lands opened up by Alexander Mackenzie's 1793 voyage to the Pacific. However, the small post it established (Rocky Mountain Fort) on the upper Peace in 1794 remained in operation for only about ten years.

In 1805 the company determined to move aggressively in order to establish their claim to the fur trade of the Peace River against any potential competition from the Hudson's Bay Company. They decided to build a substantial fort strategically located on the upper Peace that would serve as the center for the fur trade of the area as well as a base for further exploration and development of New Caledonia, that as yet largely unknown country west of the Rocky Mountains.

Archibald Norman McLeod, company partner, was entrusted with the task of building the new post, which he named for the ancestral home of the Clan McLeod on the Isle of Skye. He chose a site about fifty-seven miles upstream from Fort Forks sat the confluence of the Peace and Smoky rivers. It was on the north side of the river, on an alluvial flat at the base of gently sloping hills that rise about 400 feet above the river.

Twenty years later Samuel Black, who stopped briefly at the fort at the start of his journey of exploration into the Finlay River country, described the fort's location as follows:

The Companies Establishment at this place is finely situated on a level point at the foot of smooth Green sloping Hills, forming into Knowles & varigated by Stripes of Poplars & bush wood growing out of the Smooth brakes. The bare sloping Bases of the Hills inclining gradually & at some places pushing through the point to near the Bank of the River forming small meadows hedged & patched with bushes, the Poirier or Arrow Wood Tree [Saskatoon, i.e., *Amalanchier alnifolia*] in great luxuriance & some years bearing quantities of fruit called Poir or Pear The Point is woody the aspine & the Pine but now nearly cut down for fuel & buildings, the Soil is alluvial I believe about 30 feet above low water mark & fit for vegetable productions, Potatoes thrive well & yields 15–20 Returns. . . . The Fort is erected near the Bank of the River to the West is an extensive & placid view of the River lost in the sweep of a distant blue Hill & the points covered wt scattered Pines alternately pushing into the Bed of the River, has a fine effect:—Near the establishment is a perpendicular brake of 4–500 feet high contrasted with an equally steep & high Pine Covered hill facing on the other side of the River giving an Idea of Romantic beauty to the place:—

During the construction of Fort Dunvegan in 1806, at least 45 men were busy working at the fort site. When completed, Fort Dunvegan consisted of the "Big House," in which were the large hall where Indians were received with due ceremony, the partner's room, and the kitchen; storehouses for fur and meat; trading shop; powder house; icehouse; and blacksmith forge; as well as quarters for the men. It was 190 feet square, enclosed by a palisade with bastions set at two of the four corners.

A few excerpts from the journal kept by Alexander Roderick McLeod covering the six-month period April 18 to October 14, 1806, record typical activities in the life of the fort during this period.

During April the blockhouses and the fort stockade were constructed: "Two men sawed wood for the floorings of the block houses and bastions . . . Twelve men were busy putting up the fort pickets" after they had been "sharpened . . . knotch'd . . . and fixed . . . in the rails." Other activities included building of eleven birchbark canoes, making forty-two bags of pemmican, and preparing bales of dried meat of eighty-seven pounds each. Gardening was commenced in May: "Planted 1/2 keg of potatoes. Baptiste and Goedike were sowing onions, carot, lattuce, radish, parsley and parsnip seeds." On May 28 a fire set to clean up the wood chips and debris around the fort raged out of control, and the northeast bastion as well as sixty-nine out of one hundred five cords of wood were burned to ashes. A few Indians came in to trade during June for tobacco and ammunition. Of the thirty skins brought in "we allowed them to trade 13 skins, and the remainder we took for their debts . . ." An early frost on August 8 "froze so hard that pease, barley and potatoes were destroyed." More trading was done in October: "The Indians drank all night. The married men were given 15 to 20 skins on credit. The young men 10 to 15 skins . . ."

In the fall of 1808 Daniel Harmon arrived to take charge of the fort. The journal he kept is full of interesting information about his experiences during his two years at the fort.

His impression of his new post was that it "is a well built fort, pleasantly situated, with plains on each side of the river . . ." He added that "we have a tolerably good kitchen garden; and we are in no fear that we shall want the means of a comfortable subsistence. We have, also, a provision for the entertainment and improvement of our minds, in a good collection of books . . ." The making of canoes was a major activity at Fort Dunvegan. A journal entry for April notes: "The people, whom we sent for bark, have returned, with one hundred and eighty fathoms, which will make nine canoes, that will carry about two tons burthen, each." Numerous entries extol the fertility of the soil and the excellence of the crops produced. "We have cut down our barley; and I think it is the finest that I ever saw in any country." In October of 1810 Harmon wrote: "We have taken our potatoes out of the ground, and find, that nine bushels, which we planted the 10th of May last, have produced a little more than one hundred and fifty bushels. The other vegetables in our garden have yielded an increase, much in the same proportion, which is sufficient proof, that the soil of the points of land, along this river, is good. Indeed, I am of opinion, that wheat, rye, barley, oats, pease, & would grow well in the plains around us."

The journal entry for June 13, 1809, exemplifies the friendly understanding that Harmon had of the Indian people. "An Indian has come here, who says, that one of their chiefs has lately died; and he requests that he may be decently interred; and, also, that we would supply a small quantity of spirits, for his relations and friends to drink, at his interment; all of which I have sent, for the deceased was a friendly Indian."

John McGillivray, partner in the company, assumed charge of Fort Dunvegan in 1810, shortly after Daniel Harmon's departure for New Caledonia. He remained at the fort until 1816. His assistant was Colin Campbell, who was destined to remain on the Peace River for more than thirty years.

Fort Dunvegan successfully fulfilled the purposes for which it was established by the North West Company. Its advantageous location on the upper Peace enabled it to function as a supply depot for westward exploration and expansion. It quickly became a major trading center for fur and for the large supply of meat required for fresh provisions and for the making of pemmican, drawing from the Beaver and Sekani Indians of the area. Furthermore, its highly productive gardens contributed significantly to the overall food supply. With its union with the North West Company in 1821, the Hudson's Bay Company took over Fort Dunvegan. It continued to play much the same role in the fur trade as it had always done.

The murders by Indians in 1824 of four Hudson's Bay men at Fort St. John some 125 miles farther upstream brought about the closure of Fort Dunvegan as a punitive measure the following year. In May of 1828, however, it was reactivated with Chief Trader Colin Campbell returning to take charge. Governor George Simpson en route to the Pacific stopped at Fort Dunvegan for a day and two nights in the same year of its reopening. Chief Factor Archibald McDonald, who accompanied the Governor, wrote in his journal:

Upon such an occasion as this, it could not be supposed that the Governor would pass through the country without adverting to those outrages [the murders at Fort St. John's], and recommending proper conduct in future on the part of all the Indians of this quarter. This was done in due form through La Fleur, the Interpreter . . .

The frolics of old, from liquor, were in like manner alluded to, and in particular that which led to the death of an Indian at this place some years ago. They appeared much pleased with what is said to them. The sound of the bugle, the bagpipes, Highland Piper in full dress, the musical snuff box, &, excited in them emotions of admiration and wonder. They got a little tobacco, and a very weak drop of rum and water with sugar.

For the next fifty years Fort Dunvegan continued in its traditional role as an important center of the fur trade of the upper Peace and as a gathering depot for leather and pack cord for shipment to New Caledonia.

During the years when Campbell was in charge (1828–41), Fort Dunvegan enjoyed its most prosperous period. When he arrived back to reopen the fort on May 11, 1828, he "found the buildings in a very ruinous condition—numerous tracks of buffalos, moose, etc. around the fort." He quickly began the task of rehabilitating the buildings and restoring trade with the Indians. He wrote in his journal on May 15: "All hands busily employed about the garden, repairing the most tenable of the buildings to store the Company's property and to lodge ourselves." Ten days after his return he noted: "Finished planting and sowing our seeds, say 10 kegs of potatoes, 1 keg barley, 1/4 keg wheat with a few onions, raddish & carrot."

As soon as the fall outfit was received, the Indians received their debt in goods and supplies and left to hunt and trap. The season was a good one. Over five hundred beaver in addition to other animals were taken. When Campbell left for Fort Chipewyan, his canoes were loaded with forty-one packs of furs as well as a good supply of pemmican and corn.

The prosperity of Fort Dunvegan seemed well assured during the 1830s—game was still fairly plentiful, the beaver still existed in satisfactory numbers, and the Indians appeared contented. By the next decade, however, signs of impending trouble began to appear. The once "inexhaustible" buffalo were fast disappearing. No longer could they be counted upon as a chief source of meat and leather. Populations of game and fur-bearing animals such as the beaver were steadily and relentlessly declining. As a result, the Indians, frequently facing starva-

336

tion, unable to trap and hunt, could not bring in the furs and meat as they had formerly done.

Campbell was replaced in 1841 by Francis Butcher, clerk. During his nine years at Fort Dunvegan the food situation remained critical. Eden Colvile, who later became Governor of the Hudson's Bay Company, visited the fort in 1849. He commented in a letter written shortly afterward: "Butcher & his people lived for some time on dried suckers which appear to be about as nourishing as a pine shingle." Under Henry Maxwell, who followed Butcher in 1852, acute starvation became widespread. During the winter of 1853–54, for example, rabbits were the sole item of food available.

By the 1860s it was clearly evident that the fur trade was steadily declining. Furthermore, Fort Dunvegan was no longer required as a supply base for New Caledonia. The advent of the steamboat on the upper Fraser River and up the Pacific coast, coupled with the building of the Caribou Road, provided easier access than the old route via the Peace and across the mountains on the Leather (Yellowhead) Pass. Yet in spite of its diminished importance, Fort Dunvegan continued to operate, although on a much-reduced scale.

It was during this time that permanent missionary activity became established at the fort. The rectory of the St. Charles Mission was first built by Father Christoph Tissier of the Oblates of Mary Immaculate, about 1869. Nine years later, in 1878, the combined rectory–chapel room of St. Saviour's Anglican Mission was established by Thomas Bunn, a teacher from Fort Chipewyan. He was succeeded by the Reverend J. Gough Brick and the Reverend A. C. Garrioch, who was a grandson of the Colin Campbell who had spent more than thirty years at Fort Dunvegan, first as clerk and then as chief trader. In 1885 the St. Charles Church was erected next to the rectory by the Oblate priests Father Grouard and Father Husson. It served the Beaver, Cree, Iroquois, and Sekani Indians from the surrounding area as well as many of the resident whites. These two missions continued to be part of life at Fort Dunvegan for many years, until 1891, when first the Anglican mission shut down, followed in 1903 by the closing of the St. Charles Mission.

By 1877 Fort Dunvegan was in such a dilapidated condition, with many of the buildings actually threatening to collapse, that the decision was made to abandon the seventy-two-year-old fort and establish a new one a scant third of a mile downriver. This project was carried out by Chief Trader James McDougall so efficiently that within the space of a few years the buildings comprising the new Fort Dunvegan were all completed and functioning.

According to the Anglican missionary the Reverend A. C. Garrioch, the new fort "consisted of seven houses, three of them ordinary log buildings finished off with the approved mud-washed walls and barked roofs. These were the men's houses. The others were larger and more pretentious, having whitewashed walls and shingled roofs. One was the officers' quarters, a second was the office, another the saleshop, and the fourth was the provisions store, used also for stowing away dog-sleighs and harness. In addition to these there was also a stable, where a few head of cattle were kept over winter." By 1886 Lesser Slave Lake had become the headquarters for the Peace River district and Fort Dunvegan a mere outpost.

The beginning of the twentieth century, however, brought new life to the fort. Its strategic location on the Peace made it the favored stopping place and source of supplies needed by the increasing flood of settlers pouring into the Peace River area. For a time trade was brisk. It was also the site of a ferry service across the river installed in 1909 (a service that continued for 51 years). Hopes were even held that the railroad line then being constructed would cross the river by the fort, bringing with it settlers and economic benefits. It seemed as though once again the advantages of the fort's location were going to be realized. But it was not to be. The railroad, with its potential for prosperity, crossed the Peace twelve miles from the fort. Two years later, in 1918, Fort Dunvegan closed down, ending 113 years of operation on the upper Peace River.

Unlike many of the other fur trade forts, the site of Fort Dunvegan was easy to find, and we were able to drive right to it. The province of Alberta has acquired the site and has preserved what still remains and has marked the location of the other points of interest.

Of the original 1805–77 fort there is nothing left. The fort buildings that once stood on the flat valley floor at the base of the 400-foot hill have disappeared leaving no trace. Although the buildings are no more, the rounded tree-covered hills and the broad river flowing smoothly and swiftly eastward remain almost miraculously unchanged. What we were seeing as we looked up and down the river and across to the hills on the opposite side was exactly what McLeod, Harmon, Simpson, Campbell, and all the others saw while at Fort Dunvegan.

However, a short distance to the east one building, the lone survivor of the 1877–1918 fort, still stands. This is the dwelling of the chief factor. Rectangular in shape, surmounted with the typical Hudson's Bay Company's hipped roof, and built of hand-hewn timbers with dovetailed corners, the building is an enduring witness of its 117 years of existence. This factor's house has recently been restored and furnished to reflect its appearance during the years 1892–98, when it was occupied by Chief Trader Albert Tate, his wife, Sarah, and their five children.

The front door opens into a wide central hallway that extends from front to back, dividing the building into two halves, with a parlor and a dining room to the left and two bedrooms to the right. This hallway was more than a reception center; it was also a work area and a medical dispensary. Illustrating these various functions, coats, caps, snowshoes, and other outdoor gear hang from pegs on the wall. A large five-foot-long worktable holds the tools and equipment needed for cleaning and repairing guns and reloading shells. The factor's shotguns and rifle are conveniently close at hand on a gun rack mounted on the wall. From the post's large and indispensable medicine chest that rests on a table, the factor was able to dispense medications to the unfortunate sufferer sitting in the straight-backed chair beside the table.

The parlor is the most spacious room in the house and the one that received the greatest use. It is comfortably furnished with a sofa, several chairs, a large cupboard, an elaborate lamp on a round table, a desk, and a sewing table. A black rectangular Carron box stove provides heat. Feminine touches are present in the braided rugs, pictures on the walls, and fancy cushions on the sofa. Books, a violin, a cribbage board, and cards are also in evidence, reflecting the Tates' recreational tastes.

The dining room was reserved for formal occasions, such as Sunday meals, dinner parties, or meetings with Hudson's Bay Company officials. The six-foot table occupying the center of the room is flanked by four sturdily built side chairs, with an armchair at each end. On the open shelves of the large dresser, plates, platters, and dishes are displayed. The cutlery, serving pieces, and linens are stored in the cupboard below.

The Tates' bedroom contains a large bed over which (in the summertime) mosquito netting was carefully draped. The baby's cradle, similarly protected, is at the foot of the bed. A large armoire for extra bedding, towels, and clothing, a chest of drawers, a candlestand by the head of the bed, a washstand with ironstone basin and pitcher, and a slat-back chair complete the furnishings. Garments hang from a peg rack. In addition, the factor's traveling cassette is visible against the wall. Heat is provided by a black iron box Carron stove that projects equally through a large opening in the wall into this bedroom and the smaller children's bedroom on the other side of the partition.

The children's room is simply furnished with bed, clothes cupboard, chair, towel drying rack in front of the projecting stove, toy box, and chamber pot. Access to this room is only through the parents' bedroom.

A bit farther downstream both the rectory and the church of the Oblate mission have been restored. The magnificent paintings and decorations of Father Grouard, whose artistic talents enriched so many of the Oblate churches in the North, have been painstakingly duplicated. His *Crucifixion,* originally painted on moosehide, hangs above the altar. It is flanked on either side by two smaller works. Large paintings of Christ and of the Virgin Mary adorn the northwest and northeast walls of the nave, respectively. The entire interior of the church now glows with the blue, green, and gold colors of the beautiful designs with which Father Grouard covered the walls. An iron rectangular box stove surmounted by a barrel stove, *prie-dieu,* confession screen, credence table, pews, kneelers, and small paintings of the Stations of the Cross complete the church furnishings.

The rectory, originally built by Father Husson, has likewise been restored and furnished to reflect its appearance during the 1880s and 1890s, when it was occupied by the Oblate priests serving the St. Charles Mission. It is a two-and-one-half-story structure built of hand-hewn and squared timbers, with dovetailed corners and a gable roof. A one-story addition on the east side contains a small chapel.

In conformance with the Oblates' vow of poverty, the furnishings of both the chapel and the rectory are simple and limited to basic necessities. The tiny chapel contains an unadorned altar with tabernacle, *prie-dieu,* credence table, and chair. A cotton curtain divides the chapel from the main *salle* of the rectory.

The ground floor of the rectory proper is divided into three rooms. The largest is the main *salle,* which was the public area where the natives gathered. It is sparsely furnished with the typical box stove, benches along the walls, a clock on a small shelf, and a long narrow wall hanging depicting Father Lacombe's famous teaching catechism widely used in the Oblate missions. The other two rooms, one for the Superior of the mission and the other for an Oblate priest, are each provided with a narrow bed and mosquito netting, a washstand with pitcher and basin, a small table, and a chair. A few wall pegs and a well-worn cassette are sufficient to accommodate the priest's garments. Upstairs is a small area that served as a place where the priests could read and study. Four small bedrooms, each sparsely furnished, occupied the remainder of the second story.

Unfortunately, nothing of St. Saviour's Anglican Mission survives except a cellar depression and the cobble remains of a fireplace.

Today a modern 1,800-foot suspension bridge spanning the Peace has replaced the ferry that once linked the two sides of the river; similarly, the ferry supplanted the canoes that earlier had carried people and goods across the river. But whether bridge, ferry, or canoe, they each shared the very same location on the Peace—the location that was chosen so many years ago as the site for Fort Dunvegan.

In addition to the factor's house and the traditional crossing place of the river, something else remains of Fort Dunvegan. No one who ever visited the fort during the long time of its existence failed to comment favorably on the richness of its soil and its prolific and thriving garden crops. Today this tradition is still carried on. Extensive market gardens flourish in the same place, and cabbages, onions, carrots, lettuce, radish, parsnips, and peas are produced in abundance. Samuel Black was indeed a correct prophet when in 1824, referring to Fort Dunvegan, he wrote: ". . . the Soil is alluvial . . . & fit for vegetable productions . . ."

We were delighted to buy a few of the vegetables, and later, as we were enjoying some of the fresh peas and carrots for supper, we could imagine that we were eating vegetables whose roots, at least figuratively, had come from the garden plots of Fort Dunvegan.

Fort Good Hope

Shortly after establishing the Mackenzie River's Fort Norman and Fort Simpson in 1800 and 1803, respectively, the North West Company pushed farther downriver and in 1804 or 1805 built Fort Good Hope. For many years this was the most northerly of the North West Company's posts.

It is situated on the east bank of the Mackenzie where a small stream, Jackfish Creek, enters from the northeast. Shortly after the fort was taken over by the Hudson's Bay Company at the time of union with the North West Company in 1821, it was moved about one hundred miles farther down the river. This was done both in response to the Loucheux Indians' request for a post located more conveniently for them and in an attempt by the company to encourage trade with the coastal Inuit and to participate in the benefits from the newly emerging whaling activity.

However, the anticipated advantages of the new location were not realized, so in 1827 the fort was relocated back up the river on Manitou Island nearly opposite its original location. The post remained here until 1836, when during the spring breakup of the river a huge wall of ice that had built up and blocked the canyon of the ramparts just above Manitou Island broke loose and came roaring down the river, grinding and sweeping everything before it. It flooded the island and utterly destroyed the post. Fortunately for the inhabitants, a boat was available that enabled them to escape with their lives. The following year the post was rebuilt on its original site at the mouth of Jackfish Creek, where it has remained ever since.

The chief items for which the Loucheux Indians traded their pelts were blue and white beads. Indeed, as W. F. Wentzel of the North West Company wrote in a letter to Roderick McKenzie dated February 28, 1814:

> ... the Loucheux were near creating an uproar at Fort Good Hope on account of a deficiency in beads at the Fort; yet it would apear the Concern did not consult their own interest with the care required. For two successive years, a pressing demand had been made for beads, it being well understood that the Loucheux tribe would scarcely trade anything else, and for the want of this, their favorite article, they preferred taking back to their tents the peltries they had brought to trade; this neglect must necessarily diminish the amount of returns. These Indians are moreover very clamourous and much addicted to war and are dreaded by all the

surrounding tribes, except the Esquimaux: beads however will pacify them.

Marten was the most abundant fur animal. In its first year of operation, Fort Good Hope produced twenty packs of fine furs.

For nearly forty years Fort Good Hope was the most northerly white settlement in all of North America. It was the northern terminus of the Mackenzie brigade, which each spring made the round-trip from Fort Simpson, stopping at Forts McPherson, Norman, and Good Hope to pick up the year's harvest of furs before heading south to Fort Chipewyan and then on to rendezvous at Portage la Loche. In 1825 Sir John Franklin, at the beginning of his second journey of exploration along the shores of the Polar Sea, visited Fort Good Hope (then located at its downstream site). He wrote in his narrative:

At eleven P.M. [August 10, 1825] we arrived at Fort Good Hope, the lowest of the Company's establishments;—Our arrival at this period of the year, at least two months earlier than that of the Company's boats from York Factory, caused great astonishment to the few inmates of this dreary dwelling, and particularly to its master, Mr. Charles Dease, who scarcely recovered from his surprise until we had been seated some time in his room. But this over, he quickly put every one in motion to prepare a meal for us, of which we stood in much need, as it was then verging on midnight, and we had breakfasted at eight in the morning. This post had been but recently established for the convenience of the tribe of Indians whom Mackenzie calls the Quarrellers, but whom the traders throughout the fur country name the Loucheux. As this name is now in general use, I shall adopt it, though it is but justice to the people to say that they have bright sparkling eyes, without the least tendency to that obliquity which might be inferred from the term. The fact is, that Loucheux, or Squinter, was intended to convey the sense of the Indian name of the tribe—Deguthée Dennee, which means 'the people who avoid the arrows of their enemies, by keeping a look out on both sides.' None of the tribe was at this time at the fort; but from Mr. Dease we learned the interesting fact, that the Loucheux and Esquimaux, who are generally at war, had met amicably the preceding spring, and that they were now at peace. We procured from the store an assortment of beads, and such things as were most in request with the Loucheux, and made up a small package of clothing to be presented to each chief of that tribe, whose favour it was thought advisable by this means to propitiate, as they were the next neighbours to the Esquimaux.

Starvation was a specter that periodically threatened many of the fur forts, particularly of the far north. John McLean referred to this in his account of his years of service with the Hudson's Bay Company. He wrote: "For these three years past [circa the early 1840s] the distress of the natives in this quarter has been without parallel; several hundreds having perished of want—in some instances, even at the gates of the trading post, whose inmates, far from having it in their power to relieve others, required relief themselves." Fortunately, by 1864 enough game had returned to the area to remove the threat of starvation and to permit the fort to act as a supplier of dried meat for other posts.

Hostile attacks by disgruntled Indians occurred from time to time. Always unpredictable, the Indians, motivated by a desire to avenge some slight or ill-treatment—fanciful or real—frequently resorted to violence. John McLean recorded such an incident that occurred at Fort Good Hope in the 1840s:

> A band of these [Indians]—nine in number—made their appearance at Fort Norman this summer; and, after trading their furs, set out for Fort Good Hope, with the avowed intention of plundering the establishment, and carrying off all the women they could find. On arriving at the post they rushed in, their naked bodies blackened and painted after the manner of warriors bent on shedding blood; each carrying a gun and dirk in his hands.
>
> The chief, on being presented with the usual gratuity—a piece of tobacco, rudely refused it; and commenced a violent harangue against the whites, charging them with the death of all the Indians who had perished by hunger during the last three years; and finally challenged M. [George F.] Dechambault, the gentleman in charge of the post, to single combat. M. Dechambault, dicto citius, instantly sprung upon him, and twisting his arm into his long hair, laid him at his feet; and pointing his dagger at his throat, dared him to utter another word. So sudden and unexpected was this intrepid act, that the rest of the party looked on in silent astonishment, without power to assist their fallen chief, or revenge his disgrace. M. Dechambault was too generous to strike a prostrate foe, even although a savage, but allowed the crest-fallen chief to get on his legs again; and thus the affair ended.
>
> The Company owe the safety of the establishment to Mr. D's intrepidity: had he hesitated to act at the decisive moment, the game was up with him, for he had only two lads with him, on whose aid he could place but little reliance.

In 1859 the Oblate priest Father Grollier, who had accompanied the Hudson's Bay Company's York boat brigade from York Factory, arrived at Fort Good Hope and built the first mission nearby. At his death five years later, a second Oblate priest, Father Emile Petitot, was sent as his replacement. Under his direction, the church Our Lady of Good Hope was built.

Since its final relocation in 1836 to its present site, Fort Good Hope has continued its time-honored way of life with few changes. Trapping of beaver, marten, and mink, hunting caribou and moose, and fishing for grayling, lake trout, and whitefish are still the major activities. The Hudson's Bay Company store, later known simply as "The Bay" and in 1990 replaced by "The Northern Stores," as well as the Roman Catholic mission are still of major importance in the life of Fort Good Hope. Fort Good Hope's 185 years of existence (154 at its present location) make it one of the oldest settlements in the far north.

Fort Good Hope was one of our stops as we proceeded southbound up the Mackenzie River on the ship *Norweta*. As we tied up at the floating dock at the foot of the forty-foot cutbank early in the morning, the first hint of daylight was just showing through the stunted and scattered spruce trees. Conditions for photography were not too promising. The Indians, who normally turned out en masse to greet any arriving vessel, were still asleep in their homes.

Fort Good Hope is perched on the east bank of the Mackenzie on a long, narrow promontory formed by Jackfish Creek at its confluence with the main river. A narrow dirt road runs the length of the half-mile peninsula. The Indians have their simple log houses on the east side of the road fronting Jackfish Creek. On the west side between the road and the Mackenzie River atop the crest of the scarp are the principal buildings of the settlement, such as the school, the Hudson's Bay Company complex, the Royal Canadian Mounted Police compound, and a few large gardens. The long hours of summer sunshine and moderate temperatures are sufficient to offset the winter cold, so that, in spite of permafrost only a foot or so below the ground surface, a variety of vegetables are successfully grown. For example, in 1943 the Hudson's Bay manager grew 125 pounds of turnips, 130 pounds of beets, 380 pounds of carrots, over one hundred cabbages, and unlimited peas and lettuce, as well as beans, onion, radishes, spinach, and potatoes. The entire southern tip of the promontory is occupied by the Catholic church Our Lady of Good Hope, the cemetery, and the mission rectory.

We spent our three-hour stopover exploring the tiny community. We were a bit apprehensive of the many free-ranging dogs that checked us out much too thoroughly for our peace of mind. Apparently, however, they concluded we were harmless, so let us continue unmolested on our way down the road. We noticed small garden plots containing potatoes and greens beside many of the Indian homes. Also, next to nearly every dwelling was a canvas or skin-covered tepee for

345

smoking fish and meat. We saw several small log structures on tall posts. These were caches used to store and keep meat and fish safe from the reach of dogs and other predators. Scattered throughout the vacant fields, as well as by many of the homes, were small shelters, each with a howling dog attached to it by a long chain.

At the north end of the village were the Hudson's Bay Company buildings, instantly recognizable by their white clapboard-covered exterior and red-hipped roofs with small-paned dormer windows. Their placement reflected the company's traditional rectangular layout of their buildings. Somewhat apart was a modern metal-sided structure—the company's new store.

We finally headed back toward the southern end of the promontory. Here, perched high on the narrow point of land between Jackfish Creek and the Mackenzie, stood Our Lady of Good Hope Church. As we stepped inside the building, we were not prepared for the overwhelming splendor that confronted us. Almost every inch of the interior glowed in the soft colors of blue, rose, and gold. Large frescoes of the Stations of the Cross filled the space between the windows of the side walls. Near the entranceway were two other murals, one depicting a vision of the Virgin Mary standing on top of the ramparts as seen by an Indian man and woman in their canoe on the river below and the other showing the dying Bishop Grollier sitting up in bed in order to watch, through the open door of his log cabin, the sunrise service being conducted by one of his priests for the Indian people gathered round a large white cross on the nearby hillside.

The borders framing the frescoes, as well as the pillars, arches, altar, and sanctuary area, were adorned and embellished with a profusion of delicately painted miniatures of birds, mammals, flowers, and fruits as well as beautifully executed scrolls, fleur-de-lis, trefoils, and other decorative motifs.

This handsome interior was the work of several of the early Oblate priests, particularly Father Petitot, followed by Father Colas and, more recently, by Father Brown. Lacking linseed oil, they successfully used fish oil as a fixative for their paint and achieved many of their colors from native berries. All the interior woodwork, including the altar and chancel rail, was painstakingly carved by hand by Brothers Kearney and Ansel, using an ordinary knife and other rudimentary tools.

The rose window over the front door was ingeniously constructed by Father Seguin. He salvaged and used thirty-eight pieces of glass from a box of 150 windowpanes that arrived, shattered and broken, four long years after being ordered. The statue of the Blessed Virgin over the altar came from France and was the gift of Charles Gaudet,

Hudson's Bay manager of the post at that time (1887). The beauty of this church is so great, it has given the church such renown and importance, that, contrary to most church buildings in the North, its doors are never locked. It remains open to all and has never suffered from vandalism—a truly remarkable record!

We walked through the small cemetery adjacent to the north side of the church. A low white picket fence enclosed each grave—a long-standing Indian custom. Most were marked only with a simple wooden cross. Some of the graves displayed the most delicate and beautiful flowers and wreaths wrought entirely in tiny beads. These brightly colored pansies, lovely white-petaled flowers, and lacy wreaths, so lovingly and carefully crafted, did much to soften the stark barrenness of this graveyard.

All too soon it was time to return to our mother ship, the *Norweta*. As we walked down the sloping roadway to the river dock, we came to one of the distinctive river skiffs used on the Mackenzie. It was about twenty-four feet long, two-and-a-half feet wide at the bow, and one-and-a-half feet wide at the stern. The forward third was decked over; the bow was canted upward and square-ended. On the riverbank was the huge cache of bright red oil barrels—the trademark and lifeblood of the North.

Soon we were aboard ship and moving against the strong river current heading for the ramparts, only a few miles upstream. Our last glimpse of Fort Good Hope was of Our Lady of Good Hope silhouetted against the sky. When that, too, disappeared from sight, we knew our visit to Fort Good Hope had, indeed, finally ended.

Fort Liard

When the XY Company (which had been formed by some discontented wintering partners of the North West Company) was assimilated by the latter company in 1805, thus ending the fierce competition between the two concerns, the new North West Company was able to resume its program of expansion. Its way farther northward down the Mackenzie River was blocked by Inuit hostility; eastward were the Barren Lands, largely devoid of beaver and other furbearers; southward rival fur traders were already numerous and well established; westward flanking the left bank of the Mackenzie rose the wall of the Mackenzie Mountains. But penetrating that range was the Liard River, affording access to the fur country toward the Rocky Mountains.

Determined to take advantage of this opening, the North West Company in 1805 sent George Keith up the Liard to establish a trading post. He ascended the river about 180 miles from its mouth at the Mackenzie, and there, where the Petitot flowed into the Liard, he built Fort Liard. A short time later he pushed upstream still farther, and close to the junction of the Fort Nelson River with the Liard he built a second post, which was called Fort Nelson in honor of Lord Nelson, hero of Trafalgar. In a letter to Roderick Mackenzie, dated January 7, 1807, Keith described the Liard River as follows:

This river, denominated by the Natives, Rivière de Liard, discharges its waters into Mackenzie's river, but it is not known where it takes its sources. It is pretty broad all along, but is generally very shallow and rapid. About one and a half days march from MacKenzie's river, it becomes a continuation of rapids for upwards five leagues, and so shallow from one side of the river to the other, that some years, in the Fall, a canoe loaded with six or eight pieces, cannot proceed without making an almost continual portage. Within this distance there is only one portage, about twenty paces long, occasioned by a cascade which crosses the river. In spring and in the beginning of summer there are none, but the navigation is very difficult on account of the strength of the current. The banks all along and on each side of these rapids, are very high and perpendicular, consisting of broken rocks. There are other rapids further up, but of little consequence.

About a day's march above the rapids, the river presents a fine view to the traveller; the Rocky Mountain to the north, and a fine level country all along to the south, interspersed with small rivers and islands, neither of which of any note, except the Bis-kag-ha River, or Sharp Edge River, not far distant from the Fort, and so called from the flint stones

348

very commun in that place, and which the old inhabitants, the Na ha né tribe, made use of as knives and axes.

In spite of the fact that the Liard valley was producing the finest furs in the entire Mackenzie district, the North West Company in 1815 reluctantly decided to close Fort Liard along with its other posts on the Mackenzie. The company felt that the high overhead cost required to carry on the trade in the district made it "incapable of defraying the expenses" and that, therefore, the post would have to be abandoned. A combination of events had forced them to take this step. Two years previously, Fort Nelson had been destroyed and all its inhabitants, including Alexander Henry, post manager, and his wife and children, had been murdered by desperate and dissatisfied Indians. At about the same time, both rabbits and moose, major sources of food, had almost totally disappeared. Because of this, increased supplies of food had to be brought into the area, thereby increasing overhead costs and reducing profits. A further contributing factor was the difficulties and harassments imposed by the War of 1812, particularly regarding the importation of trade goods and the export of the furs. And, finally, the yield of furs from the entire Northwest had declined.

However, by 1818 the company, in a move to keep its rival, the Hudson's Bay Company, out of the region, reopened many of its posts. Fort Liard resumed operations in 1820. The following year, when the two companies merged, Fort Liard was taken over by the Hudson's Bay Company. It soon became a convenient base from which to carry out the exploratory expeditions that George Simpson proposed. He was determined to expand the Hudson's Bay Company's trade westward, particularly up the Liard and its tributaries, the South Nahanni and the Beaver rivers. He had heard reports of Indian tribes, known as the Nahannis, living in mountainous areas west of the Liard and Mackenzie rivers, which were rich in beaver. He wanted to find these natives and induce them to bring their furs to trade at Fort Liard. First, Chief Trader Alexander R. McLeod and, a bit later, John McLeod each penetrated far up the South Nahanni and succeeded in making contact with a few Nahannis and establishing a trade relationship with them. Murdock McPherson, the clerk in charge of Fort Liard, in 1824 undertook to explore the Liard westward and its tributary the Beaver River. He found no Nahannis but discovered that the Beaver River was well named, for its banks showed an abundance of beaver sign. In the spring of 1828 a distant tribe of Indians came to Fort Liard. McPherson called them Thekannies. They were a branch of the Sekani Indians. They brought in over four hundred beaver and requested that the company establish a post on the upper Liard located in their hunting grounds.

From 1829 to 1839 the Hudson's Bay Company continued its exploratory probes up the Liard River. In 1834 John McLeod, six company *engagés,* and two Indians completed a successful journey that took them up the Liard as far west as the mouth of the Dease. Turning south, they followed this river to its source in Dease Lake. Pushing on to the southwest, they struggled farther, eventually crossing the height of land and finally reaching the westward-flowing Stikine River, which they ascended for a considerable distance before turning back.

In 1834, in an effort to reduce costs, the company's Northern Council prohibited the importation of flour into the Mackenzie and Liard region, mandating that it be produced locally. Fort Liard enjoyed the finest climate and the longest frost-free season in the entire region and was able, therefore, to grow successfully sufficient wheat to supply its needs for flour. In addition, following Simpson's wise emphasis on the production at each fort of as much locally grown garden produce as possible, this fort was able to establish gardens that yielded barley, potatoes, turnips, cabbage, and beets—garden stuffs that sometimes meant the difference between starvation and survival.

The year 1835 brought changes to Fort Liard. Murdock McPherson, now chief trader, was transferred to Fort Simpson to assume charge of the Mackenzie River district, and Robert Campbell took over as McPherson's replacement. Two years later Campbell volunteered to establish a post at Dease Lake. Once again, Fort Liard served as a staging depot for the expedition. Its abundance of good birchbark made it a favorable location for the construction of canoes. In March of 1837 Campbell wrote in his journal: "I left the depot [Fort Simpson] in March with a party of men for Fort de Liard, where canoes for the trip had to be made & birch bark for that purpose obtained. We had the canoes finished before open water & all I wanted was canoemen & Hunters."

The mid-1840s were marked by conditions of extreme scarcity of food throughout much of the Mackenzie River district. As early as 1820 George Simpson in his *Report on Athabasca District* had recognized the great difficulty of securing adequate supplies of food for the Mackenzie district. He wrote: "There is more danger to be apprehended from Starvation here than in any part of North America, and unless the greatest precaution is taken the people must inevitably perish." His forebodings were amply justified. In a letter to James Hargrave at York Factory, J. L. Lewes, Chief Factor at Fort Simpson, wrote on

March 21, 1842: "At Fort de Liard they are not much better off—Brisbois is in a peck of troubles, short commons' at home and surrounded by starving Indians."

During this period of famine nearly three hundred Indians out of a population of about four thousand died of starvation. Many of the surviving Indians considered the fur traders responsible for this devastating death toll and reacted violently, in many cases resorting to murder and cannibalism. Those around Fort Liard showed their anger by ceasing to supply the fort with either provisions or furs.

In 1854 Robert Campbell was appointed to be in charge of Fort Liard. He wrote in his memoirs: "We made a first class trade and the winter '54 and '55 passed without anything out of the usual routine occurring except the arrival of an extra express from Sir George Simpson ordering the organization of an expedition to start in spring for the Arctic regions by the Great Fish or Back's River, to look for any trace that might possibly be found of Sir John Franklin's party."

The following year, Campbell "resumed charge of Fort de Liard where I passed a good quiet winter and made good returns!" In the spring he "forwarded the returns to the depot [Fort Simpson] and passed a monotonous summer at de Liard."

Twenty years later, from 1876 to 1882, Julian Camsell, father of the renowned Canadian geologist Charles Camsell, was in charge of Fort Liard. This was the birthplace of his famous son, and here Charles lived for the first six years of his life. From Fort Liard Camsell was transferred to Fort Simpson, where, as chief factor, he remained for the next eighteen years.

The highway recently constructed between Fort Simpson on the Mackenzie River and Fort Nelson on the Fort Nelson River enabled us to drive to Fort Liard, situated on the Liard River, without difficulty. The Liard Highway, as the road is called, cuts through a vast region of unbroken forest where poplar and giant cottonwood, the Liard of the early fur traders, are the dominant trees.

We turned off the main highway and followed a side road down a steep hill to reach our destination. Here at the mouth of the Petitot River, on a point of land between that river and the Liard, is the tiny settlement of Fort Liard, a settlement that has occupied this site for nearly two hundred years, ever since its founding in 1805. After parking our motor home, we were free to wander leisurely about, wherever our curiosity took us. There was but one main roadway, and on this were the Royal Canadian Mounted Police post, a store or two, the Fort Liard band office, the Acho-Dene craft shop, a café-lodge, and several most attractive modern homes built of western red cedar. The older buildings were located on side trails closer to the riverbank, and it was to these we turned our attention.

We were delighted to find two Hudson's Bay Company buildings, survivors of an earlier period, still standing close to the riverbank. They were boarded up and abandoned. Their white clapboard sides and red doors and roofs clearly proclaimed their proud heritage. From both the size and the placement of the windows it appeared that the building with the saddle roof had obviously been the company store. The other building had the typical Hudson's Bay hipped roof, which suggested that it was an earlier structure.

A little farther along the trail on top of the riverbank was a venerable building belonging to the early Roman Catholic church. The small belfry containing the mission bell, gambrel roof, peaked dormers, small-paned windows, and subtle curve of the roofline all reflected the French background of the Oblates of Mary Immaculate priests, who had established the mission here well over one hundred years ago.

Many of the small houses scattered here and there along the riverbank were built of hand-squared timbers with dovetailed corners. They were reached by winding little paths through the rank growth of wildflowers, bushes, and grasses. Barrels for water and fuel stood outside. One thing they all had in common—the spectacular view out over the mighty Liard River flowing by, almost at their doorstep.

We walked down a dirt rampway that led to the water's edge and watched a young Indian couple load their riverboat with supplies, gun, ammunition, ready to take off for the "bush" to hunt game for their winter food supply. We were well aware that in this country such a trip is not for sport. It is for survival.

Fort Liard today, just as it has always been, is noted for its abundant supply of birchbark. Now, however, instead of using it for building canoes, it is used for the making of birchbark baskets of all sizes and shapes. These baskets, beautifully decorated with dyed porcupine quills, are famous worldwide. We, of course, could not miss this opportunity to acquire several of them. The biggest problem was deciding which ones to buy, for they were all so lovely.

Before finally leaving Fort Liard, we walked to a vantage point at the mouth of the Petitot where we could enjoy the magnificent view overlooking the Liard. Far off in the distance upstream we could see the peaks of the Mackenzie Mountains rising into the clear sky. We remembered that it was from this spot where we were now standing that John McLeod and, a few years later, Robert Campbell, two daring trader-explorers, had set off in their fragile birchbark canoes to struggle up the terrifying Liard River, a river whose fearful reputation was well deserved. Campbell had exclaimed on one occasion: "Confound West Branch [Liard]! It must be under a spell of some malediction, a source of endless mishaps and confusion." As a result of their penetration into those mountains, the way was opened up for the fur trade. They were, indeed, intrepid men.

Fort McLeod
(McLeod Lake)

The year 1805 was marked by the establishment of the first fur trading post and permanent settlement west of the Rocky Mountains in what is now the province of British Columbia. The news of the successful U.S.-sponsored expedition of Lewis and Clark across the continent in 1803–06 had spurred the Nor'Westers into action. They feared this U.S. exploit might jeopardize their interests in the northwest. Strengthened by their recent merger with the XY Company, they were prepared to meet this potential challenge. Therefore, at the annual meeting of the company held in Fort William in the summer of 1805 it was decided to equip a small expedition of about thirty persons and send it across the Rocky Mountains following the route pioneered by Alexander Mackenzie twelve years earlier to establish trading posts, and to occupy the land in the name of Great Britain.

The man chosen for this enterprise was Simon Fraser, only twenty-nine years old but already a wintering partner in the company. In the fall of 1805, he led a force of twenty men up the Peace River as far as the foot of the fierce Peace River canyon. There he established Rocky Mountain Portage House, which was to serve both as a trading post and as an advance supply depot from which to launch his expedition across the Rocky Mountains with a minimum of delay.

After the site for this new fort had been selected on the south side of the river, Fraser entrusted the building of the post to John Stuart, one of his two clerks, while he and his other clerk, James McDougall, and a few *engagés* advanced up the Peace to continue their journey in fulfillment of their assigned mission.

At the Peace River forks, Fraser turned south into the Parsnip River, which he ascended for several days. At its confluence with the Pack River he headed up that stream and followed it to its source—a narrow lake about seventeen miles in length. The natives he encountered here were Sekani Indians, who appeared friendly. Fraser decided this would be a suitable location for his post. Accordingly, on the shore of the lake close to its outlet at the Pack River he built his trading post, which he called Fort McLeod, in honor of Archibald Norman McLeod, senior partner of the North West Company. As soon as the new post was built, Fraser arranged that a skeleton force of three, comprising La Malice and two other French-Canadian *engagés,* should remain to overwinter at the fort and to trade with the Indians. Fraser, along with

McDougall and the remainder of the party, then returned to Rocky Mountain Portage House.

It was not long, however, before discord erupted between the two French-Canadians and La Malice, left behind at Fort McLeod. The two *engagés* left the fort and, in spite of the harsh winter weather, made their way back to Rocky Mountain Portage House. Fraser sent James McDougall back to Fort McLeod to investigate the matter and to assume charge of the post. Upon his arrival, he found the post abandoned, with no trace of La Malice. That troublesome individual (destined to cause Fraser much trouble in the years ahead) eventually turned up at Rocky Mountain Portage House later in the season.

McDougall, who had been supplied with a limited store of tobacco, beads, and ammunition, undertook an exploratory trip from McLeod Lake in a southwesterly direction. After traveling three-and-a-half days, he reached a large lake, now known as Stuart Lake, which was in the heart of the country inhabited by the Carrier Indians.

The winter's trade at Fort McLeod had been most successful, and Fraser reported in his journal in 1806 that "the furs are really fine. They were chiefly killed in the proper season and many of them are superior to any I have seen in Athabasca, being quite black and being well dryed, excepting that they are not all stretched in the proper shape."

Because of the necessity of building new canoes before he could continue with his assignment, Fraser was forced to spend two weeks in June of 1806 at Fort McLeod. In a letter to the Gentlemen Proprietors of the North West Company dated August 1806 he wrote: "When we arrived at Trout Lake [Fort McLeod] our canoes were so shattered and spoiled that it was not possible to proceed any further with them, which obliged us to make new canoes there." At the end of the two weeks he was able to proceed with both his explorations and the establishment of additional fur-trading forts.

When Fraser departed from Fort McLeod, he left instructions for James McDougall, who was to be in charge during Fraser's absence. He urged McDougall to arrange that the Indians "work beaver until the beging [beginning] of February and after that to employ the best hunters to make provisions." Fraser was especially concerned about the preparation and care of the furs and cautioned McDougall to make sure that "the Indians dress the furs properly" and that "the Furs be well envelloped & that the rats and mice does not cut them in the Store."

In 1810 Daniel Harmon was transferred from Fort Dunvegan on the Peace River to New Caledonia. He was destined to spend the next nine years there. On November 1, 1810, he wrote in his journal on his arrival at McLeod's Lake Fort:

> McLeod's Lake may be sixty or seventy miles in circumference. Small white fish and trout are here taken; but those who reside here subsist, during the greater part of the year, on dried salmon, which are brought in the winter, on sledges, drawn by dogs, from Stuart's Lake.
>
> The Indians who frequent this establishment, are Sicannies, and belong to the same tribe with those who take their furs to the Rocky Mountain Portage. Their dialect differs but little from that of the Beaver Indians. They appear to be in wretched circumstances, frequently suffering much for want of food; and they are often driven to the necessity of subsisting on roots.

Almost from the time of its founding, Fort McLeod served as the post where all goods coming into New Caledonia from the east were received and where all the furs from throughout the area were brought for shipment out of the New Caledonia district. Each spring the fort became the center of much activity as preparations were made for the annual trip to the North West Company's depot at Rainy Lake, and Harmon's journal entry for Sunday, April 21, 1811, reads: "A few days since, I sent the greater part of my people to McLeod's Lake, to prepare for the voyage from that place to the Rainy Lake."

McLeod's Lake was not a prolific fishery. It yielded only small numbers of native fish, such as whitefish and trout, scarcely enough to provide for the needs of the fort. Since the drainage of the lake was eastward into the Peace River system, it could not receive the annual salmon runs, which came only into those lakes draining into the Pacific.

The Sekanies who frequented the area around Fort McLeod were unpredictable in their behavior. Constant vigilance and resoluteness were required of the traders. Harmon recorded an incident that occurred in 1811: "Monday, [July] 29. Several days since, one of our men, who remains at McLeod's Lake, came here [Stuart Lake] with the information, that there were Indians lurking around the fort, waiting, as was supposed, for a favourable opportunity to attack it. I, accordingly, went over, hoping that I should be able to ascertain who they were; but I have not been able to obtain the least information respecting them. Probably, they had not courage to make the attack, and have returned to their own lands."

John Stuart, a partner of the North West Company and in charge of the New Caledonia district from 1809 until 1824, enjoyed the annual summer trips to Rainy Lake so much that he made Fort McLeod his headquarters during much of that time. The overland route between Montreal and far distant New Caledonia was both long, hazardous, and extremely costly. In addition, frequent delays caused by unfavorable ice conditions on the river resulted in the supplies upon which the forts were dependent not reaching their destination as scheduled.

As early as 1813, Stuart attempted to find a substitute route that would be less costly. The route he discovered went by canoe down the Fraser River and by packhorses to Fort Okanagan and thence by water to Fort George, at the mouth of the Columbia. It slowly replaced the Peace River route. Heavy items such as arms, ammunition, and ironwork in particular could be brought in more reliably and cheaply by this route. However, the furs of the district continued to go out through Fort McLeod and on east via the Peace River, and goods obtained in Montreal were brought back the same way. It took some time to learn to use the new communication, and it was not until 1826 that it finally completely superseded the old one. After that year, Fort McLeod ceased to be the post of entry and exit for New Caledonia.

In 1828, seven years after the union of his company and the North West Company, George Simpson made a trip from York Factory on Hudson's Bay to Fort George at the mouth of the Columbia River in order to inspect the posts that lay along his route, many of which were forts that had been established and operated by the North West Company. In a report he prepared for the Governor and London Committee of the Hudson's Bay Company, Simpson wrote the following concerning Fort McLeod:

McLeods Lake . . . is frequented by about 30 to 40 Seccanies, whose hunting Ground is the Mountanous Country in the neighbourhood of Finlays branch. A great part of this Country was some years ago closely trapped by Iroquois, but it has since then recruited and is now in tolerable good condition. The Hunts of the few Indians who visit the Establisht. amount to about 30 Packs Furs principally Beaver, value about £ 2500.

In regard to the means of living, McLeods Lake is the most wretched place in the Indian Country; it possesses few or no resources within itself, depending almost entirely on a few dried Salmon taken across from Stuarts Lake, and when the Fishery there fails, or when any thing else occurs to prevent this supply being furnished, the situation of the Post is cheerless indeed. Its compliment of people, is a Clerk [John Tod] and two Men whom we found starving, having had nothing to eat for several Weeks but Berries, and whose countenances were so pale and emaciated that it was with difficulty I recognized them.

We knew that the location of Fort McLeod on the north side of

McLeod Lake was within the Sekani Indian reserve and that it would be necessary to obtain permission from a band council member allowing us to visit the site. We were at a loss to know whom to contact. In the early evening when the provincial campground official came to collect our camping fee, we told him of our problem and explained that we hoped to see the Fort McLeod site in order to take photos of it that would be used in a book we were writing on the early fur trade sites. Kindly offering to seek out the proper person and secure the necessary authorization for us, he was confident there would be no objections raised. He was quite correct, for he returned to our motor home late that evening with the required permission. We were most grateful both to him and to the Sekani band for their help.

So early the next morning after a hasty breakfast, we drove into the reserve. We crossed the Pack River, mentioned so frequently in both Fraser's and Harmon's journals. Soon we came to the clearing by the river's inlet at the north end of McLeod Lake, where three very old buildings, empty and abandoned, still stood—all that now remained of the old post of Fort McLeod.

One was built of hand-squared timbers dovetailed at the corners. The second was constructed of rough-hewn logs with notched and fitted corners. The third, a smaller structure with but two very small windows high up under the eaves, was constructed of horizontally laid rough-hewn timbers held in place by a vertical upright at each corner. All three were topped with hipped roofs that once were painted red, although only a hint of that color now remained. Traces of white on the building walls suggested that they were once whitewashed. The chimneys had disappeared, as had the glass or parchment that formerly filled the window openings.

We could only guess what the function of each of the three structures had been. Based on its larger size as well as on bigger windows not only on the front but also on the sides, we surmised that the middle building (the one with the dovetailed corners) might have been the post manager's dwelling. The structure to the east was more crudely constructed and had only two rather small windows high on the front wall, one on either side of the centrally located doorway. We mentally tagged this building as the store. The remaining building, considerably smaller in size, with no windows on the front, might well have been a storehouse of some kind.

The beautiful lake that the fort buildings faced extended far to the south. It was enclosed by gently rounded wooded hills. At the time of our visit in early fall, the temperature was mild, the sun shining, the sky blue, broken with a few white clouds—truly an enchanting place. It was hard to reconcile this with John McLean's 1833 description of the same spot: "A more dreary situation can scarcely be imagined, surrounded by towering mountains that almost exclude the light of day, and snow storms not seldom occurring, so violent and long continued as to bury the establishment. I believe there are few situations in the country that present such local disadvantages . . ."

Maybe beauty really is only "in the eye of the beholder." Gone forever are the bustle and activity that enlivened the post as the furs from the other New Caledonia forts were received, canoes readied, and preparations made for the long yearly journey east to Fort Chipewyan and Fort Lac la Pluie on Rainy Lake. With the departure of the brigade, headed so many times by John Stuart, Fort McLeod settled down to a period of quiet.

Today it is still quiet, the peace and solitude broken only by the appearance of a few native Sekanies walking on the path along the edge of the lake toward the modern settlement of McLeod's Lake located on the main highway a short distance to the east. We, too, were intruders as we walked about the buildings, examining and photographing them from every angle. But soon we departed. Fort McLeod was left once again to its solitary and lonely existence on the shores of McLeod's Lake.

Rocky Mountain Portage House

When Simon Fraser and a party of about twenty men left the North West post of Rocky Mountain Fort on the Peace River in the summer of 1805, they advanced upstream as far as the lower (east) end of the awesome Peace River canyon. There Fraser chose a site on the south side of the river for the construction of a post that was to serve both as a trading post, particularly for the local Sekanies, and as an advance base for his projected dual undertaking of establishing trading posts on the western side of the Rocky Mountains and exploring the supposed Columbia River to its mouth at the Pacific Ocean.

Leaving behind John Stuart, his reliable and indispensable clerk, and most of his men to carry out the task of building the new fort, which was appropriately named Rocky Mountain Portage House, Fraser, James McDougall, and a few *engagés* continued on with their reconnaissance trip along the upper reaches of the river and its southern tributary, the Parsnip, eventually advancing as far as McLeod's Lake, where they erected Fort McLeod. In the late fall Fraser and his party returned to Rocky Mountain Portage House, where they spent the winter of 1805–06. Fraser and McDougall, once again leaving Stuart behind at the post, journeyed down the Peace to Fort Dunvegan, where they enjoyed the festivities of the Christmas holidays and had the opportunity for extended discussions with Archibald Norman McLeod, a senior partner of the North West Company.

During the spring of 1806, Fraser was occupied chiefly in endeavoring to secure sufficient provisions for his summer's journey, in transporting them to the upper end of the portage, and in getting the necessary canoes repaired and constructed. John Stuart, who was the only competent builder of canoes that Fraser had, could not do much, as he was kept so busy with all his other duties at the fort.

The Rocky Mountain portage around the impassable waters of the Peace that tumbled and roared through the canyon was on the north side of the river. It was actually about twelve miles in length and, because of its difficulty, was dreaded by all who had to cross on it. John McLean on his way to a posting in New Caledonia described the portage:

> ... we reached the portage bearing their name [Rocky Mountains] on the 10th [October], the crossing of which took us eight days, being fully thirteen miles in length, and excessively bad road, leading sometimes through swamps and morasses, then ascending and descending steep hills, and for at least one-third of the distance so obstructed by fallen

trees as to render it all but impassable. I consider the passage of this portage the most laborious duty the Company's servants have to perform in any part of the territory; and, as the voyageurs say, 'He that passes it with his share of a canoe's cargo may call himself a man.'

The next day, May 21, Fraser, Stuart, and their party, with the arduous crossing of the portage behind them, proceeded on their way, ready to continue their exploration and establishment of further trading posts.

Daniel Harmon, at this time in charge of Fort Dunvegan, faithfully recorded in his journal the appearance of the men from Rocky Mountain Portage House each spring with the combined returns from New Caledonia and again in the fall with the brigades carrying the goods and supplies destined for Rocky Mountain Portage House and the forts beyond the mountains.

For example, Harmon recorded in his journal that the eastbound brigade passed Fort Dunvegan on May 22: "Messrs. J. Stuart and H. Faries and company, passed this place in four canoes, with the returns of New Caledonia and Rocky Mountain Portage; and, like many others, they are on their way to the Rainy Lake." Nearly five months later they passed the fort on October 6 on their return journey westward: "Mr. John Stuart and company, in four canoes, have arrived from Fort Chippewyan, having on board, goods for the establishment at the Rocky Mountain Portage and New Caledonia."

In 1814, after nine years of operation, Rocky Mountain Portage House was closed. Situated as it was at the head of navigation on the Peace, it had served as a key link in the Peace River–based transportation system over the Rockies into New Caledonia. Gradually, however, this route was largely replaced by one that utilized both the Saskatchewan and the Columbia rivers. This changeover removed the necessity for maintaining the post at Rocky Mountain Portage.

Rocky Mountain Portage House was briefly reopened in 1823 by the Hudson's Bay Company, and Samuel Black spent the winter of 1823–24 there making preparations for his forthcoming expedition into the Finlay River country. Four months later, in September of 1824, Black and his party, after completing their exploration of the Finlay River watershed, arrived back at the western end of the Rocky Mountain portage where they "took a promenade across the Portage counting on finding Mr. Heron at his Post but coming on the Top of the Hills overlooking the establishment saw it desolute & no appearance of human beings about the Houses:—on account of the murderers, the

Post was last spring temporary abandoned but again to be reestablished towards the fall . . ."

During the previous season (1823) George Simpson had decided to close Fort St. John, sixty miles down the Peace, and replace it with a reopened Rocky Mountain Portage House. The Beaver Indians, however, were adamantly opposed to this projected move. They were also greatly incensed at the Hudson's Bay Company's decision to cut down on the trade in liquor. So strong were their feelings that in early November they callously murdered four of the company's men as they were returning to Fort St. John after transporting some materials upriver to Rocky Mountain Portage House. The Indians then succeeded in killing Guy Hughes, who had been left alone at Fort St. John. A further unprovoked murder took place at Fort Dunvegan the following year.

Faced with these atrocities, Simpson decided to close down both Fort Dunvegan and Rocky Mountain Portage House. This would serve to effectively punish the Indians. It would also benefit the depleted populations of game and fur animals by affording them a respite from the intense hunting and trapping that had been carried on. The closure of the posts on the British Columbia section of the upper Peace remained in effect until 1858, when Fort St. John was reestablished.

Hudson's Hope

George Simpson's total withdrawal from the upper Peace River country at the time of the murders in 1823 at Fort St. John remained in effect for nearly forty years. It was not until sometime in the late 1860s that a trading post was reestablished at the eastern end of the Peace River canyon. It was located on the south side of the Peace about half a mile east of Maurice Creek, probably on or very near the site of Fraser's 1805 Rocky Mountain Portage House.

By the mid-1860s free traders and trappers had moved into the area. However, the Hudson's Bay Company in 1868 answered this threat to their domination of the trade by buying out every one of them. Also at about this same time (1869) the post was first referred to as Hudson's Hope and the old name of Rocky Mountain Portage Fort was no longer used. A satisfactory explanation for the selection of the name Hudson's Hope for the trading post has so far not been found.

A contemporary description of Hudson's Hope as it was in 1872 is given by William Francis Butler in his book *The Wild North Land:* "About the middle of the afternoon of the 25th of April [1872] we emerged from a wood of cypress upon an open space, beneath which ran the Peace River. At the opposite side a solitary wooden house gave token of life in the wilderness. The greater part of the river was still fast frozen, but along the nearer shore ran a current of open water. The solitary house was the Hope of Hudson!"

It was feared that crossing the river to reach the fort on the far side would be hazardous, and indeed it was. The small canoe brought over by Charette, manager of the post, proved grossly inadequate. Shortly after Butler and his companions were embarked, "the canoe lurched quickly to one side, shipping water as she did so . . . and we were over into the icy quick-running river." Tragedy was only averted when they were able to grab a line that was thrown across the upturned canoe. "Wet, waterlogged, numbed, and frozen, we made our way across the ice to the shore." Later Butler confessed that after he had changed his "dripping clothes for a suit of Charette's Sunday finery, when Mrs. Charette had got ready a cup of tea and a bit of moose steak, and when the notebook, letters, and likenesses . . . had all been duly dried and renovated, matters began to look a good deal better."

The post under its new name continued to serve in its traditional role as a trading post, particularly for the Sekani Indians, and as a transfer depot for goods crossing the Rocky Mountains. For example, the requisition on the Saskatchewan district for the 1879 outfit for

New Caledonia to be transported on the Peace River to Hudson's Hope included 300 pounds of common pemmican, 350 buffalo skins, and twenty pounds of sinew.

For a time, Hudson's Hope operated only as an outpost of Fort St. John. Frank Beaton from Fort St. John was factor at Hudson's Hope during the 1898–99 season. He soon realized and convinced the Hudson's Bay Company as well that the post would be much more advantageously situated if it was moved to the north side of the river at the eastern end of the portage trail. Accordingly, the very next summer the store building was dismantled, the logs floated across the river, and the store rebuilt on the north bank. In 1905 H. Taylor became factor at the post. Sometime prior to 1912 he built a rather imposing two-story dwelling, soon called the Bay House. In 1912 the post of Hudson's Hope ceased to be an outpost of Fort St. John. It also began to operate on a year-round basis instead of only seasonally (from September until June) as formerly. To accommodate the anticipated increased business, the Hudson's Bay Company replaced its small store with a new larger two-story building of squared logs. The structure had a steeply pitched roof, a center door flanked by windows on the ground floor, and windows on the front of the upper story.

George Drew, who succeeded Taylor as factor, held this position for but two years (1912–14). Relying on the fact that the business of his post was flourishing, Drew concluded that the addition of a hotel to the post complex would be a profitable venture. He made the mistake, however, of going ahead with this undertaking without first seeking company approval. When the Hudson's Bay inspector arrived and saw what had been done, the new hotel with all its furnishings was sold forthwith and Drew was summarily dismissed from the service.

He was followed by John MacDougall, an experienced fur trader who had worked for the company in both the Hudson's and James Bay area as well as at Edmonton. Following long-established company policy, he, as post manager, encouraged the establishment of a large and productive garden. During the twenties, Jack Gregg, Jack McDermott, and Andy Russell were successively factors at the Hudson's Bay post. In 1942 the old two-story square-timbered whitewashed building that had been the company store ever since 1912 was replaced by a new structure characterized by the red-hipped roof and white siding that were the traditional hallmark of Hudson's Bay Company buildings until quite recently.

The first quarter of the twentieth century marked the arrival of steamboats on the upper Peace. Stern-wheelers such as the SS *Peace River* and the SS *D. A. Thomas* as well as the motorboats *Weenusk, In-*

genika, and *B. C. Boy* began to navigate this stretch of the river with regularly scheduled runs. Hudson's Hope, because of its strategic location at the head of navigation, continued its historic function as an important terminal and transfer point for freight and passengers. Unfortunately, the steamboat era was of short duration. The Peace River itself, subject to extended periods of low water levels and constantly shifting sand- and gravel bars, was always a challenge to navigation. Also, the steady penetration of railroads and roads into the country contributed to the ultimate disappearance of the river vessels. In 1929 the SS *D. A. Thomas,* the largest and most luxurious of the Peace River steamboats (she had thirty-five staterooms and room for 300 passengers), made her last trip to Hudson's Hope. With her departure the steamboat era ended. Soon the once-busy landing at the foot of the bluff was practically abandoned, henceforth used only by the narrow riverboat providing local ferry service to the south shore.

The day we spent in the attractive small community of Hudson's Hope was a most delightful one. Upon our arrival in the morning we went directly to the Hudson's Hope museum. It is housed in the building built by the Hudson's Bay Company in 1942 as its store. It contains a most interesting collection of pictures and items reflecting life in the early days of Hudson's Hope. This building, as well as one from an earlier period, is on the seven acres that the Hudson's Bay Company acquired for the use of its relocated post when it moved from the south to the north side of the river in 1890.

The earlier Hudson's Bay building dates back to the early 1900s. It is a rectangular structure, built of hand-squared timbers, caulked with white mortar, and has dovetailed corners and a pitched roof covered with wooden shakes. Inside, the rather crude wooden counter and shelves are still in place, along with a large potbellied stove and a wooden fur press. At the extreme eastern end of the Hudson's Bay acreage is the tiny Anglican church of St. Peter's. In 1938 it acquired this site from the company for a token payment of one dollar. The church was erected by local volunteers and was constructed entirely of logs. The colorful flower beds bordering the walk leading to the church entrance add much to its charm. The lovely stretch of parklike Hudson's Bay Company land extends for nearly seven hundred feet along the bluff above the river. The view from here is magnificent. The mighty Peace flows eastward, its powerful current plainly visible. The forest-covered hills extend unbroken and seemingly endless in all directions as far as the eye can see. It is a most beautiful spot. Directly below us was the once-busy landing for stern-wheelers and motorboats. For some years it was used by the small river ferryboat, until it, too, was discontinued, replaced by the modern bridge a short distance upstream. Now all trace of the landing has disappeared.

Our chief purpose in coming to Hudson's Hope was to locate and photograph the sites of the two forts on the south side of the river, i.e., Rocky Mountain Portage Fort (1805) and its reestablished version: Hudson's Hope (circa 1875). We received directions from the friendly owner of a combined sporting goods store and gas station. Following his instructions, we crossed the Peace and followed a narrow dirt trail paralleling the south side of the river eastward until we reached the end of the road at Maurice Creek. We carefully searched this location in ever-widening circles but found nothing to indicate any suggestion of a trading post site.

We returned to Hudson's Hope just before dark, tired, hungry, and quite disappointed. However, after enjoying one of the best meals we'd ever eaten of perfectly cooked liver and onions at the Sportsman Inn, we felt greatly refreshed and our disappointment vanished. "After all," we told ourselves, "we can always come back and try again." And this was just what we planned to do. In the meantime, however, we contacted Dr. David Burley of Simon Fraser University, who had been so generous in sharing his knowledge of the early forts on the upper Peace, and from him we found that the area we should have been searching was on the east side of Maurice Creek.

So, yes, we would try again. Actually, we were glad of the need to return, for the beauty of this little town, the friendliness of its people, the availability of good food, and the hospitality offered by the free campsites in the Alwin Holland Memorial Park made a repeat visit to Hudson's Hope a most pleasant prospect.

We did return to Hudson's Hope three years later. We knew from Dr. David Burley that at this time (1991) only the general location of the 1804 Rocky Mountain Portage House somewhere on the south side of the Peace River a short distance east of Maurice Creek was known, there being as yet insufficient archaeological evidence to accurately pinpoint its site. We decided, therefore, to confine our efforts to obtaining overall views that would encompass the probable location of the post. Accordingly, we stationed ourselves behind the Hudson's Hope museum on the north side of the high bank above the Peace and focused on the entire panorama of heavily wooded hills rising from the south side of the river a short distance east of the mouth of Maurice Creek. We felt by doing so our general overall view of the area would include the site of the 1804 fort when it is finally located.

Fort St. James

After establishing Fort McLeod in 1806, Fraser returned to Rocky Mountain Portage Fort, his base on the eastern side of the Rockies. There he spent the winter making ready for his next season's explorations. The following spring the breakup on the Peace was late and it wasn't until the twentieth of May that Fraser was able to leave Rocky Mountain Portage Fort. He arrived back at Fort McLeod on the seventh of June 1807. Encouraged by the enthusiastic report of his clerk, James McDougall, who had made a three-and-one-half-day journey overland from Fort McLeod to Carrier (Stuart) Lake during the previous winter, Fraser decided to go there to investigate its suitability for a fur trade post. Instead of traveling cross-country as McDougall had done, Fraser, John Stuart, and their small party of six men in two canoes followed a long, tortuous, difficult water route that required thirty-three days to reach their destination. After threading the tangled and obstructed mishmash of streams leading from McLeod Lake to the Fraser River, Fraser's party turned up the Nechako, a large river flowing into the Fraser from the west. Of this river Fraser wrote: "The banks of the River is beautiful, in many places resembling that of the River Lac la Plui [Rainy River], and the Liard [Poplar] is the most stupendous I ever saw." At the forks of the Nechako and the Stuart rivers he ascended the latter, and finally, on July 26, he reached Carrier Lake.

His expectations had been high, but shortly after his arrival he admitted that although the lake was "a fine large Lake, . . . my ideas are far short of what Mr. McDougalls account of it would lead [me] to expect. In the Spring of the year when he was here, everything had a flourishing appearance—there were plenty of fish and fowl, and some meat and they told him that Beaver were plenty likewise. Since our arrival here we have seen upwards of 50 men—all in a starving state." He uncharitably assessed the native people living around the lake as "a large Indolent thievish set of vagabonds, of a mild disposition. They are amazing fond of goods . . . But then they are independent of us, as they get their necessaries from their neighbors who trade with the Natives of the sea coast."

Fraser and Stuart quickly set about the task of building a fort, eventually called Fort St. James, on the lake henceforth known as Stuart Lake. The site chosen was in a beautiful bay immediately northeast of the outlet of the lake.

John McLean, who was stationed at Fort St. James thirty years after its establishment, in his *Notes of a Twenty-five Years' Service in the Hudson's Bay Territory* has left a quite vivid description of the lake:

> Fort St. James, the depôt of New Caledonia district stands near the outlet of Stuart's Lake, and commands a splendid view of the surrounding country. The lake is about fifty miles in length, and from three to four miles in breadth, stretching away to the north and north-east for about twenty miles; the view from the Fort embraces nearly the whole of this section of it, which is studded with beautiful islands. The western shore is low, and indented by a number of small bays formed by wooded points projecting into the lake, the back-ground rising abruptly into a ridge of hills of varied height and magnitude. On the east the view is limited to a range of two or three miles, by the intervention of a high promontory, from which the eye glances to the snowy summits of the Rocky Mountains in the distant background. I do not know that I have seen anything to compare with this charming prospect in any other part of the country . . .

Fraser and his men now began to experience the hardships of life at a fort whose basic source of food was dependent upon the unpredictable annual run of salmon. The salmon did not appear when expected; other fish were caught, but only in insufficient numbers; wild berries constituted their chief form of sustenance. Finally, long overdue, the salmon began to arrive in September and Fraser commented that ". . . now they have thousands of them drying. I have not as yet traded many but . . . I am at a loss how to pay them. The Indians dont seem to value goods much, . . . and what is worse I am afraid that they will not make any furs." Fraser's discouragement was expressed in a letter to John Stuart dated September 29, 1806: "I assure you I am tired of living on fish and I feel quite dull and lonesome since you left me. Nothing goes on to my liking. I hate the place and the Indians."

In 1810 Daniel Harmon was transferred from his post at Fort Dunvegan on the Peace River to New Caledonia. He, accompanied by thirteen men, arrived at Fort St. James on the seventh of November. He wrote in his journal: "This fort stands in a very pleasant place, on a rise of ground, at the east end of Stuart's Lake, which I am informed, is at least three hundred miles in circumference. At the distance of about two hundred rods from the fort, a considerable river runs out of the lake, where the Natives,—have a village or rather a few small huts, built of wood. At these they remain during the season for taking and drying salmon, on which they subsist, during the greater part of the year."

In the spring Harmon reported that "this afternoon, the ice in this lake broke up. Musquetoes begin to come about; and troublesome companions they are in the wilderness." How very true this observation still is! He also noted that "as the frost is now out of the ground, we have planted our potatoes, and sowed barley, turnips, & which are the first that we ever sowed, on this west side of the mountain." Underscoring the fort's dependence on salmon, Harmon's journal entry for August 2 reads: "Our whole stock of provisions in the fort, for ten persons, consists of five salmon, only. It is impossible, at this season, to take fish out of this lake or river. Unless the salmon from the sea, soon make their appearance, our condition will be deplorable." On September 2, his journal entry is in marked contrast to the one made a month earlier. He wrote: "We now have the common salmon in abundance. They weigh from five to seven pounds. There are, also, a few of a larger kind, which will weigh sixty or seventy pounds. Both of them are very good, when just taken out of the water. But, when dried, as they are by the Indians here, by the heat of the sun, or in the smoke of a fire, they are not very palatable. When salted, they are excellent." By the end of October, Harmon could write in his journal: "We have now in our store, twenty five thousand salmon. Four in a day are allowed to each man." Still another entry reflects the importance of the salmon in the lives of both native and traders alike: "Saturday, August 15. Salmon begin to come up this river. As soon as one is caught the Natives always make a feast, to express their joy at the arrival of these fish. The person, who first sees a salmon in the river, exclaims, Tâ-loe nas-lay! Tâ-loe nas-lay! In English, Salmon have arrived! Salmon have arrived! and the exclamation is caught with joy, and uttered with animation, by every person in the village."

John Stuart, who had accompanied Simon Fraser on his epic journey down the Fraser River as well as assisted in establishing the four trading posts west of the Rockies, was named in 1809 by the North West Company to succeed Fraser as chief of New Caledonia, a post he held for the next twelve years. In 1821, when the North West and Hudson's Bay companies amalgamated, the four Fraser River area forts were taken over by the new company and Stuart, given the rank of chief factor, was retained as head of the New Caledonia district for three more years.

By this time Fort St. James had become the headquarters for the district, as well as the chief residence of the superintendent. Furs were collected here from posts throughout the district (which soon included almost all of the central interior of present-day British Columbia), and were shipped out by way of Fort McLeod and the Peace River until the mid-1820s, when the new route via the Fraser River as far as Fort Alexandria, overland by packhorse brigade to Kamloops and Okanagan, and thence by the Columbia River to the Pacific was used. The fort also quickly became the major depot for distribution of trading goods to the other posts. In addition, Fort St. James conducted an active trade with the local Carrier Indians for their furs, chiefly beaver, marten, mink, otter, lynx, and bear. William Connolly, formerly of the North West Company, was made chief trader in 1824 and chief factor in 1825, at which time he was sent to Fort St. James, where he served as head of the New Caledonia district from 1824 to 1830.

George Simpson during the course of his 1828 voyage from York Factory on Hudson's Bay to Fort George at the mouth of the Columbia River on the Pacific spent a week at Fort St. James. The journal kept by Chief Factor Archibald McDonald covering this trip contains many references to their stay at the post. McDonald under date of Wednesday, September 17, described the pomp and ceremony that Simpson mandated should accompany his arrival at any of the fur forts:

The day, as yet, being fine, the flag was put up; the piper in full Highland costume; and every arrangement was made to arrive at Fort St. James in the most imposing manner we could, for the sake of the Indians. Accordingly, when within about a thousand yards of the establishment, descending a gentle hill, a gun was fired, the bugle sounded, and soon after, the piper commenced the celebrated march of the clans—(Peace: or War, if you will it otherwise.) The guide, with the British ensign, led the van, followed by the band; then the Governor, on horseback, supported behind by Doctor Hamlyn and myself on our chargers, two deep; twenty men, with their burdens, next formed the line; then one loaded horse, and lastly, Mr. McGillivray [with his wife and light infantry] closed the rear. During a brisk discharge of small arms and wall pieces from the Fort, Mr. Douglas met us a short distance in advance, and in this order we made our entrée into the Capital of Western Caledonia.

While Simpson was at Fort St. James, he took advantage of the occasion to convene a gathering of the principal Indians of the area. After being introduced to them as the "Great Chief of the Country," he proceeded to review the various acts of violence that had occurred in the area during the past several years. Although he well realized that he could not back up his blunt words with force if the Indians challenged him, he did not hesitate to boldly point out how hopeless the Indians' situation would be if he were to wage hostilities against them. He concluded by warning them that in the event of any further violence the "Whites should be compelled to inbrue their hands in the blood of Indians," and "it would be a general sweep; that the innocent would go with the guilty,—and that it was hard to say when we would stop; never, in any case, until the Indians gave the most unqualified proof of their good conduct in future." McDonald also noted that "at the close of the harangue, the chief had a glass of rum, a little tobacco, and a shake of the hand from the Great Chief, after which the piper played them the song of peace. They dispersed, to appearance quite sensible of all that was said to them."

A year later, in a report Simpson prepared for the Governor and London Committee he estimated that the Carrier Indians of the Fort St. James area furnished annually about twenty-five packs of furs valued at about £2,000. He described the almost total reliance of nearly all the posts in New Caledonia on fish, chiefly salmon, for their sole source of food. Unfortunately, many times this failed and all were reduced to "half allowance, to quarter allowance and sometimes to no allowance at all." Simpson admitted that living conditions in New Caledonia were "anything but enviable" and that attempts to improve them by the growing of garden crops had failed due to the frequency of devastating summer frosts.

In November of 1827 Chief Factor Connolly sent his clerk, James Douglas, to a nearby lake to establish a fishery there. His efforts, however, were unsuccessful as Connolly reported that "the fish trade has entirely disappointed us, only about 1,600 having been procured, part of which the dogs have brought to the Fort by Mr. Douglas' men."

The celebration of New Year's Day made a welcome break in the rather bleak daily routine of the post. The entry in the Fort St. James journal for the fourteenth of January 1830 reads: "This day was celebrated the return of the New Year, and nothing was heard but the sounds of mirth and jollity. Feasting, carousing, dancing and singing were the order of the day."

At the end of 1830, Chief Factor Peter Warren Dease arrived at Fort St. James to take over the post and district from Connolly. Dease had already rendered valuable assistance to the Sir John Franklin Arctic expedition during the years 1825 to 1827. And after Dease's four-year stint at Fort St. James, he and Thomas Simpson, between 1837 and 1839, conducted important explorations along the Arctic coast. Company records show that the furs Dease took down to Fort Vancouver on the Columbia River in the summer of 1834 were valued at £11,000. Deducting expenses of £3,000 covering the "outfit" (trading goods), a balance of £8,000 remained—quite a tidy profit. In fact, by this time it was recognized that New Caledonia was one of the richest districts in the company's entire domain, yielding an average annual return of 8,000 beaver plus other valuable furs.

During Dease's tenure as chief factor in charge of New Caledonia, John McLean, who had many years of service at the company's eastern posts, was sent to Fort St. James to serve as clerk. McLean described the extent of his duties at Fort St. James: "The accounts of all the posts in the district, eight in number, were made up here; I had also to super-intend the men of the establishment, accompany them on their winter trips, and attend to the Indian trade."

At the close of his one year's stay at Fort St. James, McLean wrote the following words, which were a well-deserved tribute to the achieve-ments of the old North West Company:

> When the district [New Caledonia] was first settled, the goods required for trade were brought in by the winterers from Lac la Pluie, which was their dépôt. The people left the district as early in spring as the naviga-tion permitted, and returned so late that they were frequently overtaken by winter ere they reached their destination. Cold, hunger, and fatigue, were the unavoidable consequences; but the enterprising spirit of the men of those days—the intrepid, indefatigable adventurers of the North-West Company—overcame every difficulty. It was that spirit that opened a communication across the broad continent of America; that penetrated to the frost-bound regions of the Arctic circle; and that estab-lished a trade with the natives in this remote land [New Caledonia], when the merchandise required for it was in one season transported from Montreal to within a short distance of the Pacific. Such enterprise has never been exceeded, seldom or never equalled.

Peter Skene Ogden succeeded Dease as head of the New Caledonia district, serving there from 1834 to 1844. A former Nor'-Wester and a tough, enterprising, and successful trader, he was well qualified for the job. According to A. G. Morice, "he was not for ruling with a rod of iron, and he could be considerate for the lowliest of his men, though he visited misbehavior with sound corporal punishment." The same writer added further: "Though at times rather brusque, he was on the whole considerate towards his subalterns, and feeling the weight of his responsibility, he more than once insisted on prudence when dealing with obstreperous aborigines. He was impartial, and did not hesitate to lay the blame on his own men when they did not treat the Indians fairly . . ." Ogden consistently practiced a policy of prudent restraint designed to serve the best interests of the company in dealing with problems involving the native people. As he wrote in a letter to one of his men who had become involved in a fracas with the Indians:

> You must bear in mind that if unfortunately in these quarrels blood was

to be shed, the affairs of the district would be deranged to retaliate,—it is not only our duty, but our interest also, so far as circumstances will admit, to avoid coming to extremes with the Indians. Look at our numbers compared to theirs; look at the many opportunities they may have of committing murder; look at their treacherous character; look also at the weakness of our establishments in the summer and the impossibility of obtaining assistance, and then judge for yourself if it is not more prudent to avoid quarrels than to engage in them.

On the occasion of the murder of his friend Chief Factor Samuel Black, Ogden wrote a circular letter to the officers in his district warning them "how cautious and how guarded we ought to be on all occasions with Indians, and this most melancholy event, independently of long experience, teaches us never to place any trust or confidence in them. We are well aware that in this country our lives are constantly exposed, and in regulating our treatment of Indians neither too much severity nor leniency will answer; but a medium between both is the most advisable."

Unfortunately, the man chosen to replace Ogden as head of the New Caledonia district was of an entirely different character. Chief Trader Donald Manson, while zealous and energetic in his promotion of the company's interests, lacked the even disposition of his predecessor. Manson's volatile and excitable temperament, coupled with his frequent recourse to violence ("club law," according to George Simpson), soon lost him the respect and regard of both his own men and the natives alike, thereby adversely affecting the fullest realization of his management efforts. For example, his violent and unrestrained reaction in response to a fistfight with an Indian compromised the safety of his whole establishment. The resentment and hostility engendered, though superficially eased by liberal presents given by Manson to the angered natives who were besieging his post, festered in their hearts for a long time, to the disadvantage of the company.

During Manson's fourteen years at Fort St. James (1844–56), he was constantly hampered in his operations by frequent desertions of his men, as well as by the request of all his officers in charge of outlying posts to be transferred to other forts. Manson had other troubles to worry him. The returns from the district had steadily declined. An expedition sent across the Rockies to bring back "leather" (i.e., moose hides) had started back so late in the fall that it was caught by the ice in the river and forced to put the cargo *en cache,* always somewhat risky. And, finally, when his requisition for a certain quantity of accoutrements for the pack train horses was considered extravagantly large by P. S. Ogden, now a member of the company's Board of Management for the region west of the Rockies, Manson quite undiplomatically replied in a letter that "when he took charge of New Caledonia affairs he found everything of this description worn out in tatters"—a reflection on his predecessor (P. S. Odgen) that undoubtedly did not pass unnoticed by that gentleman.

Manson was relieved of his post, but subsequent explanations, plus the ill health of his replacement, resulted in his reinstatement and return to Fort St. James. However, his troubles were not ended. Desertions by his men continued, flagrant insubordination by several employees created difficulties, and the high mortality among the pack-horses used on the long and rugged overland journey between Fort Alexandria on the Fraser and Okanagan rivers was a cause of much concern. Ever since Chief Factor Connolly's departure in 1830, the number of personnel assigned to the New Caledonia district had been reduced. Much of Manson's difficulties was caused by lack of competent men to replace the chronic troublemakers and those who were incapable or unwilling to perform their duties in a satisfactory manner. It was not realistic to expect good returns from posts governed by inexperienced or careless men. Ignoring the atmosphere of unrest and the unpredictable nature of the natives, as expressed in recent deeds of violence followed by the inevitable reprisals in various parts of New Caledonia, Chief Factor Manson early in his tenure as head of Fort St. James rather rashly and prematurely had taken down the fort's palisade and bastion. This was an act that some years later he had cause to regret. Employees of the Hudson's Bay Company considered being sent to any post in New Caledonia as the equivalent of being sent to Siberia. This was partly due to the harsh living conditions and the monotonous diet of fish. It was also partly due to the reputation the district had for the rough and harsh treatment experienced from the company's officers. During Manson's time at Fort St. James as head of the New Caledonia district, it was not only he who was responsible for that reputation but also several of the officers under his direction, such as Paul Fraser, Donald McLean, and Peter Ogden. Eventually, the Governor-in-Chief, Sir George Simpson, in an official communication to Manson dated June 18, 1853, wrote at some length regarding what constituted appropriate disciplinary action properly taken by company officers:

I am sorry to state that the service in New Caledonia is very unpopular among the people in consequence of reports spread of the rough treatment experienced at the hands of the Company's officers.—'club law'—must not be allowed to prevail. We duly appreciate the necessity of maintaining discipline and enforcing obedience; but that end is not to be attained by the display of violent passion and the infliction of severe and arbitrary punishment in hot blood. When a servant is refractory or disobeys orders he should be allowed a full hearing, his case examined fairly and deliberately, and, if guilty, either taken out to the dépôt, put on short rations or under arrest—in fact, almost any punishment rather than knocking about or flogging.

I have to beg you will make the foregoing remarks known to Mr. P. Ogden, Mr. McLean, and other officers in the district, and I trust we may hear no more of these disagreeable affairs.

So strongly did Simpson feel about this matter that he addressed a private letter to Manson, saying: "You must really put a check on the 'club law' that prevails in your district. It makes the service so unpopular that it is difficult to induce men to join it. . . . We hear that McLean and Ogden use their fists very freely, and I think you should caution them on the subject."

Donald Manson had the rank of chief trader when he was sent to Fort St. James. Twelve years later when he left, in 1856, he was still chief trader. It would seem that his abilities and untiring efforts in carrying out his duties on behalf of the company were not considered sufficient to outweigh his harsh and injudicious treatment of subordinates and natives and gain for him a promotion to chief factor. So when the Board of Management turned down his request for a chief factorship, he left New Caledonia and the service of the company.

His successor was Chief Trader Peter Ogden, the Métis son of Peter Skene Ogden. He had charge of Fort St. James and the district of New Caledonia for the next fourteen years—from 1856 until 1870. During that period, the gold rush, which culminated in the Caribou Mountains in the 1860s, began with the finding of gold in the rocky crevices in the banks of the Thompson River. Soon the trickle of prospectors became a flood as they advanced up the creek beds and river valleys ever farther into the heart of New Caledonia. Inevitably their search brought them to Fort St. James. The post rapidly acquired new importance as a source of supplies, information, and emergency help for the miners and prospectors. These new customers paid in cash for the goods they bought in the company store. This marked the beginning of a gradual shift away from the company's long-established system based on a prime beaver pelt as the standard unit of trade to one based on cash. The company did not regard mining and prospecting as incompatible with trapping and was not, therefore, hostile to the appearance of miners into the country where they had been the undisputed and sole white occupants for nearly three-quarters of a century. In fact, the company endeavored to provide the miners with their needs from the shelves of their stores, thereby enhancing the profit figures in their ledgers. Another innovation was the introduction of basic foods, such as flour, rice, beans, tea, and sugar, in large-enough quantities to supply both the Indian and the miner trade. The availability of these items lessened the former complete dependence upon salmon for food. Slowly and gradually, transportation in New Caledonia was improving and expanding as trails became roads and as canoes were replaced or supplemented by steamboats and packhorses. All this made possible increased kinds and amounts of goods on the shelves of the company store.

Reflecting the drop in demand for fur in the European markets, profits from trade in furs throughout the New Caledonia district declined quite sharply during the 1880s and 1890s. In spite of this discouraging prospect, and even though the company would provide only the very minimum of money for the upkeep of the fort's buildings, somehow the officers in charge, in particular Chief Factor Alexander C. Murray, managed not only to maintain the existing buildings but even to construct new ones. However, the decline continued into the twentieth century as the fur trade steadily diminished in importance. At last, perhaps reluctantly, the order came in 1930 to abandon the old log buildings. The fur trade era they had served so well had come to an end. The company needed new buildings in which to effectively pursue its changed role as a modern retail business.

Today a smooth paved highway covers the distance from Fort George (now called Prince George) on the Fraser River to Fort St. James on Stuart Lake. Unfortunately, the beautiful Nechako and Stuart rivers, the only way in the early days to reach Fort St. James, cannot be seen from the present-day road. As we drove rapidly and easily along in our comfortable motor home, we imagined Fraser, Stuart, Harmon, Simpson, Ogden, Dease, and all the host of others laboriously paddling up or down these two rivers, eager to reach their destination and the safety and comfort of the fort or ready to begin an arduous journey over the mountains to the Peace River or down the Fraser and eventually the Columbia to the far Pacific.

The minute we stepped onto the grounds of the fort, we left the twentieth century behind us and were completely absorbed into the life of Fort St. James as it was in the early 1880s, when A. C. Murray was chief factor. This was the period to which the buildings have been restored and furnished. Today, just as it has done ever since its founding in 1806, the fort from its elevated site overlooks a magnificent vista sweeping far over the broad lake and the encircling range of rugged hills and distant mountains. This view remains virtually unchanged from what it was during the time of Fraser and all those who came after him. It still, as McLean wrote more than 150 years ago, "commands a splendid view of the surrounding country."

We walked along the wooden boardwalk to the great building on the western side of the compound. This was the general warehouse and fur store. It was a large rectangular two-story building with hipped roof and small nine-paned windows. It was a magnificent example of Red River frame construction, i.e., horizontal squared logs morticed into upright squared posts. A long wharf and tramway extended from the lake to a cargo door on the north side of the warehouse. Barrels, kegs, boxes of all sizes and shapes, crates, sacks, and bales—all stacked in orderly piles on the floor—nearly filled the cavernous interior of the warehouse. Their contents, according to what few labels and markings we could decipher in the dim light, included tea, coffee, flour, soda, Pearl oil, Graham wafers, Winchester rifles, and ammunition. On wall shelves were Hudson's Bay blankets, men's pants, yard goods, glassware, flatirons, ax heads, iron kettles, and hanks of rope; from the rafters hung an assortment of tinware, such as pans, pails, and cups. The east end of the building was taken over by the fur store. Here a multitude of small furs, including mink, marten, muskrat, lynx, and fox, as well as beaver castoreum, hung from the rafters, while beaver and bear pelts were stacked in piles on the floor. A huge screw-type fur press was also at this end of the building.

Before leaving this storehouse with its vast supply of goods, my husband was put to work. A young serving girl came to get a sack of flour needed for use in the chief factor's house. Before she could stoop to lift up the heavy sack from the pile on the floor, my husband had quickly stepped forward and tossed the bag of flour onto his shoulder, undoubtedly much to the young lady's surprise, and away they went over to the factor's residence on the far side of the compound.

The fish cache served an important role in the life of the fort. It was in this building that the vital supply of dried salmon so necessary for the fort's survival was stored. The rough Red River–type structure was erected on high posts as a deterrent to dogs and other predators. We climbed up the steep stairway leading to the door into the storage room. Inside, hanging from nails in the ceiling beams, were hundreds and hundreds of slabs of dried salmon—a most vivid reminder of the supreme importance of salmon to life in New Caledonia.

Just to the east of the fish cache was the men's house. Here lived company employees and transients, such as pack train handlers and boat crews. It was a rectangular building of squared hand-hewn logs, dovetailed corners, pitched roof, and twelve-paned windows. There was an open loft with a window at each end above the first floor, which included one main room with fireplace and two small bedrooms. Although two young female servants had been sent over to "tidy up" the men's quarters, they chose to sit and gossip, so the "tidying up" remained for the arrival of Elizabeth, a no-nonsense longtime company employee, who quickly made the dust fly as she vigorously shook out the bearskin rugs and wielded broom and dust cloth with the vigor and practice of much experience.

After leaving the men's house, we walked over to the trade store and office. Located just to the east of the great warehouse and about in the center of the fort compound, this building was quite similar to the men's house in size and construction. It was here that the furs brought in were evaluated by the clerk in charge and equivalent credit given for trade in the goods so temptingly displayed on the shelves and counter. This wide assortment of goods was really astonishing. It was truly a "one-stop" shop—the forerunner of a modern department store, where quite literally anything and everything was available: yard goods, clothes, shoes, boots, hardware, ironware, tinware, guns, ammunition, glassware, china, pots, pans, blankets, rope, saws, tools, traps, beads, food staples, and liquor. The store was well equipped to satisfy the needs of the native people and the more recently arrived miners and settlers. One end of the trade store was partitioned off to form an office where the clerk had his desk and ledgers as well as his bed.

We next wandered toward the factor's home, some distance to the east of the inner compound. On our way we had to pass the fort's large and flourishing vegetable garden, and there, back bent over, industriously yanking out weeds, was our friend Elizabeth. We paused to chat, but that did not slow her up in her attack on the weeds. When she learned we were traveling in our motor home, she thought maybe we could use a good solid head of cabbage, perhaps a few newly dug potatoes, and a couple green onions for our supper. Indeed we could, and we were delighted to add this fresh food to our larder.

Before entering the factor's residence, we paused to admire the lovely flower garden bordering the north side of the house. Laid out in raised beds, the flowers were a profusion of brilliant color, a quite pleasing change from the rather drab brown exterior of all the buildings of the fort complex.

We spent much time in the factor's home. The rooms were furnished as they had been during the years of Chief Factor Murray's residence. Living room, dining room, and bedrooms were heated by fireplaces; lighting was by kerosene lamps. The chief factor had his desk and journals in one corner of the living room. There was also a small organ in the room, which undoubtedly gave pleasure during the long winter evenings. The bedrooms all had the traditional washstand with china pitcher and basin on top and, of course, the china chamber pot discreetly hidden in the cupboard below. A large tin bathtub hung on the wall of one of the bedrooms. The tantalizing fragrance coming from the rear of the house quickly led us to the kitchen. A delicious stew was bubbling away on the big wood-burning cookstove. One of the women was busily rolling out biscuits on a flour-covered board on top of the kitchen table. We were hungry and the aroma was so appetizing, but we remembered our gift of fresh cabbage and potatoes and knew we should not be greedy. Just then Elizabeth walked into the kitchen. She had come from the hen house, where she had gathered a half-dozen or so large brown eggs. Of course we had to stop and talk a bit. As we were going out the back door to see the dairy house and chicken yard, a couple of those lovely brown eggs were put into our hands with the comment that "they would be nice for our breakfast!"

After leaving both the fort compound and the factor's residence, we walked down to the shore of Stuart Lake. It is, indeed, a most beautiful lake, as so many of the early traders stationed here had so rightly noted. Here at the water's edge, a Carrier woman was preparing freshly caught salmon for smoking and for drying. Her dexterity as she deftly and quickly cleaned and split these fish was a vivid demonstration of a skill acquired and practiced over many centuries. Some of the fish, simply gutted and split, were hung from horizontal poles for drying in the air and sun. Others were fileted with the backbone removed; the fiery red slabs were then laid on horizontal poles inside a shed to be smoked over a slow-burning fire. Once again, the importance of salmon to the culture and very existence of the people of New Caledonia was brought to mind.

Suddenly we realized that the sun had abruptly disappeared and that a squall, headed by an ever-widening curtain of rain and large tumbling black clouds, was racing down the lake toward us. The now lead-colored lake was covered with tossing whitecaps kicked up by the strong winds. We knew we had to run to reach our motor home before the storm engulfed us. But even in our hasty flight, we couldn't resist a few backward looks. By now the tourists had all fled—we had the fort to ourselves for a few precious moments. The massive warehouse, strong and sturdy, seemingly indestructible, was silhouetted against the blackening sky. The red company flag, whipping violently back and forth from the top of the tall flagstaff, was proudly defying wind and storm. We knew Fort St. James had weathered many such storms before. We knew, also, it would continue to do so for many more years yet to come.

Much later when, warm and dry in our motor home, we were enjoying our supper of the fresh eggs and the vegetables from the fort, we were still not completely back in the twentieth century. The atmosphere created by the people at the fort was so very real, it seemed as though they could not be just "playacting." They were getting their hands dirty in the garden; they were shelling peas, cooking and baking real food, operating the warehouse, selling goods in the trade store. They were friendly and neighborly. In short, they were making it possible to really experience life as it was in the earlier days of Fort St. James. It was truly living history at its best.

Fort Fraser

Simon Fraser, John Stuart, and their party of nine men reached Stuart Lake July 26, 1806, after an arduous two-month journey from Rocky Mountain Portage House. Fraser immediately set his men to work building the post that he named Fort St. James. He then devoted his efforts to obtaining sufficient provisions to enable him and his party to resume their journey of exploration down the Fraser River, which he still thought was the Columbia. However, the salmon run upon which he depended so heavily for his food supply did not appear, so he was forced to give up his river trip for that year. In a letter to James McDougall dated August 31, 1806, Fraser wrote: ". . . and having been in daily expectation of the salmons arriving, naturally led us to expect to be able to procure a sufficiency of that fish for our voyage. But now the season is so advanced and no salmon arrived that I dont expect any this year, and the Indians say it does not come up every year." Frustrated in his river exploration, Fraser lost no time in carrying out the second part of his assignment—the establishment of trading posts on the western side of the Rockies. He sent John Stuart and two men to scout out a lake called Natleh by the Indians, which was reported to be highly productive of fish. This lake was situated about forty miles south of Stuart Lake. Stuart rendezvoused with Fraser at the forks of the Stuart and Nechako rivers in early September. Stuart's impression of the lake was so encouraging that Fraser went to see it himself. He, likewise, was favorably impressed, so much so that he immediately made arrangements for a trading post to be constructed there.

At long last the run of salmon commenced, and everyone at the new post was busily occupied with the task of netting or trapping and drying the enormous numbers of fish needed for the winter's food supply. Prospects for beaver looked promising, but since the expected canoes with goods from the east failed to reach New Caledonia, Fraser had nothing to trade to the Indians for either supplies or beaver. Consequently, the fare of nothing but dried salmon at his forts must have been deadly monotonous, while the trade results were disastrous.

In the fall of 1810, Daniel Harmon was transferred from Fort Dunvegan to New Caledonia, where he was to remain for the next nine years. He spent the winter of 1810–11 at Fort Fraser, arriving there on December 29. He wrote in his journal:

This establishment is at the east end of Frazer's Lake, which received its name from that of the gentleman, who first built here, in 1806. At the distance of about a mile from this, there runs out of this lake, a considerable river, where the Natives have a large village, and where they take and dry salmon. This lake may be eighty or ninety miles in circumference, and is well supplied with white fish, trout, &.

Tuesday, January 1, 1811. This being the first day of another year, our people have passed it, according to the custom of the Canadians, in drinking and fighting.—As soon as they began to be a little intoxicated, and to quarrel among themselves, the Natives began to be apprehensive, that something unpleasant might befal them, also. They, therefore, hid themselves under beds, and elsewhere, saying, that they thought the white people had run mad, for they appeared not to know what they were about.

In a journal entry for Wednesday, January 30, Harmon described how he had handled an incident of Indian pilfering:

Two nights since, an Indian cut a hole in a window in my room, which is made of parchment, at the distance of not more than two feet from the foot of my bed, where I lay asleep, and took from a table, near it, several articles of clothing. The next morning, two other Indians brought back to me a part of the stolen property, and informed me who the thief was, and where he could be found. Soon after, accompanied by my interpreter, I went, and found the young villain, in a hut under ground, along with about twelve others, who are as great thieves as himself. I told him, that, as he was young, I hoped this was the first time he had ever been guilty of theft; and, provided he would return all the property which he had taken away, I would forgive this offence; but if he should ever in future be guilty of any misconduct toward us, he might depend on being severely punished. I then returned to our house; and, shortly after, two Indians brought me the remainder of the property which had been stolen, and I gave them a little ammunition, for having made known the thief.

In October of 1814, Harmon sent J. La Roque over to Fraser's Lake to reestablish the post there, which apparently had fallen into disrepair. Harmon, himself, following orders from John Stuart, went there a short time later to assume charge of the fort. That spring, under Harmon's direction, an attempt was made to raise some vegetables to supplement the fort's food supply. Harmon's gardening efforts appeared to have been moderately successful, for he noted in his journal in October of 1815: "We have taken our vegetables out of the ground. We have forty-one bushels of potatoes, the produce of one bushel planted last spring. Our turnips, barley, & have produced well."

Misfortune befell Fort Fraser in 1817, when it burned to the ground on October 4. The fort was subsequently rebuilt and taken over by the Hudson's Bay Company after its amalgamation with the North

West Company in 1821. George Simpson, who visited Fort Fraser during the course of his 1829 inspection trip, in a report to the Governor and London Committee, summarized his assessment of Fort Fraser as follows: "It is frequented by the inhabitants of Six Villages of the carrier Tribe, amounting to . . . Souls, whose hunting grounds are more extensive than those of Stewarts Lake, but held as private property in like manner by the Natives. It has been a rich Country both in Beaver & small Furs, but was previous to the coalition over run by Iroquois Trappers as many other parts of the District, and consequently much injured; but it has since then recruited, and is now the most valuable Post in New Caledonia yielding about 30 Packs Furs value about £3000."

During the 1830s the post was under the management of William Thew. He, unfortunately, was an exception to the usually capable Hudson's Bay post managers. He lacked totally the temperament needed for dealing not only with the native people but also with his own men. His high-handedness, autocratic ways, uncontrollable temper, and cruelty were the cause of numerous desertions by his employees and unrest and even violent outbreaks among the Indians. A. G. Morice, referring to Peter Skene Ogden's journal, described the following incident in his book *The History of the Northern Interior of British Columbia:*

> On some trivial pretext he [Thew] shortly after fell on one of the leading Indians of Fraser Lake, dubbed Saint Paul by the engagés of the fort, and gave him such a beating that, arming themselves with axes, the naturally peaceful villagers went in a body to the fort, a mile distant, broke open the gates, and rushed on the establishment, when the now fairly frightened autocrat came to a window, and, begging for his life, threw down gifts to the mob, promising at the same time to make Saint Paul a chief and compensate him for the ill-treatment he had received, words which succeeded in calming the irritation of the natives and preventing further hostilities.

Fort Fraser remained active until about 1900, continuing to trade for salmon and furs and serving the needs of the native Indians.

We experienced no difficulty in reaching Fraser Lake nor in finding the site of the fort, for it was well marked. In the large clearing at the southeast side of the lake, shallow cellar depressions, unmistakably marked by distinctive vegetative ground cover, were now all that remained of the once-busy fort. As we looked over the clearing, we tried to picture it as it was when the fort buildings stood there and, in the words lettered on the large information sign, "many historic figures such as Simon Fraser, Daniel Harmon and Peter Skene Ogden . . . passed through the fort's high gates." The spot chosen for the post was a most sightly one. It was situated on a slight elevation at the bottom of a large bay enclosed by gently wooded slopes behind which rise the lofty summits of an encircling range of hills. Close by was the small stream that flows into the Nechako River.

The first time we visited Fort Fraser we were forced to see the site and the bay under the most adverse conditions. Misty rain, fog, and low-hanging clouds almost totally shrouded the view over the lake. Obviously, conditions for photography were, to say the least, not the best. So two years later we returned, but we were doomed to disappointment once again. This time the misty rain was a drenching downpour, and the lake was practically invisible. Not satisfied until we captured the beauty of this site in our photographs, it was in 1991, on our third attempt, that our persistence paid off. We were rewarded with blue sky and sunshine, so that at last, we, too, were able to enjoy the beautiful panorama of Fraser Lake and its encircling hills.

Fort George
(Fraser River)

Continually frustrated in his hopes of receiving the supplies and additional men he needed to undertake his journey down the Great (Fraser) River, Simon Fraser impatiently waited during most of 1807, either at his most recently constructed Fort Fraser on Fraser Lake or at Fort St. James built a short while earlier on Stuart Lake. Finally, in the autumn of that year, two canoes loaded with supplies and men arrived from across the mountains. At long last Fraser could begin to take the measures necessary for carrying out his grand plan of exploration.

His first step was to build a post at the confluence of the Nechako and Fraser rivers. This was to be his advance base from which he would begin his expedition. And since it was in an area exceedingly rich in furs, it would serve as a trading post for the local Carrier Indians. He put Hugh Faries, one of the two clerks who had arrived with the canoes, in charge of the new post, which was called Fort George in honor of the then-reigning British monarch. According to Marjorie W. Campbell's description in her book *The Savage River,* "Fort George . . . was only a group of log shacks, each with a crude stone fireplace and beds made of poles and bark, all surrounded by a strong, rough stockade of pointed logs."

By early spring the many months of planning and preparation were behind Fraser. Now that he was provided with an adequate supply of dried salmon for food and with enough trading goods both to ensure the goodwill of the Indians and to pay for any necessary services or items that might be required during his trip, he could, at last, undertake his journey. Early on the morning of May 28, 1808, he, Stuart, Quesnel, a crew of nineteen men, and two Indians embarked in four canoes, departing from Fort George, and, accompanied by shouts of "bon voyage" from Faries and others left behind, headed downstream, ready to face the dangers of this trip into the unknown. Ten weeks later, on August 6, they all returned to Fort George, their journey to the Pacific successfully completed.

At the time of the coalition of the North West and Hudson's Bay companies, Fort George was taken over by the Hudson's Bay Company. Barely two years later, an incident took place at the fort that illustrated anew the unpredictableness of the natives. When James M. Yale, clerk in charge, returned to his post after a two-day visit to nearby Fort St. James, he was horrified to find that during his absence two of his employees had been brutally killed by two Fraser Lake Indians. The mutilated bodies were discovered in an outhouse, along with one of the men's axes, which had been used to commit the murders.

Charged with apparent neglect of duty, Yale was relieved of his post and sent to district headquarters at Fort St. James to await the outcome of an investigation into the charges against him by the Council of the Company. While there, he served as one of three clerks under Chief Factor William Connolly. Finally, after two years, the verdict was rendered. Yale was completely exonerated of any negligence and absolved from any blame. He returned to Fort George, reinstated as the clerk in charge of the post.

There were some years when Fort George was temporarily closed for short periods. For example, in September of 1826 George Simpson wrote in his journal kept during his canoe journey to the Pacific: "Thick morning. At Forks [i.e., of Nechako and Fraser] by five. A few minutes before, left ruins of Fort George on our right."

John McLean, who was in charge of Fort George during the year 1836–37, recorded his impression of the post: "The situation of the post is exceedingly dreary, standing on the right bank of Frazer's River, having in front a high hill that shades the sun until late in the morning, and in the midst of 'woods and wilds whose melancholy gloom' is saddening enough. Yet it has its agrémens, its good returns,—the ne plus ultra of an Indian trader's happiness—its good Indians, and its good fare; the produce of the soil and dairy." Following the Hudson's Bay Company's policy of encouraging the growing of local food products whenever possible, McLean had four acres prepared for sowing. As he wrote in his book *Notes of a Twenty-five Years' Service in the Hudson's Bay Territory,* "Seed was ordered from the Columbia, and handmills to grind our grain. Pancakes and hot rolls were thenceforward to be the order of the day; Babine salmon and dog's flesh were to be sent—to Coventry!"

Peter Skene Ogden's journal entry for January 31, 1840, reflects his satisfaction with the results of the trading at Fort George, remarking on the "considerable excess on [its] returns." New Caledonia was a country rich in furs, but even its abundant returns could not continue to pay the ever-mounting transportation costs, as the distance to be covered increased with each new fort established. As far back as 1813 the North West Company had recognized that the only way a profit could be realized from the bountiful fur resources of New Caledonia was through the discovery of a shorter transportation route that would take the furs westward to the Pacific rather than eastward to the Atlantic.

Accordingly, John Stuart set out from Fort St. James in an attempt to find a practicable way that would replace the Peace River–transmountain route to the distributing center of Fort McLeod. He pioneered a route by canoe from Fort George down the Fraser as far south as Fort Alexandria, then overland by packhorse to Kamloops at the junction of the North and South Thompson rivers, thence southward through the Okanagan valley to the Okanagan River. Here travel by canoe was resumed, following the Okanagan and Columbia rivers to Fort George on the Pacific.

It took a while for this route to become established, but by the time of the coalition of the two fur-trading companies it had largely replaced the older route. At the same time, however, the heavy items including large shipments of leather (i.e., dressed moose or caribou skins) came into New Caledonia by canoe up the Athabasca River, then by packhorse along its tributary, the Miette River, over the Yellowhead Pass to Tête Jaune Cache on the Fraser; canoes were then used for the remainder of the journey down the Fraser to Fort George. By 1826 Fort George had largely replaced Fort McLeod as the entry and exit post for New Caledonia. Through its fort gates now passed most of the goods either coming into or going out of the district.

The obvious advantages of Fort George's location at the forks of the Fraser and Nechako rivers soon made it the natural supply center for all of the central northern area of what is now British Columbia—a position it still occupies to the present day.

In 1871, with the appearance of the first small stern-wheeler, *Enterprise,* in the upper Fraser, Fort George assumed new importance as a major terminus for steamboat transport. During a relatively brief ten-year period beginning in 1909, a number of sturdy stern-wheelers made scheduled round-trips from Fort George to Tête Jaune Cache at Mile 53, the head of navigation on the upper Fraser, and from Fort George to Soda Creek, the start of navigation on the upper Fraser and the northern terminus of the packhorse trail to the Columbia River. The Fraser River was not easily conquered. Its turbulent canyons, rapids, rocks, and whirlpools took a heavy toll on the vessels attempting to navigate its waters. Eventually, however, railroads and highways reaching Fort George removed the need for continuing the perilous and uncertain steamboat transport. In 1921 the haunting whistle of the stern-wheeler, as she signaled her approach to Fort George, was heard for the last time. The steamboat era on the Fraser River had ended.

Bruce Hutchinson in his book *The Fraser* rather aptly summed up the significance of Fort George: "In some ways Fort George was the most notable white man's habitation on the river. From it Fraser started for the river's mouth and the fur brigades moved southward out of the northern trapping areas down to Kamloops and the Columbia. Steamboats plied from the fort up and down the river. Finally the Grand Trunk Pacific Railway reached here from the Rockies and made a town." Fort George, now called Prince George, is today a thriving city, the third largest in British Columbia. It continues to reap the advantages of its strategic location at the confluence of the Fraser and Nechako rivers.

Before going in search of the site of the old fur fort, we made our way to the banks of the Nechako, a most beautiful stream. At its junction with the Fraser it rippled over a short stretch of shoal water, the tiny waves sparkling in the sunshine. The site of Fraser's Fort George was on the banks of the Fraser, a short distance below the mouth of the Nechako. It was surrounded by a lovely park that extended along the west bank of the river. Close by the river's edge were a well-aged reproduction of a four-sided bastion and a small section of the log stockade wall that once enclosed the fort. It was quite impressive in its simplicity and quite enough to symbolize most effectively the great importance Fort George had in the development and growth of New Caledonia. Surrounding this historic monument was a beautifully landscaped park, with large expanses of unbroken greensward, flower beds of riotous colors, scattered shade trees, and plenty of benches for people to sit and enjoy the peace and beauty of the scene.

We sat on the grassy riverbank; on the opposite side, the river was flanked by a range of pine-covered hills. We could not agree with McLean's reference to the location as "exceeding dreary." We thought it delightful. The river flowed past steadily and smoothly southward. It looked quite peaceful, giving no hint of the horrendous rapids and whirlpools located downstream. Romantics that we were, we couldn't help feeling a real thrill as we realized we were actually at the very spot where Simon Fraser's historic journey down this mighty river nearly two hundred years ago had both begun and successfully ended. We knew we would always cherish this experience.

Fort Gibraltar

As the North West Company continued its push during the first decade of the 1800s into the upper reaches of the Fraser and Peace rivers, establishing Fort Fraser, Fort St. James, and Fort George, it was quickly realized that increasingly large supplies of pemmican would be needed not only to maintain the posts already built but also to permit the continuation of further expansion westward. It was pemmican (that form of concentrated food made from dried and pounded buffalo meat) that fueled the brigades and provisioned the distant forts. Fortunately, the company's Fort Pembina on the Red River at the mouth of the Pembina, located in the very heart of the buffalo country, was able to provide large amounts of pemmican on a sustained basis, thus making the company's aggressive expansion possible.

Secure in its possession of the products of the upper Red River valley, the company decided to erect a fort at the strategic junction of the Red and Assiniboine rivers. Such a fort would ensure their control over the flow of supplies, especially the pemmican, coming down these rivers, a vital link in the Nor'Westers' supply line stretching between Lake Superior, the Rockies, and the Athabasca country to the north. Accordingly, in 1807 John McDonald of Garth, head of the Upper Red River department, announced he would build a post at the confluence of the two rivers. McDonald wrote in his *Autobiographical Notes* under the date of 1807: "I established a fort at the junction of the Red and Assiniboil rivers, and called it 'Gibraltar,' though there was not a rock or stone within three miles." However, there is some evidence to suggest that John Wills, who succeeded Alexander Henry the younger in charge of the Lower Red River department in 1809, was the actual builder of Fort Gibraltar in 1810 and that perhaps MacDonald was only responsible for the suggestion that it be built.

The site chosen for the fort was on the north side of the Assiniboine, on a high bank overlooking the knoll on the opposite shore of the river where the old French Fort Rouge had once stood. Wilson F. Green in his *Red River Revelations* described the fort as follows: "Inside an 18-foot stockade of stout split oak logs were upwards of a dozen buildings: a 64-foot main residence, two servants' houses, store, kitchen, icehouse and number of stables for horses, cattle, other livestock and poultry. A high lookout point gave a clear view of the entire countryside in all directions. From the top of the walls, guns would be able to control traffic on both rivers." Construction of the fort was delayed by a major flooding of the Red River in 1809, so that it was not until the following year, 1810, that the complex was started. A crew of twenty men was able to complete it during the next year.

Fort Gibraltar served as the headquarters of the North West Company's fur trade and pemmican shipments from the Red, Assiniboine, and Qu'Appelle rivers and their surrounding area. On August 30, 1812, the first of several contingents of the Selkirk settlers, led by Captain Miles Macdonell, arrived to establish their colony on the banks of the Red River on land granted to Lord Selkirk by the Hudson's Bay Company. From that moment, Fort Gibraltar became also the base of operations for the North West Company's implacable opposition to the presence of these newcomers. To the Nor'Westers this attempt to establish an agricultural community in the heart of fur country athwart their main transportation waterway was a threat to their very survival.

To them this colony established by Lord Selkirk, who was a major shareholder in the Hudson's Bay Company, was merely an extension—a tool—of that company. They did not have to be particularly clairvoyant or astute to recognize the threat posed by the Red River colony, and as E. E. Rich wrote in his *History of the Hudson's Bay Company 1670–1870,* "... it would have needed great powers of casuistry as well as detailed knowledge of the Company's [i.e., the Hudson's Bay Company's] affairs for them to have accepted a distinction between Company and Colony, especially when they saw Miles Macdonell taking measures which placed their claims and their trade under challenge."

The North West Company correctly recognized that the establishment of the colony on the Red River was the first step in the Hudson's Bay Company's decision to challenge the Nor'Westers' monopoly of the rich Athabasca fur trade. According to Rich: "... the colony must play its part by interrupting the Northwesters' provision and transportation system and by forwarding the Company's supplies of men and pemmican."

At this time Alexander Macdonell, a cousin to Miles Macdonell, was in charge of Fort Gibraltar. For the first winter (1812–13) relations between the two groups were, to all outward appearances, reasonably friendly. However, when faced with the arrival of additional settlers sent over by Lord Selkirk and with a lack of sufficient supplies to feed them, Miles Macdonell, in his capacity as governor of the colony, early in the winter of 1814 issued the proclamation that precipitated the "Pemmican War." Dated January 14, 1813, the "Pemmican Proclamation" forbade the export of "any provision, either of flesh, grain, or vegetables, procured or raised within the said territory [Assiniboia], by water or land carriage." This, of course, included shipments of pemmican. Naturally, this inflamed the Nor'Westers, who neither recognized nor accepted Macdonell's authority. Furthermore, due to the War of 1812, between the United States and Great Britain, the North West Company's supply line from Montreal had been cut by the Americans, so that the burden of supplying all their posts west of Lake Superior depended on Fort Gibraltar and Fort Pembina. It was essential for the existence of all their forts that the flow of pemmican and other supplies from these two forts be maintained.

As if this embargo on pemmican shipments were not enough to arouse the wrath of the Nor'Westers, Macdonell followed it up with a high-handed notice ordering all North West Company agents to leave the territory that had been ceded to Lord Selkirk within six months. If they refused to depart, their post buildings would be destroyed. The right to fish or to cut any wood for fuel or building was also denied to them.

In May and June of 1814, as the main shipments of pemmican began to come down the Souris and Assiniboine rivers destined for Fort Gibraltar, Governor Macdonell, fearing that the Nor'Westers might be able to successfully smuggle it out of the country by a route that would bypass the Forks and thus escape his surveillance, sent his sheriff, John Spencer, accompanied by Joseph Howse, a Hudson's Bay Company trader, and three men from the Red River colony up the Assiniboine to seize the pemmican that was being temporarily stored at the North West Company's Fort la Souris. Forcing his way into the fort, the sheriff confiscated the pemmican, dried meat, and fat—in total about thirty tons of food supplies. Most of this he carried over to Hudson's Bay Company's Fort Brandon just across the river; the rest was transported down to the company's headquarters at Fort Douglas, a mile or so below Fort Gibraltar.

The Nor'Westers could not and would not let this seizure of their pemmican go unchallenged. The gauntlet thrown down by Macdonell was picked up by the North West Company. Duncan Cameron at the head of a party of armed men captured Howse as he was returning to Fort Douglas from Fort la Souris. They brought him to Fort Gibraltar preparatory to sending him off to Montreal to stand trial for larceny. However, Miles Macdonell countered by training his field guns on the Red River from Fort Douglas, which effectively prevented any passage down the river by Cameron with his prisoner. With the arrival at Fort Gibraltar of John McDonald of Garth, a wintering partner of the North West Company, a compromise was reached between the Nor'Westers at Fort Gibraltar and Governor Macdonell, which temporarily prevented further overt hostilities.

However, when the partners and agents of the North West Company, gathered for their annual rendezvous at Fort William, heard the details of the compromise, they were furious. William McGillivray, chief partner of the North West Company, felt that the company had been insulted and was determined to utilize the full strength of his organization to avenge the insult. Led by Duncan Cameron and Alexander Macdonell, the Nor'Westers began to successfully retaliate against the Governor's measures. Sheriff Spencer was arrested and removed to Fort Gibraltar before being taken to Fort William. Cameron began a campaign to subtly undermine the confidence and loyalty of the settlers. Macdonell was skillfully fanning the resentment of the Métis against the Governor's edict prohibiting them from following their traditional practice of running the buffalo.

In April of 1815, during a time when Governor Macdonell was temporarily upriver at the Hudson's Bay Company post of Fort Daer, a large number of settlers, lured by Cameron's promise of free transportation to Upper Canada and free land on their arrival there, had left the colony and moved into Fort Gibraltar. They carried with them not only their own personal belongings but also, more important, the field pieces from Fort Douglas. Upon Macdonell's return, he was served with a warrant for his arrest. The Métis and Nor'Westers, led by Alexander Macdonell, began a systematic harassment of the colony. Hostilities did not cease until Governor Macdonell agreed to accept the warrant and surrender to the Nor'Westers. On June 22 he was embarked for Fort William as the first stop on his way to stand trial in Montreal. The settlers who had accepted Cameron's offer for transportation and land in Upper Canada likewise left.

Three days later, the remaining settlers were notified that they, too, must "retire immediately from Red River, and no trace of a settlement to remain." So, two days later, on June 27, the thirteen families, numbering about sixty persons, "took to boats, saving what they could, started for Norway House (Jack River), declaring they would never return." The next day their homes were put to the torch, the crops trampled down, and the cattle, sheep, and horses driven off or slaughtered. Simon McGillivray, one of the leading North West wintering partners, wrote: "I am happy to inform you that the Colony has been all knocked in the head by the North West Company." Indeed, Cameron and Macdonell had done their work well.

However, it was still a bit premature to write off the Red River colony. There yet remained a flicker of life in the abandoned settlement.

Four men had been permitted by the Métis to remain to watch over what little was left of the company's and colony's property. Undaunted by the ruin and desolation surrounding them, they labored heroically to salvage what they could of the crops that had not been totally destroyed. They made some hay, repaired fences, and even began the construction of a new fort. Imagine their delight and relief when, late in August, they saw a brigade of canoes advancing up the river, bringing back the settlers who had been forced to leave two months earlier. Their return was due to the efforts of Colin Robertson, a former Nor'Wester, now in the employ of the Hudson's Bay Company. Robertson, aggressive and capable and supremely confident that the tables could be turned on the North West Company and its Métis allies, was able to persuade the disheartened settlers whom he found at Norway House to accompany him back to the Red River and start once again to reestablish their colony. Two months later their number was augmented by the arrival of 180 new settlers under the leadership of Robert Semple, the newly appointed Governor of the Hudson's Bay Company's territories in America, commonly known as Rupert's Land. Thus strengthened, the struggling settlement slowly but surely began to attain a degree of permanence and prosperity.

Meanwhile, Duncan Cameron at Fort Gibraltar and Alexander Macdonell in the Qu'Appelle valley were not strong enough to immediately contest the reestablishment of the colony. Determined as ever to drive out the colonists, they spent the winter rallying and enlisting as many Métis and freemen, or *gens libres,* as possible to join them in a renewed drive against the settlement. Colin Robertson, alert to any hostile moves made by the Nor'Westers and secure in the knowledge of his superior numbers, did not hesitate an instant before acting decisively. When he learned that the Hudson's Bay Company's post in the Qu'Appelle valley had received threats and was being intimidated by Alexander Macdonell, he promptly marched on Fort Gibraltar, seized the fort, and arrested Duncan Cameron. Only upon Cameron's written pledge to desist from any further hostile actions was he released, after twenty-four hours of detention, and the fort returned to him.

However, this pledge was quickly broken, and the plotting and scheming for the destruction of the colony continued throughout the winter. Robertson again acted decisively. On March 19, accompanied by fourteen men, he appeared at Fort Gibraltar, seized the astonished Cameron, and carried him off to Fort Douglas. There he was confronted with a letter he had written to a fellow Nor'Wester urging that the colony be attacked and totally destroyed. This letter, along with others of similar import, had fallen into the hands of Robertson, who had not

393

hesitated or scrupled to seize and search the North West Company's mail-carrying express canoe.

Based on this overwhelming evidence of the hostile designs of the North West Company against the colony, Robertson urged Governor Semple to capture and tear down Fort Gibraltar and to send Cameron to England for trial. At last Semple agreed. On June 11, Robertson, with Cameron as his prisoner, set off for York Factory en route for London. On the same day the Governor led a force of thirty men to Fort Gibraltar, which quickly fell into his hands. It required a week to totally tear down the fort and level it to the ground. Everything that could be rescued was floated downriver to Fort Douglas to help in the rebuilding of the colony and its new fort.

Although the Nor'Westers had lost their stronghold at the junction of the Red and Assiniboine and one of their leaders had been shipped off to England, the efforts of the North West Company to bring about the total destruction of the colony did not cease. Encouraged by the wintering partners from Fort William, Alexander Macdonell intensified his efforts to manipulate and foment discontent and resentment among the Métis against the colony.

It all came to a climax on June 19, 1816, when, in the Battle of Seven Oaks, Governor Semple and twenty-one of his settlers were killed in a confrontation with Cuthbert Grant and his Métis followers. Fort Douglas was taken over by the victorious Nor'Westers and Métis, and for the second time the settlers were dispossessed of their homes and forced to leave the colony. Dispirited, destitute, and discouraged, they embarked in canoes and once more headed downstream on their way to Norway House and York Factory and thence back home to far-off Scotland.

But once again, fate intervened. Their sponsor, Lord Selkirk who had arrived in Montreal the previous year, had finally begun his journey toward the Red River colony. While en route, he learned of the Seven Oaks disaster and the subsequent dispersal of the settlers. Outraged, he retaliated by capturing not only the great North West emporium of Fort William but also many of the wintering partners who were at the fort. Furthermore, Miles Macdonell, returning at the head of a small force of De Meuron soldiers who had been recruited by Lord Selkirk, had on January 10, 1817, successfully surprised and recaptured Fort Douglas. News of this unexpected turn of events was brought to the settlers who had been stranded at Norway House for the winter months. In addition, they were told that Lord Selkirk himself was on his way to Red River and would restore their lands to them, reimburse them for their losses, and provide guaranteed protection through the presence of the De Meuron soldiers, who were going to settle in the colony on land granted them by Selkirk. Encouraged by this news, the settlers unanimously agreed to turn back and return to Red River. This they did in June of 1817, just as soon as navigation opened on Lake Winnipeg. Never again would they be forced to flee from their homes.

The North West Company rebuilt Fort Gibraltar shortly after it was destroyed by Semple. Donald Gunn, a longtime employee of the Hudson's Bay Company dating back to 1813, wrote in his book *History of Manitoba:* "The Northwest Company fort had been razed to the ground and could not be restored, but that active and energetic body procured new materials, built new houses and stores on the old site, and commenced business anew." This second Fort Gibraltar was located on the north bank of the Assiniboine River, somewhat closer to the Forks than the original fort it replaced.

The rebuilt Fort Gibraltar was taken over by the Hudson's Bay Company at the time of its union with the North West Company in 1821, and a year later Governor George Simpson changed the name to Fort Garry. This was done both to remove the feeling of resentment still prevalent amongst the old Nor'Westers at the occupation of their post by the Hudson's Bay Company and to honor Nicholas Garry, a member of the Hudson's Bay Company's London Committee. Alexander Ross described the rebuilt Fort Gibraltar (newly renamed Fort Garry) as it appeared in 1825:

> I was anxious to see the place, I had heard so much about it, but I must confess I felt disappointed. Instead of a place walled and fortified, as I had expected, I saw nothing but a few wooden houses huddled together, without palisades, or any regard to taste or even comfort. To this cluster of huts were, however, appended two long bastions in the same style as the other buildings. These buildings, according to the custom of the country, were used as dwellings and warehouses for the carrying on of the trade of the place. Nor was the Governor's residence anything more in its outward appearance than the cottage of a humble farmer, who might be able to spend fifty pounds a year. These, however, were evidences of the settled and tranquil state of the country.

This fort served as headquarters for the Hudson's Bay Company until 1835. In that year Governor Alexander Christie moved into the newly constructed post, named Upper Fort Garry, that had been erected close to the old Fort Gibraltar site. For a few years the old fort served as part of the Hudson's Bay Company's short-lived experimental farm operation. Later it was leased by a local settler, Robert Logan. However, this was only a temporary postponement of the inevitable end.

With the demolishment in 1852 of the buildings of the old fort, now crumbling into ruin and in eminent danger of sliding into the Assiniboine, the last vestige of the North West Company's rebuilt Fort Gibraltar, which had once dominated the Forks, disappeared forever. It must be added, however, that in 1871, nineteen years after the razing of the old fort, the keen eye of Winnipeg historian Charles Napier Bell was able to detect unmistakable signs of its presence. Bell wrote:

> I took a walk down the Assiniboine from Fort Garry a few hundred yards to the traditional site of Fort Gibraltar, and there, plainly to be seen very near to the edge of the bank, were recognizable hollows representing cellars, and the mixture of semi-calcined limestone, remains of chimneys,—it was clear to us that buildings of some kind had been on that ground, though it was also evident that almost the whole area of the enclosure that had once been there had disappeared into the river through the washing away and crumbling in of the banks.—I am quite satisfied that the hollows and chimney debris which we then saw were the last remains of Fort Gibraltar.

Fifty-six years later (in 1927) Bell revisited the site and wrote: "—found that if not in the two rivers, what remains of it [Fort Gibraltar] is now buried many feet under the cinders and general refuse of the railway yard of the Canadian National."

It would seem that the site of Fort Gibraltar has vanished completely, leaving no trace. But perhaps not quite. Parks Canada, in cooperation with the city of Winnipeg, has removed the blight of commercial and industrial development that had been allowed to completely engulf the land bordering the Red and Assiniboine rivers. Now a park of beautifully landscaped grounds enhanced with lawns, trees, shrubs, and flowers, as well as a walkway, extends along both rivers. With freedom from their straitjacket of commercial structures, the rivers' natural beauty has been restored and is available for everyone to enjoy. During the course of this development, considerable archaeological work was undertaken in an attempt to locate the sites of the various forts that were once located in the general area of the Forks. This was done through an innovative and highly successful program that utilized not only trained archaeologists but also many closely supervised enthusiastic amateurs. This is an ongoing project with no final answers as yet. However, even if the exact site of each fort is not determined, this parkway will ensure that this historic area of the Forks will forever remain in its natural state and, as such, serve as an effective memorial to the North West and Hudson's Bay forts that once stood here and played such an important role in fur trade history.

The brigades of canoes, the fur traders, the Indians and Métis have long since disappeared from the confluence of these two rivers, replaced by motorized pleasure boats and by large numbers of happy people strolling along the new walkways along the riverbanks. It is only the meeting of the two rivers that remains unchanged. Here at the Forks, just as they have done for untold centuries, the waters of the Assiniboine flowing from the west meet and merge with the northbound waters of the Red.

Kootenay House

During the period 1807–11, when the Nor'Wester Alexander Henry the younger was developing the trade of the upper Red River and the North Saskatchewan and Simon Fraser was establishing his fur trading posts in New Caledonia on the upper Fraser River, David Thompson was unraveling the intricacies of the Columbia-Kootenay river system in order to open up the area for the trade of the North West Company.

Finally able to elude the Piegans, who were determined to prevent him from crossing the Rocky Mountains, Thompson and his men, accompanied by his wife and children, in May of 1807 left Rocky Mountain House on the North Saskatchewan River close to the foothills of the Rockies on the first of what were to be many trips across the mountains. Penetrating the barrier of the Rockies by the Howse Pass, he descended the Blaeberry River to its confluence with the Columbia River. Thompson, not realizing that the broad northward flowing river he had reached was the Columbia, thought it was the Kootenay. He and his party headed their canoes south (upstream) and soon reached a long widening of the river, now called Lake Windermere.

Here, on a point at the northwest corner of the lake, Thompson began to construct a trading post. However, acting upon the advice of friendly Kootenays, who pointed out that this post as situated would be practically indefensible, "as it was very far from water, and open to the insult of the Peigans, who seldom fail every year to make a visit and steal horses," Thompson abandoned the site, even though a warehouse to protect his trading goods had already been erected.

His new site was a short distance up Toby Creek, a small stream that flows into the Columbia River on the west side about a mile north of the lower end of Lake Windermere. Here he built Kootenay House. As Thompson wrote: ". . . [We] at last found an eligible spot on the Kootenay River [Toby Creek], in a commanding situation, the water quite near, a rapid river in front, with a small, nearly surrounding lake that precluded all approach but on one side."

During the remainder of 1807 Thompson and his party confined their activities to the general vicinity of their new post. Active trading with the Kootenays was carried on. In addition, Thompson made numerous astronomical observations: "In my new dwelling I remained quiet, hunting the wild horses, fishing and examining the country." Thompson described the arrival of the salmon and their spawning activity. He wrote: "At length the salmon made their appearance, and for about three weeks we lived on them; at first they were in tolerable condition, although they had come upwards of twelve hundred miles from the sea, and several weighed twenty-five pounds. But as the spawning went on upon a gravel bank a short distance above us, they became poor and not eatable; we preferred horse meat."

Sometime during the middle of September, two Piegans, who had crossed the mountains on foot, arrived at the fort. Thompson correctly surmised that they had come to assess the strength of the new fort. Thompson was not duped. As he stated in his *Narrative:* "I showed the strength of the Stockades, and Bastions, and told them I know you come as Spies, and intend to destroy us, but many of you will die before you do so . . ." Soon afterward, Thompson's fears of a hostile attack by the Piegans were realized when a formidable force of forty appeared at the gates of Kootenay House. Thompson detailed what happened in his *Narrative:*

> I had now to prepare for a more serious visit from the Peagans who had met in council, and it was determined to send forty men, under a secondary Chief to destroy the trading Post, and us with it, they came and pitched their Tents close before the Gate, which was well barred. I had six men with me, and ten guns, well loaded, the House was perforated with large augur holes, as well as the Bastions, thus they remained for three weeks without daring to attack us. We had a small stock of dried provisions which we made go as far as possible; they thought to make us suffer for want of water as the bank we were on was about 20 feet high and very steep, but at night, by a strong cord we quietly and gently let down two brass Kettles each holding four Gallons, and drew them up full; which was enough for us: They were at a loss what to do,—Finding us always on the watch, they did not think proper to risque their lives, when at the end of three weeks they suddenly decamped;—they decamped to cross the mountains to join their own Tribe while all was well with them . . .

The threat from the Piegans was not yet over. A new force of about three hundred warriors under three chiefs was assembled and once again crossed the mountains, rendezvousing on the Columbia about twenty miles below Kootenay House. As before, two men were sent to see the strength of the fort; Thompson described in his *Narrative* what happened next:

> I showed them all round the place, and they staid that night. I plainly saw that a War Party was again formed, to be better conducted than the last; and I prepared Presents to avert it: the next morning two Kootenae

399

Men arrived, their eyes glared on the Peagans like Tigers, this was most fortunate; I told them to sit down and smoke which they did; I then called the two Peagans out, and enquired of them which way they intended to return. They pointed to the northward. I told them to go to Kootenae Appee and his War Party, who were only a day's journey from us, and delivering to them the Presents I had made up, to be off directly, as I could not protect them, for you know you are on these lands as Enemies; the Presents were six feet of Tobacco to the Chief, to be smoked among them, three feet with a fine pipe of red porphyry and an ornamented Pipe Stem; eighteen inches to each of the three Chiefs, and a small piece to each of themselves, and telling them they had no right to be in the Kootenae Country: to haste away; for the Kootenaes would soon be here, and they will fight for their trading Post . . .

Thompson's ploy succeeded. The Indians accepted the tobacco and returned across the mountains. In Thompson's words, ". . . they all smoked, took the Tobacco, and returned, very much to the satisfaction of Kootanae Appee my steady friend; thus by the mercy of Good Providence I averted this danger." It should be said that it was not only the "mercy of Good Providence" that prevented this potential catastrophe but also the unfailing ability of Thompson to correctly understand the Indians' motives.

The deep snows in the mountain passes provided safety for the men in Kootenay House during the winter months of 1807–08. In the spring, as soon as travel was possible, Thompson sent off Finan McDonald with the furs that had been traded during the past winter. Thompson himself undertook a series of exploratory journeys that took him southward down Kootenay River to Kootenay Lake and back to Kootenay House, which he reached June 6. Almost immediately afterward, taking his family with him, he began the long journey eastward to the North West depot on Rainy Lake. He arrived there July 22. He and his men quickly unloaded their cargo of furs and as quickly for their return trip took on an assortment of trading goods for two canoes, each carrying twenty *pièces* of ninety pounds each. No time was taken for resting and relaxation. Much against his will, Thompson was ordered to include two kegs of alcohol in his cargo. In his *Narrative* he recounts how he carried out this order:

. . . I was obliged to take two Kegs of Alcohol, over ruled by my Partners (Messrs Dond McTavish and Jo McDonald [of] Garth[h]) for I had made it a law to myself, that no alcohol should pass the Mountains in my company, and thus be clear of the sad sight of drunkeness, and it's many evils: but these gentlemen insisted upon alcohol being the most profitable article that could be taken for the indian trade. In this I knew they had miscalculated; accordingly when we came to the defiles of the Mountains, I placed the two Kegs of Alcohol on a vicious horse; and by noon the Kegs were empty, and in pieces, the Horse rubbing his load against the Rocks to get rid of it; I wrote to my partners what I had done; and that I would do the same to every keg of Alcohol, and for the next six years I had charge of the furr trade on the west side of the Mountains, no further attempt was made to introduce spirituous Liquors.

On November 10 Thompson arrived back at Kootenay House, "where we shall winter, please God."

The winter of 1808–09 was spent in trading with the Kootenays. With the arrival of spring, preparations were made for the annual trip east to bring out the furs and obtain supplies. When on April 17, 1809, Thompson left Kootenay House at the conclusion of the winter's trading season, it was for the last time. He never again occupied the fort. As he extended his exploration of the Columbia and Kootenay rivers ever farther—eventually reaching the Pacific Ocean—and as he successfully established trading relations with more distant Indian tribes, he erected other trading posts closer to his new areas of activity.

Kootenay House was used but briefly after Thompson's departure. When his journey down the lower Columbia River to the Pacific Ocean in 1811 prevented him from making his usual trip east to Rainy Lake House to bring out his furs and obtain the goods required for the next winter's trade, three Nor'Westers were sent from Rainy Lake House to bring the supplies to him. John McDonald of Garth, with some of the trading goods, stopped at Kootenay House, which he reopened for the ensuing season. The other two, John G. McTavish and James McMillan, continued on for another five weeks before finally reaching Thompson and delivering the supplies to him. Ultimately, continued hostility from the Piegans forced the abandonment of the fort soon after 1812.

We anticipated no undue difficulty in finding Kootenay House, for we knew the site had been identified and marked with a Historic Site cairn and that it was located just below the lower end of Lake Windermere on the west side. Driving south on Highway 95, which runs along the east side of the Columbia River, we soon came to Blaeberry River. Its grayish-blue silt-laden waters from the mountain glaciers above were rushing with considerable velocity toward their confluence with the Columbia River a short distance beyond the highway. Sheer walls of rock—some exposed, some covered with tall spruce and fir

401

trees—rose from each side of the river. In the background the high peaks of the Rocky Mountains towered toward the sky.

Miraculously, the Blaeberry remained today just as it was in Thompson's day. It has not as yet been dammed, diverted, or developed. The only modern intrusion was the highway crossing it. However, by turning our backs to the road and shutting our ears to the noise of the cars as they whizzed by it was not too difficult to look up this lovely mountain stream and see David Thompson and his men with their heavily laden packhorses appear around the bend at the far end, exhausted but grateful that their arduous descent down the Blaeberry had been completed—"thank God," as Thompson would have piously added.

A bit reluctantly, we at length left this historic spot. As we continued southward following the northward-flowing Columbia, it was easy to understand Thompson's dilemma. He was searching for a southward-flowing river that would lead to the Pacific, and yet although he was traveling in a southerly direction, the river on which he was flowed to the north. Eventually, as the first man to journey the entire length of the Columbia from its source to its mouth at the Pacific he, of course, discovered the solution to the puzzle.

Before long we arrived at Lake Windermere, crossed over to the western side, and soon reached the large grassy clearing on a moderately elevated knoll that, as indicated by the government cairn, was the site of Kootenay House. A rather sparse fringe of spruce trees rimmed the area on three sides. At the base to the east was Toby Creek. Beyond it in middistance the banks of the Columbia River were visible, and behind them rose the massive wall of the Rockies with their many lofty peaks. It was, indeed, as Thompson had written, "in a commanding situation, the water quite near."

Today it is only the steady murmur of nearby Toby Creek or the chirping of a few grasshoppers that disturbs the quiet of the Kootenay House site—a sharp contrast to the warlike sounds heard over 180 years ago when the Piegans besieged the fort and only the foresight and diplomacy of Thompson saved it from destruction. The fort that once stood here on this knoll was the first post constructed west of the Rocky Mountains on the Columbia River. It was also the first of the several succeeding posts that Thompson established as he worked his way along the Columbia-Kootenay river system to the Pacific Ocean.

Kootenay Falls House

In the spring of 1808 David Thompson explored a considerable stretch of the Kootenay River from McGillivray Portage (now Canal Flats) as far as Kootenay Lake. During this trip he made contact with the Flathead and Kootenay Indians. Upon his return to his base at Kootenay House, he and his able clerk, Finan McDonald, immediately set off on the long journey eastward to the North West Company's depot on Rainy Lake in order to bring out the furs traded during the past winter and to obtain the goods and supplies required for the next season. They arrived back at the Columbia River at the end of October. Thompson then sent McDonald off with the canoes and part of the supplies to set up a trading post on the Kootenay River for trade with the Indians whom he had contacted during his earlier journey in the spring. He himself continued on his way to Kootenay House on horseback.

McDonald, however, was able to go but a short distance until the ice forming in the river prevented any further travel by canoe. He returned to Kootenay House, where he obtained horses so he could continue on his way. At someplace not too far above the Kootenay Falls he found a location suitable for his post. He and his men quickly built a log warehouse to shelter the trading goods. Then they settled down in their two leather tents for a winter of trading. Their post was intended to serve not only as a trading station for the Kootenays and Flatheads but also as a base for exploration of the Pend d'Oreille country. Sometime during the winter, McDonald sent two of his men southward on a preliminary scouting trip as far as Pend d'Oreille Lake.

The exact location of McDonald's Kootenay Falls House has not been determined with certainty. The only suggestions put forth have been based on written records, not on archaeological evidence. When in the spring of 1808 Thompson was on the Kootenay in the vicinity of the falls, he made the following observation in his journal under the date of April 27: "A fine site for a house, but on the West side of the river." Today the generally accepted consensus is that McDonald's Kootenay Falls House was on the north side of the river about ten miles above the falls near the confluence of the Kootenay and Fisher rivers (near Jennings, Montana).

In the spring of 1809 McDonald rejoined Thompson at Kootenay House, and the two then made their usual journey across the mountains to bring out the furs and obtain supplies. McDonald remained in charge of Kootenay Falls House for the next two years. In 1811 Nicholas Montour took over the post.

By this time traders from John Jacob Astor's Pacific Fur Company were advancing from their base of Fort Astoria at the mouth of the Columbia and appearing in the Kootenay River country. Their avowed goal was to drive the North West Company from the country west of the Rockies. Their plan was to set up a trading post opposite each of the posts David Thompson and his men had established for the North West Company. François Pillet was sent to build a trading fort on the Kootenay River close to Montour's Kootenay Falls House. The highly volatile and excitable nature of both men resulted in some quite lively encounters. Alexander Ross, one of Astor's men, in his *Adventures of the First Settlers on the Oregon or Columbia River* wrote: "Mr. Pillet, with some men and a supply of goods, was sent to the Cootanais to oppose Mr. Mantour on the part of the North-West. Mr. Pillet travelled a great deal, and turned his time to good account. Both were zealous traders, and they could fight a duel as well as buy a skin, for they carried pistols as well as goods along with them. They therefore fought and traded alternately, but always spared the thread of life, and in the spring parted good friends." Another Astorian, Ross Cox, described a rather farcical encounter between the two traders. "Mr. Pillet fought a duel with Mr. Montour of the North-West, with pocket pistols, at six paces; both hits; one in the collar of the coat and the other in the leg of the trowsers. Two of their men acted as seconds, and the tailor speedily healed their wounds."

Kootenay Falls House was taken over from the North West Company by the Hudson's Bay Company at the time of their union in 1821. When the western border between the United States and Canada was established by the Oregon Treaty of 1846, Kootenay Falls House was one of several Hudson's Bay posts south of the boundary for which indemnity for their loss was claimed by the Hudson's Bay Company.

Since the precise site of Kootenay Falls House is as yet unknown, we had to be satisfied with photographing a section of the Kootenay River that was in the general area of the probable location of the fort and was also well-known to Thompson, McDonald, and their men. Kootenay Falls (called the lower Dalles by Thompson) is a formidable obstacle in the river. The dangerous and difficult portage around it was described in considerable detail by Thompson in his *Narrative:*

At the lower Dalles [i.e., the falls] we had to carry everything on the right side, up a steep bank of Rock, and among the debris of high Rocks, apparently rude basalt, the slope to the River Bank was at a high angle, and our rude path among loose fragments of rock was about three hundred feet above the River, the least slip would have been sure destruction, having carried about one mile, we came to a Brook where we put up for the night. Each trip over this one mile of debris took an hour and a quarter, and cut our shoes to pieces. The banks of the brook were about two hundred feet in height, with a steep slope of debris to descend, with not a grain of sand, or earth, on them, to relieve our crippled feet. From the brook we had one mile to carry to the River, to which we descended by a gap in the Rocks; the River had steep banks of Rocks, and [was] only thirty yards in width; this space was full of violent eddies, which threatened us with destruction and wherever the river contracted the case was always the same, the current was swift, yet to look at the surface the eddies make it appear to move as much backward as forward; where the river is one hundred yards wide and upwards the current is smooth and safe.

Since we were not faced with the task of carrying canoes and heavy loads over the treacherous slopes skirting the falls, we were free to enjoy their rugged beauty. Here at the base of the lofty pine-covered hills, the Kootenay, compressed within walls of horizontally layered rock, leaped down a series of steplike rocky terraces and in swirls of white water poured through narrow chutes and rushed over foaming rapids, before finally emerging below, partially subdued and tamed.

We spent several highly delightful hours here, as we tried to meet the challenge to our photographic abilities posed by this magnificent wild spectacle. We did not forget, however, that what was a source of admiration to us was, to David Thompson and his men, a dread hazard that had to be overcome with toil and hardship. It is highly unlikely that they had either the time or inclination to appreciate the wondrous beauty of the Kootenay Falls.

Kullyspell House

As soon as David Thompson arrived back at the Columbia River about the middle of August 1809 after completing his yearly transmountain journey, he set off without delay to continue his exploration down the Kootenay River and south into the Pend d'Oreille country, where he hoped to establish a post for trade with the Indians of that area. On the ninth of September he reached the mouth of the Clark Fork River on the east side of Lake Pend d'Oreille, where he was met by a party of fifty-four Salish, twenty-three Skeetsboo, and four Kootenay Indians with their families. The next day was spent in searching for a suitable location for his trading post. A site, though not entirely satisfactory, was found on a small peninsula extending from the east side of the lake about a mile and one-half from the mouth of Clark Fork River. Building began immediately. Thompson wrote in his *Narrative:*

> The next day with two Indians [I] went to look for a place to build a House for trading; we found a place, but the soil was light, and had no blue clay which is so very necessary for plaistering between the Logs of the House and especially the roofing; as at this time of year, the bark of the Pine Tree cannot be raised to cover the Roof, for want of which, we had an unco[mfo]rtable House. We removed to the place and set up our Tents and a Lodge. On the 11th we made a scaffold to secure the provisions and goods, helved our Tools ready to commence building; our first care was a strong Log building for the Goods and Furrs, and for trading with the Natives.
>
> On the 23rd we had finished the Store House. To make the roof as tight as possible, which was covered with small Logs, we cut long grass and work[ed] it up with mud, and filled up the intervals of the small logs which answered tolerable well for Rain, but the Snow in melting found many a passage; in this manner we also builded our dwelling House; and roofed it, the floors were of split Logs, with the round side downwards, notched so as to lie firm on the Sleepers, and made smooth with the Adze; our Chimneys were made of stone and mud rudely worked for about six feet in height and eighteen inches thick, the rest of layers of grass and mud worked round strong poles inserted in the stone work, with cross pieces, and thus carried up to about four feet above the roof; the fire place is raised a little, and three to four feet in width by about fifteen inches in depth. The wood is cut about three feet in length, and placed on the end, and as it costs nothing but the labor of cutting we are not sparing of it . . .

The establishment of this trading post (called Kullyspell House after the local Indians) was welcomed by the natives of the area. They were now able to replace their bows and flint-headed arrows and lances with guns and ammunition. Thus armed, they could now face their enemies, the Piegans, on equal terms. The Piegans, naturally, blamed Thompson for this. Their memories were long and their hostility toward him implacable. This enmity was to have grave consequences for Thompson during the next several years.

While his post was being constructed, Thompson spent ten days exploring the Pend d'Oreille River in the hopes of finding a way to the Columbia that was outside the territory controlled by the Piegans. However, he was forced to turn back because of "a series of heavy Falls—the sides of the Falls steep basalt rocks." During his brief absence, forty-four Skeetshoo Indians came to the new post and traded nearly 200 pounds' weight of furs and three horses. On October 7, 1809, Thompson wrote in his *Narrative:* "Having cut the Logs for the House, we began hauling them, to the place for the House." Four days later Thompson set off with horses, two men, and a guide to meet his clerk, James McMillan, who was bringing the canoes loaded with the trading goods that they had brought to the Columbia River from east of the mountains. They met on the Kootenay River above the falls. "We separated the goods for the different Posts to trade with the Natives." Thompson was back at Kullyspell House on October 30, but three days later, leaving his clerk, Finan McDonald, in charge of the post, he moved on up the Clark Fork River about one hundred miles and established yet another trading post, this one called Saleesh House.

In April of the following year (1810) Thompson left his new post and, descending the Clark Fork River, arrived back at Kullyspell House on April 21. From there he set off once again down the Pend d'Oreille River, hoping he could follow it to its junction with the Columbia River, thus providing a feasible alternative to the old trade route to the east. He was able to descend the river about twenty-two miles, but once again, as before, the river became totally impassable beyond this point and he was forced to turn back and return to Kullyspell House. A week later, on May 9, Thompson left that post and began the long trip eastward to Rainy Lake House along the old route of the Kootenay and Columbia rivers to Blaeberry River and the Howse Pass.

Finan McDonald remained in charge of Kullyspell House on a rather intermittent basis. He was there in 1811, when he was instructed by Thompson to supply the Saleesh Indians with as much ammunition as he could spare from the stock at the post. And he was still at the fort when in November of the same year he received a letter from Thompson asking him to keep watch on the Kootenay River for the arrival of the canoes loaded with goods and supplies that John McDonald of Garth was bringing from east of the mountains.

Kullyspell House continued in operation for only a few years. During that period about four thousand pounds of dressed furs were traded. Other posts, such as Saleesh House to the southeast and Spokane House to the southwest, soon replaced it. Once abandoned, it fell into ruin. The buildings were destroyed by fire in 1832.

When we drove along Idaho Highway 200 on the east side of Pend d'Oreille Lake, we had little hope of finding the site of Kullyspell House. All that we knew was that it was about a mile and a half below the mouth of Clark Fork River on a small peninsula on the east side of the lake somewhere near East Hope. We would probably have to be satisfied with photographing the lake, showing the "general area of the fort site." We did, however, have one tangible clue. We had a copy of a picture that had appeared in the Winter 1972 issue of *The Beaver* magazine and showed "a pile of stone believed to be from the original fireplace of Kullyspell House." Nevertheless, as we neared East Hope, we kept a keen watch for any cairn or sign that might relate to the site. Suddenly, to our surprised delight, on the west side of the highway by a side road we spotted an enormous wooden sign bearing the name Kullyspell House in huge letters. We learned from reading the sign that the site of Kullyspell House was two and one-quarter miles southwest from this marker and that it was on private property. Firmly believing that "nothing ventured, nothing gained," we turned down the side road, and carefully watching our car compass and mileage indicator, we drove along the road, which, indeed, led in a southwest direction. Two and one-quarter miles brought us to the end of the road at the shore of Pend d'Oreille Lake. To our right extending along the lake was a parklike grove of majestic western pines in the midst of which, surrounded by beautifully and immaculately landscaped grounds, was a most handsome home. Leading to the house from the road where we had stopped was a blacktop driveway. A very few yards beyond the stone entrance gateposts and just to the edge of the driveway, clearly visible from the road, was a pile of stones—quite an anachronism in these otherwise meticulously maintained grounds. But to us this small pile of tumbled rocks was the treasure we were seeking. They were without question the very stones shown in the picture we had from *The Beaver* magazine. Their shapes and position in the pile were identical. We were, without doubt, looking at the stones "from the original fireplace of Kullyspell House."

We have always been scrupulous respecters of private property and NO TRESPASSING signs. In this instance, however, in spite of the

408

posted PRIVATE signs, the temptation was strong to walk the few yards down the driveway and quickly get the photographs. But instead, I summoned my courage and walked down the driveway right past the stone pile to the front door of the house, intending to seek permission to take the pictures I so desperately wanted. I guess the only explanation for this unusual boldness on my part was perhaps the euphoria the sight of the pile of stones had produced in me. Although I rang the doorbell several times, no one answered. I hope the owners of the property will graciously condone what happened next. For on my way back up the driveway, I did stop and I did photograph the pile of rocks—that small heap of stones—the remains of David Thompson's post on Pend d'Oreille Lake. Incredibly, we had succeeded in finding and photographing the site of Kullyspell House. I could still scarcely believe our good luck.

Saleesh House

Two months after establishing Kullyspell House on the east side of Pend d'Oreille Lake in September 1809, Thompson ascended the Clark Fork River and chose a site not far downstream from the mouth of Thompson River for the location of another trading post, the fourth in the chain of forts he was establishing as he slowly and methodically advanced toward his ultimate goal of the Pacific Ocean. He described the place he had chosen for his post as follows: "The House was situated in a small bay of the river, close to us was a spur of the hills which came on the River in a cliff of about sixty feet in height, beyond which to the south eastward the country opened out to a great extent of fine meadow ground, the scene of many a battle; the Saleesh Indians with their allies, when hard pressed, always made for this rock as their natural defense, and which had always proved a shield to them, and [they] shewed us, the bones of their enemies slain at different times in attempting to force this pass . . ."

Thompson and his men were in rather desperate straits. They had had no food for two days and were unable to obtain any from the few Indians in the area. Fortunately, on November 14 Jacques Finlay, a half-breed usually known as Jaco, arrived at their camp. Son of James Finlay, a merchant from Montreal and prominent in the early days of the fur trade, Jaco was well-known to Thompson. As Thompson wrote in his *Narrative:* "We were all of us very hungry, having had but little on the Road: . . . until the 14th, when Jaco, a fine half breed, arrived and relieved us. From him we traded twenty eight Beaver Tails, forty pounds of Beat Meat, thirty pounds of dried meat, and now, we all, thank God, enjoyed a good meal." With all thus fortified with food, construction of the new post was immediately begun.

According to a study based on Thompson's journals made by M. Catherine White in 1942, Saleesh House consisted originally of three principal buildings: a house for Thompson, one for the men, and a warehouse. The type of construction was that known as Red River frame, in which the buildings were constructed with upright posts into which the ends of the horizontal hewn logs forming the walls were mortised. The ends of the structures were gabled. According to White, "Thompson's house had two fireplaces and was partitioned into three rooms, one of which he used as a bedroom. It was furnished with a bed, desk, and cupboard. The windows were covered with paper, which was probably replaced by skins." James McMillan, Thompson's clerk and assistant, who suffered the misfortune of blowing off two of his fingers

410

by the accidental discharge of his gun upon his arrival at the site of the new fort, occupied one of the other rooms. On December 1, 1809, Thompson wrote: "Slept in my Room—may Kind Heaven send me Peace, Health, & Plenty in my new dwelling."

Throughout the winter months of January and February, Thompson employed numerous Indians as hunters to supply the post with the large quantities of meat needed both for daily consumption and for making the pemmican needed for the long eastward journey that had to be made each summer. A *glacière* was constructed to store the meat. Also during this time his men were kept busy drying and pounding meat, melting the fat, mixing it all together, and packing it into ninety-pound bags.

Thompson made three trips in late February and March to the large Salish camp located on the Flathead River twenty miles above its confluence with the Clark Fork River, which was fifty miles above Saleesh House. On each occasion he traded a quantity of furs and provisions. His journal entries made during his third trip (March 17 through 25) record that he traded twenty-two bales of furs of seventy to eighty pounds each and fifteen *pièces* (about 1,350 pounds) of pemmican. In addition, ten and one-half packs of furs and thirteen *pièces* (ninety pounds each) of buffalo meat were received two days after his return to Saleesh House.

At last on April 6 Thompson sent off some of his men with part of the year's returns (ten packs of furs and fifty pounds of gum) to Kullyspell House. He himself left about two weeks later with the remaining ten bales of furs and five bags of provisions. Then on the twenty-fourth the entire party left Kullyspell House to begin their long journey east to Rainy Lake House. Before leaving, he sent Finan McDonald to Saleesh House to spend the summer months there during his absence.

It wasn't until May 27 of the following year (1811) that Thompson was able to return to Saleesh House. He found the post deserted. Driven by fears of hostile Piegans, the men had set up a temporary base about twenty miles downstream. Thompson did not linger in the area. At long last, urged on by the North West partners and driven by the realization that he was, as E. E. Rich wrote, "actively aware that he was racing Americans for possession of the Coast, and of the Columbia as a fur-trade route," he pushed on with as much speed as possible. On July 15, 1811, he reached the mouth of the Columbia, where he found John Jacob Astor's Fort Astoria established but three months earlier.

Thompson retraced his way back up the Columbia, including the one remaining stretch that he had not previously traveled, thus completing his survey of the entire river from its source to its mouth.

He was back at Saleesh House on November 19, 1811. The post was quite deserted. Finan McDonald was at a Flathead camp in the vicinity trading for provisions. The buildings had been allowed to fall into a ruinous state. Thompson was without supplies or food. Therefore, the arrival on the twenty-fourth of November of "John George McTavish and James McMillan in company with fifteen men, and ten horses carrying about twelve hundred pounds weight of merchandize for trading furrs" was a most welcome surprise for Thompson. These men had been sent from Rainy Lake House to bring supplies to Thompson when it was realized there that he would not be able to make his usual trip east that summer.

Fortunately, the season, though late, continued mild and open, so Thompson could send Finan McDonald with an assortment of goods upriver to the Saleesh camp to trade for provisions. He returned with all they could spare. Thompson wrote: "All the dried provisions are of Bison meat, and must be carefully kept for the voyage of next summer; so that for the winter we depend for subsistence on the Antelopes; they are in sufficient numbers, but the hunting is precarious." Thompson also had to undertake the task of restoring the fort to its former condition of strength. He wrote in his *Narrative:* "We continued repairing, in some cases rebuilding our Houses, and by the 16th December we were all under shelter, and strange to say, the Roofs kept out the rain, but the melting of a smart shower of snow dropped through in many places."

The winter of 1811–12 was similar to the previous one. Game was scarce. Food was often in short supply or even completely lacking. This is reflected in journal entries such as "only a slight Meal today" or "no Supper." However, by the end of 1811 Thompson remarked that "the year closed thank God, with our being all well, notwithstanding much exposure to the weather and frequent want of food."

During January and February of 1812, Thompson made several rather extended journeys of exploration southward up the Clark Fork, Flathead and Missoula rivers as far as the south end of Flathead Lake. In the middle of March Thompson left Saleesh House to start his last journey back across the mountains. Thompson never returned west of the mountains. Henceforth the waters of the Athabasca, Saskatchewan, Kootenay, and Columbia would know him no more.

Finan McDonald had charge of Saleesh House for the 1812–13 season. He was soon succeeded by James McMillan, who was joined by Ross Cox, a former Astorian, now in the service of the North West Company. Cox in his *Adventures on the Columbia River* described the appearance of Saleesh House when he arrived there on December 24, 1813:

It had a good trading store, a comfortable house for the men, and a snug box for ourselves; all situated on a point formed by the junction of bold mountain torrent with the Flathead river [Clark Fork], and surrounded on all sides with pine, spruce, larch, beech, birch, and cedar—. Our hunters killed a few mountain sheep, and I brought up a bag of flour, a bag of rice, plenty of tea and coffee, some arrowroot, and fifteen gallons of prime rum. We spent a comparatively happy Christmas, and, by the side of the blazing fire in a warm room, forgot the sufferings we endured in our dreary progress through the woods.

Dating from Thompson's departure from the area in 1812, Saleesh House became known as Flathead Fort.

A few years after the union of the North West and Hudson's Bay companies in 1821, the Hudson's Bay Company built a post, also known as Flathead Fort, farther up the Clark Fork River. They occupied and operated both the old Flathead Fort (Saleesh House) and the new Flathead Fort on an intermittent basis. Possession of these forts south of the international boundary gave them a hold on the Flathead trade until their eventual withdrawal from American territory. Warren A. Ferris of the American Fur Company visited what remained of the old Saleesh House about twenty years later (1833–34). In his book *Life in the Rocky Mountains* he noted that "this establishment formerly consisted of seven hewn log buildings; but all are now going to decay, except the one inhabited by the Indians who accompanied me. They supply themselves with firewood, at the expense of the other buildings."

It was entirely owing to the kindness of Professor C. I. Malouf of Montana University that we were able to find the site of Saleesh House. We had discovered in an old issue of *The Beaver* magazine, two pictures of an archaeological dig that were captioned: "Diggings at Salish House, 1971, under Dr. C. I. Malouf of Montana University." Although more than fifteen years had elapsed, on the chance that Professor Malouf might still be at the university we addressed a letter to him there, asking if he would give us directions to the Saleesh House site. Soon we received his most helpful reply, which included a sketch map of the general area marked with as many identifying features as he could remember after an absence of fifteen years, as well as a black-and-white photograph of the crew at work on the actual site with the range of mountains in the background.

413

Supplied with this information, we confidently set off on our search. When, a short distance south of Thompson Falls, we reached a large fenced grassland bordering the Clark Fork River, which, according to our map, contained the Saleesh House site, we needed further directions. We stopped at a trailer house located at the edge of the fenced field in the hope of getting more specific information. To our surprised delight, we found from the young man who answered our knock on his door that we were, indeed, at the right location. He said the field belonged to his father-in-law, but he was certain there would be no objection to our driving across the area to the Saleesh House site by the river.

We had just driven through the farm gate and stopped to walk back to replace the gate bars when a car that had been coming down the highway slammed on the brakes and swerved into the farm lane, pulling up behind us. The driver jumped out, obviously—but understandably—somewhat angry at seeing a strange motor home brazenly passing through his farm gates onto his private property. However, we quickly explained the circumstances, and when we mentioned Professor Malouf's name and what our objectives were, he immediately and most graciously extended permission to us to go wherever we wished in the area. So to Mr. Wilson, the owner of the property, we extend our thanks and gratitude.

We drove perhaps a quarter of a mile over open grassland to reach the Clark Fork River. It was, just as Thompson had said, "a great extent of fine meadow ground." There were western pine here and there, little or no underbrush. The terrain, quite level, is only a very few feet above the river, which flows quietly and smoothly on its way toward its outlet at Pend d'Oreille Lake. But where precisely amid this large expanse of grassland was the site of Saleesh House? Referring to the black-and-white picture Professor Malouf had sent us, we were able to line up the two twin peaks showing the peculiar white areas clearly visible in his photograph with the identically marked twin peaks that we could see in the distance and thus pinpoint the location of the Saleesh House site.

We happily spent several hours wandering about this lovely spot by the river bordered by forest-covered mountains with snowy peaks barely visible in the far distance. Photographing it was a joy, for the light was perfect, the sky blue, and there was a satisfying abundance of beautifully shaped white clouds. We thought of David Thompson, Canada's greatest cartographer, of the winters he had spent here trading with the natives, enduring many days of "no Supper," expanding his knowledge of the country by his frequent journeys of exploration made from this spot, reaching lands in western Montana, northern Idaho, and eastern Washington. It was from Saleesh House that he departed in June of 1811 to make his final drive down the Columbia to its outlet at the Pacific. It was to Saleesh House that he returned nearly six months later, his task of surveying the mighty river from its source to its mouth finally completed. He had become the first white man to travel its entire length. Saleesh House was, indeed, associated with great and memorable events. Perhaps someday a proper historic marker will be erected to ensure that its location and its story will always be remembered.

Fort Vermilion

When the Saskatchewan posts, first at Pine Island (in 1793) and then at Fort George (in 1800), were abandoned due to depletion of available fur animals, the North West Company leapfrogged farther up the river into new, as yet untrapped country. It built Fort Vermilion on the north bank of the Saskatchewan opposite the mouth of the Vermilion River.

This fort was typical of the many "Fort des Prairies" established by both the North West and Hudson's Bay companies along the banks of the Saskatchewan. Located as they were on the edge of the beaver region to the north and the buffalo range to the south, they were major producers of both fur and pemmican.

In the fall of 1808 Alexander Henry the younger, who had been on the upper Red River since 1800, was sent far up the Saskatchewan to take charge of "Lower Fort des Prairies," otherwise known as Fort Vermilion, because of its location opposite the mouth of the Vermilion River. Henry described his arrival and the first days at his new post in his journal entries for September 13–17, 1808: "At sunset we sighted Fort Vermilion, in a long, flat bottom of meadow, directly opposite the entrance of Vermilion river, which falls in on the S. A large camp of Slaves began to whoop and halloo as we came down the hills, and appeared rejoiced to see us. We passed the H. B. Co. fort and entered our own, where we were warmly welcomed."

Fort Vermilion and the Hudson's Bay Paint Creek House were located side by side within the same palisade. This arrangement was not uncommon for posts trading with the often belligerent Indians of the plains, as it provided greater defensive protection for the traders. Furthermore, at this time (the very early 1800s) the rivalry between the two companies had not escalated to its later bitterness, and usually civility and a reasonable degree of cooperation prevailed between the opposing posts. Indeed, shortly after his arrival, Henry invited his Hudson's Bay Company neighbor, Henry Hallett, to breakfast in order to reach an amicable agreement respecting their trading with the natives. Each pledged not to interfere or trade with the Indians attached to the other's post.

On September 13, 1809, Henry returned to Fort Vermilion after a two months' journey from Fort William with a brigade of eleven canoes, each loaded with twenty-eight *pièces* and manned by five men. According to his enumeration in his journal, the provisions required for each canoe for the journey from Fort William until the buffalo country was reached, which was somewhere near the elbow of the Saskatchewan, were as follows: two bags of corn, two bags of wild rice, six bags of pemmican, and twenty-five pounds of grease. "This," he wrote, "shows the vast quantity of provisions we require yearly to carry on the trade in the N.W."

He found about three hundred tents of Indians, all on the south side of the Saskatchewan and on both sides of the Vermilion, awaiting his arrival, impatient to get their supplies. They wanted to cross over to the fort at once in the hopes of getting "a dram," but Henry did not permit it. He wrote in his journal: "The natives have become so troublesome that we find it necessary to keep them at a proper distance while at our establishments, and not allow them to come in numbers inside our principal fort; so that, should they be unruly, we might have full scope to defend ourselves."

There was much jealousy and ill feeling between the Cree and Blackfeet, each feeling that the other had been more favorably treated by the traders. This resulted in feelings of bitter resentment toward the trader, which, as Henry accurately predicted in his journal, "—may some day be attended with serious consequences to the establishment on this river."

Henry's brigade reached Fort Vermilion the day after his arrival. The canoes were quickly unloaded and everything carried into the safety of the fort. Henry sent word for Painted Feather and his principal men, heads of families, to come over to the fort. Henry wrote: "I gave them a nine-gallon keg of Indian rum and a fathom of tobacco, informing them at the same time what would be our system of trade this winter, what kind of skins were of value, and what otherwise. They were thankful for the present, and promised to behave well and do all in their power to hunt." The next day (September 15) was a busy one for Henry and his men. He wrote in his journal: "Early this morning we made out our assortment of goods, and packed up all that was intended for above. The Blackfeet were all sober, and wanted to trade what trash they had. I accordingly stationed three men to ferry them to and fro." Later, according to Henry, "We had a dance at my house, to which I invited my neighbor [Mr. Hallett] and his family. All were merry—our men as alert as if they had already rested for a month; but we were much crowded, there being present seventy-two men, thirty-seven women and sixty-five children, and the room being only 22 x 23 feet made it disagreeably warm."

When dealing with the Blackfoot tribe, Henry knew that constant vigilance was required. He wrote in his journal on September 21: ". . . Indians troublesome at the water-side in crossing, and wishing to steal our boats . . . However, to guard against a surprise, I was careful to keep my swivel loaded, frequently fresh-primed in their presence, and always pointed at their camp across the river, giving them to understand that, if they misbehaved, I would instantly fire the big gun and sweep their tents away. This had the desired effect, and the old men redoubled their exertions to keep the young ones in order."

By the end of September the last Blackfoot had departed for the plains to the south and west. Henry wrote on September 24: "We are heartily glad to be clear of those Slaves [i.e., Blackfeet] for some time." The Crees then started to come in to the fort, and for the first three weeks of October Henry was busy trading with them.

Trading was not the only occupation that kept Henry and his men busy during the fall months. His journal is full of the wide range of activities that the successful operation of a trading post required:

Sept. 25th: Set two men to dig away the bank, as it was too steep to haul up our firewood. Sept. 26th: All my men hard at work at the Indian house. Sept. 27th: Rain; men repairing the chimneys and doing other necessary work within doors. Sund. Oct. 1: Men repairing their saddles, etc.; to go hunting; Oct. 2nd: Sent eight men with horses to hunt buffalo on the S., as we were getting short of fresh meat. Oct. 6th: Gathered all my turnips—about 50 bushels, very large and of an excellent quality. Oct. 9th: Finished gathering potatoes—80 bushels, but small and watery. . . . Sent six men again up river for a raft of pine to make kegs for the winter and spring, when we require a quantity for trade and to contain grease. Oct. 13th: My men all at the fall work of the fort, such as building the Indian house, store, and shop, surrounding them with stockades, repairing the houses, mudding the chimneys, carting hay, etc. Oct. 20th: My men finished repairing their houses, and this evening everyone was entered and settled for the winter.

According to Henry's list of people at Fort Vermilion, 106 people (thirty servants plus their families) were accommodated in seven houses. Since these dwellings were anything but commodious, it must have been quite a "snug fit" for the fifteen or so occupants per unit.

During January and February Henry's men were often sent *en derouine*—that is, to go to the tents of the Indians deep in their winter trapping grounds and there trade for their furs. Meanwhile, the women at the fort were busy stretching buffalo hides to make pemmican bags and pack cords. February 1 Henry wrote: "Laid meat in the icehouse—550 thighs and 380 shoulders."

By the middle of February 1810 Henry, along with his Hudson's Bay neighbor Henry Hallett, had decided to abandon their respective

418

posts of Fort Vermilion and Painted Creek House and move to a new location. Together they chose a site farther up the Saskatchewan River at the mouth of the Terre Blanche River. At the same time, James Hughes also decided to close down his North West post of Fort Augustus and move down to the new location. As before, the posts of the two companies were to be within a common palisade. This new location, being more centrally located, would, as Henry wrote, "answer the same purpose as the two present establishments and save the expense of one of them; it will also draw all the Slaves [i.e., Blackfeet] to trade at one place, where we can better defend ourselves from their insults."

During the month of May preparations were made for sending the year's returns of furs down to the North West Company's great depot of Fort William and for closing the fort and moving it upstream to the new location at Terre Blanche. Apparently, the two forts thus closed were not permanently abandoned. When Gabriel Franchère reached the mouth of the Vermilion River on his way east to Montreal in June of 1814, he found both posts occupied. In his *Voyage to the Northwest Coast of America* Franchère wrote:

> Knowing that we were near a factory, we made our toilets as well as we could before arriving. Toward sundown we reached Fort Vermilion, which is situated on the bank of a river at the foot of a superb hill.
>
> We found at this post some ninety persons, men, women, and children; these people depend for subsistence on the chase and fishing with hooks and lines, which is very precarious. Mr. Hallet, the clerk in charge was absent, and we were dismayed to hear that there were no provisions on the place, a very disagreeable piece of news for people famished as we were. We had been led to suppose that if we could only reach the plains of the Saskatchewin, we should be in the land of plenty. Mr. Hallet, however, was not long in arriving: he had two quarters of buffalo meat brought out, which had been laid in ice, and prepared us supper. Mr. Hallet was a polite, sociable man, loving his ease passibly well and desirous of living in these wild countries as people do in civilized lands. Having testified to him our surprise at seeing in one of the buildings a large cariole like those of Canada, he informed us that, having horses, he had had this carriage made in order to enjoy a sleigh ride; but that the workmen having forgot to take the measure of the doors of the building before constructing it, it was found when finished much too large for them, and could never be got out of the room where it was; and it was like to remain there a long time, as he was not disposed to demolish the house for the pleasure of using the cariole.
>
> By the side of the factory of the North West Company is another belonging to the Company of Hudson's Bay. In general these trading houses are constructed thus, one close to the other and surrounded with

a common palisade, with a door of communication in the interior for mutual succor in case of attack on the part of the Indians. The latter, in this region, particularly the Blackfeet, Gros Ventres, and those of the Yellow River, are very ferocious: they live by the chase, but bring few furs to the traders; and the latter maintain these posts principally to procure themselves provisions.

By May of 1816 the posts were closed down once again—never to reopen.

We knew from studying our road map that secondary highway 897, which crosses the Saskatchewan at the mouth of the Vermilion River, should take us to the vicinity of the fort site. However, it required keen observation to spot the unmarked insignificant dirt roadway leading from the highway that actually did take us the few rods to the fort location. The clearing where the two forts once stood is situated near the edge of the high open plateau on the north side of the Saskatchewan River and directly opposite the mouth of the Vermilion River on the south bank. A woven wire fence now surrounds the site in much the same way as the original stockade enclosed the two adjacent forts. Except in the two places about three hundred yards apart where the concentration of numerous cellar holes indicates the existence of fort buildings now long vanished, all the thick growth of poplar and underbrush that had rapidly invaded the area upon the forts' abandonment has been cleared and the prairie grasses carefully mowed. The Hudson's Bay Company's Painted Post stood at the east end of the approximately two-acre clearing, while the North West Company's Fort Vermilion was located at the west or upriver end. Other than the two clusters of brush-and-bramble-covered cellar holes, there was nothing to assist the imagination in picturing the once-busy forts that had stood here. However, the plains to the south over which the unpredictable but always arrogant Blackfeet had come, the broad river flowing below, representing a safety barrier for the forts, and over which Henry's man had such trouble ferrying the Indians back and forth—these were still plainly visible from our vantage point high above the Saskatchewan. In fact, recalling the vivid written words of Henry himself, it was not too difficult to let our imagination take over and, indeed, to "see" the comings and goings of the traders and the Indians—to catch a glimpse of what life was like at the forts.

Green Lake House
Essex House

The recently formed North West Company quickly moved ever deeper into the rich fur lands of the *pays d'en haut*. It is probable that by 1789, perhaps as early as 1782, they had established a trading fort on Green Lake. A letter written to Roderick Mackenzie by Angus Shaw, dated December 16, 1789, contains the following reference to a post at Green Lake: "—Tourangeau winters at Lac Vert [i.e., Green Lake]."

Another reference is found in the journal entry for October 8, 1790, of Philip Turnor written at Île à la Crosse: "Friday Two Canadian [i.e., North West] Canoes with Seven men in each went for a Settlement in a small Lake up the Beaver River it lays on the south side of the river between it and the Sas-skash-e-wan and is called by the Indians A-quack-a-pew Sack-a-ha-gon this House is only kept up in the Winter and is only a detached post belonging to Isle-a-La Crosse."

Green Lake with its easy access to Beaver River was a highly strategic location for a trading post. The Beaver River provided an east–west waterway midway between the Athabasca to the north and the Saskatchewan to the south. It also gave access to the Churchill River by its outlet into Lac Île à la Crosse. It therefore served as a most important link between the company's Churchill River and Saskatchewan River departments.

According to David Thompson's notebooks, the site of the North West Company's Green Lake Post at the time of his visit there in the fall of 1798 was on the southwest shore of the lake. Thompson left his canoes at Green Lake House to proceed on up the Beaver River toward Lac la Biche, while he himself took horses to ride cross-country to Fort George on the Saskatchewan, where he spent a few days before riding back to rejoin his men in the canoes.

Green Lake House, in addition to gathering the furs from the surrounding regions, served as a link connecting the English (i.e., Churchill) River department with the Saskatchewan department. Canoes for Green Lake left the North West depot on Lac Île à la Crosse and ascended the Beaver River to its great bend, where they left the river to go up the small stream leading to Green Lake.

When he was in charge of the English (Churchill) River department, North West wintering partner William McGillivray arranged that the posts on the Saskatchewan River acquire sufficient surplus pemmican to relieve the acute shortage of food frequently experienced by the more northern posts. Thus when in the spring of 1795 the men of

Green Lake House were starving—existing on soup made from fish bones thrown out the previous autumn—a life-saving supply of pemmican from the Saskatchewan post of Fort George was sent to them.

Until 1799 the North West Company had no competition on the upper Churchill River. In that year the Hudson's Bay Company sent up a number of boats well equipped with goods and supplies to Île à la Crosse. From there they ascended the Beaver River. The North West Company did not let this move go unchallenged. Peter Fidler recorded in his journal on August 25, 1799: "While we waited for Mr. Auld—Mr. McTavish of the old [North West] company used every mean and rogish method in his power to persuade our pilot to leave us . . ." A few days later Fidler wrote: "A Canadian [North West] canoe with 2 men passed us on their way to Green Lake we suppose to tell the master there of our unexpected arrival and to get all the Indians out of the way if possible."

Undaunted, Auld established his post, known as Essex House, on the west shore of Green Lake at the north end near the outlet. The North West Company responded by moving their Green Lake House to the east side of the lake directly opposite their rival's post. On August 28, when Fidler and William Auld reached the site they had chosen on Green Lake (so called because of the large quantities of "green floating grass"), they were met by the manager of North West's Green Lake House. According to Fidler, "The Canadian master came to us to endeavor to drive away the Indians that we luckily found here . . . there has been a house here since or before the smallpox of 1781."

William Auld quickly realized that it would be necessary to keep his Essex House post operating on a year-round basis instead of just as a wintering post. In January of 1800 he wrote in his journal: ". . . with regard to this house at Green Lake it will be necessary to keep it up during the summer as by relinquishing it we immediately give the natives room to suspect that we don't intend to return by which they will continue their attachment to the Canadians which ought to be our constant business to weaken."

During the second year of their rivalry (1800–1801) the North West Company's Green Lake House had a complement of thirty officers and men; Essex House was staffed with eleven men. Combined returns for that same period for the posts on Île à la Crosse and Green Lake were equivalent to 12,000 Made Beaver for the North West Company and 1,800 Made Beaver for the Hudson's Bay Company.

With each successive year, friction between the two companies intensified. The North West Company, determined to prevent the Hudson's Bay Company from penetrating farther into the Athabasca country, challenged and fought each advance every inch of the way. In 1806 the Nor'Westers from Green Lake House made their move. They crossed over to the Hudson's Bay Company post, where they utterly destroyed the fort's garden; then they torched the buildings, leaving nothing but charred ruins to mark the location of Essex House. Four years later (in 1810) Peter Fidler at Île à la Crosse sent Robert Sutherland to rebuild the post. Although Sutherland was able to elude detection by the watchful Nor'Westers, his absence was soon noticed and his destination and purpose discovered. The hold over the local Indians by the North West Company was so strong that the Nor'Wester Samuel Black had only to send one man with threats to the Indians to keep them from trading at Sutherland's reestablished fort. As Fidler stated in his journal: "... on purpose to keep Indians from coming near as it is well known that even the sight of a Canadian [i.e., Nor'Wester] will so frighten the Natives as to be frightened of speakg. to us."

Sutherland's post was short-lived. As soon as he left it in June of 1811, the Nor'Westers from Green Lake House struck again. They climbed over the abandoned fort's stockades and burned the post to the ground. Once more the Hudson's Bay presence on Green Lake had been wiped out.

A few years later the Hudson's Bay Company was ready to try yet again to reestablish their post on Green Lake. This time the attempt was spearheaded by Colin Robertson, formerly of the North West Company, well versed in their aggressive tactics and prepared to meet force with force. In fact, according to John McDonald of Garth, Robertson, who had actually been in charge of Green Lake Post in 1804, had "afterwards behaved somewhat amiss," which had resulted in his dismissal from the North West Company by McDonald.

By the spring of 1815 the Hudson's Bay Company post had been reestablished for the third time on its site at the north end of Green Lake opposite the North West Company's post of Green Lake House. Robert McVicar was able to bring out four packs of furs in the spring of 1816. During the next two years the bitter struggle between the two companies for the control of the Athabascan country escalated into unrestrained violence and lawlessness, and Green Lake did not escape the turmoil. Led by the Nor'Wester Peter Skene Ogden, in charge of Green Lake House, and Samuel Black, both well-known for their aggressive behavior, the Hudson's Bay Essex House was overrun and plundered and its officers and men imprisoned. Still the Hudson's Bay tenaciously continued to maintain its presence on Green Lake. By 1818 the post was reestablished and it was even able to show a return of thirty packs of furs for that year.

In 1820 Sir John Franklin stopped off at Essex House, where John Stewart MacFarlane was in charge. Franklin commented on the Green Lake posts in his *Narrative of a Journey to the Shores of the Polar Sea in the Years 1819, 20, 21, and 22:* "These establishments are small, but said to be well situated for the procuring of furs; as the numerous creeks in their vicinity are much resorted to by the beaver, otter, and musquash. The residents usually obtain a superabundant supply of provision."

At last in 1821, with the union of the two rival companies, the strife ended and peace came to the fur trade. Hudson's Bay Company's Essex House was abandoned in favor of the North West Company's Green Lake House, whose name was retained.

Gradually the Churchill River district lost much of its earlier importance as a fur-producing area. Green Lake, however, continued to function as the outpost linking up the district with the Saskatchewan. In the years following 1821, Green Lake House assumed increasing importance as a major depot and transshipment point for the Hudson's Bay Company. Almost all the goods and supplies necessary to service the Athabasca and Mackenzie districts came through this post.

Some seventy years after the strife-filled events of 1811–18, violence once again threatened the post on Green Lake. In the spring of 1885, the Métis and Indian uprising was erupting throughout the area. Green Lake House warehouses were bulging with over one hundred tons of goods and supplies, including 200 guns and large quantities of ammunition, that were waiting for the spring breakup to be transported north. Lawrence Clarke, the Hudson's Bay Company factor, well aware of the danger of the supplies being plundered, tried to get Commissioner Irvine of the North West Mounted Police to send a detachment from Prince Albert to Green Lake to protect the post and its stores but was refused. Clarke, in desperation, organized a small force of twenty Hudson's Bay employees but was not allowed to equip them with government guns or ammunition. Nevertheless, they hastened to Green Lake, but they arrived too late—the Indians had already been there. However, due to the foresight and resourcefulness of James Sinclair, the man in charge of Green Lake House, the would-be plunderers got little of any value. The moment word reached Sinclair of the fighting at Duck Lake and Fish Creek, he quickly and quietly emptied his warehouses, caching the goods at various places along the Beaver River. When the Indians stormed into the post, he pacified them by handing out food from his few remaining supplies and successfully convinced them that he had no arms or ammunition, that, in fact, his warehouses were empty. The Indians at last departed without causing any further trouble.

Today the Hudson's Bay Company post, still located on the north side of Green Lake, continues in operation much as it has always done for nearly the past two hundred years. Green Lake is now a tiny community at the north end of Green Lake. It is located at the intersection of two modern highways that roughly parallel the entire course of the Beaver River. One, Number 155, extends from Green Lake to the river's big bend northward to Île à la Crosse, the river's end; the other, Number 55, runs from Green Lake westward to Lac La Biche, the river's beginning. With these highways as our travel routes, we were able, in the comfort of our motor home, to quickly and easily reach points along the Beaver River that Thompson, Fidler, and all the other early traders could only attain after days of wearisome and difficult paddling and poling in the winding and tortuous river.

At Green Lake we photographed the provincial marker commemorating North West Company's Green Lake House and Hudson's Bay Company's Essex House. But it was only as we stood on the bridge spanning the small river flowing out of Green Lake (just visible to the south) to the nearby Beaver River (just out of sight to the north) that we were able to catch a glimpse of what the country was like two hundred years ago. For in the whole vast area to the north, as seen from the bridge, there was no evidence of the twentieth century—no buildings, no motor boats, no utility poles, nothing. The land stretching away to the far horizon remained unchanged from the days of the fur traders. The low-lying country was flat, broken only by distant ridges of dark spruce. Just the stream quietly flowing toward its junction with the Beaver River penetrated this remote, almost forbidding wilderness. This was still the country just as the traders saw it as they traveled this section of the river. Perhaps, just perhaps, if we concentrated hard enough and called upon all our powers of imagination, we might be able to catch a glimpse of them paddling up the river toward one of the Green Lake posts.

Spokane House

Spokane House was the fifth (and last) of the posts established by David Thompson during the course of his five-year endeavor to reach the Pacific Ocean by way of the Columbia River.

In 1810 Thompson sent Finan McDonald, his capable assistant, along with Jaco Finlay to build a post west of Kullyspell House on the Spokane River. The location chosen was on a peninsula at the confluence of the Spokane and Little Spokane rivers—a beautiful, protected flatland, triangular in shape. For generations this had been a favorite gathering place for the Indians to catch and dry fish. Spokane House was situated on the east bank of the river, a mile above the mouth of Little Spokane River.

In the summer of the following year (1811) Thompson stopped at Spokane House before continuing the journey that would finally take him down the Columbia to the Pacific. He recorded in his *Narrative:* "On the evening of the 14th [June] we arrived at the Spokane House on the River of that name, where I left a small assortment of Goods to continue the trade; there were forty tents of Spokane Indians, with Jaco [Jaques Raphael Finlay], a half breed, as Clerk. We remained here two days."

Two months later (on August 11) Thompson was back at Spokane House after successfully completing his journey to the mouth of the Columbia River: "Having gone about forty miles, we arrived, thank God, at the trading Post on the Spokane River. Provisions having fallen short and our Guide assuring us we should see no Deer, nor Indians to supply us, we had to shoot a Horse for a supply." Thompson remained at Spokane House until the seventeenth of August. He wrote in his *Narrative:* ". . . the Salmon caught here were few, and poor. Several Indians of the Kullyspell and Skeetshoo tribes came to see us, but finding we had not brought a supply of goods, they returned . . ."

Eventually supplies did arrive from across the mountains and Thompson was able to send his canoe "loaded with goods, and nine men . . . down the Columbia to the Ilthkoyape [Kettle] Falls to the care of Mr. Finan McDonald for the supply of the lower posts on McGillivray's [Kootenay] the Saleesh and Spokane Rivers."

Early in the spring of 1812, Thompson began what would be his last trip east across the mountains. On March 13 he left Saleesh House, where he had wintered, and first by canoe and then overland by horseback he traveled by way of Spokane House to Kettle Falls on the Columbia. Here he and his men spent a busy week building the necessary canoes needed for the journey upstream to the mountain crossing (Athabasca Pass). By April 21 the canoes were finished and John G. McTavish and James McMillan had arrived from Spokane House with the year's trade in furs. Thompson and his brigade of six canoes quickly embarked and began their long journey homeward.

David Thompson had scarcely left the Columbia region when traders from John Jacob Astor's recently organized Pacific Fur Company spread into the area from their base at Fort Astoria, at the mouth of the Columbia River.

John Clarke, who had once been an employee of the North West Company but had entered into the service of the Pacific Fur Company, was given the task of placing forts in opposition to all those established by David Thompson for the North West Company. Clarke himself built his post right next to Spokane House, where James McMillan was in charge. Clarke had a large force of thirty-three men under his command, which greatly outnumbered that of the North West post. He was well equipped with heavy tools and a plentiful supply of materials and supplies and was soon able to erect a strong palisaded post with two bastions.

From the outset the competition for the Indians' trade was fierce and quite unscrupulous. According to Alexander Ross of the Pacific Fur Company, who visited the post for three days in December:

> I had frequent opportunities of observing the sly and underhand dealings of the competing parties, for the opposition posts of the North-West Company and Mr. Clarke were built contiguous to each other. When the two parties happened to meet, they made the amplest protestations of friendship and kindness, and a stranger, unacquainted with the politics of Indian trade, would have pronounced them sincere; but the moment their backs were turned, they tore each other to pieces. Each party had its manoeuvring scouts out in all directions watching the motions of the Indians, and laying plots and plans to entrap or foil each other. He that got most skins, never minding the cost or the crime, was the cleverest fellow.

However, Ross Cox, another Astorian, wrote that the two competing traders had a friendly agreement not to give rum to the Indians. He also said: "In other respects also we agreed very well with our opponent, and neither party evinced any of the turbulent or lawless spirit, which have so ferocious an aspect to the opposition of the rival companies on the east side of the mountains."

Late in 1812 when the Nor'Wester John George McTavish arrived back at his post of Spokane House, he brought not only goods to resupply the fort but also news of the outbreak of war between the United States and Great Britain. This had far-reaching consequences for both the North West Company and the Pacific Fur Company. For the Nor'Westers it was an opportunity to turn the state of war between the two countries to their own advantage. They saw in it a means whereby they could gain control of the mouth of the Columbia River, enabling them to establish a base there for both inland and maritime fur trade. Accordingly, they arranged for British warships to convoy their trading vessel, the *Isaac Todd*, when it sailed from London in March of 1813, with instructions to capture Fort Astoria from the Americans. For the partners of the Pacific Fur Company the news was a devastating blow. The war between England and the United States meant that Astor's vessels, upon which they were utterly dependent for supplies, would henceforth be subject to attack by English warships. Since they were daily expecting the arrival of Astor's ship the *Lark* with supplies, they decided to carry on for the ensuing year (1813), but if it failed to come, they would be destitute of supplies and would then be forced to sell out to the North West Company.

In the meantime, John George McTavish came down the Columbia to await the arrival of the North West's ship *Isaac Todd*. When it failed to arrive, he returned to his post at Spokane House. However, on the seventh of October he returned bearing a letter to Duncan McDougall, the partner in charge of Fort Astoria, from McDougall's uncle, Angus Shaw, informing him of the sailing of the *Isaac Todd* and the accompanying warships. Within a few days of his arrival, McTavish was followed by a number of other Nor'Westers, all gathered to meet the expected ships. Confronted with these facts, along with the nonappearance of Astor's *Lark* (it had capsized off the Sandwich Islands), the partners of the Pacific Fur Company recognized that their position was untenable. To prevent their fort, with all its goods and furs, from falling into the hands of the English warship and confiscated as lawful spoils of war, on October 16, 1813, they entered into an agreement with McTavish and others of the North West Company whereby they sold to them all their fur forts, their total inventory of goods, and their furs on the basis of ten percent above the original cost and charges. So when the British warship HMS *Racoon* did arrive off the mouth of the Columbia at the end of November, it was welcomed by the new owners of Fort Astoria —not Americans, but British subjects, the men of the North West Company.

With the acquisition of Clarke's Spokane House, the Nor'Westers abandoned their own post and moved into the more commodious one of their former rivals. For the next twelve years the North West Company's Spokane House was the principal distributing and wintering point for the upper Columbia, Kootenay, and Flathead trade. It was also the depot to which the company's push south into the Snake River country was attached. The Spokane district was the most prolific source of furs in the entire Columbia area. Furthermore, these furs were of the very highest quality.

However, its location was not well chosen. The Spokane River, on which it was located, was unnavigable during certain seasons of the year, which meant that horses had to be kept for overland travel from the river's junction with the Columbia. It was also much too far from the nearest and best approach to the Snake River country. As Alexander Ross wrote in his *The Fur Hunters of the Far West:*

> This [Oakinacken] was the point of general separation, although the depot for the interior was still one hundred and forty miles farther east, at a place called Spokane House. Now whatever Oakinacken might have been, Spokane House, of all the posts in the interior, was the most unsuitable place for concentrating the different branches of the trade. But a post had been established at that place in the early days of the trade and after the country had become thoroughly known, people were adverse to change what long habit had made familiar to them. So Spokane House still remained. Thence both men and goods were year after year carried two hundred miles north by water, merely to have the pleasure of sending them two hundred miles south again by land, in order to reach their destination.

He continued: "At Spokane House, too, there were handsome buildings. There was a ball room, and no females in the land so fair to look upon as the nymphs of Spokane. No damsels could dance so gracefully as they; none were so attractive. But Spokane House was not celebrated for fine women only, there were fine horses also. The race ground was admired, and the pleasures of the race. Altogether, Spokane House was a delightful place and time had confirmed its celebrity."

The disadvantages of the Spokane House location were recognized by the North West Company, but although Donald McKenzie established a new fort (Nez Percé) in a much more convenient location "more central for the general business of the interior," Spokane House was not closed down. In fact, as soon as McKenzie retired from the Columbia country, Finan McDonald, who had been placed in charge of the company's trading into the Snake River area, moved back to Spokane House and made it the main depot for his trade.

In 1821 the North West Company amalgamated with the Hudson's

Bay Company. Excerpts from the journal kept by Finan McDonald and James Birnie at Spokane House during the first years after this union detail many of the activities that took place at the fort.

In response to the need for rehabilitating the fort, a major building program was undertaken. A new store as well as bastions were constructed and renovations made to the Indian shop, provision store, and men's houses. Improvements to the "Big House" were made such as adding a new room for the "reception of Mr. McMillan" and, "so that there will be no danger for the fire for the future," raising its chimney with stone. New palisades were built enclosing not only the fort but also the fort garden and the horse yard. A gallery was added extending halfway around the fort. The necessity to obtain food was not neglected. Salmon were caught in the nearby Spokane River: "We got 27 salmon from our barrier today. The People cut away the branches along the River near the barrier, which frighten away the fish prevents them from coming up . . " Potatoes from the fort garden were dug: "Put five hands to dig up the potatoes in the garden. We have but a poor crop when compared with that of last year . . ." The Indians were exhorted by the factor "to tent off from the fort, and go in search of beaver instead of losing their time here where they do nothing but dance and gamble their property away a propensity to which they are much addicted." Horses for overland travel had to be always available. "Messrs. McMillan, Brown & Kittson with 4 men arrived from Okangan . . . They came here for horses; thirty odd being wanted for New Caledonia." A welcome break in the fort's daily routine was provided in November when "Mr. Kennedy give a ball being the custom of the place when the men leave this for their winter grounds . . ."

Spokane House was visited by Governor George Simpson in October of 1824 during the course of his journey from York Factory to Fort George (formerly Fort Astoria). As a result of this visit, during which not only Spokane House but also the other posts in the Columbia River department were subjected to his eagle-eyed scrutiny, many drastic changes were inaugurated, all designed to put the area on a profitable basis.

Simpson met at the forks of the Spokane and Columbia rivers Chief Factor Peter Skene Ogden and John Work with about thirty men who had just come up from Fort George with the outfits for the interior after the arrival of the Hudson's Bay Company's supply ship *Vigilant*. Ogden reported to Simpson that the country was in a state of peace and quietness and that the affairs of the company were going on as usual. Reacting to Ogden's remarks, Simpson rather tartly wrote in his journal under the date of October 27: "which is not saying a great deal as if my information is correct the Columbia Deptmt from the Day of its Origin to the present hour has been neglected, shamefully mismanaged and a scene of the most wasteful extravagance and the most unfortunate dissention."

Simpson decided to leave the Columbia River and make the overland journey to Spokane House so as to see for himself the condition of the post. The next day, accompanied by Dr. McLoughlin, James McMillan, Peter S. Ogden, and others, he rode to Spokane House: ". . . the distance is about 60 miles and being well mounted we got to the Establishment in the same Eveng. the road tolerably good and the Country interesting being a succession of Hills plains and points of Wood the winding course of the River bringing it frequently to our view and adding much to the beauty of the scenery.—Spokane house is delightfully situated near the banks of the Spokane & Skichen [Little Spokane] Rivers in a fine plain or valley and surrounded at the distance of two or three miles by Hills clothed with Grass and fine Timber to their summits. Here we found Messrs Finan McDonald & Kittson Clerks and a large concourse of Indians of the Spokane & Nez Percés Tribes encamped about the Fort."

At the time of Simpson's visit, Chief Factor Peter S. Ogden was in charge of Spokane House, assisted by John Work and seven other men. Ogden had succeeded Chief Factor Alexander Kennedy, who in turn had followed Chief Factor John Haldane. During the 1823–24 season, the post had shown returns of approximately nine thousand beaver, about half of which had come from the Snake River country to the south.

By the time of Simpson's departure from Spokane House three days later on October 31 to resume his journey toward Fort George, he had arranged that Finan McDonald and four other men would be in charge of Spokane House and that Ogden would lead a beaver-trapping expedition into the Snake River country. Simpson had also, in no uncertain terms, expressed his disapproval of certain wasteful practices prevalent in the Spokane district and made it fully clear that henceforth they must cease. His outrage is reflected in his journal. "The good people of Spokane District . . . have since its first establishment shewn an extraordinary predilection for European Provisions without once looking at or considering the enormous price it costs; . . . they may be said to have been eating Gold." Instead of the sixteen men and two boats sufficient for the trade for the district if "anything like respectable profits should be realized," thirty-five to forty men and five or six boats "principally loaded with Eatables, Drinkable and other *Domestic Comforts*" had been required each year. "These extra men alone

... were sufficient to run away with a large share of the Columbia profits." Since the Spokane district and ample resources for comfortable living, "abundance of the finest Salmon in the World besides a variety of other Fish Within 100 yds. of their Door, plenty of Potatoes, Game if they like it," there was no reason "why one oz. of European Stores of Provisions should be allowed . . ." Simpson's ultimatum ended all such extravagance: ". . . they had better Hoard the European provisions and Luxuries they have got now in Store as their future supplies will be very scanty barely the allowance determined on by the Honble Committee."

When Simpson reached the forks of the Spokane and Columbia rivers on his return from Fort George in April of the following year (1825), he had reached a decision that Spokane House should be closed down and removed to the Kettle Falls (David Thompson's Ilthkoyape Falls), some one hundred miles farther up the Columbia. He stated his reasons for his decision in his journal under the date of April 8:

> ... the advantages to be derived from this change are, that a very heavy expense and serious inconvenience in transporting the Outfits and returns between the Main River [Columbia] and the present Establishment by Land a distance of about 60 Miles will be avoided; that at the Kettle Falls an abundant stock of Fish may be secured for the maintenance of the Post throughout the Year; that the Post of Okanogan can be abandoned and that by a little attention to Farming a sufficient quantity of Pork Potatoes & Grain may be provided for consumption at the Post and on the Voyage so as to render them independent both of the Natives and of our Stores at the Coast.

Simpson also felt that the Flathead and Kootenay posts to the east could be supplied with equal ease from the new location with the further possibility that if the river access to them was found to be practical, the use of horses could be discontinued, which would be a great saving both in expense and trouble.

Simpson lost no time in putting his decision into effect. As soon as he reached Kettle Falls, a week later (on April 16), he made arrangements with the local chief for the use of land a short distance above the falls. Simpson chose a site for the new establishment and marked out the dimensions both for the fort and for the fort's garden plot. He wrote to James Birnie at Spokane House instructing him to send men to the new site at once to plant five or six bushels of potatoes. He was further ordered to begin the necessary preparations for the removal of the property from Spokane House as soon as possible after the arrival of the brigade upbound on the Columbia.

432

The fall and winter of 1825–26 were a busy time for Chief Trader John Work at Spokane House. In addition to overseeing the trade at the Flathead post, he had three boats under construction and was attempting to get enough lumber cut for the construction of Fort Colville, the new post at Kettle Falls. By March of 1826 the dismantling of the buildings at Spokane House was nearly completed and the iron hardware, such as latches and hinges, had been removed. On April 7 the last pack train left and Spokane House was officially abandoned.

Old Jaques (Jaco) Finlay, formerly clerk in the North West Company and long associated with both David Thompson and Spokane House, chose to remain behind with his family. He and his many sons, now hunting and trapping as freemen, were considered among the best in the country. Jaco Finlay died in 1828 and, in accordance with his wish, was buried under Spokane House's southeast bastion.

By 1833 only this southeast bastion remained. Its preservation was due to the respect felt for Finlay's grave beneath it. All the other buildings and the stockade had been used by the Indians for firewood. As late as 1836 this bastion was still standing, but by 1843 when the German naturalist Charles A. Geyer visited the site, nothing was left but a slight elevation marking the location of the chimney.

The site of Spokane House was easy to find. After leaving Thompson's Saleesh House on the Clark Fork River, we followed as closely as it was possible to do when traveling on land highways instead of waterways the well-established route of the traders to Spokane House. Highway 2 took us along the north side of Pend d'Oreille Lake, down the Pend d'Oreille River as far as Newport. Here roughly retracing Thompson's "Skeetshoo" Road, the highway turned south, paralleling the Little Spokane River to Spokane House.

The day we came to Spokane House, we were fortunate to find Jim Perkins on duty in the interpretive center. Not only was he well-informed about the history of Spokane House, but he also had the additional distinction of being a seventh generation direct descendent of that very Jaco Finlay who lay buried at the fort site.

The outlines of the North West Company's 1810 fort, the Pacific Fur Company's fort, and the subsequent Hudson's Bay Company's enlargement have been established as a result of considerable archaeological work on the site. These are represented by color-coded wooden sills following the forts' outlines; in addition, posts mark the locations of gate entrances, cellars, and the forge hearth area. In the southeast corner where the southeast bastion had once stood is a flat, unmarked concrete slab. This covers the grave of Jaco Finlay.

Today, just as in the time of Clarke, McDonald, Finlay, and Simpson, the spot occupied by Spokane House is one of beauty. The river can just be glimpsed through the trees fringing its banks. Rising in the background are the gently rounded hills—quite bare of undergrowth—well covered with widely spaced pine trees. Simpson's 1824 description—"delightfully situated near the banks of the Spokane & Skichen [Little Spokane] Rivers in a fine plain or valley and surrounded at the distance of two or three miles by Hills clothed with Grass and fine Timber to their summits"—is as true today as it was when he wrote those words 166 years ago.

The modern interpretive center houses many informative charts, plans, and drawings illustrating the layout of the three forts occupying the site. It also displays much of the wealth of material found during the various archaeological digs. Among the objects recovered were colored glass beads, brass finger rings, brass hawks' bells, Jew's harps, metal buttons, lead musket balls, lead shot, musket flints, Chinese porcelain plate and bowl fragments, glass bottles, English earthenware, nails, spikes, bolts, clay pipes, and three flintlock trade muskets.

Perhaps of particular interest—certainly to Jim Perkins, his descendant—was the uncovering of the grave of Jaques Finlay. The body had been interred in a casket of pine boards. Also in the casket were coat buttons, a pair of spectacles, five smoking pipes, a hunting knife, and a tin cup. It is to be hoped that this grave will be dignified by an appropriate identifying inscription, so that the last resting place of Jaques (Jaco) Finlay, half-breed son of James Finlay, North West Company partner; friend, interpreter, and assistant to David Thompson; clerk in the North West Company; cofounder with Finan McDonald of Spokane House; celebrated freeman hunter and trapper will not be allowed to slip into oblivion—unmarked and forgotten.

Fort Astoria
Fort George (Columbia River)

During the early 1800s, when David Thompson was systematically exploring and mapping the Columbia River from its source west of the Rockies while establishing the North West Company's claim to the area by building trading forts as he steadily progressed westward toward the mouth of the great river, an enterprising German-born American merchant, John Jacob Astor, was taking steps to expand his trading activities to include the Pacific coast and the ports of China.

Briefly, his ambitious and far-reaching scheme (backed by the tacit support of President Jefferson) called for the establishment of a series of trading forts along both the Missouri and Columbia rivers (as well as subsidiary posts on their tributaries), with the main headquarters to be at the mouth of the Columbia. This entrepôt would supply the interior posts with the goods and equipment necessary for trade. It would also receive and warehouse all the furs traded. It would be serviced yearly by a ship from New York bringing reinforcements, supplies, and trading goods. This vessel loaded with its new cargo of furs would then sail to the China coast and the port of Canton. There the furs would be sold and the money thus realized would be used to acquire a cargo of tea, silks, porcelains, and other Chinese goods for the return trip to New York, where they would be sold at a substantial profit. This three-pronged enterprise was possible only because Astor, as an American citizen, was not barred from Chinese ports, as were British subjects and commercial concerns (such as the North West Company) by the monopolistic rights of the East India Company.

To avoid costly and detrimental competition in the region west of the Rockies as well as to utilize its superior experience in fur trading, Astor offered the North West Company an opportunity to acquire a third interest in his enterprise. The Nor'Westers, however, declined, believing that their posts already established in New Caldonia and on the Columbia would give to them a monopoly of the trade west of the mountains and, furthermore, that they would have secured the mouth of the Columbia themselves before Astor could possibly arrive there.

Undaunted, Astor organized his Pacific Fur Company in 1810. He provided the capital in the amount of $200,000 and was responsible for the management of the new concern's affairs at the New York end. The partners were to carry on the enterprise from the trading posts that they were to establish. They would share in the profits according to the number of shares each held. Stock in the company was divided into one hundred equal shares of $2,000 each. Fifty were held by Astor; the remaining fifty were to be divided among the partners and associates. Among the men Astor recruited as partners were three former Nor'Westers: Alexander McKay, Duncan McDougall, and Donald McKenzie. In addition, William Hunt, David Stuart, his nephew Robert Stuart, and Ramsay Crooks agreed to become partners in the newly formed company.

Astor's plan called for sending two simultaneous expeditions to the mouth of the Columbia: one from New York by sea around Cape Horn and up the west coast to the Columbia; the other by land up the Missouri, over the Rockies, and down the Columbia to its outlet on the Pacific.

On September 8, 1810, the *Tonquin* with partners Alexander McKay, Duncan McDougall, David Stuart, and Robert Stuart aboard, carrying a cargo of assorted trading merchandise, a frame for a coasting schooner, and supplies for the establishment and maintenance of the new post, including vegetable seeds, cleared New York Harbor and eight months later, in March of 1811, dropped anchor at the mouth of the Columbia River.

The land-based expedition, under the leadership of William Hunt and Donald McKenzie, left New York in the latter part of July in 1810. After stops at Montreal and Mackinac Island to recruit the Canadian voyageurs as well as acquire all the many items, including an assortment of Indian goods, needed for the long overland trek, the party had advanced as far as St. Louis by September 3. At last, on October 21, Hunt was able to head up the Missouri with his small flotilla of three boats. Many weary months later, in January of 1812, haggard, emaciated, clothed only in tatters, some of his men reached the mouth of the Columbia River, where Fort Astoria had been established. They were followed by Hunt and the rest of his party a month later, on February 15. So at long last, after the passage of nearly nineteen months, all the partners (with the exception of Ramsay Crooks, who was still somewhere behind in the wilderness) were reunited.

Washington Irving in his book *Astoria* gives a vivid account of the reunion of the sea and overland parties: "A day was now given up to jubilee, to celebrate the arrival of Mr. Hunt and his companions, and the joyful meeting of the various scattered bands of adventurers at Astoria. The colors were hoisted; the guns, great and small, were fired; there was a feast of fish, of beaver and venison, which relished well with men who had so long been glad to revel on horse flesh and dogs' meat; a genial allowance of grog was issued, to increase the general animation, and the festivities wound up, as usual, with a grand dance at night, by the Canadian voyageurs."

During the ten months preceding the arrival of William Hunt and his men, the seaborne party on the *Tonquin,* which had reached the mouth of the Columbia in April of 1811, had been able to select a site and erect the buildings forming their trading post, which they quite appropriately named Fort Astoria.

According to Washington Irving's account in his *Astoria,* "The situation chosen for the fortified post was on an elevation facing to the north, with the wide estuary, its sand bars and tumultuous breakers spread out before it, and the promontory of Cape Disappointment, fifteen miles distant, closing the prospect to the left. The surrounding country was in all the freshness of spring; the trees were in the young leaf, the weather was superb, and everything looked delightful to men just emancipated from a long confinement on shipboard."

A somewhat more somber (and probably more realistic) picture of the construction of the new fort is found in the words of Alexander Ross in his book *Adventures of the First Settlers on the Oregon or Columbia River.* He wrote:

> From the site of the establishment, the eye could wander over a varied and interesting scene. The extensive Sound, with its rocky shores, lay in front; the breakers on the bar, rolling in wild confusion, closed the view on the west; on the east, the country as far as the Sound had a wild and varied aspect; while towards the south, the impervious and magnificent forest darkened the landscape, as far as the eye could reach. The place thus selected for the emporium of the west, might challenge the whole continent to produce a spot of equal extent presenting more difficulties to the settler: studded with gigantic trees of almost incredible size, many of them measuring fifty feet in girth, and so close together, and intermingled with huge rocks, as to make it a work of no ordinary labour to level and clear the ground. With this task before us, every man, from the highest to the lowest, was armed with an axe in one hand and a gun in the other; the former for attacking the woods, the latter for defence against the savage hordes which were constantly prowling about. In the garb of labourers, and in the sweat of our brow, we now commenced earning our bread.

Gabriel Franchère, in his *Narrative of a Voyage to the Northwest Coast of America,* recorded that after the warehouse was completed the Astorians "were busily occupied from the 16th to the 30th [May] in stowing away the goods and other effects intended for the establishment." On the fifth of June, the *Tonquin,* with much of her cargo now safely stored in the new warehouse, "got out to sea, with a good wind," and embarked on a trading voyage up the coast toward Vancouver Island. Franchère wrote: "We continued in the meantime to labor without intermission at the completion of the storehouse, and in the erection of a dwelling for ourselves and a powder magazine. These buildings were constructed of hewn logs, and in the absence of boards were tightly covered and roofed with cedar bark."

Such was Fort Astoria on July 15, 1811, when an unexpected visitor arrived. Franchère described the ". . . arrival of [a] canoe, which touched shore at a little wharf that we had built to facilitate the landing of goods from the vessel. The flag she bore was British, and her crew was composed of eight Canadian boatmen or voyageurs. A well-dressed man, who appeared to be the commander, was the first to leap ashore, and addressing us without ceremony, said that his name was David Thompson and that he was one of the partners of the North West Company." Thompson's own account as written in his *Narrative* of his arrival at Fort Astoria gives no hint of the disappointment he must have felt at seeing a rival post already established at the mouth of the Columbia. However, he did express his satisfaction at achieving his goal of reaching the Pacific: ". . . on the 15th near noon . . . brought us to a full view of the Pacific Ocean; which to me was a great pleasure, but my Men seemed disappointed; they had been accustomed to the boundless horizon of the great Lakes of Canada, and their high rolling waves; from the Ocean they expected a more boundless view, . . . and my informing them, that directly opposite to us, at the distance of five thousand miles was the Empire of Japan added nothing to their Ideas." Thompson continued his account: "The waves being too high for us to double the Point we went close to the River bank where there is a narrow isthmus, of one hundred yards, and carried across it; from thence near two miles to the fur trading Post of Mr. J. J. Astor of the City of New York; which was four low Log Huts, the far famed Fort Astoria of the United States; the place was in charge of Messrs McDougall and Stuart who had been Clerks of the North West Company; and by whom we were politely received." With the keen eye of a fur trader, Thompson commented: "This place was about seven miles from the sea, and too much exposed to the undulations of the waves; the quality of their goods for trade very low, but good enough for the beggarly Natives about them . . ."

At the end of a week, Thompson concluded his stay at Fort Astoria and commenced his return journey. At the same time, David Stuart and his small expedition left the fort on their way to establish the first of the Pacific Fur Company's interior posts. The Astorians had learned that the North West Company had erected a trading post on the Spokane River (i.e., Spokane House). Stuart's objective, therefore, was to erect a post in opposition. For the sake of safety and protection from harassment by the natives, the two parties traveled together up the Columbia for better than a week before separating, Thompson proceeding eastward up the Snake and Stuart continuing northward up the Columbia.

The men remaining at Fort Astoria, now reduced in numbers both by those on board the *Tonquin* and those in Stuart's party, alarmed by rumors of impending hostilities from the natives, immediately began to strengthen the fort's defenses. Franchère wrote: "The dwelling house was raised, parallel to the warehouse; we cut a great quantity of pickets in the forest and formed a square, with palisades in front and rear, of about 90 feet by 120; the warehouse, built on the edge of a ravine, formed one flank, the dwelling house and shops the other; with a little bastion at each angle north and south, on which were mounted four small cannon. The whole was finished in six days, and had a sufficiently formidable aspect to deter the Indians from attacking us; and for greater surety we organized a guard for day and night." Their spirits were further depressed when a wandering band of natives brought them word in early August that the *Tonquin* had been blown up and all hands lost.

However, in spite of all this discouragement, the men continued their work of completing the fort complex. By the end of September the dwelling house was finished and the men moved in. According to Franchère, it "was sufficiently spacious to hold all our company, and we had distributed it in the most convenient manner that we could. It comprised a sitting, a dining room, some lodging or sleeping rooms, and an apartment for the men and artificers, all under the same roof. We also completed a shop for the blacksmith, who till that time had worked in the open air." The small schooner was likewise finished and launched with due ceremony on October 2. Christened *Dolly,* she was the first American vessel launched on the West Coast.

By the beginning of July the food supplies brought with them were exhausted, and the men had to content themselves with fish and "very lean, very dry doe-elk" meat. As Franchère wrote: "This dry meat and smoke-dried fish constituted our daily food, and that in very insufficient quantity for hard-working men. We had no bread, and vegetables, of course, were quite out of the question." He concluded by writing: "In a word, our fare was not sumptuous." However, according to Franchère, "Christmas Day, passed very agreeably: we treated the men on that day with the best the establishment afforded. Although that was no great affair, they seemed well satisfied; for they had been restricted during the last few months to a very meager diet, living, as one may say, on sun-dried fish." New Year's Day, January 1, 1812, was greeted with a discharge of artillery; a small amount of spirits was issued to the men, "and the day passed in gayety, everyone amusing himself as well as he could."

The holidays behind them, the men resumed their regular occupations. Some cut timber for building; others made the charcoal required by the blacksmith. The carpenter constructed a barge, and the cooper made barrels for the use of posts to be established in the interior. On the eighteenth of January the arrival of Donald McKenzie and his party of ten men (part of the overland group led by William Hunt), followed on the fifteenth of February by Hunt and his contingent of thirty men, resulted in a renewal of optimism among the Astorians and promised well for the success of their venture.

In early May John J. Astor's ship the *Beaver,* loaded with much-needed supplies and trading merchandise, as well as carrying additional personnel, including another partner (John Clarke) and six clerks, arrived at Fort Astoria. Thus reinforced with both men and supplies, the partners were at last, for the first time, in a position to aggressively push forward their plans for establishing a string of trading posts in the interior. In a series of resolutions passed by the partners, David Stuart was directed to "proceed to his post at Oakinacken, explore the country northward, and establish another post between that and New Caledonia"; McKenzie was ordered to "winter on the Snake country;—and report on the state of the country"; and Clarke was sent to "winter at Spokane, as an intermediate post, between Stuart on the north and McKenzie on the south, in order to oppose and keep in check the North-West Company established there."

It was also decided that Robert Stuart would "proceed to St. Louis across land, with dispatches for Mr. Astor" and "that all these several parties, for mutual safety, advance together as far as the forks, or entrance of the great south branch [Snake]." And it was further agreed "that Mr. Hunt should accompany the ship Beaver to the Russian settlements on his coasting trip."

On the twenty-ninth of June, 1812, the four brigades, numbering sixty-two people, left Fort Astoria and headed up the Columbia toward their various destinations. The *Beaver,* although she weighed anchor the next day, due to prevailing westerly winds was not able to cross the dangerous Columbia bar to begin her coastal trading voyage until August 4. She was scheduled to return by the end of October, at which time, after offloading any surplus goods and taking on the furs accumulated at the fort, she would proceed to the markets of China, where the furs would be sold.

The men still remaining at Fort Astoria, in addition to their regular tasks, completed the construction of a house forty-five feet by thirty feet to be used as a hospital for the sick and as a lodging house for the mechanics.

The small schooner was utilized for trading voyages up the Columbia under the leadership of Franchère during October and November. These ventures were highly successful, yielding venison, wildfowl, bear meat, 750 smoked salmon, a quantity of *waptoe* root (a good substitute for potatoes), and 450 beaver skins. Finally, toward the end of November, fourteen men, led by Halsop and Wallace, were sent to establish a trading post on the Willamette, a hundred miles or so up the Columbia from Fort Astoria.

When the *Beaver* had not returned by January 1813, McDougall and the few men still at Fort Astoria were increasingly fearful that some calamity had befallen it. They were further disheartened at the unexpected return in the middle of January of Donald McKenzie, bringing news that was anything but encouraging. He had found trading prospects so poor at the post he had established on the Snake that he had decided to abandon it. Before returning to Astoria, however, he had traveled north to Clarke's establishment on the Spokane in order to confer with him. While there, they were visited by John George McTavish, North West Company partner, who rather gleefully informed them of the state of war then existing between the United States and Great Britain. He told them further that he had received a fresh supply of goods from east of the Rockies with which he proposed to mount vigorous opposition to all the Astorians' posts and, finally, that the North West Company's ship *Isaac Todd* had already sailed from London headed for the mouth of the Columbia River, where she was expected to arrive about the beginning of March.

The partners McDougall and McKenzie, confronted with this news, coupled with the nonappearance of the *Beaver* and the knowledge that they could expect no aid from the United States as all their ports would undoubtedly be blockaded by British naval power, determined that they had no alternative but to abandon Fort Astoria and the several other posts just established in the interior and as early in the spring as travel was possible return across the Rocky Mountains back to St. Louis.

McKenzie was sent back up the Columbia to inform Clarke and Stuart of this decision and to tell them to do all possible to trade for the horses and provisions that would be needed for the long journey east.

441

Both Clarke and Stuart strongly disagreed with the decision to abandon Fort Astoria. They had each had a very successful season at their respective post. They, therefore, neither took the steps required to close their posts nor confined their trading to the acquisition of provisions and horses.

As previously arranged, Clarke, Stuart, and McKenzie rendezvoused at the mouth of the Walla Walla River at the end of May. Then, in a combined brigade of two boats and six canoes loaded with 140 packs of furs, they proceeded downriver, reaching Fort Astoria on the twelfth of June. The Willamette party had returned a few days earlier, bringing out seventeen packs of furs and thirty-two bales of dried venison. As soon as it was realized that the horses and provisions needed for the journey back east had not been procured, their departure had to be postponed until the following spring (1814). Therefore, Stuart and Clarke, furnished with a new supply of merchandise, returned to their respective post in early July for another trading season.

At last on August 4 William Hunt returned to Fort Astoria aboard the American ship *Albatross*. When informed of the partners' decision to abandon the fort and withdraw from the country, he objected strongly but was unable to alter their decision. Accordingly, at the end of the month he embarked on the *Albatross* in order to find and obtain a vessel to transport both the fort's valuable accumulation of furs and the heavy goods as well as any of the men who wanted to return by sea instead of overland.

McKenzie was dispatched at the beginning of September to carry an additional supply of goods to the men wintering in the interior and to inform them of the final arrangements concluded with Hunt regarding the abandonment of Fort Astoria the following spring. A few days after his departure up the river, he returned to the fort in company with two canoes bearing the Nor'Westers John G. McTavish and Angus Bethune, as well as John Clarke, who, alarmed at the news brought by McTavish, had left his post on Spokane River and joined the Nor'Westers on their way to Fort Astoria. They were but the advance party to a brigade of light canoes under the leadership of John Stuart and James McMillan, coming down from the interior with their harvest of furs to meet the North West supply ship at the mouth of the Columbia.

McTavish delivered a letter to Duncan McDougall written by his uncle, Angus Shaw, a North West partner, informing McDougall that the North West Company ship *Isaac Todd* had sailed from London in March with letters of marque, accompanied by the British frigate *Phoebe,* which was under orders to seize the American establishment of Fort Astoria. The Nor'Westers, numbering about seventy-five men, camped at the bottom of a small cove near the fort, and there they set-tled in to await the arrival of their ship.

Faced with no hope of any reinforcements and the imminent arri-val of a British warship, McDougall on behalf of the Pacific Fur Com-pany in October of 1813 drew up an agreement with McTavish and the other North West partners whereby, in the words of Alexander Ross, "the whole of the goods on hand, both at Astoria and throughout the in-terior, were delivered over to the North-West Company, at 10 per cent. on cost and charges. . . . The whole sales amounted to 80,500 dollars; M'Tavish giving bills of exchange on the agents for the amount, pay-able in Canada." This sale would assure some financial return to Astor as an alternative to total loss following seizure and confiscation by the British.

The wily McTavish delayed signing the agreement in the hopes that the arrival of either the armed *Isaac Todd* or the British ship of war, with the inevitable seizure of the American fort as a prize of war, would release him from the necessity of purchasing it. However, he was finally outmaneuvered by McDougall and McKenzie and on No-vember 12, 1813, signed the purchase agreement.

The American colors were hauled down from the fort's flagstaff and the British flag run up, thus marking the passing of John Jacob Astor's Fort Astoria into the possession of the North West Company. So, even though David Thompson had failed two years earlier, the Nor'Westers had at last realized their goal of a fort at the mouth of the Columbia.

About two weeks later the British sloop-of-war *Racoon* of twenty-six guns, commanded by Captain Black, sailed over the bar at the mouth of the Columbia and came to anchor in Baker Bay opposite Fort Astoria. Captain Black was amazed to find that the fort was not in the hands of the enemy (the Americans) and, as such, a source of legiti-mate booty and confiscation but, rather, was in the possession of his own countrymen, the Nor'Westers, who had acquired it by simple pur-chase.

As Ross wrote, "—they [Black and his men] had made up their minds that the capture of Astoria would yield them a rich prize; but in place of golden egg they found only an empty shell." Furthermore, they had expected to find a fortress of some importance. In the words of Franchère, "The captain landed after dark; when we showed him the next morning the palisades and log bastions of the factory, he inquired if there was not another fort; on being assured that there was no other he cried out, with an air of the greatest astonishment: 'What! is this the fort which was represented to me as so formidable! Good God! I could batter it down in two hours with a fourpounder!'"

On December 12, 1813, the colorful ceremony of the British taking possession of the fort was enacted. Franchère described it in his *Narrative:*

> After dinner the Captain caused firearms to be given to the servants of the Company [i.e., North West] and we all marched under arms to the square or platform, where a flag-staff had been erected. There the Captain took a British Union Jack, which he had brought on shore for the occasion, and caused it to be run up to the top of the staff; then taking a bottle of Madeira wine, he broke it on the flag-staff, declaring in a loud voice that he took possession of the establishment and of the country in the name of His Britannic Majesty; and changed the name of Astoria to Fort George.—Three rounds of artillary and musketry were fired and the health of the king was drunk by the parties, interested . . .

December 31, 1813, marked the departure of Captain Black and the *Racoon,* and the business of fur trading was resumed by the Nor'Westers at Fort George, their newly acquired post.

Many of the former Astorians elected to enter the service of the North West Company. Among them were Duncan McDougall, who was given a partnership, and Alexander Ross and Ross Cox, who remained as clerks. David Stuart, Donald McKenzie, John Clarke, and Gabriel Franchère all chose to return east.

James Keith was placed in charge of Fort George. Under his direction men were sent to assess the fur potential of the Willamette and Cowlitz valleys. John G. McTavish continued at Spokane House and Alexander Ross at Fort Okanagan. Toward the end of November, John Stuart and Donald McKenzie set off for the interior in order to effect the transfer of the Spokane and Okanagan posts to the new owners.

On January 3, 1814, a party of fifteen men in two canoes laden with trading goods was dispatched into the interior under the command of Alexander Stewart and James Keith. Three days after their departure, Stuart and McKenzie returned to Fort George and reported that as they were descending the river they had been attacked by a group of natives just above the falls. Fearing for the safety of Stewart and Keith and their small party, reinforcements were immediately sent after them. They were too late, however, to prevent an assault by the natives, in which Stewart was severely wounded and the whole party had to retreat down the river to the safety of the fort, abandoning all their goods and supplies, including fifty guns and a large quantity of ammunition, all of which was immediately seized by the natives.

The Nor'Westers quickly organized a strong expedition to return up the Columbia to recover their goods and to punish the aggressors. A force of sixty-two well-armed men in six canoes carrying a small brass field piece, was able to effectively cower the natives (at least temporarily) and recover much of their property.

All this time the Nor'Westers were anxiously awaiting the arrival of their ship the *Isaac Todd*. Long overdue, it was not until April 23, 1814, that she finally appeared—thirteen months after leaving England. Her arrival with goods and supplies greatly strengthened the position of the men at Fort George. An unfortunate accident marred the vessel's presence at the fort. Two of her passengers, wintering partners Donald McTavish and Alexander Henry the younger, were drowned while returning to the ship in a small skiff from Fort George.

The *Isaac Todd* within a short while continued on her way to Canton with the furs from the fort. Henceforth, each year a company ship brought supplies to the fort via Cape Horn and then proceeded to the China coast with the company's harvest of furs. At last the North West's plan for securing the maritime trade of the Pacific coast with access to the China markets was being realized. The results, however, were not as rewarding as had been anticipated. The existence of the East India Company monopoly severely hampered them in the Canton market, so that the returns from these trading trips were not financially profitable.

In 1816, in an effort to improve the poor returns from the Columbia department, the North West Company sent in Donald McKenzie with authority to make changes. McKenzie, who at the time of the takeover had declined to join the North West Company and had returned east, had, however, subsequently reconsidered and joined the company as a partner.

He abolished the costly courier express canoes up and down the length of the Columbia in favor of delivery of letters by natives relayed from village to village. He also reestablished the practice of sending parties to trap the beaver streams in the large region drained by the upper waters of the Snake River. Finally, he abolished the old circuitous route to the upper forts via the Okanagan and Spokane posts and replaced it with a more central location at the mouth of the Walla Walla River for the general rendezvous.

The Nor'Westers continued to develop the route pioneered by John Stuart in April 1813. This involved the use of canoes down the Fraser, packhorses to Fort Okanagan, and canoes down the Columbia to the terminal of Fort George. Joseph Larocque, using this route, brought the first consignment of goods to Fort George in October of 1814. This short and sure route to the Pacific eventually totally replaced the former supply route via the Peace River.

The value of the company's shipments to the Columbia was increasing steadily: £15,000 in 1815; £27,000 in 1817; £29,000 in 1818. It was beginning to appear as if the Nor'Westers' faith in their Columbia venture was justified.

The war between the United States and Great Britain ended in 1814. The Treaty of Ghent, ending hostilities, was based on "status quo ante bellum," which provided that all conquests were to be returned to their original owners. Seizing upon this provision, John Jacob Astor challenged the North West Company's possession of his fort and demanded its return. The Nor'Westers strongly refuted the claim, arguing that the fort had been legally acquired by purchase, not by conquest. The Americans, however, sent an armed sloop to reclaim the fort. To avoid renewed hostilities, Lord Bathurst, Secretary of State for War and the Colonies, dispatched HMS *Blossom* with instructions for James Keith ordering that Fort George be handed over to the Americans. Simon McGillivray, a senior North West partner, proposed that the post be burned to the ground instead of being returned to Astor, but James Keith reluctantly obeyed Lord Bathurst's orders and relinquished the post, but allowed no formalities or ceremony at the transfer except for the change of flags on the fort's flagstaff.

The North West Company was not to be deterred by this setback. Supremely confident in the value of the Columbia trade, they were determined to keep their foothold on the shore of the Pacific at the mouth of the Columbia. Accordingly, they promptly built a new fort a bare three hundred yards away from Astor's American fort. The two posts existed side by side—an arrangement that was confirmed and extended by the Convention of 1818, which provided that for ten years any land claimed by either country to the west of the Rockies should be free and open to citizens of both countries and to their shipping.

Thus, when three years later in 1821 the North West Company was merged with the Hudson's Bay Company, they were able to bring to the new company this important post strategically located at the mouth of the Columbia River. Its trade with the coastal Indians was substantial, and its return for 1822 was 6,000 beaver. Although the Columbia department had proved to be less profitable than the New Caledonia department to the North West Company because of its much greater expenses, it, in the words of Arthur S. Morton "was the *point d'appui* for an attack on the lucrative maritime trade"—a consideration that George Simpson, newly placed in charge of the Hudson's Bay Company's North American affairs, quickly grasped.

446

Simpson's voyage of inspection that he undertook in 1824 took him to Fort George. He arrived there November 8, after completing a record-setting journey of eighty-four days from York Factory on James Bay. He recorded his impression of the fort and its management in his journal:

> The Establishment of Fort George is a large pile of buildings covering about an acre of ground well stockaded and protected by Bastions or Blockhouses, having two Eighteen Pounders mounted in front and altogether an air or appearance of Grandeur & Consequence which does not become and is not at all suitable to an Indian Trading Post. Everything appears to me on the Columbia on too extended a scale *except the Trade* and when I say that that is confined to Four permanent Establishments the returns of which do not amount to 20,000 Beaver & Otters altho the country has been occupied upwards of Fourteen Years I feel that a very Severe reflection is cast on those who have had the management of the Business, as on looking at the prodigious expences that have been incurred and the means at their command, I cannot help thinking that no economy has been observed, that little exertion has been used, and that sound judgment has not been exercised but that mismanagement and extravagance has been the order of the day. It is now however necessary that a radical change should take place and we have no time to lose in bringing it about.

Simpson was as good as his word, and sweeping changes were quickly made affecting both Fort George and the other posts in the Columbia department. First the number of personnel for Fort George was reduced drastically: one chief factor instead of two, two clerks instead of three, and twenty men instead of sixty-five.

The fact that of the 645 *pièces* of goods and provisions transported from Fort George into the interior only 183 were of trading goods and equipment, while the remaining 462 consisted of provisions and luxuries, did not escape Simpson's notice. He did not hesitate to end this profligacy, writing in his journal that "a very large proportion of the last item [Provisions Luxuries] is quite superfluous and unnecessary." Simpson instituted other changes. He arranged that the many old Canadian voyageurs and Iroquois who were living at Fort George should be sent back east, thereby reducing the fort's population from 150 to less than 100 and easing the strain on the fort's food supplies. Also, as was his custom, he encouraged the local production of vegetables and grain to decrease the reliance of the fort on imported foods.

Simpson was amazed at the almost total lack of knowledge of the coast both to the north and to the south of the fort. He felt that the Inland Brigade after reaching the fort in the spring, instead of idling away at company expense while waiting for the arrival of the yearly supply ship, should be utilized in exploring the country and seeking new sources for furs. In his words, "such indolence and indifference is unpardonable must be broke through this year . . ." He was appalled that "there is not a Boat at the Establishment fit to cross the River in bad Weather nor a person competent to Sail one." He regarded this as "one instance of the gross mismanagement and wretchedly bad system on which the Coy's affairs have been conducted in this quarter and which is inexcusable and unpardonable . . ." Simpson was convinced that the coastal trade was worth fighting for. He wrote: "The Trade of this Coast and its interior Country is unquestionably worth contending for . . . I make bold to say can not only be made to rival, but to yield double the profit that any other part of North America does for the Amount of Capital employed therein . . ."

During his five-and-one-half-month stay at Fort George, he reached the conclusion that important savings and gains would be realized by transferring the company's principal depot from the mouth of the Columbia northward to the mouth of the Fraser River—a location more centrally situated for both the coastal and interior trade—from which the company "could with greater facility and at less expence extend our discoveries & Establish-ments to the Northward and supply all the Interior Posts now occupied."

Simpson, facing the probability that the United States would ultimately secure title to the country south of the Columbia and that the resumption of American jurisdiction at Fort George was inevitable, took steps to select a site for a new fort to replace Fort George. The spot chosen was almost one hundred miles farther up the Columbia, on the north bank of the river. This new fort was constructed during the winter of 1824–25 while Simpson was at Fort George.

At long last, on March 16, Simpson left Fort George to begin his return journey, and those left at the fort undoubtedly drew a sigh of relief. All the valuable property from the fort had already been transported upstream to the new fort prior to his departure. Donald McKenzie and nine men remained behind for two or three weeks until the few remaining articles were removed. Finally, on June 7, 1825, the company abandoned the fort. Barely three months later the botanist John Scouler visited it and found it "entirely abandoned by the settlers, and taken possession of by the Indians who are rapidly reducing it to a state of ruin and filth."

The post remained deserted until 1829, when, in response to the appearance of American ships, Donald Manson, clerk, was sent back to

448

reopen the old fort in a move to offer the Americans more direct competition than the company's new fort upriver could provide.

Furthermore, the Hudson's Bay Company had decided that retaining actual occupation of Fort George would strengthen the company's possessory rights over the soil and bolster its claim to future compensation from the United States for the loss of these rights as well as of trading rights when the fort and any other posts south of the forty-nine-degree boundary as determined by the Oregon Treaty of 1846 would have to be relinquished.

Until the old fort could be rebuilt, Manson was forced to live in a tent. The reactivated post was never restored to anything like its former size. According to John K. Townsend, a well-known Philadelphia physician and naturalist who was there in 1834, "it scarcely deserves the name of a fort, being composed of but one principal house of hewn boards, and a number of small Indian huts surrounding it . . ."

When in 1846 the Oregon Treaty finally established the boundary between the United States and the British Northwest, Fort George was one of several Hudson's Bay Company posts located within the territory of the United States. An inventory of the fort taken to determine the amount to be used in the company's claim for compensatory reimbursement listed three dwelling houses and one store, for a total valuation of 671 pounds.

About this same time the company transferred their agent from the fort to a new warehouse located at the mouth of the Columbia on the north shore at Cape Disappointment. In 1849–50 the U.S. Army took possession of the old post, and Fort George, formerly Fort Astoria, ceased to exist as a fur trading fort.

In our quest to see the site of Fort Astoria, we had to make two attempts. The first time we were on a week's cruise of the lower Columbia and the Snake rivers. One of the ports of call was Astoria, where a bus tour of the town was scheduled. We assumed that this would certainly include a stop at the site of the old fort. Much to our dismay and complete frustration, the bus driver refused to deviate from her prescribed route through town to drive the extra two blocks that would have taken us to the fort site.

Three years later we returned to Astoria, this time driving our own vehicle. Freed from an intransigent tour bus driver, we had no difficulty reaching the Fort Astoria site. Halfway up the hillside rising from the river, on a busy street in the center of town, is a tiny park marking the location of the first American settlement west of the Rockies. A reconstructed log bastion and small section of palisade have been erected at one side of the well-kept grassed square. This small oasis is surrounded and overshadowed by present-day homes as well as commercial and municipal buildings, all of which make it no longer possible to enjoy the commanding view over the mighty Columbia that this site offered when the fort occupied the spot. In the quiet seclusion of this peaceful place, it is rather difficult to imagine the dramatic events that took place here. Astorians, David Thompson, Chief Comcomly, Nor'Westers, Governor George Simpson, Hudson's Bay men— all had been here and all had contributed to shaping the destiny of the fort.

The Columbia River flows on unchanged to its meeting with the Pacific Ocean. It is now modern freighters, luxury cruise ships, and fishing boats instead of sailing frigates, schooners, and sloops that are moored along the river. But foaming breakers still swirl and crash over the hazardous and treacherous sandbar at the river entrance, providing a vivid reminder of the many men and vessels that have been lost in their attempts to reach Fort Astoria and safe anchorage.

For the United States, the establishment of Fort Astoria on the West Coast was the culmination of an irresistible two-hundred-year march across the continent that began with the founding of Plymouth Plantation on the East Coast in 1620.

Fort Okanagan

Just a little more than three months after the Astorians disembarked from the *Tonquin* on April 12, 1811, and began the erection of Fort Astoria at the mouth of the Columbia, they sent an expedition into the interior to establish a trading post. David Stuart, partner, and Alexander Ross, clerk, led the small party of seven men. For the sake of mutual protection and safety, the Astorians traveled for some distance with David Thompson's party on their return trip back up the Columbia.

According to Ross, the Astor party traveled in "two clumsy Chinook canoes laden each with fifteen or twenty packages of goods, of twenty dollars each." Ten days later, after successfully completing the 1,450-yard portage around the Cascades, the first barrier of the Columbia, in spite of a considerable amount of harassment from the Indians, the two parties separated, Thompson's proceeding east via the Snake and Stuart's continuing on up the Columbia.

On August 31 the Astorians had advanced about six hundred miles up the main river, which brought them to the Okanagan River, which they ascended for about two miles before camping for the night.

The next day Stuart and his men descended the Okanagan until they reached a level area about one-half mile from its mouth. There they landed, took their canoes out of the water, and pitched their tents. Ross described the spot:

> This plain is surrounded on all sides by high hills, so that in no direction does the view extend far—near its [Okanagan] junction with the Columbia, it is hemmed in on the east by a sloping range of high rocky hills, at the foot of which the two rivers meet. On the south bank of the Oakinacken, half a mile from its mouth, was the site pitched upon for the new establishment.
>
> The general aspect of the surrounding country is barren and dreary. On the west the hills are clothed with thick woods—a dense forest: on the south and east, the scene is bare; but to the north the banks of the river were lined with the willow and poplar, and the valley through which it meanders presents a pleasing landscape.

Stuart and his men quickly commenced erecting a small dwelling house, sixteen by twenty feet, chiefly constructed of driftwood which was readily available and easier to procure than suitable standing timber. However, when the structure was but half-completed, some of the party returned to Fort Astoria, while Stuart and three men set off on an exploratory journey toward the headwaters of the Okanagan River, expecting to be gone about a month.

Alexander Ross was left alone at the new establishment until Stuart's return, his "only civilized companion being a little Spanish pet dog from Monterey, called Weasel." He kept busy finishing the building and putting the few trade goods he had into a kind of cellar that he made in the middle of the house. He also undertook to learn the Indian language and, "although the task was a hard one, . . . found, from my progress, that perseverance would overcome many difficulties."

It was not until the twenty-second of March 1812 that Stuart returned to Fort Okanagan. During that time Ross had traded 1,550 beaver, besides other peltries, calculated by Ross to be worth 2,250 pounds sterling in the Canton market, at a cost to the company of about 35 pounds sterling.

At about this same time, a party conducted by Robert Stuart left Fort Astoria bound for Fort Okanagan with supplies. After surviving a hostile attack by the Indians at the Columbia River narrows, the party reached Fort Okanagan the twenty-fourth of April. At the expiration of five days they, accompanied by David Stuart and two men, returned to Fort Astoria in four canoes, bringing with them 2,500 beaver skins. Once again Alexander Ross was left behind, but this time in addition to his little dog, Weasel, two men remained to assist him.

At a meeting of the Astorian partners at Fort Astoria in May of 1812—the first time all of them were reunited—it was resolved "that Mr. David Stuart proceed to his post at Oakinacken, explore the country northward, and establish another post between that and New Caledonia"; Stuart arrived back at Okanagan on August 12. During his absence, Ross with two men and sixteen horses had set off on a trading expedition up the Thompson River as far as a place called Cumcloups by the Indians. Here he successfully traded his entire small stock of goods for beaver pelts.

When Stuart with his men and trading goods left Fort Okanagan toward the end of August to winter among the Shuswap Indians about three hundred miles up the Okanagan River, he left Ross in charge. Ross passed the winter in making several trading and exploring trips as well as short visits to John Clarke at Spokane House and to Stuart with the Shuswaps.

The thirteenth of May 1813, Stuart with his men and furs arrived back at Fort Okanagan. After spending ten days packing and pressing the furs, Stuart, Ross, and all their men set out down the Columbia for the May 30 rendezvous with fellow Astorians Clarke and McKenzie at the mouth of the Walla Walla River. The combined parties all arrived at Fort Astoria on the fourteenth of June. Three weeks later, with a renewed stock of trading goods, Stuart, Clarke, and McKenzie left Fort Astoria to return to their respective winter trading posts. On the fifteenth of August Stuart and Ross reached Fort Okanagan, where Ross was to winter; Stuart proceeded on to the Shuswaps.

Ross had only been at his post a few weeks when he was surprised by the sudden arrival of a "strong party of North-Westers, seventy-five in number, in a squadron of ten canoes, and headed by Messrs. M'Tavish and Stuart, two North-West bourgeois, on their way to the mouth of the Columbia, in high glee, to meet their ship, the *Isaac Todd,* which was expected daily."

After the purchase of the Pacific Fur Company's forts, furs and assets in November of that year, Donald McKenzie and John Stuart proceeded to the interior to oversee the transfer of the property to the new owners according to the terms of the sales agreement. On December 15 they were received by Ross at Fort Okanagan, where they were soon joined by David Stuart and his men from the Shuswaps. The business of the transfer completed, the combined parties left Fort Okanagan on December 20 to return to the fort at the mouth of the Columbia, now called Fort George, where they arrived January 7, 1814.

Ross signed on with the North West Company, and each spring for the next two years he was sent back to Fort Okanagan. He spent much of his time traveling in the area between the Thompson and Columbia rivers, trading furs and seeking to acquire the many horses needed for the overland trade route being developed.

In addition to being the rendezvous for all the upper posts, Fort Okanagan was becoming increasingly important as the southern terminus for the overland brigade route first explored by John Stuart in 1813. The large number of packhorses required for the overland brigades had to be readily available and cared for at the fort.

In the spring of 1816 Ross was succeeded by Ross Cox, another former Astorian who had entered the service of the North West Company. Cox, with a large crew, undertook to rebuild and fortify Okanagan. In his book *Adventures on the Columbia River* Cox wrote: "By the month of September we had erected a new dwelling-house for the person in charge, containing four excellent rooms and a large dining-hall, two good houses for the men; and a spacious store for the furs and merchandise, to which was attached a shop for trading with the natives. The whole was surrounded by strong palisades fifteen feet high and flanked by two bastions. Each bastion had in its lower story a light brass four-pounder, and the upper loop-holes were left for the use of musketry."

Five years later, in 1821, Fort Okanagan passed into the hands of the Hudson's Bay Company when it merged with the North West Company.

Simpson, of course, did not overlook Fort Okanagan during the course of his 1824–25 trip of inspection. He arrived there Monday, November 1, 1824, and found James Birnie in charge along with two men. Simpson, in a rather lengthy discourse on one of his favorite subjects, inveighed against the unwillingness of the post factors to endeavor to become partially self-sufficient by growing their own food, noting that "those in charge have preferred the less troublesome and more costly mode of Importing them from England Boston or California and employing extra men to deliver it into their Stores. It has been said that Farming is no branch of the Fur Trade but I consider that every pursuit tending to lighten the Expense of the Trade is a branch thereof . . ." He felt the post at Okanagan ought to be maintained. It required an "Establishment only of a Clerk and two men," and it produced about six hundred beaver. Four years later (in 1828) Simpson revisited the Columbia River country and recorded his impressions in a lengthy dispatch to the Governor and London Committee of the Hudson's Bay Company. With reference to Fort Okanagan he wrote: " The next Post in the Columbia, below Colville House is Okanogan, but the few skins it yields are not worth naming. This place is maintained almost entirely for the accommodation of New Caledonia and Thompsons River, being the point at which the route from those places strikes upon the Main River . . ."

Sometime between 1831 and 1837 Fort Okanagan was moved two miles north from the Okanagan River to the north bank of the Columbia. According to Louis R. Caywood in his report *Excavations at Two Fort Okanagan Sites, 1952,* the depth of water in Okanagan "is not deep and during that time of the year when the depth drops the large York boats which were then in use could not have been properly loaded and unloaded at the steep-sided location" of the Okanagan site. Caywood added also that "during the summer dust and mosquitoes plagued the occupants of the fort, while in the winter the fine clay and silt turned into a deep mud making movement of heavy goods most difficult." However, at the new site on the Columbia River there was a good hard gravel bar and the ascent from the water to the fort site above was a gradual slope.

The new fort, according to Charles Wilkes in his *The Narrative of the United States Exploring Expedition during the Years 1838, 1839, 1840, 1841 and 1842,* was "situated on a poor, flat, sandy neck, about two miles above the junction of the river of that name with the Columbia. It is a square, picketed in the same manner as those already described, but destitute of bastions, and removed sixty yards from the Columbia. Within the pickets there is a large house for the reception of the Company's officers, consisting of several apartments, and from each end of it two rows of low mud huts run towards the entrance. These serve as offices and dwellings for the trappers and their families. In the centre there is an open space."

Although the Oregon Treaty of 1846 mandated the handing of the fort back to the United States, the Hudson's Bay Company continued to occupy it until 1860, at which time it suspended operations there and moved north of the international boundary. Not until the signing of the Treaty of 1863 did the Hudson's Bay Company finally relinquish its holdings south of the border.

As late as the 1880s sections of the fort were still standing. But appropriation of the buildings by natives, vandalism, and the great flood of 1894 eventually and effectively removed all traces of the old fort.

Today the sites of Fort Okanagan can be viewed from a high bluff overlooking the level plain at the confluence of the Okanagan and Columbia rivers. Here the state of Washington has built an impressive interpretive center housing the numerous artifacts recovered from the archaeological digs made at the sites as well as maps, pictures, and a representative assortment of trading good items. We stood on the viewing knoll outside the museum building and looked out over the panorama spread below us. At this point the course of the Columbia is largely in an east–west direction, with the Okanagan flowing down from the north. Once a remuda of the many horses needed for the overland brigades would have been grazing here. Now the flat peninsula formed by the two rivers is largely covered with the lush green of the apple orchards made possible by the miracle of irrigation. The uniformly sized trees growing in precisely spaced rows provide the only touch of color to an otherwise rather drab landscape. The words of Alexander Ross: "The general aspect of the surrounding country is barren and dreary" are as true today as when written 180 years ago. High hills, some quite bare, others supporting a scattered sparse growth of western evergreens and desert shrubs and sagebrush, rise from the banks of the rivers enclosing the peninsula.

With the construction of the Wells Dam on the Columbia in the 1960s, the two sites of Fort Okanagan were almost totally submerged by the resulting backwaters. As an aid in pinpointing the two locations of the fort, rifle-type sighting devices mounted on the viewing platform have been lined up with tall flagpoles erected as near as possible to the fort's locations.

We did not stray from the short walkway leading to the viewing overlook, for after all, as noted on Ross Cox's map of 1816, this was rattlesnake country. We were not venturesome enough to find out for ourselves if his notation was still applicable.

One vestige from the post still remains, for in the desertlike environment of this country changes are slow. The well-worn path leading from the hills to the river and to the trading post, winding over the land through the clumps of desert brush—a trail that was used for over two hundred years—is still plainly visible. Now, however, it is only the moccasined feet of the ghosts of Indians and traders that silently tread the path down to the river and to the place where the white man's trading posts once stood.

Fort Kamloops

During the winter of 1811–12, the Thompson River country, home of the Shuswap Indians, was first penetrated by a fur trader. David Stuart, partner in Astor's Pacific Fur Company, after getting the construction of his new fort at the mouth of the Okanagan River under way, proceeded north beyond the lakes at the head of the river and over the height of land, at length reaching the valley of the South Thompson River, where he spent several months among the natives of the region. During the few months that Stuart spent with the Shuswaps, he was able to trade 2,500 beaver pelts.

The following summer (1812) while Stuart was taking the furs that had been traded to Fort Astoria, his clerk, Alexander Ross, with sixteen horses, following Stuart's route of the previous winter, returned to the Thompson River for further trading. Ross described his adventure in his book:

> . . . reached the She Whaps on Thompson's River, the tenth day, and there encamped at a place called by the Indians Cumcloups, near the entrance of the north branch. From this station I sent messages to the different tribes around, who soon assembled, bringing with them their furs. Here we stayed for ten days. The number of Indians collected on the occasion could not have been less than 2,000. Not expecting to see so many, I had taken but a small quantity of goods with me; nevertheless, we loaded all our horses—so anxious were they to trade, and so fond of tobacco, that one morning before breakfast, I obtained one hundred and ten beavers for leaf-tobacco, at the rate of five leaves per skin; and at last, when I had but one yard of white cotton remaining, one of the chiefs gave me twenty prime beaver skins for it.

Later that same summer, after Stuart had returned from Fort Astoria in fulfillment of his promise to the Shuswaps, he journeyed back to their country, and there, near the forks of the north and south branches of the Thompson River, on the south bank of the South Thompson, he erected a trading post known as Shuswaps Fort.

The North West Company was not caught napping. They immediately responded to the challenge, sending in Joseph Larocque, clerk, to build Fort Thompson close to Stuart's. It may have been located on the south side of the South Thompson a short distance east of Stuart's Fort Shuswap or perhaps across the river on the point of land formed at the confluence, north of the South Thompson and east of the North Thompson.

When Alexander Ross visited Stuart at his Kamloops fort toward the end of December, he commented favorably on the relationship that existed between the two rival traders: "Mr. La Rocque, the North-West clerk in charge, and Mr. Stuart, were open and candid, and on friendly terms. The field before them was wide enough for both parties, and, what is more, they thought it so; consequently they followed a fair and straightforward course of trade."

The Pacific Fur Company was not destined to remain in existence for long. In November 1813 the entire company—forts, furs, and all other assets—was bought out by the North West Company. Alexander Ross, who entered into the service of the new owners, was retained in charge of both Fort Okanagan and its outpost on the Thompson River. From somewhat sketchy evidence it appears that the trade was carried on at Larocque's Fort Thompson, and Stuart's Fort Shuswap was abandoned and allowed to fall into ruin and oblivion. The trade in furs that had appeared to offer such rich promise by the end of ten years had dropped off drastically. Furthermore, the Indians were unpredictable and frequently hostile. In 1817 the trader in charge was shot and killed by a young native. Also, in spite of the utmost vigilance, many of the company's horses were stolen by the Indians, almost with impunity.

The Nor'Westers' Fort Thompson was becoming increasingly important as a staging depot midway on the long line of communication from New Caledonia to the north to Fort Vancouver at the mouth of the Columbia. As the overland brigade route was developed, the meadowlands and open range of the Kamloops area provided the ideal feeding and breeding grounds for the hundreds of horses needed for the fur brigades.

In 1821, through amalgamation, the Hudson's Bay Company took over the North West Company. At that time a new fort was built on the promontory formed by the confluence of the north and south arms of the Thompson River. There on the flat plain in the shadow of Mounts Peter and Paul, the fort was ideally situated to command the approaches from both branches of the river.

First reports for the Thompson River district were very encouraging. According to a letter written by Chief Trader John L. Lewes from Fort George to Governor Simpson dated April 2, 1822, "The returns of Thomsons [sic] River is Two Thousand four Hundred Beavers, an increase on the last years returns of Six Hundred,—. This—will shew that the general trade is improving."

The North West Company fort built by Larocque after an encouraging beginning soon reflected a subsequent sharp decline in fur trade returns. The post was allowed to deteriorate, and the buildings fell into ruins. In fact, when in 1821 Chief Trader John McLeod took over for the Hudson's Bay Company, he found the entire post so overrun with brush as to be almost invisible from a short distance away. McLeod cleared away the undergrowth and rebuilt some of the buildings. The fort consisted of several log structures enclosed by a fifteen-foot picket wall, reinforced by bastions at diagonal corners.

John McLeod's son, Malcolm, recorded a few of his early memories of Fort Kamloops in the notes he wrote to accompany Archibald McDonald's journal covering his trip with George Simpson from York Factory to Fort Langley in 1828:

Kamloops was always the 'capital' of the Thompson's River District. My father was in charge of the District from 1822 to 1826, and a troublesome and most arduous, as well as perilous charge it was,—. I remember the old compact and well palisaded Fort, and the 'stockades' a little distance off, large enough for three or four hundred horses, for the horse brigades for transport of 'goods in' and 'returns out' for the District, and for New Caledonia, generally numbered about two hundred and fifty horses. A beautiful sight was that horse brigade, with no broken hacks in the train, but every animal in his full beauty of form and color, and all so tractable!

John McLeod, chief trader, remained in charge of the fort from 1822 to 1826. When George Simpson made his first journey of inspection in 1824–25, his itinerary did not include Fort Kamloops. However, based on the returns from the post, he reached certain conclusions concerning the future of the establishment, which he recorded in his journal on November 1, 1824, while he was at Fort Okanagan:

The District I am concerned to say has not improved under the management of Mr McLeod; for these last two years there has been a continual outcry for more officers men goods & Provisions which the state of the trade does not authorise and if a very great amendment does not this year take place it ought in my opinion to be abandoned. . . . if the Post of Thompson's River cannot be kept up with a Gentleman and Eight or Nine Men say Ten in all and yield about 1500 Beaver it should be abandoned as we can turn the Services of our officers & men to better account in many other parts of the Country even by outfitting them as trappers.

On this same date (November 1, 1824) Governor Simpson wrote a letter to Chief Trader John McLeod that was considerably more amiable than the rather harsh comments he had recorded in his journal:

The returns of Thompsons River, I am concerned and surprised to learn, have fallen off while at the same time the expences are considerably increased within the last year or two; this may have arisen from circumstances beyond your control, but which I doubt not you will be able to account for, and I am satisfied is not occasioned by any want of zeal or exertion on your part. I however sincerely trust things will assume an improved appearance next spring:—if its affairs do not look better, my opinion as also that of Messrs McLoughlin, McMillan & Ogden is that it should be abandoned as 1700 Beaver will do little more than cover the interest on the capital employed, whereas in many other parts of the Country it can be turned to much greater advantage.

The decrease in the beaver population continued unabated. Archibald McDonald, in charge of Fort Kamloops for a brief period, explained it in his 1827 report on the trade as follows: "For this sudden falling off, there is no other pheasable [plausible] way of accounting, than the Beaver run on the verge of extermination, which the natives themselves observe, and not only deprecate this loss, but the rapid disappearance of wood animals also."

George Simpson finally visited Fort Kamloops in 1828 during the course of a journey he made by canoe from York Factory on James Bay to Fort Langley near the mouth of the Fraser River. He had high hopes of utilizing the Thompson and the lower reaches of the Fraser as a main communication route to New Caledonia if the Columbia had to be given up to the Americans. He planned to test the validity of these hopes by traveling the proposed route himself. His trip down the Thompson after he left Fort Kamloops and then down the Fraser to Fort Langley convinced him that these hopes could never be realized. He was forced to concede that a trip downstream on the Fraser would be certain death in nine cases out of ten and that passage upstream would be quite impossible. He had to admit that the "Fraser River can no longer be thought of as a practicable communication with the interior." The Columbia remained as the only feasible supply route from the coast into the interior. At the conclusion of his 1828 cross-country trip from York Factory to Fort Langley, which included his two-day stopover at Fort Kamloops and journey down the Thompson and Fraser rivers, Simpson reported to the company in London that "the post of Kamloops, or Thompsons River, is a very unprofitable Establishment."

In 1830 Chief Trader Samuel Black was transferred to Fort Kamloops from Fort Walla Walla (Nez Percés). Black was not the man to permit any depredations by the natives to go unpunished. In a letter written by Chief Factor John McLoughlin to the Hudson's Bay Com-

460

pany in London, the following incident, which well illustrates Mr. Black's character, is detailed:

> This Spring as our people was coming from Thompsons River to Okanagan, the Indians stole a Horse from them; Mr. Black sent a party after them who overtook the thieves, and made them give up the Horse, but as the man was receiving the Horse, he pulled the halter roughly from the Indian who held him; another Indian called out not to give up the Horse, immediately on which several shots were fired, and an Indian killed, but neither can say who fired first. On receiving intelligence of this, Mr. Black started with all his people to meet the Caledonia Brigade, on whome Mr. Black justly feared the Indians would attempt to revenge the death of their Countryman. Mr. Black met Mr. Ogden and his party, as he was arriving where the Indians were waiting him, when a Battle ensued, one of our men Killed, and Mr. Blacks Horse shot under him, and the firing ceased; in this instance also neither party can say who fired first, but I am happy to say, that our people were not molested in passing this Summer on their return to the Interior, and that the intercourse between our People and these Indians, is apparently on the former amicable footing.

Chief Factor Samuel Black was murdered at Fort Kamloops by a young Indian on February 8, 1841. Earlier in the year a dispute had arisen between Black and Tranquille, a chief of the Shuswaps, over the ownership of a gun. Tranquille left the fort, the matter still unsettled, and died in his camp a short time later. His widow blamed Black for Tranquille's death and managed to persuade Tranquille's nephew to take vengeance on the trader. R. M. Patterson in his introduction to Black's *Rocky Mountain Journal* described what happened next:

> The nephew reached Thompson's River on February 8, 1841 . . . The day was cold and he was taken in and given a meal and a pipe; he spent the afternoon sitting in the hall by the fire. . . . he [Black] passed to and fro through the hall, exchanging, as he did so, a word or two each time with Laprade who was picking over sprouting potatoes in the cellar which was reached through a trap door in the floor; the Indian remained by the fire, arousing, to some extent, Laprade's suspicions but, unfortunately, not Black's. Then, towards evening, two young men who had been sitting with Tranquille's nephew rose and departed. Shortly afterwards Black returned through the hall from one of his periodic excursions and stooped down to pass through the doorway into his room; the Indian rose, took his gun from its place of concealment beside the fire-place and fired; the heavy ball struck in the small of the back, travelling on upwards, and Black fell forwards without speaking a word, dead.

When Donald Manson arrived in November of 1841 to take charge of Fort Kamloops he "found the Fort here in wretched state of defence, the houses & store being completely rotten." By 1842 Chief Trader John Tod was sent to Fort Kamloops. Under his direction a new fort was constructed on the west side of the North Thompson River opposite Black's fort. The main reason for relocating the fort to the west bank of the river was to enable the overland pack brigades to reach the fort without the necessity of crossing the river. The new fort was a larger post consisting of a dwelling house, store, privy, kitchen, men's house, and several outbuildings. A fifteen-foot palisade and two bastions provided security and defense. Whip-sawn logs that were floated down the North Thompson to the site were used in the construction of the various buildings, which were both larger and more carefully built than those of the earlier post. Within the stockade there was sufficient space to hold a large number of horses, but the main corral was built opposite the fort on the south side of the river. The fort was surrounded by a considerable acreage of fenced farmlands and hay meadows.

The discovery of gold in 1857 in the rivers and streams of the Kamloops area brought an ever-increasing flood of people into the country. Responding to the changing conditions, the Hudson's Bay Company shifted their efforts from fur trading to outfitting, i.e., buying produce and supplies from "outside" and selling to the miners and prospectors. To better serve this new trade, the company fort was moved once again, this time to a site almost directly opposite on the south side of the Thompson River. This was right on the direct trail from Oregon to the gold rivers of the North.

The new post built by Chief Factor Donald McLeod was constructed of whip-sawn logs; hand-pressed sun-dried bricks were used for the chimneys. It included a gable-roofed dwelling house, a store, and a building used as a restaurant. The post no longer needed palisades and bastions for protection, but extensive fencing to enclose gardens and livestock range was still required.

This third company fort, built in 1863, stood for nearly eighty years, until 1941, when the old fort buildings were demolished to make way for an auto camp. The Hudson's Bay Company, however, followed the growth of the Kamloops settlement, and sometime shortly after the arrival of the Canadian Pacific Railway in 1885 they moved their main operation from the post on the outskirts into the heart of the town where they remain to this day.

For our visit to Fort Kamloops we were particularly fortunate to have Ken Favrholdt as our guide. Ken, formerly curator and archivist at the Kamloops Museum and Archives, had spent many years studying the early history of the area and was kind enough to share his knowledge with us. We first drove to Riverside Park opposite the confluence of the north and south branches of the Thompson River. An informative bronze tablet mounted on a granite boulder, bordered by an attractive planting of colorful flowers, marks the probable location of David Stuart's 1812 Pacific Fur Company Fort Shuswaps. We stood on the shore of the park a few yards in front of the historical marker. To our right from the east, the South Thompson flowed by us; from the north, directly in front of us, the North Thompson joined the waters of the South Thompson; then the two branches, united into one river, flowed swiftly to the west, to our left, to merge eventually with the mighty Fraser. It was not surprising that this strategic location at Kamloops was chosen as a location for the establishment of a series of fur forts.

Next we crossed to the north side of the South Thompson, to the point of land between the north and south arms of the river. This is now part of the Kamloops Indian reserve. Here on the east side of the North Thompson on a low-lying sandy flatland, the Hudson's Bay Company's Fort Kamloops of McLeod and Black stood from 1821 to 1842. A thick zone of small willows and poplars screens the large clearing from the river. Sage- and rabbitbrush and other dryland plants carpet the ground. On the east side of the clearing is the imposing and well-maintained white wooden Roman Catholic Church of St. Joseph with its tall steeple surmounted by a simple white cross rising high into the blue sky. The entire peninsula nestles at the foot of the rounded hills of the twin Mounts Peter and Paul, which dominate the skyline to the east and north. No surface evidence of the fort's existence is visible today, but it is hoped that the interest and cooperation of the native Shuswap band can be obtained to permit archaeological investigations to be made at this important site.

As we walked over the clearing, today quite deserted except for a few Indian youngsters riding their small bicycles, it was difficult to picture traders and Indians occupying this spot, busily carrying on their daily activities. In particular, we remembered that it was right here that Samuel Black, the aggressive fighter, resourceful and brave explorer of Finlay's River, shrewd and competent trader, victor of many encounters with both rival traders and hostile Indians, had been instantly killed by a shot in the back by an Indian who dared not confront Black face-to-face.

The important place horses occupied in the life of Kamloops trading posts is even today reflected in the large numbers of horses raised in the Kamloops area as well as in the well-used racetracks nearby.

Next we crossed over to the west side of the North Thompson to a spot almost directly opposite where we had just been. This was the site of the Hudson's Bay Company's 1842–62 fort. Today street pavement effectively covers all traces of the probable location of the fort buildings. Comfortable modern homes of an attractive subdivision now occupy what once were the horse corrals and hay meadows that surrounded the fort. The only very tenuous link to the past is found in the one street sign standing close to the site bearing the name "Fort." For the third Fort Kamloops (1863–84) we returned to the south side of the river just below the junction of the two branches. There a broad expanse of "blacktop" extending to and along the river for a short distance covers the fort's location.

At the end of the day we somewhat wearily made our way up the hills that border the town on the south to a fine restaurant that had not only delicious food but also a superb view over the city of Kamloops. Ken adroitly secured a window table for us, so we were able to enjoy the beautiful panorama spread below us at our leisure. From our vantage point up on the hills we could appreciate how well named Kamloops is. It is truly, as the Indian name indicates, the "meeting of the waters."

While practically nothing remains from the days of the fur traders, the encircling rounded hills, bare except for a few scattered western pines, still dominate the skyline; the two rivers meet, merge, and flow united westward to the Fraser; the yipping of the coyote is still heard in the stillness of the night; and the dry, hot fragrance of the sagebrush continues to scent the air. Much does, after all, still exist unchanged—much that would be recognized and familiar to both trader and Indian.

Several years after our first trip to Fort Kamloops, we returned to the area. This time our goal was to find the spot where, according to local tradition, the body of Samuel Black lies buried. According to this widely held belief that has been handed down from reputable sources, after Black's murder at Fort Kamloops his body was wrapped in a horsehide, placed in a coffin made of hand-sawn boards, and buried within the walls of the fort compound. Shortly afterward, it was decided that it would be more appropriate if he were to be properly buried at the company's western headquarters at Fort Vancouver on the Columbia River. His body was exhumed and loaded onto a packhorse ready to accompany the fur brigade on their journey to Fort Vancouver. While crossing Monte Creek, ten miles or so east of Kamloops, either the horse stumbled and fell into the creek or, in another version of the story, the Indian carrying the coffin slipped while walking over the single log bridge and tumbled into the stream. Whichever happened, Black's body was so completely soaked that it could not have withstood the long journey to Fort Vancouver. So there, on land gently sloping up from the little creek, Chief Factor Samuel Black was hastily buried at the foot of an enormous ponderosa pine on land that later became the ranch belonging to Senator Bostock. Somehow it seems a fitting conclusion to Black's colorful and sometimes-tempestuous career that his final burial was marked by this disastrous misadventure. Not for him was there to be a quiet burial in a peaceful cemetery with a proper monument like that which marked the last resting places of fellow traders such as George Simpson, Peter Skene Ogden, John Rowland, and James Douglas.

Once again we called upon Ken Favrholdt, our knowledgeable guide, to help us in our quest. He led us to Monte Creek, a pleasant little stream rippling along over scattered rocks and offering the promise of hidden trout. We crossed it at the spot where the old brigade trail had once done. On the hillside on the east side are still a number of magnificent ponderosa pines, but which one shelters the body of Samuel Black is not presently known. Numerous exploratory test holes have been dug in an attempt to locate the grave, but with no success thus far. However, it is expected that these efforts will continue, so that eventually the burial site will be found and the last resting place of Samuel Black can then be appropriately marked.

Fort Nez Percés/Fort Walla Walla

As a result of decisions made at the North West Company's Fort William headquarters, the board of management at Fort George was ordered to send Donald McKenzie and 100 other men up the Columbia to establish a new post at the mouth of the Walla Walla River, a short distance below the Great Forks (the confluence of the Snake and the Columbia). The company had decided that a fort at this new location, being more centrally situated for the effective pursuit of trading expeditions, would henceforth replace Spokane House as their chief interior post. The party, which included Donald McKenzie as leader, Alexander Ross, and ninety-five other men, reached their destination on July 11, 1818, and encamped on the site selected for the new fort about one-half mile from the mouth of the Walla Walla River.

Alexander Ross described the spot in his book *The Fur Hunters of the Far West:*

> The spot for Nez Percés fort was however marked out on a level point upon the east bank of the Columbia, forming something like an island in the flood, and by means of a tributary stream, a peninsula at low water.
>
> The place selected was commanding. On the west is a spacious view of our noble stream in all its grandeur, resembling a lake rather than a river, and confined on the opposite shore by verdant hills of moderate height. On the north and east, the sight is fatigued by the uniformly and wide expanse of boundless plain. On the south the prospect is romantic, and abruptly checked by a striking contrast of wild hills and rugged bluffs on either side of the water, and rendered particularly so by two singular towering rocks similar in colour, shape and height called by the natives 'Twins' situated on the east side, and they are skirted in the distance by a chain of the Blue Mountains, lying in the direction of east and west.

Ross also referred to the place chosen as "the most hostile spot on the whole line of communication. A spot which the whites, it was said, could never hold with safety." And, further, he wrote: "In the whole land this spot was among the most difficult, the most barren of materials for building,—. But plans had been formed, the country must be secured, the natives awed and reconciled, buildings made, furs collected, new territories added.—and in the dreaded spot we took up our stand to run every hazard and brave every danger."

The construction of the new fort was undertaken under extremely difficult conditions. In the words of Ross, "By far the greater part of the

466

timber had to be collected in the bush and conducted by water the distance of a hundred miles, for not a tree or shrub was on the spot itself!" In addition, the natives began to gather in alarming numbers: "They insisted on our paying for the timber we were collecting. They prohibited our hunting or fishing. They affixed an exorbitant price of their own to every article of trade, and they insulted any of the hands whom they met alone."

Eventually a conference was held between the traders and the chiefs of the different tribes whereby the traders secured from the local natives the rights to extend their trading and exploring journeys into the Snake country—the land of their inveterate enemies. As soon as this agreement was ratified by the ritual smoking of the pipe of peace, Donald McKenzie lost no time in heading south into the Snake country. His expedition consisted of fifty-five men, 195 horses, and 300 beaver traps, plus a considerable stock of trading goods. His objective was threefold: to trap, to trade, and to explore the country as a potential source of fur. The results of this first trip into the Snake country proved very favorable and promised well for future expeditions.

During McKenzie's long absence, Alexander Ross was in charge of Fort Nez Percés and responsible for the completion of the fort. Because of the presence of so many warlike tribes close by, the fortifications of Fort Nez Percés were more elaborate than normally required for trading posts. Ross described them in considerable detail. A two-tiered palisade of massive sawn planks six inches thick enclosed the fort. The twenty-foot-high lower row was surmounted by a four-foot rampart containing loopholes and backed by a wide gallery. The smooth surface of the sawn timbers prevented the natives from scaling the walls. Several water reservoirs of 200-gallon capacity each were positioned on the gallery as protection against fire, the threat most feared and dreaded. Additional defense was provided by two strong wooden bastions and a culverin over the gate. Within the fort an elaborate system of strategically placed walls equipped with loopholes and slip doors served as effective barricades against any hostile attempts. At Fort Nez Percés the Indians were never admitted within the walls of the fort except when especially invited on important occasions. All trading was carried on through an eighteen-inch-square aperture secured by an iron door in the outside wall of the trade shop, the Indians remaining on the outside, the traders on the inside. The fort was well supplied with weapons of defense, such as four pieces of ordnance from one to three pounds, ten swivels, sixty stands of muskets and bayonets, twenty boarding pikes, and a box of hand grenades: "It was therefore at once the strongest and most complete fort west of the Rocky Mountains and might be called the Gibralter of the Columbia."

June 22, 1820, Donald McKenzie returned to Fort Nez Percés after completing a second highly successful expedition into the Snake country. He soon departed for a third time on a trapping expedition into the lucrative Snake country and returned July 10, 1821, to Fort Nez Percés with an increase in fur returns and his entire party intact.

During his absence, the North West Company was absorbed by the Hudson's Bay Company by terms of the union of 1821. Henceforth, the control of all the North West forts passed to the Hudson's Bay Company. McKenzie spent the winter of 1821–22 at the fort along with Alexander Ross before leaving the country in the autumn of 1822. He was named chief factor in the new company and appointed Governor of the Hudson's Bay Company's Red River colony at the forks of the Red and Assiniboine rivers.

With McKenzie's departure, Governor Simpson ordered that another party be outfitted for the Snake country under the direction of Finan McDonald, a veteran of the old North West Company and able associate of David Thompson. McDonald's expedition was successful, but at its conclusion, instead of returning to Fort Nez Percés, he came back to Spokane House, the Nor'Westers' favorite and traditional rendezvous and depot.

John Warren Dease arrived to assume charge of Fort Nez Percés, and Alexander Ross prepared to leave the country. However, on his way out, he received a favorable offer of employment from George Simpson giving him the management of an expedition into the Snake country. Ross accepted, but instead of being outfitted from Fort Nez Percés as he had expected, he was forced to proceed to the inconveniently located Spokane House because of McDonald's earlier return there. In spite of many hardships, according to Ross, "—all things considered our returns were the most profitable ever brought from the Snake country in one year, amounting to 5000 beaver, exclusive of other peltries,—"

George Simpson visited Fort Nez Percés in November of 1824, when Chief Trader John Dease was in charge. Simpson recorded his impressions and recommendations in his journal as follows:

This post has been progressively improving for these last three years but the profit it yields is still very moderate. There is an Establishment of Eleven in all attached to it which will admit of reduction and by lopping off superfluities in the outfit I am in hopes that next year will shew a very material amendment. Its returns this season are estimated at 2000

Beaver—and it does not appear to me that there is a prospect of any considerable increase unless trappers are introduced as the Indians cannot be prevailed on to exert themselves in hunting; they are very independent of us requiring but few of our supplies and it is not until absolutely in need of an essential article or an article of finery such as Guns & Beads that they will take the trouble of hunting.

At this time Simpson felt that the Snake country expeditions could be better outfitted from Spokane House than from Fort Nez Percés; later, however, he changed his opinion. After the company's first expedition into the Snake country, Simpson and Peter Skene Ogden agreed that Fort Nez Percés should be the outfitting headquarters for future Snake trapping expeditions, since horses could be obtained there quite cheaply, transportation costs from Fort Vancouver would be lower, the distance to the hunting and trapping grounds less, and the buildup and strengthening of the fort would serve to better keep the unruly Nez Percés under control.

Simpson commented in his journal that Chief Factor McKenzie "kept a Watchful Eye upon them [the Nez Percés] and never allowed them enter the Gates of his Fort except for the purposes of Trade and then not exceeding two or three at a time . . ." Simpson found that at Fort Nez Percés, just as at the other posts he visited, "large quantities of Luxuries and European provisions are annually consumed at a prodigious cost and for no other good reason than that they are preferred to the produce of the Country which is cheap and abundant." On his return from Fort Vancouver, Simpson stopped again at Fort Nez Percés. He held a council with nine chiefs accompanied by 300 warriors. After a distribution of presents such as tobacco, ball and powder, and lengthy speeches, the Indians "promised to exert themselves in hunting, to respect the Whites, to protect us while on their Lands and begged me to assure the great chiefs on the other side of the Water, that they had not two Mouths, one for me, an other for the Camp, that they meant what they said would act up to it and that their hearts were now exactly like those of White Men." Simpson also promised that he would replace Dease the following spring according to his request and alluded once again to the wasteful consumption of provisions that he found so prevalent at many of the forts.

One of the major decisions reached by the company's London Committee as well as by George Simpson during his 1824–25 trip was that in view of the probable takeover of the country south of the Columbia by the Americans at some future time, it would be in the best interests of the Hudson's Bay Company to pursue a "scorched earth" policy, i.e., "by keeping all the frontier country hunted close, and by trapping expeditions in those countries likely to fall within the Boundary of the United States." The objective of this policy was to "scour the country wherever Beaver can be found" to the south of the Columbia River and west of the Rocky Mountains—to trap the country clean of all fur. In Simpson's words, ". . . while we have access thereto it is in our interest to reap all the advantage we can for ourselves, and leave it in as bad a state as possible for our successors."

For the next twenty years this policy of total extermination of the furbearers was aggressively followed and trapping brigades were regularly sent into the country south of the Columbia. Simpson was convinced that if these expeditions just cleared expenses, yielding no profits, they should be continued, as "the more we impoverish the country the less likelihood is there of our being assailed by opposition."

In 1825 Chief Trader Samuel Black was appointed in charge of Fort Nez Percés, where he remained until 1830. During that same period, Peter Skene Ogden was the leader of five trapping expeditions far into the country south of the Columbia River: three to the Snake country, one into southwestern Oregon and northern California, and one into the Great Salt Lake region. For all these expeditions Ogden depended upon Black at Fort Nez Percés for his outfits—particularly the large number of horses these lengthy and arduous trips required. To operate effectively while trapping, each trapper required four horses; however, the number, quality, and condition of the horses that he received was a constant source of irritation and dissatisfaction to Ogden. The importance to the success of the trapping expeditions is underscored in Ogden's comments in his journal on March of 1829: "What a decided advantage we would now have if we had good strong horses in lieu of the trash we received from Fort Nez Percés; it will again this year make a difference of nearly one thousand beaver in our returns but this I cannot prevent."

In a letter to Black at Fort Nez Percés dated August 29, 1829, Chief Factor McLoughlin wrote: "It is certainly disturbing to find horses so scarce as to be unable to purchase a sufficient number at Walla Walla [Fort Nez Percés] for Mr. Ogden's party, and I see no alternative but that he goes to the Nez Perces camp and purchase his wants. I need not say how necessary it is that you trade as many horses as you can as [without them] we will not be able to keep up our trapping parties."

Fort Nez Percés was quite properly considered a "hardship" post. According to Simpson, "A more dismal situation than that of this post can hardly be imagined . . ." He listed several of its more obvious disadvantages, such as lack of any trees, buildings made of driftwood, the desert climate, and frequent dust and sandstorms, these last a result of both the high winds along the Columbia in the Dry Belt and the over-grazing by the large bands of horses confined close to the fort buildings.

In a dispatch written in 1829 to the Governor and London Committee, George Simpson evaluated Fort Nez Percés. He wrote:

> This Post has never been very productive, as the country in its neighbourhood is not rich, and the Natives who are a bold Warlike race do little else than rove about in search of Scalps, plunder and amusement. It is necessary however, on many accounts, to keep on good terms with them, and to maintain a Post for their accommodation whither it pays or not, as in the first place, they from their numbers and daring character command the main communication [i.e., the Columbia River]; in the next place, our Snake Expedition usually passes through their Country to its hunting grounds, which they could not do if we were not on good terms with them; in the third place, we depend on them principally for an annual supply of about 250 Horses, and finally, the Trade in Furs altho' falling off pays tolerably well, as Outfit 1825 yielded about £1800 profit, Outfit 1826 £2200 Outfit 1827 £1100; the accounts of Outfit 1828 are not yet closed, but we think the profits may be estimated at about £1500. The few Furs collected here, are chiefly obtained from the Cayuses, and as their Country is becoming exhausted by the ravages of our own and the American Trappers, the annual returns, must soon diminish rapidly.

George Barnston was assigned to Fort Nez Percés in 1830 to replace Samuel Black, who was transferred to Fort Kamloops on the Thompson River. Two years later Pierre Pambrun, clerk, was given the charge of Fort Nez Percés, a post he retained until his death in May of 1841, the result of a fall from a horse. Pamburn was promoted to chief trader in 1839. According to Simpson, Pamburn was "a very active and efficient officer" who had managed to acquire "considerable influence" over the daring and warlike Indians of the neighbourhood.

When Simpson visited Fort Nez Percés in 1841 during the course of his trip around the world, his assessment of conditions there was as follows:

> At Walla Walla [i.e., Fort Nez Percés], my next place of call, the business appeared to be in a regular and satisfactory state, without any material alteration having taken place in its condition as regards profits, since last reported upon. In former years, and until very lately, this was considered to be a post of danger, being surrounded by several warlike and independent tribes, who were difficult of management, but I was grati-

471

fied to find that both the natives and the people at the establishment have improved greatly in each others' estimation, and that the latter feel in perfect security, although the complement of servants at the post is very small.

Shortly after Simpson's departure from Fort Nez Percés, the fort was destroyed by accidental fire, but without any serious loss, as both furs and goods were saved. Simpson reported that "the Indians on this occasion behaved with great propriety, manifesting much regret at the calamity, and affording every assistance in their power to save the property.... The fort was rebuilt; this time the walls and bastions were constructed of brick."

In 1846 the Oregon Treaty was signed setting the forty-ninth degree of latitude from the Rockies to the Pacific Coast as the international boundary between the United States and Great Britain. This, of course, put Fort Nez Percés and ten other Hudson's Bay Company's trading posts within U.S. territory. The Hudson's Bay Company had possessory rights to their trading establishments, for which they were entitled compensation. The company vigorously insisted that these possessory rights also included the right of trading.

The expeditions from Fort Nez Percés into the Snake country still paid off, although in diminishing returns as the exhaustion of the over-trapped country began to be felt. However, the company felt obliged to maintain and operate these posts in order to justify their claims for compensation from the United States—compensation that, according to the Company, had to cover not only the posts themselves (buildings, land, equipment) but also the value of the trade carried on at the posts. By this time some of the posts were realizing substantial profits from trade with the increasing number of settlers moving into the country in addition to a reasonable trade in furs.

In 1854 the U.S. Department of Indian Affairs denied to the Hudson's Bay Company the right to trade with the Indians in the territory of the United States, declaring that it was not an inherent corollary of the company's possessory rights to their trading establishments. Chief Factor Ogden ignored this decision and continued to trade from Fort Nez Percés. However, the growing danger from the American Indian Wars so seriously threatened the safety of the post that the American Indian agent ordered James Sinclair to close it down. Accordingly, in October 1855, after thirty-seven years of continuous operation, the post was abandoned and Fort Nez Percés was no more.

Today there is nothing left to see of Fort Nez Percés. It has suffered the same fate as so many other trading posts that were built along the Columbia River. They all have disappeared beneath the backed-up waters of dam-created lakes. What was once a mighty, vibrant, and surging river rushing along through the narrows, over cascades and rapids, is now a series of wide placid lakes, each created by one of the many dams that now control much of the entire river. A low granite stone monument at the edge of the highway beside the Columbia commemorates the nearby location of the post. Somewhat like a tombstone, it gives the name (Fort Nez Percés) and dates of "birth" (1818) and "death" (1856). A few clumps of sagebrush grow in the sand about the marker. The small stream, the Walla Walla, bordered by a narrow ribbon of green still winds down from the hills to empty into the Columbia. The surrounding barren hills of sand remain unchanged. The adjacent countryside is a bleak and barren desert. The wind blows the sand in gusts and swirls. The sun glares in the cloudless sky and reflects harshly from the broad river that flows to the west between a gap in the sere-and-brown-colored flat-topped hills that rise on each side. High overhead a hawk wheels in wide circles. As we stood beside the granite marker and surveyed the landscape before us, we were in total agreement with both Simpson and McLoughlin when they said: "A more dismal situation than that of this post can hardly be imagined," and, "Nez Percéz is such a hell I don't know what to say about it. . . ."

Fort Mackinac

John Jacob Astor was a young German immigrant who came to New York in 1784. A shrewd trader and natural entrepreneur, by buying and selling furs in the countryside around New York he was able within a few years to accumulate a considerable amount of capital. Helped by the friendly interest of Alexander Henry the elder (an experienced fur trader and survivor of the 1763 massacre at Fort Michilimackinac), Astor was introduced to the intricacies of the fur trade as well as to many of the leading fur traders of the day.

By 1808 Astor was able to organize his own company, the American Fur Company, with capital of $1 million. Next, with the tacit backing of the U.S. government, Astor in 1810 organized the Pacific Fur Company in order to carry out his grand scheme of capturing the marine trade of the Pacific coast and selling the furs in the markets of China. Astor's men successfully established Fort Astoria at the mouth of the Columbia River in 1811 but, forced by the subsequent loss of supply ships and the outbreak of the War of 1812 between the United States and Great Britain, withdrew and sold their fort and furs to the North West Company. In spite of this setback, Astor continued his fur-trading ventures. In 1811 he successfully acquired control of the Michilimackinac Company and formed the South West Fur Company, which was based on the trade of the Mississippi valley. After the end of the war in 1815, because of the passage of a law by Congress providing that "licenses to trade with the Indians . . . shall not be granted to any but citizens of the United States" Astor was able to buy out the English traders of the South West Company and reestablish the American Fur Company, which became one of the largest business enterprises of its day.

He chose Mackinac Island as the location for the base of operations for his newly formed company. His choice was a shrewd one, for this island in the straits between Lake Huron and Lake Michigan was astride the crossroads of fur trade routes leading southwest to the Mississippi and Missouri rivers as well as northwest to the *pays d'en haut*—the country beyond Lake Superior.

In addition to the large three-story fur warehouse erected in 1810, Astor in 1817, built the spacious Agency House which housed his two agents, Robert Stuart and Ramsay Crooks, (both of whom had been partners in his short-lived Pacific Fur Company), as well as one hundred or so clerks during the busy summer months. Also in the same year, next to the Agency House quarters were built for the 400 clerks who were busily engaged in trading weapons, blankets, and clothing for the Indians' fur pelts. To round out these holdings, Astor bought a building originally built in 1783 by the North West Company, which he used as his retail store from 1818 until 1834.

From this base on Mackinac Island, Astor's American Fur Company dominated the fur trade in the United States from the Canadian boundary as far west as the upper Missouri south to the Wabash and Illinois rivers. Each fall the company sent its agents to trade for furs to the Indian camps in the interior, and each spring, as soon as the ice left the rivers and lakes, they returned with their huge canoes loaded with tons of fur.

Walter Havighurst in his book *Three Flags at the Straits* wrote:

With Mackinac Island as his northern capital, he [Astor] sent traders to Indian tribes as far west as the upper Missouri. To his warehouses under the guns of Fort Mackinac came hundreds of clerks and voyageurs from Montreal, Albany and Niagara. Bateaux loaded with Indian goods made the journey, by way of the Niagara portage, up Lake Erie and Lake Huron to Mackinac harbor. At the Mackinac headquarters, Astor's agents hired the veteran traders and voyageurs and sent them into the wilderness; brigades of five to twenty bateaux went into the hinterlands to establish trading posts near the winter camps of the Indians.

Life as one of Astor's clerks has been vividly described by Gurdon Hubbard, who in 1818 signed on with the American Fur Company for a five-year term at $120 a year. When he arrived at Mackinac Island in July, he found that the village of five hundred permanent residents now swarmed with three thousand traders. Boatmen, voyageurs, and two or three thousand Indians camped all along the shore. The days and nights were noisy with their revelry. Hubbard was housed in the newly erected Clerks Quarters. He worked in the warehouse, where piles of peltry were stacked up to the roof. His job was that of "second counter," that is, tallying skins already sorted and sending them on to the pressing frame. Engulfed in the smell of musk, smoke, grease, and leather, the riches of the fur harvest passed through his fingers as he deftly counted mink, marten, fox, lynx, badger, otter, beaver, and muskrat pelts. He worked from five in the morning until the sunset gun boomed from the fort on the bluff high above the small village along the waterfront. His second summer he worked again in the warehouse. This time his task was first to beat the furs to rid them of dirt and vermin and then to press them in ninety-pound bales in the giant fur press. At the end of the day, he worked by candlelight writing up records and posting accounts. He also worked in the company's retail store. By the end of his five-year contract in 1823, Hubbard had achieved the status of a special partner in the American Fur Company.

Market Street, where Astor's buildings were located, was always thronged with traders, clerks, voyageurs, and Indians. Just a block away was the waterfront with its many taverns, all well patronized by the voyageurs. During the summer months, Indian tepees and campfires crowded the shores of the harbor. Henry Rowe Schoolcraft in his *Narrative Journal of Travels* has given an interesting account of his visit to Mackinac Island in 1820:

> Since our arrival here, there has been a great number of Indians of the Chippeway and Ottaway tribes, encamped near the town. The beach of the lake has been constantly lined with Indian huts and bark canoes. The savages are generally well dressed, in their own costume, and exhibit physiognomies with more regularity of features and beauty of expression, than it is common to find among them. This is probably attributable to a greater intermixture of blood in this vicinity. These savages resort to the island for the purpose of exchanging their furs, for blankets, knives, and other articles. Their visits are periodical, being generally made after their spring and fall hunts, and their stay is short. Some of the tribes also bring in for sale several articles of Indian manufacture, particularly a kind of rush mat of a very handsome fabric, bark baskets filled with maple sugar, called moke-ocks, with quilled mockasins, shot pouches and other fancy goods of Indian fabric, which are generally in demand as articles of curiosity.
>
> The Indian trade is chiefly conducted by the American, or South West Fur Company, under the direction of Messrs. Stuart and Crooks. Indeed the ware houses, stores, offices, boat yards and other buildings of this establishment, occupy a considerable part of the town plot, and the company furnishes employment to a great number of clerks, engagés, and mechanics, and contributes very largely to the general business activity, and enterprise of the town. The trade and operations of this company are confined principally to the northwestern territories of the United States.

The fur trade was responsible for the prosperity that the island enjoyed during the 1810s and 1820s. It has been estimated that in 1822 furs valued at $3 million were processed in Astor's Market Street warehouse. A contemporary account of Mackinac Island during this period written by Juliette Kinzie, wife of one of Astor's clerks, reflected the prosperity that prevailed on the island during this time: "It was no unusual thing to see a hundred or more canoes of Indians at once approaching the island, laden with articles of traffic; and if to these we add the squadrons of large Mackinaw boats constantly arriving from the outposts, with the furs, peltries and buffalo robes collected by distant traders, some idea may be formed of the extensive operations and important position of the American Fur Company."

Robert Stuart, Astor's representative on Mackinac Island, was related to both David Stuart, one of Astor's partners in the American Fur Company and in the Pacific Fur Company venture, and John Stuart, companion to Simon Fraser and partner in the North West Company and later a chief factor in the Hudson's Bay Company. Stuart had a violent temper and was often quite heavy-handed when dealing with his employees. However, under the influence of the Presbyterian minister, the Reverend William Ferry, Stuart managed to curb his temper and brutality. He became a deacon in the church, halted Sunday work at the warehouse, and for a while controlled the sale of whiskey to the Indians.

But all this prosperity was not destined to last. The beaver and other furbearers could not sustain indefinitely the relentless trapping to which they were subjected. Fur returns diminished steadily until finally the era of the fur trade came to an end. In 1834 Robert Stuart left Mackinac Island quite abruptly, not even bothering to remove the company records for safekeeping. The fur warehouse was closed. Market Street was deserted. The clerks left to seek employment elsewhere. The voyageurs and trappers had to move westward in search of new lands as yet untrapped. The waterfront taverns were quiet. The Indian camps disappeared from the beaches. John Jacob Astor, ever the shrewd businessman, made rich by the fur trade, simply moved his millions into New York real estate—and thereby became even richer.

The best time to visit Mackinac Island is in late May or early June. That is lilac season, a time when these glorious bushes—some tree-sized and well over two hundred years old—that grow so profusely around the white-clapboarded houses, along fences and byways, delight the eye with their beautiful colors of pale lavender, deep purple, and snowy white. Their sweet fragrance permeates the entire island. Indeed, it even spreads out over the water of the straits to meet the visitors on the ferryboats coming from the mainland. Another reason to visit the island at this time is that it is prior to the tourist season, when the island is inundated by the visitors who come each day by the thousands throughout the summer.

Since we live only ninety miles from Mackinac Island, we have been able to visit it many times. Our most memorable visit was made in early June several years ago. We had spent the night at the Grand Hotel—that hundred-year-old "Grande Dame" of all resort hotels. We had enjoyed promenading along the hotel's vast 800-foot-long open porch with its huge white columns, colorful array of American flags, and massed display of red geraniums. We had marveled at the breathtaking view over the blue waters of the Straits of Mackinac, had watched the sun sink amid clouds of brilliant color, and later, as the sky darkened, had marveled at the thousands of stars sparkling overhead and the strings of twinkling lights outlining the spans and cables of the "Mighty Mac" bridge to the west.

Early the next morning we set off from the hotel to walk along Market Street—the main roadway in Astor's day. It was Sunday. All the shops were closed, and the first ferryboat of the day was not due for several hours. Except for a few dedicated golfers headed for the nearby golf course and some early churchgoers, we had the street to ourselves. Market Street, which runs roughly in an east–west direction, is a block back from the street next to the waterfront. It is dominated by Fort Mackinac, the U.S. military post perched high on the cliffs rising above the street's east end.

We first came to the Biddle House at the west end of the street. It was a long, low colonial-style white clapboard house with two small dormer windows extending in the front from the rather steeply pitched roof. Probably built about 1780, it was purchased in 1818 by Edward Biddle, a prominent fur trader and partner in the company of Biddle & Drew, which had both a dock and a warehouse on the waterfront to handle not only its fur trade but also shipment of fish and wood.

Farther down the street we came to the first of Astor's American Fur Company buildings. This was the warehouse, a tall, narrow L-shaped building of three floors, with a pulley hoist at the peak of the roof for raising pelts to the upper levels. The narrow end fronted the street, while the wing formed an open courtyard in the rear. This, Astor's first building on Mackinac Island, was built in 1810. Hand-hewn beams, wooden dowels, and hand-wrought nails were used in its construction. This was where the furs were stored, graded, pressed, and bundled for shipment.

Next door to the warehouse was the Agency House. Built in 1817, this was the home of agents Robert Stuart and Ramsay Crooks. It was a well-proportioned, imposing white clapboard dwelling of two full stories built above a ground-floor basement. It had a garret, and four tiny dormers protruding from the pitched roof. A rather steep stairway on each side of a small landing led to the front door. The small-paned windows were symmetrically placed. The exteriors, both of this building and of the warehouse, reflected their colonial American background. Hand-hewn timbers for beams and floors, wooden dowels, hand-made

478

nails, doors with raised panels in the shape of a cross, massive iron locks, and twenty and twenty-four small-paned windows were but a few of the features that characterized its construction. Among the few furnishings preserved at the Agency House were the tall secretary-type desk used by the agents, a massive iron safe, ledgers of the American Fur Company, and a set of fur-weighing scales. Upstairs were numerous small rooms, each opening off the long central hallway. The windows in the basement were protected with hand-wrought iron bars. The Agency House was not only the home of Astor's chief agents, Stuart and Crooks (and as such was the social center for the town's elite); it was also the agents' office, where business was transacted and records and ledgers kept. In addition, during the busy summer months some one hundred clerks were housed on the upper floors. Dug into the hillside behind the warehouse and Agency House were three underground cellars where money, whiskey, and ammunition were stored. The doors to these cellars as well as the retaining walls were still visible.

A short distance away at the eastern end of Market Street was the reconstructed replica of the American Fur Company retail store. First built in 1783 by John Ogilvy, prominent in the fur trade and Montreal agent first for the XY Company and later for the North West Company, it was later acquired by Astor's company in 1818 and served as their retail shop until 1834. The general appearance of the building—its overall proportions, gently curving roof, peaked dormers, chimney at each gable end, shape and placement of windows—reflected the French tradition of its Montreal builders. It was inside this building that in June of 1821 a young Canadian voyageur, Alexis St. Martin, was accidentally shot by a customer who was examining one of the store's guns. The lad suffered a gaping hole in his stomach, which, surprisingly, was not fatal. The wound did not close, but a fold of flesh grew, like a flap, to cover the stomach opening. Dr. William Beaumont, Fort Mackinac's surgeon, who cared for St. Martin over a period of many years, was able to watch the digestive process occurring in the man's stomach simply by raising the flap of flesh. Beaumont's observations enabled him to make medical history with the knowledge he gained about the process of digestion.

As we reached the end of Market Street and the last of the American Fur Company buildings, we realized that much time had elapsed and that the island was awakening to another day of bustle and activity. But we were content. We had had our visit into the past undisturbed by any modern intrusion. Now the first ferry was due with its load of eager tourists. The loud clop-clop of horses was increasingly audible as drivers headed their open wagons and carriages toward the docks and the waterfront streets ready for the day's business. No automobiles were allowed on the island. Horses, carriages, and bicycles were the only means of transportation. No gasoline fumes fouled the clean air. Only the strong pungent smell peculiar to horses competed with the sweet fragrance from the island's many lilacs.

In addition to the buildings from the fur trade era, Mackinac Island had several other places of much interest. Perched on top of the high limestone cliff overlooking Mackinac Harbor is Fort Mackinac. This was built in 1780 when Captain Patrick Sinclair decided to move his British garrison from Fort Michilimackinac on the mainland to the island because of its superior defensive location. The Americans took possession of the fort in 1796 but lost it to the British during the War of 1812. However, by terms of the Treaty of Ghent it was restored to the Americans in 1815.

At the foot of the cliffs, below the fort and facing the harbor, was the Indian dormitory. This building erected in 1838 was headquarters for the U.S. Indian Agency at Mackinac. It served the Indians until 1846, giving them food and shelter as needed.

Mackinac Island has many natural features of great interest. On the east side of the island is Arch Rock. This is a natural bridge rising 146 feet above the lake, with a span of 50 feet. According to Indian legend, it was built by the Great Spirit, who once lived on the island.

Another place of interest is the so-called Skull Cave. Located in the interior of the island, this limestone cave littered with bones and skulls was where Alexander Henry the elder, after surviving his terrible ordeal of the massacre at Fort Michilimackinac, spent the night while hiding from hostile Indians.

Mackinac Island has much to offer the visitor—beautiful scenery, gracious hotels, gourmet dining, history, fun, enticing shops of all kinds. In addition, there are miles of trails through northern woodlands for hiker, horseback rider, or bicyclist, the total absence of mosquitoes, and world-famous fudge. No wonder the ferries are crowded as they shuttle back and forth between the island and the mainland. A visit to Mackinac Island is a most rewarding experience.

Fort Assiniboine
(Athabasca River)

At the annual meeting of the Hudson's Bay council held at York Factory on July 5, 1823, a resolution was passed "that the present Post of Lesser Slave Lake if practicable be abandoned & that a Post at McLeods Branch be substituted in place thereof." Simpson had been told by Indians that there was an ample depth of water for boats and batteaux on both the Athabasca and Pembina rivers and that for the fifty-mile portage between the two rivers horses loaded with two ninety-pound *pièces* could make the trip in four days in the autumn, six days in the spring. When this resolution was implemented, the Lesser Slave Lake post was not abandoned, and the new post was located not on the McLeod River, but on the Athabasca some distance downstream to the east at the confluence of Freeman Creek. It was called Fort Assiniboine and J. F. Larocque was put in charge.

During the course of George Simpson's 1824–25 trip from York Factory to Fort George at the mouth of the Columbia River, as a result of experiencing at first hand the extreme difficulties entailed in the Beaver River–Portage la Biche section of the route he resolved to revamp the entire transportation system. As a first step in carrying out his plan, upon his arrival at Lac la Biche he instructed Jacques Cardinal, a freeman and well-known horsekeep, to ". . . in the course of this ensuing Winter and Spring get a Horse track or road cut from Fort Assiniboine to Edmonton House Saskatchewaine . . ."

Simpson recognized that the Beaver River route was a most unsatisfactory one. The river's shallowness, or even at some seasons total lack of water, not only made passage extremely difficult but also required that only the small, uneconomical North canoes could be used. The North Saskatchewan, on the other hand, although it afforded unimpeded travel for boats and batteaux was exposed to the danger of attack from the hostile tribes of the plains. To meet this danger more men were used in the brigades than would have been necessary for normal boat transport.

Simpson's solution was to divert the Lesser Slave Lake brigade and Columbia River express from the old Cumberland House–Athabasca route via Frog Portage, Churchill and Beaver rivers, and Portage la Biche to the North Saskatchewan, where, in company with the usual Saskatchewan brigades, they would be sufficient numbers to pass through the danger zone of the open plains in safety and at no extra cost. At Edmonton the Lesser Slave brigade and Columbia express would reach the Athabasca at Fort Assiniboine by means of the horse road that had been cut by Cardinal. Once on the Athabasca, with the Beaver River section bypassed, boats could be used for the remaining travel on that river. This was a well-thought-out plan, and Simpson's reorganization of the transport system resulted in major economy for the company. Simpson relied upon boats to replace canoes whenever possible, amalgamation of brigades to provide safety with economy, careful attention to the packing of the outfits, and the use of horses for overland transport in certain areas. His plan was ratified by the council, and its merit was soon demonstrated by the fact that in the season of 1825 only forty-five men were needed instead of the seventy-nine formerly required. This represented a savings of about one thousand pounds per annum. Henceforth, the Beaver River route was abandoned.

Chief Factor William McIntosh was in charge of Fort Assiniboine when Simpson stopped off there for a day on his way west in 1824. He wrote in his journal that "Fort Assiniboine is beautifully situated on the North Bank of the Athabasca River." To implement his plan for making Fort Assiniboine the northern end of an overland portage from Edmonton, Simpson directed that "horses would of course be kept at Fort Assineboine where they can be safe from Thieves and where Hay may be had in abundance and with little trouble."

On Simpson's return east in the spring of 1825, he traveled over the newly cleared "road" between Fort Assiniboine and Edmonton House. Referring to the portage, he wrote in his journal: ". . . left Fort Assiniboine for Edmonton on Horseback . . . having gone about 12 Miles, the road tolerably good considering that it has been opened since I passed here last Fall through thick woods." The next day Simpson continued in his journal: "I am now . . . enabled to say that New Caledonia and Lesser Slave Lake can be supplied by this route instead of Athabasca and the Beaver River which will be a very great Saving in Men's Wages Provisions . . . I am satisfied that this discovery of Mine (as I alone can claim the merit thereof it never having been even dreamt of by any other) will enable us to do the Peace River business at a reduction of one third on the usual expences of that place . . ." On Monday, May 2, Simpson "reached Edmonton at 12 A.M. having come from Fort Assiniboine in about 2 Days the distance being about 80 Miles."

The statement made by Simpson that he alone could claim the credit for first realizing the advantages of an overland portage from Fort Assiniboine on the Athabasca to Edmonton House on the North Saskatchewan, while completely in character, was not entirely true. If

482

he had not been so zealous in promoting his own reputation with his company superiors in London, he might quite properly have shared the credit with John Rowand, chief factor at Edmonton. For it was on the return trip from York Factory that the difference in elapsed time between the two travel routes was dramatically demonstrated. Dr. John McLoughlin and his brigade, following the northern route (Churchill-Beaver rivers–Lac la Biche), took sixty-seven days to reach Fort Assiniboine. John Rowand and his party, on the other hand, following the North Saskatchewan, reached Fort Edmonton in fifty-two days and spent a day or so unloading cargo and two or three more days riding the eighty miles to Fort Assiniboine. There he remained four days, hoping to meet Simpson and his party also on their way west. After waiting in vain, Rowand left a note for the Governor and returned to Fort Edmonton. When Simpson received Rowand's note, he quickly realized its significance. Rowand's note, with its record of his arrival date at Fort Edmonton, quite clearly proved that the passage by the Saskatchewan required fewer days then the old Beaver River route. Its advantages were already known and utilized by John Rowand. This fact should have been acknowledged by Simpson.

Later that same year (1825), Alexander Ross on his way back to the Red River settlement from the Columbia district stopped off at Fort Assiniboine. He described the fort in his book *Fur Hunters of the Far West* as follows:

> . . . a petty post erected on the north bank of the river, and so completely embosomed in the woods, that we did not catch a glimpse of it until we was among huts, and surrounded by howling dogs and screeching children. At this sylvan retreat there were but three rude houses. Two white men, and six half-breeds, were all the men we saw about the place, and there was not a picket or palisade to guard them from either savage or bear. This mean abode was dignified with the name of fort; and with the presence of a chief factor. It is right to observe, however, that Fort Assiniboine was but a new place, in process of building.

The minutes of the council held at York Factory on July 2, 1825, provided that Fort "Assenboan" be staffed during the winter with a chief trader (James McMillan) and a clerk (George Deschambault) and during the summer with but two men, one an interpreter. It was also resolved "that Horses be provided at Edmonton for the transport of the Lesser Slave Lake Outfit and Columbia property to Fort Asseniboan at which place the requisite craft is to be in readiness to forward the same further on . . ."

Chief Trader J. E. Harriott was in charge of Fort Assiniboine for two years (1826–28). During that time an average of seventy-eight packhorses was needed to take supplies across the portage. As a year-round base of operations, the facilities at Fort Assiniboine, in addition to quarters for its men, included warehouses, root cellars, ammunition cache, and boatbuilding and repair shops.

Edward Ermatinger, traveling with the York Factory express between Fort Vancouver and York Factory a few years after Fort Assiniboine was established, stopped there for a week in May of 1827. His journal entry for May 7 reads: "Arrive at Fort Assineboine at 8 p.m. and learn that this Post has not provisions enough to furnish our men a meal . . ." The fourteenth of May he left on the overland trail for Edmonton, and his journal entries for the next eight days describe the condition of the trail and the hardships it imposed on the horses. One entry, dated the sixteenth of May reads: ". . . Our road the whole of this day had been thro' one continued mire—several horses too weak to come up with the rest, tho' light."

In 1847 Kane and his party arrived in a starving condition back at Fort Assiniboine in the month of November. He wrote gratefully and enthusiastically of the feast of whitefish that was prepared for them: "Whether it was the hunger from which I was suffering, or the real goodness of the fish, I know not now; but certainly they seemed to be the most delicious I had ever tasted, and the memory of that feast hung over me, even in my dreams, for many a day afterwards."

Fort Edmonton was the southern end of the portage between it and Fort Assiniboine. A well-coordinated and carefully planned time schedule was followed each fall to get the various packhorse brigades off so as to enable their cargos to reach their destination before freeze-up. The first to leave Fort Edmonton for Fort Assiniboine was the outfit destined for Jasper House, on the east side of the Rockies, and the Columbia and New Caledonia districts. In 1854 twenty-eight horses were required to carry the goods and provisions. Next to leave was the outfit for the Lesser Slave Lake post. This required forty-three horses.

The outfit for Fort Assiniboine followed. It needed only seven horses. This fort, which was the depot at the northern end, served as departure point for the brigades and as supplier of the necessary pemmican required for the brigades. It was a scene of great activity when the brigades were arriving preparatory to embarking on the Athabasca for their long journeys to their final destinations. In 1854 its staff consisted of an interpreter at thirty pounds per year and a servant-clerk at seventeen pounds. Fort Assiniboine, in addition to being the northern terminus of the overland portage, was also important as a fur post. Foxes of all kinds, as well as beaver, lynx, marten, and mink, were traded in sufficient numbers to make it a profitable operation.

By January of 1859, when James Hector of the Palliser expedition stopped there, he found that the post consisted "merely of a few ruinous log huts on the left bank built on a beautiful level prairie several miles in extent and elevated 30 feet above water." It was surrounded by a ramshackle palisade that Hector salvaged for firewood. By this time the post was only operating during the summer months, when the portage road was open.

For many years the Fort Edmonton–Fort Assiniboine overland portage remained a vital link in the long communication chain that stretched across the breadth of Canada. It only fell out of use when it was replaced by new routes across Panama and along the Pacific coast. By about 1880 Fort Assiniboine was closed down, its days of usefulness over.

Today there is little remaining to mark the site of Fort Assiniboine. A Historic Sites cobblestone cairn with appropriate bronze plaque identifies the fort's location on the north bank of the Athabasca. The site is, indeed, just as George Simpson wrote, "beautifully situated."

The clearing where the fort stood extends along a bend in the river. From its thirty-foot elevation there is an unobstructed view of the river winding off in both directions, bordered by spruce-covered forests. Here, in this pleasant clearing, the grass is mown, with only a fringe of prairie grasses and flowers and one or two poplar trees growing along the edge of the bank. To the keenly observant eye, it is just barely possible to detect a few faint contours and depressions in the opening that suggest the prior existence of fort structures.

A replica palisade surrounding a log building that houses a small museum and senior citizen center has been built on one side of the clearing. Inside the museum is an interesting collection of a few of the artifacts found when part of the site was excavated in preparation for the erection of a Canadian Legion building. Among the articles displayed were knife blades, a covered pail, ax heads, keys, nails, hardware, and a small shard of English blue china.

Although today all traces of the fort building have long since disappeared, the Athabasca continues to flow quietly along, unchanged from the days when it bore the traffic of the heavily laden boats arriving from and departing for the Rockies and Lesser Slave Lake. Quite miraculously, this small clearing, this section of the river, and the spruce woods bordering it remain practically the same as they were 150 years ago, when the men of Fort Assiniboine lived and worked here. We were grateful that this part of the past—untouched and unspoiled—still exists for us to experience and enjoy.

Fort William
(Lac des Allumettes)

By the early 1820s independent petty traders in considerable numbers were penetrating ever farther up the Ottawa River valley. To meet this competition and threat to the company's monopoly of the fur trade, John Siveright, in charge of Fort Coulonge, in 1823 sent John McLean to establish an outpost some miles upstream to the widening of the river known as Lac des Allumettes. McLean in his book *Notes of a Twenty-five Years' Service in the Hudson's Bay Territory* wrote: "A few hours' paddling [up the Ottawa River] brought us to an old shanty in the island of Allumette, where, to my great joy, I perceived my opponent intended to fix his winter quarters. We accordingly commenced erecting a couple of huts, a store, and dwelling-house, in close proximity to him. This being the best season of the year for the natives to hunt, it was the interest of all parties not to molest them; and we therefore employed our time in preparing suitable accommodation for the winter." McLean's trading opponent was Aeneas Macdonell, son of John Macdonell, a former partner of the North West Company from 1796 to 1815 who, after retirement now operated a store and ferry service at the lower end of the Ottawa River. The two traders kept each other under constant surveillance. In McLean's words: "The motions of our opponents must needs be attended to, . . . each morning every path was carefully examined, to ascertain that no one had started during night; . . . and every stratagem that could be devised to elude each other's vigilance put in practice, it being the 'interest' of each party to reach the Indians alone."

From 1830 to 1837 Nicholas Brown, clerk, was in charge of the Lac des Allumettes post. Endeavoring to implement George Simpson's policy of making each post as self-sufficient as possible, Brown sowed twenty-eight bushels of oats and planned "to sow 12 Bus. more which is all mixed with Hay Seed." In addition, he cleared a small acreage for potatoes and turnips.

During this same period, as E. E. Rich wrote in his book *Hudson's Bay Company 1670–1870,* "the Company could see little hope of profit, and the petty traders crept further north each year and the lumbermen hacked into the forest and the Iroquois and Algonquins took advantage of the 'extraordinary and oppressive license' . . . to hunt at will regardless of supposed tribal boundaries. Faced by roaming Indians, the easy route to Montreal, the petty traders' use of spirits, and opposition from lumbermen, the Company was well on the defensive in Ottawa River."

But ultimately the petty traders were forced from the area and the company's Ottawa posts were making enough profit to cover costs by selling provisions to the lumbermen. Simpson was able to claim by 1843 that both the petty traders and the lumbermen had been removed as a source of competition from the Ottawa River valley.

By 1844 the post had assumed the function of handling the bulk of the Indian trade of the region. George Simpson, who visited the Ottawa River posts (including Lac des Allumettes) in 1841 on his way to Red River, wrote to the Governor and London Committee: "I am sorry to say the trade is by no means as prosperous as could be wished . . . but with the best attention it is impossible that profits can be made from the fur trade, as much of the country is occupied by agricultural settlers and lumberers, all of whom give extravagant prices for any skins that may come within their reach."

In 1845 Hector McKenzie, nephew by marriage to George Simpson's wife and clerk at the former North West post of Fort William on Lake Superior, was brought down to take charge of the Lac des Allumettes district. In a move that aimed to reduce expenses McKenzie abandoned the long and correspondingly costly six-day haul to Baird's mill to obtain flour and provisions in favor of the much closer settlement of Pembroke. Governor Simpson was well pleased with this change but could not miss the opportunity of pointing out where further economies could be made: "You say, you think you have sufficient [oats from the company crop] to last till sleighing time—but as there is no work to be done before then, I do not see that the horses require oats as I presume it is not usual to pamper the horses with oats in the stable when doing nothing."

The following year (1846) McKenzie was promoted to the rank of chief trader, and a new shop and a house forty-two by thirty feet were built for him at the Lac des Allumettes post. Simpson, ever mindful of keeping costs to a minimum, instructed that in the new house there be no open fireplaces except in the kitchen. However, contrary to this directive, a fireplace was built in the living room. In a letter to Simpson reporting on the progress being made on the buildings, McKenzie wrote that the house and shop were nearly finished and added: "I have from the commencement endeavored to have every accommodation with the strictest economy." McKenzie's two-story house, which still stands, was built of logs and covered at a later date with clapboard. Three dormers project from the broad expanse of the steeply pitched roof. A ground-level porch extends across the entire front. Its flared roof is supported by sturdy fluted columns. There is a large chimney at each of the two gable ends. The many windows are large and pleasingly spaced. Inside, the rooms are spacious. Although Hector McKenzie had assured Simpson that the strictest economy had been observed in the construction of this house, it unquestionably represented a degree of elegance and spaciousness that was not common to many of the fur posts of the period.

In 1848 a post office was established at the trading post and the name changed to Fort William, a name chosen perhaps because of McKenzie's earlier connection with Fort William on Lake Superior.

The year 1848 proved to be a year of hardship for the post. In the spring there were floods: ". . . water up to the front walk in the garden & has washed away all the goose nests. . . ." However, oats, potatoes, and turnips were planted. Sales were down and the post office arrangements quite irregular. Wemyss Simpson, who was in charge of the post during McKenzie's absence, in a letter to him wrote:

> . . . no case to be had this month only having sold to the value of 13/—this five days. The crops look very bad we have nothing in the garden from Grubs, Dogs hens &. for the fence keeps nothing out & the ground is full of the former animals—the hay looks very bad & the oats quite burned up with the heat. You say you expect Stout will not have many geese we have not as yet one young one the water washed away three & the Indians or some one else stole the eggs of two more & I am afraid the Turkeys will ever remain in suspense we have eight pigs & I could get some more if you wanted them. The old white horse you bought last winter looks very bad.

As if this litany of woes were not enough, three years later the old sales shop burned down when high wines, while being drawn, were ignited by a candle. Hector McKenzie became chief factor in 1851 and for the next thirteen years remained at Fort William.

By 1853 the long-standing time-honored system of barter was no longer in general use, since much of the trade was now with tavern keepers, lumbermen, and Indians who often earned wages as boatmen or laborers. Following long-established custom, the Indians came to Lac des Allumettes each summer to meet the Jesuits from Montreal, who would solemnize their burials, baptisms, and marriages. When these were concluded, a great feast took place, followed by horse racing and games. In 1857 the Hudson's Bay Company built a wooden church for the Indians. Hector Mckenzie the following year reported that "all the Indians connected with this Post are encamped round the establishment awaiting the arrival of the Priests from Moose."

A. G. Dallas, who became Governor-in-Chief of Rupert's Land after the death of Sir George Simpson (Simpson had been knighted in

1841) proposed in 1862 that Fort William be closed and be replaced by the post at the portage around the Des Joachims Rapids farther up the Ottawa River. He visited Fort William in 1863 and described it as "a very fine and well kept establishment, with numerous and excellent buildings and 800 acres of land, having a frontage of a mile on the Ottawa River . . . the staff consists of a Chief Factor, two clerks, a head farmer, blacksmith and several labourers . . ."

Chief Factor McKenzie so strongly disagreed with Governor Dallas's decision to close down Fort William that, unable to change the Governor's mind, he resigned from the company's service in 1864. Five years later (in 1869) the company sold Fort William for $3,000 and Chief Trader Watt, who had been in charge of the post since McKenzie's retirement, established the company agency in an office across the Ottawa River in Pembroke.

Fort William is tucked away on the north shore of the widening of the Ottawa River still known as Lac des Allumettes. At Pembroke, Ontario, we crossed over the *Rivière des Outaouais* to reach Allumette Island; after following a secondary road to the north side of the island, we then crossed the narrow *chenal de la Culbute* to reach the mainland of Quebec. From that point on, it was up to us to find Fort William. Sandy roads led in all directions, no signs to direct us, no one to ask. We followed first one road, then another in our search. The countryside of woods and fields was beautiful, and we were in no hurry. Often the road we followed dead-ended at the Ottawa River and we were rewarded with unobstructed views of this magnificent waterway. Eventually we followed the right combination of sandy byways and to our great satisfaction found Fort William.

The few buildings that now comprised Fort William stood on an isolated point of lowland that extended into the Ottawa River. Close to the river's edge was an old-time general store built of brick, which was open for business. It had been built on the site of the Hudson's Bay Company's store. Attached to it in the rear was a small stone storehouse that was a part of the original Hudson's Bay store. Just to the south of the store and facing the river was Chief Factor Hector McKenzie's house. Sagging a bit and badly in need of refurbishing, it still appeared to be sufficiently sound structurally to withstand the floods of spring and the storms of winter for some years to come.

We wandered around the area trying to imagine what it was like when the Indians were coming here to trade and when the lumbermen were sailing the great logging rafts downstream past the fort. In those days Fort William must have been a very active and busy place, since it required "a Chief Factor, two clerks, a head farmer, blacksmith and several labourers" to operate it.

To the north of the store was the small, modest house formerly used by the company clerks. Today it is clapboarded and painted red. Close by a small ridge overlooking the river was a tall wooden cross that marked the small graveyard now in danger of being overrun by encroaching bushes and vines.

A short distance behind the factor's house we noticed the skeleton framework of massive timbers—all that remained of what was once a large barn. Within, in addition to a profusion of wood and iron items of many sizes and shapes all jumbled together, was a lovely old-fashioned two-seater horse-drawn red sleigh. From here we followed a trail that led up a gentle slope to a clearing in the woods where the 1858 church built by the Hudson's Bay Company still stood. It was a simple white clapboard structure surmounted by a typical Québeçois-style belfry. Apparently, the church was still used during the summer months.

To us Fort William represented a tiny isolated oasis—a place of peace and quiet—where time appeared to have paused and change had come but slowly. Although the fur trade and the lumbering days have long since ended, we felt that here at Fort William we could still hear—very faintly—echoes from the past.

Fort Pelly

As a result of the union in 1821 of the North West and Hudson's Bay companies, many trading posts became redundant. The ones that had been established along the Swan River were abolished. To replace them Governor Simpson directed that a new post be erected to serve as headquarters and distribution center for the company's Swan River district. It was to be outfitted from York Factory on Hudson's Bay. This post, called Fort Pelly, was erected in 1824. From its strategic location at the southern end of the overland portage leading from the Assiniboine to the Swan River it provided access to York Factory.

This well-used portage crosses a very low and narrow dividing ridge that separates the waters of the Assiniboine from those of Swan River. Miry Creek, which flows into Snake Creek, an effluent of Swan River, is not more than three miles from the Assiniboine. In other words, a bateau or canoe may descend the Assiniboine from Fort Pelly and reach Lake Winnipeg by Red River; a bateau or canoe may also descend Miry Creek, Snake Creek, and Swan River and reach Lake Winnipeg by Dauphin River. In addition, close by to the north were the beaver-rich parklands, while on the prairies just to the southwest were the buffalo—source of the all-important pemmican.

The site selected by Chief Trader Allan McDonell was on a flat one-quarter-mile north of the narrow point (known as the elbow or *recoude*) where the Assiniboine abruptly shifts the direction of its course from northeast to southeast. The September 21, 1824, entry in the fort's official journal describes the spot chosen for the fort: ". . . we pitched upon a small eminence for our house. The situation is in a fine valley, environed by rising grounds on the E. and W., on the N. thick woods, on the S. a continuation of the valley, through which winds the Red River [Assiniboine], and on the N.E. a fine high plateau running towards the third crossing place of the Swan River."

The site selected, Chief Trader McDonell and his crew of about twenty men immediately began the work of constructing the new post. When completed that fall, Fort Pelly consisted of a forty-by-twenty-foot store and trading shop, an officers' dwelling of the same dimensions divided into three compartments, an eight-by-twenty-foot four-room building to serve as a combined Indian hall and living quarters, a small kitchen, forge, workshop, stable, and boatyard. All this was within a 120-foot square enclosed by a palisade.

Results of the first season's trade in furs, leather, and provisions were quite encouraging. On April 25, 1825, sixteen men transported the year's returns in three boats and seven carts to Swan River for forwarding to York Factory.

Disaster struck in 1825 when the Assiniboine River flooded and, in the words of Chief Trader McDonell, "destroyed all our Crops of Potatoes and Barley and carried off one half of our establishment." The following year Chief Factor John Clarke was given charge of the post. He, never one to underestimate his own achievements, wrote in the fort's journal (1829): "Fort Pelly as it stands at present has a good dwelling house, Indian House a range of Mens House Stores and Stables well stockaded in and with Bastions, which was not the case on my takeing charge of the District it being then in a most dilapitaeted state hardly fit for any purpose with no Gardens." During Chief Factor Colin Robertson's two years at the fort (1830–32) the stockade was enlarged, a new stable was built, and in the factor's residence (the "Big House") the modern convenience of a stove was installed, replacing the open fireplace and chimney.

For the next decade (1832–42) Chief Trader William Todd was in charge of Fort Pelly. During this period, the Hudson's Bay post experienced much competition from American traders. The great advantage for the Americans was that the Assiniboines were able to reach their forts in two or three days of travel, whereas it required fourteen or fifteen days to come to Fort Pelly. Furthermore, the American traders gave higher prices for both furs and buffalo robes. This resulted in a falling off of the Fort Pelly trade. However, when trouble eventually developed between the Americans and their Assiniboine customers, the trade picked up at the Hudson's Bay post. Also during this period, the company employees were sometimes attacked by Indian raiding parties while traveling over the prairies to and from Fort Pelly.

The minutes of the Northern Council held annually at York Factory record that for the period 1824–31 the number of boats carrying the yearly outfits assigned to Fort Pelly varied from two to five, with an average of three and a half; the number of *pièces* ranged from 91 to 250, with an average of 168; and the number of servants ran from a low of eleven to a high of twenty-seven, for an average of nineteen. For 1824 the chief trader was instructed to furnish twenty kegs of salt and "as much sugar [maple] as they can supply." For 1826–28 the orders read that the chief factor "be directed to adopt measures to provide and forward for the use of the Depot such supplies of Salt Provisions and vegetables as his means permit." For the years 1829–31 the chief factor was authorized "to contract with a Freeman for the delivery of 200 to 300 Bushels Salt annually at 5s.p. Bushel."

One of the products traditionally manufactured in the Pelly area and shipped to the Red River and other posts was salt. Harmon in 1800 referred to a place near the Swan River where "there is a salt spring, by boiling down the water of which, tolerable salt is made." According to Hind (1882), the salt that was made at the Swan River was packed in birchbark containers for transportation to Red River, "where it commands twelve shillings sterling a bushel, or one hundred weight of flour, or a corresponding quantity of fish, pemican or buffalo meat, according to circumstances."

In spite of the fort's proximity to the buffalo herds, shortage of food was sometimes a problem. The buffalo roamed over a large area and sometimes went beyond the reach of the local Indians. However, in the good years when buffalo were accessible, large quantities of meat were traded at the fort by the Indians. A journal entry in 1833 reads: "Crees finished their trade which amounted to 3160 lbs. dried [meat] 1950 lbs grease 60 lbs Beat meat."

Fort Pelly relied heavily upon hunting and fishing to procure the food required for its own needs. There were several excellent fisheries where an abundant supply of fish could usually be obtained. For example, according to the fort's December 10, 1825, journal entry, the fishery in the Porcupine Hills yielded between two and three thousand fish during a ten-day period. In addition, every effort was made to grow as much garden produce as possible. In 1833 the fort journal recorded that 96 bushels of barley and 400 bushels of potatoes had been successfully harvested. Predictably, frosts, drought, floods, and grasshopper infestations all too frequently destroyed the crops.

Fort Pelly was a busy place. The enormous amounts of firewood needed to heat the buildings during the winter had to be cut, hauled, and split. Pit saws were constantly in use where men converted logs into sawn lumber. Boats, both the York boat type as well as bateaux, scows, and small boats, were made in the fort's boatyard. The carts needed for overland travel when shallow water made river travel impossible were also built.

As headquarters for the Swan River district, Fort Pelly received the goods (the "outfit") from York Factory allotted for the district; these after being sorted and repacked were transported to the respective posts. Each spring the furs and provisions that had been traded over the winter throughout the district were collected and made ready for shipment to Swan River as the first step in their journey to York Factory. Fort clerks were kept busy preparing and checking the huge volume of invoices, indents, and bills of lading that this heavy movement of goods and furs into and out of the fort entailed.

In the winter of 1842–43 Fort Pelly suffered the misfortune that

494

was the fate of so many forts. It was destroyed by fire. Chief Trader Cuthbert Cumming, who had just succeeded Chief Trader William Todd, immediately began the task of rebuilding the fort. Cumming remained at the post but one season. Then for the next ten years Fort Pelly was under the direction of a succession of men. Chief Trader William Todd returned and was in charge of the post from 1845 to 1849 and again in 1851. Finally, Chief Factor William J. Christie, son of Chief Factor Alexander Christie, came to the fort in 1852 and remained there for six years. It was during his administration that, in 1856–57, Fort Pelly was moved to a new site about one-quarter mile to the southeast. The move was dictated by the periodic flooding of the Assiniboine, which, although it did not reach the fort buildings, inundated enough of the surrounding area to cause considerable inconvenience.

Free traders posed a constant threat to the company's control of the trade. However, in spite of the competition from them, Fort Pelly traded an impressive number of furs of all kinds: muskrats, mink, marten, lynx, fisher, beaver, badger, otter, wolverine, wolves, foxes, bears, and moose.

When Captain Palliser during the course of his journey across Canada in 1857–60 visited the newly relocated Fort Pelly in October of 1857, he found the fort still in the process of construction. He commented that it reminded him of a "commodious shooting lodge, similar to those at home in the highlands of Scotland."

The crew of sixteen men assigned to Fort Pelly was busy working on the buildings for the new post. Six men were laboring in the three saw pits converting logs into lumber for buildings and for boats. Two carpenters were hard at work laying floors, roofing the newly constructed buildings, and endeavoring to get all the dwellings, storehouses, shops, and stables completed and ready for use. The blacksmith kept the fire glowing in the forge hearth and the anvil ringing as he turned out the variety of items needed both by Fort Pelly and by the other posts in the Swan River district: nails, ax heads, building hardware, fish spears, steel traps, and harness equipment. Over in the boatyard and carpenter shop, boats, carts, sleds, and toboggans were being turned out in large numbers.

By the end of 1859, when the Earl of Southesk arrived at Fort Pelly during the course of his journey through the Hudson's Bay Company territories, the post was virtually completed. The Earl recorded his impression of the fort in December of that year:

Fort Pelly, pleasantly situated on rising ground, is a new, square, white-washed cottage with small dormer windows in the roof, and offers better accommodation than any house I have seen since leaving Red River. Various out-houses for stores, etc., surround it at the back and sides, but the Saulteaux Indians of the district are so peaceable that no stockade has been thought necessary. Looking from the front windows the eye ranges over a large extent of flat country, swamp and willows first, and then an interminable border of poplars interspersed with pines.

In the immediate foreground stand the remains of the old Fort, partly occupied by the servants and partly converted into cattle-houses. Not far off flows the Assiniboine, here an insignificant stream scarce twenty yards wide, and not deep. In spring there is water enough for boats, but in summer the channel is nearly dry.

The Earl mentioned the fort's livestock and farming activities: "There is a well-shaped bull, a cross between Ayrshire and Shorthorn, there are also a number of cows, some pure Ayrshires,—about seventy altogether. They farm a little, growing potatoes and barley; turnips will also grow, but are not cultivated to any extent." He also noticed that on Sunday there was morning service at the old fort, conducted by the Reverend Mr. Settee—a gentleman of Cree origin, who had been appointed to the spiritual charge of the Swan River district by the Church Missionary Society. The earl added that "Mr. Settee is an agreeable man and a good missionary; but here, as in most places, the Indians obstinately refuse to be Christians, though many of them are ready enough to submit to the ceremony of baptism."

Chief Trader Robert Campbell was posted to Fort Pelly in 1863. Campbell, an experienced trader and explorer, veteran of hardship posts on the Yukon, Dease, Liard, Pelly, and Mackenzie rivers, was charged with the task of restoring the trade of the Swan River district to its former prosperous condition. Upon his arrival at the post, he discovered that the district had been so poorly provisioned that it had been necessary to slaughter valuable domestic cattle to provide food both for the people living at the fort as well as for the boat crews traveling to York Factory with the year's returns. Furthermore, no indents for the district outfit and men's equipment had been prepared to accompany the returns. Fortunately, buffalo were plentiful and accessible that year, so serious food shortages were averted.

At about this time, the traditional route into the interior by way of York Factory was gradually being abandoned. The growth and spread of American railways and steamship lines enabled the Hudson's Bay Company to develop a new route to Fort Garry via St. Paul, Minnesota. From St. Paul the goods were transported on the last leg of their journey to Fort Garry by river and Red River cart brigades. This new way proved both quicker and considerably cheaper. By 1861 the shipments to and from Fort Pelly for the Swan River district were utilizing the new route.

At the end of his first year's residence at Fort Pelly, Campbell was justifiably satisfied with the progress he had made. It was obvious when the district returns were packed for shipment to York Factory that each of the posts had made a good trade. One item alone consisted of more than four thousand buffalo robes. In addition to the returns shipped, a large quantity of pemmican and provisions was safely stockpiled to meet the needs of the transport brigades.

Campbell devoted much attention to the fort's herd of horses. Ever since its early days in the 1820s Fort Pelly had been a horse- and cattle-breeding station. It possessed great natural advantages, situated as it was amid the excellent pasturage of a well-watered and wood-sheltered country. It was also safely outside the range of the worst tribes of native horse thieves. Campbell continued the policy of upbreeding the native horses by crossing them with stallions, such as Melbourne, which the company had imported. This valuable stallion and his numerous offspring roamed the parklike prairies surrounding Fort Pelly under the watchful care of an Indian horse guard who made sure they did not range too far. Before long Fort Pelly's band of horses was both numerous and of a fine quality and constituted the best item of the district's trade. During Captain Palliser's 1857 visit to Fort Pelly he commented on the post's superior breed of both horses and cattle, noting that there was "a large number of brood mares, and a very fine breed of horned cattle; these wander wild in the woods, but return to the precincts of the fort to eat the hay provided for them in the winter months."

From his headquarters at Fort Pelly Campbell skillfully achieved one of the main objectives of the company, that of securing the large amounts of provisions obtained from the hunts out on the prairies. The Indians had to be properly supplied for the hunt, as well as the company men who followed the Indian and half-breed hunters and traded their goods for pemmican, dried meat, grease, tongues, and robes.

After a few years of Chief Factor Campbell's (he had been raised to that rank in 1867) energetic and capable leadership, the trade for the district was once again on a prosperous basis. In the summer of 1869, when a smallpox epidemic struck the Indians along the U.S. boundary and threatened those in the Swan River area, Campbell's prompt action in vaccinating them was so effective that no one in his district became infected, whereas in the Saskatchewan district over six hundred Indians perished from the disease.

The following year (1870) the troubles at the Red River settlement erupted into the resistance movement led by Louis Riel. Campbell, no stranger to facing hostile attacks, ordered all the posts in his district to be put on alert, to take adequate defense measures, and, if attacked, to defend themselves and the company property. At Fort Pelly he distributed caches of provisions, ammunition, and other goods around the fort, collected an ample supply of arms and ammunition in the main house to withstand any attack, and in the cellar put a sufficient amount of gunpowder to blow up the place if such an act of desperation were required. Fearing that the year's returns might be confiscated by Riel if he sent them to Red River, Campbell decided to transport them by cart to the Hudson's Bay Company post on the upper Red River in Georgetown, Minnesota, which was on the direct route to St. Paul, the railhead. Although this involved a hazardous journey over trackless prairies through Sioux country, he felt it would offer less of a risk to the company's returns. Accordingly, on April 15 Campbell, his wife and family, and a brigade of seventy carts loaded with furs left Fort Pelly headed for Georgetown and St. Paul, which they eventually reached without incident. After getting the brigade well on its way on the first lap of the journey toward Georgetown, Campbell returned to Fort Pelly and joined the brigade that took the balance of the season's returns by the Swan River route to Norway House and thence to York Factory.

The year 1870 marked the end of a two-century era. The Hudson's Bay Company surrendered its territories to Canada, retaining only its trading posts and a certain amount of land surrounding them. A few years later Fort Pelly was superseded as headquarters for the Swan River district by Fort Ellice.

Clerk Adam McBeath took charge of Fort Pelly in 1874. Under his experienced management the fort, although now simply a fur trading post, continued to function as one of the best and most profitable of the company's fur posts. Trading continued, but much of the old way of life was rapidly changing or disappearing. Steamboats carrying freight and passengers began to appear on the rivers. By 1881 the steamboat *Marquette,* a flat-bottomed stern-wheeler, succeeded in navigating the shallow, twisting Assiniboine as far as Fort Pelly.

Clerk Angus McBeath, nephew to Adam McBeath, came to Fort Pelly in 1890 and served there throughout the remaining years of its existence. By this time there were more than one hundred families in the surrounding area, and Fort Pelly became the business and social center of this growing community. McBeath and his two daughters presided in the factor's house.

In the rear was the large half-empty old-style post-on-sill warehouse of hewn logs, its walls plastered with clay, its roof covered with hand-made shakes, a relic from the earlier days, when it was crammed to the rafters with furs and trade goods. The Hudson's Bay Company ensign continued to fly proudly from the fort's flagpole, but signs of decay were beginning to be increasingly evident throughout the fort.

The coming of both steamboat and railway to the region brought an end to the need for the services provided by the trading post. The railway passed Fort Pelly just near enough to virtually destroy the mixed trade with settlers as well as the Indians who had formerly patronized the company's sales shop. Trade steadily diminished to such a low level that in June of 1912 Fort Pelly closed its doors, thereby ending its eighty-eight years of operation at the elbow of the Assiniboine River.

To find the site of Fort Pelly took considerable persistence, since there were no helpful directional signs to point the way. We knew that the fort had been located near the peak of the elbow on the east side of the Assiniboine. Therefore, relying on our indispensable car compass and a provincial grid road map, we followed a maze of side roads until eventually we found what we were seeking. By the side of the road we spotted an inconspicuous low provincial fieldstone monument bearing a plaque that identified the area as the site of the first Fort Pelly. It was a typical grassland opening in the parklands. The flat prairie extended in all directions, broken only by extensive clumps of willow and cottonwood. At the time of our visit in September, the grasses, which grew thick and tall, as well as the abundant Canada thistle, goldenrod, and pearly everlasting, had all gone to seed. Only the bright green of the low-growing wild rosebushes with their red hips and the silver-green of the wolf brush brightened the drab browns and tans of the grasslands.

The drizzling rain that was falling did not deter us from wandering about the area and photographing it from many directions. We were able to discern numerous topographical features, such as embankments, trenches, and depressions—all indicators of the earlier presence of the buildings that once stood here. However, the dense mantle of vegetation that covered the entire area served to obscure these features to a considerable extent.

Today nothing at Fort Pelly remains aboveground. Only the archaeologist's spade can uncover its remains in the soil below. The prairie opening where once the busy fort was located has reverted back to its natural state—has been reclaimed by the native grasses and flowers of the plains. Noises that once characterized the fort have stilled. It is now the song of the western meadowlark and the sparrow that is heard. Fort Pelly is indeed gone, but through the preservation of the place where it once stood its story will always be remembered.

Fort Vancouver

After eighty-four days of rapid canoe travel from York Factory on Hudson's Bay, George Simpson arrived at the company's Fort George, at the mouth of the Columbia River. Here he spent the winter of 1824–25. Although the Hudson's Bay Company was continuing to conduct their trade at Fort George, it was only on the sufferance of the Americans, since this post had been formally returned to the United States in 1818, after the close of the War of 1812.

At this time the location of the boundary between the lands claimed by the United States and Great Britain west of the Rocky Mountains to the Pacific was being fiercely disputed by the two governments. It seemed quite probable, however, that at the very least, all land south of the Columbia would become American territory. In anticipation of this, Simpson had been instructed by the Hudson's Bay London Committee to abandon Fort George (located on the south bank of the Columbia) and build a new post somewhere on the north side of the river. The directive read: "We approve of the removal of the depôt from Fort George to Fort Vancouver, and expect that much benefit will be derived from raising here all the provisions that can be required for the whole of our trade West of the Mountains."

Further urgency for this move was supplied by the persistent rumors that the United States was planning to establish a colony at the mouth of the Columbia during the spring and summer of 1825. This would inevitably result in their taking possession of Fort George. The loss of this fort would pose serious difficulties for the company's operations on the lower Columbia if no alternative trading post had been established.

So, shortly after his arrival at Fort George in November, Simpson sent Chief Factors John McLoughlin (who was to have charge of the new fort) and Alexander Kennedy upriver to look for a suitable site for the new establishment. They selected a spot just above the confluence of the Willamette and Columbia about seventy-five miles from the mouth of the Columbia. Known locally as *le jolie prairie* (Belle Vue), it was an opening in the forest about three miles long and a mile deep. It was bounded on the north by a low bluff atop a gently rising slope bordering the north bank of the river. Under McLoughlin's vigorous direction, work was begun on the new fort at once, so that by March two warehouses and a dwelling had been constructed as well as a palisade of thirteen-foot pickets enclosing the post.

In March 16, 1825, Governor Simpson left Fort George to begin his return journey east. He wrote in his journal for that date: "All the valuable property having been transported to the new Establishment at Belle Vue Point, Dr. McLoughlin accompanied us to take charge thereof leaving Mr. McKenzie, Cartie & Eight men at Fort George where they are to remain for two or three weeks until the few remaining articles are removed." Two days later (on March 18) Simpson described the new fort in his journal: "The Establishment is beautifully situated on the top of a bank about 1-1/4 miles from the Water side commanding an extensive view of the River the surrounding Country and the fine plain below which is watered by two very pretty small Lakes and studed as if artifically by clumps of Fine Timber. The Fort is well picketted covering a space of about 3/4ths of an acre and the buildings already completed are a Dwelling House, two good Stores an Indian Hall and temporary quarters for the people. It will in Two Years hence be the finest place in North America . . ." The next day Simpson recorded the christening of the new fort: "At Sun rise mustered all the people to hoist the Flag Staff of the new Establishment and in presence of the Gentlemen, Servants, Chiefs & Indians I Baptised it by breaking a Bottle of Rum on the Flag Staff and repeating the following words in a loud voice: 'In behalf of the Honble Hudsons Bay Coy I hereby name this Establishment Fort Vancouver God Save King George the 4th' with three cheers. Gave a couple a Drams to the people and Indians on the Occasion."

One of the major attractions of the Belle Vue location was its evident suitability for both the raising of crops and the pasturing of livestock. One of the first tasks undertaken after the move there was the planting of 100 barrels of potatoes. In addition, one-quarter-acre of beans and three acres of peas were sown. The thirty-one cattle, seventeen pigs, and several workhorses brought from Fort George, the nucleus for the fort's future thriving livestock production, were enjoying the abundant succulent pasture.

The one major drawback to the fort's location was its distance from water. It was necessary to keep one man constantly at work hauling water in a tank cart to the fort from the river one and one-quarter miles away.

Partly because of the unsettled ownership status of the Columbia River and partly because Governor Simpson felt that the Fraser River would provide better access to the fur-rich New Caledonia district than the Columbia, he intended Fort Vancouver to be merely a trading post subsidiary to the main headquarters he planned to construct at the mouth of the Fraser. It was thought that Fort Vancouver would maintain the company's presence on the Columbia and its agricultural activities would lend support to the British claim to the land north of the river.

However, when Simpson during the course of his second cross-country journey from York Factory in 1828 experienced for himself the wild waters of the Fraser and lower Thompson rivers, he was forced to concede that the Fraser was not navigable and that the fort that had been constructed at its mouth could not, therefore, become the center of the company's northwest trade. The Columbia River would have to remain the company's highway into the interior, and Fort Vancouver would have to be expanded into the headquarters and entrepôt for the company's transmontane operations. Simpson had reached this decision by the time he reached Fort Vancouver on October 25, 1828, at the conclusion of his journey.

During the three years that had elapsed since his first visit, much had been accomplished under the direction of Chief Factor McLoughlin. The fields had produced 4,000 bushels of potatoes and more than 3,000 bushels of various grains. Cattle had increased from 31 to 153, pigs from 17 to 200. A sawmill had been built a few miles upriver. Fort Vancouver had advanced a long way toward becoming self-sufficient.

Simpson's report to the London Committee reflected his satisfaction. He wrote that although Fort Vancouver's Indian trade was not large, it had attained the main objective for which it had been established, "that of rendering ourselves independent of Foreign aid in regard to the means of subsistence." Because of its extensive farming operations, it was no longer necessary for valuable space in the holds of the company supply ships arriving from England to be taken up with foodstuffs for the district.

It was quickly realized that for its expanded role the present fort was located too far back (one and one-quarter miles) from both the river docks and an accessible supply of water. To overcome these limitations, the fort was dismantled and moved to a new site three-quarters of a mile downstream and within 1,300 feet of the river. Work on the relocated fort was begun in the spring of 1829. Before long a massive palisade had been erected enclosing an area approximately 326 feet square. (This was later enlarged to 750 feet by 450 feet.) Within soon rose the numerous buildings required to house the fort's many and varied activities: warehouses, artisans' shops (cooper, carpenter, blacksmith), Indian shop, dispensary, men's quarters, bakery, kitchen, chief factor's dwelling, office, church, jail, and a stone-brick powder magazine. Somewhat later a three-story bastion with eight three-pound cannon was erected at the northwest corner of the palisade. Within the stockade two rock-lined wells filled through seepage from the river provided water. The main entrance to the fort was through two massive gates (wide enough for wagons and carts) in the stockade facing the river. A smaller gate in the opposite (north) wall led to the garden and orchard. A small pond just to the southwest of the fort enclosure provided water for the livestock and by means of a dredged outlet to the Columbia provided a protected anchorage for small boats and bateaux within 600 feet of the fort.

Outside the walls of the fort to the south and west were grouped a vast array of buildings on the plain between the fort and the river. The sixty or more cabins of married servants, Sandwich Islanders, French-Canadians, Iroquois, and other employees formed the nucleus of a small village. The large salmon warehouse was located at the head of the main wharf. On the west side of the pond were the numerous barns, horse and ox stables, pig sheds, and granaries required by the farming and livestock operations, while on the east side were the tan pits, cooper's shop, and blacksmith's quarters. Close by along the river-bank were the large boat sheds used for building and storing bateaux, the salt house, and the hospital.

To the north of the fort were more servants' cabins, a church, a horse-powered gristmill, and a schoolhouse. An orchard was set out just beyond the north wall. Next to it was a vegetable garden neatly laid out in rows bordered on each side with strawberry plants. Culti-vated fields extended on all sides. Indian lodges, often as many as thirty or forty, were pitched under the large oak trees outside the fort walls.

Fort Vancouver rapidly became a community of some seven hun-dred people. It soon developed into the great provisioning center of the Columbia department. It also pioneered in the successful export of lumber and salmon from the Columbia and Fraser rivers, both of which contributed significantly to the company's profits.

When Fort Vancouver was first established, Simpson clearly spelled out the objectives he expected McLoughlin to accomplish from his new post. In brief these were: end traffic in alcohol; vigorously pur-sue coastal trade and thereby eliminate the American competition; en-courage trade with the Russians; complete the construction of Fort Langley at the mouth of the Fraser River; totally trap out all the fur-bearers in the area south of the Columbia (i.e., the land likely to be-come American territory); probe southward into California with trapping expeditions; and engage in extensive farming and livestock production sufficient to supply not only the food needs for the entire district, but also a surplus for sale.

This was quite an assignment, but McLoughlin was equal to the task. One by one, he achieved these objectives. Henceforth rum was no longer a standard item of trade. McLoughlin's policy was that "we Sell no liquor to them [Indians] on any account, Selling liquor is prohibited by a positive order of the Committee." Sometimes, it is true that competition reduced this policy to: "If the Americans [or Russians] give no Liquor to Indians neither must we."

By a ten-year contract that Simpson concluded on behalf of the Hudson's Bay Company with the Russian-American Company in 1839, in return for an annual rent payment of 2,000 land otter skins, the Hudson's Bay Company acquired trade and navigation rights in Russian-held territory along the northern Pacific coast to the exclusion of the Americans, as well as the monopoly of supplying the Russians with flour, peas, barley, salt beef, salt butter, and ham, all of which would come chiefly from the extensive agricultural operations at Fort Vancouver.

McLoughlin directed the trapping expeditions under Peter Skene Ogden into the Snake River country south of the Columbia that so successfully trapped out the beaver that the competition from American fur traders was completely eliminated.

Finally, Fort Vancouver became the provisioning post both for the company ships engaged in the growing coastal trade and for the trading posts established along the northern coast. Their herds provided beef for the company ships; their grain fields and gardens supplied many of the other provisions needed by the interior posts of the New Caledonia and Columbia districts.

From these districts and from the newly established posts on the north Pacific coast such as Forts Simpson, Nass, and McLoughlin, the furs came by coastal vessel and by river canoe and bateau to Fort Vancouver. Here they were processed—sorted, cleaned, graded, and packed ready for shipment in the long passage around Cape Horn to London.

From the holds of the company's supply ships the enormous cargo of trade goods was carried into the fort's warehouses. There it was sorted and repacked for forwarding to the various interior posts by canoe and packhorse brigade and for loading into the small company vessels for the coastal trade. In addition, lumber produced by the fort's sawmill, as well as casks of salted salmon, was shipped to the Sandwich Islands. Within a few years Fort Vancouver had become, in fact, the company's provisioning and trade *entrepôt* of the Northwest.

In May of 1833 the company ship *Ganymede* docked at Fort Vancouver. One of its passengers who had made the eight-month passage from London, was Dr. William F. Tolmie, newly engaged by the Hudson's Bay Company. He described his arrival and first days at the fort in his diary:

Saturday, May 4 [1832] . . . reached our destined port after nearly an eight months pilgrimage . . . Our approach being announced to Govr. McLoughlin, he appeared in shirt & trowsers on the stair case of Common Hall & welcomed us with a cordial shake of the hand. Sat down in dining hall . . . Our fare was excellent, consisting of superb salmon, fresh butter and bread, tea & rich milk & mealy potatoes. . . . Young apples are in rich blossom & extensive beds sowed with culinary vegetables are laid out in nice order . . . From what I have seen of Govr. like him . . .

Sunday, May 5 . . . attended Episcopalian morning service read by the Govr. in dining hall. The square was now occupied with upwards of 100 horses & Canadians were busy lassoing some for use. . . . All around were herds of beautiful cattle cropping the rich herbage, . . . horses, goats & swine seen in every direction . . . on the lochs wild duck abundant . . .

Wednesday, May 8 . . . walked along the plateau by the border of wood now admiring the rich groves of lupin seen amidst the trees mixing the handsome columbines, sunflowers & a great variety of other herbaceous plants . . . glimpses of the magnificent Columbia . . . showed it to flow placidly & majestically along its southern shore . . . in the background the colossal Mount Hood . . . reared his lofty summit above the clouds. The tout ensemble was the finest combination of beauty & grandeur I have ever beheld.

Sunday, May 12 . . . the Dr unfolded his views regarding the breeding of cattle here. He thinks that when the trade in furs is knocked up which at no very distant day must happen, the servants of Coy. may turn their attention to the rearing of cattle for the sake of the hides & tallow, in which he says business could be carried on to a greater amount, than that of the furs collected west of the Rocky Mountains. Furs are already becoming scarce & the present supply is obtained by an almost exterminating system of hunting.

Over this vast and busy capital of the West, Chief Factor McLoughlin ruled with firmness, good judgment, and justice. Within the fort the social distinctions based on rank in the company's organization and hallowed by long British tradition were carefully observed.

The chief factor's dwelling, the "Big House," was a one-story hipped-roof structure seventy feet long by forty feet deep. It was elevated about five feet above the ground, leaving space for a cellar used for wine storage. The centrally located front entrance was reached by two opposing curving stairways leading to a vine-shaded porch that extended across the entire front of the house. The central doorway was flanked on each side by three four-by-six small-paned and shuttered windows. On the ground in front of the porch were two black iron cannon lending an air of authority and importance to the dwelling. A softer touch was provided by the small flower garden protected by a low picket fence on either side of the stairway at the base of the porch.

Within the "Big House" were ten rooms equally divided by a spacious central hallway. Chief Factor McLoughlin and his family occupied the rooms to the right, while Chief Trader Douglas and his family lived in the other half. A large dining hall extended across the rear of the house. Here the commissioned officers of the company, clerks, chaplains, physician, ships' captains, and visiting guests of importance ate their meals. Chief Factor McLoughlin presided from his place at the head of a table covered with white linen and set with blue-and-white Spode china, sparkling glassware, and silver. Candles in silver candelabra cast a cheery glow over the tempting and abundant array of food brought to the table from the adjacent kitchen. No hard liquor was served and wine only sparingly. The conversation was intelligent, witty, and interesting, but not participated in by the junior clerks, who, occupying the bottom rung of the organizational ladder, sat at the foot of the table and were expected to speak only if spoken to. There were no women seated at this dining table. They, even the chief factor's wife, ate their meals in their own quarters.

Chief Factor John McLoughlin was a 250-pound giant of a man, six feet, two inches tall, with shoulder-length white hair, bushy eyebrows, piercing blue eyes, and a rather stern countenance. Despite his somewhat formidable appearance, he possessed qualities of great kindness, compassion, and courtesy. Through the gates of his fort he welcomed and gave succor whenever it was needed to an increasing stream of missionaries, such as the Whitmans and Spaldings, destitute American settlers and starving immigrants, various scientists and explorers, and many others, even competing traders such as the American Jedidiah Smith.

In the 1840s relations between McLoughlin and Governor Simpson became increasingly strained, in large part due to their disagreement over the best way to pursue the company's coastal trade. Simpson advocated the use of coastal trading ships, whereas McLoughlin believed land-based forts on the coast were more effective. In addition, McLoughlin's generous extension of credit and efforts to help the American settlers get established in the Willamette valley, though at first approved by Simpson, were later harshly condemned. The final blow to their relationship was Simpson's response to the murder of McLoughlin's son at Fort Stikine in 1842. Simpson implied that young

McLoughlin was drunk and at fault and thus would not press charges against the murderers.

Matters reached a climax when on May 13, 1845, the Governor and London Committee reduced McLoughlin's sole authority at Fort Vancouver by creating a Board of Management for the fort to be composed of McLoughlin, James Douglas, and Peter Skene Ogden. At the same time, reflecting his lessened authority, they lowered his salary. McLoughlin was given no opportunity to defend his actions but forced to face a *fait accompli*. To a man of his pride and experience that was intolerable, and he could not accept such a reduction in his status, implying as it did a loss of confidence by the company in his management abilities. His response was inevitable. In a letter dated November 20, 1845, he gave notice of his resignation from the company.

For the remaining years of its existence Fort Vancouver was administered by the Board of Management, which at first consisted of three men: James Douglas, Peter Skene Ogden, and John Work.

In December of 1846 Paul Kane, the noted Canadian artist, arrived at Fort Vancouver, where he was greeted by Chief Factors Douglas and Ogden and entertained with the most liberal hospitality for about two months. Kane described the fort in the account he wrote of his travels, *Wanderings of an Artist among the Indians of North America:*

Fort Vancouver—is the largest post in the Hudson's Bay Company's dominons, and has usually two chief factors, with eight or ten clerks and 200 voyageurs, residing there.—The buildings are enclosed by strong pickets about sixteen feet high, with bastions for cannon at the corners. The men, with their Indian wives, live in log huts near the margin of the river, forming a little village—quite a Babel of languages, as the inhabitants are a mixture of English, French, Iroquois, Sandwich Islanders, Crees and Chinooks.

The Columbia is here, ninety miles from its mouth, a mile and a quarter wide; the surrounding country is well wooded and fertile, the oak and pine being of the finest description. A large farm is cultivated about eight miles up the river, producing more grain than the fort consumes; the surplus being sent to the Sandwich Islands and the Russian dominions. They have immense herds of domestic horned cattle, which run wild in unknown numbers; and sheep and horses are equally numerous. When first introduced from California, Dr. M'Laughlin, the gentleman then in charge, would not allow any of the horned cattle to be killed for the use of the establishment until their numbers had reached 600, by which means they have multiplied beyond calculation."

The Oregon Treaty of 1846 established the forty-ninth parallel as the boundary between the United States and Britain. Fort Vancouver, being on the north bank of the Columbia River, was situated in American territory. This forced the Hudson's Bay Company to reassess the fort's role as the company's main transmontane headquarters and Pacific depot. There was general agreement that the fort's location was plagued by numerous drawbacks. It was ninety miles inland from the ocean. The infamous and dangerous Columbia bar at the mouth of the river was a serious navigational hazard causing not only lengthy delay due to adverse wind but also the occasional loss of a vessel, cargo, and crew. Furthermore, the fort was not conveniently sited for servicing the northern coastal trading posts. Finally, it was subject to frequent outbreaks of intermittent fever (i.e., malaria).

In October of 1846 the Governor and London Committee informed the Board of Management that the new fort then being erected on the southern tip of Vancouver Island was more advantageous than Fort Vancouver for the Pacific depot. Three years later the committee issued orders that the company's operations be transferred from Fort Vancouver to Fort Victoria. Ogden and Douglas both argued that the new fort was not yet ready to handle the current harvest of furs or the year's shipment of supplies from England, but London remained adamant. Accordingly, on May 31, 1849, Chief Factor Douglas, accompanied by his family, left Fort Vancouver to take over his new assignment as head of Fort Victoria.

Ogden and Work were left to run Fort Vancouver. In 1849 they were able to establish a profitable market in San Francisco for their flour and lumber, but this was short-lived. The Fort Vancouver sales shop was operating at a loss due to the necessity of paying American custom duties on all their imported British goods at a stiff 35 percent on prime cost.

Fort Vancouver's days of dominance and prosperity were rapidly coming to an end. In Douglas's words, "cattle all vanished—no pork to spare—wretched crops—the Companys land covered with squatters, and no returns: What more have we to Lose?" Elsewhere in 1852 he wrote: "Prosperity has for ever fled from that post [Fort Vancouver]—and without a complete change of system it will be a burden to the trade—."

In 1853 an organizational change for the posts west of the Rocky Mountains was made by the Hudson's Bay Company. All posts in United States territory outfitted from Fort Vancouver were to constitute the "Oregon Department" and be administered by a Board of Management. Peter Skene Ogden and John Ballenden were the first members, although Ballenden was soon replaced by Dugald Mactavish. Ogden, who died in 1855, was succeeded by John Work.

Although the Oregon Treaty had guaranteed the possessory rights of the Hudson's Bay Company to the lands they occupied on American territory and to the joint use of the Columbia River, prospects for continuing a profitable operation were not encouraging. Pressure from increasing numbers of American settlers hungry for land, fierce competition from American freetraders, and the inevitable organization of American territorial government all made the company's position increasingly untenable. Squatters were steadily encroaching on company lands. There was a strongly held belief in the United States that when the Hudson's Bay Company's License to Trade expired in 1859, their possessory rights would also be terminated.

At Fort Vancouver, for example, the U.S. military reservation now occupied what had been the fort's farm- and pastureland. An army officer requested that the large salmon warehouse at the head of the company wharf be torn down to make room for an army expansion project. Without waiting for Dugald Mactavish's consent, the army proceeded with their construction. When Mactavish protested, he was told that except for the buildings within the stockade, all now belonged to the U.S. Army.

In 1860 Alexander Grant Dallas, who had become Governor after the death of George Simpson, decided it was fruitless to continue to retain possession of Fort Vancouver. The fur trade was ruined. For the year 1858 the company had made a net gain of only twenty-nine pounds from its operations in American territory. American settlers were closing in on all sides. Accordingly, on May 10, 1860, he gave the order to abandon Fort Vancouver, and by June 14 the last of the company servants had walked out through the massive gates for the final time and the fort was left empty and deserted. Six years later the aging buildings and stockade burned to the ground. Within a short time the crops planted by the army covered and destroyed the last traces of the site where for forty years the mighty Fort Vancouver had once stood.

One hundred and twenty-two years later we visited the site of Fort Vancouver. Under the auspices of the National Park Service, Historic Sites, the massive walls of the fort's reconstructed palisade rise once again on their original location on the north side of the Columbia River almost opposite the modern city of Portland, Oregon.

As we approached the fort along the dirt roadway leading to the back (north) gate, we passed between an extensive orchard and a flourishing garden "sowed with culinary vegetables . . . laid out in nice order."

Once inside the gate we were impressed with the really tremendous size of the enclosure. As yet, only a few of the many buildings that once filled the compound have been reconstructed. Archaeological evidence has made it possible to erect these replica buildings on their original location.

We walked across the southeast corner of the compound to a long rectangular building that housed under one roof both the Indian trade shop and the resident doctor's combined dispensary and living quarters.

We entered first into the Indian store. Here shelves lined all the walls and were filled with the usual assortment of yard goods, colorful kerchiefs, caps, blankets, boots, chinaware, utensils, kegs, and clay pipes. From rods suspended from the rafters hung a variety of brightly colored dresses and shirts, trousers, strings of beads of all sizes and colors, twists of tobacco, and powder horns. Trade rifles, traps, and paddles were displayed on the walls. Over the counter was the enormous balance arm used for weighing purchases. A high desk with open ledger stood off in one corner. Contrary to the usual practice followed at most trading posts, at Fort Vancouver the Indians had free access into the fort's interior and could enter the trade shop unrestricted to trade their furs for the goods so alluringly displayed there.

The west half of this building was occupied by the fort's doctor. In the dispensary the cabinets, cupboards, and shelves were filled with neatly arranged bottles and phials each meticulously labeled, mortars and pestles, apothecary scales, medical books, and a variety of surgical instruments laid out in orderly precision. Standing close by was the sheet-draped operating table. On top of a plain slant-top desk were the doctors' ledgers, where each patient's treatment was recorded. Opening directly off the dispensary was space occupied by six narrow wood-framed beds. The doctor's living quarters, which consisted of a bedroom and a combined living-dining room, took up the far end of the building.

Next we walked over to the blacksmith's shop at the southeast angle of the stockade. Within the rather gloomy interior was a huge brick forge. A large hand-operated bellows was suspended from the ceiling on each side of the forge. A bewildering assortment of blacksmith's tools hung from iron racks on the walls and in front of the forge. Also present were anvils, tempering barrels, and moulds. On a small table were displayed a sampling of the many items made in the shop. These included items used for trade such as ax heads, fish spears, awls, traps, knives of various shapes, and Jew's harps. In addition, nails, hinges, and other hardware items needed for the construction and maintenance of the fort were made.

The bakery we visited next was a whitewashed building set half inside and half outside the east palisade wall to minimize the effect of any potential fire. This gable-roofed structure, one and one-half stories high, contained two large fire brick ovens ranged side by side along one wall. At one end of the large room were flour barrels, a heavy iron beam balance, and enormous wooden mixing bins. On long wooden tables in the center of the room the bakers rolled and shaped the dough into loaves or flat biscuits. The long-handled peels and rakes were stored on the rafters overhead. These were implements used for getting loaves and biscuits into and out of the ovens and for raking out the coals when the oven, having reached the right temperature, was ready to be used for baking.

Between the bakery and a small building used as a washhouse just to the west was one of the two stone-lined wells that provided water for the fort.

Nearby along the north palisade wall was the main kitchen building. It was directly behind the chief factor's house and connected to it by a covered passageway. Within this building was a laundry room complete with box stove and copper tub for boiling clothes. The kitchen proper with its big open fireplace and brick oven occupied a most important place in the life of the fort, for here all the meals for the commissioned officers, their families, and numerous visiting dignitaries were prepared. A vast array of pots, pans, and various cooking utensils hung from the ceiling beams in front of the hearth. Canisters, crocks, bottles, and jugs filled the shelves. Barrels and water casks were pushed against the walls. At one end of the room on a low table were the wooden tubs used for washing dishes. On the wall above was the wooden rack for storing the plates. The large table in the center of the kitchen was used during food preparation. It was also where the kitchen staff ate their meals. The miscellaneous collection of dinnerware and cutlery used by them was kept in an open-shelf dresser. The pantry at the foot of the stairs leading directly upstairs to the dining hall was lined with compartmented shelves containing the lovely Spode dinner service, including plates, bowls, sauce dishes, platters, pitchers, and covered tureens, as well as silverware, silver serving dishes, crystal decanters, and an abundant supply of candles.

Today from the exterior the "Big House" looks just as it did when McLoughlin and Douglas lived there. The two cannon still symbolically guard the entrance. The two curving stairways rising to the vine-shaped porch extending across the front of the building have been faithfully reproduced. Within, a central hallway separates the living quarters of the two factors. Their living and bedroom furnishings reflect the quiet elegance and gracious living of nineteenth-century England. Polished mahogany of chairs and tables, rugs, window draperies, gilt-framed paintings, leather-bound books—all characterize these rooms. In the mess hall the long table flanked by matching mahogany side chairs was set for dinner, complete with spotless white linen, blue Spode dinnerware, sparkling glasses, and silver candelabra. Several large covered tureens and crystal decanters graced the mahogany sideboard. The only things missing were the guests and the food. These we must supply from our imagination.

We walked along the north palisade wall to the bastion erected at the northwest corner and climbed up the steep stairway to the top level. This was octagonal and fitted with square portholes to accommodate the battery of eight cannon. These cannon were seldom fired—usually only to salute arriving ships or on some ceremonial occasion. They never had to be used in any hostile action.

As we slowly headed back toward our motor home, our feet aching and ourselves somewhat wilted from the 102-degree temperature, we reflected that although we realized that everything we had seen at Fort Vancouver was a complete and total reconstruction, only the location of the buildings and stockade being original, we were, by means of these excellent reconstructions, able to capture in our imagination something of what the fort must have looked like during its days of operation. Archaeological excavations are still ongoing, revealing the sites of many of the other buildings that once were crowded within this stockade. Perhaps someday some of these, too, can be reconstructed to further round out the re-creation of Fort Vancouver. In fact, plans are well advanced for the erection of one of the large warehouses along the south of the compound.

Fort Langley

The establishment of Fort Langley in 1827 was the outcome of George Simpson's fact-finding journey to the Pacific coast in 1824 and of his increasing, albeit reluctant, acceptance of the strong possibility of American domination of the Columbia River country.

As he wrote to the Hudson's Bay Company in London, it was intended to achieve "the double object of securing a share of the Country Trade which had previously been monopolized by the Americans, and of possessing a Settlement on the Coast which would answer the purpose of a Depot, in the event of one being under the necessity of withdrawing from Fort Vancouver. It is found to meet the former of these objects, but not the latter, and therefore may now be considered as forming a branch of the Coasting Trade." Simpson also wrote in his journal: "Whether the Americans come to the Columbia or not I am of opinion that the principal Depot should be situated North of this place [Fort George] about Two or Three Degrees at the Mouth of the Frazer's or as it is sometimes called New Caledonia River as it is more central both for the Coast and interior Trade and as from thence we could with greater facility and at less expense extend our discoveries and Establishments to the Northward and supply all the Interior Posts now occupied."

Simpson realized that he lacked reliable information about the Fraser River. The need for this was imperative. Wasting no time, within ten days of his arrival at Fort George he had dispatched a reconnaissance party to explore the lower reaches of the river.

Chief Trader James McMillan accompanied forty men, including Tom McKay (Dr. John McLoughlin's stepson), Francis Annance, and John Work, left Fort George on a dreary November 18 to begin their arduous journey. Rain, wind, cold, long portages in knee-deep mud through treacherous swamps, up tree-and-brush-clogged streams, and dangerous traverses across windswept bays all were stoically endured as the party worked their way northward. At last on December 16, after twenty-eight days of incredible hardship and misery, the men in their three heavy wooden boats reached the banks of the Fraser thirty miles from its mouth. Three days later they turned downstream and soon reached its outlet to the sea. Here they took careful soundings and made detailed observations. Their mission accomplished, they returned to Fort George.

Simpson's plans for erecting a post on the Fraser received the approval of the London Committee. They made their wishes known in a

514

letter dated February 23, 1926. "We wish Frasers River to be established next season if possible," the committee wrote, "and Mr. McMillan should be appointed to the charge of it, as his reappearance among the natives may have a good effect. From the central situation of Frasers River we think it probable that it will be found to be the proper place for the principal depot . . ."

Accordingly, early in July of 1827 Chief Factor James McMillan and clerks Francis Annance, Donald Manson, and George Barnston, plus twenty-five other men, left Fort Vancouver and journeyed via the Cowlitz River and Cowlitz Portage to Puget Sound. There they proceeded to the south end of Widbey Island, where they boarded the *Cadboro*, under the command of Captain Aemilius Simpson, for the last leg of their journey. Slowly the *Cadboro* moved up the Fraser as McMillan intently scrutinized the shores, searching for a suitable location for the new post. At length close by the small stream by which two and a half years earlier he and his exploring party had first reached the Fraser, a promising site was found. McMillan's journal entry for July 30, 1827, reads: "The schooner was brought close to the shore and the horses landed by slinging them off to the bank. The poor animals appeared to rejoice heartily in their liberation. Our men at noon were all busily employed clearing the ground for the establishment. In the evening all came on board to sleep, a precaution considered necessary until we are better assured of the friendly disposition of the natives."

For the next few months the men worked without letup. The rainy season set in and many of the men sickened, weakened as they were by exhaustion, continual exposure to the damp and wet, and the monotony of a diet of fish. The men were pushed to the limit, but still they struggled on. Pickets for the palisade were cut, timbers for the bastions squared, and in the saw pits the large amount of lumber needed for living quarters and storehouses was made. And always there was the endless task of clearing the site of the big trees and thick underbrush. On August 13 the first bastion was finished and the artillery mounted in it. By the end of the month the second one was completed. At last on September 8 the defenses of the fort were finished and the men could be assured of protection from any hostile attack by the Indians who were present in the area in large numbers. According to the journal entry for that day, "Picketting of the fort was completed and the gates hung. The rectangle inside is 40 yds. by 45; the two bastions 12 ft. square each, built of 8-inch logs and having a lower and upper flooring, the latter of which is to be occupied by our artillery. The tout ensemble must have a formidable enough appearance to the eyes of the Indians, especially those here who have seen nothing of the kind before."

By the middle of the month the first storehouse was finished. The stores and equipment were then quickly unloaded from the *Cadboro* and carried into the new building. On September 18 the schooner weighed anchor, saluted the fort with a three-gun salvo, and slowly headed downstream as the fort's three guns boomed out in return salute.

September 26 marked the near-completion of the wintering house. It was thirty feet in length by fifteen in width, divided into two apartments, each with a fireplace and two windows. A month later a day of celebration was declared by McMillan in recognition of the men's tireless efforts in accomplishing so much. New Year's Day 1828 and several succeeding days were celebrated in the manner dear to the hearts of all fur traders and their men. Regales of wine and cakes, generous rations of flour, peas, meat, raisins, tea, and sugar, and liberal amounts of rum all contributed to making the day a joyous occasion. Chief Factor McMillan had good reason to enjoy the festivities, for he had accomplished much during the past five months: his fort had been built and he had traded 911 beaver and 269 land otters.

However, one problem still remained to threaten the security of the fort. This was the unremitting hostility of many of the Puget Sound and Vancouver Island Indians, particularly the Clallams and Yucultas. In the spring of 1828 the Clallams murdered Chief Trader Alexander McKenzie and four of his men as they were returning to Fort Vancouver after spending the Christmas and New Year holiday at Fort Langley. Obviously this could not go unpunished, for as McLoughlin wrote from Fort Vancouver, ". . . nothing could make us more contemptible in their eyes than allowing such a cold blooded assassination of our People to pass unpunished." A punitive force of sixty men to act in conjunction with the schooner *Cadboro* was organized to avenge the murders. This was accomplished so effectively and completely that henceforth the Clallams ceased to be a menace to the fort.

Much remained yet to be done. The days of spring and summer were busy ones. The men's living quarters were finally completed, vegetable gardens were planted and tended, chickens were carefully cared for, the abundant salmon were harvested, and trading of furs was diligently pursued. In October of that year (1828) the people at the fort were stunned by the unexpected arrival of Governor Simpson accompanied by Chief Trader Archibald McDonald and clerk James Murray Yale. They had just completed their hazardous descent of the Fraser and Thompson rivers—a feat that compelled Simpson to face the reality that ". . . from my own knowledge of Frasers River, I can positively say, that it never can be made a communication adopted for

516

purposes of inland transport." He further admitted: "I . . . consider the passage down to be certain Death, in nine attempts out of Ten."

When Simpson left Fort Langley after a brief stay, he took with him Chief Factor James McMillan, who was eager for his promised furlough. Left behind were Chief Trader Archibald McDonald, to replace McMillan, and clerk James Yale. McDonald had kept a journal during his journey with Simpson from York Factory to Fort Langley. In it he described the fort as he first saw it:

> The Fort is 135 feet by 120, with two good bastions, and a gallery of four feet wide all round. A building of three compartments for the men, a small log house of two compartments, in which the gentlemen themselves now reside, and a store are now occupied, besides which there are two other buildings, one a good dwelling house, with an excellent cellar and a spacious garret, a couple of well finished chimnies are up, and the whole inside now ready for wainscoting and partitioning, four large windows in front, one in each end, and one with a corresponding door in the back. The other is a low buillding with only two square rooms and a fire place in each, and a kitchen adjoining made of slab. The out door work consists of three fields, each planted with thirty bushels of potatoes and look well. The provision shed, exclusive of table stores, is furnished with three thousand dried salmon, sixteen tierces salted ditto, thirty-six cwt. flour, two cwt. grease, and thirty bushels salt.

For the next six years Chief Trader McDonald remained in charge of Fort Langley. He soon realized that the location of the fort was too distant from the more desirable agricultural land to permit a successful farming operation. However, he was enormously impressed with the tremendous potential offered by the salmon fishing. He calculated that the 7,544 salmon that had been traded from the Indians in 1829 at a cost of £13.17.10 in trade goods were the equivalent of a half-penny each. He enthusiastically presented his plan for development of this fishery resource to the receptive ears of Simpson and the London Committee. Eventually, with the arrival of skilled coopers to make the barrels and casks required for the proper curing and shipping of the salmon, McDonald's enthusiasm was justified. This marked the beginning of Fort Langley's enormously profitable salmon fishery. In addition to developing the salmon industry, he pioneered the beginning of a profitable export trade in timber products, producing cedar shingles and two-inch deal planks.

In 1834 McDonald was transferred to Fort Colville on the Columbia River and Fort Langley was entrusted to James Yale, a charge he retained for the next quarter-century. By 1837 Fort Langley in the first ten years of its existence had successfully traded a total of 14,651 beaver, thus making a significant impact upon the American coastal trade.

Much happened during Yale's long administration; almost the first thing he did was relocate the fort a few miles farther upstream to a location with much better access to his expanding farming operation. He was able to write to Governor Simpson in a letter dated January 15, 1840: "The affairs of Fort Langley are in as favorable a condition as could be expected. Our removal from the old place was effected by the 25th June, without aid. We had cleared, fenced and cropped a sufficiency of new ground to amply repay us for what we had abandoned and that cost several years' labor. We did not commence moving any part of the old fort until we had our square here well surrounded with pickets and bastions and a store made to receive the goods."

Yale continued to promote and expand the salmon fishery. Shipments of salted fish were now being regularly made to the Sandwich Islands. He also developed the manufacture of isinglass made from the float bladder of the sturgeon, eventually producing three to eight hundred pounds annually of this profitable item.

Fort Langley was rapidly assuming the appearance of a prosperous farming operation. Herds of cattle grazed on the lush pasture close by; the fields provided abundant hay and grain. There was now even a creamery within the fort. There was, however, one dark cloud on the horizon. The warlike Yucultas, though temporarily rebuffed by their humiliating defeat in 1829 when 270 of their best warriors in nine great war canoes were routed by James Yale and his eleven men in their single canoe, still constituted a threat to the fort. Eight years later, in 1837, the Yucultas tried again. An armada of fifty or so mighty cedar war canoes, each bearing twenty or more warriors, came boldly up the Fraser River. Fort Langley was not caught by surprise. The men were at their posts on the palisade galleries and in the bastions. The cannon were loaded with grapeshot, and all the small arms were primed. The Yucultas' canoes converged upon the fort from the far side of the river. When they were within point-blank range, the cannon erupted flame and shot, blasting the Indians and their canoes out of the water. Their destruction was complete. This, once and for all, put an end to Indian hostilities directed against the fort.

Furs were still being traded—1,025 beaver for 1839—but, as was expected, the advent of the company's coastal trading steamship *Beaver,* functioning as a mobile post, diverted many furs from Fort Langley.

The 1839 agreement between the Hudson's Bay Company and the

Russian-American Fur Company whereby the Hudson's Bay Company contracted to supply the Russian company each year with large amounts of agricultural products resulted in increasing pressure on Yale to provide a large share of these products from his fields and herds at Fort Langley.

On April 11, 1840, that dreaded enemy of all trading posts struck. Fire broke out in the blacksmith's shop and, in spite of the men's best efforts, quickly spread until the entire fort—buildings, pickets, and bastions—was ablaze. By morning nothing remained but hot ashes, smoking timbers, and blackened stockade stumps.

Yale was not one to stand by, wring his hands, and bemoan the catastrophe that had happened. He and all his men immediately began the task of rebuilding. Within an amazingly short time a 70-foot-by-108-foot protective stockade had been erected. Then one by one the buildings within the enclosure were built. So rapidly was his rebuilding accomplished that by February 10, 1841 (just ten months after the fire), he was able to write to Governor Simpson: "The whole total affairs of Fort Langley would hardly seem to have met with a check. Nearly everything that could be done in the way of farming was accomplished; the salmon fishery in due time re-established—that is in the necessary buildings, vessels for pickling the fish in, etc.—and in regard to the business of the dairy, it would appear that we may carry the feather. Have a fort far more spacious then the old one, and things inside nearly as far advanced towards a completion as Fort Langley was when you first visited it, the second year after it was established."

Under Yale's competent direction 240 acres of land had been broken and brought under cultivation; his cattle numbered 195, his pigs 180. He anticipated a harvest of 500 bushels of fall wheat, 250 bushels of spring wheat, 300 bushels of barley, 500 bushels of oats, and 600 bushels of peas, plus an abundant yield of potatoes. His new fort had been built on a much larger scale, permitting more space between each building to help prevent the uncontrollable spread of fire.

In 1844, in recognition of his accomplishments at Fort Langley, clerk James Yale was raised to the rank of chief trader. He had good reasons to be pleased as well as proud of what had been achieved at the fort.

In a report submitted in 1846 by the Board of Management (James Douglas and John Work) to the Governor and the London Committee, the prospects for Fort Langley were reviewed:

The Fur returns of Fort Langley have improved this year, and the Salmon Fishery has been also uncommonly productive, greater attention having been paid to it than usual, in consequence of the increasing demand for salt fish at the Sandwich Islands. Last year upwards of 600 Barrels were sold in course of a few months at 10 and 11 dollars a barrel, and there has been an urgent demand for a much larger quantity. To meet this we have first shipped 1,530 Barrels the whole yield of this season by the Barque *Columbia* & we hope it will sell to as much advantage as the fish of last year. This business is becoming of more importance every year the price being good and the demand likely to last, as the article has become one of the necessaries of life at the Sandwich Islands. We shall devote much attention to this fishery, and endeaver to increase our exports of Salmon to 2,000 Barrel, allowing fully for all expenses and at the present sale price will yield a considerable profit.

In contrast to this glowing assessment of Fort Langley's performance is the one submitted for the following year (1847): "Every branch of business carried on at Fort Langley exhibits a decline this year, to a greater or less extent, as compared with the prosperous result of last Outfit, in Consequence of causes which the able and indefatigable exertions of Mr. C. T. Yale, could not altogether controul." However, two years later, in 1849, Douglas was able to write: "The Salmon fisheries at Fort Langley, which have been attended with a remarkable degree of success this season, yielded 2,610 Barrels of prime fish, being an increase of 885 Barrels on the yeild of the preceding year."

In 1846 the boundary between the United States and Great Britain was established at the forty-ninth parallel and all of Vancouver Island was awarded to Great Britain. In addition, provision was made that the navigation of the Columbia River was to be open equally to both the British and the Americans. However, U.S. Customs' interpretation was that since the Columbia was within American territory, all British goods brought in by traders using the river were subject to U.S. custom duty. This ruling made it imperative for the Hudson's Bay Company to find a new route into the Thompson River and New Caledonia districts that was wholly north of the new boundary and thus not subject to U.S. Customs.

During 1846–48 numerous attempts were made to find such a route, and eventually one was established with Fort Langley as its southern terminus and Fort Kamloops on the Thompson River as its northern end. All this meant increased work for Fort Langley. As the Board of Management reported in 1848 to the London Committee:

The preparations for opening the new road to the interior for the passage of the summer Brigade threw much additional work upon the establishment of Fort Langley, as besides making the road from Kequeloose to the

Ferry, and from thence through the Portage to the lower end of the Falls of Frasers River a distance of 18 miles, through a wooded country, levelling and zigzaging the steep ascents, bridging Rivers, there were stores erected for the accommodation of the Brigades above and below the Falls, boats and skows built for the ferry, and seven large Boats for the navigation from Fort Langley to the Falls, there was the heavy transport of provisions to the latter place, and a vast amount of other work connected with that object which it required no common degree of energy and good management in Chief Trader Yale to accomplish with 20 men in the course of a severe winter.

In addition, the arrival and departure and layover (sometimes of several weeks) of the brigades disrupted the orderly daily operations of the fort. The unremitting pressure upon Yale to produce yet more from his fields and herds and to expand his already-large salmon fishery allowed no leeway for any departure from his tightly organized work-filled days. The heavy burden Yale was carrying was increased in 1849 when, as reported by Chief Factor James Douglas in a letter to the company in London:

> . . . a destructive fire broke out in the early part of last winter in the Barn Yard at Fort Langley which consumed a large quantity of grain, and the whole stock of fodder laid up for the cattle. That misfortune happening on the eve of a winter of extraordinary severity was attended with the most disastrous consequences, to the cattle, which notwithstanding every exertion made to save them, perished in great numbers, from the effects of cold and hunger.
> But of 240 heads of cattle only about 80 cows survived the winter, and Mr. Yale most gratefully acknowledges the attention of the Indians encamped in the vicinity of the Fort, who took the cattle into their houses during the dreadfully severe colds, and fed them with rushes and Pine boughs, which they collected from the forest. Without their assistance Mr. Yale is of opinion that every one of the cattle would have perished before Spring.

A source of annoyance to Yale was the blame he was receiving for the decline in the fort's fur returns. This was unacceptable to him, for he knew the cause was the siphoning off of his furs both by the coastal trading steamer *Beaver* and by the Indians going to the company's new emporium—Fort Victoria on Vancouver Island—with their furs. In frustration he wrote to Sir George in 1852 expressing his feelings and defending his fort's performance:

The greatest evils here seem to spring out of Vancouver's Island. It

would be ungenerous and to cause no salutary consequences, to cast re-
flections derogatory to the business of Fort Langley. It has resisted many
tendencies to obstruct its due course, and tho' much depreciated, Old
Langley stands still stable, the main prop of the Company's commerce on
the North West Coast of America, and can not, with any show of reason,
be reproached for anything, except, perhaps, that of affording maintenance to a rising Sodom on Vancouver's Island. . . . A great part of the fur
procured by the natives in the Interior within the Langley precincts are
taken to Fort Victoria. The Indian traders here are glad to get a few furs
to secure an ostentatious reception at the great emporium—and after
seeing the World, and tasting of its sweets into the bargain, they come
home loaded with goods.

During the early 1850's a new item for export was developed. This
was the cranberries that grew so abundantly in the lowlands of the
Fraser delta. They were shipped in wooden kegs to San Francisco,
where they found a ready market.

In 1856 the magic words "gold found on the Fraser" triggered a
rush of men to the area. Most of them on their way to this new El Dorado passed through the ponderous gates of Fort Langley impatient to
buy supplies and get whatever news they could pick up about the latest
"hot" spots. Daily in increasing numbers they arrived, overrunning the
fort compound and spreading out beyond the palisade walls. They
crowded into the sales shop and kept the clerks busy supplying their
needs. During the period of this "invasion" the volume of daily sales av-
eraged $1,500, well worth the disruption of the fort's normal schedule
of operations.

Fort Langley continued to occupy an important position as a trading and supply center during the Fraser gold rush days, even after
American steamships successfully navigated the Fraser River farther
upstream beyond Fort Langley to Fort Hope. Chief Trader Yale was
confronted with new problems: squatters eager to acquire land were
spreading onto the fort's farming and pasturelands, whiskey peddlers
in increasing numbers were openly selling their wares, and smuggling
of goods was rampant. For him the old days of company rule and orderly routine were completely shattered, never to return.

On November 19, 1858, a colorful ceremony took place at Fort
Langley. As Chief Trader James Yale quietly watched in the back of
the crowded dining hall in the "Big House," the monopolistic trading
rights of the Hudson's Bay Company, which he had done so much to
help preserve, were formally extinguished, the new crown colony of
British Columbia was officially proclaimed, and James Douglas,

stripped of his rank as chief factor of the Hudson's Bay Company, was named Governor.

This event marked the end of an era for Fort Langley as well as for its loyal and devoted chief trader, James Yale. He left the fort in 1859 and resigned from the company's service a year later.

Fort Langley continued to function, though on an increasingly reduced scale, as a fur trade provision post until 1886, when it was closed down after nearly sixty years of operation. Abandonment and neglect soon took their toll. Almost all of the fort's buildings as well as the palisade fell into disrepair and eventual ruin. Only one structure—the trade goods warehouse—remained to bear witness to the existence of the once-proud fort.

Nearly 130 years later Fort Langley was rescued from total oblivion by Parks Canada. Under its direction the one surviving building was restored and restocked with representative trade goods. In addition, relying on careful archaeological investigation, the stockade, northeast bastion, blacksmith's shop, artisan's shop, and "Big House" were reconstructed on their original sites and appropriately furnished.

Thus we were able one beautiful summer day to walk through the massive gate in the stockade and enter the spacious fort compound of a Fort Langley partially restored to its former appearance. We first entered the old trade warehouse by the east stockade wall and were immediately transported back a century and a half by the sights and smells that greeted us. Stored within this one-and-a-half-story hipped-roof building of the usual post-on-sill construction was a bewildering array of trade items of all kinds. Barrels, kegs, crates, boxes, chests, bales, and sacks, one on top of the other, lined the walls from floor to ceiling. An amazing assortment of tinware, pants, shirts, shoes, axes, shovels, rope, tobacco twists, guns, traps, blankets, buttons, dried fish, and bear and beaver pelts all stacked in overflowing piles took up most of the floor space. Hanging from the rafters were some beautiful fox and wolf skins as well as several ducks and geese. We ascended the narrow stairway to the garret above. There, in addition to more sacks and bales, were large numbers of the hundreds of wooden barrels made by the fort's cooper. Outside the warehouse was the large fur press used to compress the furs into ninety-pound bales.

The blacksmith's shop was between the trade warehouse and the northeast bastion. It had one hearth, a huge hand-operated bellows suspended from the ceiling, several anvils, and the usual blacksmithing tongs, pinchers, and other tools.

We climbed up the steep stairway to the upper level of the bastion.

The small cannon there were still pointed toward the river, barely visible through the open portholes. Today the cannon are harmless—their barrels not charged with shot or grape. But 150 years ago they were aimed and used with deadly purpose to repel the ferocious Yucultas and prevent their destroying the fort.

Next we walked across to the artisans' building on the west side of the spacious compound. This was another typical post-on-sill, hipped-roof, one-and-a-half-story, five-bayed building. Within, the carpenter and cooper were busy at work. The carpenter had obligingly constructed a small model showing the *poteau-sur-sole* (post-on-sill) method of construction that was used so frequently by builders of Hudson's Bay Company forts. His work area was well equipped with a great number of broadaxes, saws, chisels, hammers, and clamps all neatly arranged on the walls above his workbench.

The other half of the building was the cooper's domain. Here the thousands of barrels needed each year for the fort's thriving salmon fishery were made. The cooper, a large, burly man, was almost hidden by the finished barrels stacked against the walls. Near his work table in the center of the room were the tools of his trade: a hoop forming board and close by a supply of pine staves. Suspended overhead were hundreds of iron and withe hoops. The continuing success of Fort Langley's salmon export trade was dependent upon the cooper's skill in making leak-proof and properly cured barrels. He was a most important man in the Fort Langley establishment.

At last we walked over to the factor's house, situated on the crest of a gentle slope at the south end of the compound. It was an imposing building of two stories with a hipped roof. The central doorway, reached by a short flight of steps, was flanked by three symmetrically spaced windows on each of the two levels. Within were spacious rooms rather sparsely furnished. The main dining hall for the fort's officers, the factor's parlor, office, and bedroom, and the clerk's bedroom occupied the ground floor. Sleeping quarters for visiting company officers were on the second story. The kitchen (not reconstructed) is thought to have been a separate building to the rear of the "Big House."

We left the house and stepped out onto the small landing at the head of the front steps. There we paused for a moment to enjoy the lovely view spread before us. At the far end of the compound, sloping downward from the factor's house and framed between two tall Douglas fir trees, were the warehouse to the right and the artisan's shop to the left. Rising behind them were the forest-covered hills bordering the

Fraser River, with yet farther in the distance the snowcapped peaks of the coastal mountains. It was a most pleasant vista and one that Chief Trader James Murray Yale must have enjoyed many times during his twenty-five years at Fort Langley.

Dease Lake Post
Fort Halkett

When the "scorched earth" policy of trapping out areas to preclude the competition from acquiring furs was ended by the merging of the North West and Hudson's Bay companies in 1821, it was quickly recognized that a policy of conservation would have to be pursued in order to allow the depleted areas to recover. Many of the districts were put on a quota based on their fur production average for the three years 1823–25. To offset the reduced fur yield from the exhausted and quota-controlled districts, new posts were established in the frontier districts (Mckenzie River, Columbia, and New Caledonia districts) where the fur resources were as yet still potentially rich and productive.

The minutes of a council held at Norway House June 2, 1829, resolved "that a Post be established on the West Branch of the Liard River, to be named Fort Halket, this ensuing autumn for which the necessary complement of People and Outfit of Goods are furnished." To implement this order, Chief Factor Edward Smith from his headquarters at Fort Simpson outfitted John Hutchinson, clerk, and four other men who were selected for this assignment. Three and a half weeks later, on July 22, they commenced construction of the new fort. Hutchinson remained in charge there for the next several years. His successor was Chief Trader John McLeod, who devoted much of the summer of 1834 to exploring the country to the west and south of Fort Halkett. He not only discovered Dease Lake but also reached the Stikine River. A year later John Hutchinson was back at Fort Halkett. This time he was specifically charged with carrying out the order of the Northern Council, which had resolved at their June 1835 meeting "that the present Establishment of Fort Halkett be removed to Dease's Lake, Summer 1836 if possible, and that measures be concerted for the purpose of establishing a new Post on the banks of that river, at least 200 miles distant in a direct line from the height of land towards the Pacific, in the summer of 1837/38."

In the course of following these instructions, Hutchinson and his party left Fort Halkett and began to ascend the turbulent Liard River. They had proceeded but a short distance—in fact, it was only their third night out—when (according to Hutchinson's later report) they "discovered a numerous war party of Indians under arms with their visages painted black." Panic-stricken, Hutchinson and his men ran to their canoes, abandoning all their goods and supplies, and fled back down the Liard, never stopping until they reached Fort Liard.

After Hutchinson's abortive attempt, the task of establishing a post on Dease Lake was entrusted to Robert Campbell. Early in the spring of 1837 he left Fort Simpson for Fort Liard, where he arranged for the necessary birchbark canoes to be made and where he signed up his crew of canoemen and hunters. By the time he was finally able to leave Fort Liard, the river was in summer freshet, with such strong current that his onward progress was slowed so considerably that when he finally reached Fort Halkett the lateness of the season forced him to halt and spend the winter there at the abandoned post. Campbell, writing his autobiography many years later, described Fort Halkett as follows:

> Fort Halkett is situated on the bank of Smith River at its confluence with the Liard, & except in the river valley is surrounded by rugged mountains, whose hard rocky sides were beautified by occasional green slopes, & woods of the general varieties indigenous to that country, viz: Spruce, poplar, pine, birch & tamarac, while small shrubs grew in profusion. Wild fruits such as rasp- & straw-berries, blue berries & cranberries are very abundant. Our garden also yielded well. For our winter's sustenance we depended mainly on our fisheries which were established on lakes 30 miles or so away by Smith River, together with what our Indian hunters brought in. In the neighborhood are some curious warm water springs issuing from the sloping bank of the river. The water, though cold as ice in summer, is warm (but not hot) in winter and keeps a channel open all winter for miles along the bank. The water encrustates the ground it rises through as though it froze the ground, and it seems continually to have to be making new exits for itself.

Campbell and his men, after quickly restoring the fort to a condition suitable for their occupancy, settled in for the winter. At length in the fall the Indians who had formerly traded there, noting the smoke rising from the fort chimneys, came in to trade their furs for the ammunition and other supplies of which they were totally destitute. And so the winter of 1837–38 passed by uneventfully, the major happening of importance being Campbell's promotion from postmaster to clerk.

Late in the next spring (1838), abandoning Fort Halkett once again, Campbell and his party of sixteen men set off in two canoes on their way to Dease Lake. After successfully reaching their destination in the beginning of July, they "selected a suitable site for the fort about 5 miles from the mouth of the Nahany [i.e., the Dease] & at once commenced building operations."

Leaving A. R. McLeod to supervise the building of the fort, Campbell, accompanied by his interpreter Francis Hoole and his two faithful young Indians, Lapie and Kitza, left the fort site to carry out the instructions given him by George Simpson to explore the west side of the mountains. He wrote in his Journal: "We took pine bark canoes with us to the South end of the Lake, 20 miles off, & then shouldering our blankets & light equipment such as small axe, kettle, &c., we started on foot trusting to our guns to keep us in provisions."

Within a couple of days they came to a deep ravine at the bottom of which raced a raging river. A swaying flimsy pole bridge provided the only way to reach the opposite side. In Campbell's words, "It was a rude ricketty structure of pine poles spliced together with Withes & stretched high above a foaming torrent; the ends of the poles were loaded down with stones to prevent the bridge from collapsing. This primitive support looked so frail & unstable & the rushing waters below so formidable that it seemed well nigh impossible to cross it. It inclined to one side which did not tend to strengthen its appearance for safety."

The following day Campbell and his loyal companions with much trepidation successfully crossed this "flimsy bridge swaying & bending with our weight & threatening to precipitate us into the boiling waters beneath."

Undeterred by warnings from friendly Indians of the great danger in visiting the main Indian camp, Campbell pressed on. He was told that the "great chief 'Shakes' from the sea was there & Indians from all parts without number;" and "that they [the Indians] had always been told that if they ever met White people from the East side of the Mountains, to be sure & kill them as they were enemies."

About thirteen miles from the Terror bridge Campbell caught his first glimpse of the huge Indian camp from the top of a nearby hill. It was indeed immense. Campbell described it: "Such a concourse of Indians I have never before seen assembled. They were gathered from all parts of the Western slope of the Rockies & from along the Pacific Coast. These Indians camped here for weeks at a time, living on salmon which could be caught in thousands in the Stikine by gaffing or spearing, to aid them in which the Indians had a sort of dam built across the river."

Campbell, unaccompanied by his companions whom he had ordered to remain behind on the high hill, resolutely descended to the camp where he faced the noisy yelling throng that surrounded him. An opening was made to permit Shakes to approach Campbell and conduct him into a tent that provided some relief from the ear-splitting din outside. Campbell described Shakes as "tall & strongly built." He subsequently learned that this coast Indian was all-powerful among the natives on that side of the mountain. He ruled despotically over a large number of different tribes. Each year he came to this huge rendezvous in the heart of Tahltan country on the Stikine well provided with goods supplied to him by the Russians at Fort Highfield (later Fort Dionysus and still later Fort Stikine) located at the mouth of the Stikine River (present-day Wrangell). He served as the important middleman trading their goods with the Indians of the interior. His enmity, therefore, toward anyone, such as Campbell, who threatened his position as middleman was understandable.

Eventually Campbell was able to leave Shakes and the noisy throng and return unharmed to the hill where his three companions had been anxiously awaiting him. Here he "hoisted the H.B.C. flag, & cut H.B.C. & date on a tree, thus taking possession of the country for the Company." Here, too, Campbell met a remarkable woman, the Chieftainess of the Nahanies, who not only on this occasion but also on several subsequent ones, proved her friendship for Campbell and his men. She urged him not to pause on his return to Dease Lake until he had safely crossed the Terror bridge, warning him that Shakes could not be trusted not to attempt to harm him.

Shortly after his safe return to his Dease Lake Post, Campbell set off on the long and hazardous journey to district headquarters at Fort Simpson on the Mackenzie River to report on his recent trip over the mountains to the westward flowing Stikine River and his contact with the Russian or Coast Indians. In addition he planned to get some much needed supplies and provisions for his post. On his way he stopped at Fort Halkett to exchange their cumbersome spruce bark canoe (made at Dease Lake) for the much superior birchbark canoe left there in the spring. On August 20 he reached Fort Simpson only to find that his trip had been made quite in vain. As Campbell said, "Though I went there at the risk of my life it availed me little. Mr. McPherson, though glad to hear of my success, was deaf to all my entreaties for a few extra & much wanted supplies." So disheartened but undaunted, he started back up the treacherous Liard River, reaching his own Dease Lake Post in a blinding snowstorm on October 12.

From then on until the following spring, he and his men battled just to survive. Numerous entries in his Journal reflected the desperate straits he and his men faced. "The produce of our nets, on which we depended principally for subsistence, was inadequate to our daily wants, & the hunters were unable to add anything to our slender means." "Everything possible was used as food,—'tripe de roche', skins, parchment, in fact anything." "Game seemed to have deserted the country at this season."

In addition to these severe privations, Campbell was subjected to frequent harassment by the "passing & repassing of the Russian Indians, who kept us night & day in a state of alarm & uncertainty." In their weakened and emaciated state and with many of the men away from the post trying to find game, Campbell was in no position to repel these arrogant intrusions. He realized that "they [Coast Indians] were taught by Shakes & other interested parties who came up from the coast to barter with them, to regard us as enemies, & were instigated by these individuals to do us all the harm they could."

Finally May arrived, the river opened and the men could at last look forward to leaving this starvation post and returning to Fort Simpson. Campbell wrote in his Journal: "As we were now ready to start & our snow shoes were of no further use to us, we removed all the netting off them, & that along with our parchment windows, was boiled down to the consistency of glue. The savoury dish thus prepared formed the 'menu' of our last meal before leaving Dease's Lake on 8 May, 1839."

Campbell's year of misery and near-starvation at Dease Lake had accomplished little. Because of the arrangement made between the Hudson's Bay Company and the Russian-American Fur Company, it was no longer necessary to penetrate toward the coastal country from the east side of the mountains, since now access to it could be gained from the Pacific with greater facility and less expense. Dease Lake Post was, therefore, no longer needed and so was abandoned.

Our first attempt to find the site of Dease Lake Post ended in failure. We had so little to go on—just the brief entry in Campbell's Journal: "Reaching Dease's Lake in the beginning of July, we selected a suitable site for the fort about 5 miles from the mouth of the Nahany [Dease] & at once commenced building operations." Was it on the east side of the lake or the west side? Using our car mileage indicator we drove five miles from the beginning of the lake along Highway 37 that closely paralleled the east side of the lake. At the end of five miles we parked the motor home and explored the narrow zone of trees and brush that bordered the lake, but found nothing that remotely suggested a possible site for a trading post. All that we could do was photograph this upper end of the lake and accept the fact that somewhere in this vicinity on either the east or west shore Campbell's Dease Lake Post had once stood.

It was not to be until seven years later that a lucky purchase of an out-of-print book that I had long wanted provided the clue that led me to Campbell's post. The book was *Trail to the Interior* by R. M. Patterson. It included an account of Patterson's canoe trip on Dease Lake in

1948. He was using an 1887 map of the area made by George M. Dawson as his guide. He noticed that on the map the site of a Hudson's Bay Company post labeled as (abandoned 1839) was shown on the east side of the lake at the mouth of a small stream on a point of land called Sawmill Point. As he paddled down Dease Lake close to the east shore, he was on the look-out to find an area that corresponded to this location. Finally not far from the northern end of the lake he came to the curving point on the east side with the small stream emerging into the lake—exactly as shown and marked as the site of Dease Lake Post.

Patterson landed on the point on the north side of the small creek. He wrote: "I waded around in the long grass and the heavy dew, searching among the trees. Soon I came to ground that seemed to have been disturbed and then on a mount of stone that was half-buried in the drifted leaves and the humus of a hundred and ten years. That would be a hearth and a chimney; and these mounds and hollows and scattered stones were all that was left of Campbell's fort." He added that this was the place where "Robert Campbell had lunched off boiled parchment windows and the filling of his snowshoes just over a hundred years ago."

Elated at uncovering this reference that located the site of Campbell's Dease Lake Post, I soon was able to travel to Whitehorse and there make arrangements to charter a Cessna 185 for a flight to Dease Lake. With Pierre as pilot we flew over the magnificent Cassiar Mountains toward our destination. The day was perfect for flying and photography. Soon the long narrow lake cradled by snow-capped mountains came into view. It was still partially covered with ice, but the open water reflected the brilliant blue of the sky. We had no trouble locating Sawmill Point. About three miles below the north end of the lake on the east side, it was the only prominent tongue of land extending into the lake from an otherwise unbroken shoreline. It was exactly as located on Dawson's map and described by Patterson.

Although we couldn't land and search for the tumbledown pile of chimney stones that Patterson had uncovered, I was well content with the result of our flight, happy with my view of this tiny wooded peninsula curving out into the lake where Robert Campbell and his men had endured so much hardship and misery with such great fortitude and resolution.

In February of 1840 William Mowat came up the Liard from Fort Simpson to relieve Campbell of the charge of Fort Halkett, so the latter could continue his explorations beyond the headwaters of the west branch of the Liard. Campbell left Fort Halkett about the end of May. After a most successful summer during which he discovered Frances and Finlayson lakes and reached the Pelly River, he returned about the middle of September to Fort Halkett, full of enthusiasm about his discoveries and their promising fur potential.

Shortly after Campbell's return, Mowat and eight men left Fort Halkett to return to Fort Simpson. Somewhere between there and Fort Liard, the Liard River lived up to its reputation for treachery, and a mighty whirlpool engulfed the canoe, swallowing up six of the crew, including Mowat. The three survivors after three days of incredible hardship, cold, bereft of clothing, barefoot, and without food, eventually struggled back to Fort Halkett, where they were warmly welcomed and cared for.

The winter of 1840–41 was one of great privation and suffering for Campbell and his men at Fort Halkett. The men Campbell sent off to hunt for food were back in two days, blaming their early return on a sore foot one of them had developed. As Campbell wrote later: "This was most provoking and maddened me to find that I had no hand to turn upon—none of my people at the house, no fish nor anything else in my store but the little meat I had with such care husbanded for a holiday treat for my own poor men . . ." Campbell continued: "It is truly a most perplexing circumstance, and nothing can be done on this river but is attended with some evil fatality as if a malediction pervaded all our actions in that quarter . . . No person has this season laid down to rest within the precincts of this Fort without feeling the unpleasant sensations of hunger."

Chief Factor Lewes in a letter to Simpson also acknowledged the difficulties of getting sufficient food to Fort Halkett. The treacherous Liard River was dreaded by all, and there were few willing to challenge its waters. Consequently, provisioning Fort Halkett was always uncertain. Lewes considered the post to be the worst off in the whole Mackenzie River district. Everyone was suffering because of the great periodic scarcity of snowshoe rabbits, "the only means of winter subsistance with many of them . . . the consequence has been most dreadful among them, starvation even to death, murder and cannibalism."

At last, two years after his first expedition to Frances Lake, Campbell, equipped with supplies from Fort Simpson, set off from Fort Halkett on July 27, 1842, to renew his discoveries and to establish a post on Frances Lake. He left P. C. Pambrun, clerk, in charge of Fort Halkett for the duration of his absence. In the spring of 1844 Campbell left Frances Lake to bring out the fur returns to Fort Simpson. To his dismay, he found that the provisions that had been stored at Fort Halkett for him for his trip to Fort Simpson had already been eaten, "in consequence of which we were several days drifting down the river with nothing to break our fast."

On his way back to Frances Lake in the fall, Campbell because of desertions among the Indians in his crew, coupled with the fact of the Liard being "in such a state as not to be attempted by water," was not able to undertake the difficult portages and so was forced to leave half his outfit "to be stored at Fort Halkett, not a very secure or safe depot." To guard against his supplies being tampered with at Fort Halkett, John McLean, temporarily in charge at Fort Simpson, wrote a note to Pambrun in charge at Fort Halkett: "In the event of Mr. Campbell's finding it expedient to leave some provisions in deposit at your post, such deposit must absolutely be considered as sacred property and not to be touched under any circumstances or on any condition whatever."

A small garden was planted each year that Fort Halkett was in operation. It produced a small but welcome yield of barley, potatoes, cabbage, and turnips.

With Campbell's discovery of the Pelly connection to the Yukon River, providing a relatively easier route for supplying the Northwest, the treacherous Liard could be avoided, and Fort Halkett was no longer so essential as a supply post on that river. After a further thirty years of intermittent operation, it was closed down permanently about 1875.

We noticed from our road map that the section of the Alaska highway that we were traveling crossed Smith River just a short distance up from the Liard. We were confident that we could strike through the bush from the highway and by closely following the Smith downstream reach its junction with the Liard—the site of Fort Halkett. We pulled off the road and parked our motor home in a small level clearing most conveniently located on the bank of Smith River.

Full of enthusiasm and anticipation, I undertook this short "safari" by myself. Before reaching the thick spruce woods that lay between me and the Liard, I had to cross a rather large open area with a hard-packed surface where crushed gravel and other materials were stockpiled for road maintenance.

I had advanced but a short distance when I saw clearly and precisely imprinted on the bare ground the tracks of a bear headed in the same direction I was going. As I stared at the tracks, I suddenly realized that these were not just ordinary black bear tracks. (I was quite familiar with them from living in northern Michigan.) These were grizzly bear tracks! The large size of the footprints and particularly the length of the claws left no doubt in my mind. All of a sudden some of my enthusiasm for this little solo jaunt ebbed away. But resolutely I continued onward. However, when I entered the gloom of the dense woods, contrary to my normal custom of moving as quietly as possible, I made quite a racket—I hoped enough to scare all the game (especially the grizzly bears) out of the country! I kept on going for quite a while, or so it seemed to me (it was probably less than a half an hour), and I still had not reached the Liard. I decided that any longer absence might cause worry back at the motor home, so with no argument on my part, I gave up the search and turned back, disappointed that I had failed to find the site of Fort Halkett but very happy to get back to the motor home. For some strange reason I did not mention the grizzly bear tracks.

Two weeks later, as we headed east toward home, we traveled back over the same highway and came once again to Smith River. During the time that had elapsed from my first attempt, my disappointment at not finding Fort Halkett had steadily mounted. I was resolved to try again. So after parking the motor home in the same spot by the river, we set off—this time the two of us—for the junction of the Smith and the Liard.

We came to the area where the road-building materials were stockpiled. Numerous grizzly bear tracks were plainly evident, but no comment was made by either of us as we walked along. I did notice that as we began to penetrate the thick tangle of brush and the maze of downed timber, my husband, who normally walks as noiselessly as an Indian when in the woods, was coughing and knocking a stick against trees, in short, making as much noise as I was.

Eventually we emerged on the north bank of the Liard at the mouth of the Smith. What a beautiful sight greeted us! A range of low green-covered mountains bordered the Liard on the south side. Directly opposite the mouth of the Smith and extending upstream to the west the effects of an old fire were evident—exposed bare rock and a growth of young poplar instead of the usual solid dark green of spruce and fir. The flats along the Liard on the north were literally covered with rocks of all sizes, many probably deposited there by the river during its highwater rampages in the spring. Animal tracks were all over the shore. Moose, caribou, bear, lynx, wolf, and mink all had left their imprints.

Smith River is a lovely stream of fast-running clear, sparkling water. Its junction with the Liard is marked by a noisy whitecapped series of small riffles. We looked across to the other side. There, on the ground slightly elevated above the river and now covered with a luxuriant growth of spruce, birch, and poplar, over one hundred years ago had once stood the Hudson's Bay post of Fort Halkett. There the indomitable Campbell had been stationed in between his various journeys of exploration; from there the unfortunate Mowat and his five men had gone to meet their death farther downstream on the Liard, that terrible river considered by Campbell to "be under a spell of some malediction, a source of endless mishaps and confusion." All traces of the fort have long since vanished.

As we enjoyed the beautiful day and took advantage of the perfect light conditions for photographing the Fort Halkett site, it was difficult to picture the hardship and privation that once had prevailed there. The Liard was flowing quietly toward its ultimate outlet in the Mackenzie, but we were well aware that in many places it was still untamed and dangerous.

As the shadows began to lengthen over this beautiful valley, we realized it was time to leave. Occasional coughs, intermittent attempts at whistling, plus much brush snapping and cracking brought us safely back to our motor home. It was only after we were inside that we both simultaneously and a bit nonchalantly blurted out, "Did you see those grizzly bear tracks?" We shared a good laugh as well as the enormous satisfaction of having accomplished our goal of finding Fort Halkett in spite of grizzly bears—imagined or actual.

Fort Pitt

Always alert to new opportunities for increasing the efficiency and thus the fur trade profits for his company, Governor George Simpson decided in 1829 to establish a post in the buffalo country of the North Saskatchewan to utilize the Crees, who, in the words of Simpson, "would otherwise idle away their time in the Plains—but will now confine themselves to the thick woods during the winter season, where they will collect a few skins; it is also a good Situation for Leather and Provisions."

Accordingly, at the annual meeting of the Northern Council held at Norway House on June 22, 1829, it was resolved "that C.F. Rowand be at liberty to establish a Post near the Red Deer Hills if he find it expedient." Acting promptly on these instructions, Chief Factor Rowand at the end of September sent Patrick Small, a company clerk, and his family plus three men, two Indians, and four women and four children from Edmonton House to establish the new post. Within a month they had erected a small fort protected by two bastions. The first winter the small group, augmented by fourteen additional men sent by Chief Factor Rowand, was obliged to live in tents since there had not been sufficient time to construct any living quarters for themselves. The new fort was named Fort Pitt in honor of Thomas Pitt, a member of the Hudson's Bay Company Governing Committee from 1810 to 1832.

During 1830 and the spring of 1831 the men were busy completing the building within the fort stockade. A main house fifty feet long by thirty feet wide was built of squared logs, as was a store. The exterior walls were mudded and then whitewashed with a coating of white earth. Wooden flooring was laid in the fourteen-foot-square bastions, each mounting a two-pound cannon. A blacksmith shop and coal kiln were also constructed. The palisade that enclosed the buildings was fifteen feet high and 150 feet on a side and had a gallery extending the length of its inside walls. The first season was a profitable one, and Simpson could report to the London Committee that "although the post had barely had time to be known, its returns were very respectable."

Fort Pitt was established primarily to service the Crees, but its location between the territories of the Crees and Blackfeet—longtime traditional enemies—rendered it vulnerable to attack by the warlike Blackfeet, who felt the traders at the fort favored the Crees. Because of this constant danger of hostile Indian action, a large complement of men was needed to staff the post, at a considerably greater expense to the company.

In 1832, because of the increased turbulence among the Plains Indians, it was decided it would be wise to close Fort Pitt, "in consequence of the danger arising from War Parties frequenting that neighbourhood." However, in the autumn of 1833 the fort reopened with Henry Fisher, clerk, in charge and a complement of fourteen men.

The country around the fort was fertile, and from the very beginning crops were planted to help the post become as self-sufficient as possible. Barley, potatoes, and turnips were grown successfully. Indeed, Fort Pitt became quite famous for the quality and quantity of the potatoes it raised. And, of course, as it was located in the heart of prime buffalo country, there was always an abundance of meat.

Fort Pitt functioned primarily as a provision post. It traded chiefly for dried buffalo meat, pemmican, and buffalo grease from the Crees, Blackfeet, and some Métis. In addition, buffalo robes and wolf skins were traded as well as some of the finer furs, such as beaver, marten, and mink, from the more northern Indians.

However, Fort Pitt was not solely a provision post. It raised a large number of both horses and dogs, all so essential for the company's overland and winter transport system. The horses were kept at some distance from the fort in a "horse-guard" where they were under the constant surveillance and care of several men. The forage was so luxuriant and nutritious that one visitor to the fort in 1872 wrote: ". . . more horses are kept at Fort Pitt than any other post on the Saskatchewan. There are 300 now, and they increase rapidly, though the prairie wolves destroy many of the foals. All of them were in prime condition.—They cropped all their own food; and sleek and fat as they are now, they are equally so in midwinter: pawing off the dry snow they find the grasses abundant and succulent beneath."

During the 1830s and 1840s Fort Pitt carried on a profitable trade with the Crees, Blackfeet, and Métis. Constant vigilance was required, since the actions of the irascible and volatile Blackfeet were always unpredictable. The men at Fort Pitt had to be constantly on their guard. Typical was the unsuccessful attack by the Blackfeet on the Crees just outside the walls of Fort Pitt: "The Fort Pitt Crees sent upwards of thirty Blackfeet & Cercees to their long home (on boute de Sable) where they say they all go one day. One day nineteen of those wild fellows were discovered close to the Fort Pitt Cree Camp. The Call was given and in less than one hour after the whole were all killed & cut pieces their scalps flying at the end of poles, their hands and feet hanging after the horses necks and tails. The Cree women playing at ball with something else. This is all true. It was done in revenge for scalping some of their friends alive shortly before they fell in with the camp."

Among the many visitors who stopped off at Fort Pitt was the artist Paul Kane. He was there in 1848. In his book *Wanderings of an Artist among the Indians of North America,* he wrote about the enormous number of buffalo he encountered on his journey down the North Saskatchewan River from Fort Edmonton to Fort Pitt: "We reached the fort soon after dark, having been seven days on our route from Edmonton. We had killed seventeen buffaloes in this journey, for feeding ourselves and dogs. The animals had, we were told, never appeared in such vast numbers, nor shown themselves so near the Company's establishments; some have even been shot within the gates of the fort. They killed with their horns twenty or thirty horses in their attempt to drive them off from the patches of grass which the horses had pawed the snow from with their hoofs for the purpose of getting at the grass, and severely gored many others, which eventually recovered."

On his return journey to Toronto sometime later, Kane again visited Fort Pitt. He wrote: "May 27th—What with the strong current, the men pulling all day, and drifting all night, we again arrived at Fort Pitt, where we got an addition to our party of two more boats. These boats are all loaded with the furs and pemmican of the Saskatchewan district. The furs are taken down to York Factory, in the Hudson's Bay, where they are shipped to Europe; the pemmican is extended for those posts where provisions are difficult to be procured. We remained at Fort Pitt for two days whilst the other boats were getting ready."

In 1843 John Rowand, son of Chief Factor John Rowand of Fort Edmonton, replaced Henry Fisher as head of Fort Pitt. Rowand remained there for the next twelve years, attaining the rank of chief trader in 1850.

In the spring of 1854 Fort Pitt was the scene of the last act in the eventful life of one of the truly epic figures in the fur trade. Chief Factor Rowand had left his Fort Edmonton for the last time and was on his way east to begin his new life of retirement. He had stopped off at Fort Pitt to spend the night with his son. In the morning while he was standing at the river's edge waiting to embark in his canoe, a fight broke out between two of the canoemen. Immediately responding with his customary vigor, old John Rowand rushed in, attempting to break up the fray, only to fall to the ground, dead.

Hector of the Palliser expedition described the fort as he saw it when he stopped there in 1857:

It is a small fort, at least the place within the palisades is small, but it is one of the best posts for trading quantities of provisions in the whole Saskatchewan district, the buffalo never being very far distant even in summer, as the real bare prairies extend very far north in this longitude, almost reaching this place—. The fort is built upon a flat about 20 feet above the river level, which is of very considerable extent,—The Indians who trade here are Crees and Blackfeet, the latter only, however, when there is any peace as at present. Sometimes, when there is war, smart skirmishing goes on close to the fort, and not infrequently the Blackfeet attack the place itself. On account of the great number of Indians constantly around the fort much agriculture has not been attempted here.

The Earl of Southesk in a visit to Fort Pitt in 1859 commented upon the dangerous location of the fort because of its proximity to the territory of the Blackfoot and the Cree. He wrote: "Fort Pitt stands in a country which is very frequently the scene of Indian warfare, placed as it is between the territories of the Blackfoot and the Crees, and the Fort itself often becomes the centre of hostilities, war-parties lying in wait for another in its immediate neighbourhood."

By 1863 the Blackfeet began to raid Fort Pitt itself, crossing the river from the south and creating a state of fear and apprehension among the traders who had hitherto considered the region to be safe.

The year 1870 will always be remembered as that of the devastating epidemic of smallpox that swept from the Missouri through the Blackfoot and along the whole length of the North Saskatchewan, attacking indiscriminately Crees, half-breeds, and Hudson's Bay personnel. When William Butler reached Fort Pitt toward the end of November in that fateful year, he found that it was free from smallpox, but as he wrote in his book *The Great Lone Land:*

It had gone through a fearful ordeal: more than one hundred Crees had perished close around its stockades. The unburied dead lay for days by the road-side, till the wolves, growing bold with the impunity which death among the hunters ever gives to the hunted, approached and fought over the decaying bodies. From a spot many marches to the south the Indians had come to the fort in midsummer, leaving behind them a long track of dead and dying men over the waste of distance. 'Give us help', they cried, 'give us help, our medicine-men can do nothing against this plague; from the white man we got it, and it is only the white man who can take it away from us.'

But there was no help to be given, and day by day the wretched band grew less. Then came another idea into the red man's brain: 'If we can only give this disease to the white man and the trader in the fort,' thought they, 'we will cease to suffer from it ourselves;' so they came into the houses dying and disfigured as they were, horrible beyond description to look at, and sat down in the entrances of the wooden houses, and stretched themselves on the floors and spat upon the door-handles. It was no use, the fell disease held them in a grasp from which there was no escape, and just six weeks before my arrival the living remnant fled away in despair.

Butler described Fort Pitt and its surrounding as follows: "Fort Pitt stands on the left or north shore of the Saskatchewan River, which is here more than four hundred yards in width. On the opposite shore immense bare, bleak hills raise their wind-swept heads seven hundred feet above the river level. A few pine-trees show their tops some distance away to the north, but no other trace of wood is to be seen in that vast amphitheatre of dry grassy hill in which the fort is built. It is a singularly wild-looking scene, not without a certain beauty of its own, but difficult of association with the idea of disease or epidemic, so pure and bracing is the air which sweeps over those great grassy uplands."

The smallpox epidemic was not the only significant happening of the 1870s. The huge buffalo herds, long considered inexhaustible, began to decline at an increasingly rapid rate. The year 1873 was the last time that the great herds of buffalo were seen in the Fort Pitt area.

The rebellion in Manitoba of 1870 that, in effect, "crowded out [the Métis] of their country and cheated out of their holdings" aroused apprehensions among the Indian people who feared that they, too, would be dispossessed of their lands by the ever-growing spread of white settlement. At Fort Pitt the Indian bands were particularly hostile, so much so that in 1871 the trader in charge of the post reported that "of late the Indians have been overbearing in manner and threatening at times. Indeed, the white men dwelling in the Saskatchewan are at this moment living by sufferance, as it were, entirely at the mercy of the Indians." To strengthen its position at Fort Pitt, the Hudson's Bay Company appointed to the post William McKay, a longtime veteran in the company's service, "in the interests of the Company's safety and business in the Saskatchewan District at large." Chief Trader McKay (made chief factor in 1873) was well respected by the Indian people, and it was hoped he would be able to dispel the unrest among them.

In September 1876 Lieutenant Governor Archibald arrived at Fort Pitt for the ceremonial signing of Treaty Six with the Indians of the area. The treaty provided that in return for the Indians' surrendering their rights to an area of approximately 121,000 square miles, they would receive an annual payment of five dollars per person, reserves of land not exceeding one square mile for each family of five people, a small amount of agricultural tools, some livestock, and a medicine

540

chest for each band. Furthermore, in the event of famine or pestilence, aid and rations were to be provided to them. It was significant that Big Bear, leader of a band of Plains Cree, refused to sign this treaty. He held out until 1882, when, faced with starvation for his people, he reluctantly did sign.

By the end of the 1870s, the Indian people of the Northwest were starving, for not only the buffalo but even the small game had vanished from the plains. In the eighties the situation further deteriorated. The government used the issuance of food rations as a lever to force the Indians to settle on their allotted reserves and accept an agricultural way of life. Starvation, disease, hopelessness, and resentment were widespread among the Indian people. The situation was a powder keg needing only a spark to explode. Because of the potential danger, a detachment of twenty-five North West Mounted Police under the command of Inspector Francis Dickens had been sent to Fort Pitt in September of 1883.

In spite of the growing discontent and unrest among the Indians, Fort Pitt carried on its normal operations. With the advent of steamboats on the Saskatchewan, it had become one of the regular ports of call. At this time the small settlement of Frog Lake, thirty-five miles northwest of Fort Pitt, had begun to grow and even threatened to replace the older fort.

In October 1884 Chief Trader W. J. McLean took over the command of Fort Pitt. He was well aware of the dissatisfaction and resentment of the Indians. However, he always treated the members of the Cree bands with respect, which they, in turn, accorded him, despite their mounting hostility toward white people in general.

Christmas 1884 was celebrated at Fort Pitt with a splendid meal. New Year's, too, was a gala event with another bountiful feast, followed by a grand ball in the evening. W. Bleasdale Cameron in his article "Christmas at Fort Pitt" reminisced about the festivities at the fort:

By half-past eight the ball-room [i.e., dining room of the Big House] was packed to capacity by a crowd of voluble celebrants on tiptoe with excitement and expectancy: the big event of the year was about to open, for they lived for the most part lives of loneliness and isolation and rarely had an opportunity to attend such gatherings or to meet so many of their friends. And now the first dance was about to begin. The master of ceremonies then announced it, the Lancers; the couples took their places, 'Professor' Patsy Carroll mounted his 'podium', rapped for attention, and with a flourish of his baton and a crash of melody, Fort Pitt's grand New Year ball was in full swing and away. From this time forward the gaiety was fast and unconfined. With hardly any intermission dance followed dance—and there were a lot of them.

As the clock strikes midnight, the music and the dancing stop abruptly and the men are invited to the office, where the chief trader produces—apparently from thin air like a magician—a bonnie big flask of Scotch. We all have a nip and drink to the departing year and welcome to the one newly born. Then back once more to the ball-room and refreshments and to the cotillions, the waltzes, and reels, three-steps and polkas. The dance goes on until the night is old and everybody tired and ready—after voting the ball a magnificent success and thanks to the police and the Company for their hospitality—to join in making the rafters ring to the strains of 'Auld Lang Syne' and in mutual Happy New Year wishes, to don their duffle and depart.

Few of these merrymakers had any premonition of what lay ahead in the next year. At least four of those present were destined to die within the next three months, and the fort itself would soon be completely destroyed.

Discontent was steadily intensifying among the Indians. Their complaints to the government Indian agent stationed at Fort Pitt were ignored. When news of the defeat by the Métis of the North West Mounted Police at Duck Lake on March 26, 1885, reached the Crees of Big Bear's band, their long-suppressed frustration erupted in the massacre at nearby Frog Lake. Nine white men were killed, and the rest of the inhabitants of the tiny settlement were taken prisoner. When word of this tragedy came to Fort Pitt, McLean immediately ordered everyone to help in strengthening the fort to withstand the attack that all feared was imminent. Unfortunately, the fort's location on a flat overlooked by surrounding hills made it extremely vulnerable. Furthermore, its stockade had been removed, which rendered it even more defenseless.

On April 13, Big Bear's band of Crees numbering 250 warriors swarmed down the hills to the fort. Big Bear, whose moderating influence was being increasingly challenged by the warlike members of his band led by Wandering Spirit, had managed to persuade his warriors to let the police evacuate the fort and not attack it if they left. A parley was held the following day between Chief Trader McLean and Big Bear and his chiefs outside the fort and beyond the range of its guns. The meeting was abruptly terminated by the sudden appearance of three of the police riding hard toward the fort. They were returning from a scouting mission they had undertaken the previous day in spite of McLean's strong objections. The Indians, thinking they were the objects of a surprise attack by the "Red Coats," commenced firing at the

542

riders, killing one and wounding another. McLean was instantly made a prisoner.

The Indians were now thoroughly aroused and making their demands with increasing vehemence. McLean, held captive at the Indians' camp, wrote a letter to the fort urging all the civilian inhabitants of the fort (including his own family) to surrender to the Indians and informing Dickens that unless he and his force withdrew immediately, the fort would be attacked and no one within it would be spared. Dickens accepted the offer, and within a few hours the police left the post, hastened down to the river, embarked in the leaky scow moored there, and, after a hazardous trip down the Saskatchewan, reached safety at Battleford. As soon as the police had disappeared around the bend in the river, all the civilian inhabitants came out through the fort gates and walked over to the Indians and into the custody of Big Bear. He did what he could to extend his protection to the Hudson's Bay people and the other captives, many of whom were half-breeds with relatives among the Crees and others old-time traders who were still friends to the Crees.

The Indians quickly stripped the fort of all of its supplies. That done, it was put to the torch. An eyewitness described what happened when the Indians burst into the deserted fort:

Forcing the doors of the H.B. stores, the Indians rushed in. Each seized the first thing he could put his hands on. It might be a cask of sugar, a chest of tea, a princely fur, a bolt of calico, a caddy of tobacco, a keg of nails—it was all one. Off he rushed, set it down outside and hurried back for more. When he returned his first prize was certain to be gone; another—a weaker brother—had appropriated it. A woman might get hold of a fine wool shawl, some buck fancy it for his wife and she would be forcibly dispossessed. It was bedlam and war for the spoils, Indian expletives mingling with blows and outcries. Tins of Crosse and Blackwell's Yarmouth Bloaters, jars of pickled walnuts and pâte de foie gras, imported at great expense all the way from London, were slashed open with knives, sniffed at and flung on the ground. The police hospital stores were got at. The red men evidently believed all medicines in use by the police were 'comforts;' they drank them, until one old man nearly succumbed. Then they decided the enemy had tried to poison them. They hesitated to use the sacks of flour piled in tiers for the defense of the fort; the police, they thought, might have mixed strychnine with it.

The thirty-three civilian prisoners, which included Chief Trader McLean and his wife and nine children, were forced to remain with Big Bear's band for nearly two and a half months as the Indians fought rear guard actions striving to escape capture by Generals Strange and Middleton, who were pursuing them relentlessly. Eventually McLean was successful in arranging terms of peace for them in exchange for the release of the prisoners. It was not until June 24—seventy-one days after the surrender of the fort—that they made their way back. One of McLean's daughters wrote: "What a different place it looked now! The fort itself had been destroyed by fire. A large area leading down to the bank of the river was covered by military tents. . . . Drawn up at the bank lay the steamer 'Marquis.'" All that was left of Fort Pitt were two small buildings. However, by September Angus McKay, clerk, was able to reopen the post and begin the task of rebuilding. During the next few years a dwelling house, men's house, and stable were constructed.

But Fort Pitt's days of prosperity never returned. The main tide of settlement had shifted to the south of the North Saskatchewan River. By 1890 William McKay, Jr., recognized that Onion Lake, about twenty miles distant, was more advantageously located for the fur trade than Fort Pitt. He, therefore, simply moved all the buildings from the old fort to Onion Lake, where a company outpost had been established three years earlier, and Fort Pitt ceased to exist.

We followed a narrow secondary road along the north side of the Saskatchewan River to the site of Fort Pitt. On the grassy plain by the river once occupied by the palisaded fort there is now but a solitary structure. This was erected some years after the dismantling of Fort Pitt. Built of whitewashed squared logs and with a hipped roof, it serves to re-create in a small way the illusion of Fort Pitt as it once was. The location of the other fort buildings is indicated by identifying markers. Bald hills and brush-filled draws still overlook the river flatlands.

The appearance of the area is little changed from the days when Big Bear's warriors poured down from these hills intent on attacking the isolated fort below. Today the steamboats have gone from the river, the screech of the wooden carts bringing buffalo meat is no longer heard, the vast herds of buffalo have disappeared, and the Crees are living on the nearby Frog and Onion Lake reserves.

As we stood on the riverbank enjoying the peaceful scene before us, it was difficult to realize that perhaps it was on this very spot that Chief Factor John Rowand's life had ended so abruptly. The only sounds breaking the stillness were the clear, melodious song of the western meadowlark and the steady murmur of the river flowing swiftly eastward. Perhaps only the mournful cry of the coyote each evening at dusk will keep alive the memory of Fort Pitt and the people who lived and worked there.

Fort Ellice

Fort Ellice I was established by the Hudson's Bay Company in 1831 in order to retain the trade of the Assiniboines and Crees and keep them from dealing with the Americans who were infiltrating northward from their posts at the junction of the Missouri and Yellowstone rivers and at Turtle Mountain. As a further inducement to the Assiniboines and Crees, the company was forced to trade in buffalo robes, a practice long followed by the Americans.

At a meeting of the Northern Council held at York Factory on June 29, 1831, it was resolved that "in order to protect the Trade of the Assiniboines & Crees of Upper Red River from American Opposition on the Missouri . . . a new Post be established at or in the neighbourhood of Beaver Creek to be called Fort Ellice." This fort was intended to replace Brandon House, which after reopening in 1828 had closed down in 1832. The site chosen for the fort was described by Captain Palliser. "Fort Ellice [he wrote] is situated near the junction of the Assiniboine and Qu'Appelle rivers, . . . both distant about two miles. It is built on a steep thickly-wooded bank, at the foot of which flows the Beaver Creek at a depth of about 200 feet. Like most of the Hudson Bay trading posts it is built of wood and surrounded by pickets." Arthur S. Morton, who visited the site in 1940, reported that "about 100 yards to the west a perennial spring, which breaks out of the upper edge of the valley, was the source of the water-supply of the fort."

Chief Trader Dr. William Todd was its first manager; he was soon followed by James Hughes, who, in turn, was succeeded in 1833 by postmaster John Richards McKay. He remained at Fort Ellice for twenty-five years. Under his skilled and experienced direction the trade was extended greatly and among so many tribes that it was necessary to find interpreters who could speak several different languages. McKay enjoyed considerable prestige among the Indians, who were impressed by his outstanding skills as a horseman, swordsman, and marksman. His qualities of friendliness and fair play, of courage and cordiality, commanded the Indians' respect and loyalty. To them he was known as "Little Bear Skin."

Fort Ellice I, which would operate for thirty years, soon earned a reputation as one of the Hudson's Bay Company's most important posts. It built up a flourishing Indian trade and was able to provide large amounts of buffalo meat and pemmican for distant posts. It was also renowned for its good food and warm hospitality to all who came within its gates.

When John McKay retired in 1856, he was succeeded by his son, Chief Trader William McKay, who held the post until 1872. The son, a worthy successor to his father, had the tact and expertise of an accomplished trader. While always steadfastly devoted to the interests of the company, William was just and kind in his dealings with the Indians. In the opinion of those who knew him, "he was the model of what a really good Indian trader should be." Thus the tradition of capable leadership was continued.

The workforce at the fort varied from ten to thirty men. In addition, for many years Fort Ellice benefited from the service of two exceptionally capable workers: Henry Millar, overseer of the agricultural and livestock operations, and Jacob Beads, a highly skilled and versatile carpenter.

The land about the fort was fertile and well repaid the unremitting attention that was devoted to farming. Numerous entries in the fort's journal refer to cutting potatoes for seed, plowing, sowing turnips in the kitchen garden, planting cabbage, supervising the building of haystacks, cutting hay in the valley flats, "milking and attending the cows and doing sundries little jobs in the gardens."

In May of 1858 Chief Trader McKay could take pride and satisfaction in the knowledge that in his storehouses, well cooled with ice cut from the river during the winter, were 11,518 pounds of pemmican, 4,782 pounds of dried meat, and 500 pounds of grease—the products of successful buffalo hunts.

The services of Jacob Beads were indispensable. He made harness and Red River carts for the ever increasing number of brigades passing through the fort; he built York boats and bateaux to transport the cargoes of pemmican, meat, and furs to Fort Garry at the Forks of the Red River; he made snowshoes and dogsleds. As head carpenter he was responsible for the construction of all the buildings of Fort Ellice II. His many skills and fine workmanship were a legacy that was remembered and respected both by the men who had worked with him and those who followed him.

Captain Palliser commented in his report written in 1857 that, "Once it [Fort Ellice] was a very lucrative emporium, but now its principal value is derived from its importance as a post for trading provisions; two excellent ferry-boats have been placed one on each of the rivers—[i.e., Assiniboine and Qu'Appelle]; thus the whole of the trade in the country, both that of the Hudson Bay Company and also of those engaged in opposition, pass by the fort, so that the Hudson Bay Company often obtain considerable advantage from their rivals in the trade, who are frequently obliged to exchange the furs traded by them from the Indians for the common necessaries of life, which can only be obtained at this fort."

Henry Youle Hind during the course of his Assiniboine and Saskatchewan exploring expedition of 1858 visited Fort Ellice several times. He wrote in his *Narrative:* "Fort Ellice was at one period a post of considerable importance, being the depôt of supplies for the Swan River District, now removed to Fort Pelly. The buildings are of wood, surrounded by a high picket enclosure. Mr. McKay, one of the sub-officers, was in charge at the time of our arrival. Some twenty years ago, before the smallpox and constant wars had reduced the Plains Crees to a sixth or eighth of their former numbers, this post was often the scene of exciting Indian display." He also noted that "Fort Ellice, the Qu'appelle post, and the establishment on the Touchwood Hills, being situated on the borders of the great Buffalo Plains, are provision trading posts." Hind noticed that "the grasshoppers at this post had destroyed the crops last year . . . Provisions were very scarce at the post, and had it not been for the fortunate arrival of the hunters with some pemmican and dried meat, we should have been compelled to hunt or kill the ox."

By 1862 the decision was made to move the fort about a mile to the east to a site on the edge of the high plateau overlooking the Assiniboine valley.

Dr. Milton Cheadle has left a quite colorful account of his and Viscount Milton's arrival and stay at Fort Ellice during the time that the new post (Fort Ellice II) was being constructed:

Thurs. Sept. 4, 1862 . . . Arrive at Fort; gates closed. Made a great hullabaloo. Doors open; drunken Indian, with only breechcloth on, immediately seizes my hand with friendly shake. The Factor Mr. McKay appears without shoes or stockings. He had gone to bed having no candles made & just been aroused by drunken Indian. Provide us with dried meat & galette & makes us beds on floor with blanket from store.

Friday, September 5th . . . took a turn toward new Fort to see that & view some Indian & half-breed lodges. Making pemmican. Half-breeds just driven in from Fall hunt by Sioux who killed one man, two women & a boy, surprising them whilst cutting firewood.

Saturday, September 6th . . . Indians & Squaws come into Fort, especially about meal times & squat in corner. Mackay kind in giving food & tobacco. Says he makes many bad debts with them, lends them carts & horses often for plain hunt. Many drunk. Company abolished liquor traffic except at Fort Garry . . .

During the 1870s settlers commenced to move westward from the

Red River in ever-increasing numbers. Fort Ellice became the great gateway through which they passed. This made the fort a very busy place, straining its facilities to the utmost to supply both their needs and those of its Indian customers. In addition, freight from outlying posts was constantly arriving. Brigades of Red River carts, their wooden wheels and axles screeching shrilly, entered and departed through the ponderous gates of the fort on their way east or west almost daily. The fort even became the head of navigation as steamboats arrived there after laboriously following the twists and turns of the Assiniboine.

At this time the headquarters of the Swan River district were transferred from Fort Pelly to Fort Ellice, and Chief Factor Archibald McDonald came in to replace William McKay as head of the fort.

To service the ever-increasing movement of people and freight, additional buildings and warehouses had to be built. N. M. W. J. McKenzie, who succeeded Jacob Beads as carpenter in 1876, wrote a detailed description of Fort Ellice as it was when he was stationed there in his book *The Men of the Hudson's Bay Company:*

The Fort was built in a large square, the big front gates being about thirty yards from the front of the bank which was very precipitous at this point, and well wooded with small trees, ferns of all kinds, and saskatoon bushes. . . . on one side of the square was a long row of one-storey log buildings, with thatched roofs all joining each other. The carpenters shop was at one end of this row and blacksmiths' shop at the other. The doors or entrances all facing to the Fort. There was a men's house, the mechanics' house, the native servants and dog drivers' houses, also the married servants' houses, each of which . . . consisted of one large room. . . . Two tiers of rough bunks round the walls were the sleeping accommodations, while a large mud chimney, open fire place, provided ventilation. . . . on the other side of the square, in an equally long row, built in the same style, were warehouses, ration houses, dry meat and pemmican house, flour, pork and beef house, and a well appointed dairy, with a good cellar and lots of ice.

On one side of the big gate in front was the trading store and district office, and on the other side the fur store and reserve stock warehouse, each of these buildings were very long and substantial, fully one-and-a-half storeys high. . . . The main building in the Fort was the Boss's or the "big house," . . . being the quarters of the Officers and clerks. It stood well back in the square, its front being in line with the end of the long rows of buildings on either side, so that every house in the Fort could be seen from its front windows. It was a two-and-a-half-storey, 60 X 40 feet building, with a large kitchen behind, built . . . and known as a Red River frame building. It was made of 8 inch logs, 10 feet long, set in a frame. It

548

has a nice balcony and verandah, the main entrance being in the center of the building, and opening into a large recreation and council hall. The boss's private office was to the right, and the parlour or sitting room to the left. Large mess room, dining room, and private bedrooms were in the rear. Upstairs was a large hall and reading room, and bed rooms for the clerks. The same mud chimneys—two of them—only more elaborate and massive than those belonging to the other buildings were in the big house. There were four fire places on the ground floor, and another in the kitchen, as well as a large cooking range. A splendid mud oven stood outside for baking bread and cooking extra large roasts. There was also a fine well close at hand with the proverbial oaken bucket attached to a rope and chain. . . . all the houses were mudded and white washed with lime, altogether they presented a good appearance from a distance. A four foot side walk ran all around the square, and another one from the front gate to the front door of the big house. There was a nice vegetable, flower and kitchen garden of about an acre behind the house. The flagstaff stood at the front gate, and the Belfrey stood outside the Boss' private office. A high stockade enclosed the whole square, so that when the big gates were locked at night there was no danger of losing any scalps before morning.

Fort Ellice's days of glory were not destined to last forever. The disappearance of the buffalo from the plains in the 1870s signaled the beginning of its decline. Then the railroads came and their tracks, like tentacles, spread out over the prairies, supplanting the bateaux and canoes on the rivers and the Red River carts on the overland trails. Fort Ellice struggled on, but it was a futile effort, for change had brought about the end of its usefulness. One by one the fort buildings were sold to settlers for the timber. The "Big House," a monument to Jacob Bead's skill and superb craftsmanship, was the last to go. By 1900 Fort Ellice was no more. As Arthur S. Morton so aptly wrote: "When the buffalo disappeared and the Canadian Pacific Railway was built across the prairies over which they had grazed, bringing the comforts of civilization to the doors of an increasing mass of settlers, the last of the fur trade posts, Fort Ellice, passed away."

Eighty years later we set out to find and photograph the site of Fort Ellice. Our search was not too difficult. Of course, there were no helpful road signs (we were quite accustomed to that), but we were fortunate enough to encounter a young gas station attendant at St. Lazare who gave us the directions we needed. To our amazement, he knew not only the location of the fort but also its history. He told us that he had been one of a group at his high school that had made a de-

549

tailed study of Fort Ellice, which had eventually been issued as a mimeographed report.

Following a narrow dirt road, we crossed the junction of the Qu'Appelle and Assiniboine rivers—a truly significant and historic landmark in the fur traders' canoe highway. About four miles farther south, in the lovely valley between Beaver Creek and the Assiniboine, we came to the steep, deeply rutted trail that led up to the top of the plateau nearly 240 feet above the valley floor. Where once ox-driven Red River carts had labored up this abrupt uphill climb, we now slowly ascended, thanks to the powerful four-wheel drive of our motor home.

Once on top we were rewarded with a spectacular view over the lovely Assiniboine valley. On the far side, a mile away, rose a high plateau similar to the one on which we were standing. The river still "wending its winding way for miles to and fro in the parklike bottom lands" resembled a bright blue ribbon of graceful bends and loops. Some of the bottomlands have now been converted to grain and hay fields. When we were there in September, the gold and bronze of autumn were tinting the trees and bushes marking the river course and covering the slopes of the hillsides.

Of Fort Ellice nothing remains; only the trained eye of the archaeologist can detect any evidence of the fort's existence on this spot. A federal commemorative cairn has been erected about thirty yards from the brow of the plateau on the approximate position of the fort's front gates.

Although the buildings and the stockade have long disappeared, perhaps a better and more lasting memorial to Fort Ellice is the enduring beauty of this valley, which the fort once overlooked—a beauty that still exists today to delight all who see it just as it has always done.

Lower Fort Garry

In 1830 Governor George Simpson determined that a new fort should be built to replace the aging Fort Garry at the forks of the Red and Assiniboine rivers. The minutes of the annual meeting of the Northern Council held at York Factory on July 3, 1830, recorded that "the Establishment of Fort Garry being in a very dilapidated state its situation not sufficiently centrical, much exposed to the spring floods, and very inconvenient in regard to the navigation of the River and in other points of view," it was resolved, therefore, "that a new establishment to bear the same name [Fort Garry] be formed on a site to be selected near the lower end of the Rapids for which purpose Tradesmen be employed or the work done by Contract as may be found most expedient, and as stones and lime are on the spot those materials to be used instead of timber being cheaper and more durable."

A report to the London Committee cited in greater detail Simpson's reasons for this decision:

> The Establishment of Fort Garry is in a very dilapidated state, as much so as to be scarcely habitable, and lies so low what we are every successive spring apprehensive that it will be carried away by high water at the breaking up of the ice. It is moreover very disadvantageously situated, being about 45 miles from the Lake and 18 miles above the rapids.
>
> I therefore determined last Fall on abandoning that Establishment altogether, and, instead of wasting time labour & money in temporary repairs of tottering wooden buildings, to set about erecting a good solid comfortable Establishment at once of Stone & lime in such a situation as to be entirely out of the reach of high water and facilitate any extensive operations connected with craft and transport which may hereafter be entered into; and accordingly selected the most eligible Spot in the Settlement about 20 Miles below the present Establisht., laid the plan & commenced operations without loss of time, and I had the satisfaction of seeing the Walls of the principal building nearly up before my departure, and hope to see New Fort Garry (the only Stone & lime and I may add the most respectable looking Establisht. in the Indian Country) occupied next spring.

In addition to this official explanation for the building of the new fort, it is probable that Simpson was also strongly motivated by several personal desires. He wanted to provide an impressive residence for his young bride that would be away from the raw and rough environment of the trading community at the Forks. He also wanted to avoid the possibility of any awkward encounters between his English wife, Frances, and Margaret Taylor, his discarded country wife and mother of two of his children, whose marriage Simpson had hastily and conveniently arranged to a French-Canadian living in the Red River settlement at the Forks.

Furthermore, the implementation of Simpson's ambitious plans for expanding the Red River settlement's economic base by introducing new items for export, such as tallow, hemp, flax, and wool products, would require his constant presence at Red River for extended periods of time. He undoubtedly felt that his official residence should be one commensurate with both his and the company's importance and prestige.

The site selected by Simpson for the new fort was situated on the west bank of the Red River about twenty miles from its outlet into Lake Winnipeg. In the words of his young wife, it was "a beautiful spot on a gentle elevation, surrounded by Wood, and commanding a fine view of the River." Simpson's more practical appraisal was that it was "a fine level spot, where the banks of the river were high, with abundance of limestone and wood on the opposite shore." Pierre LeBlanc, the company's most capable builder, was brought down from York Factory in 1830 to supervise the construction of the new fort. According to Simpson he was "a very useful man . . . in any capacity."

The Simpsons spent a year in a house that had been renovated and refurbished for their use at Upper Fort Garry. By the fall of 1832 the "Big House" and the fur-loft retail shop of the new fort complex were completed. The Governor and his wife quickly moved into their spacious and comfortable new home. Lower Fort Garry officially became administrative headquarters for the Hudson's Bay Company in Rupert's Land.

Within a year it became apparent that the Governor's twofold expectations that the new fort would become the center for the Red River trade and provide a congenial setting for his married life were not to be realized. It simply could not and did not replace the old fort at the Forks. Lower Fort Garry's acknowledged advantages of a location below the rapids and a site well above flood level were not sufficient to offset its numerous drawbacks. Traders, Indians, and Métis bringing in the indispensable pemmican from the buffalo country along the Red, Assiniboine, and Qu'Appelle rivers balked at the extra travel required to reach the new fort below the rapids. And to the people at the Forks, accustomed to the convenient accessibility of the fort's retail sales shop, the twenty miles to the new fort's retail store imposed an irritating hardship that was quite unacceptable. In fact, in order to retain its retail trade, the company was forced to keep open its sales shop at the old fort. In short, the trading center of the Red River settlement was so firmly entrenched at the Forks that it could not be displaced by George Simpson's efforts to move it downriver.

The Governor had to face other disappointments. Both he and his young wife were suffering from ill health and the profound depression they each felt over the death of their infant son the previous year. There were musical evenings, dancing, and horse racing on the frozen river to help brighten life at the fort. But for Frances Simpson the harsh climate and the rude frontier society became unbearable. Bound by a self-imposed, iron-clad class system, the Simpsons' circle of acceptable acquaintances was extremely limited. It was only his overriding interest in the progress of the building under way at the fort that enabled the Governor to admit master carpenter and supervisor Pierre Le Blanc to his dining table "on Sundays when he has his clean things on." In a letter written to his friend J. G. McTavish, Simpson expressed his great anxiety over his wife's "very delicate health" and added: "and I myself am become so melancholy and low spirited that I scarcely know what enjoyment is—I feel that my health and strength are falling off rapidly. I am most anxious to get away from this country of which I am sick and tired." In the summer of 1833 the Simpsons left Lower Fort Garry and returned to England.

In the year following Simpson's departure, Alexander Christie, acting in his dual capacity as Governor of Assiniboia (the Red River settlement) and a chief factor of the Hudson's Bay Company, pointed out the inconvenience and inefficiency of shuttling between Lower Fort Garry to carry on the fur trade business and Upper Fort Garry to conduct the affairs of the settlement. He recommended, and Simpson agreed, that old Fort Garry at the Forks should be rebuilt and reestablished as the company's administrative center of the fur trade. By 1837 a rebuilt Upper Fort Garry was once more the Hudson's Bay Company headquarters, and Lower Fort Garry had relapsed into a subsidiary trading post and residence for company officials and important visitors.

But Lower Fort Garry was not destined to gracefully fade into oblivion. New buildings were constructed. In March 1834 Thomas Simpson, cousin and George Simpson's secretary during the latter's residence at the Lower Fort, wrote: "This place is a large stone establishment that has cost us a good few thousands, and it is yet unfinished. We are making preparations to build a large granary and provision store this summer, unless the work be stopped. The Big-wigs at home are rather cool on the subject, and I do not wonder at it." Simpson still had plans for the development of the fort and the role it was to play in the future of the fur trade. He wrote to Christie in February 1838: "The lower Fort will I consider in due time become the Principal Engagement for Farming warehousing Holding Courts and Councils & and it will be therefore be necessary to make it a place of some strength and of greater extent than the upper establishment."

During the early 1840s, several of the annual council meetings of the Northern department were convened at the Lower Fort. Various company officials enjoyed the comforts of the "Big House," as did Simpson himself whenever he spent any time at the Red River settlement. In a letter written in 1841 he said: "This is my own headquarters when I visit the settlement; and here also reside Mr. Thom, the recorder of Rupert's Land." As Alexander Ross said, "Lower Fort Garry is more secluded, although picturesque, and full of rural beauty. . . . To those of studious and retired habits, it is preferred to the upper fort." Robert Ballantyne, a new apprentice clerk on his way up the Red River to Upper Fort Garry, recorded his first impression of the lower fort: "The Stone fort is a substantial fortification, surrounded by high walls and flanked with bastions, and has a fine appearance from the river."

The sales shop continued to serve the considerable needs of the parishes of the lower Red River, supplying the imported goods and providing a market for their excess farm produce. In addition, it provided for the requirements of the local Indians and the fur trade.

The Lower Fort because of its location below the rapids in the Red River remained the staging point for the York boat brigades traveling the Portage la Loche–Norway House–York Factory route. In addition, it became the point of departure for most of the northern exploration and scientific expeditions. The list of the intrepid men who began their journey of discovery from Lower Fort Garry to the shouts of well-wishers and the salutes of the fort's cannon is an impressive one. It includes such names as Sir John Franklin, Sir George Back, Sir John Richardson, Dr. John Rae, Peter Warren Dease, Thomas Simpson, Robert Kennicott, and Lieutenant J. H. Lefroy.

In response to increasing tension between Great Britain and the United States over the Oregon boundary dispute and the rising dissatisfaction among the Red River settlers with the company's trading monopoly and their frustration at being denied the right of free trade, Simpson was able to persuade the British government to send a small military force, the Sixth Regiment of Foot, to quell any potential disturbance in the Red River colony and repel any hostile threat from below the border. In September of 1846 this force arrived at Lower Fort Garry, where they were quartered for the next two years.

During this period the massive stone walls and round bastions were completed. This work was largely done by the troops themselves, aided and supervised by Duncan McRae and John Clouston, stonemasons from the Scottish Hebrides brought out by the company in 1837. The walls were three feet thick and seven and one-half feet high and extended 450 feet along each side of the enclosure. Loopholes for the purpose of rifle fire were spaced fifteen and one-half feet apart. A round stone bastion guarded each corner of the fort's quadrangle. The northeast bastion was used as a powder magazine; the bakehouse in the northwest bastion was where large amounts of hardtack biscuit for use on the boat brigades travelling north were made; the bastion at the southwest corner was used by the soldiers as a wash house and cook house. After their departure it became a storehouse. The southeast bastion served as an icehouse.

During the late 1840s, in an effort to appease the ever restless and dissatisfied Red River settlers, the company decided that no longer should the civil government of the colony and the management of the company remain in the hands of one individual. Henceforth, the affairs of the colony would be handled by a civil governor and those of the Company by a company-appointed chief factor. This policy had long been advocated by Simpson and the London Governor and Committee, but it was not easy to accomplish. In actual practice, the company continued to dominate affairs of the Red River colony. Whenever the Governor of Rupert's Land was in the Red River settlement during a session of the Council of Assiniboia, it was he who took over as its presiding officer, not the Governor of Assiniboia. All members of the Assiniboia Council were named by Simpson subject to confirmation by the London company. Although two non–Hudson's Bay Company men had for a brief period served as Governor of Assiniboia, in 1858 the posts of Governor of Rupert's Land and Governor of Assiniboia were held once again by one person, Chief Factor William McTavish who served in this dual capacity until 1870, when Assiniboia became a part of the province of Manitoba.

This resulted in an inevitable weakening and erosion of the company's authority among the people of the Red River settlement. To meet this challenge to their position, the company decided to send over someone from London who would take up residence in the colony and, by means of his presence, reverse this trend. The man they chose was Eden Colvile, son of the Deputy Governor Andrew Colvile. He was appointed a Governor of Rupert's Land—to be a substitute for Governor George Simpson, who was now living in an imposing mansion provided by the company on the St. Lawrence just above the mighty rapids of Lachine.

Governor Colvile and his wife arrived at Lower Fort Garry in August 1850, and once again the "Big House" became the official residence for a Hudson's Bay Company Governor. During the three years the Colviles were at the lower fort, much was accomplished. First and foremost, by his tact and diplomacy the Governor did a great deal to restore the company's prestige and remove some of the animosity felt toward it. Also during his residence at the fort, he made many improvements to the landscaping within the fort enclosure. In addition, he was responsible for numerous alterations within the "Big House," which greatly added to its comfort and appearance.

When Bishop Anderson, Anglican bishop of Rupert's Land, visited Lower Fort Garry in 1852, he remarked that "the fort has been improved with much taste by the Governor and Mrs. Colvile and it began to wear much more of an English aspect; the annuals were above ground and the lawns smooth and green."

Throughout the 1850s building construction was an ongoing activity at the fort according to numerous references in the diary kept by Samuel Taylor, a builder brought over from the Orkney Islands. For example: "November, 1850 . . . The Officers' house finished inside Tuesday and a grand danse given to all hands Wednesday." "October, 1851—The Fort fireplace finished upon the 7th. The new foundation was put under the Front Store at the above time after ship time finished." "November, 1852—The new bell, Casted by C & C Mears, London, in 1850, was put up on the 12th." "November, 1856—Samuel Taylor and Murdoch Smith began to plaster the new bake-house."

In the late 1850s Simpson's plans for a major farming operation at Lower Fort Garry were finally being realized. The fort had become the southern depot for provisioning the trade. Simpson was determined that the bulk of the provisions required should be produced locally at the fort. Alexander Lillie, an apprentice clerk with much experience as a farmer in his native country, was put in charge of the farming operation of the fort. Under his direction, ground was broken on the west side of the fort. During the next ten years his farming and livestock activities increased dramatically. Eventually the fields to the west and north were producing abundant crops of wheat, oats, barley, peas, turnips, potatoes, and a variety of garden crops. In addition, his cattle provided several tons of meat each year for shipment north. In 1868, for example, 500 pounds of pork and 10,000 pounds of beef were dressed. This great expansion of the farming operation required the erection of a whole array of stables, barns, sties, grain-flailing barns, and fenced corrals and yards.

In the 1870s farming activities became progressively less important in the daily life of the fort. The company discovered that it was cheaper for them to purchase their food supply from the local farmers, who were successfully adapting to constantly improving agricultural techniques.

Lower Fort Garry from its very beginning served as an integral link in the transportation system used by the Portage la Loche–Norway House–York Factory canoe and boat brigades. The fort's shore and landing were a scene of lively activity as canoes, York boats, sloops, and steamboats arrived and departed. In the 1850s the appearance of railroads, steamboats, and carts brought about drastic changes in this time-honored transportation system. Shipment by the "southern route," that is, rail to the Mississippi River, steamboat to St. Paul, and cart brigade to Red River, was both faster and cheaper than by the traditional "northern route." Its superiority was so obvious that its adoption was inevitable. However, such a major change did not occur overnight. It was a gradual phase-out, but by 1874–75 York Factory and Norway House became obsolete as major shipping depots, and the northern route was no longer used. However, York Factory did continue to supply the posts north of Norway House. Red River became the center for the fur trade distribution system, with the major part passing through Lower Fort Garry.

This greatly increased volume of transport business required many boats. The enlarged boatyard and boat shed area was a busy place as the company shipwrights worked to turn out the York boats, sloops, and schooners required to meet the constant demand for boats and yet more boats. In 1872 the steamboat *Chief Commissioner* slid off the shipways—the first steamer built in the western Canadian interior. Two years later it was followed by the *Northcote,* which became the first steamboat to navigate the waters of the Saskatchewan River.

In 1871 an event of great significance took place just outside the west wall of the fort. About one thousand Swampy Cree and Ojibwa Indians gathered there and accepted Treaty One, whereby they ceded to the Canadian government all the land that then comprised the province of Manitoba, receiving in return annuity payments and a number of reservations designated for their use. It should be noted that in the minds of the native people signing it this treaty merely accorded access rights to their lands to the government; it did not in any way extinguish their ownership of the land. This conception is still held by many of the people affected by the treaty and remains an emotional and contentious issue to this day.

The decade of the 1860s was in all probability the time of greatest activity at Lower Fort Garry. In an attempt to provide the wide variety of goods and services needed by the company and the settlers, a quite diversified industrial complex was established along the banks of the creek that emptied into the Red River just south of the fort.

H. M. Robinson in his 1879 book *The Great Fur Land* described in considerable detail the entire fort complex, its appearance and its operation, during that period:

> Entering through the huge gateway pierced in the centre of the east wall, facing the river, the first view is of the residence of the chief trader in command, and also of the clerks and upper class of employees. . . . It is a long two-story stone building, with a broad piazzi encircling it on three sides.
>
> With the exception of the residence of the chief trader . . . the buildings of the fort follow the course of the walls, and, in facing inward, form a hollow square . . . immediately at the left of the gateway is the trading-store . . . The sales-room is a square apartment . . . the ceiling merely the joists and flooring of the second flat, . . . from which are suspended various articles of trade. Along the side walls are box shelves . . . on the floor within the counter are piled bales of goods, bundles of prints, hardware, etc., and this space within the counter comprises almost the entire room. A small area is railed off near the door, sufficiently large to hold twenty standing customers. When this is filled, the remaining patrons must await their turn in the courtyard . . . The principal articles of trade are tea, sugar, calico, blankets ammunition, fishing-gear, and a kind of cloth, very thick and resembling blanketing, called duffle. . . .
>
> Amidst this stock of merchandise . . . may be purchased the latest styles of wear, . . . huge iron pots, copper cauldrons, and iron implements, . . . together with ships' cordage, oakum, pitch, and other marine necessities. Over this dispensary of needfuls and luxuries presides an accountant and two clerks. . . .
>
> Leaving the trading-store, a succession of warehouses containing stores and supplies is next encountered. The last and most massive building near the gateway, is the warehouse of packages destined for posts inland. These are goods, imported from England and other countries, and to be used in the fur-trade exclusively. In this vast bulk of merchandise there is not a single package of over one hundred pound weight. The greater portion weigh but eighty or ninety pounds, strongly packed, the cases lined with zinc and bound with iron. The packages are of this limited weight from the necessity of 'portaging' them . . . sometimes a long distance, upon the shoulders of boatmen . . . Twice annually this warehouse is emptied by the departure of the boat brigades for the interior, and as often replenished by shipment from England. . . .
>
> The wall surrounding the fort is about twelve feet high, and flanked by two-story bastions or turrets at each corner. . . .
>
> Outside the walls of the fort . . . is situated a miniature village of

many and varied industries. In neat dwellings reside the heads of the different departments. . . . Here dwells the chief engineer of all the steam power in use . . . the farmer who directs the cultivation of the immense agricultural farm . . . the herdsman, who superintends the rearing and care of the droves of cattle, horses and other stock; . . . the miller in charge of the milling interests; the shipwright, who directs the building, launching and refitting of the company's fleet. . . . Separate a little stand the flouring-mills, brewery, ship-yards, machine shops, etc. all supplied with the latest labor-saving machinery. Scattered along the bank of the river lie moored or drawn upon the bank, the miniature navy of the company. . . . The remaining surroundings of the fort are made up of a well kept vegetable garden, extensive stock corrals and a large farm under perfect cultivation.

In 1869, after enjoying two hundred years of monopoly in Rupert's Land, the Hudson's Bay Company surrendered its Royal Charter to the Queen in return for payment of £300,000 and Rupert's Land became once more British Crown domain, which, in turn, was admitted into the Dominion of Canada. Out of this transfer was born the province of Manitoba the following year. Winnipeg, the Red River settlement at the Forks, began to grow and prosper, as the center for transportation, trade, and government shifted back and became firmly established there. The need for Lower Fort Garry and its many services steadily waned and finally ended. Lower Fort Garry, like York Factory and Norway House earlier, left behind by change and progress, became largely obsolete. By 1884 the buildings of the industrial complex, as well as the barns and stables in the farm area, had all been dismantled and removed.

However, for the fifteen-year period 1870–85 Lower Fort Garry continued to carry on its fur trading and to operate its retail sales shop. It was during this time that some of its buildings were taken over by various units of the government. The first to move into the fort was the Second Battalion, Quebec Rifles, the French-Canadian units of Colonel Wolseley's troops who had been sent to Red River to quell Riel's Rebellion in 1870. They remained about eight months. The next intrusion into the fort compound occurred in October of 1873 when the first units of the North West Mounted Police were quartered at the fort for nine months while undergoing training. They took over several buildings, including the old pemmican warehouse in the northeast corner, the men's quarters, and the new store recently erected by the company. The officers were housed in the attic of the "Big House."

Next, during the years of 1871–77, the large stone warehouse along the north wall was used as a penitentiary, first by the provincial and later by the federal government. Some years later (1885) for a brief period this same building plus the old stone men's quarters by the west gate served as the lunatic asylum for the province of Manitoba.

During all these years of partial occupation of the fort by government troops and institutions and on into the first decade of the twentieth century, the "Big House," following in the tradition established in earlier years by Governor Eden Colvile and his wife, continued to be a center of hospitality and gracious living for Hudson's Bay Company officials and their numerous guests.

During many of these years (1867–82) Chief Trader William Flett was in charge of Lower Fort Garry. He managed with calmness and competence the many diverse and sometimes conflicting activities occurring within his fort—the demands and needs of the fur trade, the outfitting of brigades, the retail sales shop, the farm, the industrial complex along the creek, the billeting of soldiers, the security requirements of the penitentiary, the upkeep and smooth running of the "Big House." His responsibility was indeed a formidable one. In an article written for *The Beaver* magazine, Flett's daughter described the daily schedule that was followed during her father's regime.

> The life at the fort was a simple but happy one. The business in a way was conducted on military lines. At six a.m. when the fort bell rang, everyone started out to their several occupations; at seven-thirty the bell rang and everyone went to breakfast. (Mr. Flett made his round of inspection between six and seven-thirty a.m.) The bell was again sounded at eight-thirty and everyone returned to work. One o'clock the dinner bell rang; two o'clock work again. At five o'clock Mr. Flett again made his rounds. At six o'clock the bell rang and everything was closed for the day.
>
> On Saturdays the bell rang at five 'o'clock, the closing hour for that day, so as to give the men time to get their supplies.

When the company was reorganized in 1871, the position of Chief Commissioner was created to replace that of Governor of Rupert's Land. The commissioners were expected to make Winnipeg their headquarters. However, they all managed to spend part of their time, particularly during the summer, at Lower Fort Garry.

For Donald Smith (afterward Lord Strathcona) and Commissioners James A. Grahame and Clarence C. Chipman, Lower Fort Garry became a favorite summer retreat—a most desirable alternative to the official residence in Winnipeg. The social elite of Manitoba and Canadian society all enjoyed the hospitality of the "Big House." The names of Vice Regents, Governor Generals, Lieutenant Governors, industrial magnates, literary men, and artists all appeared on the pages of the fort's guest book. The "Big House" had, in truth, become the center for gracious living—"a good, solid, comfortable establishment"—exactly as Simpson had once hoped.

In 1911 Chief Commissioner Chipman and his family, who for the past twenty-one years had spent every summer at the fort, returned to London, and the "Big House" was needed no more. No longer did life and laughter fill its rooms. With Chipman's departure, John Stanger, company clerk, who had operated the retail sales shop ever since 1893, was ordered to balance his books and shut down the operation. With the closing of the shop's heavy doors for the last time, Lower Fort Garry ended its eighty years of existence as a fur trade fort.

Just as in Italy all roads lead to Rome, so in Winnipeg all highways for historically minded people lead to Lower Fort Garry, although since the imaginative and exciting development of the Forks many have been attracted to that area as well. This restored Hudson's Bay Company's trading post has become a lodestone attracting thousands of visitors each year. Early one beautiful morning in late June of 1985 we drove the twenty miles north from Winnipeg to the fort. Already the enormous parking lot was rapidly filling with a steady stream of cars, tour buses, motor homes, trailers, motorcycles—the twentieth-century equivalents of the horses and carriages and carts that formerly brought people here.

We entered the fort through the main gate in the east wall. Directly in front of us was a beautiful greensward enclosed by a low decorative fence of white wooden spindles. We could glimpse the "Big House" in the center of this emerald setting at the far end of a boardwalk. A magnificent spruce tree and cannon dating from 1846, when British soldiers were billeted at the fort, flanked the open entrance gates on each side. The wooden walkway leading to the front entrance of the "Big House" was shaded by lovely trees and bordered by colorful flower beds that we often paused to admire. Lower Fort Garry was "living history" at its best. The many buildings that comprised the fort had been superbly restored and furnished with meticulous care. They are now occupied and brought to life by the talented people who reenact the daily activities of the men and women who formerly lived and worked within the fort. They performed their parts so convincingly that it was often difficult to realize that they were not, in fact, the characters they portrayed. Standing on the low veranda by the front door were "Governor Colvile and his lovely wife," who graciously welcomed us and invited us to come inside. This we did and for the next hour wandered from one room to another, happy to have this opportunity of getting an intimate glimpse of what life was like in the "Big House."

On the ground floor were the parlor, dining room, office, and bedrooms assigned to the chief factor and later the chief commissioner and their families. These rooms were all furnished with the highly polished mahogany typical of the Victorian period. Touches of elegance were evident in the spinet, silver candlesticks, crystal decanters, marble statuary, pictures, and window draperies. Elsewhere on the first floor were the large men's dining room, company office, men's gathering room, and bedrooms. These were more simply furnished—mahogany replaced by pine, silver by pewter. One thing all the rooms had in common. This was the Carron iron box stoves with their long length of black stovepipe extending with many an angle from stove to wall.

We descended to the large ground-level basement. Here the walls were of whitewashed stone, ceiling beams and floor posts were massive and rough-cut, and the windows in the three-foot-thick walls were small. In addition to the ever present box stoves with zigzagging lengths of stovepipe were well-used open fireplaces. This was, in a way, the very heart of the house, for this was where the work was done that permitted the "Big House" to function smoothly and pleasantly. Here the meals were prepared, the laundry done. Here were the various pantries, closets, and storerooms for goods and supplies, liquor, and spirits. And here, too, the house servants ate and had their quarters. We stopped to chat for a moment with two smiling women servants who were busily rolling out flat cakes and to admire the two already nicely browning on the griddle in front of the red-hot coals glowing in the fireplace. We envied the lucky workers who would get them to eat at their noon meal.

Outside just to the rear of the "Big House" was the massive stone bake oven where bread was baked.

We next walked over to the large stone building by the south wall. This was the combined retail sales shop and fur loft. This massive building of very pleasing proportion was most impressive. It had two and a half stories and had a chimney at each end and a hipped roof broken by three dormers in the front.

As we stepped into the retail sales shop, we were pleasantly greeted by a young clerk standing behind the counter that extended around the three sides of the room. Behind him was a rich and varied assortment of goods neatly piled on the box shelves that lined the walls. China, tinware, clothing, boots, hats, blankets, yard goods, traps, tobacco, beads, guns, ammunition, and, as they say today, "much much more" were on display. As we turned to leave to make room for others, we noticed that the clerk had moved to the far end of the counter, where, in a small space partitioned off by a wooden railing, he was busily making entries into his daily ledger.

The east side of the building was taken over by the fur loft and the storage warehouse. At one end of the huge warehouse area, which was filled with barrels of all sizes, crates, boxes, and burlap-wrapped bales piled from floor to ceiling, was the clerk's office, where he kept track of all the goods and supplies shipped into and out of the warehouse. Off in one corner was his small bed. Martin Pépin, who "role-played" William Lane, the company clerk who from 1848 to 1862 managed the sales shop and the loading and unloading of the York boat brigades, kindly interrupted his record keeping long enough to chat a few moments with us. We were fascinated to learn that he was a direct descendant of Pierre Falcon, who wrote the well-known Métis ballad *La Chanson de la Grenouillère,* celebrating the Métis victory at Seven Oaks. In a small way, we felt that through our conversation with Martin Pépin we had touched a living link with the past.

We went upstairs to the fur loft, where we met genial and knowledgeable Bill Romanik. He was busily engaged in compressing beaver skins in the fur press into a standard ninety-pound bale. We were quite overwhelmed at the tremendous number of lustrous furs hanging from the rafters. There were wolf, fox (red, black, silver, cross, and white), lynx, mink, muskrat, marten, and otter. Beaver pelts were stacked up in piles on the floor, as were some buffalo robes. Ermine with their distinctive black-tipped tails were hung up in bunches of a dozen. Beaver castors dangled from a rope stretched along the wall. Close to the press was a large balance scale used for weighing the furs. At a little table in front of the small dormer window in the loft Bill kept his tally book, where he carefully accounted for all the furs received and shipped. We couldn't resist stroking a few of the lovely furs as we moved past them toward the stairway to the ground floor. And in the true spirit of a fur trader, we were trying to calculate their value in terms not of "Made Beaver" (the fur trader's unit of value) but current dollars. The only thing we knew with certainty was that there was a fortune in furs stored in the company's fur loft.

The last building within the fort's walls that we visited was the men's house. This sturdy hipped-roof stone building was where many of the men servants of the company were quartered. As might be expected, its accommodations were quite simple. Low, narrow beds plus each man's small wooden chest containing his personal possessions sufficed to furnish the bedroom. The foreman, however, had the luxury of a room to himself, with the additional comfort of a wide bed, an armchair, and a table with a portable writing desk on top. Advantage was taken of the bare walls as a place to hang rifles, powder flasks, snowshoes, antlers, hats, and the long sashes favored by the voyageurs. The small kitchen was equipped with a two-tiered box stove that served the dual purpose of cooking and heating. There was also a bake oven in the huge chimney that formed one end of the room. Crude wooden tables, stools, and benches plus an assortment of iron and tin utensils completed the furnishings. Wool socks and towels drying on a line stretched across the kitchen added a touch of realism that brought life to the room.

We next turned our steps to the buildings outside the fort enclosure, first stopping at the old blacksmith's shop just beyond the south wall. Here a giant of a man with a Santa Claus beard of snowy white was pounding away at his anvil. Always glad of an excuse to pause in his strenuous work, he came to the doorway to chat with us for a few minutes. We were particularly interested in the cumbersome wooden cagelike structure with its chains and wide leather straps that stood just outside his shop. This, he explained, was a shoeing rack and harness for horses and oxen.

We followed the riverbank southward, and a short distance beyond the blacksmith's shop we came to the farm manager's cottage. Surrounded by a rail fence, this simple dwelling with its freshly whitewashed and hand-squared log walls was a beautiful example of early Red River frame construction. It was originally the home of James Fraser and typical of the river lot farmhouses of the Red River settlement. It had been moved to this site from its original location in Winnipeg in 1970.

Close behind the farm manager's home was the stone dwelling that was built about 1840 and occupied successively by a number of company employees. These included John Black, recorder of Rupert's Land; Chief Factor Alexander Christie, the Governor of Assiniboia; Chief Factor John Ballenden; and Chief Factor Donald Ross and his wife, Mary, of Norway House. Chief Engineer E. R. Abell and his family lived in it during the 1860s. Sturdy and "four-square," hipped-roofed with one massive chimney in the center front, this home was sited so that it commanded a sweeping view of the river. It was shaded by a single box elder or maple tree and enclosed by a wooden fence. There was a thriving well-kept kitchen garden behind the house (we could not see a single weed!) and a line of bright white washing blowing in the breeze, all attested to excellent housekeeping and industrious habits.

As we stepped inside the house, we were warmed by the fire crackling in the fireplace and by the cordial welcome from the mistress. She was sitting by the window busy at the never-ending sewing and mending. We complimented her on the vegetable garden, and she agreed it had indeed done well this past season—no late frost and sufficient rain and, most important, no invasion of grasshoppers.

After resting for a short while, we took our leave and continued along the bank of the river. Below us was the landing where in former days canoes, York boats, and steamers had beached. Now the trail leading down to the river was no longer crowded with men bent low under their heavy loads transporting the goods and furs back and forth from the warehouses to the canoes and boats. Today two empty York boats tied up at the river's edge were the sole reminder of the great number that once lined the shore.

Reluctantly we turned away from the Red River—a river so beautiful and so significant in the life of the fur traders and early settlers alike. We walked toward the west through the area of the industrial complex that had once flourished along the old creek. The foundations of many of the buildings still remained. The great variety of industries carried on here was most impressive. Signs identified a malt house, distillery, lime kiln, gristmill, sawmill, and York boat building shed.

At last our day at Lower Fort Garry came to a close. Thanks to the enlightened and dedicated efforts of Parks Canada and its staff, who re-created so realistically the people who had lived and worked at the fort, we had been able to step back in time and for a brief moment catch a glimpse of what life at the fort had really been like so many years ago.

Bow River Fort/Piegan Post

In the summer of 1832 the Hudson's Bay Company was compelled to face the fact that their trade with the Piegans was being seriously threatened by the American Fur Company from their forts on the upper Missouri River. Indeed, it was reported that the Piegans had traded 3,000 beaver during the previous winter to the Americans at their post at the junction of the Marias and Missouri rivers. For many years the Hudson's Bay Company had refused to comply with the Piegans' request for a post in their hunting territory, insisting that the Piegans come to Rocky Mountain Fort on the North Saskatchewan. Now, however, with the presence of the Americans close to their hunting grounds, the Piegans no longer needed to make the longer journey to Rocky Mountain House. If the Hudson's Bay Company was to regain the Piegan trade, they had to give them the fort in their home territory that they had been demanding for so long.

According to the minutes of the annual meeting of the Northern Council held July 9, 1832, at York Factory, "The recent defection of the Piegan tribe rendering it unnecessary to maintain the Rocky Mountain House which was originally established for their convenience, *It Is Resolved* 34. To abandon that post and to establish a new post to be called the Piegan Post on the borders of the 49th parallel of latitude, with a view to attract that tribe and to prevent other Indians who are in the habit of frequenting the Honble Company's Posts in the upper part of the Saskatchewan from crossing the line."

To implement this resolution, Chief Factor John Rowand (in charge of the Saskatchewan district) and Henry Fisher, who had been at Rocky Mountain House during the previous winter, went up the Bow River and selected a site for the post. The place they chose was on a plateau on the north side of the river at the mouth of Old Fort Creek. Rowand returned to Fort Edmonton; Fisher remained to oversee the building of the new fort.

Chief Trader John Edward Harriott was transferred from the Columbia district to take charge of the new post. Harriott, who had spent many years on the Saskatchewan, chiefly at Fort Carlton, was a highly experienced trader well regarded by fellow traders and Indians alike. In the words of George Simpson, Harriott was "a finished Trader. Speaks Cree like a Native and is a great favourite with Indians; has much influence likewise with the people and is generally esteemed by his colleagues. Strong, active and fit for Severe duty. Mild tempered, well disposed, and bears an excellent private character."

Accompanied by Patrick Small, clerk, and sixteen men, Harriott arrived at the Bow River post on October 10. Fisher and his crew of ten men, wasting no time, had the new fort nearly completed. It was a five-sided stockaded complex of considerable size. The rear or western wall was roughly parallel with the edge of the ravine at the bottom of which still flows Old Fort Creek; the south wall faced the Bow River. The main entrance was in the front or eastern wall, while the north end of the compound was in the form of an acute angle. The buildings were ranged along the southern and western walls as well as in a line forming the base of the triangle of which the two northern walls were the sides, and all faced inward upon a central courtyard. A bastion was at the southwest angle of the stockaded enclosure. The Indian hall was located at the southeast corner of the fort.

Harriott sent Small and four men back to Edmonton. This left Harriott, in addition to Fisher, twenty engaged men, among whom were Colin Fraser (sometime piper for George Simpson) and Hugh Munro, plus four free half-breeds, to conduct the winter's trading. Harriott was not too optimistic about the prospects. In a letter written to his brother-in-law, John McLeod, Harriott had expressed his doubts about the success of the post, fearing that the number of beaver he would be able to trade would not be large. As it turned out, his fears were confirmed.

Only forty tents of Piegans came to trade at the new fort. The majority had already traded most of their beaver to the Americans. In spite of his best efforts, Harriott was not able to divert their trade from the American forts to Bow River Fort. However, the Blackfeet, Bloods, and Sarcee "upwards of 500 tents" converged on the new fort eager to trade there, but Harriott, following company policy, which mandated that they should take their trade to Fort Edmonton, "refused to open his wicket" and was forced to turn them away. After a disappointing winter, the post was closed for the summer. Harriott summed up his first season at Bow River Fort in the following words: "I never passed such a troublesome winter before in the Indian country and what is most distressing, nothing to show for it."

The post was reopened in August of 1833. Once again Harriott was in charge, assisted by Fisher and twenty other men. Hoping to secure the Piegan trade, Governor Simpson had hired "Jimmy Jock" Bird to establish contact with the Piegans and persuade them to bring their skins to the new fort. Jimmy Jock, half-breed son of Chief Factor Bird, was married to the daughter of a Piegan chief and had lived with the Indians for many years and acquired much influence with them. But Jimmy Jock failed to deliver. It is not clear whether it was because, as he claimed, the Piegans were defeated in battle by the Bloods and prevented from coming to the fort, or as Harriott had forecast, sufficient trade just did not exist, or Jimmy Jock reneged on his pledge to the company (as he had been known to do on other occasions). The result was that the season's prospects were so poor that Harriott decided in January of 1834 to abandon the post and reopen Rocky Mountain House. He wrote: "There being no advantage to be reaped by remaining at this place . . . I have determined on leaving it and retreating to the old Rocky Mountain House to secure the Trade of the Blood Indians where we shall be able to bring them more to our terms than at this place."

The lack of success in diverting the Piegan trade from the Americans, coupled with the constant danger to lives and property due to the post's exposed location in the territory of the volatile and frequently hostile Blackfoot and the very high trade cost, combined to end any further attempts to reestablish Bow River Fort.

Twenty-five years later, the Earl of Southesk camped by the ruins of Old Bow Fort on his way to Fort Edmonton. He described the spot as follows:

> The ruins of Bow Fort stand on a high bank overhanging the river,—here very rapid and about fifty yards wide. Looking eastward down the vale, the eye ranges far over extensive prairies, bounded by low hills, whose features are partly hidden by a few small woods occupying their slopes and spreading into the valley beneath. The colours of the foliage were most lovely in rich autumnal tints—gold, olive, green and crimson, according to the different varieties of trees that were grouped into clumps, or mingled together in the groves.
>
> The plains are all strewn with skulls and other vestiges of the buffalo, which came up this river last year [1858] in great numbers. . . . They are now rapidly disappearing everywhere; what will be the fate of the Indians, when this their chief support fails, it is painful to imagine.

The site of Bow River Fort is within the Stoney Indian reserve. To visit it we needed permission from the Stoney Indian band council. Through the good offices of Ian Getty of the Nakoda Institute, who presented our request, that permission was graciously granted. We drove west from Calgary along the secondary road on the north side of the Bow River. Just east of Old Fort Creek we turned south on a side road that led to the Stoney park and ceremonial lodge and to the Bow River Fort site.

It would be difficult to find a more beautiful spot. To the east as far as we could see stretched the open grassland plateau high above the waters of the Bow River. To the south beyond the river rose a range of rolling bluffs whose slopes were green with spruce and fir or yellowish-green with prairie grass and sagebrush. To the west, the broad valley narrowed dramatically as the wall of the Rocky Mountains closed in, leaving only a narrow gap through which the young Bow River, released from its source high in the mountains, made its tumbling way—the beginning of its long journey eastward to eventually unite with the Oldman River to form the South Saskatchewan. What an awesome sight this was! The mountains were like a storm-tossed sea of granite waves, each peak striving to reach higher and ever higher toward the blue sky overhead.

The site chosen for the fort was a most strategic one. About one hundred feet below the plateau were the Bow River on the south and Old Fort Creek on the west, while to the east stretched extensive open grasslands. Today the site is enclosed by a simple two-rung pole fence. Within this enclosure are the mounds, depressions, and piles of stone and rubble—all that is left of Bow Fort. We walked over the area, taking many photographs and trying to fit these remains into the layout of the five-sided fort as described by early observers. And not for the first time did we regret our lack of archaeological training—training that would have enabled us to better understand and interpret the significance of these visible evidences of the fort's existence.

We wandered over to where the southwest bastion had once been and looked down at the Bow River just below us. A sparkling white-capped rapid interrupted the smooth flow of the river. To our right Old Fort Creek issued out of its dark spruce-covered ravine to join the Bow, and towering over all were the mighty Rockies, their appearance changing constantly as the big fleecy clouds that drifted by momentarily shut out the light from the sun. For quite some time we just stood, quietly enjoying this unspoiled grandeur that we were privileged to see. It was difficult to turn away from it.

As we slowly walked toward our motor home, for the first time we noticed some animals in the far distance to the east. Probably cattle or horses, we thought, but yet there was something strange about them. We decided to investigate. As we approached closer, we discovered, much to our delight, that they were buffalo grazing on the grassland just as their ancestors had once done in such vast numbers over one hundred years ago. Their great dark brown burly forms slowly moving across the prairie were a link with the past—a wonderful bonus we had not expected.

The site of Bow River Fort is not marked with any official cairn or tablet. Perhaps the prairie flowers—the pale pink of rose, yellow of goldenrod, and white of daisy—that brighten the sere grass and sage-brush covering the fort ruins are sufficient to preserve the memory of its former existence here.

Fort Nisqually

Several factors were responsible for the establishment of Fort Nisqually at the southern end of Puget Sound. The first was Governor Simpson's strongly held conviction that agriculture was one of the keys to reducing the high cost of trading west of the mountains. Second, it was imperative to acquire and maintain a strong presence north of the Columbia River to reinforce Great Britain's claim to the land north of that river. Furthermore, the company's promotion of colonization accompanied by production of wool, tallow, and hides would serve to offset some of the criticism and attacks by the British Parliament on the company and help secure the renewal of their License of Exclusive Trade. Finally, it was considered desirable to have a post located midway between Fort Langley near the mouth of the Fraser River and Fort Vancouver on the Columbia. Such a post would provide a measure of safety for the Hudson's Bay men traveling over the Cowlitz Portage between the two forts.

With all this in mind, Chief Factor John McLoughlin instructed Chief Trader Archibald McDonald, when returning from Fort Langley to Fort Vancouver, to examine the area around Puget Sound as to its suitability for agricultural development.

McDonald's report was highly favorable. "For thirty miles along the coast and as many if not more towards the interior, it is a fine prairie country interspersed with islands of oak and other wood," he said. He also reported that the soil was equal to that at Vancouver and in the deep water of Puget Sound vessels of any kind could come to within a few yards of shore.

In the first entry in the official journal for Fort Nisqually, dated May 30, 1833, McDonald wrote: ". . . while on a trading expedition down Sound last Spring [1832] with 8 or 9 men, I applied about 12 days of our time to the erecting of a storehouse 15 feet by 20 and left Wm Ouvre and two other hands in charge." This was the beginning of Fort Nisqually.

A year later McDonald returned to Fort Nisqually to commence the task of establishing the post. Dr. William Tolmie, who accompanied him, described their arrival in his journal dated May 30, 1832:

At 5M [McDonald] & I started in advance at a brisk canter & arrived at Nisqually shortly after noon, having crossed several plains intersected the belts of wood & two steep hills where obliged to dismount. Forded the Nisqually about 3 miles from its mouth, . . . but rapid & broken. Passed some pretty green hills, sprinkled with young oaks & winding away to

571

westward, continued along the same plain which extended still as far as the eye could reach to Northward & descending a steep bank arrived at the proposed site of Nisqually Fort on a low flat about 50 paces broad on the shores of Puget's Sound—the most conspicuous object was a store half finished next a rude hut of cedar boards—lastly a number of indian lodges constructed of mats hung on poles in a the shape of a cartshed. Welcomed by a motley group of Canadians, Owyhees & Indians, & parties of the latter were squatted around the fire, roasting mussels.

Later on the same day McDonald showed Tolmie where he proposed to locate the fort on top of the bluff just south of the creek; the farm was to be a short distance inland. According to Tolmie's journal: "The fort is to be erected along the bank of a streamlet [Sequalitchen], which in its devious course through plain presents points well adapted for Millseats, & the most fertile spots in the comparatively barren prairie are to be ploughed for a crop of potatoes & pease, this season. M. [McDonald] is doubtful whether to erect the store houses at the mouth of the streamlet, or 150 yards to S.ward, where one is already nearly completed." In addition to the storehouses it was also planned to erect corn and sawmills, a threshing mill, and a bridge across the stream. A small garden, about forty yards square, was planted just east of the post.

Chief Trader McDonald had expected to meet the company ship *Vancouver,* which was transporting trading goods and materials for the construction of Fort Nisqually plus seed and supplies for the farm, upon his arrival at the fort site. It was nearly two weeks before the *Vancouver* finally appeared. The much-needed building supplies were off-loaded, as well as various trading goods. During the next week Chief Trader McDonald was able to trade 380 beaver. He was also able during his three weeks at the fort to witness the completion of a small house constructed on the farm site about one-quarter mile up the creek, as well as to mark out locations for the mills, the bridge, other necessary buildings, and the stockade to enclose the fort.

It had originally been intended that Dr. Tolmie would sail on the *Vancouver* farther north to Millbank Sound to take charge of Fort McLoughlin, which was located there. However, when Pierre Charles, a valued and longtime company servant, gashed his foot most terribly with an ax, it was decided that Tolmie should remain at the fort in order to administer proper medical care. He was also, upon Chief Trader McDonald's departure, to be in charge of the fort until the new replacement arrived.

Tolmie received detailed instructions from McDonald regarding the completion of the fort and the erection of the stockade, all of which he carefully noted in his journal: "The people are at present building a frame house for their own accommodation, at the south end of the store, between it and Pierre's shed—the space in front of both houses is to be picketed in, only leaving sufficient room for a path between stockades & high water mark—a line of stakes running along the foot of the bank from the corners of each is to connect the houses behind, and another row extending from the front corners of houses to the anterior range of pickets will complete an inclosure comprehending all the space between & in front of houses to the pathway which must be left. There is to be a gate in the middle of front line."

On June 21, Chief Trader McDonald left for Fort Vancouver, leading three horses loaded with the 380 beaver he had traded, and Tolmie began what was to be a long career as a fur trader.

A week later Chief Trader Francis Heron arrived to assume charge of Fort Nisqually. Although quite disgruntled at being transferred from the comforts of the well-established Fort Colville, Heron nevertheless energetically began the task of continuing the construction and development of Fort Nisqually.

Although the fort was intended as a fur post, farming and livestock raising were prime objectives as well. Because of this, Chief Trader Heron quickly decided that the store, built earlier on the shore where it was convenient for fur trading, should be removed to the farm on the uplands where the fort was built. Under his direction the work of constructing the fort on the prairie bluff about one-half mile from Sequalitchew Creek was vigorously pushed forward.

The first structure erected by Heron served the purpose of combined dwelling and storehouse until it was dismantled and replaced at the end of the year, when the more permanent men's house and the storehouse were completed. A high picket fence enclosing all doorways and windows was built between the two buildings. This was designed to enable the men "better to withstand an attack, likewise in some degree a security against many petty depredations of the Indians living nearby." The courtyard formed by the enclosure was where "the Indians can remain while waiting their turn to trade." In addition, the construction of two bastions was begun.

Chief Trader Heron's stay at Fort Nisqually was brief. He had been there barely a year when on May 18, 1834, his successor, William Kittson, arrived to assume charge of the fort. Exemplifying the old adage that a "new brome sweepeth cleane," Kittson, after completing a critical survey of his new surroundings, immediately began to make changes. At his direction, the buildings within the stockaded area were either relocated or rebuilt. The only structures that received his approval were the two bastions. By the time his improvements had been completed, Fort Nisqually was quite changed in appearance. It now consisted of a dwelling house for Kittson and his family, a separate kitchen, a store, a men's house partitioned so as to provide separate quarters for married men and their families, and an Indian hall. In addition, a cellar for the storage of potatoes was dug, a stable built, and an Indian house constructed outside the stockaded area to shelter visiting Indians.

During this period of rebuilding, Kittson did not allow the normal trading and farming activities of the fort to be neglected. By the efficient use of his staff of seven men, the furs were traded, baled, and transported to the company's headquarters at Fort Vancouver. Crops were planted and harvested; prairie and marsh grass was cut, cured, and stored as hay. On June 11, 1834, the first cattle (three cows with their calves and a bull) arrived at the fort. These were the beginning of a herd that would eventually number in the thousands.

During his second year at Fort Nisqually, Kittson, in addition to trading and farming, devoted much effort to the improvement and expansion of the farm facilities. A fifty-foot-by-twenty-five-foot barn, a small grain storehouse, a pig sty, and a milk house were constructed. The fort's livestock was increased by the arrival from Fort Vancouver of four cows with their calves, four oxen, and five plowhorses. The fort's defenses were strengthened by the construction of a bastion over the front gate, bringing the number of such structures to three.

From its founding in 1832 Fort Nisqually had been intended to serve not only as a fur trading post but also as a center for extensive farming operations and as a convenient post for the company's coastal vessels. Its trade in furs, though initially promising, began to decline a few years after the establishment of the fort. Chief Factor James Douglas in a letter to Governor George Simpson commented: "The Trade of Fort Nisqually Pugets Sound, has been on the decline since the close of Outfit 1835; and whatever may be the cause, it is still in active operation, as there is a further reduction on the Returns of this year; ascribed by Mr. Kittson who is in charge, to the prevalence of disease among the natives, and the wars existing between several of the Tribes inhabiting the Sound, who display in their mutual intercourse an uncommon bitterness of hostility."

To offset this negative aspect of Fort Nisqually's performance, Douglas praised the farming operation, writing: "Tho' the soil arround Fort Nisqually is of an inferior quality, the Post derives much benefit from its farm, it is tilled by the regular establishment of men belonging to the place, without any additional expense, except the very moderate cost of implements." Under Kittson's able management, the fort's farming efforts assumed an ever-increasing importance. Although rainfall and weather temperature could not be controlled, crop yield from a soil that was quite barren and sandy was greatly improved by the use of the natural fertilizer supplied by the livestock. By 1839 Kittson had several acres ready for cultivation near the small lake by the fort as well as about a mile farther on the level prairie near the banks of the Sequalitchew Creek.

Chief Factor James Douglas recognized Kittson's achievement in a report he wrote on October 14, 1839, to the company's London headquarters: "He [Kittson] has also been more successful than usual in farming: all former attempts in this way were in a measure defeated, through the unproductive character of the soil, which is hardly fit for tillage, in its natural state, the produce having been seldom found to exceed two to one seed: This year Mr. Kittson contrived to manure a small wheat field, and was rewarded with a crop of 250 Bushels, a result attesting the capabilities of the soil when materials for enriching it are within reach. I mention this circumstance because it is not generally supposed that provisions to maintain a large establishment of people could be raised at this Post . . ."

In 1838 the fort's livestock was increased by the arrival of 634 sheep shipped from San Francisco. Fence building became a major continuing activity as the increasingly large numbers of farm animals had to be confined in fenced enclosures. In addition, fences were required to protect the various crops. Farming, livestock tending, trading furs, remodeling and repairing buildings and equipment, plus the daily tasks of carrying water from the creek to the fort and the providing of firewood for the buildings, kept the men at Fort Nisqually busy. There was little time for leisure.

From 1837 on when the company steamship *Beaver* first docked at Fort Nisqually, the post became a regular port of call for the company coastal vessels. At about this time the Puget Sound Agricultural Company was formed as a subsidiary to the Hudson's Bay Company. Its purpose was twofold: (1) to strengthen British claims to land north of the Columbia River; (2) to gain substantial profit from supplying Russian Pacific coastal posts with meat and other farm products as provided by an agreement made between the Russians and the Hudson's Bay Company.

The Puget Sound Agricultural Company's Cowlitz Farm lacked adequate grazing grounds, but nearby Fort Nisqually had extensive acreage of such lands. Therefore, in 1839 the Hudson's Bay Company gave the agricultural company joint ownership of the fort. Fort Nisqually soon became its chief station, devoted primarily to grazing and stock farming, while the Cowlitz Farm concentrated on production of wheat, barley, oats, peas, and potatoes. However, all fur trading remained under the control and jurisdiction of the Hudson's Bay Company.

By the fall of 1840 William Kittson's health had deteriorated so severely that he was obliged to leave Fort Nisqually and return to Fort Vancouver to seek medical care. He died there in December of the following year.

In a progress report written to the London Committee in November of 1841, Governor Simpson had this to say regarding Fort Nisqually:

> ... I have great satisfaction in saying that the journey [from California to Fort Vancouver in the Columbia] was accomplished with less loss than might have been expected, as 3,200 sheep and 551 cattle were safely conveyed to the banks of the Columbia, from whence they were forwarded to Nisqually.
>
> There is a large extent of fine pastoral land in the neighbourhood of Nisqually, covered with a tufty, nutritious grass, peculiar to the country. The soil, however, being light and shingly is not so well adapted for tillage, but by proper attention it may be improved. It is not here intended to raise more grain, or other farm produce, than may be necessary for the maintenance of the establishment, and for provender for the sheep during the worst of the rainy season and while the ewes are bearing and rearing their lambs. As yet little more than 100 acres have been broken up, producing about 1500 bushels wheat, oats and pease, besides potatoes and barley.
>
> There are in all, 4530 sheep and about 1000 cattle belonging to the Puget Sound Company at Nisqually ...

Four years later the number of cattle had increased to 2,280 and of sheep to 5,872.

For the next few years Fort Nisqually was under the charge of Alexander C. Anderson (1840–42) and Angus McDonald (1842–43). During that time farming and trading were carried on as usual. It was during this period that the *Beaver* was berthed at Fort Nisqually for an overhaul that required the replacement of rotten bottom planking and the installation of new boilers. Also, a new lighter of about 150 tons to be towed by the *Beaver* was constructed by the ship's crew as well as a big warehouse on the beach at the foot of the roadway leading up to the top of the bluff where the fort was located. This much-needed structure designed to receive the cargo off-loaded from the ships replaced the earlier one that had been dismantled by Chief Trader Heron ten years earlier.

In December of 1842 the London office had written to Chief Factor McLoughlin that "while Dr. Tolmie was here, we had much conversation with him on the subject of farming, to which he seems to have given a good deal of attention, and as it is desirable that the services of a Medical Gentleman should be available at the settlements of the Pugets Sound Company at Nisqually and the Cowlitz where a numerous agricultural population are assembling, you will station him at Nisqually, where he will combine the duties of his profession with those of Indian trader and superintendant of farming operations, . . ." In compliance with this order Chief Factor McLoughlin "placed Dr. Tolmie in charge of Nisqually to manage Puget Sound affairs at that place, a charge for which I am happy to say I consider him fully qualified, and in which he takes great interest." So in May of 1843, Dr. William Tolmie returned to take charge of Fort Nisqually, where he was to remain for the next sixteen years.

Almost immediately he decided that the fort should be both enlarged and removed to a location nearer a freshwater supply. The site chosen was about a mile east of the existing fort on the south bank of Sequalitchew Creek. It was close to some of the fort's extensive fields already under cultivation. Some of the buildings from Kittson's fort were dismantled and reassembled at the new site; others were left standing to be removed later.

When the new fort was completed several years later, it included a dwelling house for the chief officer and his family, one for the men, and two storehouses. Close by were built all the many buildings required by the fort's extensive farming livestock operation, such as barns, horse and oxen stables, calf shed, slaughterhouse, building for sheep-shearing and beef curing, piggery, and dairy.

The dwelling house used by Dr. Tolmie was known as the "Tyee House." Built earlier by William Kittson, it was moved from its original site to the new fort. It contained two main rooms: an eighteen-foot-long-by-twelve-foot-wide dining room and a bedroom, with a small room built onto the south end of the building. It was not until 1848 that bastions and a stockade were erected to provide the fort with security from potential hostile attack. Each bastion contained a small swivel gun with a one-pound ball capacity, plus a supply of musketoons, blunderbuses, and flintlock trading muskets.

During Tolmie's first years at Fort Nisqually, the scope of the farming operation was greatly expanded. The number of regular employees required rose from seven to twenty-nine; in addition, a large number of Indians were employed as day laborers. The farm's animal and grain products found ready markets in Russian Alaska, Spanish San Francisco, and the Sandwich (Hawaiian) Islands. Wool from the fort's large flocks of sheep, which in 1849 numbered 12,419, was sent to the company in London. A contemporary account of Fort Nisqually has been left by Paul Kane, the artist, who visited the fort in 1847:

> April 7th—We found some difficulty in crossing the Nasqually River, as the rains had flooded it, and we were obliged to adopt the usual plan where canoes cannot be obtained, that is, swimming at our horses' tails, and floating our things over in skin baskets. A couple of hours brought us to Nasqually, which was established by a company called the Puget's Sound Company, for grazing and farming. When I visited it, it had about 6000 sheep and 2000 horned cattle. Its site is beautiful, on the banks of the eastern end of Puget's Sound. The land is inferior to that in some other parts of the same district, the soil being gravelly; the grass, however, grows luxuriantly, and the mildness of the climate adapts it well for grazing purposes, as it is never necessary to house the animals. The wool, which is good, finds its way to the English market by the Company's ships, and the cattle are slaughtered and salted for the Sandwich Islands and the Russian dominions.

In 1846 the treaty between the United States and Great Britain was signed establishing the forty-ninth parallel as the boundary between the two countries. A provision in the treaty confirmed the British rights to the use of the lands south of the forty-ninth parallel presently occupied by the Hudson's Bay and Puget Sound Agricultural companies pending a final adjustment. For Fort Nisqually this meant that although it was now in American territory, it would for the time being remain under British rule. The farming and raising of livestock continued uninterrupted.

The land owned by the Puget Sound Agricultural Company under the management of Fort Nisqually extended from the Nisqually River north to the Puyallup River and from the Cascade Mountains west to Puget Sound. Small farms or "stations" were set throughout these extensive prairie grasslands. Each was assigned to a single worker who remained at his station in order to care for the sheep and cattle in his area.

In the years following the Oregon Boundary Treaty of 1846 a steady stream of American settlers began to come into the lower Puget Sound region. Many of them came to the store at Fort Nisqually to trade. Most had little capital and few as yet had surplus farm products.

Utilizing the abundant cedar trees of the region, they began to make cedar shingles, which they traded for the food and clothing items they needed. The fort acquired an enormous inventory of shingles. When Dr. Tolmie asked Chief Factor James Douglas whether he should continue accepting the shingles, he was told not to stop the trade, since the settlers were dependent upon it for their survival. Ultimately the big building boom in San Francisco absorbed their entire inventory of shingles, yielding a handsome profit for the company.

By 1850 ten Americans had staked off land claims within the boundaries of the Puget Agricultural Company's holdings. Although served with a written notice by Dr. Tolmie stating that they were trespassing on company land, the squatters ignored the notices, refusing to move. By 1853 the number had risen to fifty. The encroachment was not limited to land. The company's cattle and sheep were also taken almost at will. Dr. Tolmie was powerless to resist; the squatters had the upper hand, for they knew the courts were sympathetic to their claims.

Another source of harassment for Fort Nisqually was the levying of custom duties. It became apparent that the American collector of customs was prone to act in a manner quite arbitrary and strongly biased against the British company. For the Hudson's Bay Company trying to keep their trade lanes open between Fort Victoria and Vancouver Island (British territory) and Fort Nisqually in American territory, it was another obstacle with which they had to contend.

On September 29, 1850, the U.S. Congress passed the Donation Land Law, which entitled any male U.S. citizen over eighteen years of age to a half-section (320 acres) of unsurveyed public land in the Oregon country. This was interpreted as a green light for the invasion of lands held by the Puget Sound Agricultural Company. By the early 1850s Edward Huggins, the young clerk at Fort Nisqually, had served notices on as many as seventy people who, in response to the Donation Land Law, had moved onto company land. These notices clearly stated that these people were squatting on land to which the Hudson's Bay Company had been guaranteed possessory rights according to the terms of the Oregon Treaty of 1846. The squatters were even staking out land claims that included the long-established Indian village at the mouth of Sequalitchew Creek and their burial grounds on the bluff above.

This irresistible influx of settlers onto company land made it apparent that appraisal of the lands and buildings along with an official survey of the company holdings must be made to establish a basis for the determination of compensation upon their eventual relinquishment to the United States.

In spite of the problems caused by squatters and tariff hassles, farming was carried on as normally as possible under the circumstances. The California gold rush of 1848–49 had caused a shortage of dependable employees, so the company was forced to rely more on Kanakas, Spanish, and Indian workers, most of whom were not as productive or reliable.

The Territory of Washington was created in 1853, and one of the first things the new Governor (Isaac Stevens) did was to make a series of treaties with the Indians whereby they would cede title to their lands and agree to live on designated reservations in return for certain services furnished by the U.S. government. The Indians were given no voice in the location of the reservations, and when they attempted to express their dissatisfaction and to secure land more suitable to their traditional way of life, incidents occurred resulting in bloodshed and the Puget Sound Indian War of 1855–56.

Dr. Tolmie endeavored to remain neutral throughout this conflict. His relations with both the Indians and the U.S. military force at nearby Fort Steilacoom had always been friendly. He sought to avoid getting embroiled by withdrawing his Indian workers from their farm stations, where they might be targets for undisciplined soldiers or angry settlers. At the same time, he asked for a small contingent of soldiers from Fort Steilacoom to reinforce his few men at Fort Nisqually in the event the Indians might attempt to overrun the post in order to obtain ammunition. In spite of his attempts to remain neutral, he was unfairly accused by some of siding with the Indians. This was probably the result of the anti-company and anti-British sentiment felt by many of the settlers who resented the continuing British presence on American soil.

After the renovations to Chief Trader Tolmie's Tyee House were completed in 1852 (which included remodeling and the addition of a veranda), work was started in 1853 on a new house for the clerk, Edward Huggins. A. M. Daly, a discharged American soldier, was given the job of building and overseeing the other carpenters in the construction of the house. The fort journal recorded that "the house [was] to be built in the Yankee style." It was built of sawed lumber obtained from the first water power mill constructed upon Puget Sound. It was a large (fifty feet by thirty feet) one-story house with an attic and an eight-foot-wide veranda. Inside, it was partitioned into two large rooms (parlor and dining room, each twenty-seven and a half feet by sixteen feet) plus two bedrooms and hall. The fireplaces were faced in brick.

By the mid-1850s, although the farming operation was still continuing in spite of many frustrating obstacles, the fur trade had declined drastically. Only one or two brigades a year arrived with furs for shipment from the fort. On December 3, 1853, Dr. Tolmie received notification "that Governor Stevens had received orders to stop the Hudson's Bay Company trade with the Indians." This really had little impact on the fort, however, because the company's trade was now chiefly with the U.S. Army at nearby Fort Steilacoom and the increasing number of settlers in the area. On July 29, 1859, Dr. William Tolmie, who had by now been promoted to the rank of chief factor, and his family left Fort Nisqually and moved to Fort Victoria. Although no longer at his old fort, he still had supervision of its farming operations. Upon Tolmie's departure, clerk Edward Huggins was given charge of the routine activities of the fort.

Twelve years later (in 1871) the Puget Sound Agricultural Company and the Hudson's Bay Company surrendered their possessory rights and claims in return for $650,000 compensation awarded them by the United States. Fort Nisqually both as a Hudson's Bay Company fur trading post and as a farming operation of the Puget Sound Agricultural Company ceased to exist.

Huggins had become a naturalized American citizen in 1859. As such he was eligible to acquire land in the new territory. He filed a preemption claim that enabled him to retain ownership of the Fort Nisqually buildings and some of the land surrounding them. He remained in his old house at the fort and continued to farm and raise livestock. He also kept the sales shop open and even traded in furs for a few years. In 1906, when seventy-five years old, he sold the farm, and Fort Nisqually's last tenuous tie with the Hudson's Bay Company and the Puget Sound Agricultural Company was completely severed.

The new owner was the E. I. Du Pont Powder Company. They occupied the site for nearly seventy years, during which time they carried on the manufacture of black powder and other high explosives. By 1930, only two of the original Fort Nisqually buildings were still standing: the factor's house and a granary, and they were scheduled for imminent destruction to make room for projected expansion by the company. Fortunately, before the two buildings were demolished interested civic and historically minded groups led by the Washington State Historical Society and the Tacoma Young Men's Business Club arranged with the Du Pont Company for the acquisition of the two structures. They were removed to nearby Point Defiance Park in Tacoma, fifteen miles distant. There they formed the major components of an ambitious project—namely, the reconstruction of Fort Nisqually complete with its various buildings, bastions, and stockade.

So when we set out to see Fort Nisqually, we headed for Tacoma and Point Defiance Park. The reconstructed fort occupied an elevated wooded knoll overlooking Puget Sound. A rugged stockade with two bastions on opposite corners completely surrounded the compound. We entered the fort through the massive main gate. Arranged around the open square were numerous buildings all carefully located according to their original positions as determined by old records that contained a description of the fort with the relative location and ground size of each building.

To the left of the entranceway was the factor's house. It, one of the two Fort Nisqually structures that had been moved from its original site, seemed to fit comfortably in its new surroundings. Shaded by several large trees, the low one-story building with its veranda across the front presented an inviting and attractive appearance. Inside, one of its two large rooms—the dining room—had been furnished to reflect the time of Edward Huggins's occupance. Blue-and-white English china, crystal wine decanters, candlesticks, and a large covered tureen graced the large dining table, which was flanked by eight mahogany side chairs. The other room, which was originally the parlor, was now a combined museum and gift shop.

On the other side of the compound facing the factor's house was a range of small buildings, including store number three, a granary-warehouse, store number two, and an office-clerk's living quarters. All these buildings were total reconstructions except the granary-warehouse, which was the second of the two surviving Fort Nisqually structures.

Lined up close to the stockade wall behind the factor's house were several other reconstructed buildings, including the new kitchen and the laborers' dwelling house. An object of particular interest was the large iron boiler from the Hudson's Bay Company steamship *Beaver*—a reminder of the fact that the *Beaver* docked regularly at Fort Nisqually and that in the early 1840s it underwent a major overhaul there, including being fitted with a new boiler.

Reconstructed Fort Nisqually makes a significant contribution to the perpetuation of the history of the fur trade. Historical accuracy has prevailed through the entire project. No effort was spared to ensure that the location of the buildings, the methods of construction, and the materials and tools used were authentic. And, of course, the presence of the two original Fort Nisqually buildings saved from destruction adds to the authenticity and value of the reconstructed fort.

At the time we visited this fort in Point Defiance Park, we were unaware that the true site of the original Fort Nisqually was known and that it was a large tract of land now owned by Weyerhaeuser Real Estate Company. As soon as we learned this, we knew we would never be satisfied until we had visited this place. Mr. Robert L. Shedd, vice president, graciously gave us the necessary permission. So one beautiful day in September a few years later, we returned to Puget Sound—this time to see the site of the original Fort Nisqually. At the gates leading into the 3,200-acre tract, now known as Northwest Landing, we were met first by Mr. Vern Moore, manager, and later by Mr. Jack Myers, maintenance supervisor, who cheerfully conducted us to the areas where Fort Nisqually of 1833 and of 1843 had once stood.

Weyerhaeuser had purchased the land from Du Pont in 1976 for the purpose of developing it into a planned community that will include not only an industrial and office area but also space designated for residential, recreational, and civic uses.

In developing their master plan, Weyerhaeuser recognized the historical importance of the Fort Nisqually sites. They earmarked these for permanent preservation and protection. They also hired a competent archaeologist to investigate the sites. As a result of this work carried on over a three-year period, the perimeters of the two fort sites were determined and then delineated by horizontal log markers. An extra bonus was the abundance of artifacts such as beads, Spode china, snuff bottles, clay pipes, coins, and farming utensils that were uncovered.

The area occupied by both the forts of 1833 and 1843 is basically a flat, open plain covered with typical prairie grasses, broken only by a few scattered trees and bushes. In the distance thick forests of spruce, fir, and hardwoods mark the shallow ravines and draws. A road cuts through the middle of the 1833 fort site. A small monument placed by the Du Pont Company identifies this location. Only a huge fir and a locust tree interrupt the smooth expanse of prairie grass within the fort's perimeter.

A short distance to the northeast is the site of the 1843 Fort Nisqually. In the same manner as was done for the 1833 site, the perimeter of this fort has been determined and is now marked by logs. Prairie grasses cover the entire site. Prominent against the skyline are several large locust trees. These had shaded the factor's house when it was located here under their sheltering branches. Close by is Sequalitchew Creek—once the source of freshwater for the fort. It is now hardly recognizable as a waterway, it is so overgrown with vegetation.

We next went to the edge of the prairie plateau—to the high bluff rising steeply from Puget Sound. On the shore far below us not only the first temporary warehouse and shelter for the new Fort Nisqually but also the wharf for the company ships had been hastily erected. Close to where we were standing, we saw traces of the steep trail leading from the beach up to the plateau—the trail up which all the cargo off-loaded from the ships had had to be carried to the large warehouses on top of the bluff, a truly herculean task!

From our vantage point on the bluff we could look far out over beautiful Puget Sound. The *Beaver,* the *Cadboro,* and all other Hudson's Bay Company coasting vessels had long since disappeared. Today their place is taken by the sailboats and pleasure yachts that cruise the blue waters of the sound.

As our visit to Fort Nisqually ended, we left with a satisfied feeling reassured by the knowledge that its sites will be respected and protected by the new owners; that as "Northwest Landing" the land that once saw a vibrant fur trading and farming operation will once again support a thriving, productive community.

Upper Fort Garry

During the troubled years of 1815–16 the Forks (the junction of the Red and Assiniboine rivers) continued to experience increasing acts of violence between Selkirk settlers and their close supporter the Hudson's Bay Company on one side and the North West Company on the other. First the Nor'Westers, after forcing the settlers to leave their Red River colony, totally destroyed the colonists' Fort Douglas. A year later, retaliation came when the settlers, who in the meantime had returned and were under the organization of the colony Governor, Robert Semple, captured the North West Company's Fort Gibraltar. A few months later "the greater part of the N W Co. House and buildings and stockades were pulled down and conveyed to Fort Douglas," where they were used in the rebuilding of that fort. On June 19, 1816, the inevitable confrontation (known as the Battle of Seven Oaks) occurred. Twenty-one settlers and three Métis were killed.

A year later, as a result of the report of Colonel William B. Coltman, appointed by the Governor-General of Canada, all property and land at the Forks was ordered to be restored to its former owners. The North West Company lost no time in rebuilding Fort Gibraltar II just a bit south of its original site. Peter Fidler in his journal for 1819 described how they had "enclosed the whole with excellent sawn oak piquets 14 feet above ground set very close together like a continued wall about 100 feet square." According to Robert Coutts of Parks Canada, "The only known representation of Fort Gibraltar II is a sketch by Peter Rindisbacker made in 1820. . . . It depicts a fairly large comfortable establishment situated immediately adjacent to the junction of the Red and Assiniboine. A number of substantial buildings are shown in the drawing and two large houses have mansard roofs, stone or brick chimneys, and dormer windows. A bastion appears to be located in the southwest corner of the fort."

When the two rival fur companies merged in 1821, the new Hudson's Bay Company decided to abandon Fort Douglas and move into the North West Company's rebuilt Fort Gibraltar II. This fort had the superior advantage of being located on the point between the Red and Assiniboine rivers. Governor Simpson issued instructions to put the "New North West Fort in order so as to remove into it next fall." For the next nine months the work of remodeling and rebuilding the fort proceeded at a rapid rate. The post journal recorded that on September 14, 1822, repairs for the sales shop were begun; eleven days later, it was ready to receive the company's stock of trade goods. By early January of 1823 Chief Factor John Clarke and Chief Trader Thomas McMurray had moved into the newly remodeled fort, which now became the official headquarters for the reorganized Hudson's Bay Company. Simpson changed the name from Fort Gibraltar II to Fort Garry in honor of Nicholas Garry, a company director who had come over from England to facilitate the details of the merger of the two companies. Simpson also felt the name change would help remove feelings of resentment still existing among the Nor'Westers at the occupation of their fort by the Hudson's Bay Company.

Fort Garry was not a very impressive place. Alexander Ross in his book *The Fur Hunters of the Far West* described its appearance in 1825, when he first saw it on his return from west of the Rocky Mountains:

> I was anxious to see the place, I had heard so much about it, but I must confess I felt disappointed. Instead of a place walled and fortified, as I had expected, I saw nothing but a few wooden houses huddled together, without palisades, or any regard to taste or even comfort. To this cluster of huts were, however, appended two long bastions in the same style as the other buildings.
>
> These buildings, according to the custom of the country, were used as dwellings and warehouses for carrying on of the trade of the place. Nor was the Governor's residence anything more in its outward appearance than the cottage of a humble farmer, who might be able to spend fifty pounds a year. These, however, were evidences of the settled and tranquil state of the country.

At this time Fort Garry included a retail sales shop, warehouse, dwelling house, icehouse, root house, and powder magazine.

Disaster struck in 1826, when the worst flood ever to strike the region wiped out almost the whole settlement. Fort Douglas was completely destroyed, and Fort Garry was badly damaged. Simpson commented on the difficulty of keeping "the Dirt and Filth which collects in heaps from our muddy and crumbling walls" out of the goods in the store. When in June the floodwaters finally receded enough to allow Fort Garry to be reoccupied, the post was a "complete pile of ruins ... there being no homes yet habitable for [their] reception." Chief Factor Donald McKenzie set his men to repairing and rebuilding the damaged fort. The July 1828 minutes of the Northern Council recorded: "40. The Establishment of Fort Garry being in a very delapidated state That C.F. McKenzie be authorized to expend a sum not exceeding £100 towards its repairs."

But the deterioration seemed irreversible. At the council meeting two years later (in 1830) it was written in the minutes: "The Establishment of Fort Garry being in a very dilapidated state, its situation not sufficiently centrical, much exposed to the spring floods, and very inconvenient in regard to the navigation of the River . . ."

It was at this time that Governor Simpson made the decision to relocate the company headquarters farther down the Red River just below the rapids. Lower Fort Garry (known locally as the Stone Fort) was built, and in 1832 Simpson and his young wife moved into the new fort. Only a clerk and his helper were left to operate the sales shop required to serve the needs of the people living at the Forks. James McMillan in charge of the nearby company farm reported the Forks "very dull, as the usual stir of Ft. Garry is now down at the new establishment where the Govr makes his headquarters, and the Good Old Fort gone to ruins." The number of *pièces* assigned each year to Fort Garry and the Colony Shop during the ten-year period 1821–32 varied from 364 to 700.

Simpson had decided to discontinue going after the Indian trade in their home territories, but instead to funnel it to the Colony Shop. In a report to the London Committee he explained his decision:

> I consider it would be advisable in different points of view that the Compy. should not follow up the Indian Trade by establishing Posts as formerly in the District but that the business thereof should be confined to the Colony Shop or Store which under good management will certainly realise profits at the present Tariff of advance. The demands of the Settlement will I think in future be equal to one thousands pieces of Goods or the cargoes of Fourteen Boats and as it does not appear that any of the Colonists are likely to open public Stores it will be necessary for the Company to provide that quantity.

In 1826 Chief Factor Donald McKenzie already in charge of Fort Garry since 1823 was appointed Governor of Assiniboia. He served in this dual capacity until 1833 when he left Fort Garry shortly before his retirement. James Hargrave who served as accountant at Fort Garry from 1822–1827 in a letter to Cuthbert Cumming characterized McKenzie as follows:

> Your old Bourgeois is a jolly and plump as ever - rolling about in his inexhaustible good humour, happy himself - and making every one happy around him. He has now as you know the management of both the Colony & Coys affairs here, - and it would do your heart good to see him deciding cases ensconsed in his elbow chair, covered with a buffalo robe, and crowned with the very identical broad scotch bonnet that he used to sport of yore. Titles and dignities made no change either on his outer or

inner man. The same ample suit of grey the same piles of socks - and leggins as capacious as to a pemican Bag still decorate his visible and material parts - to sum up all he is, as you used to call him, still Sir John Falstaff.

It did not take long to recognize that the removal of the company's headquarters from Fort Garry at the Forks to Simpson's Lower Fort Garry was a mistake. Alexander Christie, who had succeeded Donald McKenzie as chief factor of the Fort and Governor of Assiniboia, cited the inconvenience and inefficiency of being obliged to travel to Lower Fort Garry to transact Hudson's Bay Company business in his role as chief factor and then return to the Forks to administer the affairs of the colony as required by his position as Governor of Assiniboia. The colonists, as well, had bitterly resented the move downriver, since it forced them to undergo the hardship of traveling the extra distance to sell their produce and buy the manufactured goods they required.

Governor and Chief Factor Christie urged that the company move back to the Forks in order to better serve the needs of the settlers and to reinforce company authority and control of the growing settlement. His arguments prevailed with the London Committee. Accordingly, preparations began in the winter of 1834–35 for the building of a new stone fort at the Forks. The site chosen was the north bank of the Assiniboine a quarter-mile west of the rapidly disintegrating Fort Garry I. It was oriented so that its main gate faced the Assiniboine. Pierre Le Blanc was brought up from Lower Fort Garry to oversee the stonework.

By 1838 James Hargrave was able to report to the Governor: "The new fort is completed and securely walled in, with two excellent Bastions which completely sweep every side and render it the securest as well as the best finished Fort the Company has in Rupert' Land." Two additional bastions were built before 1845. The new Upper Fort Garry was "a quadrangle of 240 x 250 feet, with stone walls 15 feet high and four corner bastions." Alexander Ross, fur trader and contemporary historian of the Red River settlement, described Upper Fort Garry II in his book *The Red River Settlement:*

> This fort has therefore been rebuilt on a more elevated site than it formerly occupied, and on an improved plan. Its form is nearly square, being about 280 feet from east to west, and 240 from north to south. It is surrounded by a stone wall of 15 feet high, and of considerable thickness; having two large gates on the north and south sides, and four round towers of blockhouses at each corner, with port and loop holes for cannon and musketry. In the inside of the wall is a gallery which runs round the

fort, and which affords a pleasant walk, and an extensive view of the surrounding country. The principal dwelling-house—a large and commodious building—occupies the centre of the square, behind which, and near the northern gate, stand the flagstaff and belfry. There are also houses within the walls, for the accommodation of the officers and men attached to the fort; together with stores and granaries, and—would it were not necessary to add—a jail and court-house for the colony. It was a neat and compact establishment, and reflects great credit on Mr. Governor Christie, under whose eye the work was accomplished.

According to Robert Coutts, in his *The Forks of the Red and Assiniboine: A Thematic History, 1734–1850:*

The layout of the buildings within the fort followed a basic 'H' configuration. . . . A row of buildings along the fort's western wall stored furs, trade goods and plains provisions, as well as the supplies for Red River that had been imported from England via York Factory. These buildings included the inland depot, a fur store and pemmican warehouse. . . . On the east side of the UFG [Upper Fort Garry] compound were a number of structures, including the sales shop. Access to this store by fort personnel and local inhabitants accounted for a number of structural changes to the fort over the years: side entrances or 'postern' gates were added, and later the southeast portion of the wall was demolished to allow direct access to the shop from outside the fort. Also along the east wall were the Recorder's house and the Men's House, both built in 1839. The Main House or officers' quarters was constructed between 1835 and 1837 and was located roughly at the center of the fort quandrangle.

Robert M. Ballantyne, a young clerk newly arrived at the fort in the early 1840s, painted a lively picture of his surroundings. In his book *Hudson's Bay* he wrote:

Fort Garry, the principal establishment of the Hudsons' Bay Company, stands on the banks of the Assinaboine river, about 200 yards from its junction with Red River. It is a square stone building, with bastions pierced for cannon at the corners. The principal dwelling-houses, stores, and offices, are built within the walls, and the stables at a small distance from the fort. The situation is pretty and quiet; but there is too much flatness in the surrounding country for the lover of the grand and picturesque. Just in front of the gate runs or rather glides the peaceful Assinaboine. . . .

On the left extends the woodland fringing the river, with here and there a clump of smaller trees and willows surrounding the swamps formed by the melting snows of spring, where flocks of wild-ducks and noisy plover give animation to the scene, while, through the openings in

589

the forest, are seen glimpses of the rolling prairie. . . . Soon after my arrival, I underwent the operation which my horse had undergone before me, viz. that of being broken in; the only difference being, that he was broken in to the saddle and I to the desk. It is needless to describe the agonies I endured while sitting, hour after hour, on a long-legged stool, my limbs quivering for want of their accustomed exercise, while the twittering of birds, barking of dogs, lowing of cows, and neighing of horses, seemed now to invite me to join them in the woods; and anon, as my weary pen scratched slowly over the paper, their voices seemed to change to hoarse derisive laughter, as if they thought that the little misshapen frogs croaking and whistling in the marshes were freer far than their proud masters, who coop themselves up on smoky houses during the live-long day, and call themselves the free, unshackled 'lords of the creation'!

The place of labor for Ballantyne and the other clerks—the counting room—was furnished with "two large desks and several very tall stools, besides sundry ink-bottles, rulers, books, and sheets of blotting paper."

In its dual role as trading fort and the settlement's administrative center, Upper Fort Garry was a busy place. The arrival and departure of the boat and cart brigades, the spring and fall buffalo hunts, and the planting and harvesting of crops were the major events that controlled life at the fort.

The tasks required from the company's laborers were numerous and varied: construction and repair of buildings, palisades, barns, stables, and fences; cutting and hauling of firewood; plowing, weeding, and harvesting on the nearby experimental farm; pressing the furs into ninety-pound bales; and receiving, sorting, packing, and expediting the tons of supplies, trade goods, and country produce that passed through the fort's warehouses. The skilled tradesmen—carpenters, coopers, and blacksmiths—were never idle. The demand for the kegs and cassettes used to transport trade goods and supplies to the interior posts was never satisfied.

As Robert Coutts has so aptly written in his history of the Forks:

Duties at a major administrative and transhipment post such as Upper Fort Garry involved a great deal of clerical work, the 'dull and insipid calculations' which inevitably accompanied the movement of goods and furs. Not only were detailed inventories recorded of the outfits going to each post, but exact lists were kept of what was in each piece or bundle. One copy of this list, called a packing account, was sent to the receiving post in order to confirm orders and indents. Clerks and their apprentices spent many hours entering the type and amount of various commodities into the post ledger, requisitioning items for the northern posts, purchasing country produce, engaging trip men, outfitting the plains hunters, maintaining inventories of furs and saleshop goods, and keeping the accounts of local settlers up to date.

In addition to the laborers, tradesmen, and clerks required to carry on the work of the fort, local Métis were also hired to man the company's boat and cart brigades and to bring in the fresh and dried meat so essential for survival of the interior posts.

The relationship between the Hudson's Bay Company at Upper Fort Garry and the Red River settlers was at the beginning largely one of mutual benefit. The farms of the settlers, the buffalo hunts of the Métis, and the number of Métis and English half-breeds available for hire supplied the company with much of the country food needed for its northern posts and the manpower for its far-reaching transportation system. The colony, in return, relied upon the company not only for all its goods and supplies but also as a buyer of its surplus farm products and as an employer of importance. However, it was not long before the settlers of Red River began to chafe under the company's iron-fisted economic monopoly of all aspects of the trade in furs. Resentment soon spread to the company's control of much of the political, legal, and social life in the community. Eventually the company had to bow to mounting pressure from the settlers and, in spite of their charter rights, allow, albeit unofficially, others to engage in the fur trade in the Red River region.

Upper Fort Garry was the residence not only of the head official of the Hudson's Bay Company. It was also headquarters for the Council and Governor of Assiniboia.

By 1850 the fort was becoming so overcrowded that enlargement was imperative. During the three-year period 1851–54 the walls were extended northward about 329 feet, which more than doubled the size of the enclosed area. These new walls were built of oak timbers, three feet thick with a packed earth core. A new, spacious two-story house for the use of the company official in charge of the fort was also built at this time. It was located in the center of the newly extended area, where it fronted an attractive landscaped oval garden encircled by a driveway leading to the massive stone gateway in the north wall. Other buildings included in the enlarged fort were a flour storehouse, clerks' quarters, and a large warehouse known as Fort Garry Depot.

This latter building was under the management of Chief Trader William Anderson, who had had many years of similar duty at York Factory. In this depot were stored Canadian and American goods as well as a large supply of English goods required not only for the settlers but also to outfit the Métis, who traded all over the plains. Room was found within the new enclosure for an ample kitchen garden.

In 1852, just twenty-six years after the disastrous flood of 1826, another flood inundated the Forks. Water rose six and one-half feet in the fort buildings. The two buildings and one bastion—all that were still standing of old Fort Garry I—were unable to withstand the flood-waters swirling around them. The bastion toppled into the river, to disappear from sight. The two surviving buildings were so weakened by the flood that as soon as the water receded they were torn down, thus removing the last traces of Fort Garry I—previously known as Fort Gibraltar II.

As described in James J. Hargrave's book *Red River,* Upper Fort Garry in 1861 was a collection of buildings surrounded by an oblong wall built partly of stone and partly of logs. The stone portion had four bastions each used as magazines for the storage of various items. Within the walls in addition to the imposing house where the Governor maintained his residence and where the officers took their mess, was Bachelor Hall which housed many of the company staff and which included the large general hall, or public room, where the men gathered for relaxation, such as card playing, reading from the available books, or exercising their usually rather questionable talent on a musical instrument (most frequently a violin).

Fort Garry serving both as the residence of the Governor and as the central point of the Northern Department was unquestionably the most important post in the Department. It was here that "trading goods for cash, furs or country produce, of forwarding the outfits for certain large districts to their destinations in the interior of the territory, and of banking and transacting a variety of general business with the inhabitants of the settlement took place." In order to handle this wide range of activities, a bonded warehouse, a sale shop, a general office, and sundry stores for pemmican, provisions and other articles of a special nature were needed, each with its own staff of clerks, warehousemen and laborers.

The people living in the fort formed a rather tightly knit community subject to company imposed regulations. A rigid schedule was adhered to for both the conducting of business and for meals: breakfast—7:30 or 8:00; dinner—2:00; supper—6:00; business hours 9:00–6:00, except 2:00–3:00 when offices were closed.

Upper Fort Garry in its role as headquarters of the Hudson's Bay Company and as the seat of government for the settlement was the undisputed social center of the settlement. Its hospitality was extended to the many illustrious visitors—sportsmen, scientists, English nobility, clergy, company dignitaries, plus retired chief factors and chief traders who passed through its gates. The occasional balls and dinners at the fort to which the elite of the settlement were invited were the social highlights of the year.

Christmas and New Year's were appropriately celebrated at the fort. According to Margaret Arnett MacLeod,

> . . . the main building of the fort was painted in startling colors. The long messroom had a huge fireplace at one end which, when piled at night with great crackling logs, lit it brilliantly to the farthest corner.
>
> Here many a sumptuous Christmas dinner was served, and eaten with great jollity. One of the fort cattle was usually sacrificed to the holiday spirit and huge smoking roasts of beef graced one end of the table. There were great platters of fish browned in buffalo marrow and great platters still of game. But the real delicacies of the season were boiled buffalo hump, dried moose nose, smoked buffalo tongue and beaver tail; while among the epicures of the country, the most esteemed dish for the Christmas table was an unborn buffalo calf boiled whole.

Another dinner was described by Charles Mair in a letter written November 27, 1868: "We had a pleasant stay at Fort Garry, and received all sorts of entertainment. They live like princes here. Just fancy what we had at a dinner party there. Oyster soup, white fish, roast beef, roast prairie chicken, green peas, tomatoes stewed, and stewed gooseberries, plum-pudding, blanc mange, raisins, nuts of all kinds, coffee, port and sherry, brandy punch and cigars, concluding with whist until four o'clock a.m. There is a dinner for you, in the heart of the continent, with Indian skin lodges within a stone throw."

The New Year's balls at the fort were gala events. Again according to Margaret Arnett MacLeod, "Guests presented themselves at the small night gate [of Fort Garry] where all the icy winds that blew seemed to sweep around the fort walls. The ancient porter was notoriously slow in shuffling down the long board walk to answer their ring, and old ladies recall how, as girls, dressed in all their finery but with feet clad in dainty white moccasin slippers, they practised their steps on the frozen ground to keep warm." At the ball on New Year's Eve, 1859, after enjoying a sumptuous supper the dancers broke with long-established tradition, for "the hornpipes, jigs, strathspeys and reels, which usually put life into the heels of young Red River, gave way to polkas, gallops and quadrilles which were danced with grace and spirit."

In 1869 the political unrest, dissatisfaction, uncertainty, and apprehension concerning the proposed surrender of Hudson's Bay Company's lands to the English government for immediate transfer to the Canadian government resulted in the Rebellion of 1870, under the leadership of the Métis Louis Riel. On November 2, 1869, in a surprise move he and his followers occupied Upper Fort Garry over the protests of William Mactavish, Governor of Assiniboia, and Dr. William Cowan, chief trader in charge of the fort. By the end of the month Riel had gained complete control of the fort, had placed both the Governor and Dr. Cowan under arrest, had broken into the company's warehouses for supplies, pemmican, and ammunition, and had seized the official record books of the government of Assiniboia. Governor Mactavish, who was gravely ill, was powerless to resist.

On November 19 of the same year the Governor of the Hudson's Bay Company in London formally signed the Deed of Surrender by which the company's two-hundred-year-old charter was relinquished to the English Crown, thereby effectively terminating the company's jurisdiction and monopolistic trading rights within Rupert's Land.

By February of 1870 Riel had succeeded in establishing his interim Provisional Government, of which he was president. He moved into Dr. Cowan's house inside the fort, establishing it as his official "Government House." Both Governor Mactavish and Dr. Cowan were released from their arrest. On April 8 Riel, satisfied that his interim Provisional Government was effectively established and functioning, handed the keys to the fort back to Governor Mactavish.

The Hudson's Bay Company resumed business and by the end of the month was able to reopen its sales shop. Life at the fort and at the settlement returned to its normal cycle of activity: outfits were packed and dispatched to the inland posts; company currency was once more circulated; crops were planted and preparations made for the spring buffalo hunt.

At last, on June 23, 1870, the confusion and uncertainty that prevailed at Red River were ended. By an Order in Council of that date, the holdings of the Hudson's Bay Company in Rupert's Land and the Northwest were transferred to the Dominion of Canada, effective July 15, 1870, and the province of Manitoba, comprising the Red River settlement, was established. The rule of the company had come to an end. Henceforth it would operate solely as an independent trading concern subject to the jurisdiction of the Canadian government. On September 2, 1870, Lieutenant Governor Archibald arrived at Red River to assume his duties as head of the new province. He established his residence in Upper Fort Garry, in the former home of Governor Mactavish, which the Canadian government leased for Archibald's use from the Hudson's Bay Company.

Following the incorporation of the Red River settlement into the city of Winnipeg in 1873 came many changes to Upper Fort Garry. First some of the stone walls were torn down so that access to the company's sales shop at the southeast corner of the fort could be had without the necessity of going through the fort's main gate. A few years later the stone bastions were demolished and four of the warehouses removed to the company's nearby mill. The final blow came in 1882 when the entire south section of the fort (which included the sales shop) was razed so that Main Street could be extended in a straight line to meet the new bridges over the Assiniboine River. And so to avoid the jog in the street that bypassing the fort would have caused, a place that would have been of permanent historic value was ruthlessly destroyed.

With the demolition of the fort's sales shop, the company's retail business was transferred to a new red brick department store on Main Street, where it remained for forty-four years, until it was moved in 1926 to the imposing stone structure it now occupies on Portage Avenue.

The Governor's house built at the time of the 1850 enlargement of the fort was sold in 1888 for $100. It and whatever buildings that still remained were taken down and reerected elsewhere in the city. Soon all that remained of the once-proud Upper Fort Garry, the Hudson's Bay Company's fur trade capital, was the imposing stone gate in the north wall. In 1897 it was saved from destruction and presented to the city of Winnipeg by the company.

Today in the heart of the bustling city of Winnipeg, close to the busy intersection of Assiniboine and Main streets, in a small park shaded by a few beautiful trees, the old stone fortresslike gate still stands—a permanent and poignant reminder of the link of the present modern metropolis to its fur trade beginnings and heritage.

Standing within the massive gateway through which had passed so many of the officials, settlers, traders, and visitors from far and wide—all of whom had played important roles in the creation of Winnipeg from the tiny settlement at the Forks—we were able to glimpse beyond the trees and see, on the far side of Main Street, the southwest corner of the imposing three-story red brick Hudson's Bay House, which until 1989 was the company's main headquarters in Canada.

The move from Upper Fort Garry, which had been the company's administrative center for over fifty-five years, to their new headquarters was a short one—literally just across the street. We thought it quite appropriate that the symbolic tie between the old fort and the new building was not completely severed, for archaeological investigation had shown that the southwest corner of their new building overlapped the site of the company's old retail sales shop once included within the stone walls of the fort. This tie remained unbroken until 1989. It was then that the proud house flag of the Hudson's Bay Company was lowered for the last time from the staff atop their headquarters building, marking its sale to new owners and the transfer of the Hudson's Bay Company's operations to Toronto. This departure of the Hudson's Bay Company from the City of the Forks, where it had played such an important role in the city's founding and development, brought to an end a chapter in Canadian history that had lasted nearly a century and three-quarters.

Fort McPherson

A decade or more after the bitter rivalry and competition between the North West and Hudson's Bay companies had ended in their 1821 amalgamation, the fur trade had more or less stabilized in all but the Mackenzie, Columbia, and New Caledonia districts. These represented new frontiers—new sources of rich furs—as yet largely unexplored and unexploited. Their potential led the Hudson's Bay Company to promote major journeys of exploration for the purpose not only of expanding their trade but also acquiring geographical knowledge of these new areas. While admittedly the chief object of these exploratory expeditions was to locate new sources of fur, the company was also motivated by the need to give the older, continuously exploited districts a respite from trapping and the opportunity to recover.

In 1839 John Bell, clerk, was ordered by Governor Simpson to ". . . proceed down the Mackenzie River in a boat manned by 5 servants and 2 hired Indians and ascending Peels River from its mouth endeavour if time and circumstances will admit to trace that stream to its source. Your principal aim will be to select a commodious situation for an Establishment, and to acquire knowledge of the resources of the country in its vicinity for its support." Bell left his post of Fort Good Hope on June 25 and, after three days going down the Mackenzie River, reached the mouth of the Peel. He ascended this river first by York boat, then, as the river narrowed and increased in velocity, by canoe and by foot for nearly two months. He thought he had finally reached the river's headwaters, but in fact, it was the source of the Snake River, a tributary of the Peel, that he had reached. At a junction of the two rivers about 180 miles up the Peel, he had unknowingly followed the tributary stream rather than the main river. On his return down the Peel, Bell found a location suitable for a trading post about a day and half's journey upriver from the Mackenzie.

A year later, on June 3, 1840, John Bell again set out from Fort Good Hope accompanied by Alexander Isbister, twelve Orkneymen and Canadians, plus four Indian families, who would serve as the post's "home guards"; that is, they would do the hunting, dressing skins, and other chores about the fort. On June 7 the party reached the spot that Bell had chosen for the new fort the previous summer. Bell wrote in the post journal: "Its elevation above the present level of the River is considerable, but not withstanding I entertain some fears of the waters rising in the spring. That is perhaps the only objection which can be urged against it as a site for a Fort but that objection from the uniformly Low & swampy Country through which this River flows is unfortunately impossible to be obviated."

The new post was at first called Peel River Post but later named Fort McPherson after Chief Factor Murdock McPherson. It consisted of a trading shop, the manager's residence, and men's quarters, all enclosed by a wooden palisade. By September construction of the fort was completed and trade commenced. Indians from the Peel and Rat rivers were among the first to bring their furs to the post.

Bell's returns for his first year were most promising. In a letter in August of 1841 to his friend James Hargrave at York Factory, Bell described the first season at his newly established post: "I am happy to inform you that my success in trade has been more successful, having since last autumn procured 1450 Beavers, 1000 Mar [marten] besides some other Furs of less value, forming in all 45 Packs of 85 lbs. ea.—I have at present a fine rich field to work in, and trust in a few years hence to render Peels' River one of the most valuable Posts in this District." The items apparently most in demand by the Kutchin Indians were beads and tobacco.

The following year, Bell's fears regarding the vulnerability of the fort site to floodwaters were justified. On May 26, 1842, the breakup of the ice in the Peel had jammed, forming a dam that forced the water to overflow its banks. The water spread into the fort enclosure and into the buildings. The men quickly moved the stores to a higher spot behind the post. Bell, mindful of an earlier disastrous flood at his former post of Good Hope, had the foresight to bring a large wooden boat to their elevated refuge just in case they had to evacuate the area.

The winter of 1841–42 had been one of hardship for all the posts in the Mackenzie district, and Fort McPherson had been no exception. In another letter to James Hargrave dated August 22, 1842, Bell wrote:

I am likely to be short of last year's quantity of Beaver, from an unforeseen circumstance which I did not expect. The distant Indians from whom the greater part of the Beavers are procured had last winter and spring suffered great privations, which reduced them to the necessity of eating a good many Beaver to keep them from Death's door. When the Party cast up here in May last they looked more like MacBeath's Ghost than human beings! What gave me great pain was our own scarcity of Provisions at that time which would not permit me to assist the Miserable wretches as I could have wished. We are in fact struggling hard to obtain our livelihood at this place during the long and dismal winter. In the summer we catch a sufficiency of Fish for the use of the Establishment, in the fall they are not so abundant, and in Winter they vanish altogether from the River. Large animals are by no means scarce, but the Indians are such miserable hunters that they cannot always kill them.

The majority of the furs that were brought to Fort McPherson came from the west across the Richardson Mountains, a range in the Mackenzie Mountains. The Kutchins, also known as the Loucheux, who inhabited the Peel River and Mackenzie delta, had become the middlemen between the Hudson's Bay posts and the Indians west of the Richardson Mountains, who came to the Peel River Post only rarely or not at all, although they were the source of most of the furs that were traded there.

So optimistic were Bell's expectations for this fort that Chief Factor John Lee Lewes, in charge of the Mackenzie district, in a letter to his friend James Hargrave wrote that "this post [Fort McPherson] if well supplied will be the brightest Feather in the Cap of Mckenzie's River."

John Bell mounted several attempts to find a river passage through the Richardson Mountains that would provide a practical route to the rich beaver country on the western side. He managed to make his way up the Rat River through McDougall Pass and down the Bell River to the Porcupine, a major tributary of the Yukon, but which Bell thought was just a branch of the Bell. Here, deserted by his Indian guide and short of provisions, Bell was forced to turn back, returning to Fort McPherson on July 24. He had regretfully concluded that though the land west of the mountains was "rich in Beaver and large animals," it could not be profitably exploited. He expressed this feeling to his good friend James Hargrave in August of 1842: "What a pity it is [Bell wrote] that a water communication does not exist to enable us to form an Establishment in that apparently rich Country. I fear we cannot succeed in transporting our Goods for the trade through such an abominable track where I could hardly travel with My Gun on My shoulder, scrambling up and down Mountains & deep vallies where goats and Deer could hardly get footing!!" A second attempt was made from Fort McPherson in June of 1843 but again resulted in failure due once more to the desertion of the Indian guide. Bell recorded in the post journal: "The unexpected failure of this second attempt in discovering a practicable overland track by which we might be able to transport goods for carrying on the trade beyond the western Mountains, has blighted my fond hopes."

It was quite apparent that the Kutchin Indians were not going to help the company expand its operations over the mountains, thereby destroying their advantageous position as middlemen, which they presently occupied.

John Bell was nothing if not persistent. Three years after his last attempt, he tried again to find a way over the Richardson Mountains. This time, however, he abandoned the idea of an all-water route across the mountains and accepted the inevitability of an overland portage for part of the distance.

On May 27, 1844, Bell left Fort McPherson accompanied by two of his men and two Indians. It took five days of strenuous climbing to get across the mountains and reach the banks of the Bell River on the west side. There they stopped to hunt for provisions and to construct a birch-bark canoe. They descended the Bell in a few days' time, reached the Porcupine, and continued westward on this river until, on June 16, they reached the mouth of the Porcupine and entered a large river, nearly two miles wide and dotted with small wooded islands. Bell learned from three western Kutchin Indians he encountered that the name of this great river was the Yukon. They told him further that "... the country is rich in Beaver, Martens, Bears, and Moose deer, and the River abounds in Salmon, the latter part of the Summer being the season they are most plentifull, when they dry enough for winter consumption. The Salmon ascends the River a great distance but disappear in the fall."

Shortly after his return to Fort McPherson, Bell made arrangements to have an outpost established at the western end of the portage across the Richardson Mountains. Its function was twofold: located in excellent caribou country, it would provide both meat and leather for Fort McPherson; it would also serve as a halfway house for the goods transported across the mountains from Peel River that were consigned for the Yukon.

In 1849 Bell was transferred to Fort Liard and Augustus Peers took charge of Fort McPherson, a post he held until his sudden death in 1853 at the early age of thirty-three. It was during this period that Chief Trader Robert Campbell's journey of exploration from Fort Selkirk confirmed his belief that the Pelly and Yukon were the same river. Campbell left his fort on the Pelly on June 5, 1851, and headed downstream, carried swiftly along by the strong current. The river widened the farther north he went, but he encountered no treacherous rapids or dangerous canyons. Three days later Campbell arrived at the Hudson's Bay post of Fort Yukon, where he remained but one day. The next morning, following the route pioneered a few years earlier by John Bell, Campbell hastened up the Porcupine River, over the Richardson Mountain portage, and down to the Peel River and Fort McPherson.

Campbell's successful journey had demonstrated that the dangerous Liard River route could now be replaced by the Mackenzie–Peel–Porcupine–Yukon river route. This was officially acknowledged in a letter from Eden Colville, Governor of Rupert's Land, to the company in London dated March 16, 1852: "Mr. Campbell, in June last descended the Pelly to the Youcon post in seventy hours, and estimates the distance to be about 420 miles. . . . We may therefore consider the West Branch [Liard] Route and the post at Frances Lake, which has lately been the scene of so many disasters, as definitely abandoned."

Because of successive flooding nearly every spring, the fort in 1852 was moved downriver about four miles. This time the site chosen was on the west side of the river because of its 100-foot elevation. The Indians, however, pointed out that from that side it would be impossible to see the approach of Eskimo war parties, which periodically descended upon the Indian settlement on the Peel River, whereas the east side afforded a clear view for many miles downstream. The company, recognizing the validity of the Indians' argument, constructed the new Fort McPherson on a high bank on the east side of the Peel—the site it has occupied ever since. Chief Trader Charles Gaudet took over Fort McPherson shortly after the death of August Peers.

After 1859 the feuding between the Loucheux (Kutchin) and the Inuit subsided, and Fort McPherson grew into the most important center in the Mackenzie delta. Trade with the Indians flourished. In 1851, for example, the returns for the fort amounted to £ 14,443. Marten was one of the most important furs traded.

In 1871, John Firth, a remarkable lad of seventeen years, made his first appearance at Fort McPherson. He came from Stromness in the Orkney Islands. After a few years at Fort McPherson, he was transferred to La Pierre's House at the western end of the Richardson Mountain portage and then to Rampart House on the Yukon River. Finally, in 1893, he was sent back to take charge of Fort McPherson, where he remained the rest of his life. He was chief factor there for twenty-seven years, until his retirement from the company in 1921. George M. Mitchell visited the fort in 1898 and described John Firth in his book *The Golden Grindstone:* "John Firth had come out as a boy and had risen from dog-runner to factor through sheer excellence, honesty and force of character. He looked like a man of granite—square, broad, and powerful—and there was a formidable quietness about him which had a compelling effect on Eskimo and Indian. They felt that his cool grey-blue eyes were looking right into their thoughts, and minded their manners accordingly."

Gradually change came to Fort McPherson. In 1887 the big

601

wooden York boats that had to be tracked upstream were replaced by steamers. These held sway for nearly sixty years. Their annual arrival at the fort loaded with supplies and mail was the year's highlight, eagerly anticipated by all the people from the fort and the village. The arrival and departure of the boat were signaled by the customary *feu de joie* fired from the men lined up on the riverbank.

By 1860 an Anglican mission was established in Fort McPherson, and under its influence practically the entire population became members of that faith. The Anglican church built in 1920 still stands and plays an active role in the life of the community.

The great gold rush of 1897–98 brought major changes to Fort McPherson and ended forever their isolation from the world "outside." As many as six hundred eager prospectors converged on the company post preparatory to ascending the Wind and Rat rivers in their attempts of reach Dawson City—the El Dorado of their dreams. It was thus that a link—even though somewhat tenuous—was forged between Fort McPherson and Dawson City. The native Loucheux were in demand as guides, and gradually many of the Peel River Indians diverted their trade from Fort McPherson to the fast-growing city on the Yukon. Although trade at the fort dropped off drastically, the post continued to remain open, but the outposts of La Pierre's House and Rampart House were closed.

In 1903 a detachment of the North West Mounted Police under the leadership of Sergeant Edward Fitzgerald was stationed at Fort McPherson. Eight years later Inspector Fitzgerald, three constables, and an Indian guide set out from Fort McPherson on what was supposed to be a routine 1,000-mile patrol from the fort to Dawson City on the Yukon River. Plagued by unprecedented cold weather, incompetence of the guide, and plain bad luck, the patrol ended in total disaster, with the death of Fitzgerald and his three constables. The men's bodies were finally recovered by a search party led by Corporal Dempster. They were brought back to Fort McPherson, where they were buried in the little cemetery beside the Anglican church.

The bizarre story of the "Mad Trapper," known as Albert Johnson, began in the summer of 1931 when Johnson arrived at Fort McPherson and asked for mail. There was none for him. He next bought a substantial grubstake, paying in cash, and then disappeared into the bush after vaguely indicating that he was headed for the Rat River country. Six months later, in December, Indians complained to the Fort McPherson police that a trapper living in a cabin near the mouth of the Rat River was interfering with their trapline. That started a chain of events resulting in a six-week manhunt that only ended with John-

602

son's death after he had killed one policeman and seriously wounded two others.

Fort McPherson has successfully survived the economic ups and downs brought about by changes in transportation and the influx of prospectors, missionaries, whalers, police, and traders. It has remained a central gathering point for the Peel River Loucheux and an important trapping center for mink, marten, and muskrat. That is what it has been during its long 150 years of existence, and that is what it is today. With the completion in 1979 of the Dempster Highway from just east of Dawson City to Inuvik near the mouth of the Mackenzie River on the Beaufort Sea, access to Fort McPherson is now no longer confined to riverboat or airplane.

We started up the Dempster Highway one beautiful morning in early September. The many dire warnings we had heard of the sharp shale sections of the road leading to punctured tires, its greasy slippery surface when wet, its narrowness, and the steep embankment on each side, plus the frequency of sudden storms at the higher elevations, all had made us somewhat apprehensive of what we might encounter, but it did not dampen our enthusiasm or our determination to undertake the 800-mile round-trip.

The warnings of potential hazards were accurate, but through careful driving at a very moderate speed we suffered no mishap. Actually, the biggest danger came from the big trucks, many of which, showing little courtesy or concern for safety, roared by, raising clouds of dust and stones (many of which left their mark on our windshield). We invariably pulled over as close to the edge of the road as we dared whenever one of these monsters came into sight, and I, especially, sitting on the side of our motor home that appeared to overhang the edge of the steep drop-off, always drew a deep sigh of relief when they were safely past.

The highway winds across the barren lands following the Klondike, Blackstone, Ogilvie, and Eagle river valleys, through the Richardson Mountains, to the flatlands bordering the Peel and Mackenzie rivers to Fort McPherson on the Peel and Inuvik on the Mackenzie. The country is indescribably beautiful; a veritable Oriental carpet of soft yellow, pink, red, peach, mauve, and scarlet spreads over the rolling tundra as far as the eye can see. The dark green of stunted spruce borders the sparkling waters of the rivers racing to join the Yukon to the west or the Peel and Mackenzie to the east. In the distance the mountains of the Richardson, Ogilvie, and Mackenzie ranges provide a glorious backdrop. Many of their summits sparkle brilliantly as the sun strikes their snow-covered peaks. The urge to photograph—to attempt to capture some of this splendor on film—was irresistible, and our progress was interrupted by a succession of stops to get yet one more view or vista that we simply had to "shoot."

Eventually we reached the halfway point at Eagle Plains, where there were accommodations including a motel, RV campground, restaurant and, most important, a garage fully equipped to repair the ravages of the highway. At this point there was a large sign by the side of the road that advised whether the highway was open to travel for the rest of the distance to Fort McPherson and Inuvik. We were lucky—no storms, washouts, or vehicle accidents blocking the road had occurred, so we were able to continue on our journey the next morning. Soon we came to Peel River and were taken across to the east side on a small ferry. Fort McPherson is just a few miles off the Dempster Highway.

Today, as it has been for the last 150 years, it is located on a high bank on the east side of the Peel River. After leaving our motor home by the modern Hudson's Bay store, we wandered along the main street, grateful for the wooden boardwalk that protected us from the omnipresent mud. Since it was Sunday, both the "Bay" and the Fort McPherson Canvas Shop were closed. We passed a building now tightly boarded up, which was obviously a Hudson's Bay store of an earlier time, for it conformed to the company's traditional substantial appearance of rectangular shape and hipped roof.

The square turret of the Anglican church rose above all the other small houses in the village and served as a prominent landmark. We walked over to the riverbank where the church had withstood the winter storms for the last seventy years. At one side was the well-kept cemetery. Every grave was marked by a plain cross or simple stone or wood slab; each was enclosed with a low white picket fence. Near the center of this small graveyard and surrounded by a chain and four posts was the last resting place of Inspector Fitzgerald and his three constables, who perished in their ill-fated patrol to Dawson City. The graves were marked by four identical low headstones, while in the center of the enclosed plot was a large white cross with the four men's names inscribed on the base.

We left the cemetery and slowly walked along the footpath on top of the high bank. Below, close to the dirt track leading down to the river, a number of boats were drawn up on shore. Most were the typical river type—long and narrow with square stern and upward-sloping square bow. Each had its outboard motor or "kicker" on the stern. There were also a few canoes quite dwarfed by the big riverboats.

The view across the river was magnificent. Far to the west rose the lofty Richardson Mountains, many of whose summits were crowned with snow. In the foreground a broad spruce-covered flat extended from the Peel back to the foot of the mountains. Already the tamaracks scattered among the spruce were beginning to show the golden tints of autumn. Overhead puffy white clouds slowly moved across brilliant blue sky. It was a scene of great tranquillity and beauty. Small wonder that the people of Fort McPherson had remained so attached to this site for over 150 years. We also noticed that, just as the Loucheux had pointed out so many years ago, the view from the east side downriver was, indeed, clear and unhindered—a strategic advantage no longer of any importance now that Indian and Inuit live in peace with each other. From a commanding spot on the bluff overlooking the river and close to the church, a Canadian historical plaque commemorates the founding of Fort McPherson by Hudson's Bay Company trader John Bell in 1840.

We were reluctant to leave Fort McPherson and resolved to return when we could visit their successful canvas shop. We also admitted to an overwhelming desire to see the country of the Bell and Rat rivers, which Bell and Campbell had done so much to develop. We promised ourselves that next time when we returned we would retrace their route over McDougall Pass between the Yukon and Fort McPherson—admittedly not on foot as they traveled, but by the twentieth-century magic of the airplane.

Three years elapsed before we were able to fulfill this promise. In late August of 1991 we retraced our way up the Dempster Highway to Inuvik on the Mackenzie River near the shores of Beaufort Sea. There we checked in at the Inuvik Air Charter Ltd. float base. Prospects for a chartered flight over the Richardson Mountains were not encouraging. The weather outlook was dismal—cold, strong winds, heavy snow squalls, low ceiling, with extremely limited visibility. We had no choice but to wait it out until conditions for flying improved. So we parked our motor home by the plane dock and passed the next several days in the warm dispatcher's building, chatting with Bob Milner, base manager, listening to local weather forecasts over the radio, drinking gallons of strong coffee, and every few minutes scanning the skies for signs of a break in the cloud cover.

Finally, on the third day, the forecast was favorable. We wasted no time. In quick order, our Cessna 185 was gassed up and we climbed aboard and fastened our seat belts as Rob Ziesman, our pilot, warmed up the engine, and within minutes we were roaring down the lake into the wind and soon were flying high above the Mackenzie delta—ready to fulfill our dream of retracing the route over the mountains taken by Bell and Campbell 150 years ago.

We had a detailed topographical map on which we had charted the course we wanted to follow. From Inuvik we headed south–southwest, crossing several of the main channels of the Mackenzie River flowing north through the vast delta on their way to the Beaufort Sea. This flat delta with its maze of hundreds of lakes of all sizes interconnected with a bewildering number of large and small winding waterways stretched endlessly toward the far horizon.

We soon reached the southern edge of the delta where the Peel River, a major tributary, flowed in from the west to mingle its waters with those of the Mackenzie. Up the Peel we flew. We had just glimpsed Fort McPherson far ahead of us on the river's east bank when we reached the mouth of the Rat River, which empties into the Peel from its source high in the Richardson Mountains to the west. We flew above this river following its twists and turns and loops as its winding course cut deep into the high treeless plateau that stretched from the foot of the mountains to the Peel River valley. The dull yellowish-tan drabness of the barren plateau was relieved only by the blue waters of numerous small lakes scattered over its surface and in the river bottoms and along the bordering sides of the plateau by the vivid green of trees along with a few splashes of bright gold—a forerunner of autumn soon to come.

On we went, following the meandering Rat as it led us ever closer to what appeared to be a solid wall of forbidding mountains. The jumbled sea of jagged peaks that we were now rapidly approaching extended in all directions. The sight was an awesome one. Indeed, the impression of sheer massiveness, of brute strength, was quite overwhelming. On this day their forbidding aspect was softened somewhat and given a rare beauty by the dusting of white that a recent snowfall had left on their sharp peaks.

Suddenly, abruptly, and indeed, we thought, quite miraculously—just as the waters of the Red Sea parted—so did the mountain barrier before us to reveal a pass leading through it. This was McDougall Pass, long known to native people, first traveled by fur traders John Bell and Robert Campbell, who recognized it as the key to a practicable transportation system between the Yukon and Mackenzie rivers. This passageway through the mountains is a treeless plateau bordered by towering mountains. It straddles the height of land between the Mackenzie and Yukon watersheds. Its barren surface is broken by a cluster of several small ponds. One is the source of the eastward flowing, Mackenzie-bound Rat River; from another the Bell River begins its westward course into the Porcupine and ultimately into the Yukon River. It didn't take long to fly through the pass and emerge on the western side of the Richardsons. We then followed the Bell as it twisted and cut its way out of the mountains through the high plateau barrens to finally reach the Porcupine River, a major tributary of the Yukon.

A considerable distance down the Bell from the pass, we came to the approximate location of La Pierre's House. This small post situated at the head of navigation for the boat brigades served as the depot at the western end of the portage over the pass for the storage and trans-shipment of supplies and furs.

From the mouth of the Bell we flew westward a short distance following the Porcupine, but all too soon we had to give the signal to Rob to turn back and begin our return to Inuvik. If funds had been unlimited, we would have continued down the Porcupine to its junction with the Yukon—to the site of Fort Yukon—but this we simply could not afford.

Our bird's-eye view from the comfort of an airplane, flying high above the long and arduous route over the Richardson Mountains, did not blind us to the incredible toil such a track demanded when followed by the fur traders. They took its hardships as a matter of course. They were much relieved that it would now replace the dreaded and notorious Liard River as the route to serve the interior trading posts.

As Campbell wrote in a letter to Chief Trader Anderson dated August 6, 1851, shortly after he reached Fort Simpson on the Mackenzie River at the successful conclusion of his first journey over the Richardsons:

> This I trust will be the finale of the countless miseries and hardships wantonly and to no earthly purpose endured for the three years we have now been on the Pelly. The road is now open and I beg to leave it with you to turn it and the ample resources and production of the country to advantage. There is not a portage, or I may say a rapid, from here to the forks Lewes [i.e., the Yukon] and Pelly nor any other impediment to put the winter transport over the mountains and with abundance of provisions to maintain its people and carry on its business.

(Interesting details of his journey are provided in Campbell's journal.)

> The water [of the Porcupine] was very high, weather very warm, with the sun continually overhead, as we were now within the Arctic Circle, mosquitoes very troublesome, so much that the reindeer [i.e., caribou] were often seen swimming in the river to rid themselves of their pestiferous attendants. . . . We arrived at the head of the navigation,

Lapierre's House, the Depot for the goods carried over the mountains in winter on dog sleds from the head waters of Peel River, an affluent of the mighty McKenzie. The fur packs were stored there to be transferred in winter, and the Youcon outfit which had been rendered there from Peel River during last winter was loaded into the Youcon boat and sent back on the return trip at once.

Monday 23rd. Mosquitoes tormenting us all day . . . We had good tracking all the afternoon.

Saturday 28th. About noon it was thunder and lightning began to rain in torrents wh. [which] obliged us to lay by with the boat. Mr. Murray and myself came off across land to the fort or House [i.e., La Pierre's] and reached it in 1 3/4 hour . . .

Tuesday July 1st. . . . We put ashore to sleep . . . warm with clouds of mosquitoes tormenting us to deaths door.

Thursday 3rd July. We were on the road again at 6 p.m.—had fine head winds the fore part of the night and came in well—crossed the height of land about midnight. The view of the country magnificent . . . but though it looks at a distance and beautiful swelling green plains, on closer inspection it is all deception to [?] over a pimply and swampy surface—Put ashore in a winter hut at 5 or 6 a.m. for rest—flies becoming troublesome throughout the morning come about 9 pipes.

Saturday 5th. Put ashore at the first wood we saw since we left the hut our last resting place—by the time we had cooked and ate it began to rain and left us without shelter. We creeped under small Indian huts of willow and moss—got wet to the skin and shaking with cold—left again with having had a rest at 2 p.m . . . put ashore . . . where tired of rain without wood for either fire or wood to shelter us left for the river . . . at 2 a.m. we reached an Indian hut opposite the Fort—no 'hallowing' could rouse them—enjoyed a good drying (being wet to the skin) and sleep among the hospitable Indian family.

Sunday 6th July. About 10 a.m. Indians crossed from the Fort with a boat and soon after I received a hearty welcome from Mr. and Mrs. Reess at Fort P. River [i.e., Fort McPherson].

Our trip over the Richardson Mountains had been a memorable one. True, it had been costly in terms of money, but the returns had been well worth it. For the space of a few hours we had been able to travel—in spirit—with Robert Campbell and share with him his great achievement. We could say, just as he wrote, that "the view of the country magnificent grand of expanse of Mts. hills and swelling dell and vallies in all green and [?] state of nature. It is the finest savage country I ever saw . . ."

Frances Lake Post
Pelly Banks Post

The signing of the favorable agreement of 1839 between the Hudson's Bay Company and the Russian-American Company regulating the trade of the Pacific Northwest coast allowed George Simpson to turn his attention to the unknown country west and north of the upper Liard River. The man he chose to undertake the task of exploring this region was Robert Campbell.

Accordingly, at the end of May 1840 Campbell, with seven other men, left Fort Halkett on this new assignment and headed westward up the Liard River. Some distance past the mouth of the Dease River, he turned up the right branch of the Liard. This Campbell named Frances River in honor of Lady Frances Simpson, the Governor's wife. After several days ascending this river, Campbell reached its source—a large body of water surrounded by hills and mountain ranges. This, too, Campbell named after the Governor's wife.

Frances Lake is shaped like a giant wishbone, with lofty mountains separating the two arms of the lake. Each side of the wishbone is about thirty miles long and a mile wide. Campbell proceeded up the west arm for about twenty-five miles. At a small island near the lake's northern end he stopped long enough to drop off three of his crew, whom he supplied with the canoe, guns, and nets so they could set out the nets for fish as well as hunt for game while he and the rest of his men proceeded on foot in their attempt to find a navigable river draining to the west.

Campbell followed a narrow river, quite unnavigable, that entered the lake from the west in the vicinity of the island. It was tough going. For three days they pushed and slogged through tangled river brush, marshes, and stretches of spongy morass. Finally, after struggling for twenty-five miles, they broke through to the eastern end of a narrow ten-mile-long lake. Utilizing the bark of available pine trees, they built two canoes, which, though crude, enabled them to travel in relative comfort the length of the lake (to which, along with the stream they had just followed, Campbell gave the name Finlayson in honor of Chief Factor Duncan Finlayson).

When the western end of the lake was reached, the party proceeded on foot once more. Encouraged by encountering several westward-flowing small streams, Campbell realized that they had, in fact, crossed the divide between Mackenzie river system and the as-yet undiscovered system of westward flowing rivers. Doggedly he and his men pushed on. Eventually they reached a small westward-flowing creek whose twisting course they followed. (Today it is known as Campbell Creek.) At last from the top of a high ridge they were rewarded with the sight, far off, of a large river flowing to the northwest.

They lost no time in covering the distance to the river. There, standing on the riverbank, they observed the customary ceremony—hallowed by long tradition—that always marked a new discovery. Using water from the river (which Campbell had promptly christened the Pelly after John Henry Pelly, London Governor of the Hudson's Bay Company), toasts were drunk to Her Majesty the Queen and to the Honorable Hudson's Bay Company. Then Campbell took possession of the area in the name of the company by raising its flag and by carving its claim on the bark of a nearby tree. This done, and confident that his mission had been successfully accomplished, he and his men began their return journey, retracing their way back to Frances Lake and then to Fort Halkett, which they reached about the middle of September.

Campbell wrote the account of his discovery of the Pelly River in his journal:

On a small Island—the only one there is—in the West branch, which is situated on the N. extremity of this branch I left 3 of the men with a canoe & nets & guns to fish & hunt round there & wait our return, while I went off on foot with Hoole & the 3 Indians, carrying our blankets, &c on our backs & our guns in our hands, to cross the mountains in quest of any river we might find flowing from the West side. Traversing a rough wooded country along the base of hills, we ascended the valley of a river, which enters Frances Lake nearly opposite the little Island; for the last 10 miles of its course, it cuts its tortuous way, a foaming torrent through a rocky chasm. We traced it to its source in a lake 10 miles long & about 1 mile in bredth, whch with the river I named Finlayson's Lake and river (after Chief Factor Duncan Finlayson . . .). The lake is situated so near the watershed that, in high floods, its waters flow at one end down one side the mountains, & at the other end, down the other side.

For 3 days on this trip we had neither the luck to kill nor the pleasure to eat; but having managed to make pine bark canoes we paddled to the W. end of Finlayson's lake & shortly after that we got deer & beaver more than sufficient for our wants, on the 6th day of our journey . . . we had the satisfaction of seeing from a high bank a large river in the distance flowing Northwest. I named the bank from which we caught the first glimpse of the river "Pelly Banks" & the river "Pelly River," after our home Governor, Sir H. Pelly. Descending to the River we drank out of its pellucid water to Her Majesty & the H. B. Co.

We constructed a raft & drifted down the stream a few miles, &

threw in a sealed tin can with memoranda of our discovery, the data, &c, with a request to the finder, if perchance the can should fall into anyone's hands, to make the fact known. After taking possession in the name of the Company by marking a tree "H.B.C." with date, & flying the H.B.C. ensign the while overhead, we traced our steps to Frances Lake, highly delighted with our success;

It was to be two years before Campbell returned to Frances Lake, this time charged with the twofold task of establishing a trading post on the lake and exploring Pelly River to its mouth. He left Fort Halkett on July 27, 1842, with two York boats. He reached Frances Lake about three weeks later and immediately began building his post at the junction of the east and west arms of the lake. His first winter was marked by a severe scarcity of food—a condition with which Campbell was all too familiar. Two entries in the fort's journal reflect the harsh conditions prevailing during that first winter.

December 31 Thus closes upon us the year 1842, with only 106 fish in store, 8 bags in the depôt, not an ounce of any kind of meat; the last was issued on this evening and makes with all our other bonbons but a sorry fare for our people for their New Year's Day. The prospects before me for commencing another year with its joys and woes is not very cheering, but a gracious Providence is our aid and is sufficient for us.

[Jan. 12, 1843] Four of us passed the day as usual from its early dawn till the close, visiting the setting nets some of which are at least 7 miles distant, and the result of our day's toil was only 3 small fish. Thus from 23 nets, requiring the attendance and hard toil of four of us, is inadequate to procure a sufficiency for our daily support, that our situation is becoming more and more forlorn and dreary. How we are to get through the winter in this wild region God only knows. He alone can prosper our condition and in his providence I confide. I was obliged again to issue out a ration of pemmican to the people and which with the best economy I can use cannot take us long.

Earlier in the fall Campbell realized that the food supply was going to be critical. He wrote in his journal: ". . . our fisheries proving insufficient to meet our daily wants much less to allow us to lay aside fish for the winter. . . . Then came better times, the Indians finding us out and spreading the news that we were stationed at Frances Lake, & gladly coming in to trade furs & provisions with us."

Gradually the Frances Lake post took shape and the necessary buildings were erected. They were not many. The most important ones were a thirty-by-twenty-foot store/warehouse and quarters for the men, each measuring thirty by sixteen feet. In one of the latter Campbell had a small room partitioned off for his own use. In February the men were cutting pickets for the stockade and "Lapierre fixing the shop." Later in the spring Lapierre began to square posts for the bastions, and wood for flooring in one of the men's houses was prepared. On May 6 the framework of the lookout over the front gate was erected, and a few days later the forty-five-foot flagstaff was mounted over the gate. By the end of the month, the stockade and four bastions were completed. When Campbell returned to the fort in late July at the conclusion of his journey down the Pelly River, he was gratified to see that during his absence Lapierre had "roofed all the houses, procured bark and covered them with it, built a kitchen, etc."

In October of 1843, when the boats arrived at Frances Lake from Fort Simpson bringing dispatches and the annual outfit, they also brought a young clerk, William Hardisty, who was to serve as assistant to Campbell.

The ensuing winter was a repetition of the previous one. As soon as ice conditions permitted, Campbell left Frances Lake to bring the year's returns to the company headquarters at Fort Simpson. On his return he noted in his journal: "I returned in the fall with the outfit to my winter quarters at Frances Lake & found Mr. Hardisty & all at the fort well, but the fisheries in no way improved."

That same fall Campbell sent Hardisty over to Pelly Banks to open up trade with the *Gens du Couteaux* (Knife) Indians, who had consistently and adamantly refused to make the arduous journey over the mountainous height of land to Frances Lake to trade their furs. His venture was successful, but their "constant enemy, want of provisions," forced him to curtail his stay and return to Frances Lake toward the end of January of 1845.

The following spring (1845) Campbell was again ordered to make the long journey with the fort's returns down the hated Liard River to Fort Simpson. He wrote that just as in the previous year "towards spring the Indians killed a great number of deer & brought in fur & meat which enabled us to better our condition & also to make a good trade." Campbell was back at his Frances Lake post by the middle of October. "Painfully disappointed at the limited outfit forwarded by the officer in charge [at Fort Simpson] to meet our trade requirements & other necessities in a remote & little known region." However, in the words of his journal, we "immediately set about our arrangements for the winter. We got through it pretty comfortably & made a very good trade, considering the small number of Indians who had yet found us out."

By 1846 Frances Lake Post was sufficiently well established so that Campbell was able to undertake the construction of a more permanent post on Pelly Banks. In May of that year, leaving William Hardisty in charge of Frances Lake, Campbell crossed over the mountains and height of land, "a distance of 120 miles or more through bogs and swamps that are all but impassable in the summer season," to Pelly Banks. There on the site where three years earlier his men had thrown up a simple shelter and had built the canoe used for Campbell's first exploratory journey down the Pelly River, the post of Pelly Banks was built. Campbell's journal entry was brief: "We got our buildings up in the course of the summer & had occasional visits from Indians for supplies & trade."

According to Theodore J. Karamanski in his book *Fur Trade and Exploration,* "The Pelly Banks Post was a well-built fort with a stockade, store, and dwelling house, but it was a difficult post to maintain. After the year's outfit had been brought by boat along the Liard and Frances rivers to the Frances Lake Post, it had to be cached until winter, when it was hauled on dog sleds to Pelly Banks."

Campbell spent the 1846–47 season at Pelly Banks, and his assistant, Hardisty, assumed charge of the Frances Lake Post. A good trade was realized at both places. This promising condition was repeated the following year, the only difference being that at Frances Lake James Stewart had replaced Hardisty, who had been granted leave because of poor health. Campbell recorded in his journal that after placing James Stewart in charge of Frances Lake for the winter, "I crossed the mountain to Pelly Banks . . . tedious fatiguing walk . . . with the balance of the men, including a boat builder. In course of the winter I got 2 boats & a skiff built ready for the summer's operations. We passed a busy winter, not only free from want, but in comfort, & made a flourishing trade both at Pelly Banks & at Frances Lake, as more Indians were finding us out & were only too glad to come & trade."

It was always difficult to provide for the needs of Pelly Banks, but the post had to be maintained, for it was a vital link in the route from Frances Lake to the Pelly River country. As Campbell wrote in 1847: "Of the present arrangement, until a better route is found to Pelly River, it will be impossible to throw up Pelly Banks for the two reasons that it is required as an *entre-depôt* for the goods and furs, and the Pelly Indians will not now more than formerly consent to resort to the lake [Frances]."

Satisfied that his two forts were now firmly established, Campbell felt free to leave them so that he could comply with the wishes of Governor Simpson and build a new fort down the river he had discovered four years ago. He, however, had strong reservations about clerk Pierre C.

Pambrun, who had been sent to take charge of the two forts during his absence, writing: "Mr. P. was well-known to posses neither the judgment nor the foresight nor the energy requisite at a remote & isolated charge like that, where everything so much depended on his own efforts." Unfortunately, subsequent events were to prove his fears well founded, for it didn't take long for the almost criminal ineptitude of P. C. Pambrun to drastically affect the fortunes of the two posts that had been entrusted to him. From his new post at the forks of the Pelly River (Fort Selkirk) Campbell sent two men to Pelly Banks to pick up the annual outfit that Pambrun was to convey across the mountains from Frances Lake to Pelly Banks on dog sleds during the winter. When Campbell's men returned with a "trifling part of our outfit" Marcette, the guide, reported that "at Pelly Banks he had found everything in confusion and the people in want . . ." Campbell noted in his journal that this was "as I had anticipated. The outfit they had been unable to render across the mountains as we used to do; part of it was left scattered & abandoned along the route, & part was still unmoved on the other side . . . All this was the result of not looking ahead & making proper provision in advance." In Campbell's words, Pambrun "neglected the instructions & advice given him for his guidance . . . wasted all the provisions on hand . . . and failed to use the ways & means at his disposal to increase his supplies." At Frances Lake they were "in a starving condition." Campbell did not hesitate to ascribe this hardship to "the result of sheer neglect of duty after the warning & advice I had given . . ."

The following year (1849) was a repetition of the previous one—"the result of not looking ahead & making proper provision in advance." Conditions went from bad to worse at Pelly Banks under Pambrun's supervision. He and his people were "in misery, no proper fishery & nothing laid by for the winter." When two of Campbell's men arrived there on their way to Fort Simpson, they were appalled at what they found. According to Campbell's account, "they found [Pelly Banks] in a truly deplorable state. The Fort all but one small house had been burnt down in the early part of winter. They discovered Mr. P. & Lapie camped close by, emaciated to skin & bone, after passing through dreadful suffering all winter."

But there was even worse to record: "The 2 men Forbisher & Debois died of starvation & several of the Indians around; & pitiably sad to relate, some of the poor wretches had been driven by their unspeakable sufferings to commit some acts of cannibalism."

Campbell added: "This distressing state of affairs . . . should not have occurred had ordinary care been taken of the previous winter's nets, which had been left at the different fisheries & which had been allowed to rot."

Dr. John Rae in a letter written in August 1850 provided further details of the tragic happenings at Pelly Banks:

Mr. Pambrun, finding that the boats did not arrive [from Fort Simpson], sent his two men to fish, while he endeavoured to support himself by hunting. On the 30th Novr., when all parties were thus employed at a distance, the house caught fire and was completely consumed with about £800 worth of Furs and all the private property: three packs of Furs and a little powder being all that was saved. During the winter the party suffered much from hunger and want of sufficient clothing until the 5th of March, when having eaten all the skins one of the men (a Canadian named Dubois) died of starvation, and the other (an Orkneyman named Forbister) shared the same fate 20 days after-wards, having first eaten all or greater part of his dead Companion. Mr. Pambrun by hunting succeeded in keeping himself alive, until joined by Mr. J. Stewart and a man from Fort Selkirk with whom he came down to Fort Simpson . . .

Almost unbelievably, in view of his past performance, P. C. Pambrun was reappointed to the charge of the Frances Lake post for the 1850–51 season. This was a disappointment to Campbell. He had counted on the post remaining in the hands of his capable assistant, James Stewart, who had spent the fall at the post and had succeeded in restoring it to its former habitable condition. With Stewart at the fort, Campbell knew that "in that case there would be no repetition of the mismanagement of the past 2 years; but on the other hand that I could count on the goods being forwarded in winter as we used to do, & rely on finding them intact at Pelly Banks, instead of scattered all along the route from the 'cache.'"

Campbell returned to Frances Lake post in April of 1851 to pick up supplies designated for his new post (Fort Selkirk). He rather caustically noted in his journal: "We found Mr. P. & two men well but without provisions.—As I had expected, we found that but a small portion of our outfit had been crossed to Pelly Banks."

Robert Campbell's journey in the summer of 1851 quite conclusively demonstrated the feasibility of the Pelly–Yukon–Porcupine–Peel river route to Fort Simpson on the Mackenzie. Almost immediately the dreaded Liard River was abandoned. No longer would the voyageurs have to brave its treacherous whirlpools and foaming rapids. As Campbell had predicted in a letter to his friend Chief Factor Donald Ross at Norway House, written some months before his epic journey: "It takes generally between 40 & 50 days to perform the hard voyage coming up to Frances Lake [via the Liard River]—Now the voyage for below [the lower Mackenzie River] they may perform sleeping in their boats to the Mouth of the Peel, from which one day's tracking will bring them to the Fort [Fort McPherson]."

The outlook for the future continuance of both Pelly Banks and Frances Lake was not promising. In late 1850 Chief Trader John Bell, in charge of the Mackenzie River, district wrote to Governor Simpson:

A fatality appears to attend this voyage [to Frances Lake]. More untoward circumstances and accidents have happened upon it than in any other in this district, perhaps I may even say in the Northern Department, but it is not on the voyage alone [i.e., on the Liard River] that there is a risk of life, for the awful tragedy which happened last winter at Pelly Banks shows that no dependence can be placed upon the provision resources of the mountain posts except by forwarding a large supply of pemmican which can only be done at a ruinous cost, as the returns of Fort Selkirk and Frances Lake far from cover the expenses of keeping them up. The prospects of returns from that quarter are as poor as can well be. . . . Mr. Pambrun thinks that if he can collect two packs for next Spring it will be as much as he can do. The abandonment of Frances Lake would be a positive benefit to the district as it would remove the heaviest drain upon our provision resources and do away with a wintering ground which, from the starvation so frequently experienced there, our men hold in actual dread and abhorrence.

An even more convincing reason for the abandonment of the forts was found in the company's account ledgers. During the years 1848 to 1850, the two posts at Frances Lake and at Pelly Banks, plus the recently established Fort Selkirk, showed not a profit but a net loss of over fourteen hundred pounds. By 1852 both the Frances Lake Post and the Pelly Banks Post had been abandoned, their short term of operation written off as being neither feasible nor profitable.

After the total destruction of Fort Selkirk by the Chilkat Indians in August of 1852, a disheartened Campbell made his way back to Fort Simpson by way of Frances Lake and the Liard River. The last references to the two posts are found in his journal: "Tuesday 28th [September 1852] Arrived at the desolated Pelly Banks about noon—" A week later he reached Frances Lake Post.

Tuesday 5th [October] Come off down the lake—had fine aft wind—reached the Fort [Frances Lake] about 3 p.m. where we to set a net and pass the rest of the day and night but to my surprise and vexation found the Fort all burnt down—the stockades cut down and everything appearing as if no small savage pains had been taken to destroy it which must have been done in the course of the sumr (summer). Great God has they wrath against us for our sin caused Thee let the Savage vest their rage against us and the work of our hands intended for their good—oh that thou would but instruct and guide me in the path of carefulness Thou knowest that this has been my constant and earnest desire. Come off at once from the eyesore seing the finest Fort in the Distric in ashes—Killed a partridge behind the Fort and found a large Swedish turnip fresh and green growing behind the kitchen which I took for supper when we camped a mile—(?) down the river . . .

Even though we realized that only the general locations of the Frances Lake and Pelly Banks Posts were known, we wanted to visit this area so closely associated with Robert Campbell's exploits. To follow his travels up the rivers, across the lakes, and over the mountainous height of land to the Pelly River required travel on foot and by canoe that, unfortunately, was beyond our capabilities. So we resorted to that modern miracle, the airplane. We chartered a Cessna 185 at Watson Lake on the Liard and soon were flying over the remote region explored by Campbell and his men a century and a half ago. As we looked down upon the rugged terrain, the foaming rapids and steepsided canyons of the rivers, the windswept lakes, and the jumbled mass of rounded mountain peaks of the high Yukon plateau, we marveled at the incredible endurance of the men who routinely overcame these awesome obstacles.

We followed up the Frances River from its mouth at the Liard to its source in Frances Lake. The river is lovely, just as Campbell described it, flowing in "serpentine curves—through a valley well wooded with Pine & Poplar, the mountains on both sides increasing in altitude as we advanced, & showing lovely slopes of bright verdure facing the South." We noticed many stretches of whitewater rapids and several narrow rock-walled canyons, all challenging obstructions that faced the voyageurs.

Frances Lake is a beautiful, quite uniquely shaped body of water. Its V-like formation is clearly evident from the air. On the far (north) side opposite the river, the two sides of the V come together in a point. A broad, rugged plateau of mountaintops and valleys separates the two arms of the lake. Simpson's Tower, the highest peak rising from the plateau, dominates the skyline.

We knew that the site of Frances Lake Post was somewhere in the vicinity of the junction of the two arms of the lake, for according to Campbell's journal "the Party . . . had built a rough shanty at the foot of

617

Simpson's Tower on the point at the forks of the Lake." To enable us to photograph the location from all directions, our pilot obligingly circled several times over the area.

Leaving the point behind, we headed up the length of the west arm. Gentle hills sloped to the lake, their sides mantled with the green of spruce and pine. Rising behind them to the south were the low mountains of the Campbell range.

Finlayson's River emptied into the west arm near its upper end. We followed the course of this stream as it cut its "tortuous way" through the plateau in a series of rapids and "foaming torrents," then meandered and twisted through spruce swamp and muskeg to its source in the east end of Finlayson Lake. This is another long, narrow body of water, bordered on each side by spruce forests and high plateaus. In the far distance to the north we could see a continuous wall of mountain peaks. Finlayson Lake straddled the height of land so that during periods of high water its waters at each end flowed out of the lake in opposite directions.

After reaching the eastern end of this lake, we flew over the rugged plateau that divided the watersheds of the Pelly and Mackenzie rivers. Guided by our topographical map, we were able to pick up Campbell's Creek—an insignificant stream flowing westward, the one Campbell had followed to its outlet at the Pelly. We, too, followed its course as it cut its way through spruce ridges and muskeg to reach its final destination in the Pelly River. This was the spot, somewhere near in this general area, where the Pelly Banks Post had been established.

From our vantage point high in the sky we enjoyed the marvelous panorama of the Pelly valley. It was a land of forested ridges, myriad lakes of all sizes, and muskeg-and-spruce-covered bottomlands. The broad Pelly cut across the entire landscape, winding its way in graceful curves and loops toward the western horizon. Just as he had done at Frances Lake, our pilot circled several times over the general area around the mouth of Campbell's Creek so that we could cover the location from all directions. At last, satisfied that we had successfully followed in Campbell's "footsteps" on his long journey from the Liard to the Pelly River, we gave the signal to the pilot to begin the return flight to Watson Lake.

We were well pleased with our trip. We had viewed beautiful and interesting scenery, much of it largely unchanged from Campbell's day; we had seen and photographed the approximate locations of his two trading posts; and, finally, we had gained a greater appreciation of the incredible hardships and hazards that the fur traders had to over-come as they pushed their way upriver, through swamps and over mountains, in the accomplishment of their trade and exploration missions.

Fort Victoria

The decision by the Hudson's Bay Company to move their principal de-pot west of the Rocky Mountains from Fort Vancouver on the Columbia River to the southern tip of Vancouver Island was not a sudden one. In fact, as early as 1834 the drawbacks of the fort's location had become increasingly apparent. One of the most important was the existence of the deadly bar across the mouth of the Columbia—a barrier that all vessels had to cross to reach the fort ninety miles upriver. Vessels, along with crew and cargo, were on occasion lost on this dreaded bar, and almost always ships were delayed, sometimes for weeks, waiting for the turbulent waters to quiet sufficiently to permit passage of the ships with safety, thereby, in Simpson's words, "deranging the best lade plains." In a letter dated December 8, 1835 the Governor and Committee in London wrote to Chief Factor McLoughlin:

> We have again to draw your attention to the object of removing your Principal Depot from the Columbia River to the Coast, . . . easy of access, as we consider the danger of crossing the Columbia Bar too great a risk to be run by the Annual Ships from and to England, with the Outfits and returns. . . . we are desirous that the Ships from England should go into the Columbia as seldom as possible, and that the Imports and Exports of the West Side the Mountains, should be taken to and from the New De-pot on the Coast in like manner as has heretofore been done in regard to Vancouver.

A second drawback was the frequent incidence of outbreaks of malaria that were thought to be attributable to the fort's location.

Chief Factor McLoughlin was not at all receptive to the idea of this move to Vancouver Island and succeeded for some time in avoiding any implementation of the company's proposal. In 1839 he did visit the southern tip of the island, where Chief Trader James Douglas had ear-lier found what he considered a good location for the new depot, but McLoughlin assessed it as "not a nice place suitable to our progress."

Also by 1842 Governor Sir George Simpson had decided in favor of carrying on the Pacific coastal trade by means of the company steam-ship *Beaver* instead of from land-based coastal forts such as Taku, Stikine, and McLoughlin, established earlier under the direction of Chief Factor McLoughlin. This change in company policy required the building of a depot suitable for the needs of maritime shipping—one lo-cated closer to the center of the coastal trade. Clearly, the Columbia

River, with its dangerous bar at its mouth, and the ninety miles' distance upriver to Fort Vancouver were not acceptable.

Other considerations influencing Simpson in his decision to move the Company's main western depot to Vancouver Island were: first, his belief that the steadily increasing number of Americans settling in the nearby Willamette Valley posed a threat to the security of Fort Vancouver; and, second, the fact that the boundary between British territory and the U.S. Oregon country when finally determined might quite possibly be well north of the Columbia River. Vancouver Island, however, was sure to remain secure within the territorial limits of Great Britain.

The Council of the Northern Department at their annual meeting at Norway House in June 1842 approved Governor Simpson's proposal that a new depot be built on Vancouver Island. Accordingly, in 1842 Governor Simpson issued specific orders to Chief Factor McLoughlin that could not be ignored. He was instructed to undertake the construction of the new depot on the southern end of Vancouver Island. Chief Trader James Douglas was sent to the island to select a site suitable for the post. The spot he chose was on the inner basin of present-day Victoria Harbor.

In a letter written to his friend James Hargrave, Douglas described the location chosen as follows:

> The site we intend to build upon, is well adapted to the purpose of settlement; it lies about half a mile off the main strait of De Fuca, in a snug sheltered cove from 5 to 10 fms deep, accessible at all seasons to vessels, which may anchor within 50 feet of the bank on which the Fort will stand. A narrow canal passes the Fort and runs 5 miles into the interior of the Island, affording, at one point, a water power of incalculable force, and abundance of Pine with other valuable timber on its banks. The place itself appears a perfect 'Eden', in the midst of the dreary wilderness of the North west coat, and so different is its general aspect, from the wooded, rugged regions around, that one might be pardoned for supposing it had dropped from the clouds into its present position.

The first of March 1843, Chief Trader Douglas left Fort Vancouver to begin his twofold assignment of constructing the new fort on Vancouver Island and of dismantling two of the far northern coastal posts: Taku and McLoughlin. Douglas was able to substantially augment his force of fifteen men by promising the local Songhee Indians a two-and-one-half point blanket for every forty cedar pickets they cut. This was a blanket weighing two-and-one-half pounds. In the corner of every blanket was a woven stripe known as a point that indicated the blanket's weight—one stripe equaling one pound. March 16 the actual work of cutting the posts for the stockade commenced. Although McLoughlin had thought a fort of modest size would be sufficient, Douglas had other ideas, which he expressed in a letter dated March 10, 1843, to Simpson: "I am confident that the place from its situation and accessibility, will eventually become a centre of operation, either to ourselves or to others who may be attracted thither, by the valuable timber and exhaustless fisheries of that inland sea.

"I would therefore purpose to make the stores roomy and substantial, and the Fort on a plan of at least 300 feet square, so that when it is up we may not be put to the expense and derangement of incessant changes and extensions."

When the work of building the fort was well under way, Douglas left to sail up the north coast to oversee the dismantling of the company's two trading posts (Taku and McLoughlin) and to bring back their officers, men, and supplies.

By the beginning of June, Douglas was back at the fort site. He was accompanied by Chief Trader Charles Ross and Clerk Roderick Finlayson, along with the entire complement of fifty men from the abandoned forts. With this increase in the labor force and aided by exceptionally favorable weather, the work of building Fort Victoria proceeded rapidly. In fact, by October so much had been accomplished, including the completion of the palisade and an octagonal bastion, that Chief Trader Douglas was free to return to Fort Vancouver to resume his duties as assistant to Chief Factor McLoughlin. Chief Trader Charles Ross was given charge of the new fort. Roderick Finlayson was named second in command.

Progress reports to Governor Simpson from both Douglas and Ross provided convincing evidence of the rapidity with which the fort complex was being constructed. Douglas was able to write on November 16, 1843:

It is in form a quadrangle of 330 by 300 feet intended to contain 8 buildings of 60 feet each, disposed in the following order say 2 in the rear facing the harbour and 3 on each side standing at right angles with the former leaving the front entirely open. The outhouses and workshops are to be thrown in the rear of the main buildings and in the unoccupied angles, so as not to disturb the symmetry of the principal square. So much for the plan now for the progress made in carrying it out. On the 21st September when we last heard from Ross the Pickets and defences were finished, and two of the buildings completed so far as to be habitable, and they were engaged in hauling out the logs of a third building.

In keeping with Simpson's new policy of insisting that each fort be as self-sufficient as possible, Ross had not neglected to make a small start toward raising food crops for the fort. He wrote: "The farming is as yet little more than in embryo—there being only about five acres under cultivation and about the same quantity prepared for the Plough." Trade in furs was carried on, resulting in a return for the first year of between three and four hundred skins, mostly beaver and otter.

The sudden and unexpected death of Chief Trader Charles Ross on June 27, 1844, resulted in Roderick Finlayson, just twenty-six years old, being entrusted with the charge of the fort. This post he held for many years, discharging his duties with great competence and earning the respect of all who knew him.

By 1846 Finlayson had succeeded in bringing 300 acres under cultivation, so that by the following year the yield from the fort's fields was 1,000 bushels of wheat, 400 of peas, 700 of oats, and 3,000 of potatoes. Livestock brought from Fort Nisqually began to furnish dairy products. A six-acre orchard was laid out. It was soon found necessary to expand the fort. The stockade was pushed north by 135 feet, two new stores were completed, and a 100-foot warehouse was built on stone pilings at the harbor's edge.

In 1846, during a stopover at Fort Victoria of HMS *Herald,* one of the passengers made the following observations regarding the Hudson's Bay Company's trading policies as carried out at their new fort:

> . . . a trading house, in which smaller bargains are concluded, and tools, agricultural implements, blankets, shawls, beads, and all the multifarious products of Sheffield, Birmingham, Manchester and Leeds are offered at exorbitant prices. There being no competition, the Company has it all its own way; it does not profess to supply the public; indeed, although it does not object to sell to people situated as we were, yet the stores are for the trade in furs, to supply the native hunters with the goods which they most value, as also for the use of its own dependents, who, receiving little pay, are usually in debt to the Company, and are therefore much in its power. In fact, the people employed are rarely those to whom returning home is an object; they have mostly been taken from poverty, and have at all events food and clothing. The work is hard, but with health and strength this is a blessing rather than otherwise.

In May of 1848 the vessel *Vancouver,* after unloading at Fort Victoria the annual supplies for the fort and the Northwest coastal trade, was wrecked on the infamous Columbia bar en route to Fort Vancouver. This was the last straw for the Governor and London Committee. They informed the Board of Management (James Douglas, Peter Ogden, and John Work) at Fort Vancouver that wrecks on the Columbia bar had become much too frequent and the "serious evil" of winds and tides at the river's entrance increased the danger to shipping. Therefore, they issued a directive that, effective immediately, all vessels from England were to proceed directly to Fort Victoria, there to discharge goods for that post and the Northwest coast before proceeding to Fort Vancouver. Furthermore, they directed that all furs and other returns collected at Fort Vancouver during the winter of 1848 be taken to Fort Victoria for shipment to England. Although Douglas argued that facilities at Fort Victoria were as yet inadequate to handle the increased amount of supplies and shipping, the committee would not reverse their decision.

Another event also contributed to the company's decision to make Fort Victoria their main Pacific headquarters. Because of the loss of the Oregon Territory resulting from establishment of the forty-ninth parallel as the international boundary by the 1846 treaty, the island of Vancouver assumed new importance for the company. They felt that control of the island was essential in order for them to maintain secure access to the northern coastal region as well as to New Caledonia. Therefore, they had applied to the British government for a grant to the island.

The British government was motivated by a strong desire to establish their presence in the area now formally acknowledged as theirs by terms of the 1846 treaty. Lacking the financial means themselves to underwrite the founding of a colony, they were quite willing to turn to the Hudson's Bay Company to achieve their objective by utilizing the company's vast resources—substantial amounts of capital, strategically located trading posts, and well-equipped trading vessels, plus a corps of experienced men.

The Hudson's Bay Company's application, therefore, was favorably received and approved. Letters Patent dated January 13, 1849, were issued making the Hudson's Bay Company proprietors of the entire island subject to the payment of a token yearly rent of seven shillings. In addition, the company contracted to transport colonists from Great Britain and to sell them land at one pound per acre. The proceeds from such sales (less 10 percent for the company) were to be applied to the general needs of the colony.

Although both the British government and the Hudson's Bay Company considered James Douglas as by far the most qualified man for the post of Governor of the new colony, it was felt politically expedient to have a noncompany man for the position. This was due to the strong anticompany and antimonopolistic trading sentiments held by many at that time. Richard Blanshard, a young lawyer with no administrative experience, was appointed as Governor. Until he arrived at Vancouver Island, James Douglas was to act as interim Governor.

In a letter addressed to the Board of Management at Fort Vancouver, the Governor and London Committee wrote, a bit undiplomatically, to say the least, that Douglas should take up permanent residence at Fort Victoria since "it appears to us that Mr. Douglas can be better spared from Fort Vancouver at present than Mr. Ogden." The letter continued to say that Douglas would be commissioned as Governor *pro tempore* by the British government: "We say pro tempore because it is not improbable that those persons, who may settle on the Island may not be content that a Gentleman, having so deep an interest in the Fur trade, should hold the situation of Governor of a Colony, which is to be free and independent."

Douglas was not enthusiastic over this new appointment, and he resented the reference to his being "better spared from Fort Vancouver" than his colleague Peter Skene Ogden. Nevertheless, Douglas swallowed his chagrin, and on May 31, 1849, he and his entire family moved out of the "Big House" at Fort Vancouver and, traveling over the Cowlitz Portage to Fort Nisqually, proceeded across the Straits of Juan de Fuca to Fort Victoria. He brought with him 636 pounds of gold dust and twenty packs of otter for a total value of about thirty thousand pounds. With his arrival and establishment of permanent residence, Fort Victoria effectually superseded Fort Vancouver as the company's main Pacific depot and headquarters.

The new Governor, Richard Blanshard, did not reach Fort Victoria until March 11, 1850. It was not until six months later that his house was sufficiently completed so that he could take up his residence in it. According to Chief Factor Douglas, the house had been constructed at a cost of less than sixteen hundred dollars. It was forty by twenty feet, with a kitchen eighteen by twelve feet attached and a house twenty-four by eighteen feet for his servants: "It has a neat appearance and is on the whole the best finished building in Oregon."

Richard Blanshard held the office of Governor for only two years, and of those two years he was present on Vancouver Island but seventeen months. During that short period Blanshard found that his Governorship had little real substance. His duties were restricted to civil government of the colony and to military matters. He was to receive no salary until revenue was generated through the sale of land to potential settlers and royalties from the island's coal deposits. There were, as yet, no colonists to govern and no infrastructure of law courts or police or military force to enforce any decrees he might issue. He quickly recognized that all real authority was vested in James Douglas, who as chief factor of the Hudson's Bay Company controlled the economic life and even existence of the new colony. It was truly an impossible situation for anyone—even one more experienced in administration than the young Governor. He was immediately confronted with several crises to resolve.

When he unwisely declined to turn over to the American garrison two of its men who had deserted and successfully escaped to British territory by stowing away on a company vessel, he precipitated retaliatory action by the Americans, involving seizure of a company vessel, impoundment of its cargo, and closure of Fort Nisqually as a port of entry for British ships. Only after considerable and protracted diplomatic effort and at a cost of $12,669.25 was this contretemps finally settled.

Trouble was erupting among the men brought over from Great Britain to work the coal mines at Fort Rupert newly established at the northern end of the island. Unrest was rampant, the miners protesting against harsh treatment and unacceptable rations. A complete breakdown of law and order seemed imminent. Three men who had deserted from the company's service were murdered by Indians. Blanshard went to Fort Rupert on board HMS *Daedalus* determined to bring the murderers to justice. The attempt was quite futile. The only thing accomplished was the total destruction of a deserted Indian camp. Still Blanshard made a second attempt the following year, resulting in a similar failure.

The Governor's handling of the affair was contrary to the Hudson's Bay Company's long established and successful policy of diplomacy and negotiation as well as avoidance of confrontation when dealing with the Indians. The British government in their reprimand to Blanshard made it plain that it did not support his action, feeling that it had been both imprudent and ineffective, failing to achieve its objective of bringing the guilty to justice.

By this time Richard Blanshard had had enough. He was suffering from severe attacks of ague; he was disheartened and disillusioned. He wrote to the British government asking for his immediate recall and release from office. It must have been with a sense of profound relief when in September of 1851 he was finally able to leave Vancouver Island and sail homeward to England.

Chief Factor James Douglas was named to succeed Blanshard as Governor of Vancouver Island, effective September 1, 1851. In his acknowledgment of his appointment he wrote: "Though I feel highly honored by this new mark of confidence . . . I beg to say that my appointment . . . affords me anything but pleasure . . . I greatly fear that it will be out of my power to discharge the responsible duties of the office, either with satisfaction to myself, or advantage to the Colony. I also feel assured that it will lead me into expenses which my limited income cannot afford."

James Douglas was well suited by temperament and training to fulfill the duties of his new position as Governor. However, the assumption of this new responsibility required that he simultaneously advance the best interests of both the colony and the company—a task not always simple or easy when those interests were contradictory.

The expansion of agriculture was encouraged with the establishment of four farms by the company's subsidiary, the Puget Sound Agricultural Company, in outlying areas. These farms, totaling about ten thousand acres, were Viewfield, Colwood, Craigflower, and Constance Cove. They were each well stocked with sheep, cattle, and pigs. They soon began to produce dairy products as well as grain crops of wheat, barley, and oats, in addition to potatoes, carrots, turnips, and other vegetables. Much of the grain raised was exported to the Russian colonies in Alaska.

A trickle of settlers was beginning to arrive on the island. Eighty were brought out in 1850 followed by 165 the following year. Retired company men were encouraged to buy and settle on acreage in the close vicinity of the fort. By 1852 they formed the core of the colony: Douglas himself purchased 395 acres; Chief Trader James Todd, 109-1/2; Chief Trader Roderick Finlayson, 103; Captain Charles Dodd of the company's SS *Beaver,* 203; Chief Trader William Tolmie, 268; George Blankinsop (Chief Trader in 1855), 105; and Captain William McNeill (Chief Factor in 1856), 150. As Margaret Ormsby wrote in her introduction to *Fort Victoria Letters 1846–1851:* "The fur traders had taken the place of the small class of gentlemen farmers that the Company had intended at the beginning to send out to the colony of Vancouver Island." Their land purchases at £1 per acre had mounted to £1,378 in revenue for the colony.

One of Richard Blanshard's last acts as Governor had been his appointment of a council. It consisted of James Douglas, John Tod, and James Cooper. This constituted the first tentative step toward self-government. Roderick Finlayson replaced Douglas on the council when the latter became Governor.

Eventually and inevitably the next step in self-government was taken. The British government recognized that "British subjects could not be kept permanently under the authority of a government which they had no part in selecting," in the words of Derek Pethick in his book *Victoria: The Fort.* In 1856 Douglas was instructed to make the necessary arrangements for the election of an assembly. The ownership of 300 pounds' worth of property was prerequisite to holding office, ownership of twenty acres to voting. On August 12, 1856, the new House of Assembly, consisting of seven freely elected members, convened. Dr. John Sebastian Helmcken was elected Speaker. Henceforth the people of Vancouver Island were to have a voice in their government.

During this period the fort continued to be the administrative center for the island. A contemporary account (circa 1855) described its appearance as follows:

> The site of the fort was an oak opening. The ground to the extent of an acre was cleared, and enclosed by a palisade, forming a square, on the north and south corners was a tower, containing 6 or 8 pieces of Ordinance each, the north one served as a prison, the south one for firing saluts, when ever the governor visited any place officerly. In the centre of the east and west sides were maine gate ways, each had a little door, to let people out or in after hours. On the right entering by the front or south gate, was a cottage, in which was the post office, it was kept by an officer of the Company a Captain Sangster. Next in order was the smithy. Next and first on the south side was a large store house, in which fish oil &. were stowed away. Next came the Carpenter's shop. Close to this was a large room provided with bunks for the Company's men to sleep in. Next, and last on that side, was a large building, a sort of barrack for new arrivals. Between this corner and the East gate was the Chaple and Chaplin's house. On the other side of this gate was a large building which served as a dineing room for the office adjoining this was the cook house and pantry. On the 4th side were a double row of buildings for storing furs, previous to shipment to England, and goods before taking their place in the trading store. Behind these stores was a fireproof building used as a magazine for storing gunpowder. On the lower corner was another cottage in which lived Mr. Finlayson and family, who was then Chief Factor. On the other side at the front or west gate, was the flag staff and bellfry. The central part of the enclosure was open, and always kept clean. Through this inclosure, ran the main road leading from the 2 gates.

The Governor's own home, enclosed by a small stockade, was located about two hundred feet north of the palisaded fort.

Throughout the next several years, Fort Victoria experienced a slow but steady growth. Its population had reached about three hundred. Although the fur trade was still of significant importance, the company had begun to diversify increasingly into other enterprises based on the island's abundant natural resources. Sawmills were built to utilize the magnificent stands of timber, farming was actively encouraged and expanded, the coal deposits discovered near Nanaimo were exploited, and a salmon fishery was established.

This quiet existence came to an abrupt end in July 1858, when word of the discovery of gold on the Fraser and Thompson rivers reached Fort Victoria. Overnight Fort Victoria was transferred from a staid, well-ordered trading establishment to a place of near-bedlam, besieged night and day by hordes of impatient and frequently unruly men "strangers of every tongue and country, in every variety of attire" who converged on Fort Victoria—the gateway to the "Promised Land" of the gold strikes.

In the words of Alfred Waddington, who was in Fort Victoria in 1858:

> Never perhaps was there so large an immigration in so short a space of time into so small a place.
>
> As to goods, the most exorbitant prices were asked and realized; for though the Company had a large assortment, their store in the Fort was literally besieged from morning to night; and when all were in such a hurry, it was not every one that cared to wait three or four hours, and sometimes half a day, for his turn to get in.
>
> When the older inhabitants beheld these varied specimens of humanity streaming down in motley crowds from the steamers and sailing vessels, and covering the wharves, as if they had come to take possession of the soil, they looked on in silent amazement, as if contemplating a second irruption of barbarians.

During a short twelve-day period from June 27 to July 8, 5,500 passengers disembarked on the company wharf. Again quoting Waddington: "Shops, stores, and wooden shanties of every description, and in every direction were now seen going up . . . In six weeks 225 buildings, of which nearly 200 were stores, . . . had been added to a village of 800 inhabitants . . . Besides which the whole country around the town was covered with tents, resembling the encampments of an army."

Governor and Chief Factor James Douglas met this invasion head-on with decisive action. There was no time to consult either the British government or the Honorable Company in London. He had to act on his own responsibility. The situation facing him was formidable. It required that he protect the economic and trading rights of the Hudson's Bay Company, that he maintain the political rights of the British government, and that he ensure that Vancouver Island and New Caledonia on the mainland remain firmly under British control in spite of the huge wave of Americans pouring into the country.

In a series of decrees Douglas declared that all gold mines in the

629

Fraser and Thompson districts belonged to the British Crown and that licenses for mining there would have to be obtained from proper government authorities in Victoria. Next he issued a proclamation reaffirming the Hudson's Bay Company's legal and sole rights "to the trade with Indians in the British Possessions on the north-west coast of America, to the exclusion of all other persons, whether British or Foreign." Boats and their cargoes "not having a license from the Hudson's Bay Company, and a sufferance from the proper officer of the Customs at Victoria, shall be liable to forfeiture, and will be seized and condemned according to law."

Further, Douglas felt that in view of the influx of such an enormous number of people, "maybe one hundred thousand," the whole country should "be immediately thrown open for settlement, and that the land be surveyed and sold at a fixed rate not to exceed twenty shillings an acre." This was in complete accord with the policy of British Colonial Secretary Sir Edward Bulwer-Lytton, as expressed in a dispatch to Douglas dated July 1, 1858, urging "the peopling and opening up of the new country, with the intention of consolidating it as an integral and important part of the British Empire."

The year 1858 was notable for more than the Fraser River gold rush. In that year the British House of Commons created the colony of British Columbia, which absorbed the old fur trade district of New Caledonia. Also at that time, reflecting a growing and increasingly antimonopolistic sentiment in Great Britain, which presaged the end of the Hudson's Bay Company's special status as holder of exclusive trading rights in British North America, the government decided that no longer should the office of Governor of the colony and of Chief Factor of the Hudson's Bay Company be held by one person.

James Douglas was offered the Governorship of the new colony of British Columbia. He was to retain his position as Governor of Vancouver Island, but he would have to resign as chief factor and sever all his connections with the Hudson's Bay Company. He agreed to the terms and accepted the offer. On November 19, 1858, in a ceremony held in the main hall of the factor's house at Fort Langley, James Douglas, no longer a "commissioned gentleman of the Honorable Hudson's Bay Company," was sworn in as Governor of British Columbia. So ended thirty-seven years of service with the company, in which he had risen from the rank of clerk to that of one of the most respected and influential of the company's officers. Alexander G. Dallas, son-in-law of Douglas, was named as the new chief factor for Fort Victoria.

January 1, 1859, brought another milestone in the steadily diminishing influence of the Hudson's Bay Company in British North America. On that date Queen Victoria signed a royal proclamation terminating the Crown Grant of 1849 that had given sole ownership of Vancouver Island to the company. This meant that all of the island reverted to the Crown with the exception of land acquired by the company by right of possession prior to 1846, when the Oregon Treaty confirmed British title to the island. It was the company's position that the site of Fort Victoria and its several outlying farms belonged in this category. The total such land claimed by the company amounted to 3,084 acres. This comprised the area known as the Hudson's Bay Company's reserve. It included the townsite of Victoria (where the fort was located) and extended from the waterfront inland for more than a mile, plus the lands occupied by their farms.

As Arthur S. Morton wrote in his *History of the Canadian West:* "These were the most eligible areas for cultivation . . . Thus, in a somewhat natural way, the heart of the colony, with outlying farm areas, was in the hands of the Company, and without the payment of a single pound to the development of the Colony. Newcomers must go farther afield . . . When parts of these outer lands were thrown open for sale, officers of the Company made first purchases. Out of this situation arose the implacable hostility of incomers to the Great Company."

The company put in a claim to the British government for £40,290—the amount they had spent in promoting colonization of the colony of Vancouver Island. In addition, they pressed their claim for recognition of their ownership of the 3,084 acres that they had occupied prior to 1846. By terms of an agreement reached in 1862, the government honored the claim for reimbursement for colonization expenses and, with a few minor exceptions relating to one of the farms, the company's land claims were also acknowledged.

Other changes took place. As the trade in furs steadily declined, the fort assumed a new and important role as a merchandising outlet—stocked to serve and supply the needs of the growing number of settlers, farmers, and miners. New buildings of all kinds began to appear. There were hotels, stores, saloons, churches, warehouses, a bank, a custom house, a post office, and a House of Assembly. The old fort compound still survived, but its former position of isolated dominance was increasingly threatened as new construction crowded ever closer.

Its death knoll was first sounded on April 16, 1859 in an article appearing in the *Gazette* that referred to the fort stockade as "an eyesore to our people and a serious hindrance to the prosperity of the south end of the town, by cutting off communication between the upper and lower portions, and we shall be but too glad to chronicle its demolition."

The great northeast bastion was the next structure to fall, as the

631

fort was slowly being dismembered, building by building. The newspaper *Colonist* on December 15, 1860, recorded the event: "The old picket fence that has so long surrounded the fort yard is fast disappearing. Piece after piece—it is taken down, sawed up, and piled away for firewood. Yesterday afternoon workmen commenced removing the old bastion at the corner of View and Government streets, and before today's sun gilds the western horizon, the wood comprising it will no doubt have shared the ignoble fate of the unfortunate pickets. Alas! poor bastion. Thy removal should be enough to break the heart of every Hudson Bay man in the country." Four years later the end came to the old fort. In November of 1864, the *Colonist* chronicled its final demise: "Bit by bit all traces of the Hudson Bay Company's old fort are being obliterated. The work of demolition of the remaining fort buildings has been going on gloriously during the past few days."

The year 1864 witnessed not only the disappearance of the old company fort. It also saw the retirement of Sir James Douglas as Governor. His services to the colony and his outstanding merit had been recognized the previous year by the British government, which had conferred upon him the "Second Class of Knight Commander of the Most Honorable Order of the Bath." The March 12, 1864, *Colonist* summed up his twenty-one-year career on Vancouver Island in the following words:

> The best answer to Sir James' accusers is the publication of the despatches relative to the Crown lands, which show how thoroughly the Governor performed his duty toward the Crown and the public of his Colony when the interests of the Hudson Bay Company came in conflict with those of the colonists. Many held the opinion, previously to the publication of these despatches, that the Governor had leaned toward the Hudson Bay Company more than his position as Governor justified him in doing. Human nature is weak, and those who are so ready to accuse Sir James of unpatriotic conduct, in all probability judged him by their own standard of morality, and did not give him credit for that zeal for the interests of the country, which it has since been proved that he warmly exerted upon this most trying and important occasion.

The razing of the fort did not by any means end the Hudson's Bay Company's presence in Victoria. Anticipating the eventual demolition of the fort buildings, the company in 1859 built a large new store and warehouse just west of the old fort on Wharf Street facing the harbor and the company wharf. The red brick building was four stories high, with both a basement and a subbasement. Its walls were twenty-two inches thick; the framework was of hand-hewn Douglas fir; the windows were iron-barred and equipped with iron shutters. In preparation to meet all contingencies, including the possibility of Indian attack, supplies of food and ammunition were stocked in the subbasement, which had an escape tunnel leading from it under the city. This was the center for the company's extensive trading activities. Here their fleet of schooners and steamships docked to discharge or take on their cargoes of furs, goods, provisions, and supplies. Eventually, in 1901, the company sold its fleet and withdrew from the shipping business.

At length the warehouse itself became outmoded and obsolete. It was demolished in 1937. A modern new department store was built in 1921 as its replacement. This building, now five stories high and occupying a full city block, is the latest in the succession of company buildings stretching back to the first one erected in 1843. As of this writing (1992), the Hudson's Bay Company has been a vital and progressive presence in Victoria for almost 150 years.

The wrecking ball and bulldozer did their work well when the old buildings of Fort Victoria were demolished to make way for "progress." Today there is no trace remaining of the historic fort. However, its memory is perpetuated by a large circular bronze medallion—a replica of the Hudson's Bay Company's seal—embedded in the sidewalk of busy Bastion Square. This marks the location of the northeast bastion of the old fort. The octagonal shape of the bastion is delineated by a row of bricks laid in the pavement, while within the circumscribed space others extend diagonally outward from the bronze seal at the center. Each brick bears the name of a company man involved in the fort's early history or of one of the Indian chiefs of the neighboring tribes who signed treaties giving the company ownership of the fort site.

The people of this flower-filled city have not forgotten their beginnings. The names Douglas, Blanshard, Dallas, Ross, Tod, Tolmie, Helmcken, Ogden, and Finlayson all are used to mark streets, parks, cemeteries, harbors, and land points. Wharf, Bay, and Fort streets as well as Bastion Square itself bear mute witness to the presence of the once-thriving company fort—a fort that during its existence dominated the life of the tiny settlement and helped it become the beautiful vibrant city it is today.

As part of our quest to find reminders of the early days, we visited the old Quadra Street cemetery, today almost overshadowed by the magnificent Anglican cathedral that towers beside it. In this quiet oasis in the heart of the city, ancient trees spread their sheltering branches over the old-style tabletop monuments which mark the graves of many of the company men, including John Work, Charles

Ross, James Yale, Charles Dodd, David Cameron, and John Helmcken. The inscriptions have been partially obliterated by time as well as obscured by luxuriant growth of ivy. Quite appropriately, a small stone marker bearing the Hudson's Bay Company seal and giving dates of the deceased's service with the company has been placed at the foot of each of these monuments.

To see Sir James Douglas's grave, we had to drive to Ross Cemetery, located in the southeast section of Victoria. The day we went, it was raining steadily. But, undeterred, we donned rain gear and, following directions received from the cemetery superintendent, soon found what we were seeking. A tall, imposing monument of polished rose granite enclosed by a low wrought-iron fence marked the burial plot containing the graves of Sir James Douglas, his wife, Lady Amelia, and their son, James William Douglas. Drooping boughs of an enormous spruce tree almost completely hid the site from view. This, coupled with the heavy downpour, made picture taking quite a challenge. However, once again (as has been the case so many times) Zeiss lens proved equal to the task and we were able to secure adequate photographs.

There are two buildings dating from the 1850s that have managed to survive modern "gung-ho" city planners and developers. The first is the Helmcken House, built in 1852. Still modestly occupying its original site, it is today almost overshadowed by the great Parliament Buildings of British Columbia.

Dr. John Sebastian Helmcken was married to Cecilia, a daughter of James Douglas. Dr. Helmcken was the Hudson's Bay Company's doctor and also a leader in the early formation and subsequent development of Victoria. His simple home contains much of its original furnishings, such as the massive mahogany linen press, spool bed, horsehair chair, doctor's medicine chest, and medical library.

The other building remaining from the Hudson's Bay Company's era is Craigflower Manor. This was one of the four farms established by the Puget Sound Agricultural Company, a satellite of the company, in fulfillment of the Crown's requirement that in return for its grant of Vancouver Island the Hudson's Bay Company had to promote and encourage colonization.

Craigflower Manor was built in 1853. Under the supervision of Kenneth McKenzie, who was brought over from Scotland to be bailiff and overseer, the farm was successfully established and developed to include a sawmill, flour mill, brick kiln, smithy, slaughterhouse, general store, and twenty-one well-built homes for the farmworkers. Livestock of all kind and crops from the extensive acreages of well-tilled fields provided some of the abundant agricultural products required to meet the needs of the Hudson's Bay Company.

The manor house is a beautifully proportioned and well-constructed rectangular building of two stories. Its roof is of the simple ridge type, with a chimney at each end. Many of its architectural features reflect a Georgian influence, such as the simple classic pediment and pilasters embellishing the main entrance. The front door is studded with heavy iron nails; two ponderous hand-wrought decorative hinges extend across its entire width. On the ground floor are a parlor, dayroom, study, dining room, pantry, and kitchen. A graceful stairway with a hand-shaped and polished handrail of madrona wood leads from the central hallway to the second-story bedrooms. All the rooms have been restored to their original condition and are well furnished with furniture and accessories appropriate to the 1850s. A few articles actually belonged to the McKenzies.

Outside, we paused to admire the flourishing kitchen garden. Vegetables of all kinds were planted in neat rows and bordered by beds of colorful flowers. The waterway, today known as the Gorge, flows right by the manor. It was down this long, narrow inlet from the harbor that the farm's products were easily transported to the Hudson's Bay Company wharf at its lower end.

Craigflower Manor soon became a social center for the surrounding area, perhaps partly due to the presence of four young daughters who were rapidly reaching marriageable age. Its successful farming operations were convincing proof of the feasibility of the colonizing effort. No longer would Fort Victoria remain a fur trading post only. Henceforth its development and transformation into a settled community of landowners became inevitable.

Fort Selkirk

Soon after Frances Lake and Pelly Banks Posts had been satisfactorily established, Robert Campbell received instructions to establish a third trading post, which was to be built at the forks of the Pelly and Yukon (then known as the Lewes) rivers. Five years earlier, when he had just descended the Pelly as far as its junction with the Lewes, he had been much impressed with the forks as a site for a trading fort. At that time he wrote:

> The Forks is one of the finest sites for an establishment anywhere to be seen . . . The spot chosen for it is between the two rivers but on the bank of the Pelly—the fine level plain, behind which at some little distance rises a beautiful green hill of considerable altitude covered with verdure and forming a crescent around this level bottom to near the Lewes . . . the whole affording excellent grazing and pasture ground for cattle.
>
> A little above the said spot for building is a fine point of large wood for the purpose and, with little trouble, [timber] could be rafted down to the door or taken in boats from a cluster of well-wooded islands at the confluence of the rivers. Directly opposite this on the right bank of the Pelly rise the ramparts, some hundred [150] feet high.

Early in May of 1848 Campbell embarked at Pelly Banks to carry out his new assignment. He had with him his assistant James G. Stewart and eight other men, plus some of his Liard hunters. Campbell and his party reached the forks on the first of June, his boat, skiff, canoes, and raft all intact. They quickly selected a site and "proceeded with the erection of the building in earnest & got on rapidly, naming the new post Fort Selkirk."

The local Indians soon gathered, "coming & going freely among us—all very friendly & strictly honest—gazing with wonder at the work of putting up a building, never having seen a house before—in fact nothing in the shape of a dwelling place but their leather tents."

In August a group of Chilkats about twenty in number arrived at Fort Selkirk. They had drifted down the Lewes (i.e., Yukon) from near its headwaters. They acted as middlemen in the trade between the Hudson's Bay Company coastal ships and the Indians of the interior. It was a role the Chilkats guarded most zealously. Their "thieving propensities" so flagrantly displayed while at the fort were but a forerunner of the havoc they would bring to the post four years hence.

Meanwhile, work on completing the fort was "getting on apace." Campbell's Liard hunters and other local Indians were bringing in provisions in sufficient quantities. Due to the gross mismanagement and negligence of the man left in charge at Pelly Banks and Frances Lake, the supplies and provisions left there for Fort Selkirk were not available. This meant a lean and bleak winter for those at Fort Selkirk.

As Campbell wrote in his memoirs: "We made every preparation with our limited means to face the winter. Our twine & nets we used to the best advantage, establishing several fisheries at Lakes in different quarters in the mountains . . . As it turned out our efforts, hunting & fishing, met great success, as we passed the winter enjoying an abundance of country produce; but we were not in a position to make any big fur trade for want of goods."

The following summer the Chilkats appeared once again. They brought letters from Captain Charles Dodd of the Hudson's Bay Company coastal trading vessel *Beaver;* upon their departure they carried letters from Campbell for delivery to the captain.

The winter of 1849–1850 was a repetition of the previous one, characterized by lack of supplies. This was due to the nonarrival at Fort Frances Lake of the boats from Fort Simpson bringing the year's outfit of provisions and trading goods. Fortunately, however, "the produce of our fisheries & hunters was amply sufficient to keep us in comfort through the season. Flour, Tea, & such luxuries were beyond our reach, except on rare occasions; & trade without goods was of course limited."

Campbell continued to be plagued by a chronic shortage of supplies. The constant lack of goods prevented any trading "except on a very small scale." In the spring of 1851 he was delighted to receive permission from Governor Simpson to undertake exploration of the Pelly River downstream from Fort Selkirk "as far as I might deem advisable." Campbell had long suspected that the Pelly and the "Youcon" (i.e., Yukon) were the same river. Now he was going to have the opportunity to prove it. So on June 5 Campbell set off on his journey of discovery and recorded his progress in his diary:

> We travelled night & day. The river increased in size & beauty as we advanced, its waters swelled by many tributaries from the mountains on either side. After a time the ranges of mountains skirting the river on both sides recede, the river widens, & for miles wanders among countles islands. After travelling about 45 miles after entering this level stretch of country, we had the satisfaction of coming in sight of the fort. . . . It turned out to be Fort Youcon, situated at the confluence of the Porcupine river. . . . I had thus the satisfaction of demonstrating that my conjectures from the first . . . in which hardly anyone concurred . . . were correct & that the Pelly & the Youcon were identical.

The distance between Fort Selkirk and Fort Youcon was computed by Campbell to be 320 miles, a distance he had covered in a little more than three days. He proceeded up the Porcupine River and its tributary, the Bell, to La Pierre's House; then over the Richardson Mountains by way of McDougall Pass and down the Rat, Peel, and Mackenzie rivers, eventually reaching Fort Simpson on the fourth of August. Here he picked up his outfit of supplies and trading goods and headed back over the same route he had come. On October 17 he was safely back at Fort Selkirk, well pleased with his success in demonstrating the superiority of this route over that of the Liard River for supplying his fort. He summarized his feelings in his diary entry for that day as follows: "I cannot express my gratitude to kind Providence for the success of my summers voyage and our safe arrival here by water with the necessary supplies I took in hand to render."

By the end of 1851 Campbell had decided that Fort Selkirk must be moved to a new location. The flooding caused by ice jams during the breakup of the river each spring made its present site most undesirable. The new site chosen was about two-and-a-half miles downstream from the forks on the left bank of the Lewes (i.e., Yukon). Apparently, this was the spot Campbell had chosen for his first fort, but because he was uncertain what the disposition of the numerous Indians might be, he had chosen to build "the first fort in thick woods on the very point of confluence of the two rivers" as better situated for defense.

The site for the relocated fort was a fine plain whose banks were a safe height above the river. During the winter, in addition to maintaining their numerous fisheries Campbell's men were "generally sawing and getting wood for our new Fort."

During the early spring of 1852 Campbell and his men were busy erecting the fort. By the end of April, with the exception of the enclosing stockade, most of the work was complete. Campbell wrote in his diary for April 30: "Nothing has been procured from our hunters or any other quarter in provision since the last date [April 3] consequently our stock is now very small—we have been very busy removing our old fort to the new site and today we finished re-erecting it on a more extensive scale dwelling house 50 feet long—mens house 52 and store 50 feet—with kitchen of 14 feet sqr in wh. chimney was put up today—"

With the use of the new Yukon–Porcupine–Mackenzie route providing a dependable way for servicing Fort Selkirk, its future seemed secured. With adequate goods for trading and the small amount of necessary supplies needed to supplement the game and fish available locally, Campbell felt confident that at long last Fort Selkirk could become an important and profitable post. But it was not to be.

By the first part of August 1852 only a few men remained at the fort. The local Indians had left for their summer hunt, and Stewart and four men had departed to undertake further exploration of the Yukon River. Only Campbell and a couple of men were left. On August 19 they paddled the short distance up the Pelly to the site of their abandoned first fort in order to cut some hay in the clearing. The next morning they were startled by the sudden appearance of five rafts of Chilkats rapidly coming down the Lewes (i.e., Yukon). Quickly dropping their scythes and rakes, Campbell and his men raced down to their canoe and, paddling furiously, tried desperately to reach the fort ahead of the Chilkats. They did not succeed, and when they reached the fort, all was confusion.

As Campbell later wrote: "The Fort being so large and not yet picketed round it was impossible for so few of us to keep an eye everywhere. They in short had us entirely in their power." He continued: "But though I temporized and used every conciliatory appearance to soothe them they were like a volcano every moment ready to burst out."

During the night Campbell stationed two of his men within the store, one in the kitchen in the rear, while he himself remained inside the dwelling house. The account in his diary described what occurred: "The night passed irksome enough—some of the infernal devils were on the move the whole night trying the store doors and windows [?] to open them and get inside. Early the next morning, Saturday 21st August 1852 they were on the move bent on mischief of every description than even yesterday . . ." Campbell "wished to take shelter in the store and defend ourselves to the last extremity but then we had no water and they could set fire to the other end of the house and burn us out . . ."

At that moment a boat and two canoes carrying some of the fort's hunters came into sight. The savages began "yelling like fiends armed with guns and knives and as the Boat passed along the bank they rushed into the water and dragged it shore. . . . Ere the Boat had touched the shore the fiends had everything out of it tearing it from each other and the yelling and uproar was tremendous." Campbell ran down to the river to try to prevent bloodshed, "but in less than two minutes they had pillaged everything . . ."

Next, when Campbell headed back toward the house, "three of the demons sprung with their cocked guns from the Hall door before me [and] hold [held] them within a few feet of my heart others [held] my arms and other sprung on [me] with their daggers for running me

639

through . . . the blood dripping from the blade on my arm as the blow was evaded. They were all yelling like fiends—the uproar would beggar description—smashing and crashing everything in the house."

One of the Chilkats rushed up to Campbell and, shoving his blunderbuss at his chest, pulled the trigger. Fortunately for Campbell's survival, it missed fire. Another, armed with a long knife, lunged at him, but two less bloodthirsty Chilkats pulled him aside just in time to avoid the deadly thrust.

It was obvious the Chilkats "were determined on our destruction or expulsion." Soon the savages swarmed around Campbell and forced him down toward the bank. In the ensuing scuffle his pistols were snatched from his belt. Amidst a wild melee of rampaging Chilkats, Campbell jumped into the boat at the foot of the bank and shoved off, quickly gaining the safety of the river.

As he wrote later: "Like people burnt out we got off with the boats with nothing but what [we] happened to have upon us." Campbell and the few men who had escaped with him drifted downstream about five miles. They were "now without anything to eat or a blanket to cover us—many without even a Capot . . ."

The next day Campbell, reinforced by a few friendly Indians from a nearby camp, started back for Fort Selkirk, determined to exact full retribution. However, when they reached the fort, they found it deserted.

Campbell wrote in his diary: "the villans had already left with their booty. They left a scene behind them that nothing will describe—The door open, windows cut out. The store and house from end to end slewed over with everything that can be imagined with filth, etc. [?] ball, shot, meat, geese, fish, pans, kettles [?] rice, raisins, sugar, flour, feathers, knives, paper, leather, letter, etc. etc. God Almighty what a syte in the abode of peace and comfort a few days ago."

Undaunted, Campbell wished to set off in instant pursuit, but the Indians who had accompanied him, citing the head start the Chilkats had as well as their superiority in arms and number, refused to go. They would not be persuaded to change their minds, so Campbell had no alternative but to abandon his chase.

The fort had been thoroughly "trashed" by the Chilkats. They had left "not even a grain of powder, nor hardly anything of clothing—not so much as a sock was left—cassettes, boxes, etc. smashed to atoms . . ."

"Without a grain of powder or an article of clothing or a single blanket among us" Campbell knew it would be impossible to survive the winter at the fort unless they could get emergency help from either Stewart or Fort Yukon. They packed "what little refuse" they could salvage and the next day (August 25) left the fort and slowly headed downstream. When, five days later, they finally reached Stewart's camp on the Yukon, they quickly saw that the latter had no surplus supplies that could be spared to enable them to remain at Fort Selkirk over the winter. Campbell had no choice: the fort had to be abandoned for the winter. He sent Stewart with six of his men and some of the Indian hunters along with four boats and two canoes and the pitiful amount of goods that had been rescued from the fort to winter at Fort Yukon.

A disheartened Campbell accompanied by his two men set off in a birchbark canoe for Fort Simpson by the old route of Frances Lake and the Liard River. Forty-six days later they reached Fort Simpson.

Although Campbell pleaded eloquently for the men, arms, and supplies necessary to enable him to reestablish Fort Selkirk, his request was denied. The decision had already been reached that both Fort Selkirk and Fort Yukon were to be permanently abandoned. Chief Trader James Anderson summed up his reasons for arriving at this decision in a letter to the Governor and council.

2. If we do send back it must be with the determination of punishing these scoundrels, which will require a stronger force than I have at command and could be more efficiently done at the sea coast by the steamer [*Beaver*].

3. I have an unshaken conviction that this post can never pay, from the long period the returns take to reach market; from the low tariff which must be adopted to compete with the Chilkats; from the large establishment of officers and men which must be kept up and which would require to be increased to guard against retaliation; and from the apparent poverty of the country.

So for the next forty years the high plateau by the forks of the Pelly and Yukon remained deserted. Within a few years Campbell's fort, reduced to the remains of a few tumbled-down log buildings, became little more than a memory.

The discovery of gold in the Klondike in 1896 coupled with the advent of the stern-wheelers plying the Yukon from Whitehorse to Dawson gave rise to the rapid rebirth of the settlement of Fort Selkirk. Five hotels, an Anglican and a Roman Catholic church, several trading stores, a sawmill, a school, a post office, and a Royal Canadian Mounted Police post now occupied the flatland above the river. Fort Selkirk's future seemed assured. However, when the rush to the Klondike and the accompanying gold rush had subsided, Fort Selkirk's fortunes declined dramatically.

It was not until the late 1920s that it began to recover some of its former vitality. A new Anglican church was built, the Royal Canadian Mounted Police reopened their post, and in 1936, just eighty-four years after Campbell had been driven out of his fort, the Hudson's Bay Company returned and built a store within a few yards of the original fort site. Hopes bounced back for the future of Fort Selkirk.

But once again the looked-for prosperity did not last. The completion of the highway between Whitehorse and Dawson in 1955 ended the era of the stern-wheelers on the Yukon. Not only the availability of transportation by road but also the increasing use of airplanes doomed Fort Selkirk's existence as a viable community. No longer needed to service the needs of the gold rush, nor of the paddle-wheelers, nor of the settlements along the river, Fort Selkirk quietly slipped back into the obscurity of a Yukon River ghost town.

Fortunately, however, Fort Selkirk was not destined to fade away into total oblivion. Thanks to a joint effort sponsored by the Selkirk band of Tuchone Indians and funded by the Heritage Branch of the Yukon government and Yukon College, many of Fort Selkirk's buildings are today being stabilized and renovated. Archaeological research has unearthed evidence that this site had been used as a native gathering and campsite within at least the past one or two thousand years. It now appears that Fort Selkirk is to be spared the fate of many ghost towns, where only mounds of building timbers slowly rotting under the rank growth of brush and vine are left to mark the existence of a once-thriving community.

The only way we could reach Fort Selkirk was by a small riverboat or by chartered plane. We had made tentative plans to fly from Dawson City, but on the day of our proposed flight weather was so unpromising we knew that good photography would not be possible.

Accordingly, we drove down south as far as Minto, a former paddle-wheeler stop on the banks of the Yukon about twenty-five miles south of Pelly Crossing where the Klondike Highway crosses the Pelly River. There we had the good fortune to contact Pat Van Bibber, who operates a resort on the Yukon and who agreed to take us to Fort Selkirk in his riverboat. Van Bibbers have lived on the Yukon and Pelly rivers for generations. Both Pat's grandmothers were Tuchone Indians.

Early the next morning, first fortified by one of Jerry Kruse's hearty breakfasts served at his well-known Midway Lodge nearby, we piled into the twenty-four-foot narrow square-ended river skiff powered by two fifty-horsepower motors. In addition to Pat and ourselves we had as a passenger Chief Danny Robert of the Tuchones, who stays at Fort Selkirk during the summer months. His task is to keep track of the visitors to the site and watch over the general security of the area.

Our trip down the Yukon was a delight. A range of rounded hills bordered the swiftly flowing river. Beautiful bald eagles were common; in fact, we saw at least twelve of the majestic white-headed birds. In addition, we were fortunate to see a group of nine snow-white Dall sheep resting on a bare area near the summit of one of the hills. Highlighted by the bright sunshine, their dazzling whiteness was spectacularly resplendent.

Pat showed us iron rings low down in the rocky cliffs bordering the river that were used by the paddle-wheelers to aid them as they winched their way over certain sections of strong current and rapids.

We stopped at what was once the Blanchard Wood Landing on the right bank of the Yukon and halfway between Minto and Pelly Crossing. This was one of the many "wooding stops" along the river where the enormous number of cords of wood required by the wood-burning paddle-wheelers were cut and stacked by men working under contract to the steamship company. The remains of an old homestead log building were still visible, although it would not be long before they would be reclaimed by the soil and undergrowth of the surrounding woods. This, Pat told us, had been his mother's home. He said he could remember the bustle and excitement when the stern-wheelers edged in to the bank and the frantic race to load the cordwood down the steep bank onto the boat in the shortest possible time. Now all was quiet, but it was not empty of life, for as we poked around the roofless cabin we discovered we were almost walking in the unmistakable footprints of a large bear. We were looking for good photographic angles; he was probably looking for the ripe berries that were so abundant on the profusion of vines rapidly encroaching on the small clearing.

As we approached the junction of the Yukon and the Pelly, we noticed the numerous low-lying islands in the widened Yukon that partially obscured the actual confluence of the two rivers. The Yukon, now strengthened and enlarged by the Pelly, made a wide bend to the west as it swept along with powerful current towards its ultimate destination of the Arctic Ocean. In the distance we could see the buildings of Fort Selkirk scattered along the plain atop the Yukon's left bank.

The setting was magnificent. Across the river from Fort Selkirk a range of rounded hills, much like a mighty palisade, followed the westward course of the Yukon as far as we could see. A short distance upstream to the east, this lofty barrier wall ended abruptly, its sheared off eastern face marking the entrance of the Pelly River valley.

In a matter of minutes we had beached our boat and were soon walking along the very plain where Robert Campbell had established his 1852 post. Of course no above-ground evidence has survived, but recent archaeological work has been able to pinpoint its location, which lies in the very shadow of Tuchone Chief Danny Robert's small cabin.

The buildings still standing at Fort Selkirk date from the approximately fifty-year period beginning with the 1898 gold rush, including the stern-wheeler river transportation era and ending in the 1950s with the completion of the Klondike Highway. Lined up in a row along a reddish dirt roadway and facing the river, the buildings of Fort Selkirk, in various stages of renovation, cling to their precarious hold on survival.

At the eastern edge of the settlement the concrete foundation and front steps are all that remain of the store built by the Hudson's Bay Company when they returned to Fort Selkirk in 1936, eighty-four years after Campbell had been forced to flee his post. It is interesting that the company's new store was situated but a few yards from the site of the 1852 fort.

Midway along the roadway the large store built in 1910 by Taylor and Drury, a major competitor of the Hudson's Bay Company, has managed to survive the onslaught of weather and time. Within the building the long counter and the shelves, once loaded with goods of all kinds, are now bare but can quickly be stocked once again, even if only in imagination.

Between the two stores are numerous log buildings, some roofless, some covered with grass sod, others with an assortment of shingles, all in varying stages of repair. These include a garage, a Hudson's Bay Company machine shop, a mounted police post, a large stable, and several cabins used by trappers, traders, and outfitters for a river freighting operation.

To the west of the Taylor and Drury store are the small school building built in 1892, the Anglican rectory, which according to tradition was built by George Carmack, whose discovery of gold on Bonanza Creek precipitated the great Klondike gold rush of 1898, and St. Andrew's Anglican church, built in 1929 to replace an earlier structure built in 1893. Several other cabins and houses, including one owned by Ira Van Bibber, a well-known trapper and hunter who used it when he came to Fort Selkirk from upstream on the Pelly River to sell his furs and buy supplies, straggle along as far as the western end of the road. Nestled back in the woods well behind the front-line buildings is the St. Francis Xavier Catholic church. Built in the early 1900s, it was first located near the riverbank but was moved to its present site in 1942.

For several happy hours we slipped back in time as we wandered in and out of the Fort Selkirk buildings. Within the small one-room schoolhouse, the scarred wooden desks, the small box stove in the center of the room, and the blackboard on the front wall were all in place, just waiting for the noisy arrival of the children.

We opened creaking doors and stepped into cabins—once homes full of life and activity but now silent and empty. A few simple tables and chairs, a rickety stool, a scarred bench, a narrow iron bedstead, the omnipresent rusting barrel stove, a battered trunk, crude bed frames fastened to the walls—these were all that now remained from that day more than forty years ago when the men and women walked out of their homes for the last time.

Time has laid but gentle hands on the two churches. St. Andrew's with its wooden steeple tower has been largely spared the ravages of more than fifty years of neglect. Inside the church, its walls sheathed with wood now glowing with a soft patina, the altar with its beautifully carved Christian symbols of IHS, Alpha and Omega, the chancel rail, the pews, and the large heating stove with its tall stovepipe stretching upward to the high ceiling all were in perfect order—ready to welcome its congregation and resume its role as a house of worship.

Likewise in St. Francis Xavier the altar, adorned with tabernacle, cross, sacred pictures, and even a bouquet of dried flowers, seemed to be quietly waiting for people to file in and fill the empty pews.

At last lengthening shadows warned us that it was time to leave Fort Selkirk and begin our return trip up the Yukon back to Minto. First, however, we walked the half-mile along the dirt road to the extreme eastern end of the plain where the Yukon Field Force had been stationed during the height of the Klondike gold rush. Only one building remained standing, but the foundations of barracks, storehouse, officers' mess, bakery, guardroom, and combined hospital and quartermaster's stores were still visible.

The last thing we saw as we finally headed out into the strong current was Tuchone Chief Danny Roberts sitting on the small porch in front of his cabin, his small black dog curled at his feet, looking out over this beautiful land where his forebears had hunted, trapped, and traded in friendship with Robert Campbell. The cries, shouting, and din of the throng of maddened Chilkats who shattered the peace of this very place 140 years ago have long since faded away. Even the memory of the violence has receded into the past. Today peace and tranquillity have been restored and the Tuchone continue to maintain their watchful guardianship over their traditional homelands.

Fort Rupert
(Vancouver Island)

In 1836, when Dr. William Tolmie was stationed at Fort McLoughlin, he learned of the existence of an outcropping of coal less than one hundred miles away on nearby Vancouver Island. It appears that while some Indians, who had come to his fort to trade, were watching the fort's blacksmith working at his forge, they asked where he obtained the "soft black stone" he was using in his forge. His reply, explaining that it required a six-month ocean voyage to bring it from far off Wales, was received with astonished hilarity by the natives. When asked the reason for their mirth, they told the rather incredulous blacksmith that a good supply of the "soft black stone" was easily available less than one hundred miles away on the northern tip of Vancouver Island. Of course, Dr. Tolmie was immediately informed of this astonishing and very welcome news. He, in turn, passed along the information to Dr. John McLoughlin, chief factor of Fort Vancouver. Shortly afterward the company steamer *Beaver,* ordered to check out the report on her next coastal trading voyage, was able to verify it by locating surface seams of coal along the northern tip of Vancouver Island.

The ink was scarcely dry on the Letters Patent dated January 13, 1849, whereby the Hudson's Bay Company became proprietors of Vancouver Island, charged with the responsibility of establishing a colony there, when preparations were made to build a post at the northern end of the island in order to take advantage of its coal deposits. Governor Sir George Simpson, never slow to grasp an opportunity to embark on new ventures that offered advantages for the company, was quite enthusiastic about the possibility of the availability of coal on Vancouver Island. In a letter to Chief Factor Peter Skene Ogden dated April 17, 1849, Simpson wrote: "From the frequent applications made to me on the subject [of the coal mine] and from the large fleet of Steamers about to proceed to the Pacific from the United States it is quite evident that the Coal trade will soon become of great importance."

Simpson even believed that the cost of establishing the colony of Vancouver Island could be largely defrayed by the royalties on the coal that the company would receive. And Sir John Pelly, London Governor of the company, even more optimistically felt the royalties would be sufficient to pay the salaries of the new colony's Governor and other public officers.

Fort Rupert was erected primarily to develop the coal deposits of the area, but it was also expected to take over the trade in furs that had been lost when Fort McLoughlin was closed in 1843. Chief Trader William McNeill, formerly captain of the company's steamship *Beaver,* was named as head of the new post. His son-in-law, George Blenkinsop, was McNeill's second-in-command. The fort's complement of men numbered about forty, and included those withdrawn from the recently abandoned Fort Stikine as well as an additional twenty men (half-breeds, French-Canadians, Kanakas [Sandwich Islanders]) recruited from Fort Vancouver.

The site chosen for the post, which was to be named Fort Rupert, was on the shores of a small bay called Beaver Harbour. It faced to the northeast, overlooking the waters of Queen Charlotte Strait and the Coast Mountains of the mainland to the east. Charles Beardmore, clerk at the fort, in a letter to Dr. Tolmie wrote in 1849 that the site selected for the fort was by the side of a stream and that "the pickets are up, the Trading House under Weigh, Masters' Palace erected and I have made for myself a snug little log house where I mean to reside for the winter." He added that the front pickets had been whitewashed and that the beach was full of clamshells and the woods full of salal berries.

A year later Dr. John Helmcken, stationed at Fort Rupert, wrote his impressions of his surroundings in a letter to a friend in far off London: "Here I am in a fort 80 yards square, situated on the borders of the densest forest this earth can produce, with only about three acres of cleared land, which has been made with an awful deal of trouble, in order to grow potatoes, and a few other vegetables, upon which we have to depend." He added that the post had fifty sheep, six cows and calves, and six horses. Native game, such as deer, birds, and fish, was present in abundance.

In order to mine the coal, the Hudson's Bay Company in 1848 arranged to bring out a group of miners from Scotland. They were mostly from one family—that of John Muir. He was appointed Oversman of the group. They reached Fort Victoria on June 1, 1849, six months after leaving London on December 9 of the previous year. At last, "after a very tedious passage," they reached Beaver Harbour on the twenty-fourth of September.

From the very beginning, problems arose that disturbed the smooth working relationship between the miners and the post's officers. First of all, the miners were unable to locate any promising or significant workable seams of coal. They were able to spot only small ribs of coal about two inches thick, and even the surface deposits went no deeper than eighteen inches. Their second grievance was that they were expected to help with the construction of buildings within the fort

647

and to assist in digging the fort's well. The miners felt this was laborers' work and not what they were contracted to do. One of John Muir's sons, Andrew, expressed their feelings as follows: They had come to Vancouver Island "to work coal not to look for it and do all manner of work and I consider the Company has broken our agreement as we were only to work as labourers in the event of the coal not succeeding. Now we never saw a coal at all and on speaking about it we were told we should have to work at anything we were put."

Another issue of contention was the refusal of the fort officer to provide the miners with protection when they were at work at the coal pit that was located outside the stockade. They had asked for a picket fence to be built around the pit, but this was refused. According to miners, the Indians "have come down and threatened to shoot us." The miners also asked for clay to line the pit walls as a safeguard against cave-in, but this, too, was refused. Reflecting their dissatisfaction and discontent, the miners' complaints increased. Now, in addition to their grievances regarding the type of work they were required to perform, they complained about shortness of food rations and the confiscation by the fort's officers of the fish and meat brought to them by the Indians.

On May 2, 1850, the company vessel *Beaver* arrived at the fort. The next morning Captain McNeill summoned all the miners to a meeting. Then, backed both by George Blenkinsop, his assistant, and Charles Beardmore, clerk, McNeill threatened the miners and peremptorily ordered them to return to work. The miners held firm, not only refusing to accede to Captain McNeill's ultimatum but also demanding "to be fairly tried by English law." Two of the miners, Andrew Muir, son, and John McGregor, nephew of John Muir, were put in irons, imprisoned in the fort's bastion, and kept on bread and water. Adamant in refusing to return to work, the two men were determined to make an issue of the whole matter and "would do no more until their case was tried and settled."

By this time chaos had replaced the orderly routine of the fort. Little work was being done; no digging of coal by the miners; the nearly three thousand Indians assembled on the nearby islands were showing signs of increasing hostility; and like a powerful magnet, news of the California gold strike was successfully luring people to the new El Dorado. On May 23 the American ship *Massachusetts* docked at Fort Rupert to take on a cargo of coal; the following morning the British barque *England* arrived for the same purpose.

Sometime prior to this, three crewmen had jumped a Hudson's Bay Company ship when it was docked at Fort Victoria and had taken refuge on the *England*. During the time the *England* was docked at Fort Rupert, the three men hid in the nearby woods, until the time of her sailing. Blenkinsop, determined to find the deserters and bring them to the fort, enlisted the aid of the Indians. They were successful in finding the hideaways, whom they promptly killed. Whether Blenkinsop promised the Indians ten blankets "for each of their heads should they bring them back only their heads" or the offer was simply ten blankets "per head," i.e., for each man, has never been satisfactorily determined. At any rate, two expeditions were mounted in ships of the Royal Navy to search out and apprehend the Indians who had killed the three crewmen. Although the effort was a failure, punishment was inflicted on the tribe of the killers by totally destroying their village at Bull Harbour. Eventually it was the Indians themselves who executed the killers and brought their bodies to Fort Rupert.

Sometime during this period of turmoil and confusion, Andrew Muir, John McGregor, their families, and several other of the miners surreptiously left Fort Rupert and took refuge in the woods until they could safely slip aboard the *England* and proceed to San Francisco.

With their departure, coal mining came to a stop at Fort Rupert. Andrew Muir was nothing if not persistent in his efforts to seek redress of what he considered had been the wrongful treatment he had received. He was eventually vindicated when the Hudson's Bay Company in London, upon receiving reports of the trouble at Fort Rupert, realized that their officers there had exceeded their legal rights and had violated the miners' rights as British subjects. Governor Pelly wrote a sharp rebuke to Chief Factor Douglas at Fort Victoria in which he emphasized that Captain McNeill, George Blenkinsop, and Beardmore had no legal right whatsoever either to imprison the miners or to put them in irons. Eventually, many of the Muirs and McGregors moved to the Nanaimo area, where, shortly after 1851, steps were taken to develop the more promising coal deposits that had been discovered there.

The end of the coal mining at Fort Rupert did not mean the end of the fort. In 1856 Hamilton Moffat, while working as a surveyor for the company, stopped off at Fort Rupert. He "admired the well kept garden outside the stockade" and observed that "part of the fort was encroaching onto the Indian village. Bastions stood at two corners opposite each other. These two Bastions were squared at the bottom, octagonal at the top, with loop holes for muskets at the top. Four cannon stood ready at the bottom of the bastions." Moffat noticed that the building housing the officers was ninety feet by forty feet and that a stockade surrounded the living quarters, which included four large houses. The miners' houses were located in the center of the stockade enclosed area, and standing beside them was a huge stone fireplace that served as a communal kitchen.

An active trade in furs and salmon had developed to justify the continuing existence of Fort Rupert. Moffat commented that "Salmon were bought from the Indians at One Salmon for One leaf of Tobacco" and used for food supplies at other company posts. The salmon, sometimes smoked, was shipped to Fort Victoria in barrels. A vivid description of Fort Rupert has been left by Dr. John K. Lord, naturalist with the British Boundary Commission, who visited the post in 1857:

> The Trading Post is a square enclosed by immense trees—a platform about the height of an ordinary man from the top of the pickets, is carried along the sides of this square . . . The entrance is closed by two massive gates, an inner and outers; all the houses—the chief trader's, employees', trading house, fur room and stores—are within the square. The trade room is cleverly contrived so as to prevent a sudden rush of Indians; the approach from outside the pickets is by a long narrow passage, bent at an acute angle near the window of the trade room, being only of a sufficient width to admit one savage at a time (the precaution is necessary in as much as, were the passage straight, they would inevitably shoot the trader).
>
> At the angle nearest the Indian Village are two bastions, octagonal in shape, and of a very doubtful style of architecture. Four embrasures in each bastion would lead the uninitiated to believe in the existence of as many formidable cannons; with rammers, sponges, neat piles of round shot and grape . . . Imagine my surprise on entering this fortress to discover all this a pleasant fiction: two small rusty carronades, buried in the accumulated dust and rubbish of years, that no human power could have loaded, were the sole occupants of the mouldy old turrets.

Commander R. C. Mayne visited Fort Rupert in 1857. He became interested in the details of the trading carried on at the fort. Seeing the great abundance of the salmon, he wondered why more was not purchased from the Indians, cured, and sold in the Sandwich Islands. He learned that at one time "3000 salmon were used annually as manure for the garden" at the fort, which resulted in a garden from which "the product of vegetables and flowers is yearly most luxuriant." Mayne also compiled figures for the number of skins traded, their equivalent in trade blankets for tobacco leaves, the total cost of trade goods, and the total value of the skins in England. He calculated: "If then we add the cost of furs 600 pounds for the expense of the post, we have 1260 pounds against 5405 pounds (the total value of the skins in England), showing a profit of more than 4100 yearly on this establishment, which is considered by the Company as one of their least profitable stations." The great timber resources of Vancouver Island also caught Mayne's eye. He stated categorically that "we came upon no place there [i.e., in British Columbia] where such fine spars were to be found, and with such facilities for shipping as at . . . the neighbourhood of Fort Rupert."

Hamilton Moffat assumed charge of Fort Rupert in 1857. At this time there were "only 5 men there, exclusive of the cook and watchman." Even with this small staff, trading was good, for fort records showed satisfactory fur returns in beaver, marten, and otter. In addition, firewood and wooden shingles were shipped out in the company ship *Beaver*. The following year (1858) 500 marten skins, as well as additional wooden shingles and fish oil, were sent out.

Interesting light is shed on the Indians' unshakable preference for certain specific trade goods. According to Moffat, his native customers would not accept three-point blankets in trade; they would accept only two-and-one-half-point blue ones. He finally had to clear his shelves of the spurned three-point blankets by sending them to Fort Victoria, since "they have been here for years and are of no service."

By 1862 trade was falling off. The arrival of whiskey peddlers at the fort brought the inevitable demoralization of the Indians. At this same time, the deadly smallpox spread to the post, and in spite of Moffat's best efforts (he "vaccinated more than 100 Indians") five died. Moffat pleaded for materials to permit him to make much-needed repairs to the fort, but nothing was sent. He wrote: "I am in terror lest a stiff breeze of wind may at any time level an entire side."

In 1864 the roster for Fort Rupert was F. N. Compton, clerk; Robert Hunt, trader; and five laborers. Robert Hunt had come from England in 1849 to work for the company as a laborer. He married a Tlingit chief's daughter, fathered eleven children, and moved to Fort Rupert. By 1857 he had been promoted to Indian trader; twenty-four years later he had attained the rank of company postmaster at Fort Rupert.

When the company withdrew from Fort Rupert in 1882, Hunt was allowed to occupy, free of rent, the fort buildings "on condition of making the necessary repairs at his own cost, and taking care of the premises for the Company." The next year Hunt retired from the company, and two years later (in 1885) he was able to buy the trading post and surrounding five acres of land for $1,500. For many years thereafter Hunt and his family lived in the company's old buildings and continued to operate successfully what had once been the company store. His store ledgers show that the two-and-one-half-point blue blankets were still being stocked to satisfy his customers' traditional preference for this item. Each blanket was valued at one large black bear skin. The furs most often traded at his store were marten, otter, raccoon, fur and hair seal, wolf, mountain lion, black bear, elk, and deer. It is noteworthy that beaver pelts were not listed. Fish oil continued to be a popular item of trade. In May of 1889 much of the old fort was destroyed by fire. Hunt recorded that "Big House, fowl house, cook house and closet got burnt to the ground at 2:30 a.m. How it got on fire no one seems to know." Robert Hunt died in 1893, age sixty-five. For many years afterward succeeding generations of his family have remained at Fort Rupert and successfully carried on his business.

By the early 1940s all the fort had succumbed to the ravages of time, fire, and vandalism. Today the huge rough-hewn stone chimney from the factor's house is the only surviving structure left to mark the location of Fort Rupert—"the newest and best built station of the Hudson's Bay Company I have seen" according to Commander R. C. Mayne.

However, the fame of Fort Rupert does not depend on the existence of this relic from the past, interesting though it is. Its legacy is the enduring outpouring of superb native carvings—traditional masks, massive totem poles, and ceremonial objects—that Hunt and his gifted descendants created and continue to produce to the present day.

Our drive up the beautiful east side of Vancouver Island was a most enjoyable experience. Meals were a gourmet treat of seafood; the scenery was magnificent. The snow-covered tops of the lofty Coast Mountains on the mainland sparkled against the brilliant blue sky. We were not fortunate enough to see any of the killer whales that frequent the waters of Johnstone and Queen Charlotte Straits. A good excuse for a return trip!

Halfway up the island we took the brief ferry ride to Quadra Island. There we enjoyed seeing the totem poles and the excellent collection of native art housed in the Kwakiutl Indian Museum. Farther up the island, we took another short ferry trip across Queen Charlotte Straits to Alert Bay on Cormorant Island. It was an overcast day, the clouds blocking out the Coast Mountains and nearly reaching down to the water. And still no killer whales for us to see!

The totem poles were in the Nimpkish cemetery, which bordered the main street along the waterfront. Bearing witness to a proud tradition, these poles—some tall, some short; some erect, some tilting sideways; some bright with the vivid colors of new paint, some the soft silver-gray of age—all faced toward the straits to the west. All were examples of masterful carving, and all told a proud story of family tradition. Obeying the NO TRESPASS signs, we could only see the totem poles from the sidewalk outside the cemetery but were grateful to get even this close to them.

We also visited the impressive U'mista Cultural Center. This magnificent building completed in 1980 replicates a traditional Kwakiutl Big House. There in the hushed quiet and subdued light of the large sunken great hall, the precious head masks, the ceremonial rattles, the "coppers," and many other sacred items that were once ruthlessly torn from their owners by shortsighted and arrogant government agencies are now, at least some of them, at long last safely back home in the custody of the Kwakiutl people.

At Fort Rupert, after a few inquiries, we were able to find the Hudson's Bay Company fort's massive stone chimney. It stood in a small clearing not far from the water. As we photographed the structure and the adjacent area, we noticed the slight ridges and depressions that probably marked the foundations of the fort's early buildings.

After leaving the site of the company's Fort Rupert, we drove slowly along the road by the harbor. No longer were canoes pulled up on the clamshell shingle. A short distance away we overtook a young lady walking along the road. We stopped to chat and learned that she was on her way to tend the grave of her grandfather Robert Hunt. This was the Robert Hunt who was patriarch of the long line of distinguished artists who still make their homes around Fort Rupert. He lies buried in a small picket-enclosed graveyard just off the harbor road at the top of a slope overlooking the fort site. The modest totem pole marking his place of burial faces both the ocean and the fort where he lived and worked for forty-three years.

The final bonus of our Fort Rupert trip was the opportunity of visiting the large open-sided carving shed and watching one of Hunt's grandsons working on a huge totem pole. Other totem poles in various stages of completion were lying on sturdy sawhorses within the carving shed. Outside were several mammoth cedar logs. On one we noticed the name "Hunt" along with the log's dimensions—3'5-1/2" x 38' painted on the butt end.

Located close by the same ridge overlooking the harbor was the partially completed frame of a massive traditional house. The two pairs of heavy internal house posts carved to represent family crests and totems had been placed at the front and rear of the house. They supported the four heavy round beams that spanned the width and length of the building. We gazed in wonder and admiration at this

653

example of native ingenuity and craftsmanship. Indeed, we felt particularly fortunate that we had been afforded this great opportunity of catching a glimpse, brief though it was, of the magnificent Pacific Northwest Indian culture.

Touchwood Hills Post

Chief Factor William J. Christie had not occupied his new post at Fort Pelly, main headquarters for the Swan River district, before he realized the necessity for establishing a post where the cart brigades traveling the long Fort Ellice–Carlton trail could reprovision. Touchwood Hills was a logical choice. It was roughly halfway between Fort Ellice on the Assiniboine River and Fort Carlton on the North Saskatchewan River. It was on the edge of good buffalo country and was also on the near edge of the Carrywood Plain and the Great Salt Plain. In addition, it was in an area equally rich in buffalo and muskrats.

Christie entrusted the task of establishing the new fort to Thomas Taylor, who was well qualified for the job. He had been reared in the Hudson's Bay Company tradition. His mother was the daughter of Chief Factor George Keith. Taylor had been educated in Montreal and then had served as an apprentice clerk, first under Sir George Simpson at Lachine and later under Governor Ballenden at Fort Garry. Furthermore, he was fluent in Cree, Saulteau, French, and English.

Early in September of 1852, Taylor and five men journeyed to Big Touchwood Hills and began to build the first Touchwood Hills post. The factor's house was located at the far end of the open square. It faced the main gate in the south stockade. A large reception hall occupied the central portion of the building. At one side were quarters for the factor and his family, which consisted of a bedroom and living room, while on the other side was a bedroom. A covered passageway led from the hall to the separate kitchen building in the rear. The men's houses joined in a row were located along the west wall. The interpreter's house was in the northeast corner, and the trading store and provision store were lined up side by side along the east wall. Palisades enclosed the entire compound.

Henry Hind visited the Touchwood Hill Fort in 1858 during the course of his Assiniboine-Saskatchewan expedition. He described the fort and its surroundings in his *Narrative:*

> Touchwood Hills Fort, August 16th [1858]—Arrived at the fort after sunset last evening. It is situated on the south-east flank of the range near the foot of a hill from which an extensive view of the country is obtained.
>
> The garden, or rather the remains of a garden, in the rear of the fort, produces every variety of vegetable grown in Canada, but the efforts to cultivate it are almost abandoned in consequence of the depredations committed by Indians from the prairies, when they arrive in autumn with their provisions for trade, such as buffalo meat and pemmican. A

few of the lakes near the fort are known to contain fish, and it is probable that all of the large fresh water lakes in this beautiful region also abound in them. The officer in temporary charge of the post stated that the people here had only known of the existence of white-fish in the Last Mountain Lake for three years; they are now taken there in the fall, and it is probable that the fishery recently established will become of great importance to this part of the country. . . . Mr. Hoover, the officer in charge at the time of my visit, told me that he had first observed white-fish under the ice in November of 1854, and since that period they have established a fishery which provides the fort with an ample supply for winter consumption. The white-fish weigh on an average 7 lbs., but 10 lbs. each is not uncommon.

The timber on the Touchwood Hills is nearly all small and of recent growth, fires years ago having destroyed the valuable forest of aspen which once covered it. . . . So luxuriant and abundant is the vegetation here, that horses remain in the open glades all the winter, and always find plenty of forage to keep them in good condition. The cows are supplied with hay, the horses are worked during the winter, either journeying to Fort Pelly or to the Last Mountain Lake to fetch fish. Buffalo some-times congregate during the winter in the beautiful prairie south of the fort in vast numbers.

After about ten years, the fort was moved to a new site a few miles to the south in the Little Touchwood Hills. This second Touchwood Hills post remained at this location for the next fourteen years. Thomas Taylor continued to be in charge.

In 1876 Touchwood Hills Fort was relocated for the third (and last) time. The move was a short distance to the northeast, convenient to the Carlton Trail and its intersection with the Qu'Appelle Trail. Here the fort remained for the next thirty-three years, until it was finally closed down in 1909. This last post was built by clerk Angus McBeath, who then operated it for sixteen years. A short time after his retirement, N. M. W. J. McKenzie took over, in 1895.

The Touchwood Hills posts had been set up originally as subsidiary outposts of Fort Pelly, which supplied them with their trading goods and to which they sent their returns. However, the posts, while never very large—either in buildings or in personnel—rapidly became a major source of furs and provisions (mainly pemmican) for the district. They outgrew their dependency status and became independent posts, carrying on a thriving business serving the needs of settlers and railway contractors as well as the Indians who still lived by hunting and trapping. They not only continued to supply and service the cart brigades but also became important and well-known stopping places for travelers on the Carlton Trail.

In his book *The Men of the Hudson's Bay Company* McKenzie has written an interesting account that sheds much light on life at the Touchwood Hills Post during its last fourteen years of operation. He wrote: "The Post Office was in the store, where we received a weekly mail by stage. My private office was in the dwelling house. The store and warehouse was well equipped, most of the supplies for the winter being then in stock and as yet being unopened, pending my arrival, which made stock taking much easier and quicker."

The local Indians of the area were settled on four reserves, each with its own farm instructor. Cattle and grain raising were well established, and "the quality of the cattle very much improved by the importation of pure bred bulls." According to McKenzie "The majority of the Indians were doing well, and a large number of steers were disposed of annually." He further noted that "quite a number of the Indians still continued hunting in the winter, it being a good district for furs of all kinds, which were still fairly plentiful, especially in the Spring. For several years muskrats were very numerous and their skins came in very handy for the purchasing of supplies before farming operations began."

The Touchwood Hills post was a busy place. McKenzie wrote:

There were always plenty of customers at the store, and a good profitable business was being done. The settlers and ranchers in the locality generally came in once a week for their mail and gave us a busy day in the store, as well as in the house, as many of them coming long distances stayed with us for lunch and we were always glad to see them. Many of them did not see a soul from one week's end to another, except when they had a look at themselves in their mirror, so we were never short of company of one kind or other at the Post, and plenty of passers-by in the summer time, travelling east and west, who invariably stopped at the store to replenish their wants . . .

During 1907–08, when the Grand Trunk Pacific Railway was being constructed along a route that passed about two miles south of the Touchwood Hills post, McKenzie enjoyed a particularly busy season "supplying all these surveying parties and their men, outside of all the regular trade of the Post. It gave the business of the Post a large volume of increase for the time." McKenzie wrote: "We were doing a big business, and I had a string of freighters continually on the road. . . . during that two years I could sell the goods as fast as I could get them in." But McKenzie recognized that "as soon as construction was over and the engineers' camps moved away all the trade of the Post would go flat, at the present site. The settlers would all go to do their business at the different railway stations, so there was nothing for the Company to do but either build a new place at one of the stations, or close the Post up."

The Hudson's Bay Company made the decision to close down the Touchwood Hills post and to that end directed McKenzie to reduce his stock as much as possible. That spring of 1909 the trade had been good. According to McKenzie, "Thousands of rat skins were piled up everywhere, a good opportunity to reduce the stock which was now pretty low except in the necessary spring trade articles. There was every possibility of a good profitable clean up before the end of the outfit." On May 31, 1909, Touchwood Hills Post was officially closed down. In McKenzie's words, "I had everything closed out and satisfactorily finished on the 31st of May, and Touchwood Hills Post and all its former greatness had passd away."

Today the site of the 1876–1909 Touchwood Hills Post has been rescued from oblivion by the province of Saskatchewan. A historic marker has been erected to properly identify the site. The area occupied by the post is kept mowed, which makes it very easy to see the cellar depressions and the ridges marking the building foundations. Each of the buildings is identified by a sign and its outside dimensions shown by stones placed at each corner.

A heavy growth of young aspen borders the clearing to the north. To the south the gently rolling grasslands broken only by wooded islands stretch to the far horizon. The buffalo that once roamed these plains in sight of the post have long since vanished. Now the yellow of the canola, the blue of the flax, and the gold of grain have largely replaced the green of the grasslands. It is difficult to imagine that this small clearing, so quiet and peaceful today, was once a busy trading post on which Indians, settlers, construction workers, travelers, and cart brigades all converged with their furs for trade and their demands for goods and supplies. But that, like the buffalo and unbroken grasslands, was long ago. Now it serves to keep alive the memory of the important part Touchwood Hills played in both the fur trade and settlement of Canada's West.

Fort Qu'Appelle

It was not until about 1813 that the Hudson's Bay Company moved into the Qu'Appelle valley in order to oppose the North West Company. The small fort they erected was merely an outpost of their major establishment of Brandon House on the Assiniboine River.

The following year (1814), both companies moved to a new location on the north bank of the Qu'Appelle River about half a mile west of Big Cut Arm Creek. Alexander Macdonell of the North West Company and John Richard McKay of the Hudson's Bay Company not only built their forts in close proximity; they also made an agreement not to interfere with each other's trade. According to a letter written by James Sutherland of Brandon House dated February 28, 1815, "At Qu'Appelle Mr. McKay and the Canadians [Nor'westers] have by mutual consent abandoned their old Houses and erected new ones in the Vicinity of each other, and have agreed not to interrupt or molest the Indians in bringing their Trade to whatever House they may be inclined; this has been done and will be advantageous for our People."

This friendly arrangement was soon broken. Tension between the two companies steadily mounted, exacerbated by events taking place at Lord Selkirk's Red River settlement at the forks of the Red and Assiniboine rivers. The Nor'Westers, convinced that Selkirk's colony was just a ploy on the part of the Hudson's Bay Company to ruin their trade and cut off their supply routes, were determined to drive the Hudson's Bay people out of the region. When John McKay and his brigade of twelve men returned in the fall of 1815 to their new post, Fort Qu'Appelle I, they found nothing but charred ruins. Alexander Macdonell and his men had burned it down to the ground sometime during the summer. Nothing daunted, McKay immediately began to rebuild.

About a week later Macdonell and his brigade of thirty-six men returned to their Fort John. Almost immediately he sent down an ultimatum to McKay ordering him to remove to another location and threatening that if he refused, he (Macdonell) "would come down with his own men and cut the few stockades" that McKay had already erected. When McKay ignored this threat and continued with the job of rebuilding his post, Macdonell tried other tactics. He trained two cannon (which had been carried off from the Red River colony's Fort Douglas) on the Hudson's Bay post. In addition, he had his men conspicuously engaged in arming themselves and bringing out ammunition from the fort's store. But McKay was not to be intimidated and, aided by the support of loyal Indians, managed to keep Fort Qu'Appelle functioning successfully throughout the winter. When McKay and his brigade left the fort in the spring to bring the year's return of furs down to Brandon House, Macdonell struck. McKay and his men, greatly outnumbered, were taken prisoner, their furs confiscated, and the Hudson's Bay post once again totally destroyed.

After this setback, the Hudson's Bay Company moved a short distance to a new location, this time on the Assiniboine River about a mile and one-half above the mouth of Beaver Creek. The small post the company built here was known both as Beaver Creek House and as Fort Qu'Appelle. Influenced by the growing hostility of the Indians, the North West Company likewise abandoned their post and within a few years built a new fort 200 yards from the Hudson's Bay post on Beaver Creek. When the union of the two companies was effected in 1821, both posts on Beaver Creek were merged. By 1824 Governor Simpson reported to the Governor and London Committee that the region had been trapped bare and that the post was no longer profitable. It was, therefore, closed down that year.

Thirty years elapsed before the Hudson's Bay Company moved back into the Qu'Appelle area. About 1855, on the upland prairie just a little south of the present town of McLean, they established Fort Qu'Appelle II as an outpost of Fort Ellice. This fort was primarily a provisioning post, processing the huge amount of buffalo meat into pemmican—that indispensable item so necessary to fuel the brigades as they made their increasingly extended journeys into the fur country. The fort consisted of a trading store, trader's house, men's quarters, and stable. Chief Trader Archibald McDonald was in charge of the post. Archaeological work done by T. Petty at the site in 1949 indicated that the post was "of some size." It also revealed that "there were several holes indicating basements more or less filled in by ploughing; a number of chimney heaps consisting of great strewn patches of fire clay which retained the impress of the stones. These formed a rough pattern of a three sided square. . . . we could find no trace of stockade."

The Earl of Southesk, Dr. Hector, Captain Palliser, and Professor Hind were but a few of the many who enjoyed the hospitality dispensed at the fort.

Fort Qu'Appelle II continued to operate at this location until 1864. At that time it was decided to move it north to the Qu'Appelle River.

As it meanders down the broad valley toward its junction with the Assiniboine River, the Qu'Appelle River widens out into a series of lakes known today as the Fishing Lakes. The site chosen for Fort Qu'Appelle III was a strategic one. It was located only 100 feet from the ford (known as Water Horse) used for crossing the river. There, on the south side of the Qu'Appelle between the second and third lakes, the new fort was established by Peter Hourie, company postmaster. Situated at the crossroads of a network of well-established trails leading in all directions to the widespread company trading posts, Fort Qu'Appelle III was a busy place—a major rendezvous for the large number of Red River cart brigades as well as a popular stopover for the increasing numbers of traders, missionaries, scientists, government and company officials, and well-heeled dilettante hunters from abroad. The major business of the fort was the procurement of buffalo for processing into pemmican. In addition, buffalo robes and other furs were traded. During the 1860s and 1870s trade prospered.

After two years Hourie was replaced by Chief Clerk Archibald McDonald (soon to be made chief trader and eventually chief factor), who ran the post from 1866 through 1872. He was joined in 1867 by a newly hired company employee, Isaac Cowie, who came to the fort as an apprentice clerk. In his book *The Company of Adventurers*, Cowie described in detail the appearance of the fort. It was an enclosed area of about 150 feet square surrounded by a 12-foot-high whitewashed stockade. In the middle of the north wall was the gate wide enough to accommodate passage of the heavily laden carts. At the rear of the square opposite the gate was the one-story forty-by-thirty-foot master's house, built of squared logs and, like all the other fort buildings, thatched with colorful yellow straw. Instead of the customary buffalo parchment, its windows were of glass. The west end of the house served both as an office and as a reception area for Indians coming to trade. The east end contained the messroom and the master's quarters. Behind and connected by a short passage was a smaller building in which the kitchen, cook's bedroom, and nursery for the master's children were located.

On the west side of the square was a range of connected log houses divided into five thirty-foot-by-thirty-foot apartments by log walls carried up to the ridgepole. The floors were planed wood, the walls were clay-plastered and whitewashed, and the ceilings were of dry skins resting on poles. Each apartment was provided with an open chimney for cooking and heating.

Directly across on the opposite side of the square was a range of connected buildings occupied by the provision stores and the trading and fur-handling activities. At the south end of the row was a dairy room, while at the north end was the "tack" room storage for all the equipment—the *agrets*—required for the many sleds and carts used in hauling the goods and furs that passed through the fort. Security was provided for all these buildings not only by strong doors and locks but also by the complete absence of any chimney or other sources of heat, for the fear of fire in a fort that stocked gunpowder was compelling and constant. The intense and bitter cold that prevailed in the unheated trading room, fur loft, and shops was just one more hardship the men of the fort had to endure.

To the rear of the fort outside the stockades was a kitchen garden of approximately the same size as the fort compound. It was protected by a ten-foot-high picket fence. Behind the garden was a ten-acre field enclosed by a rail fence, one half planted to potatoes, the other half seeded to barley. A hay yard occupied land to the west of the garden. The log icehouse was located just outside the northeast corner of the stockade. Its deep cellar preserved the fresh meat and fish in the summer and the frozen fish in the winter.

Fort Qu'Appelle III during its peak years, in addition to the trader in charge, was staffed with an apprentice clerk, an interpreter and apprentice interpreter, four canoemen, a watchman, a carpenter, a cattlekeeper-woodcutter, and four laborers. Food rations for the fort personnel were figured on the basis of a daily allowance of "twelve pounds fresh buffalo meat, or six pounds dried buffalo meat, or three pounds pemmican, or six rabbits, or six prairie chickens, or three large whitefish, or three large or six small ducks." A woman's allowance was one-half that of a man, while that for a child was one-quarter.

As part of his training, Cowie was soon introduced to the fort's numerous account books. It was his task, along with the trader in charge of the post, to make the proper entries into these books and maintain them with meticulous accuracy. There were six of them: a day book, an Indian debt book, a fur receipt book, a book for the receipts and expenditures of provisions, the post accounts, and the *Journal of Daily Occurrences.*

Cowie made many interesting and quite penetrating observations of life as he experienced it at Fort Qu'Appelle. Regarding the intricacies of trading with the Indians, he wrote:

From the time the fort gates opened at sunrise till they closed at sunset the Indians thronged the hall, singly and in family groups, and Mr. McDonald listened and talked to them with admirable patience, and managed them with tact and firmness. The natives were no fools, and quick to notice any flaw or inconsistency in an argument against them. Moreover they were all intensely jealous of each other, and strove to have similar favors, in the shape of debt and gratuities, bestowed upon each as had been given to those more deserving in the opinion of the master. No such favors could be given without being publicly proclaimed and boasted about by the recipients and their families; so it taxed all the diplomatic ability of the trader to smooth over and explain such matters.

Cowie described the way the furs were prepared for shipment as follows:

When the trading parties . . . arrived I had to take account of the goods returned and the robes and furs for which the rest of the outfits had been expended, also the Indian debts paid and the supplies given to servants there. And then commenced the lively scene of packing the robes and furs in the big lever press in the middle of the square. Before being pressed into packs, each containing ten, folded hair side in, the robes had to be beaten of the dust and mud clinging to them, in the same way as carpets are beaten with sticks. The men worked in pairs, one catching the head and the other the tail end of the robe, which was folded in the middle with the hair out. Day after day the resounding whacks of the beaters kept up from morn till eve . . .

Each pack had attached to it a wooden stave on which were branded its consecutive number, weight and '67—H.B.F.Q.' meaning Outfit 1867, Hudson Bay, (F) Swan River district, (Q) Fort Qu'Appelle. The furs were also hung up on lines like a wash to get rid of the dust in the wind, and the larger and stronger hides beaten like the robes. The finer and weaker-skinned furs were parcelled up in strong-hided summer bear-skins, and several bundles of these made up the pack to about ninety pounds weight. Each of these fur-packs was of assorted skins, and as many packs as possible made up of a uniform number of assorted skins. This was done for the same reason as assorted bales of 'dry-goods' were made up at York Factory and assorted cargoes shipped into the interior from there by boats—to avoid the risk of all the articles or furs of one kind being lost in case of accident.

Some idea of the incredible number of buffalo that covered the prairies during the 1860s is given by Cowie. "They blackened the whole country [he wrote], the compact, moving masses covering it so that not a glimpse of green grass could be seen. Our route took us into the midst of the herd, which opened in front and closed behind the train of carts like water round a ship . . . The earth trembled, day and night, as they moved in billow-like battalions over the undulations of the plain. Every drop of water on our way was foul and yellow with their wallowings and excretions."

During the troubled and unsettled period of the transfer of the Hudson's Bay Company landholdings to the government of Canada in 1870, Fort Qu'Appelle III escaped being pillaged thanks both to the resolute action taken by McDonald and Cowie, who quickly built a strong palisade of vertical logs outside the existing stockade, and to the loyalty of the local Cree Indians.

In 1872 Isaac Cowie's period of apprenticeship came to an end and he was given full charge of Fort Qu'Appelle III, replacing Archibald McDonald, who, now a chief trader, was assigned to head the Swan River district. At this time new ways of conducting the trade were introduced, largely at the instigation of Donald A. Smith, Chief Commissioner. First, instead of sending men from each post to winter and trade directly with the Indians, the Métis, who were spreading out over the plains in increasing numbers, were equipped with goods for trade with the Indians. At first this worked well and significantly increased the returns for Fort Qu'Appelle. But as Cowie explained, "As the post only got credit in the annual accounts at the tariff fixed in the year 1834 and not at the prices at which the pemmican and robes were actually purchased, it showed a loss of at least six cents on every pound of pemmican and of five dollars on every robe purchased, so that the bigger the trade we did the greater was the 'apparent loss' in the balance sheet." Cowie continued rather bitterly: "As the returns of trade in 1872 at Fort Qu'Appelle amounted to $100,000 at the old tariff of 1834, the 'apparent loss' was very large, and was actually used as an argument [?] by those who had the power to cut down my carefully-prepared requisitions, to do so in the most senseless manner." Because of this new policy of dealing with the Indians through the use of Métis as middlemen, the company, deprived of its former direct contact with the natives, lost much of its ability to influence or control them. Another major change in trading practices was the order issued to the company officers in charge of the posts to cease advancing the Indians' "debt" (i.e., credit) on their hunts.

As soon as he had closed the books for the 1873–74 season, Isaac Cowie left both Fort Qu'Appelle and the service of the Hudson's Bay Company. He felt that after seven years "I had received neither the reward nor the support which I had been led to expect and which I had well earned amid many privations and dangers."

His successor was William J. McLean, who remained in charge of Fort Qu'Appelle III for the next eight years. During Chief Trader McLean's tenure as head of Fort Qu'Appelle, N. M. W. J. McKenzie was sent to the post to oversee the construction of a new sales shop, office, and clerks' quarters. He wrote in his *The Men of the Hudson's Bay Company:* "I started building the new store very early in the Spring and before midsummer we had it completed and the new stock moved in, with ample accommodation both in room and supplies for the large increase in customers that had taken place during the year. A very large business was being done. It kept four clerks busy in the store all the time. . . . I started building the office, with clerks' quarters upstairs, immediately after the new store was occupied and had it finished throughout, ready for occupation before Christmas . . ."

As a result of a widespread rumor that the railway was coming to the fort and the small settlement that had grown up around the fort was to be made the capital of the newly formed North West Territories, the business of the post boomed. People flocked in, all hoping to cash in on these rosy prospects. Few hunters went out to the prairies for buffalo, now only to be found in greatly diminished numbers far to the west. And the company did not send its customary trading outfits out to the plains. Freighting the vast amount of supplies needed to satisfy the steadily increasing needs of the fort and the rapidly growing settlement became the dominant activity. The squeal of the wooden Red River carts was heard night and day as the brigades travelled the well-worn trails across the prairies. Although Fort Qu'Appelle did not become the capital and the railroad bypassed it twenty miles to the south, nonetheless it grew into a village in a surprisingly short time. According to McKenzie, by 1882 "it had several stores, blacksmith shop, flour mill and doctors, a school, lawyers, splendid hotel, restaurants, and everything else that goes to make up a well-appointed village." It was in 1882 that Fort Qu'Appelle III was made headquarters for the Swan River district and Chief Factor Archibald McDonald returned to assume charge. Chief Trader McLean was transferred to Fort Ellice.

A good description of Fort Qu'Appelle as it was in 1883 has been furnished by Ernest Read, a former clerk of the company. He wrote:

When I first saw the fort in 1883 the factor's residence was on the east side; the large packing plant and fur house were in the centre at south. A two-storey frame building stood in the southwest corner, the lower floor of which was used as an office, the four rooms above, used as bedrooms for the staff, opened on a wide hall which served as our sitting-room and was heated by a huge box stove. We had some jovial times there, especially when a Scot named Stewart played his bagpipes. To the north of this building was the coach-house, with ice-house underneath. Outside the palisade were the stables, and near them the whip-saw pit. The new trading store, with its innovation of a deep front for displaying goods, was also outside the palisade, to the north.

With the outbreak of Riel's Rebellion in 1855, Fort Qu'Appelle took on new importance. It became the rendezvous for the troops rushed from the east under the command of General Middleton, who made the fort his base of operations for his campaign against Riel. Middleton took over for his headquarters one of the fort buildings previously used as a school for the children of the post. It was from Fort Qu'Appelle that on April 6, 1885, General Middleton and his force of 402 men and 120 wagons began their march northward along the old Carlton Trail toward their fateful confrontation with Louis Riel and his Métis at Batoche.

With the arrival of more and more settlers in the Qu'Appelle valley and the virtual disappearance of the buffalo, the Hudson's Bay Company changed its focus from the supply and fur trade to that of retail merchandising. As a result of the rapid growth of the village, the company trading store just outside the fort's palisade soon became inadequate. Accordingly, in 1897 Chief Factor McDonald built a modern brick sales store within the village limits. At the same time the two-story office and staff building was moved from the fort compound and relocated just to the rear of the new store.

With the company business now transferred to the new location, it was no longer necessary to maintain the old fort. Soon the palisade rotted and fell down; the other buildings likewise succumbed to neglect. Before too many years had passed, the only structure still remaining of the original fort was the tiny building, constructed of logs reinforced by willows and chinked with clay, that had served as a school for the fort's children and later as General Middleton's headquarters.

Chief Factor Archibald McDonald remained at his post at Fort Qu'Appelle until his retirement in 1911. In 1897 he built his own home near the site of the fort's old packing plant and fur house. There he lived until his death in 1914, admired and respected by all, whites and Indians alike. For forty-five of his fifty-seven years of service to the Hudson's Bay Company he had guided the fortunes of Fort Qu'Appelle. With his death, the long line of Hudson's Bay Company chief factors came to an end.

Today the memory of the once busy and important fort is perpetuated in the town's name, Fort Qu'Appelle, as well as in the name Company for one of its main streets. It is also preserved by the survival of one of the fort's early buildings. Still standing on its original site close to the banks of the Qu'Appelle River, this tiny building—used at various times as fort office, school, and General Middleton's headquarters—was almost miraculously rescued from oblivion. It has been renovated and now contains a most interesting display of items relating to the early history of the fort and the town. It forms part of the modern Fort Qu'Appelle Historical Museum.

Fort Qu'Appelle is a most friendly town. We stopped in at the local bakery for coffee and a Danish and soon were chatting with two local ladies who were likewise enjoying their morning coffee and Danish. When they learned of our interest in the early history of Fort Qu'Appelle, they most graciously offered to show us several points of interest. So, under their kindly guidance, we saw the beautiful stone Anglican church built in 1885 and still very much in use and the tall monument erected on the site where Treaty Four was signed in 1874. By this treaty Crees and Saulteaux ceded forever to the Canadian government their rights to forty-eight million acres of their land.

After leaving our two friends, we walked down Company Avenue and soon spotted another reminder of the Hudson's Bay Company's presence in the town. It was the two-story brick retail store that Chief Factor McDonald had built in 1897. As of the date of our visit (1980) the building was empty, its storefront windows boarded up, but we were able to make out "1897" and the "Bay" still faintly legible on the pediment above the upper story—all that was still discernible of its once-proud sign.

Perhaps the most enduring memorial to Fort Qu'Appelle is the Qu'Appelle valley itself. This lovely valley remains today much as it was when over 125 years ago Peter Hourie erected his fort on the banks of the Qu'Appelle River. Today, as then, the gently rounded hills separated by ravines of green or yellow or red, according to the season, enclose a broad valley of lush green meadow and marsh through which the Qu'Appelle peacefully meanders its way eastward toward the Assiniboine. We heartily agreed with N. M. W. J. McKenzie, who called it "one of the most picturesque and beautiful locations in all the North West."

Last Mountain House

As long ago as 1858, Chief Trader William Christie from his Saskatchewan district headquarters at Fort Pelly recommended that a new trading post be built west and south of Fort Pelly somewhere in the vicinity of Last Mountain. He felt that a new post was needed in order for the company to more effectively meet the competition coming from the increasing number of independent freemen trading for furs in the area.

However, it was not until 10 years later that his recommendation was implemented. By that time, it was apparent that Touchwood Hills' days as a major source of buffalo meat, robes, and pemmican were coming to an end. No longer did the vast herds of buffalo roam within gunshot of the fort. They were now only to be found in diminished numbers somewhat farther to the south.

In the fall of 1869 Joseph McKay, postmaster, and a crew of men were sent from Fort Qu'Appelle to build the new post. They were expected to have it completed before snowfall and the beginning of the trading season.

The east side of Last Mountain Lake was the location chosen for the new post. It was close to the buffalo herds and was also only a "short" day away from the Indians. The site selected for the post was on the prairie uplands about one-half mile inland from the east side of Last Mountain Lake near its southern end. It was on a bald, level promontory between a series of coulees. A spring (which still flows today) was conveniently located close by. The trees and brush growing in the adjacent ravines provided the material necessary for building the log cabins and for firewood. Not only the fieldstones needed for chimneys and hearths but also the white clay used for "mudding" the houses was found in abundance in the surrounding area. Another advantage the site possessed was the prolific growth of "prairie wool"—a prime natural grass fodder for livestock—making it practicable for the fort to pasture a few horses as well as oxen and a cow. The post had no stockades since they would have required more timber then the coulees could supply. However, the several ravines flanking the plateau provided adequate defense for the fort.

Joseph McKay and his men had wasted no time. In the incredibly short space of a few weeks they had managed to build the new post, so that by November 7, when Isaac Cowie arrived to assume charge of the post, all the buildings were completed with the one exception of the master's house, which was still roofless and floorless, a condition that was soon remedied. Conforming to the usual pattern of Hudson's Bay Company posts, the buildings were situated on the sides of a rectangular courtyard (105 feet by 100 feet). The master's house dominated the open space from the northeast end. It was a story-and-a-half Red River frame building measuring thirty-five feet by twenty feet. The main house was used as the trading hall, where the Indian chiefs were received by the master. Here, after the obligatory speeches were made, the ceremonial pipe smoked, and presents exchanged, the actual business of trading was conducted. A large fireplace made of fieldstone occupied the center of the room. Since the postmaster assigned to the fort, Joseph McKay, was a married man with a family, a small lean-to type structure had been added to the west side of the main building for his accommodation.

The men's house was a long building occupying the northwest side of the courtyard. It was divided into three apartments, each with its own fireplace and outside door. The roof was of sod, covering closely laid poles extending from the ridgepole to the top of the walls.

The post store was on the southeast side of the quadrangle. This building housed all the trade goods, including the black powder used by the flintlock guns. The floorboards were merely laid on the joists, no nails being used. This was done both to reduce the cost, since nails were a scarce and expensive item, and to minimize the danger from accidental explosion of the gunpowder stored in the cellar. The cellar underneath the building was floored with clay on which a matting of bark was spread in order to keep the supplies dry.

The barn, a large, low building, thirty feet by twenty feet, also on the southeast side of the courtyard, was located between the storehouse and the master's house.

The ice cellar occupied a small spot on the south side of the quadrangle. It was excavated six feet deep, well into the sand underlying the topsoil. The twelve-foot-by-eight-foot space was cribbed with three- and four-inch diameter logs. It was roofed over with a thick layer of sod and hay covering the roof poles extending from the ridgepole. Access into the ice cellar was provided by a hatch in the roof. This ice cellar was indispensable to the functioning of the fort. Here the meat, fish, and furs were safely stored.

The Red River frame type of construction was used in building Last Mountain House. The post-on-sill method was employed for the important structures, such as the master's house and the storehouse, while the post-in-ground was deemed adequate for the walls of the men's house, the barn, and the lean-to addition to the master's house.

As a measure of defense, the rear and end walls of all the buildings

669

were constructed without any openings. All doors and windows were placed on the front facade of the buildings, i.e., the side facing the open courtyard. In addition, the buildings were placed quite close together.

After surviving a night lost in a blizzard, Isaac Cowie encountered a family of Cree Indians who guided him to his new post of Last Mountain House. He described his arrival there in his book *The Company of Adventurers:*

> Next morning, the storm having ceased, the old hunter sent his son to guide me straight across the plain to my destination, at which we arrived in the evening. . . . The buildings of the Last Mountain House were arranged in the usual manner on three sides of a square. The site was near a spring on the top of the bank of the uplands, on a bare spur between the two deep-wooded ravines which ran down to the lake. The stores on the south side and the row of men's houses on the north side were finished, but the master's house, which Joe and family and I were to occupy, was roofless and floorless still. He and his men had done a wonderful lot of good work in the short time they had been at it, and our dwelling was soon habitable.

Last Mountain House's first season of operation (1869–70) was a most successful one, and large amounts of pemmican, buffalo robes, tongues, tallow, and leather as well as furs were traded. An entry in the fort's *Journal of Daily Occurrences* records that for the season just ended (in a period of ninety-four days) 1,000 buffalo robes had been acquired.

Cowie gives a rather amusing account of the manner in which he and his interpreter, Andrew McNab, handled an attempt by an unruly Saulteaux Indian to break into the post's storehouse. The Indian had demanded credit from Cowie, but since he was not one of the Indians belonging to Last Mountain House and, more especially, since he was known to have a bad reputation, his request was summarily denied. According to Cowie:

> As soon as he saw that he could get nothing from me, he sprang up and said defiantly, 'Then I will break open the store and help myself.' While he went out to carry out his threat, followed by Andrew, I went to my bedroom to get and load my revolver. By the time I reached the front door the Indian had shouldered a heavy length of firewood and rushing at the store gave it a battering blow. As he backed off to give it a second I covered him with my pistol, intending to shoot to kill if he burst the door. That brief interval gave McNabe the chance to intervene in the line of fire, and, first wrenching the log from the Indian's shoulder, he headed

him for camp, and set him off our premises well on his way by a series of well-directed and vigorous kicks, as if he were playing football with him.

At the conclusion of the first year's season, largely because of the increasing tension and unrest at the Red River colony, Cowie was instructed by Chief Trader Archibald McDonald "to return to Qu'Appelle with all the goods, furs and provisions and all hands, leaving some friendly Cree to look after the buildings and save them from being burnt by the Indians, as was their practice in the case of all wintering houses on the plains which we left in spring."

Cowie returned to Last Mountain House in the fall of 1870 to reopen the post for the 1870–71 season. Unfortunately, the buffalo had moved far off beyond the reach of his hunters. The summer hunt had been a failure, and prospects for the fall and winter promised to be equally disastrous. The acute shortage of pemmican was felt throughout the entire district. All that Last Mountain House had accumulated the previous year was requisitioned to supply the northern brigades on their run between Norway House and Portage la Loche.

Last Mountain House was in operation for only two winters. Some time after the conclusion of the 1870–71 season, the post was completely destroyed by fire. The heat was so intense that the chinking clay was baked to the hardness of brick. The post was not rebuilt. Its location was no longer advantageous for trade. The buffalo herds had moved farther off to the southwest; there were no longer enough trees left in the ravines for the construction of a post; and, finally, the number of wolf, fox, lynx, and muskrat skins brought in for trade was steadily diminishing. The closing of Last Mountain House marked the virtual end of the fur trade in the area.

Thanks to the efforts of the Saskatchewan Department of Natural Resources, the site of Last Mountain House was rescued from destruction by a proposed development of a commercial gravel pit. In 1964 the site was acquired by the province, and soon afterward careful archaeological investigations were made of the area. Based on these, the layout of the post and the size and function of each of the buildings were determined. In addition, a wealth of artifacts was recovered, such as trade "seed" beads, gunflints, musket balls, lead shot, lead foil from the lining of tea chests, and quantities of broken table china and cutlery.

Situated beside a major highway, its location indicated on the provincial road map, Last Mountain House was very easy to find. Late in the afternoon we reached the small cluster of log buildings that comprised the reconstructed Last Mountain House. Rather unbelievably, we had the place to ourselves—we were free to wander about, undis-

671

turbed in our attempts to absorb the atmosphere and, in our imagination, bring the fort back to life. The buildings were just as Cowie had described them. Best of all, they did not look new (as do so many reconstructed buildings). They were weathered and somewhat crude; in other words, they appeared just as they probably did when Joseph McKay and his men built them. A vivid connecting link to the existence of the fort is the spring of clear water still flowing and still being used today, just as it was well over one hundred years ago.

We decided to avail ourselves of the hospitality of Last Mountain House by spending the night there in our motor home, which we parked at the edge of the clearing. There we had a magnificent view of the bald rolling prairie broken only by ravines, colorful with the green and gold of early fall. The prairie extending to the far horizon was empty—gone were the herds of roaming buffalo; gone was the smoke lazily spiraling upward from Indian camps only a "short" day's distance away.

As the darkness of night replaced the faint glow of twilight, the stars appeared, brightening the sky with their brilliance; and as is always the case in the plains country, they seemed so close as to be almost within reach. We sat outside, quietly, without speaking, just enjoying the beauty of this spectacle. Suddenly the yipping and barking of the coyotes broke the silence. For us, this was all that was needed to make our stay at Last Mountain House an unforgettable memory—one to be treasured always.

Fort McMurray
Athabasca Landing

With the advent of the railroad and the steamboat in the mid-1800s, the Hudson's Bay Company's traditional transportation system was dramatically and permanently changed. Trains replaced Red River carts; stern-wheelers supplanted York boats and canoes. The areas first affected by these new arrivals were within the general limits of the North and South Saskatchewan, Assiniboine, and Red river systems. It would be another twenty years or more before they penetrated the Peace and Athabasca river country.

The Hudson's Bay Company, however, astutely realized that the trains' and stern-wheelers' inevitable appearance in the north country was only a matter of time and resolved, therefore, to be in a position to utilize them whenever they became available. As a first step in implementing this policy, the company decided to build a post at the junction of the Athabasca and Clearwater rivers (near the foot of the rapids on the Athabasca). This location was considered to be one of great strategic importance, since it would control the traffic down the Athabasca to its outlet in Lake Athabasca, across the west end of that lake, and down the Slave River to Fort Fitzgerald, as well as a considerable distance up the Peace River. The May 9, 1870, entry in the Fort Chipewyan journal reads: "Got Mr. Moberly ready and he started in the Evening with a boat manned by 8 men who were to assist him in beginning a new Post at the Forks of the Athabasca and Clearwater Rivers—The boat is to proceed on to Portage La Loche with the rest of the Brigade and Mr. Moberly will remain and get the necessary buildings up during the Summer."

Henry John Moberly's account in his book *When Fur Was King* supplies more details about his assignment. He wrote that after the ice had cleared Lake Athabasca he

> left Fort Chippewyan on the 11th of May . . . A blizzard the last three days of the trip made travelling anything but pleasant, but as the wind was fair we carried on and landed, in a foot of snow, at the mouth of the Clearwater River.
>
> I chose a site for the fort in a thick poplar wood, and the weather having turned fine we began clearing the ground.

While doing this, Moberly was surprised to discover traces of a previous post. Subsequent investigation suggested that this long-forgotten post had been abandoned eighty-six years before as a result of the death from smallpox of almost all the local Indians.

Moberly's account continues: "Two of my first tasks, while the labour of the boat crews was available, were squaring logs for the houses and the planting of a garden. . . . I set the men to work and we built this first summer a temporary house for myself, a good store, men's house, and carpenter's shop. In the ensuing winter we had logs squared, boards sawn and everything in readiness to put up a good officer's house as soon as warm weather arrived."

Catastrophe struck the new fort the following spring when the store as well as all the squared logs ready for building the new house were destroyed by fire. Moberly wrote: "To reconstruct the store and finish the other buildings kept me fully occupied the remainder of that summer and the following winter, but by next spring [1872] all was completed and we had a comfortable post."

According to Moberly, the "country about Fort McMurray was rich in both game and fur-bearing animals." He noted that he was able to kill a large number of beaver. From the two small bands of Chipewyans and Crees trading at the fort he was able to get "forty to forty-five ninety-pound packs of fine furs in the course of a winter."

The tar oil oozing so abundantly from the banks of the Clearwater and the Athabasca did not escape Moberly's notice, just as it had not escaped the keen observation of Peter Fidler and Alexander Mackenzie nearly one hundred years ago. Moberly wrote: "Down the Clearwater . . . from Portage la Loche at its head for eighty or ninety miles and for an equal distance down the Athabasca, tar oil oozes from the banks. Along the shores in cold weather it is hard and looks like gray rock. On warm days it becomes soft and might be cut with a knife. At a few places the tar flows quite freely, and the Hudson's Bay Company collected all they required for their boats in the North. The crude product is boiled to evaporate the oil, when it becomes the best of tar."

In the spring of 1874 the additional responsibility for the operation of the thirteen-mile Methye Portage (Portage la Loche) was given to Moberly. He immediately undertook the task of upgrading and improving this famous portage, which had been used for ninety-two years, ever since Peter Pond had first walked across it. Moberly's first step was to construct a road along its entire length that would permit haulage by ox-drawn carts. He pastured the thirty-seven or so oxen required for the job on the rich grassland at the mouth of the Clearwater River.

Moberly described his new assignment: "The outfits for Athabasca, Peace River, Mackenzie River and the Yukon all passed here

674

[Portage la Loche], as well as all the furs, caribou tongues, leather, etc., traded during the previous year. While the brigades were crossing I was kept busy; checking cargoes as they arrived, apportioning loads for the boats, reporting on the condition of cargoes. The boats from Hudson Bay, Red River, Cumberland and Green Lake brought goods from the south; those from Peace River, Peel River, Mackenzie River and Athabasca brought furs." Henry Moberly remained in charge of Fort McMurray and the Methye Portage until March 1, 1878, when he was transferred to Fort Vermilion on the Peace River. His clerk, James Spencer, took over Fort McMurray.

Two events occurred in 1883 that changed forever the old transportation system used for so long in the North. The first was the arrival in Calgary on August 11 of the Canadian Pacific Railroad. The second was the building at Fort Chipewyan of the stern-wheeler *Grahame*—the first steamboat to ply northern waters. These two events revolutionized northern transport.

For some time prior to this, the Hudson's Bay Company had been endeavoring to find new, easier routes for transporting their goods to the North. They were already utilizing the steamboats on the Saskatchewan, but getting from that river to the Athabasca was the problem. There was no easy way. An additional problem was caused by the disappearance of the buffalo that had supplied the pemmican—that indispensable food required by the voyageurs.

Beginning in 1881, as the company officials watched the steady progress of the railroad across the prairies toward Calgary, they decided to try a radically new route to reach the North—one based on the use of the railroad. In brief, their plan was to ship the goods by rail to Calgary; then north to Edmonton by freight wagons; from there along the 100-mile pack trail to Athabasca Landing on the Athabasca River. The remainder of the distance would be by scow down that river to Fort McMurray, where stern-wheelers would be available to transport the goods to their northern destinations.

To put this plan into effect, a great deal of preliminary work was required. First, it was necessary to improve the Athabasca Landing Trail from Edmonton to Athabasca Landing. The advantages of this trail as the most direct link between the North Saskatchewan and the Athabasca rivers were quite apparent to the Hudson's Bay Company. As early as 1877 an order from the Northern Council had directed that a trail be blazed from Fort Edmonton in a direct line due north to the big bend in the Athabasca River known as Athabasca Landing, where the company had had a small post ever since 1848. Under Chief Factor Roderick MacFarlane's energetic direction, the work of upgrading this trail was undertaken. Corduroy was laid over the worst muskeg, bridges were built where necessary, and ferries were provided to cross the major rivers. The result was full of potholes, uprooted tree stumps, sandhills, and marshy sloughs, but, nonetheless, a usable cart road emerged over which for the next several decades, passed large numbers of wagons loaded with freight for the North, as well as traders, surveyors, missionaries, settlers, and prospectors.

In addition to the constant upgrading of the Landing Trail necessary to keep it in a passable condition, MacFarlane ordered that a warehouse be constructed at Athabasca Landing to store the goods. He also provided for the construction of the many scows required to carry the freight down the Athabasca to Fort McMurray.

The company in 1883 sent Captain John H. Smith to Fort Chipewyan to supervise the construction of the stern-wheeler *Grahame*. This vessel was 130 feet long by 24 feet beam with a cargo capacity of 200 tons. By 1884 it was operating between Fort McMurray and the head of the rapids on the Slave River.

The successful adoption of this new transportation system made the Red River cart brigades obsolete; soon the far-reaching squealing and screeching of their wooden wheels turning on the wooden axles became only a memory. In addition, the infamous Portage la Loche was bypassed. As James G. MacGregor wrote in his *Paddle Wheels to Bucket-Wheels on the Athabasca*, "For over a hundred years the old Methy Portage had been the northern voyageurs' 'bête noir.' Now this hated Long Portage had started its decline and within a few years grass would grow over the old trail and fireweed and raspberry canes would intertwine with the spokes of cracking, useless old Red River cart wheels."

The portion of the new route between Athabasca Landing and Fort McMurray was not free of hazards. The greatest one was the Grand Rapids 165 miles downstream. Here, in a fall of ninety feet, the Athabasca cuts through a ridge of sandstone. A small island at the head of the rapids splits the river into two channels, each a raging rock-filled torrent racing past the island before ending in the relatively calm waters at its foot. Agnes Deans Cameron, who made the trip down the Athabasca in 1908 in a Hudson's Bay Company's scow, has left a vivid picture of the Grand Rapids in her book *The New North:*

The great flood (Kitchee Abowstik) is divided into two channels by an island probably half a mile in length, with its long axis parallel to the flow of the river, and this island solves the question of progress. The main channel to the left is impassable; it is certain death that way. Between the island and the right shore is a passage which on its island side, with nice manipulation, is practicable for empty boats. Then the problem before us is to run the rough water at the near [i.e., upstream] end of the island, tie up there, unload, transfer the pieces by handcar over the island to its other [i.e., downstream] end, let the empty scows down carefully through the channel by ropes, and reload at the other end.

She noted other interesting features of the area: "The river has weathered the banks into vertical cliffs four or five hundred feet high, imbedded in which are wonderful cheese-shaped nodules, some the size of baseballs, some as big as mill-stones. The river-bed is strewn thick with these concretions from which the swift current has worn the softer matrix away, and many of the stones are as spherical as if turned out by a hand-lathe. The sandstone banks opposite the island are overlain with a stratum of lignite three or four feet thick, which burns freely and makes acceptable fuel." There are many rapids in the remaining eighty-seven miles to Fort McMurray, but though hazardous, all could be run by the scows with only a few casualties.

The Grand Rapids was an obstacle that could not be run by loaded scows. It was necessary to land the scows at the head of the island—in itself a rather tricky maneuver and unload the cargo, which was then taken to the foot of the island. During the two to four days this took, everyone camped on the island. When all the freight was assembled, it was reloaded into the empty scows, which had been lined down the east channel—no easy task and not always accomplished without some loss. The scows then continued down the remaining eighty-seven miles to Fort McMurray, running the many rapids that occurred along this stretch of the river—sometimes with loss of cargo, occasionally with loss of life.

The scows and scowmen played a vital role in the functioning of the company's new transport system. James G. MacGregor commented that "scows were glorified packing boxes, flexible and capable of carrying some twenty-five tons. They were flat bottomed, about fifty feet long, eight feet wide on the bottom, flaring out to twelve feet across the top, with a square bow and stern." According to Agnes Cameron, "The scow is made of green wood, and its resilence stands it in good stead as, like a snake, it writhes through tight channels or over ugly bits of water." She added that "the oars are twenty feet long. It takes a strong man to handle the forty-foot steering-sweep which is mounted with an iron pivot on the stern." During the peak years of activity at Athabasca Landing, as many as a hundred scows a year were built. MacGregor wrote: "In the earliest years these were made of lumber whip-sawn from timber growing nearby, but eventually from planks sawn by a regular mill. At the height of The Landing's fame the shipyards on both sides of the river hummed with activity as the men, framing, planking, caulking or tarring, turned out scow after scow, meanwhile repairing occasionally to the Grand Central Hotel for refreshment." Just as the voyageurs who crossed the Methye Portage could boast of their prowess and proudly say, "*Je suis un homme du Nord*," so, too, these men, mainly Crees and Métis from Lac la Biche, were an elite group comprising the famous Athabasca Scow Brigade. MacGregor characterized them as "a hardy adventurous corps" for whom "no toil was too arduous, no rapids too awesome to run."

The 250-mile journey ended at Fort McMurray. There the cargo was transferred from the scows to the stern-wheeler *Grahame* for transport northward. Since most scows were not needed for a return trip upstream, they were sold for about ten dollars each and broken up for the lumber they contained. Their scows sold, the scowmen themselves had to make the long and difficult journey on foot back either to Grand Rapids to assist other crews or to Athabasca Landing.

A very few scows, perhaps a mere dozen, out of the hundred or so that comprised the downstream brigade, were required to transport the light cargo of furs south to Athabasca Landing. This meant tracking the scows the entire distance against the strong current—no easy job. In MacGregor's words,

> No toil was more frustrating, disheartening or laborious then tracking scows from Fort McMurray to The Landing. For tracking was the name given to the method of having men walk along the shore hauling a craft upstream by means of a long rope. . . . Tracking a canoe required considerable effort, tracking a York boat upriver was a discouraging ordeal, but tracking a great lumbering box-car of a thing called a scow up the Athabasca was a man-killing job. . . . [The men] parcelled their time into spells of an hour for pulling and five minutes for resting. Three spells made up the time between meals and usually they had five meals a day. To fuel these human engines, each of the five meals was a heavy one. On one occasion, according to Harrison Young, a Hudson's Bay Company factor, sixteen trackers 'had consumed eight bears, two moose, two bags of Pemmican, two sacks of flour, and three sacks of potatoes.' Only the very strongest man could eat like that, but only the strongest could endure this most brutal form of labour.

The Hudson's Bay Company continued to modernize and improve the various components of their new transportation system. In 1885 they not only established a trading post at Athabasca Landing; they

678

also built several much larger warehouses to handle the increasing volume of freight that accumulated there. A few years later they erected two warehouses on Grand Rapids Island to store the freight until it could be safely transported across the island and loaded into the waiting scows. In addition, to ease the movement of the goods from one end of the island to the other in 1889 the company built a tramway with wooden rails encased in sheet metal, so the freight could be loaded on hand-pushed trucks and trundled down to the lower end of the island. Finally, in 1891, the convenience of a dock on the island was provided.

When the railroad reached Edmonton from Calgary in 1891, traffic on the Athabasca Landing Trail increased dramatically. The steady stream of freighting wagons was augmented by a tide of homesteaders, all headed north toward Athabasca Landing, the distribution point for both the Lake Athabasca region and the Peace River district. The company bore the expense of maintaining the trail until 1897, when it was surveyed by the government, to be declared a public road the following year.

In 1887 the company hired Captain John Segers to build the stern-wheeler *Athabasca*. It was launched at Athabasca Landing and put into service the following year. Its task was primarily to carry freight on the Athabasca River between Athabasca Landing and the Grand Rapids. With the appearance of this stern-wheeler on the river, the only section still dependent upon scows for transport was that between Grand Rapids and Fort McMurray. The Hudson's Bay Company's new transportation route for the North—made possible by railroad and paddle-wheeler—was, by the end of the 1880s, working quite smoothly and efficiently.

Fort McMurray, in spite of its strategic site, did not grow and prosper. As late as 1889 it consisted merely of a tumbledown cabin and trading store on the top of a high and steep bank. The company decided to abandon the location, dismantle the fort, and establish it downstream at the mouth of the Little Red River (now called Mackay River). This new post, named Fort MacKay, temporarily supplanted Fort McMurray, but not for long. Independent traders began to come into the area around the forks of the Athabasca and Clearwater and, liking what they saw, built their posts there. This, of course, did not go unnoticed or unchallenged by the Hudson's Bay Company. They returned to the junction of the two rivers and built a new trading fort with J. J. Loutit as the factor in charge. According to James G. MacGregor's account J. J. Loutit was "A martinet in his devotion to the Company's discipline, punctilious in his observances of the Company's orders and integrity, and meticulous in his dress, he ruled his staff and his customers. One of his concessions to his modicum of native blood was the moccasins which he always wore. His only other concession was perhaps some undue deference every few weeks to his Scottish ancestors' fondness for whiskey. Aside from his moccasins, his attire was always sartorially perfect and every year he made a trip to Edmonton where one of the best of the city's tailors catered to his strict requirements."

Athabasca Landing during this period was experiencing a real boom. Both the Hudson's Bay Company and J. K. Cornwall, founder of the Northern Transportation Company, were building new paddle-wheelers for service on the Athabasca River and on Lesser Slave Lake. The riverfront was alive with activity. The shipyards resounded with the noise of saw and hammer and mallet; in increasing numbers the heavy freight wagons rumbled down the steep hill to the riverside warehouses. The high-pitched whine of the sawmills turning out lumber for the scows was incessant. And overall the deep-throated whistles of departing and arriving stern-wheelers echoed from the surrounding hills. Crowds of traders, settlers, deckhands, freighters, scowmen, and prospectors converged upon Athabasca Landing, which had truly become the great gateway to the North and the distribution point for the Lake Athabasca district to the north and the Peace River country to the west. This flow of freight and people increased when, in 1912, the railway finally reached Athabasca Landing, thereby eliminating the need for freighting along the always rather difficult Landing Trail.

Unfortunately, Athabasca Landing's period of prosperity was short-lived. The penetration northward by the railroads brought about the decline. By 1914 the Edmonton, Dunvegan and British Columbia Railroad had reached Lesser Slave Lake, thus effectively rendering transport by steamboat from Athabasca Landing unnecessary and unprofitable. Two years later the same railroad reached the Peace River at Peace River Crossing. This meant that goods and people could now be shipped to Peace River Crossing by rail, carried down the Peace by stern-wheeler, portaged past the barrier of the Vermilion Chutes, and reloaded onto steamboats out of Fort McMurray for the final journey northward. Such a route bypassed not only Athabasca Landing but also the dreaded Grand Rapids and the section of the river run by scows.

The final blow to Athabasca Landing's importance as gateway to the North was struck about 1921 when the Alberta and Great Waterways Railroad succeeded in laying track from Edmonton to the outskirts of Fort McMurray. The route followed by the railway was laid out to strike the Athabasca River at Fort McMurray, thereby avoiding the Grand Rapids and the rapid-filled section of the river below it. This was the *coup de grâce* for Athabasca Landing and its steamboat operations.

During much of the period when activity at Athabasca Landing was at its peak, Fort McMurray was continuing its rather uneventful existence as a trading center and transfer terminal for the Athabasca scow brigades and the northbound Athabasca stern-wheelers. However, a significant event that marked a turning point for its future occurred in 1908. That year the first of many attempts to capture the oil from the vast Athabasca oil sands was undertaken. Oil derricks began to appear along the river. It would be many decades before these efforts would be successful.

For the next nine years the oil fever was rampant, as many companies were formed to exploit the tar sands. Fifteen wells were actually drilled in the Fort McMurray–Fort Mackay area, but none proved successful. Through it all, Fort McMurray remained relatively untouched by all the activity, its progress, according to James G. MacGregor consisting "of the addition of only two or three shacks on the point of land between the two rivers."

But the winds of change had begun to blow over this small settlement of crude buildings. In 1910 the Northern Alberta Exploration Company, exploring for salt, drilled two wells in the vicinity of Horse River on the outskirts of Fort McMurray. At a depth of about 600 feet they reached a layer of table salt 100 feet thick, with a second one of about the same thickness less than 100 feet beneath it. Such a huge salt deposit promised to bring in big returns. Also at about this same time, there was a rush to stake oil leases along the waterfront from Fort McMurray as far downstream as Fort MacKay. J. K. Cornwall, builder of stern-wheelers, driller of oil wells, and energetic promoter, subdivided the entire flat lying between the Athabasca and Clearwater rivers into a town site.

Slowly, as though waking from a long nap, Fort McMurray began to stretch and grow. A few settlers took up quarter-section homesteads, and the favorable land both on the flats and the higher bench was in considerable demand. Sawmills utilizing the timber growing along the Clearwater were set up. Next came a school, the Royal Canadian Mounted Police, and the arrival of S. C. Ells, a geologist, who was to contribute so greatly to the eventual successful extraction of the oil from the tar sands.

During the World War I years, interest in the tar sands declined. The arrival of the railroad at Peace River Crossing reduced Fort

McMurray's importance as the gateway to the North. Nonetheless, the Hudson's Bay Company and its chief competitor, Lamson-Hubbard Fur Company, as well as Cornwall's Northern Transportation Company, steadily continued their well-established operations.

In 1918 a devastating flood inundated the entire town site of Fort McMurray. Tepees, shacks, and log cabins were all swept away by the raging ice-filled waters of the Athabasca River. Goods and supplies stored in the large warehouses were either badly damaged or totally destroyed.

In 1926 the Alberta and Great Waterways Railway finally reached Waterways, its terminal on the Clearwater River, only two or three miles east of Fort McMurray. Now, at least during the summer shipping season, Fort McMurray awakened and became a scene of frenzied activity. For it was here at its water and rail terminals that cargo brought down from the North by the stern-wheelers of the Hudson's Bay Company and the Northern Transportation Company was exchanged for the freight brought up from the south by the Alberta and Great Waterways Railway.

Three years after the arrival of the railroad, the airplane came to Fort McMurray. Both Western Canada Airways and Commercial Airways Company established bases there. So now it was not only an end-of-steel town but also the air terminal for the North.

The thirties saw increased activity in the Fort McMurray–Waterways area as the result of a short-lived mining boom and the discovery of uranium and gold deposits in Lake Athabasca and Great Slave Lake. The population climbed to 974. Most of the people were employed in some phase of the shipping business, such as warehousemen, stern-wheeler hands, or boat and barge builders.

During the 1940s the effects of the newly constructed Mackenzie Highway were beginning to be felt at Fort McMurray. The truck transportation over that highway was making serious inroads on Fort McMurray's long monopoly of northern shipping. The Hudson's Bay Company decided to end its Athabasca shipping operation—something it had been carrying on for two-thirds of a century, ever since it launched the *Grahame,* the very first stern-wheeler on the Athabasca River. It sold its entire fleet of stern-wheelers, tugs, and barges to the Northern Transportation Company, which then became the only remaining survivor of all the companies whose vessels had once plied the Athabasca.

Fort McMurray's days of sluggish growth were soon to end. During the 1950s and 1960s, engineers and geologists were hard at work trying to discover a feasible method for extracting the oil from the tar sands. Finally, after years of experimentation by many dedicated people, the great enigma of the tar sands was solved and, by an equally great effort, the millions and millions of dollars needed to finance the venture were obtained.

On September 30, 1967, in the words of James G. MacGregor, "the great jig-saw puzzle, the world's first commercial oil sands venture, started turning out synthetic crude oil and piping it away to market." At last, Fort McMurray's history of nearly one hundred years of frustration and patience had finally paid off. Its future seemed assured.

We decided we would travel to Athabasca Landing by the modern equivalent of the old Athabasca Landing Trail. As we sped swiftly and comfortably along Highway 2 heading north from Edmonton, we recalled the hardships the early travelers had endured as they traveled the same route. It almost made us feel as though we were cheating a bit to be spared the torment of the flies and mosquitoes, the perils of potholes and muskeg, that they had suffered.

We drove down the steep hill leading to the riverfront, the heart of the town now, just as it had always been, ever since its founding. We looked in vain for any vestige—no matter how slight—of the shipping age when shipyards were busy and stern-wheelers and scows lined the banks of the river. All traces have long since completely disappeared, their place taken by the stores, service stations, and grain elevators required by the needs of today.

Fortunately, however, one small spot still remains along the riverbank untouched by modern encroachments. It's a tiny patch of land left in its natural state of native grasses and bushes—a setting most appropriate for the provincial cairn located there commemorating Athabasca Landing's role as the "Jumping-off point for the vast northland." From this small oasis we could see the low wooded hills that bordered both sides of the river. We could step to the very edge of this broad stream and dip our hands into its historic waters. (And being sentimentalists, this we did.) We were able to look downstream to our right and see that big bend curving to the north beyond which the stern-wheelers and the scow brigades disappeared from sight as they pursued their northward journey.

We noticed a wooden building of rather aged appearance whose display in the front store window of traps, guns, snowshoes, and mounted animals attracted our interest. We entered the store, and here we found that thin link with the past for which we had been searching. It must have been our good fortune that led us into this old-time place where furs were still being bought and sold and trappers being outfitted. The interior of the store was a bit dusty and dim. The old-fashioned counters and shelves were full of the great variety of items such as traps of all sizes, guns, ammunition, knives, rope, cooking utensils, etc., needed by the trapper and trader. Numerous mounted furbearers in realistic poses looked down on us from the walls. A few skins were also visible. Since there were no other people in the store, we were able to chat with the owner. We learned that since the death of her husband she had been carrying on this outfitting and fur-buying business, which he had established many years ago. For us, this unusual woman was perpetuating a steadily vanishing way of life that reached back toward the time when fur trapping and trading were a basic activity at Athabasca Landing. Through her, we felt we had been—at least for a short while—in touch with the past.

Upon leaving Athabasca Landing we continued northward toward Fort McMurray. After driving about forty miles, we came to La Biche River. The small size of this stream quite surprised us, in view of its importance as a major link in the historic Île-à-la-Crosse–Beaver River–Lac la Biche–La Biche River–Athabasca River canoe route of the early fur traders.

When we visited Fort McMurray in 1984 it was a modern city of 35,000 people whose average age was twenty-five. Its fortunes were geared primarily to the two giant companies Syncrude and Suncor, which were successfully exploiting the great Athabasca tar sands in their huge operations a short distance downriver. A few relics from Fort McMurray's early days had been rescued from destruction and are now assembled in the city's Heritage Park. To us, the most interesting were the log cabin built in the early 1900s by George Golosky, who had been employed at the Hudson's Bay Company's trading post and who had hauled freight from Athabasca Landing to Fort McMurray; the North West Mounted Police barracks built in 1919; the Northern Transportation Company's *Radium Scout,* built in 1940 for use as a yarding boat to move barges in the docking area; and the stern/paddle-wheeler *Slavie.*

For our trip to Waterways, now a subdivision of Fort McMurray, we were fortunate to have Bob Duncan, a longtime resident of Fort McMurray and an authority on its local history, as our guide. As we drove through the small cluster of buildings that formed old Waterways, we sensed that the fingers of time had touched it but gently. Scattered among homes of modern construction were many of a much earlier date. One, in particular, caught our attention. A few streets back from the riverfront was one doughty survivor. It was a log cabin, long abandoned and neglected, which, happily, is now being stabilized and protected.

Down by the riverfront, the railroad tracks still lay along the banks of the Clearwater River, the goal they reached in 1926. Across the street directly opposite the freight terminal, we noticed a rather forlorn-looking building with the high false front so typical of early days. Its white paint was faded and peeling, its windows and door boarded up. This was once the Hudson's Bay Company's store, its days of usefulness now long since ended. Nearby Bob Duncan pointed out a building somewhat altered but still recognizable as a Hudson's Bay Company's building because of its general shape and hipped roof. This had once been the home of the company factor.

We could not leave Waterways without pausing by the Clearwater. We walked across the tracks and past the freight terminal to the river, then stood in a small clearing on the riverbank resplendent with the gold of goldenrod and the purple of vetch. By keeping our backs to the town we could eliminate the sight of all buildings and see the river free of any evidence of man's presence. Against a background of low wooded hills the dark water of this historic stream flows in a great bend toward its junction with the mighty Athabasca only a few miles distant. This small section of the Clearwater was the vital eighty-mile link from the Methye Portage to the Athabasca River and the rich fur lands of the North. We thought of all those who had passed on this river right in front of the very spot where we were standing: Peter Pond, David Thompson, Peter Fidler, Alexander Mackenzie, George Simpson, to name but a few—a regular *Who's Who* of the fur trade. Undoubtedly these hills had once resounded to the chansons of the voyageurs as they rhythmically paddled their fur-laden canoes upstream to the portage and again downstream in canoes heavy with cargo of trading goods and supplies. Today, except for occasional use by canoeist and fisherman, the waters of the Clearwater flow by silently and empty. The river's exciting past is preserved only in books and in memory, brought to life only in imagination. But maybe the golden leaves that float on its surface each fall all the way from the portage are a silent reminder and tribute to its former days of glory.

The Athabasca River, like a strong magnet, drew us to its banks many times during our stay in Fort McMurray. We watched this historic stream flowing steadily and powerfully toward the far north, and wished we, too, could travel on its broad waters and experience at least a small part of the journey made by the early fur traders. So we were delighted when we located a man with a jet boat who agreed to take us the fifty or so miles down the river as far as Fort MacKay and Bitumount. Our day-long trip was a delight, and while admittedly a noisy jet boat bouncing rapidly over the water is not a silent canoe or even a slow-moving paddle-wheeler or barge, we were able to see many miles of the river in their natural state, as yet untouched by man.

A short distance north of Fort McMurray, tall stacks, storage tanks, concrete buildings, and massive embankments enclosing the tailing settling ponds dominated the west side of the river. These were but a part of Syncrude's and Suncor's huge tar sand operation. Once past this twentieth-century intrusion, we continued downstream on a pristine river flowing unimpeded northward through a wild country little changed over the centuries. The river for much of its length was bordered by limestone cliffs, topped by the unbroken boreal forest. Extensive erosion and weathering had shaped long stretches of these bluffs into a series of bold promontories separated by deep ravines filled with trees that though sloughed off from the cliff sides still continue to grow. In other sections erosion had split the cliff face into a series of similarly shaped cliffs divided only by a narrow crevice. In many places large sections of the entire tree mantle had totally sheered off, exposing the bare rock face. The telltale signs of the presence of tar were abundant. Sometimes it was a viscous black gob at the base of the cliff at the water's edge; other times it was a dark stain running down the rock face. For some stretches of the river the limestone cliffs gave way to a more level lower terrain characterized by magnificent stands of giant cottonwood trees.

After several hours we reached Fort MacKay. This tiny settlement dated back to 1898, when the Hudson's Bay Company dismantled Fort McMurray and replaced it with a new trading post, which they named Fort MacKay in honor of Dr. William M. Mackay, an eminent physician and chief trader of the company's entire Athabasca district. The company maintained this post here for only ten years before moving back to Fort McMurray. The settlement, however, continued to survive.

We left the boat at the foot of the embankment and walked up the dirt roadway leading to the top of the bluff. The small Roman Catholic church and rectory, neat, trim, and well painted, faced the river from the well-worn path along the edge of the plateau. The other buildings were scattered more or less at random throughout the clearing. There were a few modest houses of modern construction, but most were simple cabins made of hand-hewn squared logs, their roofs covered with an assortment of corrugated metal, rolled asbestos roofing, and shingles of various shapes. Many of the doors and windows of the cabins were boarded over, perhaps because their owners were out in the bush for fall trapping or fishing. We noticed one rather large tepee of the type used for smoking fish and game in front of one of the newer homes. In fact, the settlement seemed almost deserted—no curious onlookers at-

686

tracted by the arrival of strangers. Even the usually omnipresent dogs were absent. The abundance of wildflowers growing everywhere in colorful profusion did much to brighten and beautify this otherwise rather drab small collection of buildings that constituted present-day Fort MacKay. The glorious purple fireweed dominated the display, but the tall, graceful spikes of white and yellow sweet clover, pink and white alsike clover, goldenrod, yarrow, and cow parsnip all contributed their share of color.

After leaving Fort MacKay, we proceeded down the river and before long came to Bitumount. This group of abandoned buildings was the plant of International Bitumen, a company founded by Bob Fitzsimmons in 1927. It was here that, utilizing the principle of separation of the tar sands by water, the first bitumen was successfully produced in commercial quantity—8,400 gallons—in 1929. From the ownership of Fitzsimmons the plant was taken over and operated by a series of different interests, ending with the government of Alberta. Bitumount's separation plant was operating successfully, but at a terrific cost. In 1950 the government concluded that the plant could not be operated on a profitable commercial basis. Also at this time, the discovery of the great oil field at Leduc made unnecessary any attempt to continue this very expensive operation.

Bitumount today is an industrial ghost town. The separation plant, refinery, storage tanks, network of overhead pipes, tall stacks, warehouses, repair shop, office, and men's quarters all have managed to partially survive the onslaught of time and weather. Windows are broken; doors sag open; pipes and stacks are rusty; paint is peeling; siding and roofing are missing. Rusty machinery, parts, and tools lie everywhere—some on the ground outside, some still in place in the building where they once operated, some still on the workbenches in the big repair shop. The broken-down hulls of workboats, barges, and even a small river skiff—the *Golden Slipper*—are slowly rotting away, their deplorable state hidden by the rapidly encroaching growth of grass and brush. This place, the birthplace and forerunner of the successful tar sand operations upstream near Fort McMurray, is now a protected historic site—a recognition truly deserved.

After spending an hour or so exploring Bitumount, we embarked in our jet boat and soon were speeding upstream to Fort McMurray. We were well pleased with our river trip, for it had enabled us to see a portion of the Athabasca River that had remained untouched and unchanged—to see it for ourselves just as it had once appeared to the voyageurs and fur traders.

While still at Fort McMurray, we made arrangements to charter a plane to take us the eighty-seven miles up the Athabasca River to the Grand Rapids. We wanted to see and photograph these legendary rapids, still a most formidable obstacle in the navigation of the Athabasca. The morning of our trip was clear and sunny—perfect for photography. We told our pilot, Steve Wilson, that we wanted to trace the course of the river. This he did, skillfully following every curve and hairpin bend as we flew south toward the Grand Rapids.

The Athabasca River valley winds through a rolling tableland of unbroken forest. The bluffs bordering the river are mostly tree-covered right to the water's edge, only occasionally broken by headlands of bare rock. Signs of tar seeping from the banks were commonplace, even in a few places staining the river for a noticeable distance. From the height at which we were flying, the numerous rapids appeared like wavy white lines stretching across the brown-colored water of the river. We knew this was far from the truth, for the river in this eighty-seven-mile stretch drops about four hundred feet and these rapids, harmless though they appear from the air, are dangerous and over the years have exacted their toll of men, cargo, and scows.

At last we could see the Grand Rapids ahead of us—no harmless white wavy lines were these. A half-mile-long wooded island split the river into two channels. The one to the east, wider than the one to the west, appeared to be much more violent, its white water foaming and tossing wildly, frightening yet awesomely beautiful. The west channel, full of exposed rocks and boulders, seemed less turbulent. However, its calmer appearance was deceptive, for it was a lethal trap. It was the more dangerous-looking east channel that the scowmen used for tracking their empty scows past this dreaded rapid. Our pilot banked the plane and flew low over the rapids, so we could better see at close range their tremendous power. With some difficulty, we managed to both shoot pictures of the white turbulence below us and at the same time keep our stomachs in place.

After this tour de force, we headed back toward Fort McMurray. Before terminating our flight, Steve gave us a bird's-eye view of the whole Fort McMurray area. Over the present-day city we flew, then on to old Waterways on the Clearwater, on down that river past the Northern Transportation Company rail and barge terminal, past the flats where Fort McMurray had its beginnings, to the river's end at the forks—the historic junction of the Clearwater and the Athabasca rivers. It was a perfect ending to a memorable trip.

Fort Fitzgerald
Fort Smith

The shrewd and farsighted Chief Factor Roderick MacFarlane, in charge of the Hudson's Bay Company's Athabasca district, was quick to grasp the implications that the inevitable westward expansion of the railroad and the advent of the steamboat would have upon the company's northern transportation system. He established three posts at strategic points along the Athabasca-Slave waterway: Fort McMurray (1870) at the junction of the Clearwater and Athabasca rivers and below the Athabasca rapids; Grahame's Landing, known later as Smith's Landing and, after 1912, as Fort Fitzgerald (1872) at the head of the Slave River rapids; and Fort Smith (1874) at the foot of the Slave River rapids. It required the passage of ten or twelve years before the soundness of MacFarlane's actions was evidenced.

Extending over a sixteen-mile stretch of the Slave River, during which the river drops 117 feet, a series of rapids created by a granite bar, a westerly projection of the Canadian Shield, constitutes the only impassable barrier to continuous navigation along the entire 1,600 miles between the Grand Rapids of the Athabasca and the Arctic Ocean. These rapids in the words of Sir John Franklin, who portaged past them in 1819, "are produced by an assemblage of islands and rocky ledges, which obstruct the river, and divide it into many narrow channels. Two of these channels are rendered still more difficult by accumulations of drift timber; a circumstance which has given a name to one of the portages [Portage d'Embarras]. The rocks which form the bed of the river, and the numerous islands, belong to the granite formation."

Each of the rapids has its own individual characteristics as well as its own name. The Cassette Rapids opposite Fort Fitzgerald have a drop of twenty-seven feet. They owe their name to an unfortunate mishap that occurred prior to 1819. As the company canoe was crossing the river to the east side to bypass the rapids, the wooden cassette containing the Hudson's Bay Company's entire payroll for the posts of the northern district was lost overboard. As a consequence, an order was promptly issued forbidding any canoe carrying the payroll cassette from running turbulent water; henceforth, they must bypass the rapids by five land portages.

Mountain Rapids, so called because of the steepness of its portage, has a drop of forty-one feet. A climb of about 125 feet on the west bank is needed to reach the top of the point of land that the portage crosses.

In his account of his 1789 voyage to the Arctic Ocean, Alexander Mackenzie described this portage:

> The landing [he wrote] is very steep, and close to the fall. The length of this carrying-place is eight hundred and twenty paces.
>
> The whole of the party were now employed in taking the baggage and the canoe up the hill. One of the Indian canoes went down the fall, and was dashed to pieces. The woman who had the management of it, by quitting it in time, preserved her life, though she lost the little property it contained.

Franklin referred to the Mountain Portage as being "appropriately named, as the path leads over the summit of a high hill. This elevated situation commands a very grand and picturesque view, for some miles along the river, which at this part is about a mile wide."

In contrast to the erroneous location on maps by modern cartographers that shows Pelican Rapids upstream from Mountain Rapids, they were correctly identified by Mackenzie and Franklin as the rapids downstream from Mountain Rapids. The Pelican Rapids are now, as they were then, the home of a nesting colony of white pelicans. Here on isolated rocky and wooded islets in the middle of the rapids below the Mountain Rapids is the world's northernmost pelican breeding site, as well as the only known one situated amid rapids. Fortunately for the survival of these magnificent birds, the mantle of federal government protection has been given them, and all human disturbance within a 1,900-foot zone both above and around the nesting islands has been prohibited. This small colony, which now numbers about six hundred adults, was noted by all who traveled the Slave River. Both Alexander Mackenzie and Sir John Franklin referred to this white pelican rookery in their written accounts of their journeys.

Father Pierre Duchaussois, O.M.I., who in 1922 visited both Fort Fitzgerald and Fort Smith, described in his book *Mid Snow and Ice* the pelicans of Slave River:

> Over obstructions spreading out for twenty-five miles, the powerful river [i.e., Slave], on its way to the North, tumbles down in three great cataracts which not even the severest winter can lay to rest. On the precipitous rocks around, one may see the pelicans—hardly distinguishable from the foam—seizing the fishes which are carried past. Here also is their aerie or breeding-place, the only one known in the Arctic regions. On sunny days, flocks of pelicans rise from out the spray in solemn flight, and go soaring on their great white wings above the woods, and the fort, and the mission, and the neighbouring houses. But their cries are al-

ways drowned—very suitable word—in the never-ceasing roar of the rapids.

The fourth and lowest set of rapids downstream is opposite Fort Smith and named Rapids of the Drowned. They have a drop of nineteen feet. The origin of their name dates back to a tragedy that occurred in 1786, when two canoes under the direction of Cuthbert Grant, Sr., were journeying down the Slave River to Great Slave Lake to set up a trading operation. Sir John Franklin in his *Narrative for the Years 1819–1822* related the details of the accident:

Two canoes arrived at the upper end of the portage, in one of which there was an experienced guide. This man judging from the height of the river deemed it practicable to shoot the rapid, and determined upon trying it. He accordingly placed himself in the bow of his canoe, having previously agreed, that if the passage was found easy, he should, on reaching the bottom of the rapid, fire a musket, as a signal for the other canoe to follow. The rapid proved dangerous, and called forth all the skill of the guide, and the utmost exertion of his crew, and they narrowly escaped destruction. Just as they were landing, an unfortunate fellow seizing the loaded fowling-piece, fired at a duck which rose at the instant. The guide anticipating the consequence, ran with the utmost haste to the other end of the portage, but he was too late; the other canoe had pushed off, and he arrived only to witness the fate of his comrades. They got alarmed in the middle of the rapid, the canoe was upset, and every man perished.

Both Grahame's Landing (i.e., Smith's Landing and later Fort Fitzgerald) and Fort Smith were established not as fur trading posts but rather as important links in the new transportation system brought about by the advent of steamboats. Situated at each end of the impassable rapids, they would serve now only as relay depots for large volumes of freight that had to be transported by land past the rapids, but also as transfer centers for the unloading and reloading of the cargo from the steamboats tied up at the head and foot of the rapids. Grahame's Landing occupied a clearing in the spruce forest about one-quarter mile wide by one-half mile long. It was bounded by a granite bluff on the north, woods on the west, and the Slave River on the east. A small creek cut across the southern end of the opening. Fort Smith was situated opposite the foot of the rapids. It occupied the plateau atop a high sandy scarp that rose 150 feet above the river. At the base of this bluff was a lower terrace about 150 yards wide.

For the first ten or twelve years of their existence, these two outposts did little more than maintain their presence at their strategic locations. It was only canoes, York boats, barges, and scows that traveled the Slave River, sometimes running some of the rapids, other times following the calmer backwaters and "carrying places" to the east, which skirted the turbulent waters.

This period of inactivity ended June 15, 1884, with the arrival of the Hudson's Bay Company's stern-wheeler SS *Grahame* at Grahame's Landing. From that moment on, the two tiny outposts came to life and began to fulfill the purpose for which they had been established. The *Grahame* had been built the previous winter at Fort Chipewyan. She was 130 feet long, with a beam of 24 feet; her cargo capacity was 200 tons. As James G. MacGregor wrote in his *Paddle Wheels to Bucket-Wheels on the Athabasca:*

> The Grahame came up to the builders' expectations. She made her first trip from Fort Chipewyan to Grahame's Landing on June 15, 1884 and covered the 120 miles downstream in seven and one-half hours. . . . The Indians along the river had been astonished at this smoking, sparking, splashing monster. She had made another trip shortly afterwards, this time up to Fort McMurray in thirty hours, and had returned downstream in fifteen hours.
>
> From then on, as she thrashed up and down the Athabasca, the "Grahame" was the pride of the North.

Pleased with the success of the *Grahame,* the Hudson's Bay Company quickly undertook the construction of a second vessel. This was the *Wrigley,* built in 1886. It was propeller-driven, with a length of ninety feet and a fourteen-foot beam. It was designed to run from Fort Smith at the foot of the Slave River rapids, across Great Slave Lake, and down the Mackenzie River to the Arctic Ocean. In still another step to improve the efficiency of the Athabasca–Slave–Mackenzie route, the company in 1888 built the stern-wheeler *Athabasca* to run from Athabasca Landing to Grand Rapids.

These steamboats were all of very shallow draft, designed to navigate in as little as three feet of water. They were made stern-wheelers rather than side-wheelers in order to be better able to back off the frequent sand- and gravel bars that obstructed their passage. They all burned wood—enormous quantities of it. This necessitated frequent "wooding" stops to pick up the wood previously cut and piled at convenient points along the riverbank. The *Wrigley,* however, was quite different from the other stern-wheelers. She was not only smaller, but she also required a greater depth of water and was driven by a propeller rather than by a paddle wheel. These modifications were necessary because she was designed for service on Great Slave Lake and the Mackenzie River.

With the construction of these three vessels, the company had effectively put into place a feasible water transport system spanning the 1,854 miles from Athabasca Landing to the mouth of the Mackenzie River. Of course, the two obstacles of the Grand Rapids in the Athabasca and the rapids in the Slave River still prevented continuous passage along this lengthy waterway. But, nonetheless, the Hudson's Bay Company was sufficiently confident of the reliability of its transport system to be able to publish a rate schedule for passenger and cargo. In fact, as James G. MacGregor wrote, "Much of the farness had gone out of the far North."

The growing rise and importance of the steamboats required that transportation over the two portages bypassing the Athabasca Grand Rapids and the Slave River rapids be improved. The company constructed warehouses, a pier, and even a tramway to expedite the passage of cargo and passengers over the half-mile island portage that bypassed the Grand Rapids. For the sixteen-mile portage bypassing the Slave River rapids the company constructed a cart trail through the woods on the west side of the river between Grahame's Landing and Fort Smith. At first the haulage of freight was by oxen plodding along pulling small two-wheel carts loaded with the furs brought down from the North to Fort Smith and returning with the goods and supplies that had been brought up from the south to Grahame's Landing. Somewhat later the oxen and carts were largely replaced by horses and large four-wheeled wagons. Still later, after 1920, came trucks, trailers, and tractors.

The trail was full of ruts and potholes, but perhaps the worst discomfort that had to be endured was caused by the voracious mosquitoes and "bulldog" flies (which, incidentally, persist to the present day). Human passengers as well as horses and oxen were driven almost insane by the flies' bloodthirsty attacks. Agnes Deans Cameron, who crossed the portage in 1908, wrote in her book *The New North:* "On the Bloody Portage we overtook five teams of oxen which had been more than twelve hours trying to make sixteen miles and were bleeding profusely from the fly-bites. Finally two of them succumbed and a relief team had to be sent out from Fort Smith." In 1892 Elizabeth Taylor rode across the portage from Grahame's Landing to Fort Smith in a lumber wagon pulled by oxen. She commented: ". . . mosquitoes, gnats, and bulldogs were quite up to my expectations. I have never seen anything like them. Even the half breed carters wore head nets."

In the 1920s Mickey Ryan appeared on the scene, and under his energetic direction and with the expenditure of much of his earnings from various freighting operations he upgraded the portage trail into a bona fide road. He established a Halfway House midway on the portage. Here hay and feed were available for the horses. Wagons left outside overnight need not be unloaded, and hearty hot meals were provided for the carters. Halfway House as Ryan's operational headquarters, soon grew to include a house, big frame barn, granary, and bunkhouse for the teamsters. In addition, there were a log office where the business was transacted and a log blacksmith shop where Mickey's brother, Pat, shod the horses and kept their harness in repair.

By 1925 Mickey Ryan had improved the portage trail so much that he was able to transport people in the comfort of passenger car or bus instead of by horse and wagon. In 1932 the constantly improved trail—now more properly called a road—permitted the use of trucks, and tractors and trailers for hauling the freight over the portage.

During this period of the gradual transition of the Smith portage from a trail, to a cart track, to a road, the Hudson's Bay Company was expanding and modernizing its fleet of steamboats in its northern service. In 1915 the stern-wheeler *Fort McMurray* replaced the *Grahame.* That doughty vessel, for so long (thirty-one years) the company's northern flagship, had yielded up her engines for the construction in 1921 of the *Athabasca River* and now lay beached on the riverbank of Fort McMurray, an empty hulk—silent witness to her former days of splendor. The *Athabasca River* was 146 feet long, with a 36-foot beam and a cargo capacity of 150 tons. She replaced the *Fort McMurray* and was used for the next twenty-six years (until 1947) in the run from Fort McMurray to Fort Fitzgerald. In 1924 the company acquired the stern-wheeler *D. A. Thomas* from the Alberta and Transportation Company, which had used her on the Peace River. This vessel, 167 feet long with a 40-foot beam, was put into service between Fort McMurray and Fort Fitzgerald. The largest of the company's steamboats was the 200-foot stern-wheeler *Distributor,* which for many years made the passage between Fort Smith and the Arctic Ocean.

For seventy-five years the Hudson's Bay Company maintained and operated a fleet of vessels and barges on its northern waters. It was logical that as settlers, missionaries, prospectors, and developers moved into the country, the company's ships, originally built to deliver the goods and supplies and pick up the fur returns from its own trading posts, would service their needs also.

However, changes in the transportation system serving the North brought about by the building of the Mackenzie Highway, the extension of the railroad to Hay River on Great Slave Lake, and the increasing use of aircraft influenced the company to terminate its shipping operations. Accordingly, in January of 1958 the Mackenzie River Transport (the shipping division of the Hudson's Bay Company) sold its entire fleet of steamboats, tugs, and barges along with all onshore facilities to its chief competitor, J. K. Cornwall's Northern Transportation Company (NTCL). Henceforth no ships flying the proud flag of the Hudson's Bay Company plied the northern waterways.

Commencing in 1884 with the arrival of the steamboats and the resulting increase in river traffic, after ten or twelve years of dormancy, the two small outposts of Grahame's Landing and Fort Smith came to life. At Grahame's Landing, southern terminal at the head of the Slave River rapids, the Hudson's Bay Company had a trading store and a staff house, as well as a large warehouse and wharf, all at the northern end of the settlement, located just below the granite bluff that extended across the north side of the clearing. In addition to the company buildings, two large storage sheds belonging to two other trading companies (Northern Trading and Marine Operators) and a wharf were located on the riverbank somewhat south of the company's holdings. Several small independent stores, a Catholic church and mission house, a school, and a hotel comprised the rest of the settlement. About 150 Indians and Métis made their home at Grahame's Landing. During the fall and winter months they moved into the bush to hunt and run their traplines, but in the summer they were busy stevedoring, handling the freight from the many stern-wheelers that docked at the trading companies' wharves. In addition, there was work as teamsters hauling freight over the portage; and finally, of course, the portage road was always in need of maintenance and improvement.

In 1912 the name of the settlement was changed from Smith's Landing (which name had replaced Grahame's Landing some years previously) to Fort Fitzgerald to commemorate an Royal Canadian Mounted Police officer who had lost his life while leading the patrol from Fort McPherson on the Peel River to Dawson on the Yukon River. Misfortune did not spare the community. In 1918 an influenza epidemic decimated the Indians living there. Fifteen years later, in 1933, and again in 1959, fire completely destroyed the small village.

At this same time the emergence of Hay River as the new railhead on Great Slave Lake and the building of the Mackenzie Highway provided new means of access to the North that bypassed the Slave River rapids. As a result, Fort Fitzgerald became obsolete, its reason for existence ended. Its riverfront, no longer the center of life and bustling activity, became silent, its wharves empty. With its source of employment dried up, the settlement of Fort Fitzgerald was gradually

695

deserted, as its inhabitants—both white and Indian—moved elsewhere. Finally in 1965 the end came. Almost totally abandoned by all its former inhabitants, Fort Fitzgerald was completely closed down—left to revert to its original wilderness state.

Fort Smith, however, was not destined to share the fate of Fort Fitzgerald. From the simple house and few outbuildings erected at the time of its founding in 1874 by the Hudson's Bay Company, Fort Smith, commencing with the arrival of the *Wrigley* in 1886, emerged from its quiet existence and began to grow. The portage road from Fort Fitzgerald cut across the length of the small settlement from its southeast corner to the edge of the 150-foot bluff before descending a deep and well-worn cut in the sandbank to reach the lower land shelf just downstream from the last of the rapids.

Along this lower level on the waterfront, the Hudson's Bay Company built a loading dock and large distributing shed and warehouse. Somewhat later, the Northern Trading Company and the Yellowknife Mining Company likewise located their wharves and warehouses on the riverbank.

On top of the bluff close to the portage road the principal buildings of the settlement were located. These included the Hudson's Bay Company's store, a large hotel, a Royal Canadian Mounted Police post, a café, a school, a small Roman Catholic church built by the Oblates of Mary Immaculate, and a cemetery. On the south side of the settlement the Catholic church had a large reserve of land granted them on which were located their church and a large three-story hospital, as well as a barn and various other mission buildings. The majority of the Indians had their simple homes on the church reserve.

During the years from 1884 through 1965 Fort Smith fulfilled its role as the transfer point for the northern traffic. At its busy docks the vessels of the Hudson's Bay Company and of the Northern Transportation Company loaded and unloaded their cargoes of southbound furs and northbound supplies, goods, and provisions.

Fort Smith was a lively place as long lines of heavily laden Red River carts pulled by plodding oxen stirred up the dust as they moved along the portage road. Later (at least by 1911) horses and large freight wagons rumbled through the settlement on the well-traveled portage road—dusty if the weather was dry, muddy if the weather was wet. At the height of the period when horses were used for the haulage, it was estimated that at least two hundred were required for the service. Finally, in the early 1920s, it was trucks, tractors, and trailers emitting the strong fumes of gasoline that made their noisy way through the community.

Fort Smith continued to hold its place as the major terminal for northern river transportation for seventy-nine years. In 1965 the Northern Transportation Company, which had acquired the Hudson's Bay Company's fleet in 1957, moved its entire transportation operation from Fort Smith to Hay River on Great Slave Lake. This move was dictated by the arrival of the Canadian National Railroad at Hay River in 1960, which enabled movement of freight and passengers to and from Great Slave Lake and all points north without recourse to the Slave River route and its impassable rapids.

Fort Smith, just like Fort Fitzgerald, was no longer needed as a transfer shipping point. Henceforth, no more steamboats would be docking at its riverside wharves. The trading companies' warehouses and docks, abandoned and idle, quickly disintegrated or were dismantled. Before long, they disappeared, leaving no trace except perhaps to the keen eye of the archaeologist.

Fortunately, however, the departure of the steamboats did not mean the end of Fort Smith. From as early as 1921, it became the federal administrative center for the entire Mackenzie district. Over the succeeding years, it became the headquarters for a number of governmental agencies, such as Lands and Forests, Wood Buffalo and Nahanni National Parks, Canadian Wildlife Service, Health and Welfare, and Communications, to list but a few. An airport was constructed as well as a radio station. And a most important contribution to the educational opportunities of the area was made with the establishment of Thebacha College. Both the Roman Catholics and the Anglicans built churches.

By the mid-1950s the Mackenzie district office of the Department of Indian Affairs and Natural Resources, responsible for the administration of the western Arctic, was headquartered at Fort Smith. It remained there until 1969, when it was phased out and its function transferred to the Territorial Government in Yellowknife. Fort Smith continued, however, to be the regional headquarters for the Fort Smith region, the largest and most diversified of the four regions included in the North West Territories.

The proliferation of government agencies helped provide the employment that had been lost with the ending of the steamboat era. Instead of fading into oblivion as had Fort Fitzgerald, Fort Smith grew in importance, advancing from the status of hamlet to village to town by 1966. It expanded in all directions as new buildings were constructed to meet the needs of its growing population. Fort Smith had succeeded in becoming a stable community—in making the transition from a small settlement dependent upon the steamboat for its existence to a viable town based on a diversified base of government, business, and education.

Our visit to Fort Smith and Fort Fitzgerald was enriched by our good fortune in having Jacques van Pelt as our mentor. Profiting by his helpful suggestions, we were able to meet many remarkable people and see places of interest that we would otherwise have missed. Jacques, founder and director of Sub-Arctic Wilderness Adventures, had been born in Holland. He is a man of many talents, skilled in nature touring and wilderness travel and an ardent advocate and fighter for sound environmental practices. During the more than three decades he has lived in Fort Smith, he had become an authority on the Slave River Basin—its natural and human history, past and present. In addition to all these attributes, he makes the best bannock we ever ate.

In the course of our wanderings around Fort Smith, we found the small cemetery near the old Roman Catholic Church of St. Alphonse built in 1923, located not far from the edge of the high escarpment bordering the river. Among the many simple headstones and plain white crosses, the rather elaborate and intricately wrought iron crucifix that marked the grave of Catherine Ryan, Mickey Ryan's wife, was quite noticeable. One section of the cemetery is reserved for the last resting place of the Oblates of Mary Immaculate. These priests, commencing in 1876 with the establishment of their mission, contributed much to the early development of Fort Smith. At the time of our visit (1984), there were twenty-two graves, each marked with an identical simple white headstone surmounted by a small white cross. We paused by the freshly mounded sand over the grave of Brother Sareault, who had died just prior to our arrival in Fort Smith. For over twenty years he had been the pilot of the Oblate's mission ship, the *Santa Anna,* as it traveled up and down the Mackenzie River, now increasingly known by its native name of *Deh Cho.*

A long, narrow, rectangular three-story building was all that remains of the original Oblate mission complex. Noticeable because of its distinctive mansard roof and small pointed dormers, features reflecting the Oblate's French heritage, this structure originally constructed as a hospital was used as the Diocesan Religious Education Center until 1989, when it was demolished.

Close by were several farm buildings, holdovers from the time when the Oblates cultivated large acreages of vegetables and grain. Close to the walls of the old mission building we noticed a flourishing garden of potatoes, planted in orderly precision, absolutely weedless and in full bloom—abundant proof that the Oblates were carrying on their long tradition of agricultural excellence. However, in 1990 the garden was discontinued, thus breaking one more link with the past. It is a bit ironic that after destroying and removing all traces of the Oblates' presence, the government of the North West Territories and the local residents of Fort Smith are now planning to establish a Mission Heritage Park on the site.

We walked along the old portage road, now a paved highway and dignified by the name of Portage Avenue, through the center of town. The new metal-sided flat-topped building of the Hudson's Bay Company occupied its original site on the portage road not too far from the river. Since 1987, however, the store is no longer a part of the Hudson's Bay Company but is now owned by the North West Company, which acquired all the Hudson's Bay Company's stores north of sixty degree latitude at that time. At the rear of the store we spotted a survivor from earlier days. It was a square white building with a few small windows just below the eaves and topped with a red hipped roof—all familiar hallmarks of Hudson's Bay Company buildings. Some time after our visit we learned that this relic of former times had been torn down.

Continuing on down Portage Avenue, we came to the Anglican church built in 1936. Its wooden bell tower, with the turreted top and the tall Gothic windows along the side of the church, attests to its English pedigree. The Anglican Hall next to the church is a former Hudson's Bay Company building easily recognizable by its shape, placement of windows, and hipped roof.

In the early evening we turned our steps toward the riverfront. If we had hoped to find any remnants of the warehouses and wharves that once crowded the area, we were disappointed. No trace remains. What the passage of time, neglect, abandonment, and the assault of weather did not accomplish a massive landslide in 1968 achieved. Today except where the landslide stripped off the trees and brush, leaving nothing but bare shifting sand, the sides of the escarpment as well as the lower terrace are clothed only with native grasses, a profusion of sweet clover, and scattered bushes. Upon the bluff beside the old cart trail skirting its edge, an old building belonging to Northern Transportation Company still stands. The large warehouses and sheds, the steamboats, the barges, the stevedores, the teamsters have all gone, but the Rapids of the Drowned, treacherous and impassable, still exist, their steady roar a constant reminder of their enduring presence.

Before leaving Fort Smith, Jacques took us to see his friend David King Beaulieu, a lifelong resident of the small settlement on the Salt River at its junction with the Slave and the place where his forebears had lived for many generations. The Métis, François Beaulieu, was one of the intrepid voyageurs who accompanied Alexander Mackenzie on his trip down the Mackenzie River in 1789. His son played a prominent role as a fur trader, and his grandson, Etienne, known as King Beaulieu, worked zealously in aiding Bishop Grandin to establish the Roman Catholic faith among his people. Commencing in 1852, it was in the modest home of "Patriarch" Beaulieu on the banks of the Salt River that a room was reserved for the use of missionaries coming from Fort Resolution on Great Slave Lake to celebrate mass and to give instruction to the Indians who assembled there. Both Father Gascon and Bishop Grandin learned the Chipewyan language at this place. This mission remained at Salt River until 1876, when it was transferred to Fort Smith.

To this day, there are many Beaulieu descendants in the Slave River region. We were fortunate in being able to spend several hours with David King Beaulieu, grandson of "King" Beaulieu. We found him sitting in an old chair outside his cabin built close to the edge of the bank above the Salt River. He was a heavyset man strong and rugged looking. Unfortunately, as we later learned, his appearance of strength was deceptive, for already a deadly cancer was at work within him.

We sat on a bench in front of his cabin. Off to one side was a rack over a smoldering fire where steaks and haunches of bear meat were slowly being smoked. We listened enthralled as he reminisced about his life. He spoke of his need for salt to preserve his game and fish. Formerly he was able to obtain an abundant supply from the nearby Salt Plains, but since their inclusion within the boundaries of Wood Buffalo Park that source had been cut off. All too soon it was time to leave, but first we bought several of the smoked bear steaks for our lunch. The last we saw of David Beaulieu, he had his rifle cradled in his arm and was scrambling down the bank to his boat moored below in order to go down the river to a place where he had spotted moose tracks the previous day. He told us that he hoped to be able to follow the tracks and get the moose—a most welcome addition to his winter's meat supply.

On our way back to Fort Smith, Jacques took us to a place of incredible beauty. After walking a short distance on a trail through the woods, we came to a large clearing extending to the edge of an abrupt escarpment. Below us spread out to the far horizon in all directions were the magnificent Salt Plains of Wood Buffalo National Park, which is now designated as a World Heritage Site. We stood entranced and speechless for many moments, feasting our eyes on this glorious panorama.

In the foreground, the yellowish-green carpet of grass was only broken by numerous rivulets and many narrow fingerlike dark green islands of low brush and slender spruce trees thrusting their spirelike tops skyward. The colorful samphire, a sure indicator of the presence of salt (an item in great demand by the native people for preserving their meat and fish), provided scattered splashes of brilliant red. It was almost as if the dark islands were ships with spruce tree masts afloat on a sea of grass. In the far middle distance the plains extended unbroken in all directions. Still farther beyond the open plains were more islands of brush and spruce.

To our great delight we spotted between two and three hundred buffalo at the extreme edge of the open plains. Even though a long way off, their dark bodies were clearly conspicuous against the pale green of the grassland. By using the telescope that Jacques set up we were able to observe the movements of these giant animals. Some were quietly grazing; others were sleeping; while still others were wallowing on their backs. Sometimes the whole herd would move a short distance before stopping and resuming their grazing. We were able to distinguish the calves from the adults and even saw a wolf crouched nearby. While Jacques was busy about the campfire preparing our lunch, which included grilling the bear steaks, we stood by, gazing at this wondrous scene before us, knowing we probably would never again see its equal.

Early one morning we left Fort Smith and started down the old portage trail to Fort Fitzgerald. The sandy road wound through stands of jackpine and poplar for about eight miles before coming to the large clearing once occupied by Mickey Ryan's Halfway establishment. At the time of our visit in 1984 all that remained of the home, stables, blacksmith shop, office, bunkhouse, and other outbuildings was the barn. This log structure was in a ruinous condition and could not last the onslaughts of time and weather much longer. A section of the original Ryan portage road, now just a rarely used two-rutted road with grass center, emerged from the woods to pass in front of the barn and continue across the clearing.

We walked up to the slightly elevated knoll where Mickey Ryan's home had stood. From this vantage point we were able to see, through the intervening spruce trees, the Slave River and the rapids. A large clump of wild roses in full bloom—the focus for swarms of noisy bees—provided the only signs of life in a place that had once been a scene of much activity. It was somewhat difficult to people this peaceful field with the horses, the wagons, the teamsters, and the trucks that had formerly thronged the yards and corrals of Ryan's Halfway House.

We continued on to Fort Fitzgerald and entered the site of that old settlement from its northwest corner. With the exception of a very few houses in the northwest corner, the large clearing once occupied by Fort Fitzgerald, with a population of 2,500, was now completely vacant. Nothing remained of its homes, church, stores, hotel, warehouses, or wharves.

We walked along the riverbank hoping to find something—anything—that would recall Fort Fitzgerald's days as a busy steamboat terminal. We did notice that some of the iron sheet piling that had once lined the riverbank was still in place, as was the slip used for vessels transported over the portage. Near the northern edge of the clearing, close to the prominent granite ridge in the general area occupied by the warehouses and wharf of the Hudson's Bay Company, we stumbled upon the remains of two old buildings close to the river. Large sections of flooring, worn and battered, were still visible, even though partially hidden by the thick growth of willows and alder.

We scrambled to the top of the granite bluff, and a short distance back, in an area grown up to young poplar and spruce and almost concealed by grass and brush, we came to an Indian cemetery. Each grave site was marked with a small weathered wooden cross and enclosed with a low picket fence. Instead of the customary fence, a small low wooden spirit house protected a few of the graves. Perhaps the large number of graves was the result of the devastating influenza epidemic that struck Fort Fitzgerald in 1918.

Before leaving Fort Fitzgerald we paused for a while at the edge of the granite bluff. From this vantage point we could see the entire site extending to the south. Even though it was now empty and silent, we knew that once the Hudson's Bay Company buildings, their wharf, a hotel, and the Roman Catholic mission had occupied the land just below us along the base of the ridge; that the Northern Trading Company, its wharf, several small stores, and the Roman Catholic church had been located only a short distance farther upstream. Although all these buildings had long since vanished, to be preserved only in memories and pictures, the granite ridge, the cemetery, the Cassette Rapids, the river itself—all a part of old Fort Fitzgerald—remained, unchanged and everlasting.

The highlight of our visit to Fort Smith and Fort Fitzgerald was our two-day canoe trip down the scow channels on the east side of the Slave River. Jacques was the organizer and leader of our small brigade of two canoes. In fact, he was our *bourgeois*. John and Christine Bayly of Yellowknife, we two Americans, and Geoff Langille, assistant guide, were the other *voyageurs*. We were going to retrace the historic waterway that skirted the Slave River to the east and bypassed the rapids.

This intricate system of quiet backwaters was the one used by the canoes and scows of all who traveled the Slave River.

Early one morning we drove over the old "West Bank" portage road to Fort Fitzgerald, our starting point. Our departure was delayed for a short time due to an unfortunate mishap. While busily engaged in loading the canoes, we somehow failed to notice that the dogs that had gathered around us, had, driven by hunger, ripped open Jacque's portage pack and devoured the hamburger intended for our noonday meal. The dogs looked so hungry, we did not begrudge them our lunch. Christine rose to the occasion and, producing needle and thread, managed to repair the damage and restore the portage pack to its former usefulness.

Our two canoes set off for the far eastern side of the river. As we paddled across well above the foaming waters of the Cassette Rapids, I thought of the tragedies and mishaps that had happened in this very stretch of water—the drowning of two Oblate priests in 1908, as well as the loss of the cassette containing the Hudson's Bay Company's payroll many years earlier.

The strong current of the river running toward the rapids was very noticeable but was successfully countered by vigorous paddling, and before too long we arrived at the eastern side of the Slave. There, leaving the roar of the rapids and the powerful river current behind us, we entered an enchanted realm of peace and quiet, of gentle streams, small waterfalls, and dancing rapids. The channels we followed were bordered in many places by the bald colorful rocks of the Canadian Shield; elsewhere the spruce forest extended to the water's edge. The quiet was broken only by the soft murmur of the canoe bow breasting the water or the drip of water droplets from the paddles. On rare occasions we surprised a beaver who responded with a loud slap of his broad tail before diving underwater. By common consent we all remained silent, saving our voyageurs' songs for the evening campfire.

We portaged around the places where these streams changed their placid flow to tumble over a rocky ledge to form a beautiful little waterfall or to cascade in lovely riffles over a series of rocks and boulders. At these spots the portages were along well-trod trails worn deep into the soft moss-and-needle-covered ground. It was over these very trails that the native people and the explorers and fur traders such as Alexander Mackenzie, Peter Pond and John Franklin—to name but a few—had walked, their voyageurs, of course, carrying the canoes and the heavy backpacks, combating the mosquitoes and blackflies just as we were doing. Their pace was undoubtedly far faster than ours, but then we were making frequent stops to enjoy the beauty of the woods through which we were passing, to identify the flowers and birds that we saw, and to take pictures.

Perhaps the most beautiful spot of all was where we ate our noon-day meal. We called it "The Place Where the Waters Meet." Three streams emerging from rockbound channels united to form one glori-ous river that raced and leaped in foam and spray as it descended for some distance before subsiding and resuming its normal placid flow. At the very point where the three streams united, a single boulder of huge size thrust upward, forcing the water to flow past it on each side. One face of this massive rock was sheared off absolutely straight as though split off by some sort of Herculean ax; the other face retained its normal convex contour. Of course, we immediately dubbed the boul-der "Split Rock," both because of its shape and because of the way it split the waters of the river. The second set of rapids—Pelican Rap-ids—we missed seeing because of intervening islands bordering the east channel down which we were paddling.

By late afternoon we had reached our night's campsite at the foot of the Mountain Portage carrying place mentioned by Alexander Mack-enzie in his daily journal. This was on the east side of the river facing the beautiful island-studded Mountain Rapids and below the twenty-foot Mountain Falls. The strength of these rapids is so violent here that we wondered how these tiny islets could withstand its tremendous force. Our campsite was on a small sandy beach, providing an ideal spot for sleeping bag and tent. Soon Jacques had the "kitchen" set up, well protected by a tarp, and the fire burning. Caribou steak was the *piéce de resistance*—very delicious—but for me the bannock wrapped around a stick and roasted over the coals somewhat like a hot dog until golden brown was the supreme delight, particularly when eaten with liberal amounts of butter and jam. After the fresh air and the labor of paddling and portaging, we all slept soundly. Neither the constant roar of the Mountain Rapids, the trembling of the ground beneath us, nor the visit of inspection to our tents during the night by a black bear (as shown by his tracks clearly visible in the sand next morning) was able to disturb us.

After breakfast we faced crossing the main river back to the west side in order to make the arduous portage up the very steep embank-ment necessary to bypass the Mountain Rapids. This portage up what seemed like a mountain to all who had to use it was the reason for the rapids' name on both sides of the river. The paddle across was a strenu-ous one, the powerful current contesting every stroke as we slowly pro-gressed westward on a diagonal course. During this long traverse, we enjoyed the sight of several white pelicans circling high in the sky, as well as many Bonaparte and herring gulls resting on the small rocky island.

Finally, safely arrived at the foot of the portage, we disembarked. We looked at the well-worn trail. It went up and up and up—175 feet to the top. In the early 1900s a capstan with oxen and later with horses was used to pull the boats to the top of the portage. For us, however, there was only man—and woman—power. Fortunately, we had a sufficiency of strong backs, so eventually we had the canoes and baggage over the portage and back down to the river's edge.

For some time the wind had been steadily increasing to the point of becoming somewhat of an obstacle and even a hazard. A council was called and it was decided to abort the remaining part of the trip, which required another crossing of the river to the east side before returning below the Rapids of the Drowned to Fort Smith on the west bank. Somewhat reluctantly we all agreed this was a wise decision, even though we were disappointed that we could not complete the entire journey. Accordingly, keeping very close to the west bank of the river, we paddled downstream to a pullout near Fort Smith's water intake pump station. Jacques had cautioned us not to miss this landing, since it was very close to the head of the Rapids of the Drowned. Our strokes were well spaced and vigorous, but the strong pull of the current and the nearness of the first waves of the rapids made my heart beat a little faster, and I, for one, was quite happy to step out of the canoe onto the safety of the riverbank.

Our trip along the historic canoe and scow channels and portages of the Slave River had been a wonderful experience. The beauty of the country through which we traveled, the good fellowship of our companions, and the knowledge that we had actually followed in the footsteps of so many historic figures of the past all became memories we will always cherish.

Jacques had one more treat in store for us. He and his wife, Ruth, entertained us all for a splendid farewell dinner, which included an apple pie that merited equal praise with Jacques's bannock. It was the perfect ending for a marvelous adventure.

Grand Rapids House and Portage

The only obstacle to interrupt the smooth flow of the North Saskatchewan River on its 1,000-mile passage from its source in the Rocky Mountains to Lake Winnipeg was the Grand Rapids. Just two miles from its mouth at the northwest corner of Lake Winnipeg, the river cuts through high limestone cliffs and drops 74.2 feet in four miles in a series of turbulent and dangerous rapids.

The Indian or voyageur in a birch bark canoe was forced to walk along the river's edge and line his frail craft upstream against the strong current by means of a towline. Returning downstream, the canoes would usually shoot the rapids *demi-chargé,* that is, with only half their cargo. Even with this reduced load, the passage was perilous and not without some fatal mishaps. The south channel was the one used for the perilous descent. The loads were deposited at the foot of the rapids and then the empty canoes lined upstream to pick up the remaining half of their lading and repeat their hazardous descent.

Alexander Henry the elder, on his way to Amisk Lake in 1775 wrote in his *Travels and Adventures in Canada and the Indian Territories:*

> On the first of October, we gained the mouth of the River de Bourbon, Pasquayah, or Sascatchiwaine, and proceeded to ascend its stream. The Bourbon is a large river, and has its sources to the westward.... At four leagues above the mouth of the river, is the Grand Rapide, two leagues in length, up which the canoes are dragged with ropes. At the end of this is a carrying-place of two miles, through a forest almost uniformly of pine-trees. Here, we met with Indians, fishing for sturgeon. Their practice is, to watch behind the points where the current forms an eddy, in which the sturgeon, coming to rest themselves, are easily speared.

Four years later Philip Turnor, surveyor for the Hudson's Bay Company, en route from Cumberland House to York Factory recorded in his journal for the seventeenth of June 1779:

> Thursday at 5-1/4 AM got underway being a small Pond at the bottom of the Carrg place formed by nature and creek of about 10 yds long which leads into the fall the Canoes are loaded in it and go on to the fall through this creek, some of the Indians thinking the So side of the Fall the best to shoot crossed about 1/2 Mile below the carry-place, Mr Joseph Hansom in attempting to follow them was drove upon a Stone in the middle of the fall the Canoe overset and he drowned, his Canoemate an Indian saved himself by regaining the Canoe and drove about 3 Miles before he was

706

taken up, an Indian likewise in attempting to cross was overset by the swell and drowned likewise, Mr Hansom was taken up about 3 Miles below where he was overset having never sunk, we tried to bring him too again but without success, the Canoes was taken up about 5 Miles below the place where they were overset with little Loss of goods, at 1-1/2 PM we Intered Mr Hansom upon a Point on the No side of the River in the most Christian like maner we could, the Indian not found . . . in my opinion the whole misfortune may be imported to their not listning to . . . an old leader who forbid them attempting to cross, it not being customary, but to shoot intirely on the No side, only four Canoes in which was any of the Honble Company's Servants inn crossed, the others all followed the Leader without damage he being very carefull this day went 3 Miles from E to NE and put up at the bottom of the Fall, the whole length of the Fall about 5 Miles exceeding rapid from top to bottom, the Land on both sides very bold mostly Rockey and coverd with Pine.

In the 1780s the Hudson's Bay Company began to use York boats on the Saskatchewan. These were too heavy and cumbersome to line up the rapids. They had to be hauled over the rough terrain of the portage through the woods. In order to facilitate their passage, Thomas Holmes and Edward Umfreville laid down a succession of green logs across the portage trail so that the boats could be pushed and rolled over the pathway. When Alexander Henry the younger, of the North West Company, arrived at the Grand Rapids in 1808, he commented in his journal: "On my return I found the canoes had arrived, and the people were busy carrying the baggage over the portage. This is upward of a mile long, but would be a very good road, were it not that the H. B. Co. from York Factory, with large boats, are in the habit of laying down a succession of logs from one end to the other for the purpose of rolling their boats over. This is a nuisance to our people, frequently causing accidents which endanger their lives."

Henry's journal entry for August 20, 1808, records his impression of the Grand Rapids:

We crossed to the W. side, [of Lake Winnipeg] and proceeded up river with poles to the foot of the first rapids, where we took towing-lines up the Grand rapids. Here we saw the vast numbers of pelicans that resort to the foot of these rapids, where I am told there is an abundance of fish of various kinds, particularly sturgeon. Loaded canoes generally discharge half their load, and make two trips; but as my canoe was light we went on without loss of time, and after a tedious walk along a rough, ugly shore, with loose stones, and perpendicular banks of clay, we arrived at Grand Rapids portage. The opposite [south] shore is almost a continuous high bank of limestone of different colors. Before the canoes arrived I went to see as much as I could of the falls or rapids that occasion this portage. I did not find them nearly so bad as I had been given to understand. There is no particular fall, but a succession of descents, especially on the S. side, where I would not hesitate a moment to run down a canoe with half her cargo.

During the month of June 1819 the Grand Rapids portage was the scene of one of the many incidents that characterized the escalating violence between the North West Company and the Hudson's Bay Company. In retaliation for what he perceived to be the "massacre" of Seven Oaks, when Governor Robert Semple and nineteen settlers had been killed by a band of Métis led by Cuthbert Grant, Governor William Williams determined to strike a blow at the North West Company that would severely hamper their operation. He decided to ambush the North West partners as soon as they reached the end of the portage trail past the Grand Rapids. He positioned cannon to cover the landing place where the canoes put ashore to reload their cargoes. He himself and his supporters concealed themselves by the end of the trail at the foot of the rapids. His plan was 100 percent successful, as one by one he captured the unsuspecting partners as they emerged from the woods ready to reembark in their canoes. In all, he captured five partners (John D. Campbell, Benjamin Frobisher, Angus Shaw, John George MacTavish, and William McIntosh) plus several clerks, servants, and guides.

After enduring eight days of harsh confinement on nearby Devil's Island, the Nor'Westers were transported to York Factory on Hudson's Bay for eventual transport to England. Of the five partners only two were actually sent to England, where they were quickly set at liberty. Of the remaining three, one died during his escape from York Factory, one escaped en route from Grand Rapids to York Factory, and one was released by his captors at York Factory.

S. H. Wilcocke in his *Narrative of Circumstances Attending the Death of the Late Benjamin Frobisher, Esq.* wrote a detailed account of the Grand Rapids episode in the year immediately following the event: "The only practicable route to an [sic] from Athabasca . . . is through the north western outlet of Lake Winnipeg leading through Cedar or Bourbon Lake, to the River Saskatchewan." Close to the eastern end was the Grand Rapids, an "extremely difficult" stretch of water that for "more than a mile is wholly impracticable for loaded canoes." Goods and passengers were obliged to use the portage around the rapids that bordered the north side of the river. To carry out his plan of capturing the North West Company partners on their return from the Athabasca country, Governor Williams set up an ambush at the east end of the portage. He stationed a four-pound canon and two swivels on a point of land overlooking the foot of the rapid and positioned his barge with additional artillery in the middle of the river so as to command the canoes coming downstream. On June 18 as two North West partners, John D. Campbell and Benjamin Frobisher, emerged from the portage, completely unaware of the trap into which they were walking, they were surrounded and captured by Williams's men. Campbell and Frobisher were hauled over to a small island midstream in the Saskatchewan and "placed under strict confinement in a tent . . . out of which they were not allowed to stir, though the heat was intense and the mosquitoes very numerous." Five days later two more North West Canoes carrying three partners reached the Grand Rapids passage, and once again the ambush was successful. This time it was Angus Shaw, John G. Mactavish and William McIntosh who were the victims. They, too, were "confined in the island at the foot of the rapid with a guard placed over them, who had orders to shoot anyone who should show a disposition to escape."

This daring exploit on the part of the Hudson's Bay Company was not long in being avenged by the Nor'Westers. The very next year, 1820, the scenario was repeated, only this time the ambush was prepared by the North West Company and it was Colin Robertson of the Hudson's Bay Company who was captured. Eight partners, six clerks, and over fifty *engagés* were assembled at the Grand Rapid ready to spring the trap. In the words of Marjorie Wilkins Campbell in her book *The North West Company:*

> When Robertson finally appeared, Henry McKenzie, in charge of the engagés, was ready for him. With a great whoop, his men rushed at Robertson. Ignoring his protests, they took his gun and pinioned his arms behind him . . .
> The Nor'Westers laughed at Robertson's protests; Frobisher had been a popular and competent fur-trader. With grim satisfaction they hustled him off to the tiny island where the Nor'Westers had suffered . . . the previous year. Their only disappointment was in not being able to arrest William Williams too.

The union of the two companies in 1821 brought an end to these bitter skirmishes, and the only enemies encountered on the Grand Rapids portage trail henceforth were the swarms of voracious mosquitoes and blackflies.

Gradually changes occurred that forced the company to modify its traditional transportation system. It was becoming increasingly difficult to find enough canoemen willing to join the York boat brigades for their long arduous journeys. As a result, Red River carts largely replaced the boat brigades that formerly plied the Saskatchewan River. The high labor costs of both boat brigades and cart trains were an economic burden that was increasingly difficult for the company to assume.

Fortunately, the advent of the railroad and the introduction of the steamboat furnished the Hudson's Bay Company with a less labor-intensive and thus correspondingly less costly means of transportation.

The 1870s saw the railroad reach Fort Garry (Winnipeg); it also saw the Hudson's Bay Company's first steamboat on Lake Winnipeg. This was the SS *Chief Commissioner,* a one-funnel screw steamer, used between Fort Garry and Grand Rapids. Its design was not suited for the waters of Lake Winnipeg, so it was replaced in 1875 by the SS *Colville,* a one-deck caravel-type vessel with a gross tonnage of 16,441. The company built two steamboats for use on the Saskatchewan River, the *Northcote* in 1874, a stern-wheeler 150 feet long, with a twenty-eight-and-a-half-foot beam, twenty-two-inch draft, and gross tonnage 461.3; and the *Lily* in 1877, a two-decked stern-wheeler, 100 feet long, with a twenty-four-foot beam, fourteen-inch draft, and gross tonnage 207. With the acquisition of this fleet of lake and river vessels for the company's transportation supply system for the Northwest, it was imperative that the difficulties occasioned by the Grand Rapids be lessened as much as possible.

The Grand Rapids was the only major obstacle to continuous navigation on the Saskatchewan River, just as the Grand Rapids on the Athabasca and the Slave Rapids on the Slave were to the uninterrupted passage on those rivers. In all three places much effort was expended to devise ways of circumventing the rapids by means of improved portages and tramways. As soon as the steamboats were placed in service on Lake Winnipeg and the Saskatchewan River, the portage trail around the rapids was upgraded to a dirt road, so that carts could be used to transport the freight from the lower landing at the Lake Winnipeg end to the upper landing at the head of the rapids. This road was so rough that the teams could never take full loads. This of course increased the number of trips and thus the length of time required to transport the ship's cargo across the portage. The cost was one cent per pound.

In May of 1877 Walter Moberly was given a $16,500 contract by Commissioner Grahame of the Hudson's Bay Company to construct a three-and-one-half-mile, three-and-one-half-foot narrow-gauge tramway that would bypass the rapids. Completion date was October 1. Moberly was a distinguished civil engineer, who had earlier surveyed much of the route east of British Columbia's Fraser Canyon that was followed by the Canadian Pacific Railway and who had discovered Eagle Pass through the Monashee Mountains of eastern British Columbia.

Moberly lost no time but immediately began surveying the right-of-way and clearing the undergrowth thirty-three feet on either side of the proposed track center to serve as a firebreak. The road bed was built up to a height of two to three feet with locally quarried stone and dirt fill. Cross-ties of spruce and tamarack were ax-hewn and flattened on two sides. These were laid down 2,400 to the mile. The rails were spiked directly to the ties, no tie plates being used. Sixty-pound iron "U" rail was used, even though it had already been superseded in the United States by the more effective "T" rail. To provide a smooth pathway for the horses, the grade was packed throughout with ballast even with the tops of the ties. Two twenty-five foot bridges were built over two small streams and a ten-foot deep cut made through an old beach line. Four solid oak tramcars with iron fittings and undercarriage, each costing $137, constituted the "rolling stock"; the "motor power" was provided by three horses. At each end of the tramway a storehouse was built as well as a suitable wharf for the steamboats. In addition, at the upper terminal a cookhouse was set up to serve the needs of the men working on the tramway. This was also the location of the Grand Rapids House, a small fur trading post.

According to Chief Trader Alexander Matheson, the total cost was $17,389, a mere 5 percent over the contract price. He considered the tramway well worth the cost, for now the steamboats could be discharged and loaded in one day; cargo could be transported across the portage for one-half cent per pound—exactly one-half of the previous cost. The horse-drawn tramcars were able to haul loads of 6,000 pounds per trip. Matheson wrote: "The Tramway has been a great boon to us, enabling us to do away with most of the men and horses required under the old plan, while transport by it has been so expeditious that the men and horses kept for it are available for numerous other purposes."

The success of the tramway in conjunction with the steamboats on Lake Winnipeg and the Saskatchewan River reestablished the Saskatchewan River as a major route in the company's transportation system for its northern and western districts. For over twenty years this combination of an efficiently operating tramway and steamboats enabled the company to prolong the steadily decreasing fur trade in the northwestern regions long after its disappearance in the Red River district and the southwest.

During the latter half of the nineteenth century, it was not only furs and trade goods that passed over the tramway. Pioneer families with all their belongings on their way to settle the western prairie lands as well as small shipments of wheat, flour, and coal were carried across the portage on the tramcars. During the 1885 Riel Rebellion supplies for the Canadian troops and even some of the soldiers were transported on the tramway.

As the railroad inexorably extended its tentacles ever farther north and west, the era of the steamboats came to an end and with it the need for the tramway was greatly reduced. It remained in use until the end of World War I; only a trickle of freight was passing over its tracks. As far back as 1901 the buildings at each end of the portage were in a dilapidated condition. Much of the warehouse space was empty. The company's annual report for 1909 stated that "the importance of Grand Rapids as a Fur Trading Post has ceased to exist and as there is no prospect of its being made remunerative, its operation is being discontinued." And so the tramway and buildings were sold for $800.

For the next forty years the tramway was used sporadically by tourists from the excursion boat MS *Kenora,* but even that use ceased and the tramway slowly progressed toward oblivion as its nails and rails rusted and its ties rotted away. The rapids continued to leap and tumble and roar largely unchallenged by boat or canoe. Then came the 1960s and the building of one of man's mighty monuments, the $140 million dam erected on the Saskatchewan near its mouth at Lake Winnipeg. With the closing of the floodgates in the completed dam, the waters of the river steadily rose and soon submerged the Grand Rapids, stilling forever their thunderous roar.

The tiny village of Grand Rapids in the middle of a small Indian reservation at the mouth of the Saskatchewan was easy to find. We spent several hours wandering around this interesting settlement. Thanks to the helpful information we received from several friendly people, we were able to go directly to the site of the lower terminal of the tramway and of the company wharf on a small tongue of land still known as Hudson's Bay Point.

An open expanse of grassy turf extended along the riverbank, unbroken save for a small coppice of poplar trees and, at the far end, a few stately spruce. The rays from the late-afternoon sun revealed with great clarity the contours of the old tramway rail bed, as well as other mounds and depressions formed by the warehouses that once stood here. At the foot of the bank, we were able to see and photograph a few of the old hand-hewn and notched beams, remnants of the company wharf, which still protruded from the bank into the river.

Across the dirt road that bordered the clearing, the tramway right-of-way, even though greatly overgrown with brush, was distinctly visible leading into the woods. In fact, only a few feet from the road some of the original rail was still in place.

As we stood there looking at this historic survivor of early days, we fortunately encountered the person through whose backyard this section of the tramway ran. When he learned of our interest in the fur trade and realized the long distance we had traveled to see this site, he returned to his house and came back a few minutes later carrying an eleven-and-one-half-inch section of the original tramway rail. To our surprise and delight, he presented it to us as an appropriate token of our visit to the site of the Grand Rapids tramway.

We next drove the short distance along a sandy road through woods of second-growth poplar—probably part of the old cart trail—to the foot of the dam. The high face of this massive structure dwarfed the white pelicans that, just as in the days of Alexander Henry, still dived for food in the river. In recognition of the historic significance of the area, a display featuring a tramcar on a section of original rail had been installed here.

We drove on farther past the lake created by the damming of the river toward Cross Lake, which formerly marked the approach to the beginning of the Grand Rapids. We stood on the shore looking out over this vast expanse of water; tiny wavelets rippled at our feet; driftwood littered the shoreline; a few gulls wheeled overhead. The scene was one of calm and peace. We reflected that buried deep beneath these impounded waters, obliterated forever, fated to survive only in fading memories and in history books, were not only the rapids that once roared and raced and challenged man's skills and sometimes took his life but also the portage trail over which the proud partners and gentlemen of the fur trade had walked and which was as well the scene of ambushes and other acts of violence brought about by the bitter struggle between two rival fur companies. The past had, in truth, been completely effaced by the present.

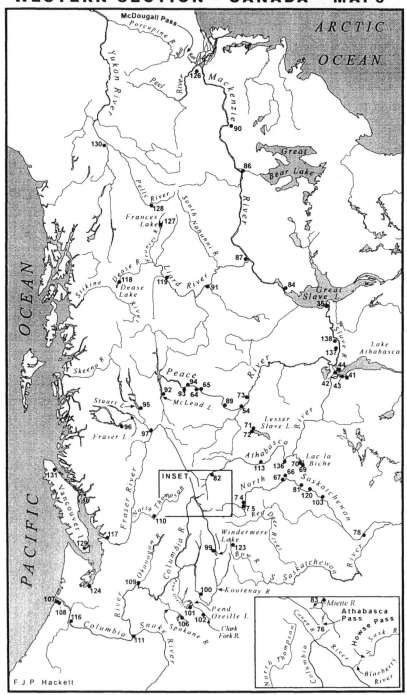

McDougall Pass

ARCTIC

OCEAN

Porcupine R.

Yukon River

Peel River

Peel R.

Rat R.

126

Mackenzie

River

90

130

Great
Bear Lake

86

Pelly River

128
Frances
Lake

127

South Nahanni R.

Dease River

118
Dease
Lake

Frances R.

119

Liard River

91

87

84

Great
Slave L.

35

Lake
Athabasca

Stikine

River

138

137

44

42 43

41

Skeena R.

Peace

94
93 64 65

92

95

McLeod L.

73

89

54

River

Stuart L.

Slave R.

Lesser
Slave L.

River

71

72

Fraser L.

96

97

Athabasca

113 136

Lac la
Biche

70

69

66

67

81

120

103

131

Vancouver I.

82

North

74

75

Red Deer River

78

117

INSET

North Thompson

110

129

124

Windermere
Lake

99

123

Bow R.

S. Saskatchewan

River

109

Columbia R.

Okanagan R.

Fraser River

100 ← Kootenay R.

83

Miette R.

Athabasca
Pass

76

Howse Pass

North Thompson

Canoe R.

N. Sask. R.

107

108

116

Columbia

Snake River

Spokane R.

101

106 102

Pend
Oreille L.

Clark
Fork R.

Columbia R.

Blaeberry
River

111

PACIFIC

OCEAN

Pend Oreille R.

F.J.P. Hackett

714

Fur Trading Forts—Western Section Canada

35. Fort Resolution
41. Fort Chipewyan I
42. Nottingham House
43. Fort Wedderburn
44. Fort Chipewyan II
54. Fort Forks
64. Rocky Mountain Fort
65. Fort St. John
66. Fort Augustus
67. Edmonton House
69. Red Deer Lake House/Fort Lac la Biche
70. Greenwich House
71. Lesser Slave Lake Fort
72. Fort Grouard
73. McLeod's Fort (Peace River)
74. Rocky Mountain House
75. Acton House
76. Athabasca Pass
78. Carlton House
81. Fort de l'Isle
82. Jasper House
83. Henry's House
84. Fort Providence
86. Fort Norman
87. Fort of the Forks/Fort Simpson
89. Fort Dunvegan
90. Fort Good Hope
91. Fort Liard
92. Fort McLeod (McLeod Lake)
93. Rocky Mountain Portage House
94. Hudson's Hope

95. Fort St. James
96. Fort Fraser
97. Fort George (Fraser River)
99. Kootenay House
100. Kootenay Falls House
101. Kullyspell House
102. Saleesh House
103. Fort Vermillion
106. Spokane House
107. Fort Astoria
108. Fort George (Columbia River)
109. Fort Okanagan
110. Fort Kamloops
111. Fort Nez Percés/Walla Walla
113. Fort Assiniboine (Athabasca River)
116. Fort Vancouver
117. Fort Langley
118. Dease Lake Post
119. Fort Halkett
120. Fort Pitt
123. Bow River Fort/Piegan Post
134. Fort Nisqually
126. Fort McPherson
127. Frances Lake Post
128. Pelly Banks Post
129. Fort Victoria
130. Fort Selkirk
131. Fort Rupert (Vancouver Island)
136. Athabasca Landing
137. Fort Fitzgerald
138. Fort Smith

Epilogue

We might be forgiven for thinking that any institution that had not only survived but also grown and prospered for more than three hundred years was indestructible. Such a one was the Hudson's Bay Company—that "Governor and Company of Adventurers of England Trading into Hudson Bay"—whose jurisdiction at one time extended over nearly one-twelfth of the world's land surface. From its founding in 1670 right down to the present it has continuously been engaged in a wide range of business ventures. This long period of uninterrupted existence has made it the world's oldest commercial enterprise.

However, as the poet Edmund Spenser wrote: "But Times do change and move continually." To better meet the problems posed by the 1970s and 1980s, the company severed its historic time-honored bonds to the life and economy of the Canadian North. In 1987 it sold all its stores and holdings north of the sixtieth parallel, electing to focus its operations in southern Canada. Ended forever was its presence in the land it had served and dominated for 317 years.

Also at this same time the company began its withdrawal from the fur business by selling its fur auction houses in London and New York. This process was completed four years later when, in 1991, it ceased handling all fur garments in its retail stores. Thus the company whose founding and early fortunes were based on the harvest and trade in furs irrevocably cut all ties with the fur trade. The company seal with its motto "pro pelle cutem" (a skin for a skin), now became irrelevant.

Seizing this opportunity to fill the void created by the departure of the Hudson's Bay Company, a consortium of several business interests plus a group of former company employees bought the Hudson's Bay Company assets north of the sixtieth parallel and organized into a company, which they named the North West Company. This choice of name was a deliberate attempt to continue unbroken Canada's historical link to its fur trade past. Through the interest and efforts of George Whitman, former vice president of public relations for the Hudson's Bay Company, the ownership of this name was traced to Imperial Oil Company, which held the legal rights to its use. Whitman arranged for a meeting with the company president and in an amicable discussion had no difficulty securing the release of the name in return for a token payment of one dollar. Thus a North West Company could once again operate in the Canadian North.

It had been 171 years since the old North West Company had been thoroughly humiliated by Lord Selkirk (a major Hudson's Bay Company shareholder). He had captured Fort William, the North West's stronghold and principal headquarters, and had seized their chief wintering partners, whom he ignominiously bundled off in overcrowded canoes for Montreal to stand trial. Five years later, as a result of the union of 1821, Fort William was turned over to the Hudson's Bay Company.

Reminiscent of the vigorous action that characterized its namesake, the new North West Company immediately began to move aggressively to revitalize its northern operations. It is continuing to play a major role in the region's fur-based economy. Harvesting of fur is a traditional way of life that has always been essential to the well-being of the local people. The company's purchase of their furs brings not only much-needed cash into the communities but also the benefits of self-reliance. Just as the old company was ever in the forefront of pushing forward into unexplored lands and meeting new challenges, so this present North West Company is ready to grasp new opportunities.

It seems quite fitting—perhaps a bit of "poetic justice"—that the new North West Company has acquired for its own headquarters the magnificent edifice that was formerly the Hudson's Bay Company's bastion of power. Today it is the house flag of the North West Company that flies over the building in Winnipeg. Perhaps now, at long last, the proud spirits of the old Nor'Westers, those "Lords of the North"—the McGillivrays, McTavishes, and McKenzies—can rest in peace, no longer tormented by humiliating defeat but, instead, gladdened by the resurgence of their old company. Truly, as the modern saying goes, "what goes around comes around."

Quite appropriately, a corner of the imposing headquarters building on Main Street occupies part of the site of the old Hudson's Bay Company retail shop of Fort Garry to the west, while to the east it overlooks the site of the North West Company's Fort Gibraltar less than one thousand feet away. It is a solid link that keeps the chain of the historical heritage of Canada and its fur-trade past unbroken.

One other link in this historical chain remains. Over the years when the Main Street building was the Hudson's Bay Company headquarters, it became the repository for a priceless collection of paintings, silver, and other objects of great historical interest in addition to splendid examples of Inuit art. Many of them were gifts to the company from the Kings and Queens of England. The paintings were portraits of figures prominent in the company's long history.

Then in 1991 an archaeologist J. V. Chism uncovered and identified traces not only of Gillam's and Grosseillier's original fort of 1668 (Charles Fort I) but also of the later one of 1681 (Charles Fort II).

It was several years before I was able to return to Rupert House (now known by its Cree name of Waskaganish). Through the courtesy of Chief Billy Diamond who furnished me with copies of J. V. Chism's reports containing the maps showing the precise location of the two forts, I was anticipating seeing and photographing these extremely important historical spots.

I was taken to the beautiful modern Auberge Kanio-Kashee built *after* Chism's discoveries had been made and told that the eastern wing of the building covered the site of the 1668 Charles Fort. Even as I stood in shocked disbelief, bulldozers were leveling the rich soil in preparation for landscaping around the building—obliterating forever any trace of the fort's existence.

I was next driven to St. Peter's Anglican Church situated on the high knoll overlooking the bay and river at the western edge of Waskaganish. It was under this church and the adjacent cemetery that Chism discovered the traces of Charles Fort II (1686).

Later on my flight home, I reflected on my rather frustrating visit. I wondered why the Auberge could not have been located just a few hundred yards downriver, thereby sparing this truly historic spot. Had Chism's brilliant work been done in vain? Were none of his discoveries to be appropriately marked and preserved for future generations? Maybe to the Cree people whose home this land has always been, the beginnings of the fur trade and the coming of the Hudson's Bay Company were not such significant events. Perhaps they are not so much interested in the past as they are in the future. For them their continued successful existence for many centuries is what is really important.

So in 1995, twenty years after my husband and I had begun our search, I finally ended our fur trade odyssey where it had begun, in Rupert House. These Charles Fort sites, even though buried as they were under a motel and a church, were nonetheless tangible witnesses to the fur trade's very beginnings on the shores of Rupert River.

References

Allen, Robert S.
1983 *Peter Fidler and Nottingham House, Lake Athabasca, 1802–1806,* History and Archaeology Occasional Paper 69. Ottawa: National Historic Parks and Sites Branch, Parks Canada, Environment Canada.

Anderson, William Ashley
1964 *Angel of Hudson Bay: The True Story of Maud Watt.* Toronto: Clarke, Irwin & Co., Ltd.

Babcock, Douglas R.
1990 *Opponents and Neighbors: A Narrative History of Fort George and Buckingham House, 1792–1800,* Alberta Community Development Historic Sites and Archives Service.

Baldwin, Douglas
1976 *The Fur Trade in the Moose-Missinaibi River Valley, 1770–1917,* Historical Planning and Research Branch. Ontario Ministry of Culture and Recreation. Research Report 8.

Ballantyne, Robert M.
1848 *Hudson's Bay, or, Every-Day Life in the Wilds of North America During Six Years' Residence in the Territories of the Honourable Hudson's Bay Company.* Rutland, VT: Charles E. Tuttle, Reprint, Edmonton: Hurtig, 1972.

Barka, Norman F., & Anne Barka
1976 *Archaeology and the Fur Trade: The Excavation of Sturgeon Fort, Saskatchewan.* History and Archaeology 7. Ottawa: National Historic Parks and Sites Branch, Parks Canada, Department of Indian and Northern Affairs.

Bell, Charles Napier
1927 "The Old Forts of Winnipeg, 1738–1927." *Transactions of the Historical and Scientific Society of Manitoba* NS 3. Winnipeg: Dawson Richardson Publications.

Bell, Charles Napier, ed.
1928 "The Journal of Henry Kelsey, 1691–1692." *Transactions of the Historical and Scientific Society of Manitoba* NS 4. Winnipeg: Dawson Richardson Publications.

Binns, Archie
1967 *Peter Skene Ogden,* Portland, OR: Binfords & Mort.
Blegen, Theodore C.
1937 "Fort St. Charles and the Northwest Angle." *Minnesota History* 18(3).
Bond, C.C.J.
1966 "The Hudson's Bay Company in the Ottawa Valley." *The Beaver* (Spring):4–21.
Bowsfield, Hartwell, ed.
1979 *Fort Victoria Letters, 1846–1851.* Introduction by Margaret A. Ormsby. Winnipeg: Hudson's Bay Record Society, Vol. 22.
Brady, Archange J.
1984 *A History of Fort Chipewyan.* Athabasca, Alberta: Gregorach Printing Ltd.
Brown, Alice E.
1963 "The Fur Trade Posts of the Souris Mouth Area." *Transactions of the Historical and Scientific Society of Manitoba* 3rd Series, 17–18.
Bryce, George
1882 "The Assiniboine River and its Forts." *Transactions of the Royal Society of Canada* 3rd Series, 10 (Section 2): 69–78.
1898 Sketch of the Life and Discoveries of Robert Campbell, Chief Factor of the Hon. Hudson's Bay Company. *Transactions of the Historical and Scientific Society of Manitoba* 52. Winnipeg: Manitoba Free Press, April 14, 1898.
Buck, S.J.
1924 "The Story of Grand Portage." *Minnesota History Bulletin* 5:14–27.
Burpee, Lawrence J.
1931 "Grand Portage." *Minnesota History* 12:4.
Burpee, Lawrence J., ed.
1907 Journal of Anthony Hendry, 1754–55. *Transactions of the Royal Society of Canada* [3rd] Series, [I](Section II): 307–64.
1910 *Alexander Hunter Murray's Journal du Yukon, 1847–48.* Publications des Archives Canadiennes 4. Ottawa: Government Printing Bureau.
1927 *Journals and Letters of Pierre Gaultier de Varennes de la Vérendrye and His Sons, with Correspondence between the Governors of Canada and the French Court, Touching the Search for the Western Sea.* Champlain Society Publication 16. Reprint, New York: Greenwood Press, 1968.

Butler, William Francis

1874 *The Wild North Land: Being the Story of a Winter Journey, with Dogs, across Northern North America.* Montreal. Reprint of 1874 edition: Edmonton: Hurtig, 1973.

1875 *The Great Lone Land.* London. Reprint, Edmonton: Hurtig, 1968.

Cameron, Agnes Deans

1912 *The New North: Being Some Account of a Woman's Journey Through Canada to the Arctic.* New York; London: D. Appleton and Co.

Campbell, Susan

1976 *Fort William: Living and Working at the Post.* Fort William Archaeological Project. Toronto: Ministry of Culture and Recreation.

Campbell, Robert

1808–53 *Journals 1808–1853.* Seattle, WN: [s.n.], 1958.

Carpenter, Cecelia Swinth

1986 *Fort Nisqually Tacoma, Washington.* A Takoma Research Publication.

Caywood, Louis R.

1954 *Archaeological Excavations at Fort Spokane, 1951, '52, and '53.* National Park Service. U.S. Department of the Interior.

1954 *Excavations at Fort Okanogan, 1952,* National Park Service, Region Four. San Francisco: U.S. Department of the Interior.

Chalmers, John W.

1960 *Fur Trade Governor: George Simpson, 1820–1860.* Edmonton: Institute of Applied Art.

Chalmers, John W., ed.

1971 *On the Edge of the Shield: Fort Chipewyan and Its Hinterland.* Boreal Institute for Northern Studies Occasional Paper 7. Edmonton: University of Alberta.

Chalmers, John W., ed.

1974 *The Land of Peter Pond.* Boreal Institute for Northern Studies Occasional Paper 12. Edmonton: University of Alberta.

Champagne, Antonio

1964 "Grand Rapids: An Old Historical Spot 1727–1760." *Transactions of the Historical and Scientific Society of Manitoba* 3rd Series, 19.

Cheadle, W. B.

1862–63 *Cheadle's Journal of Trip Across Canada, 1862–1863.* Ottawa: Graphic, 1931. Reprint of 1931 edition, Edmonton: Hurtig, 1971.

Cocking, Matthew
  1772–73 "An Adventurer from Hudson Bay: Journal of Matthew Cocking from York Factory to the Blackfeet Country, 1772–1773." Lawrence J. Burpee, ed. *Proceedings and Transactions of the Royal Society of Canada*, 3rd Series, 2:89–122.
Cole, Jean Murray
  1979 *Exile in the Wilderness: The Biography of Chief Factor Archibald McDonald, 1790–1853.* Don Mills, ON: Burns & MacEachern.
Colvile, Eden
  1956 *London Correspondence Inward from Eden Colvile, 1849–1852.* E.E. Rich and Alice M. Johnson, eds. London: Hudson's Bay Record Society, Vol. 19.
Coues, Elliott, ed.
  1965 *Journals of Alexander Henry and David Thompson.* 2 vols. Minneapolis: Ross and Haines, Inc.
Coutts, Robert
  1988 *Forks, the Red and the Assiniboine: A Thematic Study 1734–1850.* Canada Parks Service, Environment Canada. Microfiche Report Series 383.
Cowie, Isaac
  1913 *The Company of Adventurers: A Narrative of Seven Years in the Service of the Hudson's Bay Company During 1867–1876 on the Great Buffalo Plains with Historical and Biographical Notes and Comments.* A reprint of articles published in the Manitoba Free Press, February 17-December 14, 1912. Toronto: William Biggs.
Cox, Ross
  1957 *Adventures on the Columbia River.* Norman, University of Oklahoma Press.
Crouse, Nellis M.
  1928 "The Location of Fort Maurepas." *Canadian Historical Review* 9 (September).
Davidson, J.A.
  1960 "Fort Prince of Wales: the Preposterous Fortress of the North." *Canadian Geographical Journal* 61:4 (October).
Davies, K.G., ed
  1961 *Peter Skene Ogden's Snake Country Journal, 1826–1827.* Introduction by Dorothy O. Johansen. London: Hudson's Bay Record Society, Vol. 23.

1965 *Letters from Hudson Bay, 1703–40.* Introduction by Richard Glover. London: Hudson's Bay Record Society, Vol. 28.

Dempsey, Hugh A.

1973 *A History of Rocky Mountain House.* Canadian Historic Sites Occasional Papers in Archaeology and History 6. Ottawa: National Historic Sites Service, National and Historic Parks Branch, Department of Indian Affairs and Northern Development.

Dick, Lyle

1975 *Pine Fort.* Winnipeg: Historic Resources Branch.

Douglas, R., and J.N. Wallace, eds.

1926 *Nicolas Jérémie, Twenty Years of York Factory, 1694–1714.* Translated from the French edition of 1720. Ottawa: Thorburn and Abbott.

Emerson, J.N., H.E. Devereux, and M.J. Ashworth

1981 *Études du Fort Saint Joseph, Ontario,* Histoire et Archeologies 14. Ottawa: Parcs Canada.

Epp, Henry T., and Tim Jones

1969 "The Methy Portage: Proposal for a Saskatchewan Historic and Nature Trail." *Blue Jay* 27:2 (June).

Faries, Hugh

1965 "The diary of Hugh Faries." *Five Fur Traders of the Northwest.* Charles M. Gates, ed. St. Paul: Minnesota Historical Society.

Fidler, Peter

1913 "Peter Fidler: Trader and Surveyor, 1769–1822." J.B. Tyrrell, ed. *Transactions of the Royal Society of Canada,* 3rd series 7:117–27.

1792–93 *Journal of a Journey Over Land from Buckingham House to the Rocky Mountains in 1792 & 1793.* Lethbridge: Historical Research Centre, 1991.

Franchère, Gabriel

1969 *Journal of a Voyage on the North West Coast of North America during the Years 1811, 1812, 1813, and 1814.* Trans. Wessie Tipping Lamb. W. Kaye Lamb, ed. Champlain Society Publication 45. Toronto: Champlain Society.

Francis, Daniel, and Toby Morantz

1983 *Partners in Furs: A History of the Fur Trade in Eastern James Bay, 1600–1870.* McGill-Queen's University Press.

Franklin, Sir John

1823 *Narrative of a Journey to the Shores of the Polar Sea in the Years 1819, '20, '21, and '22.* Reprint, New York: Greenwood Press, 1969.

1828 *Narrative of a Second Expedition to the Shores of the Polar Sea in the Years 1825, 1826 and 1827.* Reprint, Rutland, VT: Charles E. Tuttle, 1971.

Fraser, Simon

1890 "Journal of a Voyage from the Rocky Mountains to the Pacific Coast, 1808." *Les Bourgeois de la Compagnie du Nord-Ouest* . . . L.R. Masson, ed. Quebec. Vol. 1. Reprint, New York: Antiquarian Press, 1960.

1960 *The Letters and Journals of Simon Fraser, 1806–1808.* W. Kaye Lamb, ed. Toronto: Macmillan Company.

Furniss, O.C.

1943 "Some Notes on Newly-discovered Fur Posts on the Saskatchewan River." *Canadian Historical Review* 24:3 (Sept.) 266–72.

Galbraith,, John S.

1976 *The Little Emperor: Governor Simpson of the Hudson's Bay Company.* Toronto: Macmillan of Canada.

Garry, Nicholas

1822–35 "Diary of Nicholas Garry, Deputy-Governor of the Hudson's Bay Company from 1822–1835: a Detailed Narrative of His Travels in the Northwest Territories of British North America in 1821." *Transactions of the Royal Society of Canada* 2nd Series, 6(1900): 72–204. Read May 29, 1900.

Gates, Charles M., ed.

1965 *Five Fur Traders of the Northwest Being the Narrative of Peter Pond and the Diaries of John Macdonell, Archibald McLeod, Hugh Faries, Thomas Connor.* St. Paul: Minnesota Historical Society.

Glazebrook, G.P. de T., ed.

1938 *The Hargrave Correspondence, 1821–1843.* Champlain Society Publication 24. Reprint, New York: Greenwood Press, 1968.

Godsell, Philip H.

1936 "Old Fort St. John." *Canadian Geographical Journal* 12:2 (February): 91–100.

Graham, Andrew

1969 *Andrew Graham's Observations on Hudson's Bay, 1769–1791.* Glyndwr Williams, ed. London: Hudson's Bay Record Society, Vol. 27.

Grant George M.

1873 *Ocean to Ocean: Sandford Fleming's Expedition through Can-*

ada in 1872. Toronto: James Campbell & Son. Reprint, Coles Publishing, 1970.

Grover, Sheila

1975 *Physical Description of Pine Fort (Geographical Setting).* Winnipeg: Historic Resources Branch.

1975 *Physical Description of Pine Fort (Construction Methods).* Winnipeg: Historic Resources Branch.

1975 *Red River Trade During Second Occupation of Pine Fort.* Winnipeg: Historic Resources Branch.

Hargrave, James

1821–43 *The Hargrave Correspondence, 1821–1843.* Ed. G.P. de T. Glazebrook. Champlain Society Publication 24. Toronto: Champlain Society, 1938. Reprint, New York: Greenwood Press, 1968.

Hargrave, Letitia

1947 *Letters of Letitia Hargrave.* Margaret Arnett MacLeod, ed. Champlain Society Publication 28. Toronto: Champlain Society. Facsimile reprint, New York: Greenwood Press, 1969.

Harmon, Daniel Williams

1957 *Sixteen Years in the Indian Country: The Journal of Daniel Williams Harmon, (1800–1816). W. Kaye Lamb, ed. Toronto: Macmillan Company.*

Hearne, Samuel

1934 *Journals of Samuel Hearne and Philip Turnor between the Years 1774 and 1792.* J.B. Tyrrell, ed. Champlain Society Publication 21. Toronto: Champlain Society. Reprint, Toronto: Greenwood Press, 1968.

Hendry, Anthony

1907 "Journal of Anthony Hendry, 1754–55." Lawrence J. Burpee, ed. *Transactions of the Royal Society of Canada* 3rd series, 1:307–64.

Henry, Alexander (the Elder)

1809 *Travels and Adventures in Canada and the Indian Territories Between the Years 1760 and 1776.* New York: I. Riley. March of America Facsimile Series 43. Ann Arbor: University Microfilms Inc.

Henry, Alexander (the Younger)

1965 *Henry's Journal, 1799–1814.* Elliot Coues, ed. 2 vols. Minneapolis: Ross and Haines, Inc.

Historic Sites Service Staff

1968 *Thematic Study of the Fur Trade in the Canadian West,*

1670–1870. Agenda Paper 1968–69. Ottawa: Historic Sites and Monuments Board of Canada.

Ingram, George C.

1970 *The Big House, Lower Fort Garry.* Canadian Historic Sites Occasional Papers in Archaeology and History 4. Ottawa: National Historic Sites Service, National and Historic Parks Branch, Department of Indian Affairs and Northern Development.

1970 *Industrial and Agricultural Activities at Lower Fort Garry.* Canadian Historic Sites Occasional Papers in Archaeology and History 4. Ottawa: National Historic Sites Service, National and Historic Parks Branch, Department of Indian Affairs and Northern Development.

Irving, Washington

1967 *Astoria.* Clatsop Edition, Portland, OR: Binfords & Mort.

Isham, James

1949 *James Isham's Observations on Hudson's Bay, 1743 and Notes and Observations on a Book Entitled A Voyage to Hudson's Bay in the Dobbs Galley, 1749.* E.E. Rich and Alice M. Johnson, eds. London: Hudson's Bay Record Society, Vol. 12.

Jérémie de la Montagne, Nicolas

1926 *Twenty Years of York Factory 1694–1714.* Trans. From the French edition of 1720. R. Douglas & J.N. Wallace, eds. Ottawa: Thorburn & Abbott.

Johnson, Alice

1961 "Hudson's Bay Company on Rainy River 1793–95." *The Naturalist* 12:4 (Winter):9–12.

Johnson, Alice, ed.

1967 *Saskatchewan Journals and Correspondence: Edmonton House 1795–1800; Chesterfield House 1800–1802.* Introduction by Alice M. Johnson. London: Hudson's Bay Record Society, Vol. 26.

Johnston, John

1890 "An Account of Lake Superior (1782–1807)." *Les Bourgeois de la Compagnie du Nord-Ouest* ... L.R. Masson, ed. Quebec. Vol. 2. Reprint, New York: Antiquarian Press, 1960.

Kane, Paul

1859 *Wanderings of an Artist among the Indians of North America: From Canada to Vancouver's Island and Oregon through the Hudson's Bay Company's Territory and Back Again.* Reprint, Edmonton: Hurtig, 1968.

Karklins, Karlis

1981 *The Old Fort Point Site: Fort Wedderburn II?* Canadian Historic Sites Occasional Papers in Archaeology and History 26. Ottawa: National Historic Parks and Sites Branch, Parks Canada, Environment Canada.

1983 *Nottingham House: the Hudson's Bay Company in Athabasca, 1802–1806.* History and Archaeology Occasional Papers 69. Ottawa: National Historic Parks and Sites Branch, Parks Canada, Environment Canada.

Keith, George

1890 "Letters to Mr. Roderic McKenzie (1807–1817)." *Les Bourgeois de la Compagnie du Nord-Ouest . . .* L.R. Masson, ed. Quebec. Vol. 2. Reprint, New York: Antiquarian Press, 1960.

Kelsey, Henry

1928 *Journal of a Voyage and Journey Undertaken by Henry Kelsey through God's Assistance to Discover and Bring to a Commerce the Nawatame Poets in Anno 1691.* Charles Napier Bell, ed. Transactions of the Historical and Scientific Society of Manitoba, NS 4. Winnipeg: Dawson Richardson Publications.

Kenney, James F., ed.

1932 *The Founding of Churchill: Being the Journal of Captain James Knight, Governor-in-Chief in Hudson Bay from the 14th of July to the 13th September, 1717.* Toronto: J.M. Dent & Sons Ltd.

Kenyon, Walter

1962 "Fort Albany, Second Season of Excavation." *Ontario History* 54:2(June).

Kenyon, Walter, & J.R. Turnbull

1971 *The Battle for James Bay.* Toronto: Macmillan of Canada.

Kidd, Robert S.

1971 *Fort George and the Early Fur Trade in Alberta.* Provincial Museum and Archives of Alberta Publication 2. Edmonton.

Klaus, J.F.

1961 "Fort Pelly: an historical sketch." *Saskatchewan History* 14:3(Autumn):81–97.

Lamb, W. Kayne, ed.

1957 *Sixteen Years in the Indian Country: The Journal of Daniel William Harmon, 1800–1816.* Toronto: Macmillan Company. Based on Daniel William Harmon's *Journal of Voyages and Travels in the Interior of North America,* Daniel Haskel, ed. Originally published, Andover: Flagg and Gould, 1820.

1960 *The Letters and Journals of Simon Fraser, 1806–1808.* Toronto: Macmillan Co.

1969 *Gabriel Franchère's Journal of a Voyage on the North West Coast of North America During the Years 1811, 1812, 1813, and 1814.* Translated by Wessie Tipping Lamb. W. Kaye Lamb, ed. Champlain Society Publication 45. Toronto: The Champlain Society.

1970 *The Journals and Letters of Sir Alexander Mackenzie.* Ed. W. Kaye Lamb. Toronto: Macmillan of Canada.

Le Tourneau, J.A. Rodger

1975 *The Grand Rapids Tramway.* Winnipeg: Historic Resources Branch.

1977 "The Grand Rapids Tramway—a Centennial history." *The Beaver* (Autumn): 47–54.

McDonald, Archibald

1828 *Peace River: A Canoe Voyage from Hudson's Bay to Pacific, by Sir George Simpson, (Governor, Hon. Hudson's Bay Company) in 1828: Journal of the Late Chief Factor, Archibald McDonald.* Originally published, Ottawa: J. Durie & Son; Montrèal: Dawson Brothers; Toronto: Adam Stevenson, 1872. Facsimile Reprint of 1872 edition, Malcolm McLeod, ed., Edmonton: M.G. Hurtig. 1971.

MacDonald, Graham

1992 *A Good Solid Comfortable Establishment: An Illustrated History of Lower Fort Garry.* Winnipeg: Watson & Dwyer.

MacDonald, Janice E.

1983 *The Northwest Fort: Fort Edmonton.* Edmonton: Lone Pine.

McDonald of Garth, John

1890 Autobiographical Notes (1791–1816). *Les Bourgeois de la Compagnie du Nord-Ouest* . . . L.R. Masson, ed. Quebec. Vol. 2. Reprint, New York: Antiquarian Press, 1960.

Macdonell, John

1890 Extracts from Mr. John McDonnell's journal (1793–1795). *Les Bourgeois de la Compagnie du Nord-Ouest* . . . L.R. Masson, ed. Quebec. Vol. 1 Vol. 2. Reprint, New York: Antiquarian Press, 1960.

1965 The diary of John Macdonell. *Five Fur Traders of the Northwest.* Charles M. Gates, ed. St. Paul: Minnesota Historical Society.

McDonnell, John. See Macdonell, John.

McGillivray, Duncan

1929 *The Journal of Duncan McGillivray of the North West Com-*

pany at Fort George on the Saskatchewan, 1794–95. Toronto: Macmillan of Canada.

1929 *Some Account of the Trade Carried on by the North West Company.* Ottawa: Public Archives of Canada.

MacGregor, James G.

1966 *Peter Fidler: Canada's Forgotten Surveyor, 1769–1822.* Toronto: McClelland and Stewart.

1974 *Paddle Wheels to Bucket-Wheels on the Athabasca.* [Toronto]: McClelland and Stewart.

1978 *John Rowand, Czar of the Prairies.* Saskatoon: Western Producer Prairie Books.

McKay, Elsie

1959 *The Stone Fort: Lower Fort Garry.* [Selkirk, MB: Printed by Enterprise Publishers].

McKelvie, B. A.

1947 *Fort Langley: Outpost of Empire.* Toronto: Southam Company, Reprint, Toronto: Thomas Nelson & Sons, 1957.

Mackenzie, Alexander

1970 *The Journals and Letters of Sir Alexander Mackenzie.* W. Kaye Lamb, ed. Toronto: Macmillan of Canada.

McKenzie, James

1890 Extracts from his journal (1799–1800). Athabasca District. *Les Bourgeois de la Compagnie du Nord-Ouest* . . . L.R. Masson, ed. Quebec. Vol. 2. Reprint, New York: Antiquarian Press, 1960.

McKenzie, N.M.W.J.

1921 *The Men of the Hudson's Bay Company, 1670–1920.* Fort William: [Times-Journal Presses].

McKenzie, Roderic

1890 Reminiscences of the Honorable Roderic McKenzie being chiefly a synopsis of letters from Sir Alexander Mackenzie. *Les Bourgeois de la Compagnie du Nord-Ouest* . . . L.R. Masson, ed. Quebec. Vol. 1. Reprint, New York: Antiquarian Press, 1960.

Mackie, Hugh T.

1968 Excavations of Fort Rivière Tremblante. *The Blue Jay* 26:2 (June): 101–05.

1972 *Preliminary Report, Pine Fort, 1972.* Manitoba Museum of Man and Nature Occasional Paper 1. Winnipeg: Manitoba Museum of Man and Nature. Cover Title: *Pine Fort, Northwest Company Post: A Preliminary Report.*

McLean, John
1932 *Notes of Twenty-five Years' Service in the Hudson's Bay Territory.* W. Stewart Wallace, ed. Champlain Society Publication 19. Toronto: Champlain Society, Facsimile reprint, New York: Greenwood Press, 1968.

Macleod, J.E.A.
1931 Old Bow Fort. *Canadian Historical Review* 12:4(Dec): 407–11.
1933 Piegan Post and the Blackfoot Trade. *Canadian Historical Review* 24:3(Sept): 273–79.

MacLeod, Margaret Arnett
1957 *Lower Fort Garry.* [Winnipeg: s.n.].

MacLeod, Margaret Arnett, ed.
1947 *The Letters of Letitia Hargrave.* Champlain Society Publication 28. Toronto: Champlain Society. Facsimile Reprint, New York: Greenwood Press, 1969.

McLeod, Archibald N.
1965 The diary of Archibald N. McLeod. *Five Fur Traders of the Northwest.* Charles M. Gates, ed. St. Paul: Minnesota Historical Society.

McLoughlin, John
1941 *Letters of John McLoughlin from Fort Vancouver to the Governor and Committee.* E.E. Rich, ed. 1st Series (1825–1838). London: Hudson's Bay Record Society, Vol. 4. Kraus Reprint of 1943 edition, Nendeln-Liechtenstein, 1968.
1943 *Letters of John McLoughlin from Fort Vancouver to the Governor and Committee.* E.E. Rich, ed. 3rd Series (1839–1844). London: Hudson's Bay Record Society, Vol. 6. Kraus reprint of 1943 edition, Nendeln-Liechtenstein, 1968.
1944 *Letters of John McLoughlin from Fort Vancouver to the Governor and Committee.* E.E. Rich, ed. 3rd Series (1844–1846). London: Hudson's Bay Record Society, vol. 7. Kraus reprint of 1944 edition, Nendeln-Liechtenstein.

McMorran, G.A.
n.d. *Souris River Posts in the Hartney District.* Pp. 47–62.

Malcolmson, Robert W.
1964 *Fort Espèrance.*

Mallory, Enid S.
1963 "The Life of Lower Fort Garry." *Canadian Geographical Journal* 66:4 (April): 116–23.

Masson, L.R.
1890 *Les Bourgeois de la Compagnie du Nord-Ouest: récits de voyages, lettres et rapports inédits relatifs au nord-ouest cana-*

dien: publié avec une esquisse historique et des annotations. 2 vols. Québec: s.n. Reprint, New York: Antiquarian Press, 1960.

Merk, Frederick, ed.
1968 *Fur Trade and Empire: George Simpson's Journal Entitled Remarks Connected with the Fur Trade in the Course of a Voyage from York Factory to Fort George and Back to York Factory 1824-25, with Related Documents.* Rev. ed. Cambridge, MA: Belknap Press of Harvard University Press.

Messer, Margaret
1950 Philip Turnor, island surveyor. *Saskatchewan History* 3:57-63.

Miquelon, Dale
1970 *A Brief History of Lower Fort Garry.* Canadian Historic Sites Occasional Papers in Archaeology and History 4. Ottawa: National Historic Sites Service, National and Historic Parks Branch, Department of Indian Affairs and Northern Development.

Mitchell, Elaine Allan
1977 *Fort Timiskaming and the Fur Trade.* Toronto: University of Toronto Press.

Moberly, Henry John
1929 *When Fur Was King.* With William Bleasdell Cameron. Toronto: J.M. Dent & Sons.

Morice, A.G.
1978 *The History of the Northern Interior of British Columbia.* Smithers, BC: Interior Stationery.

Morris, J. L.
1942 "Old Fort Garry in 1881 and 1939." *Canadian Geographical Journal* 24:1(Jan):52-55.

Morton, A.S.
1929 *The Place of the Red River Settlement in the Plans of the Hudson's Bay Company, 1812-1825.* Annual Report of the Canadian Historical Association.
1941 "Five Fur Trade Posts on the Lower Qu'Appelle River, 1787-1819." *Transactions of the Royal Society of Canada* 3rd Series, 35: 81-93.
1942 "The Posts of the Fur Traders on the Upper Assiniboine River." *Transactions of the Royal Society of Canada* 3rd Series, 36: 101-14.
1973 *A History of the Canadian West to 1870-71: Being a History of Rupert's Land (The Hudson's Bay Company's Territory) and of*

the North-west Territory (including the Pacific Slope). 2nd ed. Toronto: University of Toronto Press. Originally published, London; New York: T. Nelson & Sons Ltd. [1939].

Morton, W. L.

1956 *Alexander Begg's Red River Journal, and Other Papers Relative to the Red River Resistance of 1869–1870*. Champlain Society Publication 34. Toronto: Champlain Society. Reprint, New York: Greenwood Press, 1969.

National Park Service

1981 *Fort Vancouver*. Handbook 113, Washington, DC.

Noble, William C.

1973 *The Excavation and Historical Identification of Rocky Mountain House*. Canadian Historic Sites Occasional Papers in Archaeology and History 6. Ottawa: National Historic Sites Service, National and Historic Parks Branch, Department of Indian Affairs and Northern Development.

Nute, Grace Lee

1943 *Caesars of the Wilderness: Médard Chouart, Sieur des Groseilliers, and Pierre Esprit Radisson, 1618–1710*. Reprint, St. Paul: Minnesota Historical Society Press, 1978.

Ogden, Peter Skene

1950 *Peter Skene Ogden's Snake Country Journals, 1824–25 and 1825–26*. E.E. Rich and Alice M. Johnson, eds. London: Hudson's Bay Record Society, Vol. 13.

1961 *Peter Skene Ogden's Snake Country Journals, 1826–1827*. K.G. Davies ed. London: Hudson's Bay Record Society, Vol. 23.

1971 *Peter Skene Ogden's Snake County Journals, 1827–28 and 1828–29*. Gyndwr Williams, ed. London: Hudson's Bay Record Society, Vol. 28.

Patterson R.M.

1966 *Trail to the Interior*. Toronto: Macmillan of Canada.

Payne, Michael

1989 *The Most Respectable Place in the Territory: Everyday Life in Hudson's Bay Company Service, York Factory, 1788 to 1870*. Ottawa: National Historic Parks and Sites, Environmental Canada.

Peel, Bruce

1950 "Cumberland House." *Saskatchewan History* 3:2(Spring):68–73.

Pethick, Derek

1968 *Victoria: The Fort*. [Vancouver]: Mitchell Press.

Pond, Peter
1965 The narrative of Peter Pond. *Five Fur Traders of the Northwest.* Charles M. Gates, ed. St Paul: Minnesota Historical Society.

Pritchett, John
1942 *The Red River Valley, 1811–1849: A Regional Study.* New York: Russell & Russell.

Reid, C.S. "Paddy"
1977 *Mansion in the Wilderness: The Archaeology of the Ermatinger House.* Research Report 10. [Toronto]: Ontario Ministry of Culture and Recreation, Historical Planning and Research.

Reid, C.S. "Paddy," ed.
1980 *Northern Ontario Fur Trade Archaeology: Recent Research.* Archaeological Research Report 12-0706–1226. Toronto: Historical Planning and Research Branch, Ontario Ministry of Culture and Recreation.

Rich, E.E.
1958 *The History of the Hudson's Bay Company.* Vol. 1 (1670–1763). London: Hudson's Bay Record Society Vol. 21.

1959 *The History of the Hudson's Bay Company.* Vol. 2 (1763–1870). London: Hudson's Bay Record Society, Vol. 22.

1967 *The Fur Trade and the Northwest to 1857.* The Canadian Centenary series 11. [Toronto]: McClelland and Stewart.

Rich, E.E., ed.
1938 *Journal of Occurrences in the Athabasca Department by George Simpson, 1820 and 1921, and Report.* Introduction by Chester Martin. London: Hudson's Bay Record Society, Vol 1. Reprint, Kraus Reprints, 1968.

1939 *Colin Robertson's Correspondence Book, September 1817 To September 1822.* Introduction by E.E. Rich. London: Hudson's Bay Record Society, Vol. 2. Reprint of 1939 edition, Kraus Reprints, 1968.

1941 *Letters of John McLoughlin from Fort Vancouver to the Governor and Committee.* 1st Series, 1825–1838. Introduction by W. Kaye Lamb. London: Hudson's Bay Record Society, Vol. 4. Reprint, Kraus Reprints, 1968.

1943 *Letters of John McLoughlin from Fort Vancouver to the Governor and Committee.* 3rd Series, 1839–1844. Introduction by W. Kaye Lamb. London: Hudson's Bay Record Society, Vol. 6. Reprint, Kraus Reprints, 1968.

1944 *Letters of John McLoughlin from Fort Vancouver to the Governor and Committee.* 3rd Series, 1844–46. Introduction by W.

Kaye Lamb. London: Hudson's Bay Record Society, Vol. 7. Reprint, Kraus Reprints, 1968.

1947 *[Simpson's 1828 Journey to the Columbia] Part of Dispatch from George Simpson Esq. Governor of Rupert's Land to the Governor and Committee of the Hudson's Bay Company, London, March 1, 1829.* Introduction by W. Stewart Wallace. London: Hudson's Bay Record Society, Vol. 10. Reprint, Kraus Reprints, 1968.

Rich, E.E., & Alice M. Johnson, eds.

1949 *James Isham's Observations on Hudsons Bay, 1743 and Notes and Observations on a Book Entitled A Voyage to Hudsons Bay in the Dobbs Galley, 1749.* Introduction by E.E. Rich. London: Hudson's Bay Record Society, Vol. 12.

1950 *Peter Skene Ogden's Snake Country Journals, 1824–25 and 1825–26.* Introduction by Burt Brown Barker. London: Hudson's Bay Record Society, Vol. 13.

1951 *Cumberland House Journals and Inland Journals.* 1st Series, 1775–1779. Introduction by Richard Glover. London: Hudson's Bay Record Society, Vol. 14.

1952 *Cumberland House Journals and Inland Journals.* 2nd Series, 1779–1782. Introduction by Richard Glover. London: Hudson's Bay Record Society, Vol. 15.

1954 *Moose Fort Journals, 1783–85.* Introduction by G.P. de T. Glazebrook. London: Hudson's Bay Record Society, Vol. 17.

1955 *A Journal of a Voyage from Rocky Mountain Portage in Peace River to the Sources of Finlay's Branch and North West Ward in Summer 1824* [by Samuel Black]. Introduction by R.M. Patterson. London: Hudson's Bay Record Society, Vol. 18.

Rich, E.E., & Alice M. Johnson, eds.

1956 *London Correspondence Inward from Eden Colvile, 1849–1852.* London: Hudson's Bay Record Society, Vol. 19.

Robertson, Colin

1939 *Colin Robertson's Correspondence Books, September 1817 to September 1822.* E.E. Rich, ed. London: Hudson's Bay Record Society. Vol. 2. Kraus reprint, Nendeln-Liechtenstein, 1968.

Ronda, James P.

1990 *Astoria and Empire.* Lincoln: University of Nebraska Press.

Ross, Alexander

1849 *Adventures of the First Settlers on the Oregon or Columbia River.* London: Smith, Elder and Co.

1855 *The Fur Hunters of the Far West: A Narrative of Adventures in the Oregon and Rocky Mountains, 1810–1813.* London: Reprint, Norman, OK: University of Oklahoma Press, 1956. American Explorations and Travel Series, 20.

1856   *The Red River Settlement: Its Rise, Progress and Present State. With Some Account of the Native Races and Its General History, to the Present Day.* London: Smith, Elder. Reprint, with new introduction by Jay Edgerton, Minneapolis: Ross and Haines, 1957.

Rye, Laurence M.

n.d.   *Reminiscences of a Parry Sound Colonist.*

Sandercock, W. Clark

1933   "Where History Was Made: Fort Ellice, Fort Pelly, Touchwood Hills House, Fort Qu' Appelle." *Canadian Geographical Journal* 7:4 (Oct):153–62.

Saskatchewan. Department of Natural Resources

1973   *Last Mountain House Historic Park.*

n.d.   *Fort Pitt Historic Park.*

Saskatchewan Tourism and Renewable Resources

1976   *Fort Carlton Historic Park.* Historic Booklet 1.

n.d.   *Fort Pitt Historic Park.* Historic Booklet 7.

Schultz, John

1894   "A Forgotten Northern Fortress." *Transactions of the Historical and Scientific Society of Manitoba* 47. Winnipeg: Manitoba Free Press.

Smythe, T.

1968   *Thematic Study of the Fur Trade, 1670–1870.* Ottawa: Historic Sites and Monuments Board of Canada.

Southesk, Earl of

1875   *Saskatchewan and the Rocky Mountains.* Edmonton: Hurtig, 1969.

Spargo, John

1950   *Two Bennington-born Explorers and Makers of Modern Canada.* Bradford, VT: Green Mountain Press.

Spaulding, Kenneth A., ed.

1953   *Robert Stuart's On the Oregon Trail, 1812–1813.* Norman, OK: University of Oklahoma Press.

Stager, John K.

1962   *Fur Trading Posts in the Mackenzie Region up to 1850.* Occasional Papers in Geography, May 3, 1962: 37–46. Canadian Association of Geographers. B.C. Division.

Stenson, Fred

1985   *Rocky Mountain House National Historic Park.* Toronto: NC

Press, Parks Canada, and the Canadian Government Publishing Centre.

Stewart, David A.
1930 "Early Assiniboine Trading Posts of the Souris Mouth Group, 1785–1832." *Transactions of the Historical and Scientific Society of Manitoba* NS, 5.

Thompson, David
1916 *David Thompson's Narrative of his Explorations in Western America, 1784–1812.* J.B. Tyrrell, ed. Champlain Society Publication 12. Toronto: Champlain Society.

Tjompson, Edwin N.
1969 *Grand Portage: A History of the Sites, People and Fur Trade.* Washington, DC: National Park Service.

Tranter, G.J.
1946 *Link to the North.* London: Hodder and Stoughton.

Turnor, Philip
1934 *Journals of Samuel Hearne and Philip Turnor between the Years 1774 and 1792.* J.B. Tyrrell, ed. Champlain Society Publication 21. Toronto: Champlain Society. Reprint, Toronto: Greenwood Press, 1968.

Tyrell, J.B., ed.
1913 Peter Fidler: trader and surveyor, 1769–1822. *Transactions of the Royal Society of Canada* 3rd series 7:117–27.
1916 *David Thompson's Narrative of His Explorations in Western America, 1784–1812.* Champlain Society Publication 12. Toronto: Champlain Society.
1931 *Documents Relating to the Early History of Hudson Bay.* Champlain Society Publication 18. Toronto: Champlain Society. Reprint, Toronto: Greenwood Press, 1968.
1934 *Journals of Samuel Hearne and Philip Turnor.* Champlain Society Publication 21. Toronto: Champlain Society. Reprint, Toronto: Greenwood Press, 1968.

Umfreville, Edward
1790 *The Present State of Hudson's Bay: Containing a Full Description of that Settlement, and the Adjacent Country; and Likewise of the Fur Trade, with Hints for its Improvement, & c. & c.* 1954 edition. Ed. W. Stewart Wallace. Toronto: Ryerson Press. Originally published, London: Charles Stalker, 1790.

Usher, Peter J.
1971 *Fur Trade Posts of the Northwest Territories, 1870–1970.* Ottawa: Northern Science Research Group, Department of Indian Affairs and Northern Development.

Vickers, Chris
1949 "The Pine Fort on the Assiniboine River." *Canadian Historical Review* 30:66–68.

Voorhis, Ernest
1930 *Historic Forts and Trading Posts of the French Regime and of the English Fur Trading Companies.* Ottawa: Department of the Interior, Natural Resources Intelligence Branch.

Wallace, J.N.
1929 *The Wintering Partners on Peace River: From the Earliest Records to the Union in 1821; With a Summary of the Dunvegan Journal, 1806.* Ottawa: Thorburn and Abbott.

Wallace, W. Stewart, ed.
1932 *John McLean's Notes of a Twenty-Five Years' Service in the Hudson's Bay Territory.* Champlain Society Publication 19. Toronto: Champlain Society. Originally published in 1849 in 2 vols. London, England: Richard Bentley. Facsimile Reprint of 1932 edition, New York: Greenwood Press, 1968.

1934 *Documents Relating to the North West Company.* Champlain Society Publication 22. Toronto: The Champlain Society.

1954 *The Pedlars from Quebec, and Other Papers on the Nor'-westers.* Toronto: Ryerson Press.

Weiler, John
1973 *Michipicoten: Hudson's Bay Company Post, 1821–1904.* Historic Sites Branch, Ontario Ministry of Natural Resources Research Report 3. Toronto: Ontario Ministry of Natural Resources.

Wentzel, W.F.
1890 "Letters to the Hon. Roderic McKenzie, 1807–1824." *Les Bourgeois de la Compagnie du Nord-Ouest* . . . L.R. Masson, ed. Quebec. Vol. 1. Reprint, New York: Antiquarian Press, 1960.

White, M. Catherine
1942 "Salish House." *Pacific Northwest Quarterly* (July):251–63.

Wilcocke, Samuel H.
1890 Narrative of circumstances attending the death of the late Benjamin Frobisher, Esq., a partner of the North-West Company. *Les Bourgeois de la Compagnie du Nord-Ouest.* . . L.R. Masson, ed. Quebec. Vol. 2. Reprint, New York: Antiquarian Press, 1960.

Williams, Glyndwr, ed.
1969 *Andrew Graham's Observations on Hudson's Bay, 1767–1791.* Introduction by Richard Glover. London: Hudson's Bay Record Society, Vol. 27.

1971 *Peter Skene Ogden's Snake Country Journals, 1827–28 and 1828–29.* Introduction by David E. Miller and David H. Miller. London: Hudson's Bay Record Society, Vol. 28.

1973 *London Correspondence Inward from Sir George Simpson, 1841–42.* Introduction by John S. Galbraith. London: Hudson's Bay Record Society, Vol. 29.

1975 *Hudson's Bay Miscellany, 1670–1870.* Introduction by Glyndwr Williams. Winnipeg: Hudson's Bay Record Society, Vol. 30.

Wilson, Clifford
1970 *Campbell of the Yukon.* Toronto: Macmillan of Canada.

Wonders, W.C.
1974 "Athabasca Pass: Gateway to the Pacific." *Canadian Geographical Journal* 58:3 (Feb):20–29.

Wright, J.V.
1967 *The Pic River Site.* Contributions to Anthropology. National Museums of Canada Bulletin 206. Ottawa: National Museums of Canada.

Index

surrenders: Charter, 559, 594; US possessory rights, 581
Hudson's Bay House, 595
Hudson's Hope, 363–366
Huggins, Edward, 579, 580–581
Hughes, Guy, 216, 219, 362
Hughes, James, 222–224, 282, 419, 545
Hungry Hall House, 157–159
Hunt, Robert, 651–652, 653
Hunt, William, 436, 440, 442
Husson, Fr (O.M.I.), 337, 340
Hutchins, Thomas, 111
Hutchinson, Bruce, 387–388
Hutchinson, John, 526

Iberville, Pierre LeMoyne, Sieur de, 2, 23
Imperial Oil Company, 716
Indians
    alcohol and, 103, 362
      demand for, 235, 259; violence over, 183, 237, 257, 362
    American Indian Wars, 472
    intertribal wars of, 24, 50, 52, 118–120, 160–162, 196, 215–216, 223, 228, 254–257, 343, 407, 417–418, 536–538, 601
    Puget Sound Indian War (1855–56), 580
    relations with traders
      co-operative, 467, 521, 637
      hostile, 183, 207, 222–223, 236–237, 399–401, 411, 458, 461–462, 466–467, 528–530, 540, 599–600, 660
      violent, 54–55, 63–65, 102–103, 118–120, 125–126, 155, 157, 161–162, 216, 242, 270, 272, 335, 349, 362, 386–387, 398, 444–445, 452, 493, 516, 518, 526, 539, 257, 616–617, 626, 639–641

starvation, 343–344, 350–351, 598–599, 614–616
See also names of individual groups, e.g. Blackfoot, Gros Ventre, Mandan, Sioux, etc
influenza, 695
Ingenika (Peace River motorboat), 364–365
International Bitumen, 687
Inuit, arctic coast, 307, 342, 343, 348, 601
Irving, Washington, 321, 325, 436–437
Isaac Todd (NWC trading vessel), 428, 441, 442, 445, 453
Isbister, Alexander, 597
Isbister, Joseph, 63–64
Isham, Charles, 129
Isham, James, 24, 30, 129–130, 280
Island House, 283
Isle of Scotland, 283

Jacobs, Ferdinand, 24, 30, 65–66
Jasper House, 227, 286–293
Jay's Treaty, 92–93, 191, 316
Jesuits at Lac des Allumettes, 489
Johnson, Albert, "Mad Trapper," 284, 602–603
Johnston, Jane, 77–78
Johnston, John, 77

Kane, Paul
    visits: Carlton House, 273; Edmonton House, 226, 232; Fort Assiniboine (Athabasca River), 484; Fort Nisqually, 578; Fort Pitt, 538; Fort Vancouver, 508; Jasper House, 288; Rocky Mountain Fort, 256
Kearney, Brother (O.M.I.), 346
Keith, George, 136, 348–349
Keith, James, 144, 444, 446
Kelsey, Henry, 24, 28, 61
Kennedy, Alexander, 431, 501–502

Macdonell, Miles, 204, 267, 269, 390–392
Macdougall, John, 364
MacFarlane, Roderick, 145, 675–676
MacGregor, James G., 225, 676, 677–678
MacIntosh's Post, 214
MacKay, John Richard, 126–127
Mackay, William M., 686
Mackenzie, Alexander, 145, 151, 164, 166, 282
    at: Fort Chipewyan, 134–135; Grand Portage, 92; Methye Portage, 169–170
    disapproves rum trade, 103
    explorations of, xviii, 122, 179–180, 213, 294–295
    on Frog Portage name, 80
    notes oil sands, 674
Mackenzie, Roderick, 135–136, 151, 164, 166, 316
Mackenzie River Transport (HBC subsidiary), 695
Mackinac Island, 477–480
Mackinac Island State Park Commission, 39
MacLeod, Margaret Arnett, 593
Macri, Doreen, 34
Macri, Mike, 32, 34
Mactavish, Dugald, 510
MacTavish, John George, 136, 708–709
Mactavish, William, 594
Made Beaver, 66
Mair, Charles, 593
malaria at Fort Vancouver, 509, 620
Malouf, C.I., 413
Manchester House, 117–120, 183
Mandan, 207
mangeurs de lard (pork eaters), 299
Manson, Donald, 373–375, 448–449, 462, 515
Marine Operators (trading company), 695
Marlboro House, 130
Marquette (steamboat), 498

Marten, Humphrey, 24, 65–66
Martin, Jeff, 68
Martin, "Snowbird," 147–148
Massachusetts (American coal carrier), 648
Massacre Island, 51–52
Masson, L. R., 135
Matheson, Alexander, 711
Mattawa House, 116
Maxwell, Henry, 337
May, Wilfrid Reid "Wop," 284
Mayne, R.C., 650–651
McAuley, Joseph Richard, 88–89
McAuley, Lily, 34–35, 88
McBean, John, 224
McBeath, Adam, 305, 498
McBeath, Angus, 498–499, 656
McDermott, Jack, 364
McDonald, Angus, 576
McDonald, Archibald, 144–145, 216, 335–336, 370
    at: Fort Ellice, 548; Fort Kamloops, 460; Fort Langley, 516–517; Fort Nisqually, 571–573; Fort Qu'Appelle, 660–661, 665, 666; Last Mountain House, 671
McDonald, Finan, 400, 403, 407–408, 411–412, 429, 468
    at Spokane House, 426, 431
McDonald, John, 319
McDonald, John, of Garth, 119, 125, 182–184, 250, 282, 389, 401
    and Pemmican War, 391–392
McDonell, Allan, 492–493
McDougall, Alexander, 41
McDougall, Duncan, 436, 438, 441–443, 444
McDougall, James, 337, 354, 355, 360
McFarlane, Stewart, 424
McGillis, Hugh, 211, 319
McGillivray, Archibald, 214
McGillivray, Duncan, 119–120, 160–162, 174–175, 182, 184, 251, 282

759

Wandering Spirit (Cree warrior), 542
Wapiscogamy House, 111–112
War of 1812, 76, 192–193, 349, 391, 428, 441
   See also Treaty of Ghent (1814)
Warner, Glenn, 312
Warner, Trish, 312
war(s), European
   effect of on fur trade, 196
   Hudson Bay campaigns of, 11–12, 23, 24, 30–31
war(s), Indian. See Indians, intertribal wars of
Washington State Historical Society, restores Fort Nisqually buildings, 581
Waterways, 684–685
Watt, (Chief Trader), 490
Watt, James C., 3, 4
Weenusk (Peace River motorboat), 364–365
Wells Dam, 455
Wentzel, W.F., 295, 342
West, John, 269
Western Canada Airways, 682
Weyerhauser Real Estate, 582–583
White, Catherine M., 410
Whiteknife, George, 147
Whiteknife, Sally, 146
Whitman, George, 716–717
Wilcocke, S.H., 708–709

Wilkes, Charles, 454–455
Williams, William, 708–709
Wills, John, 389
Wilson, Steve, 688
Winnipeg, City of, 559, 595
Wolseley, Garnet, 559
Wood, J.J., and Mrs Wood, 8
Work, John, 431, 433, 508–510, 514, 519–520
Wrigley (HBC steamboat), 309, 692–693, 696
Wylie, Horace, 146–147
Wylie, Marjorie, 149–150, 152–153
Wyman, Nora, 284–285
Wyman, Thomas, 284–285

XY Company, 137, 202

Yale, James Murray, 385, 516–523
Yale House, 214, 216–217, 220
Yellow Quill Trail, 209
Yellowknives (Indians), 294
York boats, 17, 67, 118, 145, 308, 602, 707
York Factory, 12, 23–27, 66, 97, 177, 267, 324, 708
   governors of, 24, 26
Yorstone, 203
Young, Harrison, 678
Yucultas (west coast Indians), 516, 518